THE NEW URBAN SOCIOLOGY

Fourth Edition
THE NEW URBAN SOCIOLOGY

Mark Gottdiener
University at Buffalo

Ray Hutchison
University of Wisconsin–Green Bay

WESTVIEW
PRESS
A Member of the Perseus Books Group

Find us on the World Wide Web at www.westviewpress.com.

Westview Press books are available at special discounts for bulk purchases in the United States by corporations, institutions, and other organizations. For more information, please contact the Special Markets Department at the Perseus Books Group, 2300 Chestnut Street, Suite 200, Philadelphia, PA 19103, or call (800) 810-4145, ext. 5000, or e-mail special.markets@perseusbooks.com.

Every effort has been made to secure required permission to use all images, maps, and other art included in this volume.

Designed by Trish Wilkinson
Set in 10 point Adobe Garamond

Library of Congress Cataloging-in-Publication Data

Gottdiener, Mark.
    The new urban sociology / Mark Gottdiener, Ray Hutchison. — 4th ed.
        p.   cm.
    Includes bibliographical references and index.
    ISBN 978-0-8133-4425-6 (alk. paper)
    1. Metropolitan areas—United States. 2. Suburbs—United States.
3. Urbanization—United States—History. 4. Sociology, Urban—United States.
5. Sociology, Urban. 6. Urbanization. I. Hutchison, Ray. II. Title.
HT334.U5G657 2010
307.76—dc22   2010011487

10 9 8 7 6 5 4 3 2 1

Mark Gottdiener dedicates this fourth edition to the memory of his parents, Moritz and Aranka Gottdiener.

Ray Hutchison dedicates this fourth edition to Dulce Reyes Hutchison, whose journey from Manila to Chicago brought our global world together, and to Leilani, Heather, and Jessica, who will complete the new global world of the twenty-first century.

CONTENTS

PREFACE TO THE FOURTH EDITION

Occasionally, a colleague among urban sociologists will ask, "Say, what's so 'new' about *The New Urban Sociology* after all these years?" It sounded frivolous at first, but we have come to realize that this is a serious question, although not in the way the questioner intended, if not an attempt to state a criticism. It is a great pleasure to produce a fourth edition of this text that began as an idea of Mark Gottdiener's in 1991 and was first published three years later. Ray Hutchison joined the project as coauthor for the second edition, and later, alarmed at the excessive cost of hardcover books in this area, we switched publishers and arranged for a third edition to be put out by Westview in a paperback format. We have all been very pleased at the response to that change and the continued use of our text in the classroom.

So, what is still "new" about *The New Urban Sociology?* Our original formulation of the new paradigm directly attacked the previous dominant approach of urban ecology that was grounded in neo-Classical economics with the market of many buyers and sellers as supreme along with its neo-Liberal political and planning prescriptions that weighted market solutions heavily despite government subsidies. The new urban sociology replaced this view with the more realistic one of an economy and political system hegemonically controlled by large, powerful interests that moved to make their concerns the most important in our universally acknowledged "mixed" economy, where government intervention usually favored those powerful interests and not level-playing-field markets. To suggest, as some have, that our view, along with the theory of Henri Lefebvre, and the political economy based on our perspective, are not still "new" means that much of the rhetoric and ideological attacks against better planning, better control over our urban environments, and better management of job creation and profit making no longer have adherents among writers of urban sociology texts competing with ours. This is clearly not the case. The new urban sociology remains the best explanatory paradigm for the urban crisis, both current and past, despite the publication and use of other textbooks that retain elements of previous and discredited "free market" paradigms.

Other aspects of our approach also have yet to take hold in a way that would undercut the newness of the "new" perspective. Despite the overwhelming reality of how everyday life is organized today in the United States and increasingly in developed countries elsewhere as a regional, expanding space that we call the *mutlicentered metro-politan region,* many urbanists persist in placing the term *the city* exclusively at the center of their analysis. They speak of *world cities, edge cities, megacities.* Anyone with a rudi-mentary knowledge of maps and spatial reasoning who can chart places of residence, lo-cations of businesses, airports, and manufacturing and retailing sites can easily see the immense regional spread of socioeconomic activity as well as the formation of mini-centers that have taken over many of the functions of the classical, historical central city itself. To be sure, the City of London is still the financial center of the United Kingdom, but the City of London is not the city of London, because the latter is an increasingly multicentered metropolitan region encompassing a vast area of homes, businesses, recre-ational, and government minicenters. Clearly as well, New York City must be consid-ered globally central, but when people who should be better informed of spatial urban characteristics speak of it as a world city, they are almost exclusively talking about Man-hattan, and even more specifically, Wall Street and its attendant services and spin-off businesses. Looming as an immense regional agglomeration outside Manhattan is a vast expanse of urbanized, multicentered space encompassing parts of New Jersey, Connecti-cut, and even the edge of the Philadelphia region in Pennsylvania, as well as the rest of the New York State areas around the five boroughs of the city. In short, what remains still "new" to some people is the basic need to grasp the size and internal dynamics of this new form of urban space that we call the multicentered metropolitan region.

Lastly, when urbanists ask us to explain what is still "new" about our new para-digm, introduced in the 1990s, we often point to simplistic, sound-bite sociology that has crept into explanations for spatial dynamics in place of deep-level analysis that un-derstands fully the contributions of Henri Lefebvre and his academic followers. How can people still speak of a "growth machine" after decades of deindustrialization and global labor sourcing? How can they believe there is a one-to-one correspondence be-tween the "use value" of property allegedly enjoyed by consumers versus the "ex-change value" enjoyed by developers, when, ever since 1930s real estate reforms, the major economic investment of Americans is their home and the prospect of future in-creases in its exchange value? How can urbanists speak of the importance of cities for all people when most Americans, according to the census, have lived in suburbs since the 1970s, and when the federal government can make such a mess of the devastation of New Orleans by Hurricane Katrina that, almost a decade later, middle-income and poor people remain displaced from their beloved region and its way of life? And given all the alternative approaches advertised by other urban sociology textbooks in com-petition with ours, how can they begin to truly help students understand the current economic meltdown when it can be explained directly, easily, and quite usefully by reading *The New Urban Sociology*'s approach to the role of real estate speculation and investment, Henri Lefebvre's *second circuit of capital*, in bringing about such crises and a failure of the market?

In this fourth edition, we have updated the material in previous editions to cover the persisting importance of understanding the "new" approach in order to explain the housing crisis, the failures of the market and influence-controlled government intervention, the contradictions of use versus exchange value, the fallacy of the "growth machine," the falseness of the old, urban ecology paradigm, and the critical need for more social justice in dealing with persisting social, political, and economic problems of everyday urban life in the massive, multicentered metropolitan region. New immigrants, new forms of employment, new growth poles like airports, new cultural forms, new political struggles, new changes in the global positions of countries like India, Brazil, and China, new patterns of global labor sourcing and transnational corporate dynamics, new issues of social justice and environmental concerns, and the like, continue to make this edition of the *New Urban Sociology* as relevant today as it was when the first edition came out over twenty years ago. We hope that it will be as useful in the classroom as have previous versions of this new paradigm.

We offer our heartfelt thanks to the many people who have adopted this text for classroom use. We strongly appreciate all the feedback sent to us by teachers in the trenches of academia who have employed our text and found it most student-friendly and enjoyable to teach. We are so very thankful for your patronage and hope that this version, because it updates tables with the latest census data, and because it deals with the most contemporary of urban issues today, such as the need for affordable housing and continued infrastructure neglect of our regional spaces as well as the new cultural patterns of settlement, will continue to satisfy your teaching needs.

ACKNOWLEDGMENTS

The development of *The New Urban Sociology* through four editions has been an extended project. It could not have been accomplished without the crucial help provided by a number of people. We wish to thank friends in academia and beyond for their support: Andrew Austin, Bob Antonio, Marcelo Cruz, Karen Dalke, David Diaz, Joe Feagin, Kevin Gotham, Harvey Kay, Bruce Haynes, Chigon Kim, Nestor Rodriguez, Eric Monkkonen, Peter Muller, Adam Parrillo, Mario Small, Leonard Wallock, and Talmadge Wright in the United States; Phil Gunn, Lena Lavinas, Sandra Lincioni, Circe Monteiro and Sueli Schiffer in Brazil; Jens Tonboe in Denmark; Lorenzo Tripodi in Germany; Alexandros Lagopoulos and Nikos Komninos in Greece; Mark Clapson and Chris Pickvance in England; Gabrielle Manella and Simone Giometti in Italy; Dorel Abraham in Romania; Lynn Smith in Scotland; Milan Prodanovic and Sonya Prodanovic in Serbia; and Richard Wolff in Switzerland. Students at the University of Wisconsin-Green Bay have provided valuable comments and editorial support, including Randy Roethle and Tanya Krall (third edition) and Lora Boncher, See Colin Quintana, and Emily Vetting (fourth edition).

We thank the editing/design/production team of Sandra Beris, Nancy King, and especially Alex Masulis at Westview.

We would like to thank our colleagues who served as reviewers for earlier editions: Brian Aldrich, Winona State University; Brian Barry, Rochester Institute of Technology;

Craig Calhoun, then at the University of North Carolina, Chapel Hill, and now at New York University; Robert L. Carroll, University of Cincinnati; Scott Ford, Florida State University; Anthony Filipovitch, Minnesota State University at Mankato; Karl Flaming, University of Colorado–Denver; Judith Friedman, Rutgers University; Kevin Fox Gotham, Tulane University; Geoffrey Grant, South Dakota State University; George Kephart, Pennsylvania State University; Jerry Lembcke, College of Holy Cross; Anthony Mendonca, Community College of Allegheny County; Charles Price Reavis, CUNY–John Jay College of Criminal Justice; Nestor Rodriguez, University of Houston; Thomas Shannon, Radford University; Steven L. Vassar, Mankato State University; and J. Talmadge Wright, Loyola University.

THE NEW URBAN SOCIOLOGY

We live in an urban world. At the beginning of the twenty-first century, more than 3 billion persons—about half of the world's population—lived in urban areas. By 2030 this number is expected to increase from 3 to more than 5 billion persons—some 60 percent of the total world population. Most of this increase will occur in the developing world, much of it in megacities where many if not most persons live in shanty-towns, and with incomes below the poverty level (United Nations, 2007). This will be the first urban century in human history, and the well-being not just of families and households but of human society more generally will depend upon our creating a safe and just urban environment—something that human populations have not been particularly adept at doing. A beginning point in this very significant challenge is the study of urban sociology, which will give us the tools for understanding not just how urban regions grow and develop but also for understanding the impact of urban life on persons living in cities, suburbs, and metropolitan regions, and the even greater impact of world urbanization on human societies and the natural environment. This is the goal of our textbook, and this is your subject of study for the next several months.

URBAN REGIONS

People most often speak about the city or the suburban town they live in but rarely about the region. Yet the best way to understand urban growth is to appreciate that it is regional in scale. We might say that we are from Arlington Heights, but we work, shop, attend schools, go to churches, synagogues, or mosques, and pursue recreation in an increasing variety of locations, all within an expanding metropolitan area. Urban texts in the past have addressed this issue, but they do not take it to heart as the central organizing principle of the discussion as this text does. In Eric Bogosian's brilliant film *Suburbia*, actress Parker Posey portrays an L.A. record promoter on tour who grew up in the affluent Southern California suburbs. When asked by a group of small-town teenagers where she is from, she replies, "I come from an area." We understand that the words *city* and *suburb* fail to connect with the more contemporary reality of daily life.

1

The metropolitan regions of the United States contain an incredible array of people. Our life opportunities vary according to social class, race, gender, ethnicity, age, and family status, among other factors. These important social variables, which are often treated as the traditional subject matter of sociology, in reality interact with locational, or spatial, factors such as the clustering of homes according to family income, the journey to work or school, the diverse ways people pursue a particular lifestyle, the particular patterning of our social networks, the regional search for cultural experiences. In this text we will capture the reality of contemporary urbanism by studying the patterns of everyday life embedded within the urban and suburban settlement spaces that make up the multicentered metropolitan region. These settlement spaces are given special cultural meanings and value by the people living within them. Discovering how these settlement spaces have come to be, the role that economic, political, and social institutions play in creating and changing these spaces, and the processes by which these spaces are given meaning by local inhabitants are all part of the *sociospatial perspective* of the new urban sociology.

If we flew over our metropolitan regions, we would be struck most strongly by the immensity of scale. Urbanized development characteristically extends for one hundred miles around our largest cities. The built-up region contains a mix of cities, suburbs, vacant space, industrial parks, intensely farmed agricultural land, shopping malls, and recreational areas—all of which are interconnected and bridged by communication and commuter networks including highways, rail, telecommunications, and satellite or cellular-based links. The satellite image of the United States at night shown in Figure 1.1 shows the extensive regional development of urban areas across the country. Along the eastern seacoast, the Boston-New York-Washington megalopolis described by Jean Gottman is clearly visible. Similar urban agglomerations can be seen at the southern end of Lake Michigan (the Milwaukee-Chicago-Gary region), and the coastal urban developments in Florida (Miami to Orlando along the east coast, Naples to St. Petersburg on the west coast). The population of these urbanized areas numbers in the millions. Interestingly, most of the people residing in metropolitan regions live in suburban communities outside the large central cities. The dominant position of the suburbs relative to the central cities has existed since at least the 1970s, when census figures brought this change to our attention. At present, some 90 percent of all Americans live in metropolitan regions. But this pattern of urban growth, and the dominance of the suburban region, was not characteristic of cities in the past.

At one time, cities were highly compact spatial forms with a distinct center (the central business district) that dominated, in both an emotional and economic sense, the urbanized area surrounding it. Once inhabitants went outside the city, they would be traveling in the countryside. As the famous urban historian Lewis Mumford observed in *The City in History*, cities served as both huge magnets and containers that concentrated people and economic activities or wealth within well-defined,

FIGURE 1.1 Satellite Image of the United States at Night Showing Metropolitan Areas.
SOURCE: NASA.

bounded spaces. Table 1.1 lists the fifteen most populated cities in the United States. Many of the figures are impressive, such as a total of more than 8.2 million persons for New York City and 3.8 million for Los Angeles.

The numbers demonstrate the great variability in urban growth, with cities like Houston and Phoenix each growing by more than 230,000 persons in less than a decade, while Philadelphia lost nearly 70,000 and Detroit more than 30,000 persons. But these numbers alone do not fully illustrate the massive growth of metropolitan areas and urban regions in the United States. Compare Table 1.1 with Table 1.2 (page 9), which shows the metropolitan regions associated with these large cities. The New York metro region, for example, contains 18 million people, while the area around Los Angeles is home to 16.4 million residents. Even cities that have lost population—such as Philadelphia and Detroit—are in fact part of expanding metropolitan regions, which allows these areas to continue to rank among the top population centers in the country.

Today the city has exploded. No longer is there any one focus or "downtown," as there was in the past. People live and work in widely separated realms. Most of the U.S. population is urban, so most people live in or near some city. But fewer people each year live within the large central cities that were the population foci of the past. Instead, what we now call home is the expanding regions of urbanization that are

TABLE 1.1 Most Populated Cities in the United States, 1980–2007.

	1980	1990	2000	2007	1990–2000	% change	2000–2007	% change
New York City	7,077,000	7,323,000	8,008,000	8,275,000	686,000	9.4	267,000	3.3
Los Angeles	2,967,000	3,485,000	3,695,000	3,834,000	209,000	6.0	139,000	3.8
Chicago	3,005,000	2,784,000	2,896,000	2,837,000	112,000	4.0	–59,000	–2.1
Houston	1,595,000	1,631,000	1,954,000	2,208,000	256,000	15.1	254,000	11.8
Philadelphia	1,688,000	1,586,000	1,518,000	1,450,000	–68,000	–4.3	–68,000	–4.5
Phoenix	790,000	989,000	1,321,000	1,552,000	332,000	33.6	231,000	17.4
San Diego	876,000	1,111,000	1,223,000	1,267,000	112,000	10.1	44,000	3.5
Dallas	904,000	1,007,000	1,189,000	1,240,000	182,000	18.1	51,000	4.4
San Antonio	786,000	997,000	1,145,000	1,329,000	147,000	14.8	184,000	14.7
Detroit	1,203,000	1,028,000	951,000	917,000	–77,000	–7.5	–34,000	–3.6
San Jose	629,000	783,000	895,000	940,000	112,000	14.2	45,000	4.9
Indianapolis	701,000	732,000	782,000	795,000	50,000	6.9	13,000	1.7
San Francisco	679,000	724,000	777,000	765,000	53,000	7.3	–12,000	–1.5
Jacksonville	541,000	635,000	736,000	806,000	101,000	15.8	70,000	9.5
Columbus	565,000	636,000	712,000	748,000	75,000	11.8	36,000	4.9

SOURCE: U.S. Bureau of the Census, *Statistical Abstract of the United States.*

associated with an ever-changing array of cities, towns, suburbs, and exurban areas. This new form of settlement space is called the *multicentered metropolitan region* (MCMR), and it is the first really new way people have organized their living and working arrangements since the beginning of the industrial age. In contrast to the characteristics of the bounded city, this new form of urban space can be typified by two features: It extends over a large region, and it contains many separate manufacturing areas, retail centers, and residential areas, each with its own abilities to draw workers, shoppers, and residents. The urban region can best be understood as composed of different *realms*. Realms are differentiated according to four factors: physical terrain, physical size, the level and kinds of physical activity within the realm (most particularly the kinds of minicenters), and the character of the regional transportation network. Commuting flows are particularly critical both for the creation of metropolitan regions with many different centers and for the connection and interaction of people within the regions (Muller, 1981). In addition to the physical features of the region, it is important that people living within each realm have a shared sense that they occupy an urban space that is different from other areas within the metropolitan region.

For example, Los Angeles contains six distinct realms within a region of approximately fifty square miles and a metropolitan population in 2003 of more than 16 million persons. The six urban realms that comprise the Los Angeles region, shown

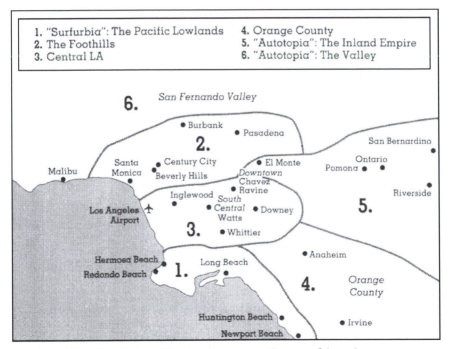

FIGURE 1.2 The Urban Realms of Los Angeles. SOURCE: Courtesy of the authors.

in Figure 1.2, are central Los Angeles (the old city center), the San Fernando Valley (the "valley"), the Pacific foothills (Santa Monica to Pasadena), the Pacific lowlands (Hermosa, Redondo Beach), eastern Orange County (a separate metropolitan region that is exclusively suburban), and the San Gabriel and Pomona valleys (extending eastward and including Pomona, Ontario, and San Bernardino).

DEFINING THE METROPOLITAN REGION

For much of U.S. history, it was sufficient to report information about the population of the central city. Most economic and commercial activity was focused in and around the central business district. By the early 1900s, suburban and regional growth, including planned suburban communities, satellite cities, and other developments, began to challenge the dominant role of the city as employers sought to escape crowded conditions. And the increasing numbers of immigrants, confronted with housing shortages in the cities, began spilling over into the suburban communities. As early as 1920, the U.S. Bureau of the Census sought to capture regional and multicentered growth within metropolitan areas by using the term *metropolitan district* (McKelvey, 1968). For the 1940 census, a new category was created: the *standard metropolitan area* (SMA), which included a city with a population of at least 50,000 persons and the surrounding suburbs and towns. In 1959 this definition was expanded to better reflect the regional growth patterns that included population in centers in two or more counties. The *standard metropolitan statistical area* (SMSA) was defined as a county or counties with a central city of 50,000 or more (or twin cities with a combined population of 50,000 or more) as well as adjacent counties linked economically and socially with the central city.

Box 1.1

Defining the Metropolitan Region

The term *metropolitan region* was first used by the U.S. Census in 1920 to describe the growing cities and suburban areas; since that time, there have been many modifications to capture the dynamic forces at work within metropolitan regions.

Standard metropolitan area (SMA) was the first term used for official metropolitan areas, as defined by the then Bureau of the Budget in 1949 for the 1950 decennial census. It was replaced in 1959 with the term SMSA.

Standard metropolitan statistical area (SMSA) replaced SMA for the official metropolitan areas defined by the then Bureau of the Budget, and was used until MSAs, CMSAs, and PMSAs were introduced in 1983.

continues

Standard consolidated statistical area (SCSA) was a forerunner of the CMSA. An SCSA was a combination of two or more SMSAs that had substantial commuting between them and where at least one of the SMSAs had a population of 1 million or greater. SCSAs were first defined in 1975 and used until June 1983.

Consolidated metropolitan statistical area (CMSA) is a geographic entity defined by the Federal Office of Management and Budget (OMB) for use by federal statistical agencies. An area becomes a CMSA if it meets the requirements to qualify as a metropolitan statistical area (MSA), has a population of 1 million or more, if component parts are recognized as primary metropolitan statistical areas (PMSAs), and if local opinion favors the designation.

Metropolitan statistical area (MSA) is a geographic entity, defined by the OMB for use by federal statistical agencies, based on the concept of a core area with a large population nucleus, plus adjacent communities having a high degree of economic and social integration with that core. Qualification of an MSA requires the presence of a city with 50,000 or more inhabitants, or the presence of an MA (see below) and a total population of at least 100,000 (75,000 in New England). The county or counties containing the largest city and surrounding densely settled territory are central counties of the MSA. Additional outlying counties qualify to be included in the MSA by meeting certain other criteria of metropolitan character, such as a specified minimum population density or percentage of the population that is urban. MSAs in New England are defined in terms of cities and towns, following rules concerning commuting and population density.

Primary metropolitan statistical area (PMSA) is a geographic entity defined by the OMB for use by federal statistical agencies. Metropolitan statistical areas (MSA) with a population of 1 million or more may contain one or more PMSAs if "statistical criteria are met and local opinion is in favor." A PMSA consists of a large urbanized county, or a cluster of such counties (cities and towns in New England) that have substantial commuting interchange.

Metropolitan area (MA) is a collective term, established by the OMB and used for the first time in 1990, to refer to metropolitan statistical areas (MSAs), consolidated metropolitan statistical areas (CMSAs), and primary metropolitan statistical areas (PMSAs).

SOURCE: U.S. Bureau of the Census.

This is determined by measuring the extent to which people in outlying counties travel to work to the designated SMSA. If enough people commute to work from outside city boundaries, the county they reside in becomes part of the SMSA. In 1983 the SMSA was relabeled *metropolitan statistical area* (MSA). While the number of MSAs in the United States continues to grow (the number increased from 254 to

258 between the 1990 and 2000 censuses), two states, Wyoming and Vermont, do not contain any. The seventy-three largest MSAs were designated *primary metropolitan statistical areas* (PMSAs). Because county boundaries vary widely across the United States (except in New England where there are no counties), the usefulness of the MSA classification is somewhat questionable. In the 2000 census, for example, New Jersey is the most urbanized state, with 100 percent of its population living in MSAs. But it is followed by Arizona (88 percent) and Nevada (86 percent), states with just one or two large population centers and where most of the state is rural.

But the regional growth and the sociospatial integration of cities proved to be even more extensive than the social, economic, and political links suggested by the MSA concept. The U.S. Office of Management and Budget created yet another term, the *standard metropolitan consolidated area* (SMCA) to better capture the expansion of the multinucleated urban regions. The SMCA was used for the first time in the 1980 census. It is defined as having a population of at least 1 million persons in two or more PMSAs *and* represents a higher order of integration for metropolitan areas that contain several adjacent metropolitan areas, such as the Los Angeles/Orange County/Riverside/San Bernardino complex in Southern California or the New York/New Jersey/Connecticut complex on the East Coast. Each of these regions contains more people than the entire country of Canada. In the 2000 census, there were eighteen consolidated metropolitan statistical areas in the United States. They are prime illustrations of the concept of the multinucleated metropolitan region that is so important for the new urban sociology.

Table 1.2 reveals important aspects of metropolitan growth in the United States. First, the urban system includes a significant number of metropolitan areas that have large populations rather than only one or two as is often found in developing nations. Second, the population living in the suburban region is often much greater than that of the older central city. Philadelphia had a population of 1.5 million persons in 2007, but its metropolitan region contained some 5.8 million persons, nearly four times as large. The city-suburban population disparity is not simply an artifact of population decline in older industrial cities, however, as we see a similar pattern in the relatively newer Sun Belt cities as well. For example, Phoenix had a population of 1.6 million in 2007, but the total metropolitan area included a population of more than 4.2 million, and Dallas had a population of 1.2 million, but its total metropolitan area included 6.1 million persons—more than five times that of the central city. (Atlanta, one of the most rapidly growing metropolitan areas in the country, had a metropolitan population of 5.3 million persons, but the central city does not rank in the top fifteen in the country.) Third, while metropolitan areas across the Northeast and Midwest have grown slowly or even lost population since the 1970s, the multinucleated metropolitan regions of the South and Southwest grew rapidly during this period (although they have suffered substantially from the recent housing crisis). This illustrates the Sun Belt shift, discussed in Chapter 6. For example, the Los Angeles, Dallas, Houston, San Diego, and Phoenix

TABLE 1.2 Most Populated Metropolitan Regions in the United States, 1980–2007.

	1980	2000	2007 Est.	2000–2007 % Change
New York-NJ-Long Island	17,412,203	18,356,506	18,815,988	10.3
Los Angeles-Anaheim-Riverside	11,497,549	16,374,000	12,875,587	7.9
Chicago-Gary-Hammond	7,973,290	9,158,000	9,522,879	10.4
Dallas-Fort Worth	2,930,568	5,222,000	6,144,489	11.8
Philadelphia-Trenton	5,680,509	6,188,000	5,827,962	9.4
Houston-Galveston-Barzoria	3,099,942	4,670,000	5,629,127	12.1
Miami-Ft. Lauderdale	2,643,766	3,443,501	5,413,212	15.7
Washington-Arlington-Alexandria	3,250,921	4,923,000	5,306,125	10.8
Atlanta-Sandy Springs-Marietta	2,138,136	3,431,983	5,271,550	15.4
Detroit-Warren-Livonia-Ann Arbor	4,762,764	5,456,000	4,817,595	8.8
Boston-Cambridge-Quincy	3,662,888	5,819,000	4,482,857	7.7
San Francisco-Oakland-San Jose	5,367,900	7,039,000	4,203,898	6.0
Phoenix-Mesa-Scottsdale	1,509,175	2,563,582	4,179,427	16.3
Seattle-Tacoma-Bellevue	2,093,285	3,265,139	3,309,347	10.1
Minneapolis-St. Paul-Bloomington	2,137,133	2,723,137	3,208,212	11.8
San Diego-Carlsbad-San Marcos	1,861,846	2,644,132	2,974,859	11.3
St. Louis	2,376,968	2,547,686	2,802,282	11.0
Cleveland-Elyria-Mentor-Akron	2,834,062	2,903,808	2,795,827	9.6
Baltimore-Towson	2,199,497	2,553,000	2,668,056	10.5
Pittsburgh-Beaver Valley	2,423,311	2,394,702	2,355,712	9.8

SOURCE: U.S. Bureau of the Census, *Statistical Abstract of the United States*. *Note:* MSAs are metropolitan statistical areas; CMSAs are consolidated metropolitan statistical areas; NECMAs are New England county metropolitan areas, which are based on townships and require a separate way of aggregating areas in the metropolitan region.

metropolitan regions have all seen double-digit population increases in each decade since 1970.

MEGACITIES AROUND THE WORLD

The world's urban population was estimated at 1 billion in 1960, 2 billion in 1985, and more than 3 billion in 2007. It is expected to increase to 5 billion by 2030—a 60 percent increase in just 25 years. The United Nations estimates that more than 50 percent of the world's population now lives in urban areas, and this number is expected to increase to more than 60 percent by 2030. *For the first time in human history, a majority of the world's population lives in urban areas.* At the current rate of growth, the urban population will double every 38 years, with almost all of the growth occurring in cities and metropolitan regions in the developing world. Migration from rural areas and the transformation of rural settlements into urban places will account for much of the increase (United Nations, 2009).

Not every country in the world is experiencing the same mix of cities, suburbs, and multinucleated centers that is characteristic of regional metropolitan growth in the United States, but all countries are subject to a process of urban development that produces gigantic cities and regional urbanization. Only 78 cities across the globe had populations of 1 million or more in 1950. In 1975 there were 65 metropolitan areas with 10 million or more persons, and by 2000 this number had increased to 251. The growth of large metropolitan regions is also expected to accelerate. In 2015 it is anticipated that there will be 358 urban agglomerations with populations of at least 10 million persons and that more than a third of the world's urban population will live in slums (United Nations, 2003).

Box 1.2

What Does It Mean to Be Urban?

Countries define their urban populations in many ways, which makes comparisons across countries and regions very difficult. Here is a sampling of the definitions for "urban" used in Africa, North America, Europe, and Asia:

Africa
Botswana: Agglomeration of 5,000 or more inhabitants where 75 percent of the economic activity is nonagricultural

Equatorial Guinea: District centers and localities with 300 dwellings and/or 1,500 or more inhabitants

Ethiopia: Localities of 2,000 or more inhabitants

Malawi: All townships and town planning areas and all district centers

Sudan: Localities of administrative and/or commercial importance or with population of 5,000 or more inhabitants

Zambia: Localities of 5,000 or more inhabitants, the majority of whom all depend on nonagricultural activities

North America
Canada: Places of 1,000 or more inhabitants, having a population density of 400 or more per square kilometer

Costa Rica: Administrative centers of cantons

Cuba: Population living in a nucleus of 2,000 or more inhabitants

Greenland: Localities of 200 or more inhabitants

Honduras: Localities of 2,000 or more inhabitants, having essentially urban characteristics

Mexico: Localities of 2,500 or more inhabitants

continues

Europe

France: Communes containing an agglomeration of more than 2,000 inhabitants living in contiguous houses or with not more than 200 meters between houses

Iceland: Localities of 200 or more inhabitants

Poland: Towns and settlements of an urban type, e.g., workers' settlements, fishermen's settlements, health resorts

Portugal: Agglomeration of 10,000 or more inhabitants

Spain: Localities of 2,000 or more inhabitants

Switzerland: Communes of 10,000 or more inhabitants, including suburbs

Asia

Cambodia: Towns

China: Cities only refer to those designated by the state council. In the case of cities with district establishment, the city proper refers to the whole administrative area of the district if its population density is 1,500 persons per kilometer

Indonesia: Places with urban characteristics

Israel: All settlements of more than 2,000 inhabitants, except those where at least one-third of the households, participating in the civilian labor force, earn their living from agriculture

Japan: City *(shi)* having 50,000 or more inhabitants with 60 percent or more of the houses located in the main built-up areas and 60 percent or more of the population engaged in manufacturing, trade, or other urban type of business

Turkey: Population of settlement places, 20,000 and over

SOURCE: United Nations, *Demographic Yearbook 2005*, Table 6.

Our projection of population growth in megacities and urban regions is based upon information from the United Nations. To compile this information, the UN uses information about urban populations provided by countries around the world. But what does it mean to be urban? As we can see from the information in Box 1.2, countries have very different definitions of their "urban" population. In some cases, the definition of urban place is based upon a population threshold, such as agglomerations or localities of 2,500 or more inhabitants (Mexico and the United States), although some countries have higher thresholds (10,000 or more inhabitants in Portugal, 20,000 in Turkey), while others have lower thresholds (just 200 or more inhabitants in Iceland and Greenland). In other cases, the definition of urban place is based upon economic activity (agglomerations of 5,000 or more inhabitants where 75 percent are engaged in nonagricultural work in Botswana), political definition (administrative centers in

Costa Rica, townships and town planning areas in Malawi), or combinations of political and population factors (communes of 10,000 or more inhabitants in Switzerland). The wide range of definitions presents some problems, as living in a town of 10,000 persons in Portugal may be very different from a community of 2,500 in Mexico. This is one of the topics we study in Chapter 3.

Urban growth is distributed very unequally across the globe. According to census estimates from the UN, the largest urban agglomerations in the developed nations will grow slowly, whereas those in other areas of the world will experience explosive growth. Thus, estimates of population growth for the period 2010–2025 for Tokyo, Osaka, New York, Los Angeles, Moscow, and Paris suggest that these urban agglomerations will experience relatively slow growth. In contrast, Mumbai (Bombay), Calcutta, Dhaka, and Delhi (all in India) and Karachi (in Pakistan) are expected to grow by some 4 to 8 million persons each, and São Paolo, Mexico City, and Manila by 2 to 3 million persons. Table 1.3 shows the fifteen largest megacities in the world and their projected populations to the year 2025.

TABLE 1.3 World's Largest Urban Agglomerations, 1975–2025.

Urban Agglomeration	Population (Millions)			Average Annual Rate of Change (percent)	Population Residing in Agglomeration, 2007, as percentage of	
	1975	*2007*	*2025*	*2005–2010*	*Total Population*	*Urban Population*
Tokyo, Japan	26.6	35.7	36.4	0.4	27.9	42.1
New York, United States	15.9	19.0	20.6	0.7	6.2	7.6
Mexico City, Mexico	10.7	19.0	21.0	0.8	17.9	23.2
Mumbai (Bombay), India	7.1	18.9	26.4	2.0	1.5	5.6
São Paulo, Brazil	9.6	18.8	21.4	1.3	9.8	11.5
Delhi, India	4.4	15.9	22.5	2.5	1.4	4.7
Shanghai, China	7.3	15.0	19.4	1.7	1.1	2.7
Calcutta, India	7.9	14.8	20.6	1.7	1.3	4.3
Dhaka, Bangladesh	2.2	13.5	22.0	3.3	8.5	32.0
Buenos Aires, Argentina	8.7	12.8	13.8	0.8	32.4	35.2
Los Angeles, United States	8.9	12.5	13.7	0.7	4.1	5.0
Karachi, Pakistan	4.0	12.1	19.1	2.4	7.4	20.7
Cairo, Egypt	6.4	11.9	15.6	1.7	15.8	36.9
Rio de Janeiro, Brazil	7.6	11.7	13.4	1.2	6.1	7.2
Osaka-Kobe, Japan	9.8	11.3	11.4	0.1	8.8	13.3
Beijing, China	6.0	11.1	14.5	1.8	0.8	2.0
Manila, Philippines	5.0	11.1	14.8	1.6	12.6	19.6
Moscow, Russia	7.6	10.5	10.5	0.2	7.3	10.1
Istanbul, Turkey	3.6	10.1	12.1	1.6	13.4	19.7
Paris, France	8.6	9.9	10.0	0.2	16.1	20.8

SOURCE: United Nations Department of Economic and Social Affairs, *Urban Aggomerations 2007*.

Although the potential benefits from urbanization cannot be overlooked, the speed and scale of what some have called the third urban revolution presents many challenges. The rapid growth and overwhelming sprawl of cities in the developing nations has been given a new term—*hyperurbanization* (see Chapter 12). New groups of policymakers and organizations are emerging to take up responsibilities of urban governance in developing nations around the globe. As national governments in many developing countries have decentralized their functions and reduced support for social programs, responsibility for poverty, health, education, and public services is increasingly being placed in the hands of untested municipal and regional governments. While the acceleration of urban growth in developing countries suggests staggering social costs for many persons around the world, the continuing growth of multinucleated metropolitan regions in the United States and other developed nations also presents serious challenges for policymakers, governments, and those of us who live in the urban world.

A NEW APPROACH TO URBAN SOCIOLOGY

How did these changes come about? What is daily life like in a multinucleated metropolitan region? How do everyday activities there differ from those in the past? How has the city construction process, or *urbanization*, given way to the regional process of concentrated central city development, dispersed minicentered districts, and sprawling suburbanization? What is metropolitan culture like in the new regional spaces, and how does it differ from city life of the past? The answers to these and other questions are the subject of this book. Our discussion is about urban sociology, but it is not about the city alone, as is often the case in the urban sociology literature. In the pages that follow, we take an integrated perspective that complements the regional focus of the multinucleated metropolitan region.

We consider everyday life in the suburbs (suburban settlement space as well as in the city or urban settlement space). But there is much more. The new urban sociology has three additional dimensions: the shift to a global perspective, attention to the political economy of pull factors (government policies including mortgage guarantees for lenders, tax deductions for homeowners, and the like) in urban and suburban development, and an appreciation for the role of culture in metropolitan life and in the construction of the built environment.

GLOBAL CAPITALISM AND THE METROPOLIS

The patterns of everyday life that we observe in the contemporary metropolis are the consequence of the complicated and continuing interaction of economic, political, and cultural forces that have not always been studied in urban sociology. In recent years, urbanists have come to appreciate just how important the link is between cities or suburbs and changes in the economy. Prior to the 1970s, discussions about urban political economy assumed that the most critical influence on urban growth and development was the behavior of local business people. A resident of a town might open up a store or factory. The owner would be known by others in the area. Jobs would be created, and local residents would apply for and fill them. Products of factories might be sold nationally, but locals would take pride in homegrown commodities and support the businesses of neighbors with their patronage, often because there was no place else to go. This was the way of life described in *Middletown*, the classic study of the American industrial town in the 1930s (Lynd and Lynd, 1929). But times have changed and seem to be changing even more quickly in the twenty-first century. Robert and Helen Lynd documented important changes in Middletown as local businesses came under the control of national companies—and their book *Middletown Revisited* was published more than seventy years ago (Lynd and Lynd, 1937)!

Now economic activity in metropolitan communities is increasingly controlled by decisions made at the global level. Businesses are owned and managed by people from distant locations. The local television repair shop, for example, may represent a manufacturer, such as Sony, whose headquarters are in another country, say Japan. The television sets themselves may be assembled in Korea or Malaysia. Finally, the selling and repair of the company's product may be supervised by foreign representatives of the manufacturer living in the United States. Reversing this example, many U.S. companies, such as Motorola and Proctor & Gamble, engage in manufacturing, marketing, and administrative activities overseas; corporate profits for U.S. companies in China were reported at more than $2 billion for the first half of 2006. In short, economies today are linked across the globe, and the small, family-run business with connections to the local community has given way to the multinational corporation and the global flow of investment as the dominant economic forces.

The global perspective has important implications for the study of metropolitan regions. Prior to the 1970s, urban sociologists saw changes in the city as emerging from the interaction of many local interests in a shared and common space. The *ecological* approach, as it is called, meant that the organization of the city was not caused by "the planned or artificial contrivance of anyone" but emerged full-grown out of the "many independent personal decisions based on moral, political, ecological, and economic considerations" (Suttles, 1972:8). Today we possess a different understanding of urban organization as being caused by the actions of powerful interests, many of which have their home bases in places far removed from local communities. Their decisions, for example, to open a plant in one location, close one down in another, buy up farms to build houses, or tear down existing housing to create mini-malls or apartment buildings are all so important that they affect the well-being of the entire community.

The perspective adopted in this text, however, does not suggest that all important influences on metropolitan development derive from the global level. Important economic and political forces also arise from within local communities that can account for change. In the following chapters, therefore, we will consider the contribution to metropolitan development of all sociospatial levels: the global, the national, and the local. It is the interplay of the forces from the different levels within the local space that is the most interesting.

Since the 1970s, urban scholars have paid increasing attention to the relationship between capitalism and the metropolis (see Chapter 4). Competition among businesses that may not have a direct effect on urban space has been overshadowed by the competition among different places for their share of global investment (see Chapters 5, 12, and 13). Local populations and community well-being are also affected by changes in employment, the level of economic activity, and growing lifestyle disparities between low-skilled or semiskilled workers and professionals living in the metropolis (see Chapter 10). All of these aspects constitute a new dimension to the study of urban sociology.

SUPPLY-SIDE FACTORS IN URBAN DEVELOPMENT

Prior to the 1970s, urban scholars looked at city and suburban growth as an expression of individual desires. For example, people moved from the city to the suburbs, it was believed, because they preferred the lifestyle in the suburbs. Or investors picked a particular plot of land to develop because they liked its size and location. Individual actions based on individually held beliefs or needs might be termed the *demand side* of market activity because they express the ways in which people and business act on their own desires. Urban sociology prior to the 1970s viewed growth almost exclusively in this manner.

At present, we are aware of several factors that operate to promote development in specific ways and thereby mold individual desires through incentives. These factors represent the *supply side* of market activity resulting from individual choice. Powerful social forces can create opportunities that persuade people to follow courses of action that they otherwise might not. Two important supply-side sources of incentives in the development of metropolitan regions are government and the real estate industry.

The Role of Government in Urban Development

The abstract model of capitalism represents economic systems as involving limited government intervention. This is not the case for modern economies. The United States, like other industrialized nations, has an economy that is influenced not only by government regulations but also by the direct spending of government tax dollars on particular public projects. The combined action of laws or regulations and direct investment provides incentives for both businesses and individual consumers to behave in certain ways.

When city dwellers who are renters decide that they want to move to the suburbs, they are expressing their personal preference. This decision may be occasioned by demand-side factors such as problems with the public schools and high rents that in effect push them out of the city. Our suburban movers likely have chosen a suburb with single-family homes that are affordable within their household budget. Because of government tax incentives on mortgage payments, it pays to own your home rather than rent. Government programs provide an enticement that pulls people in the direction of homeownership in the suburbs.

In every case the decision to move to the suburbs is a complex one that is prompted by both demand- and supply-side factors. For years urban sociologists focused on individual decisions and neglected the supply-side factors. The housing crisis of the past decade has focused attention on the way government at the local, state, and federal levels has operated to create opportunities and incentives that channel behavior in specific ways. In subsequent chapters we will see how this "political economy," the linked actions of business and government in urban development, promotes the growth of the multinucleated metropolitan region.

Another major and recent change in the population distribution of the United States has been the rise of the Sun Belt. By the time of the 2000 population census, the majority of Americans lived in the Sun Belt and western states. This transformation represents a phenomenal shift of residential location. Historically, the Midwest and the East Coast contained the majority of the U.S. population, and this remained true until the post–World War II period.

According to the old urban sociology, the shift to the Sun Belt would have been explained by technological factors, such as inexpensive airline travel and demand-side preferences for a mild climate. To be sure, these factors are part of the equation. However, the pull factors created by the political economy of the United States and its government spending cannot be ignored. They are, in fact, the major reasons for Sun Belt growth because this federal outlay created millions of jobs that provided the base for Sun Belt growth and expansion. One aspect alone tells a good part of the story. Beginning with World War II, the United States spent billions of dollars on military installations in locations in the West and in the Sun Belt. California, Florida, Georgia, and New Mexico, among others, were recipients of vast sums of spending. Even Las Vegas, which had been growing as the country's gambling mecca after the war, benefited from large-scale government spending that created jobs—first, with the construction of Boulder Dam, and then with the placement of the gigantic Nellis Air Force base in the region. Later, the Korean and Vietnam wars reinforced this pattern. The states of Texas and Florida benefited greatly from the NASA space program, as we know from the familiar names of "Houston Control" and "Cape Kennedy." The old urban sociology simply ignored the effects of government spending and tax incentives, that is, the *political economy* of urban development in the United States. But the sociospatial perspective considers this factor to be of central importance.

The Role of the Real Estate Industry in Development

With some notable exceptions (Hoyt, 1933; Hughes, 1928; Form, 1954), early urban sociologists neglected the critical role the real estate industry plays in metropolitan development. Recall from the discussion above that at one time, urban organization was viewed not as the product of any particular interest but as the interplay of many separate interests (the ecological approach). Presently, we understand that the opposite is often the case. Special interests such as global corporations or even investment firms can make or break a town depending on where they decide to invest new capital. But the single most important source of special interests in the development of the metropolis is the real estate industry.

The real estate sector includes corporations and banks, as well as land developers and construction companies, that invest in the development of land use and housing, including the land and the built environment themselves. The construction of new spaces proceeds through the actions of all those individuals, financial conduits, and corporations that make money from the change (or turnover) in land use. Because a great deal of money can be made through this type of activity, real estate interests are powerful special actors in the development of the metropolis, and their influence is greatly felt.

At any given time and on any piece of land, real estate forces can converge to turn over the existing use and engage in development that changes the utilization of local space. All of this is done in the pursuit of profit that comes as a consequence of development. In recent decades, mortgages have been bought and sold as investments on national and even international markets as speculative investments, and the resulting collapse of the derivative markets has led to the collapse of funding mechanisms for the auto industry, of international banking institutions, and the investment funds of many towns and cities across the United States. Thus, in addition to understanding the political economy of production, it is important to understand the political economy of real estate.

THE IMPORTANCE OF CULTURE
IN METROPOLITAN LIFE

The discussion of urban issues often involves economic and political concerns. As we have seen, some of the more important aspects of the new urban sociology emphasize a greater attention to political economy. But this is not all there is to the new approach. People live in a symbolic world that is meaningful to them. They possess sentiments and ideas and attempt to communicate with others using common concepts.

Social interaction in human societies is organized through the direct use of spoken or written language. A significant part, however, employs expressive symbols that are used to convey meanings. One of the principal sources of symbolic life involves aspects of the built environment. Cities and suburbs are the sites of many subcultures—ethnic, religious, racial, gender specific, and age related. Neighborhoods within the metropolis can readily be identified by objects that are signs of subcultural status. For example, ethnic areas of the city advertise themselves by the signs in front of restaurants, bakeries, specialty shops, and religious institutions (see Chapter 8). Architecture is often used to convey images of power and wealth, and in the United States, government buildings using classical architecture are intended to display democratic ideals (see Figure 1.3). People use such signs to orient themselves as they engage in metropolitan life.

The study of culture and the role of objects as signs constitute a significant part of the new urban sociology. Sociologists have studied metropolitan life as culturally meaningful for some time. What is new and different is the way such meanings are associated with objects in addition to words. For example, cities often try to develop an image that boosts attention in order to attract investment and tourists. A variety of images have been used, such as signs of industry ("Motor City"), signs of regional

FIGURE 1.3 Urban Semiotics and the Built Environment. Many government buildings in the United States make use of architectural elements from classical Greek architecture and are meant to recall ideas of Athenian democracy. Learning how to read the urban environment is an example of urban semiotics. As shown in the photograph above, the U.S. Supreme Court building, situated on a hill with an entry reminiscent of the Parthenon, is meant to convey an image of power and democracy (although the supreme court judges are not, in fact, elected officials). SOURCE: Photo courtesy of Heather Hutchison.

growth ("the Twin Cities"), signs of vision ("the city of tomorrow"), and signs of prosperity and enjoyment ("the city of leisure"). Slogans such as these are often linked to images or objects, such as a skyline or a graphic logo of some kind. In this way, a particular symbolic identity is created for a place that gives the impression that it is special. The study of culture that links symbols to objects is called *semiotics*, and the special subfield that studies the built environment in this manner is called *spatial semiotics*. Chapter 4 discusses this approach in more detail.

In the past, approaches to urban sociology have neglected the symbolic aspect of space, although some interesting early exceptions exist (see Wohl and Strauss, 1958). The perspective we will follow integrates the symbolic nature of environments with more traditional factors that make up social behavior, such as class, race, gender, age, and social status. Space, then, is another compositional factor in human behavior. We call this new perspective on metropolitan life the *sociospatial* approach.

THE SOCIOSPATIAL APPROACH

Typical urban sociology textbooks present several alternative ways of understanding sociospatial phenomena, or they present none at all and simply describe a succession of topics. Our text, while reviewing alternatives, takes a definite conceptual stand. We subscribe to the Lefebvrian turn in urban studies—including geography, urban planning, political economy, and sociology—which we have developed as the "sociospatial approach" to urban sociology.

In the past, urbanists have regarded space as only a container of social activities. But this view is limited. Space not only contains actions but also constitutes a part of social relations and is intimately involved in our daily lives. It affects the way we feel about what we do. In turn, people alter space and construct new environments to better fit their needs. Hence, a dual relationship exists between people and space. On the one hand, human beings act according to social factors such as gender, class, race, age, and status within and in reaction to a given space. When a city converts a vacant lot into a basketball court, the type of activity and interaction of groups of persons within that space will change. On the other hand, people create and alter spaces to express their own needs and desires.

The sociospatial perspective is developed around the study of everyday life in contemporary urban society. It recognizes that the urban and suburban settlement spaces that make up the built environment are situated within a larger metropolitan region. We adopt a regional perspective to study the older central cities, suburban communities, and new growth poles that make up the metropolitan region of the twenty-first century. We call this new form of social space the *multicentered metropolitan region*. We ask how and why multicentered metropolitan regions in the United States and across the globe came to be structured the way they are. The characteristics of our perspective are summarized in Box 1.3.

Box 1.3

The Sociospatial Perspective

The sociospatial perspective focuses our attention on how everyday life in the mult-inucleated metropolitan region is affected by the political economy of urban life—the interplay of cultural, political, economic, and social forces both within and outside of urban communities:

1. The urban and suburban settlement spaces that comprise the built environment are part of a larger metropolitan region. It is necessary to adopt a regional perspective to understand the multinucleated metropolitan regions of the twenty-first century.
2. The multinucleated metropolitan region is linked to the global system of capitalism where decisions influence the well-being of local areas made from the metropolitan, the national, or even the international level.
3. Metropolitan development is affected by government policy and by developers, financiers, and other institutions in the real estate industry that create incentives and opportunities that mold the behaviors, preferences, and choices of individual consumers.
4. Everyday life is organized according to cultural symbols and material objects that are part of the built environment; these symbols and objects are likely to have different meanings to different individuals or groups. We call the study of these symbols and objects urban semiotics.
5. The spatial arrangements found in urban and suburban settlement space have both manifest and latent consequences. They influence human behavior and interaction in predictable ways but also in ways the original planner or developer may not have anticipated. But individuals, through their behaviors and interactions with others, constantly alter existing spatial arrangements and construct new spaces to express their needs and desires.

The sociospatial perspective emphasizes the interaction between society and space. Within the multicentered metropolitan region, groups differ from one another with respect to lifestyle, attitudes, beliefs, and access to political power and influence, and consequently they have more or less influence on decisions about how social space is allocated and structured within and across the metropolitan region. To class, gender, race, and other social characteristics that define difference among groups in contemporary society we add the element of space itself. The spatial arrangements found in urban and suburban settlement space have both manifest and latent consequences: They influence human behavior and interaction in predictable ways but also in ways the original planner or developer may not have anticipated. Individuals and groups, through their behaviors and interactions with others, constantly alter existing spatial arrangements and construct new spaces to express their needs and desires.

The sociospatial perspective connects the dual relationship between people and space with the social factors that are the bases of individual behavior. The most fundamental concept of this approach is *settlement space,* which refers to the built environment in which people live. Settlement space is both constructed and organized. It is built by people who have followed some meaningful plan for the purpose of containing economic, political, and cultural activities. Within it, people organize their daily actions according to the meaningful aspects of the constructed space. In subsequent chapters we will discuss how sociospatial factors determine the construction and use of settlement space. Over time we will also see how change has occurred and how the built environment is in turn molded by sociospatial factors.

KEY CONCEPTS

multinucleated metropolitan region
standard metropolitan statistical area
standard metropolitan consolidated area
megacity
global capitalism
demand-side factors
supply-side factors
political economy
built environment
urban semiotics
sociospatial perspective
settlement space

DISCUSSION QUESTIONS

1. What is meant by the concept of the "multinucleated metropolitan region"? How is the multinucleated metropolitan region different from urban development of the past? Why is the metropolitan regional perspective important for understanding urban growth around the globe?

2. The authors suggest that most of the time we do not consciously think about or identify the metropolitan region from which we come. What are some of the characteristics of the metropolitan region in which you grew up?

3. The authors believe that other approaches to urban sociology, which focus upon urban neighborhoods and urban ethnic groups, are no longer useful for understanding metropolitan life in the United States. Why do they hold this point of view?

4. The sociospatial approach to urban sociology emphasizes the links with the global system of capitalism, the actions of the real estate industry, government policies, pull factors of development, the social organization of urban and suburban settlement space, and the importance of culture. Pick two of these factors and explain how they have influenced the development of the multinucleated metropolitan region in which you live.

5. The concept of "space" is important in our understanding of metropolitan life. List two important characteristics of this concept and discuss their significance for our understanding of daily life in urban and suburban settlement spaces of the multinucleated metropolitan region.

THE ORIGINS OF URBAN LIFE

Five thousand years of urban history and perhaps as many of proto-urban history are spread over a few score of only partly exposed sites. The great urban landmarks Ur, Nippur, Uruk, Thebes, Helopolis, Assur, Ninevah, Babylon, cover a span of three thousand years whose vast emptiness we cannot hope to fill with a handful of monuments and a few hundred pages of written records.

LEWIS MUMFORD, *THE CITY IN HISTORY*

The origins of urban life—the period when humankind was transformed from hunters and gatherers to city dwellers—is shrouded in the distant past. Yet we know that cities and urban civilizations appeared in many different areas of the world independent of one another in the relatively recent past. Urbanization, or the building of and living in compact, densely populated places, appeared as early as 10,000 years ago. Continuously used, densely populated settlements can be found in the Middle East dating back over 6,000 years and in the Indus Valley in India dating back over 4,000 years. Other centers of ancient urban life include the Minoan civilization of Crete (1800 BC) and the cities of China (circa 2000 BC). The origins of the earliest urban settlements are shown in Table 2.1.

The population of ancient cities tended to be small by present-day standards. The great city of Ur, home of Abraham, likely had a population of 65,000 in 2000 BC, when it was the largest city in the world. At its peak in the fifth century BC, classical Athens, the birthplace of Western art, architecture, and philosophy, had no more than 150,000 inhabitants. Until the late Middle Ages, no European city could compare with ancient Rome, which housed more than 1 million people in the first century AD.

Lewis Mumford, the great scholar of urban history and culture, has suggested that the first human settlements were cities of the dead—the Thanatopolis. The dead were the first to have a permanent dwelling (the caverns and mounds where Paleolithic hunters buried their dead). Men and women would return to these ritual

TABLE 2.1 World's Earliest Cities.

Region	Location	Approximate Date
Mesopotamia	Tigris and Euphrates rivers	3900 BC
Egypt	Nile River valley	3200 BC
India	Indus River valley	2400 BC
Eastern Mediterranean	Crete	1600 BC
China	Yellow River valley	1600 BC
Mexico	Yucatan Peninsula	200 BC

SOURCE: Ivan Light, *Cities in World Perspective* (New York: Macmillan, 1983), 13. Population estimates rounded to nearest 10,000.

spaces to worship ancestors, and it is here that humankind first drew pictographs and paintings of not only animals for the hunt but also formalized figures of men and women. Mumford writes (1961:10): "The first germ of the city, then, is in the ceremonial meeting place that serves as the goal for pilgrimage: a site to which family or clan groups are drawn back, at seasonable intervals, because it concentrates, in addition to any natural advantages that it may have, certain 'spiritual' or supernatural powers, powers of higher potency and duration, of wider cosmic significance, than the ordinary processes of life."

Several ancient cities possessed remarkable structural features that made urban living not only possible but also quite comfortable. The residential space of Mohenjo-Daro in ancient India was built on a grid street system that made maximum use of space and included an open sewer system for the elimination of waste and rainwater. Baked clay sewer pipes and roofing tiles have been unearthed at the site of this early city that are identical to the materials used in modern construction. Two-story houses were constructed around a central courtyard with balconies on the second floor. The courtyard provided private space for families but also allowed for the circulation of air through the building—important for the hot climate of the region. Jericho, in ancient Israel, possessed a system of canals that facilitated the irrigation of fields outside the city. However, it is easy to overemphasize these special cases. Many, if not most, ancient cities were plagued by unsanitary housing conditions and streets, and these problems would increase as cities grew in size.

The citizens of the early towns lived an urban life that was fragile. Precariousness was, perhaps, an inevitable consequence of the growth of cities. According to Gideon Sjoberg, cities were the sites of power. In order to be secure, it was necessary for early cities to exercise their strength and dominate the hinterland (the relatively less developed area outside the boundaries of the large city). Then, in order to prosper, it was necessary to expand the hinterland sphere of domination. As sites of wealth, ancient cities were protected by fortifications, and warfare between cities was quite common (Sjoberg, 1960). Average town citizens lived under the constant threat of attack by roving bands of warriors or armies from other towns. Often victors simply killed off or enslaved defeated city populations and then burned the city to the ground. In the book of Judges in the Old Testament, we read, "And he took the city, and slew the people that was therein, and he beat down the city, and sowed it with salt" (Judges 9:45). Once salt has been spread on farm fields, the land can never again be used to grow crops.

We have many accounts of the destruction of early cities in the writings that have come down to us from the earliest urban civilizations. The section of the Old Testament called Lamentations was written by the prophet Jeremiah, who was a court official in

---

Box 2.1

Lamentations of Jeremiah (Old Testament)

How doth the city sit solitary, that was full of people! How is she become as a widow! She that was great among the nations, and princess among the provinces, how is she become tributary!

She weepeth sore in the night, and her tears are on her cheeks; she hath none to comfort her among all her lovers; all her friends have dealt treacherously with her, they are become her enemies.

Judah is gone into captivity because of affliction, and because of great servitude: she dwelleth among the heathen, she findeth no rest: all her persecutors overtook her between the straits.

The ways of Zion do mourn, because none come to the solemn feasts: all her gates are desolate: her priests sigh, her virgins are afflicted, and she is in bitterness.

Her adversaries are become the head, her enemies are at ease; for the Lord hath afflicted her for the multitude of her transgressions; her young children are gone into captivity before the adversary.

And from the daughter of Zion all her beauty is departed: her princes are become like harts that find no pasture, and they are gone without strength before the pursuer.

Jerusalem remembereth in the days of her affliction and of her anguish all her treasures that she had from the days of old; now that her people fall by the hand of the adversary, and none doth help her, the adversaries have seen her, they have mocked at her desolations.

Is it nothing to you, all ye that pass by? Behold, and see if there be any sorrow like unto my sorrow, which is done unto me, wherewith the LORD hath afflicted me in the day of his fierce anger.

For these things I weep; mine eye, mine eye runneth down with water; because the comforter is far from me, even he that should refresh my soul; my children are desolate, because the enemy hath prevailed.

SOURCE: Lamentations 1:1–7, 1:12, 1:16 (*Old Testament*, King James version).

Jerusalem when the city was conquered by the Babylonian ruler Nebuchadnezzar in 587 BC. In Lamentations, the ancient Hebrews lament the loss of their city from their exile in Babylonia (see Box 2.1). In *The Trojan Women*, the Greek author Euripides wrote about the destruction of the ancient city of Troy. The actual destruction of Troy is not included in Homer's great epic *The Iliad* but instead comes to us from the *Posthomericus* (*The Fall of Troy*) by Quintus Smyrnaeus, a fourth-century AD poet in the city of Smyrna. After their defeat by the Greeks, the Trojan men were killed or taken into slavery, and the women were parceled out to the victors. The scene is described by Quintus Smyrnaeus:

> *Troy's daughters therewithal in scattered bands*
> *They haled down seaward—virgins yet unwed,*
> *And new-made brides, and matrons silver-haired,*
> *And mothers from whose bosoms foes had torn*
> *Babes for the last time closing lips on breasts.*
> *Each hero led a wailing Trojan woman to his ship.*
> *Here, there, uprose from these the wild lament,*
> *The woeful-mingling cries of mother and babe.*

In *The Trojan Women*, Hecuba, the former queen of Troy, speaks to the audience and describes the events in Troy shortly after the capture of the city (see Box 2.2). These two stories illustrate the unhappy fate of the inhabitants of the early cities in the face of war among competing city-states.

The domination of urban settlements by successful rulers in search of increased wealth and treasure led, in turn, not only to increased trade and commerce, but also to continued conflict as the new city-states sought to exercise power over the countryside. Early urban existence constituted a drama involving such interwoven spheres of everyday life as agricultural production, regional and foreign trade, military conquest and rule, and the pursuit of arts and sciences based on the relative success of economic and political activities. In his great work *The City in History*, Lewis Mumford asks us to consider the implications of this history when he notes that the civilizations that survived this period of human history were those that were the most warlike and able to destroy their competitors (Mumford, 1961).

Most discussions of early cities focus on the division of labor and economic activities around which the concentrated population was organized. In this way, city life is presented as a progression from limited to complex specialization of work and functional organization. Not only were cities the locus of agriculture, trade, and manufacturing; they created *social spaces* that had religious meaning and significance. Cities did not simply appear because certain fundamental economic activities had matured. Cities had to be produced, or constructed, by humans through the conscious intent of individuals and groups. In ancient societies, urban settlements were built using a

Box 2.2		

The Fate of the Trojan Women

Lift thy head, unhappy lady, from the ground; thy neck upraise; this is Troy no more, no longer am I queen in Ilium. Though fortune change, endure thy lot; sail with the stream, and follow fortune's tack, steer not thy barque of life against the tide, since chance must guide thy course.

Ah me! ah me! What else but tears is now my hapless lot, whose country, children, husband, all are lost? Ah! the high-blown pride of ancestors! How cabined now, how brought to nothing after all. What woe must I suppress, or what declare? What plaintive dirge shall I awake?

Ah, woe is me! The anguish I suffer lying here stretched upon this pallet hard! O my head, my temples, my side! Ah! could I but turn over, and he now on this, now on that, to rest my back and spine, while ceaselessly my tearful wail ascends. For 'en this is music to the wretched, to chant their cheerless dirge of sorrow.

Ah! hapless wives of those mail-clad sons of Troy! Ah! poor maidens, luckless brides, come weep, for Ilium is now but a ruin; and I, like some mother-bird that o'er her fledglings screams, will begin the strain; how different from that song I sang to the gods in days long past, as I leaned on Priam's staff, and beat with my foot in Phrygian time to lead the dance!

Oh! do not bid the wild Cassandra leave her chamber, the frantic prophetess, for Argives to insult, nor to my griefs add yet another. Woe to thee, ill-fated Troy, thy sun is set; and woe to thy unhappy children, quick and dead alike, who are leaving thee behind!

Ah me! ah me! Whose slave shall I become in my old age? in what far clime? a poor old drone, the wretched copy of a corpse, set to keep the gate or tend their children, I who once held royal rank in Troy.

O my country, O unhappy land, I weep for thee now left behind; now dost thou behold thy piteous end; and thee, my house, I weep, wherein I suffered travail. O my children! reft of her city as your mother is, she now is losing you. Oh, what mourning and what sorrow! oh, what endless streams of tears in our houses! The dead alone forget their griefs and never shed a tear.

SOURCE: Euripides, *The Trojan Women* (Oxford University Press, 2009).

shared set of symbols and a model of space that was inherently meaningful to each group (Lagopoulos, 1986). Early cities, such as Ur in ancient Sumer, were produced using cosmological codes that mandated geometrical relations between the city and the heavens, such as an east-west axis, and within the city through geometrical arrangements of the buildings. In this way, the built environment of even the earliest urban settlements had important social, political, and religious connections that created a sense of shared history and identity among the urban inhabitants.

Religious codes distinguished between sacred and profane spaces and endowed particular structures and spaces with the protection of the gods. Around 500 BC, the Etruscans, ancestors of the Romans, built cities by first plowing a "sacred furrow" as a large enclosure in a religious ceremony. The city could be built only within this space, signifying the sacred domain, separated from the profane space of the rest of the world. Only later, in fourteenth- and fifteenth-century Europe, did cities first appear without religious or cosmological codes guiding the construction of space. At this time, and continuing to the present day in Europe (and the United States), the meaning of a building (such as a bank) corresponded to the function it performed in the society with no necessary connection to any particular social or religious meaning. In contrast, in the earliest human settlements, and through at least the time of the medieval city, there was a strong connection between buildings and the way individuals living within the city conceived of the meanings of those buildings (such as the sacred treasuries at Delphi and Olympus in ancient Greece; Pedley, 2005).

As the sociospatial perspective suggests, the ancient city was the combined product of political power, economic functions, and overarching symbolic meanings that expressed deeply held beliefs of the inhabitants.

ANCIENT URBANIZATION

Social scientists are interested in the origin of cities because the process of early urbanization holds insights into the origins of social structure. In particular, the origin of the first urban communities provides clues for understanding how complex social relations arose and how strong bonds were maintained among residents who were often unrelated. The best-known theory of the rise of cities was proposed by V. Gordon Childe (1950, 1954). According to Childe, the first cities developed a form of social organization that differed from rural society in many respects and provided the social basis for modern life.

Childe viewed the development of society in terms of distinct stages and considered the emergence of urban life as a critical evolutionary phase in the rise of modern civilization. City building was part of an "urban revolution" that also brought a set of special social relations that are characteristic of modern life. The first step toward an urban society occurred when hunting and gathering societies shifted to food production in relatively stable and sedentary groups. Once the urban revolution began, civilization progressed and evolved to more complex forms of social life sustained by an urban economy based on trade and craft production. It is principally from Childe that we have derived the idea that urbanization develops through specialization of work and the separation of different functions through increasing interdependence of societal tasks. These social relations were considered different from those found in rural society, and they provided the basis for modern civilization.

Childe's theory of early urbanization was quite influential and may be accurate as a descriptive interpretation of ancient city life based on evidence from cities in Mesopotamia. But it is important to recognize that what Childe has done is to describe

---

Box 2.3

The Urban Revolution

In his essay, "The Urban Revolution," V. Gordon Childe noted that the development of the first cities was marked by a number of important innovations, including the following:

Increased population size and density: By 3000 BC, Ninevah, Ur, Uruk, and other Sumerian cities each had as many as 20,000 persons, larger than other human settlements up to that time.

Concentration of agricultural surplus: Farmers living within the region controlled by the city paid a tithe, or tax, to an "imaginary deity or a divine king" to support soldiers, priests, and other officials.

Public works and monuments: Irrigation projects built by the state (through labor required of all citizens) allowed farmers to produce an agricultural surplus; the cities were dominated by temples (ziggurats) rising from a stepped brick platform.

Specialization of labor: The production of an agricultural surplus freed individuals to perform the specialized tasks required of artists, craftspeople, merchants, soldiers, and priests.

Invention of writing: Systems of writing and numerical notation were necessary for record-keeping to keep track of commercial accounts and tax payments.

Social stratification: Priests, military leaders, and other officials formed a ruling class and were exempt from manual labor; workers and craftspeople were "relieved from intellectual tasks" but were guaranteed safety within the city.

Development of the arts: Artists and craftspeople developed sophisticated styles and traditions in the decorative and fine arts with the depiction of persons and animals.

Development of sciences: Sciences were developed to predict, measure, and standardize to assist in the production of agriculture and the keeping of tax records (arithmetic, geometry, and astronomy).

Membership: Participation in the community was based on residence and was no longer dependent on kinship.

Long-distance trade: Raw materials not available in the local area were imported for craft production and religious ceremonies.

SOURCE: V. Gordon Childe, "The Urban Revolution," 1950.

the findings of contemporary discoveries in early cities: It is not a theory of the origins of urban life. Note that it is not possible to find any one feature of the early city (described in Box 2.3) as an essential prerequisite for the development of any other feature. Like other models of its day, it asserted an evolutionary view of development according to which civilization passes first through the stage of hunting and gathering, then to agriculture, and finally to urban-based economies, with an ever more complex and interdependent form of social organization leading to a contemporary "modern" stage.

Other evidence, however, suggests a discontinuous process of development. Archeologists have known for some time that signs of civilization, such as the production of pottery in quantity or the use of writing, coexisted with the development of agriculture rather than appearing at the later stages of agriculturally based societies as evolutionary theories maintain. Because of the need to create a livelihood on marginal agricultural lands, early residents of towns innovated alternative economic activities, including trade, full-time craft work, and even religion, yielding products that could be exchanged for essential goods, thereby providing the basis for a city-based economy that could survive on trade. And many early cities disappeared because of the depletion of natural resources required to support concentrated populations.

While the social division of labor and its growing complexity certainly contributed to urban development, economic factors alone did not produce the first cities. The market by itself can never provide adequate control or guidance—that is, *regulation*—for social organization. In fact, the classical sociologists Emile Durkheim, Karl Marx, and Max Weber all showed that everyday actions in a market society generate problems and conflict that call for regulation by political and cultural means. "The most important of such problems were the construction of trust or solidarity (stressed by Durkheim), the regulation of power (Marx and Weber), and the provision of both meaning and legitimation for social activities so prized by Weber" (Eisenstadt and Shachar, 1987:50).

CLASSICAL CITIES

The earliest cities in Mesopotamia and in China were built according to complex belief systems and symbolic codes, as shown by city gates devoted to specific deities that were oriented to the cardinal points of the compass (north, east, south, and west), and a street layout that would prevent spirits from moving directly to the center of the city. In ancient Greece, cities were constructed according to a cosmological code that incorporated sacred spaces and religious symbols linked to the pantheon of Greek gods. The city of Athens was built to honor the goddess Athena, and all buildings followed geometrical design principles in accordance with the "golden mean." In the center of the circle that encompassed the city was the *agora*, which was not simply the marketplace but the public hearth or *hestia koine*, the center of the community. Over a period of two hundred years, the agora at the base of the acropolis took form as public buildings—courts, libraries, temples, gymnasium—gradually closed in the open area, creating an enclosed space where the public life of the city was focused. The public hearth was considered to be the *omphalos*, the center of the world.

Visitors would pass through the agora along the Pan-Athenaic Way, walk past the *stoa* (public marketplace), and then ascend the *propylaea*, the gateway to the sacred temples at the top of the acropolis, designed and built by the architect Mnesicles from 430 to 420 BC. Robin Rhodes (1995:53) describes the ascent of the acropolis: "Its architecture, in concert with the Panathenaic procession, progressed step by step from the west, from the realm of the secular, the human, the realm of stories, of human explanation, to the elemental religious experience of divine epiphany at the east side of the tenemos, at the front of the major temples to Athena."

Most striking of all, as visitors walked up the great stairway on the Acropolis, they would pass the columns of the first temples, destroyed by the Persian armies in 480 BC, which were built into the walls of the new stairway as a reminder of this earlier history.

FIGURE 2.1 Restoration of the Acropolis at Athens. Following the destruction of Athens by the Persian army in 480 BC, the temples on the Acropolis were rebuilt, and a ceremonial entrance (the propylae) was added. Pieces of the earlier temples were used in reconstructing the north wall, visible to Athenians from the city below. The entire structure became a monument to the city's history. SOURCE: P.V.N. Meyes, *A General History for Colleges and High Schools*, Rev. Ed. (New York: Ginn & Co., 1906).

Active participation in all parts of public life was the central organizing concept for Athenians, and urban space within Athens was overlaid by a political code that supplanted the earlier cosmological/religious one. The radial street network emanating from the center of the *omphalos* would connect all citizens to the central public space. This development is very different from both the early grid network found in cities in the Indus Valley and the haphazard organic growth of urban settlements in Mesopotamia. Radial development was dictated not by the economic concern of easy access to the market but by the political principle that all homes should be equidistant from the center because all Athenian citizens were equal. Within the center were placed the citizen assembly hall, the city council hall, and the council chamber, all structures linked to the institution of city politics.

Classical Rome was constructed using a different model, one that developed from an imperial code that stressed grandeur, domination, and (eventually) excess. The construction of urban space in Rome was based not on the political equality of its citizens but on the military power of the state and, later, the ambitions of the emperors. Functional space within the Roman forum was embedded in a larger, meaningful space governed by political and cultural symbols.

Initially, the buildings of the Republican Forum at the center of Rome were built on a human scale and formed the focal point for social interaction, public ceremony, and political activity within the city. As the empire expanded and the republic was replaced first by a dictatorship and then by a monarchy, Rome was refashioned by the imperial code to a gargantuan scale. The city of Rome became a physical representation of the empire itself. Monuments and public buildings were constructed to honor the personal accomplishments of each emperor. At its height in the third century, imperial Rome contained a population of more than 600,000 people, many of them slaves (including secretaries, clerks, accountants, and foremen in addition to laborers). It encompassed a total area of 8 square miles, much of which was given over to public space. The majority of the population lived in the 46,000 *insulae* (apartment buildings) within the city; these buildings were typically three stories tall and contained five apartments, housing five to six people each. There were only 4,000 private homes within the city. Eight aqueducts brought the more than 200 million gallons of water needed to service 1,200 public fountains, 926 public baths, and the public latrines. The streets were narrow, twisting, and dark, averaging 6 to 15 feet wide; the largest street was just 20 feet wide. The city fire department consisted of some 7,000 men. The *circus maximus*, where chariot races took place, seated more than 100,000 people and was surrounded by taverns, shops, and eating places. The famous Colosseum rose more than 180 feet above the city and seated more than 80,000 people.

Rome was very different from Athens and other Greek city-states in that it was the capital of the first urban civilization, with roads linking the city to administrative centers across Europe and the Middle East. These cities served as centers of political power, economic control, and cultural diffusion. By AD 200, more than 5 million people lived in Roman cities. As the empire prospered, the 1 million or more residents of Rome lived off the great wealth that poured into the city. Eventually the center became known for its decadence and idleness. At one time, a full 159 days out of the Roman year were declared public holidays! Of these, ninety-three days, or one-fourth of the entire year, were devoted to games at the emperor's expense. Alongside this parasitic existence emerged immense urban problems that we commonly associate with the modern city: the deterioration of housing, widespread poverty, public corruption, and a dangerous lack of proper sanitation facilities and other services for the residents.

With the expansion of the empire, Rome increasingly became a city of contrasts, with vast differences between the rich and the poor, a society wedded to spectacle and consumption rather than commerce and trade. By AD 300 the emperor Constantine moved the capital of the empire to Constantinople, and Rome began a long period of decline. The ebb and flow of human civilization, and of the urban centers that serve as the symbolic markers of those civilizations, is both remarkable and sobering. In many cases we have only the briefest of archeological evidence and written information about the earliest urban civilizations. Babylon, perhaps the best known of the Old Testament cities, lay buried for centuries beneath the sands of Iraq. Baghdad, the largest and wealthiest city of the early Middle Ages, was destroyed in the 1300s and has never achieved the dominance and influence of the earlier era. As shown in Table 2.2, the history of urban civilizations represents an ongoing cycle of growth and decline and, in many cases, permanent end due to the ecological damage that urban civilization has brought to many areas of the globe.

URBANIZATION AFTER AD 1000

After the decline of centralized control from the Roman Empire beginning in AD 500, urban space in Europe was reclaimed by the countryside and a new form of feudal relations developed. Towns needed to defend themselves in the absence of a central authority. Many became small, fortified settlements—like the walled hill towns of central Italy—while in northern Europe, small towns survived only in the shadow of the medieval castle. The level of urbanization was low in Europe during the Middle Ages, and few places exceeded 10,000 in population. In contrast, the cities of Asia, the Near East, and what is now Latin America prospered during this same period.

Most historians contend that the cities that emerged after AD 1000 were the products of powerful national rulers and the success of regional trade rather than the result of social relations that were uniquely urban in nature, as Childe's theory might suggest. City life remained precarious and dependent on social relations that emanated from state power. It was not until the seventeenth century, with the rise of capitalism

TABLE 2.2 Population History of Selected Cities.

Location	Population	Notes
Rome		
AD 100	650,000	World's largest city
600–800	50,000	Invasion by Germanic tribes
1000	35,000	
1300	15,000	Exile of Popes to Avignon
1500	35,000	
1600	120,000	Pope Sixtus and the Rebirth of Rome
Mexico City		
1500	80,000	Capital of Aztec Empire
1524	30,000	Destruction by Spanish conquistadors
1600	75,000	Colonial center of Spanish Empire
Baghdad		
765	480,000	Following establishment of Caliphate in 750
900	1,100,000	Largest city in the world; first city of 1,000,000
1400	125,000	Sacked by Tamerlane in 1401
1650	30,000	
Peking		
1200	150,000	
1300	400,000	Capital of China
1500	670,000	World's largest city
1800	1,100,000	World's largest city
London		
1700	350,000	
1800	1,000,000	Second largest city in the world
1900	6,480,000	Largest city in the world
New York		
1800	80,000	
1900	4,240,000	Largest city in United States
1950	19,800,000	World's largest city

SOURCE: Ivan Light, *Cities in World Perspective* (New York: Macmillan, 1983). Population estimates rounded to nearest 10,000.

in Western Europe, that urban life appeared to be propelled by forces emerging from within cities themselves. In China, for example, towns were organized by the state under the infallible rule of the emperor and for the principal purpose of administration. These were secular kingdoms united under a political hierarchy to harness the economic wealth of the countryside. Under the imperial capital, the provincial capitals were dispersed throughout the kingdom, and under these were clustered the still smaller county capitals of the Chinese empire. Commerce and trade combined with the power of the state to produce the great towns of the Orient.

Much the same story characterized the Middle East, which also contained places with populations that eclipsed those in Europe after AD 1000. With the coming of Islamic hegemony, cities appeared that solidified the control of territory under the Muslim rulers, or caliphs. Islam also took over older cities built by the Romans, such as Constantinople. To these it added two types of "new" towns across North Africa and the Near East: *Villes créés* were fortress cities constructed by Islamic rulers as administration centers, and *villes spontanées* arose as trading centers constructed without preconceived plans but sanctioned by the caliph. Ibu Batutah, the famous Arab traveler of the fourteenth century who journeyed from his home in Morocco to India and China and back, noted the presence of numerous caravanseries along the route from Bagdad to Mecca, dating from the eighth century. The Seljik sultan 'Alä al-Dïn Kayqubäd (1220–1237), renowned for the rich architectural legacy and court culture that flourished under his reign, constructed many caravanseries along roads linking the Anatolian capital to important trade routes. At the peak advance of the Ottoman Empire under Süleyman the Magnificent (1520–1566), a number of subcapitals emerged, including Bursa in Asia and Edirne in Europe. Both cities had remarkable *vaqufs* with mosques, bazaars, *medresas*, *imarets*, and the caravanseries to accommodate traders, pilgrims, and an increasing number of visitors (Hutchison and Prodanovic, 2009). Thus, Islamic society possessed a robust system of cities and communication, but these were all products of state-directed territorial expansion and administration. As in the Chinese case, the rulers needed cities to control the territory and commerce of the hinterland.

The experience of India during this same period (from 1000 to 1700) demonstrates the combined role of royal administration on the one hand, and the importance of local trade on the other, in the sustenance of Oriental cities. As elsewhere in Asia and the Middle East, the size and well-being of Indian cities were a consequence of the power of central state authority rather than of social relations emanating from the urban community itself. Fernand Braudel (1973:413) provides an interesting illustration of the dependency of the city on the power of the state in his examination of India during the seventeenth century: "The example of India shows how much these official towns were bound up with the prince—to the point of absurdity. Political difficulties, even the prince's whim, uprooted and transplanted the capitals several times. . . . As soon as its prince abandoned it, the town was jeopardized, deteriorated and occasionally died."

When a Mogul prince left Delhi on a journey to Kashmir in 1663, the whole town followed him because they could not live without his favors. An improbable crowd formed, estimated at several hundred thousand people by a French doctor who took part in the expedition. Can we imagine Paris following Louis XV during his journey to Metz in 1744?

Finally, in Latin America, the Aztec and Inca civilizations achieved impressive heights during this same period. Indeed, the first Spanish conquistadors to enter the city of Tenochtitlan were overwhelmed: Although many undoubtedly had visited

Cordoba and Granada, among the largest cities in Europe, none had ever seen a city as vast as the capital of the Aztec Empire. Hernán Cortés (1485–1547), the leader of the Spanish forces, described the city in a letter to Charles II (see Box 2.4).

Box 2.4

Hernán Cortés's Letter to Charles V (1520)

This great city of Temixtitlan [Mexico] is situated in this salt lake, and from the main land to the denser parts of it, by whichever route one chooses to enter, the distance is two leagues. There are four avenues or entrances to the city, all of which are formed by artificial causeways, two spears' length in width. The city is as large as Seville or Cordova; its streets, I speak of the principal ones, are very wide and straight; some of these, and all the inferior ones, are half land and half water, and are navigated by canoes. All the streets at intervals have openings, through which the water flows, crossing from one street to another; and at these openings, some of which are very wide, there are also very wide bridges, composed of large pieces of timber, of great strength and well put together; on many of these bridges ten horses can go abreast.

This city has many public squares, in which are situated the markets and other places for buying and selling. There is one square twice as large as that of the city of Salamanca, surrounded by porticoes, where are daily assembled more than sixty thousand souls, engaged in buying and selling; and where are found all kinds of merchandise that the world affords, embracing the necessaries of life, as for instance articles of food, as well as jewels of gold and silver, lead, brass, copper, tin, precious stones, bones, shells, snails, and feathers. There are also exposed for sale wrought and unwrought stone, bricks burnt and unburnt, timber hewn and unhewn, of different sorts. There is a street for game, where every variety of birds in the country are sold, as fowls, partridges, quails, wild ducks, fly-catchers, widgeons, turtledoves, pigeons, reed-birds, parrots, sparrows, eagles, hawks, owls, and kestrels; they sell likewise the skins of some birds of prey, with their feathers, head, beak, and claws. There is also an herb street, where may be obtained all sorts of roots and medicinal herbs that the country affords. There are apothecaries' shops, where prepared medicines, liquids, ointments, and plasters are sold; barbers' shops, where they wash and shave the head; and restaurateurs that furnish food and drink at a certain price.

Every kind of merchandise is sold in a particular street or quarter assigned to it exclusively, and thus the best order is preserved. They sell everything by number or measure; at least so far we have not observed them to sell anything by weight. There is a building in the great square that is used as an audience house, where ten or twelve persons, who are magistrates, sit and decide all controversies that arise in the

continues

market, and order delinquents to be punished. In the same square there are other persons who go constantly about among the people observing what is sold, and the measures used in selling; and they have been seen to break measures that were not true.

Among these temples there is one which far surpasses all the rest, whose grandeur of architectural details no human tongue is able to describe; for within its precincts, surrounded by a lofty wall, there is room enough for a town of five hundred families. Around the interior of the enclosure there are handsome edifices, containing large halls and corridors, in which the religious persons attached to the temple reside. There are fully forty towers, which are lofty and well built, the largest of which has fifty steps leading to its main body, and is higher than the tower of the principal tower of the church at Seville.

SOURCE: Hernán Cortés, Second Letter to Charles V, 1520.

Yet, as the example of the Aztec civilization in Mexico shows, these places were closely connected to the agricultural relations of the hinterland and could not be considered modern cities. According to Murray Bookchin (1974:7–8):

> An illustration of the earliest cities can be drawn from descriptions of the Aztec "capital" of Tenochtitlán, encountered by Spanish *conquistadores* only three centuries ago. At first glance, the community is deceptively similar in appearance to a modern city. . . . The city's resemblance . . . rests on its lofty religious structures, its spacious plazas for ceremonies, its palaces and administrative buildings. Looking beyond these structures, the city in many respects was likely a grossly oversized pueblo community.

As Bookchin points out, the horticulturally based activities of the family clans organized social relations within the city. These clan-based social orders reached into the very heart of city life. Integration around the agricultural economy was so complete that Aztec cities did not develop money but retained a barter system. Just as in the Orient, commercial and craft activities carried on within Tenochtitlán could not explain either its immense physical space or the size of its population. The principal role of the city was to serve as the center for the Aztec rulers and their administrative functions.

It was not until the late Middle Ages in Europe that towns acquired political independence from the state. For Max Weber, the key to city life was the creation of an independent urban government that was elected by the citizens of the city itself. Classical Athens and early Rome were two examples. Weber believed that in the late Middle

Ages, Europe also developed cities of this type. The urban community consisted of three elements: a fusion of the fortress and the marketplace where trade and commercial relations predominated; a legal court of its own that had the authority to settle local disputes; and partial political autonomy that allowed residents to elect authorities who could administer daily affairs (Weber, 1966).

If European cities of the later Middle Ages enjoyed autonomy, it was relatively short lived. By the eighteenth century, nation-states had acquired control of territory, and the commercial-trading economy was global in scale, thereby making individual places dependent on one another. Weber's remarks about the city were meant to suggest that there may once have been uniquely urban social relations that characterized city life and helped to transform society from a rural, agriculturally based system of social organization to one that is considered "modern." For example, urban life was sustained by a mode of social organization that, when compared to rural areas, consisted of greater emphasis on specialized jobs, the decline of family authority and the rise of contractual and political relations, and a replacement of the strong ties binding people together based on kinship with those based on the interdependence of sharing the same fate as the city. In addition to Weber, other classical sociologists developed ways of studying the contrast between premodern and modern societies. Ferdinand Tönnies, for example, called this the shift from *gemeinschaft* to *gesellschaft*, or the change from a traditional society based on trust and mutual aid to a modern one in which self-interest predominates. Emile Durkheim considered modernization to be a change from a society based on mechanical solidarity, or a low degree of specialization, to one based on organic solidarity, or a high degree of specialization and interdependence. We will return to these ideas in Chapter 3.

THE MEDIEVAL ORDER
AND THE RENAISSANCE CITY

Just as classical cities developed around the agora and the forum, the medieval city also included an important symbolic space in the center of the city. Buildings on each side of the central square represented the dominant social, economic, and political interests in medieval society: the cathedral, the town hall, and the merchants' hall and trade guilds. Medieval cities often competed with one another for economic and political dominance, and many were protected by city walls. Because the walls prevented the cities from expanding outward, the cities built upward, and by the late Middle Ages, four- and even five-story buildings overhanging crowded streets were not uncommon. As trade prospered, cities grew more crowded—and so did the problems of poverty, crime, poor sanitation, and ultimately disease. Daniel Defoe, in *A Journal of the Plague Year* (1722), described the ravages of the great plague that devastated London in the seventeenth century, when houses containing persons suffering from the Black Death were boarded up by city authorities with the victims still inside!

By the mid-1500s, Rome had been restored to its position as the capital city of the Catholic world, and it grew in size and significance as trade and commerce in cities across Europe produced a new merchant class with the wealth and leisure time necessary to support pilgrimages to this most holy of sites. But continued growth and an aging infrastructure produced a medieval city of narrow streets, overcrowded housing, and massive traffic problems; in the last decades of the sixteenth century, nearly 450,000 pilgrims traveled to Rome each year. Pope Sixtus V (1585–1590) began an ambitious plan of urban redevelopment. Edmund Bacon (1967:117) described the plan that would create Renaissance Rome:

> Sixtus V, in his effort to recreate the city of Rome into a city worthy of the church, clearly saw the need to establish a basic overall design structure in the form of a movement system as an idea, and at the same time the need to tie down its critical parts in positive physical forms which could not easily be removed. He hit upon the happy solution of using Egyptian obelisks, of which Rome had a substantial number, and erected these at important points within the structure of his design.

The seven holy pilgrimage sites within the city were linked by broad boulevards, providing for a new sense of movement and spatial ordering within the city. This

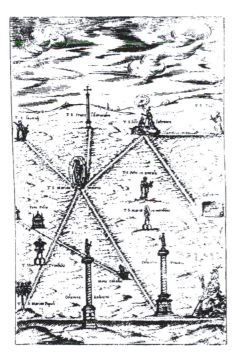

FIGURE 2.2 Creating Renaissance Rome. Pope Sixtus V's plan for the redesign of Rome involved linking the four major basilicas (St. Peter, St. Mary Major, St. John Lateran, and S. Maria del Popolo) with new roads and installing obelisks to guide pilgrims from one site to another; the plan is based upon a semiotic approach to the city and to urban design. SOURCE: Print by Giovanni Francesco Bordini (1588).

plan for urban redevelopment was celebrated in engravings by the leading artists of the day. Implementing this plan would take more than sixty years and result in the destruction of neighborhoods of crowded medieval housing, but it produced a new city that would attract pilgrims from across Europe. New squares were built and monuments erected to symbolize the power of the church.

The redevelopment of Rome served as a model for urban planning during the Renaissance. New squares would be constructed with monuments to historical events and public figures; boulevards would connect these urban spaces with one another and direct traffic through the city. Older housing, now a crowded eyesore, would be demolished to make way for urban development. The design of the new metropolis would be replicated in Renaissance cities across Europe in the 1700s and would serve as a model for urban planning in many other areas of the world, including Detroit and Washington, D.C. (Girouard, 1985).

The change in urban fortunes is clearly shown in Table 2.3, which shows the largest city in the world in each century from 1200 BC to 1850—a documentary history of the development of urban civilization across the globe. In the first half of the table, the cities and civilizations correspond to what we have learned in high school and college courses on Western history: Babylon was the largest city in Mesopotamia in biblical times, Memphis the largest city in ancient Egypt, and Rome the largest city of the Roman Empire. But urban life during the Middle Ages shifted to the great Muslim empires of the Middle East (Baghdad and Damascus in 900 and 1100) and then to North

TABLE 2.3 World's Largest Cities, 1200 BC to AD 1900.

	City	Present Location	Estimated Population
1200	Memphis	Egypt	50,000
600	Ninevah	Iraq	120,000
450	Babylon	Iraq	200,000
200	Patna	India	400,000
100	Rome	Italy	650,000
350	Constantinople	Turkey	300,000
600	Constantinople	Turkey	500,000
800	Changan	China	700,000
900	Baghdad	Iraq	1,100,000
1000	Córdoba	Spain	450,000
1100	Kaifeng	China	440,000
1200	Hangchow	China	250,000
1300	Hangchow	China	430,000
1400	Nanking	China	490,000
1500	Peking	China	670,000
1600	Peking	China	710,000
1800	Peking	China	1,100,000
1850	London	Great Britain	2,320,000

SOURCE: Adapted from Ivan Light, *Cities in World Perspective* (New York: Macmillan, 1983).

Africa and Spain (Córdoba in the 1200s and 1300s) and then to the great Chinese civilizations of the 1500s through 1700s. The rise of first European and later American cities did not occur until the advent of the Industrial Revolution in the 1800s.

In retrospect, it seems clear that the force that propelled the development of cities in Europe after the late Middle Ages did not involve the same process of urban growth that led to the urban civilizations of earlier centuries. When we examine the historical record put forward in Table 2.3, we realize that the expansion of urban civilization in Europe was a direct consequence of the rise of capitalism and industrialization. It is this change that defines the development from the relatively autonomous urban community in Europe of the seventeenth and eighteenth centuries to the large industrial and postindustrial cities that we know today.

CAPITALISM AND THE
RISE OF THE INDUSTRIAL CITY

Throughout the world, especially in North Africa, Asia, and the Near East, cities were the sites of vigorous trade and the economic activities associated with commerce. However, trade by itself did not sustain the rise of cities in Western Europe. Distinguishing the developing towns of the late Middle Ages from other such places was the emergence of capitalism based on a money economy.

The economy of the feudal manor, for example, was characterized by *simple commodity production*; that is, craft products were produced for exchange, and the owners were the producers of the products. Exchange took place among owners/producers and could be facilitated using any object or service that was equivalent according to the cultural judgment of the society. This barter system prevailed for several hundred years in Europe after the fall of Rome and existed elsewhere in the Middle East and Asia.

In the later Middle Ages, beginning in the twelfth century, the general and accepted use of money and a fully developed commodity market within the city that was regulated by local government allowed the people with capital to hire both labor and resources to produce goods. The classical sociologist Karl Marx was the foremost student of the rise of capitalism. He called the type of economy made possible by capital and city regulation of markets *extended commodity production*. That is, unlike simple commodity production, which ended in the exchange of goods or services, extended production began with money, or capital and, after production and exchange, ended with still more money, which was then invested in a new cycle of accumulation.

In this manner, commercial relations supported the accumulation of capital, and cities with such economies began to prosper beyond anything experienced up to that time. In addition, social and cultural relations changed in the cities to sanction the pursuit of wealth through the accumulation of money. For example, the early Catholic church prohibited the loaning of money, except within restricted guidelines, and limited the role of banks (see Vance, 1990). In the sixteenth century, the Protestant

Reformation swept away these cultural and social restrictions on the free flow of investment, providing a cultural basis for capitalist development (Weber, 1958). Once that point had been reached, the accumulation process spilled out into the surrounding area as the new money-based capitalist economy penetrated relations in the countryside. The history of the Occidental city, as Braudel, Weber, and Marx all agreed, became the history of capitalism.

The full impact of the changes described by these three authors may be best understood by looking at the location and size of the largest cities in Europe from 1050 to 1800 (roughly the period from the onset of the Middle Ages to the start of the Industrial Revolution). The population figures presented in Table 2.4 illustrate the shift of economic activity and urban life from southern Europe to the north. In the early Middle Ages, the largest urban areas were found in the Moorish empire in Spain and in the early Italian city-states. By the 1500s the influence of the Moorish empire was declining, and the early textile manufacturing cities of the north were ascending. Soon thereafter, the port cities of the Hanseatic League made their appearance. By 1800, the metropolitan centers of the new European powers and the cities of the industrial north predominated.

TABLE 2.4 Largest Cities in Europe, 1050 to 1800.

1050		1200		1330		1500		1650		1800	
Córdoba	150	Palermo	150	Granada	150	Paris	225	Paris	400	London	948
Palermo	120	Paris	110	Paris	150	Naples	125	London	350	Paris	550
Seville	90	Seville	80	Venice	110	Milan	100	Naples	300	Naples	430
Salerno	50	Venice	70	Genoa	100	Venice	100	Lisbon	150	Vienna	247
Venice	45	Florence	60	Milan	100	Granada	70	Venice	140	Amsterdam	217
Regensburg	40	Granada	60	Florence	95	Prague	70	Milan	120	Dublin	200
Toledo	37	Córdoba	60	Seville	90	Lisbon	65	Amsterdam	120	Lisbon	195
Rome	35	Cologne	50	Córdoba	60	Tours	60	Rome	110	Berlin	172
Barbastro	35	Leon	40	Naples	60	Genoa	58	Madrid	100	Madrid	168
Cartagena	33	Ypres	40	Cologne	54	Ghent	55	Palermo	100	Rome	153
Naples	30	Rome	35	Palermo	51	Florence	55	Seville	80	Palermo	140
Mainz	30	Bologna	35	Siena	50	Palermo	55	Florence	74	Venice	138
Merida	30	Toledo	35	Barcelona	48	Rome	55	Vienna	70	Milan	135
Almeria	17	Verona	33	Valencia	44	Bordeaux	50	Granada	70	Hamburg	130
Grenada	26	Narbonne	31	Toledo	42	Lyon	50	Marseille	70	Lyon	109
Speyer	25	Salerno	30	Bruges	40	Orleans	50	Copenhagen	65	Copenhagen	101
Palma	25	Pavia	30	Malaga	40	London	50	Genoa	64	Marseille	101
Leon	25	Messina	30	Aquila	40	Bologna	50	Bologna	63	Barcelona	100
London	25	Naples	30	Bologna	40	Verona	50	Antwerp	60	Seville	96
Elvira	22	Genoa	30	Cremona	40	Brescia	49	Brussels	60	Bordeaux	96

Population in thousands.

SOURCE: Adapted from DeLong and Shleifer (1993) and based on the work of Bairoch, Batou, and Chèvre (1988) and Russell and Cox (1972).

As Adam Smith and Karl Marx noted in their complementary works, *The Wealth of Nations* and *Das Kapital*, industrial capitalism would forever change the nature of social relations and set in motion the powerful economic forces that resulted in global capitalism and the emerging world city. Occupations became specialized, and the division of labor grew ever more complex as mercantile capitalism was replaced by industrial capitalism. Aided by emergent nation-states, the political and legal relations of capitalism began to dominate the countryside in Europe. To be successful, the emerging forms of capitalism required the legal justification of private property, and this would result in the "commodification" not just of urban space but of many other aspects of society. All this buying and selling meant that many new markets were formed and existing ones expanded, providing people with even more ways to make money.

Land, for example, that was once held only by the nobility and the church, became a commodity that could be purchased by anyone with money. A real estate market developed that divided up and parceled out land for sale. A second market, this one for labor, emerged as the serfs, who had been bound to their masters by feudal traditions, were freed only to become commodities in the new system of wage labor. As feudal relations of dependence and reciprocity were broken down by capitalism and the pursuit of monetary accumulation, immense numbers of people were forced out of rural farming areas and into cities, where they looked for work by selling their labor for a wage on the labor market. They would become the urban *proletariat*, as Marx defined them: Persons who possessed only their labor to sell.

With the coming of the Industrial Revolution, this "urban implosion," or shift of population from rural to urban places, reached truly astounding proportions. According to Lewis Mumford (1961), the cities of the late eighteenth century contained relatively few people, numbering less than 600,000. By the middle of the nineteenth century, capitalist industrialization had created cities of a million or more across Western Europe. The most dramatic changes were experienced in England and Wales because it was there that the scale of industrialization and capitalist development was most advanced. According to Geruson and McGrath (1977:25), urban counties in Britain grew by 30 percent between 1780 and 1800 and again by approximately 300 percent between 1801 and 1831. Commercial and industrial counties experienced a net population increase of 378,000 between 1781 and 1800 and an additional 720,000 between 1801 and 1831. At the same time, agricultural counties lost 252,000 people during the first period and lost 379,000 between 1801 and 1831.

Census figures at the time of the nineteenth century were not always accurate. Nevertheless, Braudel (1973:376) suggests that around the turn of the century, several regions in Europe tipped their population balance from rural to urban, especially in England and the Netherlands, a truly momentous occurrence. In short, for the first time in history, several nations changed from populations that were predominantly rural to ones dominated by urban location, and this is why the urbanization process in Western Europe after the 1700s was so significant.

By the seventeenth century, destitution had been accepted as the normal lot in life for a considerable part of the population. Without the spur of poverty and famine, people could not be expected to work for starvation wages. Misery at the bottom was the foundation for luxury at the time. As much as a quarter of the urban population in the bigger cities, it has been estimated, consisted of casuals and beggars; it was this surplus that made for what was considered, by classic capitalism, to be a healthy labor market, in which the capitalist hired labor on his own terms or dismissed workers at will, without notice and without concern for what happened to the worker or the city under such inhuman conditions. In a memorandum dated 1684, the chief of police of Paris referred to the "frightful misery that afflicts the greater part of the population of this great city." Between 40,000 and 65,000 were reduced to outright beggary. There was nothing exceptional about Paris.

By the middle 1800s, Western Europe possessed many industrialized cities. What was life like there? The cities that emerged in the nineteenth century, unlike the ancient places, were not conceived according to some overarching symbolic meaning, such as religious or cosmological codes. Development was a haphazard affair. Individual capitalists did what they willed, and real estate interests operated unchecked by either legal code or cultural prescription. Land was traded like other goods. About the only clear pattern that emerged involved the spatial separation of rich and poor. The industrial city of Western Europe became the site of a clash of classes: the workers against the capitalists. Observing the excesses of the time and the utter devastation visited on working-class life by the factory regime of capitalism, Karl Marx (1967) recognized that class struggle would become the driving force of history. It was left for Friedrich Engels, Marx's close friend, to document in graphic terms the pathological nature of uneven development characterizing urban growth under capitalism in *The Condition of the Working Class in England in 1844* (Engels, 1845).

In a chapter titled "The Great Towns," Engels describes the typical slum found in the industrial city:

> Every great city has one or more slums, where the working class is crowded together. True, poverty often dwells in hidden alleys close to the palaces of the rich; but, in general, a separate territory has been assigned to it, where, removed from the sight of the happier classes, it may struggle along as it can. These slums are pretty equally arranged in all the great towns of England, the worst houses in the worst quarters of the towns; usually one- or two-storied cottages in long rows, perhaps with cellars used as dwellings, almost always irregularly built. These houses of three or four rooms and a kitchens form, throughout England, some parts of London excepted, the general dwellings of the working class. The streets are generally unpaved, rough, dirty, filled with vegetable and animal refuse, without sewers or gutters, but supplied with foul, stagnant pools instead. Moreover, ventilation is impeded by the bad, confused method of building of the whole quarter, and since

many human beings here live crowded into a small space, the atmosphere that prevails in these working-men's quarters may readily be imagined.

Engels's description of Manchester is more graphic: "The people of Manchester emphasize the fact whenever anyone mentions to them the frightful condition of this Hell upon Earth; but what does that prove? Everything which here arouses horror and indignation is of recent origin, belongs to the *industrial epoch."* Engels's account includes rivers polluted with the intestines of slaughtered cattle and other manufacturing waste, which came from the giant factories that settled over residential areas of the city, as described in Box 2.5.

Box 2.5

Manchester During the Industrial Age

Friedrich Engels included a description of Manchester in his study of the English working class in 1884:

The south bank of the Irk is here very steep and between fifteen and thirty feet high. On this declivitous hillside there are planted three rows of houses, of which the lowest rise directly out of the river, while the front walls of the highest stand on the crest of the hill in Long Millgate. Among them are mills on the river, in short, the method of construction is as crowded and disorderly here as in the lower part of Long Millgate. Right and left a multitude of covered passages lead from the main street into numerous courts, and he who turns in thither gets into a filth and disgusting grime, the equal of which is not to be found—especially in the courts which lead down to the Irk, and which contain unqualifiedly the most horrible dwellings which I have yet beheld. In one of these courts there stands directly at the entrance, at the end of the covered passage, a privy without a door, so dirty that the inhabitants can pass into and out of the court only by passing through foul pools of stagnant urine and excrement. This is the first court on the Irk above Ducie Bridge—in case anyone should care to look into it. Below it on the river there are several tanneries which fill the whole neighbourhood with the stench of animal putrefaction. Below Ducie Bridge the only entrance to most of the houses is by means of narrow, dirty stairs and over heaps of refuse and filth. The first court below Ducie Bridge, known as Allen's Court, was in such a state at the time of the cholera that the sanitary police ordered it evacuated, swept, and disinfected with chloride of lime.

The view from this bridge, mercifully concealed from mortals of small stature by a parapet as high as a man, is characteristic for the whole district. At the bottom flows, or rather stagnates, the Irk, a narrow, coal-black, foul-smelling stream, full of debris and refuse, which it deposits on the shallower right bank. In dry weather, a

continues

Box 2.5 *continued*

long string of the most disgusting, blackish-green slime pools are left standing on this bank, from the depths of which bubbles of miasmatic gas constantly arise and give forth a stench unendurable even on the bridge forty or fifty feet above the surface of the stream. But besides this, the stream itself is checked every few paces by high weirs, behind which slime and refuse accumulate and rot in thick masses. Above the bridge are tanneries, bonemills, and gasworks, from which all drains and refuse find their way into the Irk, which receives further the contents of all the neighbouring sewers and privies. It may be easily imagined, therefore, what sort of residue the stream deposits. Below the bridge you look upon the piles of *débris*, the refuse, filth, and offal from the courts on the steep left bank; here each house is packed close behind its neighbour and a piece of each is visible, all black, smoky, crumbling, ancient, with broken panes and window-frames.

The newly built extension of the Leeds railway, which crosses the Irk here, has swept away some of these courts and lanes, laying others completely open to view. Passing along a rough bank, among stakes and washing-lines, one penetrates into this chaos of small one-storied, one-roomed huts, in most of which there is no artificial floor; kitchen, living and sleeping-room all in one. In such a hole, scarcely five feet long by six broad, I found two beds—and such bedsteads and beds!—which, with a staircase and chimney-place, exactly filled the room. In several others I found absolutely nothing, while the door stood open, and the inhabitants leaned against it. Everywhere before the doors refuse and offal; that any sort of pavement lay underneath could not be seen but only felt, here and there, with the feet. This whole collection of cattle-sheds for human beings was surrounded on two sides by houses and a factory, and on the third by the river, and besides the narrow stair up the bank, a narrow doorway alone led out into another almost equally ill-built, ill-kept labyrinth of dwellings.

Such is the Old Town of Manchester, and on re-reading my description, I am forced to admit that instead of being exaggerated, it is far from black enough to convey a true impression of the filth, ruin, and uninhabitableness, the defiance of all considerations of cleanliness, ventilation, and health which characterise the construction of this single district, containing at least twenty to thirty thousand inhabitants. And such a district exists in the heart of the second city of England, the first manufacturing city of the world. If any one wishes to see in how little space a human being can move, how little air—and *such* air!—he can breathe, how little of civilisation he may share and yet live, it is only necessary to travel hither. True, this is the *Old* Town, and the people of Manchester emphasise the fact whenever any one mentions to them the frightful condition of this Hell upon Earth; but what does that prove? Everything which here arouses horror and indignation is of recent origin, belongs to the *industrial epoch*.

SOURCE: Friedrich Engels, *The Condition of the Working Class in England in 1844*.

Engels was not alone. Many books were written in the nineteenth century cataloging the hardships caused by industrialization, including Henry Mayhew's *London Labour and the London Poor* and Charles Booth's *Life and Labour of the People in London*. These works, and many more, described what Booth called "the problem of poverty in the midst of wealth."

In the chapters to follow, we will see that many of the ideas associated with modern life have their origins in observations made about industrial cities. The problem of uneven development—the graphic contrast between the wealthy and the poor, for example, and the contradictions between progress and misery—remains very much at the center of the urban dynamic in cities around the globe. On the one hand, the city represented hope to all those laboring under meager conditions in the countryside. It was the site of industrialization and the great dream of modernization and progress. On the other hand, the powerful forces of urbanism dwarfed the individual and crushed the masses into dense, environmentally strained spaces. In time, the built environment of the industrial city would replace that of the feudal town. The city rhythm, so unlike that of the country, would replace earlier cycles of life dominated by nature. Life was worth only as much as the daily wage for which it could be exchanged. The processes of urbanization and capitalism that created large cities in Europe during the nineteenth century also thrived in the United States at the same time, and in many ways, U.S. cities were governed by the same dynamic.

KEY CONCEPTS

Thanatopolis
agora
Childe hypothesis
rise of capitalism
simple commodity production
extended commodity production
urban implosion
forum
industrialization

IMPORTANT NAMES

V. Gordon Childe
Lewis Mumford
Gideon Sjoberg
Max Weber
Karl Marx
Friedrich Engels
Henry Mayhew
Charles Booth

DISCUSSION QUESTIONS

1. V. Gordon Childe's description of the urban revolution is often said to be an evolutionary theory. What does this mean? What factors did Childe believe were necessary for the urban revolution to take place? What evidence have other scholars used to critique his theory?

2. The roles of culture and political power were important for the development of both Athens and Rome, yet these forces produced two very different patterns of urban settlement. What might account for the differences between Athens and Rome, and for the changes that took place in the development of republican and imperial Rome?

3. Early cities were built by groups using a distinctive set of symbols and a model of space meaningful to the group. Explain how the redevelopment of Renaissance Rome by Pope Sixtus V followed these same ideas.

4. The well-known saying that "city air makes one free" dates from the development of European cities in the medieval period. What does this saying represent? Why was it important for European cities to develop political autonomy from the surrounding economic and political system?

5. The rise of the industrial city in Europe is linked to the development of capitalism. Discuss two characteristics of early capitalism and show how this influenced the growth of the industrial city.

6. Urban historians have long debated whether capitalism resulted in better living conditions for the average worker. What evidence do we have from the development of the industrial city to answer this question?

CHAPTER 3

THE RISE OF URBAN SOCIOLOGY

A special inquiry devoted to urban phenomena was the premier achievement of early U.S. sociology. The first sociology department in the country was founded by Albion Small at the University of Chicago in 1893. Robert Park joined the department in 1914 and quickly took on a prominent role. Albion Small and Robert Park had something in common. They had both traveled to Germany as graduate students to take courses with Georg Simmel. In the 1890s only France and Germany had professional sociologists. Emile Durkheim, a sociologist at the Sorbonne in Paris, had developed a growing reputation in France. Max Weber, the German scholar who wrote on law, politics, religion, society, and much more, was acknowledged as the leading social thinker of his day. And another important sociologist, Georg Simmel, had a growing reputation as the most innovative social philosopher on the continent.

The first generation of sociologists shared a special concern with the impact of urbanization on European society. The political revolutions of the 1800s brought an end to earlier ideas that the social and political order reflected a divine plan. What exactly would the new social order, created by widespread changes in the economic and social structure, look like? In the wake of the social and political changes brought about by the French Revolution, questions about how social order itself could be maintained were not simply a matter of idle speculation. These questions were essential to understanding the very nature of the new industrial society that was transforming European cities.

Ferdinand Tönnies (1855–1936) is one of the early German social philosophers who addressed these questions. In *Gemeinschaft und Gesellschaft* (published in 1887 and often translated as "Community and Society," although "Community and Association" more accurately reflects the original meaning), Tönnies sketched out an evolutionary view of the development of human society. The great period of industrialization that transformed European societies beginning in the late 1700s signified a change from community to association. Tönnies saw that the transition from community (where individual families have long histories, individuals interact with one another on a personal basis because they often work together or are related to one another, and all jobs are interdependent on one another) to society (where individuals often interact with others whom they do not personally know and work at jobs that are seemingly unrelated to one another) resulted in a weakening of social ties and the loss of a shared sense of belonging to a meaningful community. His ideas (summarized in Box 3.1) are often used to highlight differences between village life of the preindustrial period and urban life of the industrial period, and between small-town life and that of the large city more generally.

Emile Durkheim (1858–1917), who was the first chair of sociology at the Sorbonne in Paris in 1883, also wrote about the changes brought about by industrialization. In *The Division of Labor in Society*, Durkheim discussed many of the same issues presented in Töennies's earlier essay, this time under the labels of *mechanical solidarity* and *organic solidarity*. In the preindustrial village, individuals were held together by the

---

Box 3.1

Gemeinschaft and Gesellschaft

In his seminal work analyzing the social changes that accompany the transition from the traditional community to the modern urban society, Ferdinand Töennies described the forms of Gemeinschaft and Gesellschaft in the following terms:

The very existence of *Gemeinschaft* rests in the consciousness of belonging together and the affirmation of the condition of mutual dependence which is posed by that affirmation. Living together may be called the animal soul of *Gemeinschaft*, for it is the condition of its active life, of a shared feeling of pleasure and pain, of a shared enjoyment of the commonly possessed goods, by which one is surrounded, and by the cooperation in teamwork as well as in divided labor. Working together may be conceived of as the rational or human soul of Gemeinschaft. It is higher, more conscious cooperation in the unity of spirit and purpose, including, therefore, a striving for common or shared ideals, as invisible goods that are knowable only to thought. Regarding being together it is descent (blood), regarding living together it is soil (land), regarding working together it is occupation (Beruf) that is substance as it were, by which the wills of men, which otherwise are far apart from and even antagonistic to each other, are essentially united.

The city is typical of *Gesellschaft* in general. It is essentially a commercial town and, in so far as commerce dominates its productive labor, a factory town. Its wealth is capital wealth which, in the form of trade, usury, or industrial capital, is used and multiplies. Capital is the means for the appropriation of products of labor or for the exploitation of workers. The city is also the center of science and culture, which always goes hand in hand with commerce and industry. Here the arts must make a living; they are exploited in a capitalist way. Thoughts spread with astonishing rapidity.

SOURCE: Ferdinand Töennies, *Gemeinschaft und Gesellschaft*, 1957 [1887].

mechanical bonds of kinship and social interdependence—mechanical because they were predetermined and could not be changed as long as the individual remained within the local village. In the industrial city, individuals were no longer bound by the mechanical bonds of kinship; instead they could work at new types of jobs and have greater opportunities for interaction with a wider range of people. These were organic bonds that flowed naturally from the increased social differentiation brought about by the division of labor. If these terms seem to be counterintuitive (we often think of work in factories as being mechanical), it is important to realize that Durkheim was convinced that the new industrial economy was an improvement over the limited opportunities of feudal society, and he may have deliberately chosen words with a positive connotation to represent the modern city. Durkheim was certain that the new industrial order would replace the earlier ways of life: "With the coming of the industrial economy, village society has disappeared, never to come again."

Friedrich Engels (1820–1895), the German scholar, saw things very differently. Engels's father was a wealthy industrialist, and he sent his son to Manchester, England, to manage the family's business interests in the new industrial city. Engels's observations on everyday life under industrial capitalism are found in *The Condition of the Working Class in England in 1844*. This seminal work in urban sociology devoted a chapter to "The Great Towns" (see also Box 2.5). According to Engels, the evils of industrialization and capitalism were intensified by the space of the city. This is a perspective to which we will return in the next chapter.

The most influential European thinker influencing urban sociologists in the United States during this early period was Georg Simmel (1858–1918). Simmel viewed the city in cultural terms and wrote about how urban life transformed individual consciousness: Everyday existence within the city altered the way people thought and acted compared to traditional society. Robert Park and Albion Small were familiar with Simmel's work and brought this "interactive" perspective back to the University of Chicago. In the United States, the work of the early Chicago School was less concerned with historical and comparative studies in the manner of Weber and more focused on social behavior and interaction within the urban milieu in the manner of Simmel.

Any thorough discussion of the development of urban sociology in the United States must begin by explaining the important difference between the two organizing topics in the field: urbanization and urbanism. *Urbanization* refers to the origins of cities and the process of city building. It studies the way social activities locate themselves in space and according to interdependent processes of societal development and change. The analyses are often historical and comparative. When we study the process of urbanization, we are interested in charting the rise and fall of great cities and urban civilizations. Our discussion of the emergence of cities, the largest cities in the world, and the changing location of large cities in Europe presented in Chapter 2 was about urbanization. *Urbanism*, in contrast, studies the ways of life that may be found within the urban community. It deals with culture, with meanings, symbols, patterns of daily life, and processes of adjustment to the environment of the city, but also with social conflict and political organization at the street, neighborhood, and city levels.

While both Max Weber and Friedrich Engels emphasized the relation between the historical development of the city and its ways of life, Georg Simmel was more concerned with patterns of activity and ways of thinking that were found in the city. The work of the early Chicago School followed Simmel closely and focused on patterns of activity within cities rather than addressing the topic of city formation or U.S. urbanization. Yet for Simmel, the study of life within the city was not meant as an "urban sociology." Simmel was instead concerned with *modernity*, or the transition from a traditional society characterized by social relations based on intimacy or kinship (known as "primary" relations) and by a feudal economy based on barter to an industrial society situated within cities and dominated by impersonal, specialized social relations based on compartmentalized roles (known as "secondary" relations) and by a money economy based on rational calculations of profit and loss. For Simmel, the subtle aspects of modernity were displayed most clearly within the large city or metropolis and through consciously directed behaviors. Simmel gives us a social psychology of modernity that Robert Park took to be the sociology of urbanism, or "urban sociology."

GEORG SIMMEL ON THE CITY

What was it like to confront modernity and why was Simmel so impressed with the city as the vehicle for change? Consider, if you will, a German farmer from Bavaria. His life was tuned to the daily rhythms of agriculture. Nature and his own physical labor provided the boundaries within which the farming endeavor was framed. The regime of labor on the land was early to bed because darkness meant little work could be done, and early to rise because it was necessary to use every second of daylight for work—even dawn and twilight. This farmer was immersed in a social world of primary kinship relations. His principal contacts were members of his family, both immediate and extended. Perhaps several generations and families lived together in the same location and worked the land. Beyond this primary network, the farmer would interact with individuals who aided his enterprise. Most typically he visited a local service center, perhaps a small town. There he was surely involved in a network of people who knew him well. In this kind of traditional society, it was entirely possible that no money changed hands while farm produce and needed commodities were exchanged. Barter, credit, and informal agreements among known persons characterized the social relations of this world.

As Simmel might suggest, suppose this individual—call him Hans—lost the farm and his family in some personal tragedy. With a small amount of money, he now traveled to Berlin to begin a new life. He went to this modern city precisely because it offered him an alternative to the traditional rural existence of farming. Karl

Georg Simmel

Georg Simmel was born on March 1, 1858, in the very heart of Berlin, at the intersection of Leipzigerstrasse and Friedrichstrasse. This was a curious birthplace—it would correspond to Times Square in New York—but it seems symbolically fitting for a man who throughout his life lived at the intersection of many movements, intensely affected by the crosscurrents of intellectual traffic and by a multiplicity of moral directions. Like "the stranger" he described in his brilliant essay of the same name, he was near and far at the same time, a potential wanderer who had not quite overcome the freedom of coming and going. Simmel was a modern urban man, without roots in traditional folk culture.

After graduating from *Gymnasium*, Simmel studied history and philosophy at the University of Berlin with some of the most important academic figures of the day. By the time he received his doctorate in 1881, Simmel was familiar with a vast field of knowledge extending from history to philosophy and from psychology to the social sciences. Deeply tied to the intellectual milieu of Berlin, he played an active part in the intellectual and cultural life of the capital, frequenting many fashionable salons and participating in various cultural circles. He attended the meetings of philosophers and sociologists and was a cofounder, with Weber and Töennies, of the German Society for Sociology.

Simmel taught at the University of Berlin, where he became a Privatdozent (an unpaid lecturer dependent on student fees) in 1885. His courses ranged from logic and the history of philosophy to ethics, social psychology, and sociology. He was a very popular lecturer and his lectures soon became leading intellectual events, not only for students but for the cultural elite of Berlin. Simmel was somewhat of a showman, punctuating the air with abrupt gestures and stabs, dramatically halting, and then releasing a torrent of dazzling ideas. In spite of the fascination he called forth, however, his academic career turned out to be unfortunate, even tragic. Many of Simmel's peers and elders, especially those of secondary rank, felt threatened and unsettled by his erratic brilliance. Whenever Simmel sought an academic promotion, he was rebuffed.

Simmel was a prolific writer. More than two hundred of his articles appeared in a great variety of journals, newspapers, and magazines during his lifetime, and several more were published posthumously. He published fifteen major works in the fields of philosophy, ethics, sociology, and cultural criticism, including his seminal work, *The Philosophy of Money*, in 1900. His influence on the further development of both philosophy and sociology, whether acknowledged or not, has been diffuse yet pervasive, even during those periods when his fame seemed to have been eclipsed. Among Americans who sat at his feet was Robert Park. No one who reads Park's work can overlook Simmel's profound impact.

SOURCE: Lewis A. Coser, *Masters of Sociological Thought*, 1971.

Marx, writing in the nineteenth century, would have focused on Hans's conversion to an industrial worker. He would have taken us into the factory with Hans and described his encounter with abstract capital (the machine), with the relations of production (the factory building, the assembly line, and the daily schedule of work), and with class relations (interaction with the workers and the boss). Simmel, writing in the early twentieth century, virtually ignored this entire domain of the factory, which could be termed the immediate environment of capitalism, and focused instead on the larger context of daily life, the extended environment—namely, the city.

Hans stands on the corner of a large boulevard in Berlin teeming with daytime auto traffic. He has to dodge the steady stream of pedestrians just to stand still and watch, since everything else is in constant motion. At first shock, Hans would be paralyzed by the "excess of nervous stimulation," according to Simmel. Haven't we all had a similar experience upon visiting a large city? Loud noises from traffic, people in the crowds calling after one another, strangers bumping us as they pass without an acknowledgment, and more—noise, noise, and noise. Hans would find himself in a totally new environment that demanded an adjustment and a response.

According to Simmel, small-town life required Hans to develop strong, intimate ties to those with whom he interacted. In the city, the excess of stimulation requires a defensive response. These are the characteristics of urbanism noted by Simmel. Hans would (1) develop what Simmel called a "blasé" attitude—a blurring of the senses, a filtering out of all that was loud and impinging but also irrelevant to Hans's own personal needs. Emotional reserve and indifference replace acute attention to the details of the environment.

Hans would require the satisfaction of his needs. Yes, he would encounter capitalism and, no doubt, sell his labor for a wage, as Marx had observed. Simmel agreed with Marx about the necessity of that transaction, which would (2) reduce the quality of Hans's capabilities simply to the quantity of his labor time—the time he spent at work for a wage. It would make his work equivalent to a sum of money, no more, no less. That sum of money exchanged for Hans's labor time would be all the employing capitalist would provide. Hans would quickly see that absolutely no concern for his health-related, spiritual, communal, sexual, or any other type of human need would be involved in his relationship with his employer. In short, the world of capitalism was (3) an impersonal world of pure monetary exchange.

Simmel, unlike Marx, showed how the impersonal money economy extended outside the factory to characterize all other transactions in the city. Hans would use his paycheck to buy the necessities of life, but in these transactions, too, impersonal or secondary social relations prevailed. Unless he went to a small store and frequented it every day, he would simply be viewed as (4) an anonymous customer being provided with mass-produced items for purchase. As a city dweller, he might find himself more frequently going to a department store where (5) a mass spectacle of consumption would be on display.

In all these transactions, Hans would have to be very careful. His weekly paycheck could go only so far. He would have to count how much each item cost and then budget accordingly. This (6) rational calculation would be at the heart of his daily life. Everything would be measured by him, just as costs were carefully measured at the factory. Rational calculation of money would require knowledge and technique. If Hans mastered it successfully along with gaining mastery over the consumer world of the city, he could look down at his country-bumpkin cousins. City life, for Simmel, was a life of the intellect, and everywhere, it was the relation between the money economy and the rational calculation needed to survive in the world of capitalism that prevailed. Those in the city who could not master the technique of money management would surely be lost.

We are not finished with the example of Hans. In the traditional society of the country, the rhythm of life was provided by nature. The city environment required (7) adjustment to a second nature—the orchestration of daily activities as governed by clock time and as played out within a constructed space. All life in the city followed the schedule of capitalist industrialization or modernity. If Hans didn't own a watch before coming to the city, he now needed one. Time and money constituted the two types of calculation necessary for survival in the second nature of the urban milieu—the built environment of concrete, steel, and glass that is the city.

Finally, Simmel also commented on the qualitative value of an experience like Hans's. He did not see the transformation as something that was necessarily bad. Hans would be cast in a calculating and impersonal world, but he would also be (8) freed from the restrictions of traditional society and its time-bound dictates. He would be free to discriminate about the types of friends he chose, about the job he took (within strong constraints, of course), and about where he lived. To Simmel, modernity meant the possibility of immense individual freedom in addition to constraint.

For Simmel, the freedom of the city meant, above all else, that Hans would be free to pursue and even create his own individuality. Provided he had the money, of course—an actuality that Marx would doubt—Hans could cultivate himself. He could dress according to some distinct fashion, develop hobbies he could share with others, perhaps take up the violin and join a neighborhood string quartet; he could enjoy a certain brand of cigar or shoes or attend night classes at the university—even Simmel's own lectures. Could Hans and Simmel eventually have met? The city allowed for the possibility of attaining such cultural freedom, and the signs of individual cultivation—the clothes, cigars, friends, lovers, discussion groups, opera, art, novels—were collectively the signs of modernity that we may also call urbanism.

LOUIS WIRTH AND URBANISM AS A WAY OF LIFE

As we have seen, Georg Simmel had an important impact on the development of urban sociology in the United States. Albion Small and Robert Park attended lectures by Simmel while they were studying in Germany, and Park included some of the first English translations of Simmel's work in the sociology textbook (titled *The Science of Society*) used at the University of Chicago. Louis Wirth was born in Germany but was sent to live with relatives in Omaha, Nebraska, where he attended high school before coming to the University of Chicago. Wirth's doctoral research reflected his knowledge of the development of Chicago's Jewish community. Published in 1926 with the title *The Ghetto*, Wirth's work describes the Maxwell Street neighborhood where recently arrived Russian immigrants had settled (the ghetto) and the area of second settlement where the older German immigrants had moved (Deutschland). Wirth became a faculty member in the sociology department at the University of Chicago and was one of the important figures in the later development of the Chicago School.

Louis Wirth was inspired by the work of Simmel. The Chicago sociologists came to view spatial patterns in the city as the result of powerful social factors, such as competition and the struggle for survival among individuals and groups within the city. Thus, Robert Park and his associates viewed urban space as a container, a built environment that encloses the action. Wirth's idea was different. He emphasized the way the city, as a spatial environment, influenced individual behavior. Wirth wanted to know what it was about the city itself that produced unique behaviors that might be called an "urban way of life." Given his study emphasis, Wirth naturally returned to Simmel. However, while Simmel (along with Weber and Marx) attributed much of the city way of life to the influence of larger systemic forces, especially capitalism and its money economy, Wirth aimed for a general theory that ignored forces having origins outside the city. He studied the characteristics of people in the city and how life there might produce a distinct "urban" culture. Hence, "urbanism," or an urban way of life, became the dependent variable to be explained.

In his important essay "Urbanism as a Way of Life" (1948), Wirth focused on three factors. Urbanism was produced in relatively large and densely populated settlements containing groups of persons of different backgrounds; that is, urbanism was a product of large *population size*, *density*, and *heterogeneity*. Wirth's approach was an important advance because he provided a set of factors that could be analyzed statistically according to their effects. It was a theory with true predictive power. Given a sample of cities, the higher each one scored on the three factors of size, density, and heterogeneity, the more one could expect it to house a true urban culture.

Wirth's theory was impressive for the time because of its predictive potential. Problems arose when he tried to define what precisely an urban culture would be like. Recall the example of Hans. Simmel gave us a detailed picture that contained both negative and positive aspects. Essentially, Simmel viewed the city as simply different. In his formulation, Wirth stressed the dark side of Simmel's vision: Urbanism as a culture would be characterized by aspects of social disorganization. Most central to Wirth's view was the shift from primary to secondary social relations. Wirth tended

Box 3.3

Urbanism as a Way of Life

Louis Wirth did not believe that there was a specific number that magically created an urban space (compare this idea with the definitions of urban from Chapter 1). Instead, he believed that cities differ from rural areas because of three factors—the size, density, and heterogeneity of the population—that interact with one another to produce a specific urban way of life. Here are some of the effects of the variables as Worth described them:

The effect of size: The greater the size of the population, the greater the specialization and diversity of social roles we find within the city—and so too the diversity of the population itself. Because the population lacks a common identity, competition and formal mechanisms of social control would replace primary relations of kinship as a means of organizing society. Because human relationships are highly segmented, there is increased anonymity and fragmentation of social interaction. These effects can be liberating (one has greater anonymity and can do as one likes) but may also lead to anomie and social disorganization.

The effect of density: The increased density of the urban population intensifies the effects of large population size, increases competition among individuals and groups, and thereby creates a need for specialization. Greater density produces greater tolerance for living closely with strangers but also creates greater stress as groups that do not share a common identity come into contact with one another. Increased competition leads to mutual exploitation, while greater density leads to the need to tune out excessive stimulation.

The effect of heterogeneity: Individuals in the city have regular contact with persons and groups that differ from them in many ways: ethnicity, race, and social status, as described above. Increased heterogeneity leads to greater tolerance among groups as ethnic and class barriers are broken down. But the effect also is to compartmentalize individual roles and contacts, and, as a result, anonymity and depersonalization in public life increase.

The increased size, density, and heterogeneity of urban areas leaves us with an urban environment where individuals are alienated and alone, where primary groups have been splintered. The individual is now subject to the influence of the mass media and mass social movements where the individual must "subordinate some of this individuality to the demands of the larger community."

to see urban anonymity as debilitating. More specifically, the effects of the three factors on social life can be expressed as a series of propositions, as indicated in Box 3.3.

Wirth's work has been exhaustively tested, mainly because it was so clearly stated (Fischer, 1975). The core assertion that size, density, and heterogeneity cause a specific set of behaviors considered urban has not been borne out. If we look at the propositions presented in Box 3.3, many of the assertions appear to be accurate descriptions of social interaction in the large city, and they help to provide a more detailed picture of what urbanism as a culture is like. However, while the theory contains some truth, we cannot be certain that these factors produce specific results. Cities merely concentrate the effects of societal forces producing urban culture. Surely we know that small towns are affected by many of the same social forces as the central city, although the types of behaviors that we observe in these environments may differ in type and intensity.

Finally, Louis Wirth held strongly to the view that the true effects of urbanism would occur as a matter of evolution as cities operated on immigrant groups to break down traditional ways of interacting over time. He did not see the larger city acting as an environment to bring about immediately the change he predicted. These things would take time, perhaps a generation. "Urbanism as a Way of Life" would inspire other urban sociologists to analyze the development of new suburban lifestyles ("Suburbanism as a Way of Life"; see Fava, 1980) and to compare urban and suburban lifestyles ("Urbanism and Suburbanism as Ways of Life"; Gans, 1968). We will return to the topic of urbanism and continue discussing the refinement of Wirth's ideas up to the present in Chapter 8. Wirth's work also inspired a subsequent generation to plow through census data and derive the statistical regularities of urban living. Much urban research is similarly conducted today.

THE CHICAGO SCHOOL OF URBAN SOCIOLOGY

While it is common to date the origin of urban sociology at Chicago to Robert Park's arrival in 1914 and his subsequent work with Ernest Burgess, the idea of the city as a laboratory for social research came much earlier (Hutchison, 2009). Charles Henderson, one of the founding members of the department, applied for funds for a systematic study of the city in the 1890s, and W. I. Thomas began his research on *The Polish Peasant in Europe and the United States* in 1908. An early (1902) description of the graduate program in the *American Journal of Sociology* stated:

> The city of Chicago is one of the most complete social laboratories in the world. While the elements of sociology may be studied in smaller communities . . . the most serious problems of modern society are presented by the great cities, and must be studied as they are encountered in concrete form in large populations. No city in the world presents a wider variety of typical social problems than Chicago.

Robert Park and Human Ecology

Robert Park (1865–1944) attended the University of Michigan and began his career as a newspaper reporter, first for the *Minneapolis Journal* and later for the *New York Journal*. Because he was assigned to the police beat at the newspapers he would have to pound the streets to develop leads and check facts for his news articles. He returned to graduate school at Harvard University and traveled to Germany, where he took courses with Georg Simmel and received a degree from the University of Heidelberg. In 1912 Park organized a conference on race relations at Tuskegee Institute. He was approached by W. I. Thomas, who taught at the University of Chicago. Thomas wanted to know if Park would come to the university and join other scholars in the newly formed department of sociology (Blumer, 1984; Mathews, 1977).

Box 3.4

Robert Park's Fascinating Career

Robert Park was born in Redwing, Minnesota, in 1864. His father did not want to send him to college, insisting that he was not "the studious type," but Park saved money from a summer job working with a railroad crew to pay for his college tuition. He graduated from the University of Michigan, where he took courses with John Dewey, and began his career as a newspaper reporter, first in Minneapolis and later in Denver, New York, and Chicago. Despite a successful career in the newspaper business, including serving as city editor for two Detroit newspapers, Park decided to return to graduate school.

He received his MA in philosophy from Harvard University in 1899 and then moved his family to Berlin, where he attended lectures by Georg Simmel, and later received his PhD from Heidelberg University. Returning to the United States in 1903, he became secretary of the Congo Reform Association and wrote a series of articles that exposed the atrocities of the Belgian government in its African colony.

While working with the Congo Reform Association, Park met Booker T. Washington, the most influential black American leader of the day and the founder of the Tuskegee Institute, and decided that he was sick and tired of the academic world and wanted to "get back into the world of men." Washington invited Park to become the publicist for the Institute, and for the next decade Park served as Washington's personal secretary, revising papers and speeches. Park used his spare time to investigate lynching in the American South and to write about race relations in the United States.

In 1912 Park organized the International Conference on the Negro at Tuskegee. One of the scholars he invited was W. I. Thomas from the University of Chicago.

continues

Box 3.4 *continued*

The two became friends, and Thomas invited Park to come to Chicago to teach. Park arrived in Chicago in 1914 and began the work that we are familiar with from the Chicago School of Urban Sociology. Because of Park's connections with Washington and Tuskegee, the University of Chicago attracted a number of black students and produced the first generation of African American sociologists in the United States, including E. Franklin Frazer, Horace Cayton, and St. Clair Drake (this at a time when black students were not allowed to attend many universities). Another of Park's students, Charles Johnson, wrote the final commission report on the Chicago Race Riots of 1919.

Charles Johnson moved to Fisk University in Nashville, Tennessee, where he would serve as president of the historically all-black school. When it came time to retire from the University of Chicago (in 1936 at the age of 72), Johnson invited Park to come to Fisk, and together they established an urban laboratory to conduct studies of race relations in American cities. Park died in Nashville in 1944, and in 1955, Fisk University named a new dormitory Park-Johnson Hall in honor of his work.

Robert Park's contributions before and after his years at the University of Chicago have largely been overlooked, as if he discovered urban sociology there and left it behind when he retired. But in reality he spent his long and exciting career engaged with the city, with sociological study, and with the African American community before and after his years in Chicago.

In 1914, at age forty-nine, Park joined the faculty of the University of Chicago on a part-time basis. Park's approach to the sociological study of the urban environment was clear: He urged his students to "get the seat of their pants dirty" by getting out into the neighborhoods of the city, studying the many different groups of people who had come there. While Park worked with W. I. Thomas on a study of immigrant adaptation to the urban environment and on his own study of the development of the immigrant press in the United States, he and Ernest Burgess conducted undergraduate classes and graduate seminars that required students to go into the community, collect data from businesspeople, interview area residents, and report back with their information.

From the very first, the Chicago School sociologists adopted a conceptual position that we know as human ecology—the study of the process of human group adjustment to the environment. Whereas European thinkers such as Weber, Marx, and Simmel viewed the city as an environment where larger social and economic forces of capitalism played themselves out in a human drama, Chicago School sociologists avoided the study of capitalism per se, preferring instead a biologically based way of conceptualizing urban life. For them urban analysis was a branch of human ecology.

Their ideas brought them closest to the work of the philosopher Herbert Spencer, who also viewed society as dominated by biological rather than economic laws of development. Economic competition, in this view, was a special case of the Darwinian struggle for survival. All individuals in the city were caught up in this struggle and adjusted to it in various ways.

According to Park, the social organization of the city resulted from the struggle for survival that then produced a distinct and highly complex division of labor, because people tried to do what they were best at in order to compete. Urban life was organized on two distinct levels: the biotic and the cultural. The *biotic level* refers to the forms of organization produced by species' competition over scarce environmental resources. The *cultural level* refers to the symbolic and psychological adjustment processes and to the organization of urban life according to shared sentiments, much like the qualities Simmel studied.

In Park's work, the biotic level stressed the importance of biological factors for understanding social organization and the urban effects of economic competition. In contrast, the cultural component of urban life operated in neighborhoods that were held together by cooperative ties involving shared cultural values among people with similar backgrounds. Hence, local community life was organized around what Park called a "moral order" of cooperative, symbolic ties, whereas the larger city composed of separate communities was organized through competition and functional differentiation. In his later work, however, the complex notion of urbanism as combining competition and cooperation, or the biotic and the cultural levels, was dropped in favor of an emphasis on the biotic level alone as the basic premise of urban ecology. This led to some of the earliest critiques of the ecological perspective, faulting it for ignoring the role of culture in the city, or what Simmel would call the important influence of modernity, and for neglecting the basis of community (Alihan, 1938), which was social and not biological.

Other members of the early Chicago School translated the Social Darwinism implicit in this model into a spatially attuned analysis. In 1924, Roderick McKenzie (one of Park's students) published an article titled "The Ecological Approach to the Study of the Human Community" that gives the definitive statement of this approach: The fundamental quality of the struggle for existence was position, or location, for the individual, the group, or institutions such as business firms. Spatial position would be determined by economic competition and the struggle for survival. Groups or individuals that were successful took over the better positions in the city, such as the choicest business locations, or the preferred neighborhoods. The less successful would have to make do with less desirable positions. In this way the urban population, under pressure of economic competition, sorted itself out within the city space. McKenzie explained land-use patterns as the product of competition and an economic division of labor, which deployed objects and activities in space according to the roles they played in society. Thus, if a firm needed a particular location to perform its function, it competed with others for that location. The study of urban patterns resulting from that process would be studied by a new group of sociologists known as ecologists.

Burgess's Model of Urban Growth

Ernest Burgess developed a theory of city growth and differentiation based on the social Darwinist or biologically derived principles common in the work of Park and McKenzie. According to Burgess, the city constantly grew because of population pressure. This, in turn, triggered a dual process of central agglomeration and commercial decentralization; that is, spatial competition attracted new business and commercial activities to the center of the city but also repelled other activities to the fringe area. This process forced other activities out and away from the core, and so the fringe itself was pushed farther out from the city, and so on.

The city continually grew outward as activities that have lost out in the competition for space in the central city relocate to peripheral areas. This sorting and survival of the fittest led, in turn, to further spatial and functional differentiation as activities were deployed according to competitive advantages. In Burgess's theory, the city would eventually take on the form of a highly concentrated central business district that would dominate the region and be the site for the highest competitive land prices, while the surrounding area would comprise four distinct concentric rings. A copy of Burgess's map for the city of Chicago is shown in Figure 3.1 (the original map is displayed in the office of the sociology department at the University of Chicago).

The importance of Burgess's model cannot be overemphasized. First, he explained the pattern of homes, neighborhoods, and industrial and commercial location in terms of the ecological theory of competition over "position," or location. Competition produced a certain ordering of space as well as a certain social organization in space. Both of these dimensions were pictured in the concentric zone model. Those who could afford it lived near the center; those who could not arranged themselves in concentric zones around the city center.

Second, Burgess's model explained the shifting of population and activities within the space of the city according to two distinct but related processes: centralization and decentralization. His theory explicitly related social processes to spatial patterns—a most important link for all theorizing about the city that was to follow and a view that is quite compatible with the aims of the new urban sociology.

Finally, Burgess revealed that the characteristics of the social organization of the urban population were spatially deployed. A gradient running from the center to the periphery characterized the attributes of the urban population. Individual traits such as mental illness, gang membership, criminal behavior, and racial background were found to be clustered along the center/periphery gradient of the city. Cutting across the urban form from the central business district (known as the CBD) to the out-

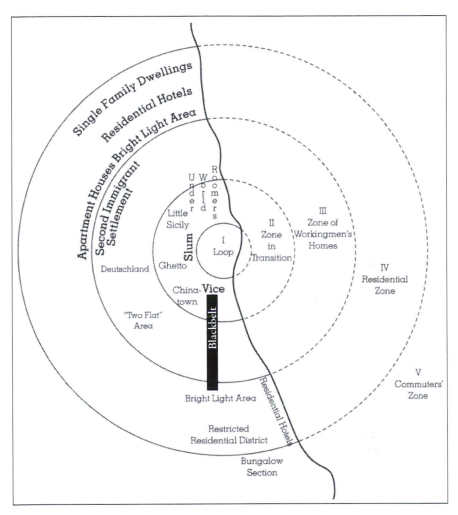

FIGURE 3.1 Burgess's Model of Concentric Zones. Ernest Burgess's model of the growth of the city shows concentric zones moving away from the central area; it also takes into account natural features (the lakefront) as well as areas of concentrated activities (such as the "Bright Light Area" on the north) and the location of ethnic communities (such as Little Sicily on the north and the Black Belt on the south). SOURCE: Reprinted courtesy of University of Chicago Press.

skirts, Chicago School researchers, using census data, found that the incidence of social pathology decreased, while homeownership and the number of nuclear families increased. The inner zones, therefore, were discovered to be the sites of crime, illness, gang warfare, broken homes, and many other indicators of social disorganization or problems.

In practice, however, research on the internal structure of cities would contradict Burgess's view of concentric zones. The first critique of Burgess's model was proposed by Homer Hoyt (1933) and was called "sector theory." Hoyt argued that cities were carved up not by concentric zones but by unevenly shaped sectors within which different economic activities tended to congregate together, that is, agglomerate. Hoyt suggested that all activities, but especially manufacturing and retailing, had the tendency to spin off away from the center and agglomerate in sectors that expanded outward. Thus, the city grew in irregular blobs rather than in Burgess's neat circles.

Other models argued that cities had multiple centers rather than a single urban core. Chauncy Harris and Edward Ullman (1945) suggested that within any city, separate functions and their particular needs require concentration within specific and specialized districts. Thus, within cities, similar activities often locate in the same area, forming agglomerations, or minicenters. Cities often grow asymmetrically around these multiple nuclei. The idea of multiple nuclei as the shape of the city further developed Hoyt's break from Burgess and is similar to the current multicentered approach used in this book (see Chapter 1).

A common assumption of all of these models is that the city remains the central place that dominates all other areas. In recent years this way of thinking about urbanized areas has been replaced by the regional perspective, which stresses the relative independence of multiple centers within the larger metropolitan region. While ecologists were concerned with location and with thinking of social activities as located in space, their biologically based explanation for perceived activities and spatial patterns has been rejected in favor of the new urban sociology (see Gottdiener and Feagin [1988] for an earlier analysis of this change in theoretical paradigms).

The Chicago School Studies

The work of the early Chicago School dominated urban sociology in the prewar years. For about a decade, beginning in the early 1920s, a veritable flood of work poured out of the sociology department. Surveying the books alone (that is, not including MA and PhD theses produced at that time), the following list gives some idea of the range of studies and accomplishments of the Chicago School. Many of these works are classics in our field of study:

> Roderick D. McKenzie, *The Neighborhood: A Study of Columbus, Ohio* (1923)
> Frederick Thrasher, *The Gang: A Study of 1,313 Gangs in Chicago* (1927)
> Louis Wirth, *The Ghetto* (1928)
> Ruth S. Cavan, *Suicide* (1928)
> Harvey W. Zorbaugh, *The Gold Coast and the Slum* (1929)
> Clifford R. Shaw, *The Jackroller* (1930)
> Paul G. Cressey, *The Taxi-Dance Hall* (1932)

Walter C. Reckless, *Vice in Chicago* (1933)
Norman Hayner, *Hotel Life* (1936)

This marvelous output was produced with a similar stamp. It took an important social phenomenon, such as suicide, and located the distribution of its incidence in the space of the city. Chicago researchers then analyzed it in terms of the relation between the individual and the larger social forces of integration/disintegration. Most often this meant that social phenomena were explained as products of social disorganization, particularly the breaking up of primary social relations through city living, as Wirth's theory suggested. As a result, the Chicago School would later be criticized for reinforcing a negative view of city life.

Despite their limitations, we can appreciate the importance of these early efforts. First, Chicago School researchers explicitly connected social phenomena with spatial patterns; that is, they thought in sociospatial terms. Second, they took an interactionist perspective. Individuals were studied in interaction with others, and the emergent forms of sociation coming out of that interaction were observed closely. Finally, they tried to show the patterns of adjustment to sociospatial location and developed a rudimentary way of speaking about the role of individual attributes in explaining urban phenomena. It was true that they focused almost exclusively on social disorganization and pathology; the breakup of family relationships, for example, was given much more attention than questions of race or class.

One early project of the Chicago School was the creation of mappings of the city of Chicago that divided the city into seventy distinct community areas. The importance of spatial analysis in the Chicago School studies can be seen in the map shown in Figure 3.2, which shows the location of taxi dance halls in Chicago in the period 1927–1930. Most of the Chicago School studies made use of a common base map of Chicago or Ernest Burgess's map of concentric zones; some, the early Delinquency Areas (Shaw, Zorbaugh, McKay, and Cottrell, 1929) would overlay the concentric zones on the base map. Paul Cressey's *The Taxi-Dance Hall: A Sociological Study in Commercialized Recreation and City Life* examined a particular social institution—the taxi dance hall—that developed to provide entertainment for single men in the industrial cities. It included not just the mapping of the location of the taxi dance halls (shown in Figure 3.2) but also maps that showed where the customers who frequented the dance halls lived, and where the young women who worked in the dance halls lived. The taxi dance halls were located in rooming-house areas of the city, as were the patrons of the dance halls, while the taxi dancers (the young women) lived in immigrant neighborhoods on the north side of the city. Cressey's own ethnographic work in the dance halls further explains that the patrons were recent immigrants who lived in the single-room apartments of the rooming house districts.

Other studies took a similar spatial approach to the study of urban phenomena. Harvey Zorbaugh's study, *The Gold Coast and the Slum*, made extensive use of maps

FIGURE 3.2 Location of Taxi Dance Halls in Chicago, 1927–1930. Many of the Chicago School studies used the base map of Chicago to locate the groups and institutions that were discussed in the research; in this example, Paul Cressey mapped the location of taxi dance halls in Chicago. SOURCE: Reprinted courtesy of University of Chicago Press.

to show where wealthy households (measured by persons listed in the social register in one case) lived along the Chicago lakefront (known as the Gold Coast), and areas where there were high delinquency rates and criminal activity (in the Slum). Interestingly, one of Zorbaugh's maps shows a street intersection labeled Death Corner—the same location where the Cabrini-Green public housing project would be constructed over a twenty-year period beginning in the 1940s (Francis Cabrini Rowhouses in 1942, the Cabrini Extension in 1958, and the William Green Houses in 1962).

Box 3.5

Street Gangs in Chicago, 1927

In the 1920s most street gangs were composed principally of recent immigrants to this country. Thrasher's census of street gangs in Chicago (included some 25,000 members in a city of 2 million) showed that roughly 17 percent were known as Polish gangs, 11 percent were Italian, 8.5 percent were Irish, 7 percent were black, and so on, with the largest percentage of all gangs composed of "mixed nationalities." While roughly 87 percent of all gang members were of foreign extraction, they were organized by territory, not by ethnicity. According to Thrasher, the gang phenomenon was explained in part by the lack of adjustment opportunities for immigrants, in part by the carryover of Old World antagonisms, and also by the need to defend territory against "outsiders."

Thrasher's study demonstrates sociospatial thinking. As Robert Park comments in his introduction, "The title of this book does not describe it. It is a study of the gang, to be sure, but it is at the same time a study of 'gangland,' that is to say, a study of the gang and its habitat, and in this case the habitat is a city slum."

Park grounded Thrasher's study in a biological metaphor by his use of the word *habitat*. Today we would adopt the sociospatial perspective and say *territory* or *space*. Gangland is the city space where gangs lived. Their influence was felt all over. What Thrasher did was locate gangs in their space. In fact, he found "three great domains" of gangdom—the "northside jungles," the "southside badlands," and the "westside wilderness." Using Ernest Burgess's map of Chicago (see Figure 3.1), Thrasher provided details for each of these areas and the gangs they contained. Within gangland, "The street educates with fatal precision" (1927:101). The northside covered an area directly north of the Chicago Loop on the Burgess map and behind the wealthy neighborhoods that lined the shore of Lake Michigan. It was home to the "Gloriannas," the location of "Death Corner" and "Bughouse Square," and a gang so threatening that Thrasher disguised its real name.

The westside was the most extensive slum area producing gangs, and it encompassed the area west of downtown, spreading out both northward and southward.

continues

Box 3.5 *continued*

The westside was home to the "Blackspots," the "Sparkplugs," the "Beaners," and the "hard-boiled 'Buckets-of-Blood'" (1927:9). The South Side of Chicago, with its stockyards and miles of railroad yards, was dominated by Poles and Italians, and gangs were known as the "Torpedoes" and the "So-So's." Also on the South Side, black gangs of the time were the "Wailing Shebas" and the "Wolves."

In a city divided by neighborhoods, Chicago pulsed with the give-and-take confrontations among the various gangs. Only the relative scarcity of killing weapons such as handguns kept the constant confrontations from erupting into the type of carnage characteristic of many cities today. For students of contemporary urban sociology, there can be no better example of spatially sensitive research than Thrasher's original study. Moreover, it is doubtful, in today's urban environment, that anyone could carry out the kind of exhaustive census on street gangs that Thrasher was able to accomplish. Certain parts of his study are now outdated, but like the pyramids, it remains an inspiration across time.

Another way to appreciate the achievements of the Chicago School is by returning to the original case studies. A particularly vivid ethnography is Frederick M. Thrasher's 1927 study called *The Gang: A Study of 1,313 Gangs in Chicago*. Thrasher spent eight years tracking down the youth gangs of Chicago and identified more than a thousand groups that he called gangs. Today media coverage tends to associate street gangs with black or Hispanic teenagers in the inner city and lament their violent ways, as exemplified by such films as *Boyz N The Hood* and *Locas*. Thrasher's work takes us back to the city of some seventy years ago when gangs were as much of a problem, but their members were almost all white. Thrasher's study is described in more detail in Box 3.5.

Roderick McKenzie and the Metropolitan Community

Roderick McKenzie was principal investigator on urban trends for President Herbert Hoover's Committee on Recent Social Trends, and author of the chapter titled "The Rise of Metropolitan Regions" in *Recent Social Trends* (1933). McKenzie used this opportunity to apply the principles of urban ecology to a regional metropolitan approach. He viewed the development of the metropolitan region as a function of changes in transportation and communication that produced new forms of social organization. These stages of development were the pre-railway era (before 1850), the railway era (1850–1900), and the motor transportation area (1900 to present). McKenzie considered technological change to be the key variable in producing spatial patterns in urban society, as he states in his introduction to *The Metropolitan Community*:

Formerly independent towns and villages and also rural territory have become part of this enlarged city complex. This new type of super community, organized around a dominant focal point and comprising a multitude of differentiated centers of activity, differs from the metropolitanism established by rail transportation in the complexity of its institutional division of labor and the mobility of its population. Its territorial scope is defined in terms of motor transportation and competition with other regions. (1933:6–7)

McKenzie's ideas were recognized as a significant contribution to the field at the time. In some respects, his approach may be viewed as a precursor to the general concept of the multicentered metropolitan region emphasized by the sociospatial approach. McKenzie spent the last seven years of his life working on a manuscript that set forth a more systematic statement of the principles of urban ecology. Perhaps because this work was left unfinished, he is sometimes overlooked even by contemporary urban ecologists. It is interesting to speculate on the reasons for this oversight. In the 1950s, a new field of study, regional science, began investigating metropolitan regions from the perspective of economic geography, an approach with less appeal to urban sociologists. McKenzie's focus on the metropolitan region conflicted with the more general tendency of urban sociologists to focus their research and writing, as well as fieldwork, on the central city. A serious consideration of his regional perspective would have led urban sociology out of the city and into the suburban region, something that would not happen for several decades but is a central focus of this text.

FROM HUMAN ECOLOGY TO URBAN ECOLOGY

In 1945, Walter Firey published a study of land use in Boston titled "Sentiment and Symbolism as Ecological Variables." He noted that large areas of land in downtown Boston were reserved for noneconomic uses. Parks and cemeteries, as well as a forty-eight-acre area in the center of the city that had formed the original "commons" of the community, had never been developed. In addition, an upper-class residential neighborhood known as Beacon Hill retained its privileged position as a home to wealthy and established Boston families despite its location near the downtown area. Each of these observations ran counter to Burgess's concentric zone model. Firey suggested that "sentiment" and "symbolism" were important ecological factors that influenced spatial patterns of development in urban space (Firey, 1945). Although other sociologists have offered little systematic elaboration of the ideas Firey presented in this important piece of research, his work is often referred to as the "sociocultural school" of urban ecology.

After World War II, the ecological approach enjoyed something of a renaissance as ecologists examined how demographic patterns had changed in American cities. By 1950, it was found that the U.S. population had matured and spread across metropolitan regions. In addition to altering population dispersal, the war years had changed the locational patterns of U.S. industry. Many industrial plants dispersed to the countryside during the 1940s. As a result of the war effort against Japan, heavy industry was also decentralized and relocated to the West. Los Angeles in particular became both a focal point for the burgeoning aerospace industry and an important port for trade with the Pacific Rim markets. All of this restructuring and change called for new research that would chart the emergent patterns of metropolitan development.

Social Area Analysis

Social area analysis is associated with the work of Eshrev Shevky and Wendell Bell (1955). This method of urban analysis ranked areas within a city or metropolitan area on the basis of the social characteristics of the population, including social status (education, occupation, and income) and family status (number of children, whether the

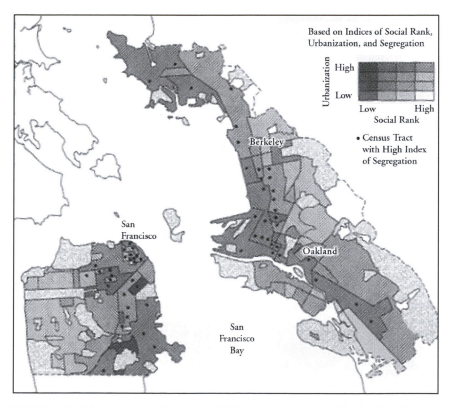

FIGURE 3.3 Social Area Analysis. Shevky and Bell's social area analysis of the San Francisco Bay Area shows the spatial location of social class and ethnic groups by contrasting regions of high social status (light areas) with regions of high urbanization (darker areas). SOURCE: Reprinted courtesy of Greenwood Press.

mother worked, and type of dwelling unit). Areas that scored high on social status and family status (typically suburban communities) could be compared with areas that scored low on the same measures. Social area analysis produced detailed maps showing the location of class and ethnic groups in the San Francisco Bay Area, as shown in Figure 3.3; especially noticeable in this mapping are the minority neighborhoods in Richmond, Oakland, and San Francisco, as well as the upper-class suburban neighborhoods in the foothills of the East Bay. But as a more general contribution to urban ecology and urban sociology, social area analysis was found to be lacking. It was a descriptive methodology, this time with a visual application, but it did not provide an analytical model that could explain why particular groupings of sociological variables (ethnicity, social class, and family status) might be mapped in one area of the metropolitan region and not in another.

Factorial Ecology

The development of new computer technologies brought sweeping changes to the field of urban ecology. Urban sociologists no longer had to limit their research to field studies of urban communities; now they could assemble data for entire cities and look for associations among, for example, the educational levels, incomes, and employment status of urban and suburban residents. Factorial ecology made use of these techniques and, through the 1950s and 1960s, produced a large number of studies that greatly increased our knowledge of the structure of cities, not just in the United States but around the world.

In the usual model, data concerning the social, economic, and family status of urban residents is examined for commonalities among households living in different areas of the city. Each census tract or community area has specific information as to the educational levels, incomes, and employment status of area residents (economic status); the age, marital status, and presence of children (family status); and racial and ethnic characteristics (urbanism). A computer-generated analysis of this information then reveals the structure of urban areas. The factorial analysis of data for American cities and their suburbs indicated that economic status is the most important determinant of residential location, followed by family status and then social status. Because of their increasing focus on these variables and an associated decrease in the field research and community studies, which employed a very different sort of research methodology, urban sociologists working in this tradition became known as urban ecologists rather than human ecologists.

Having examined the ecological structure of urban areas in the United States, it was only a matter of time before urban ecologists turned their attention to the structure of cities in other areas of the world (see Schwirian, 1974). In a sense, they were out to prove a very important point: Urban ecology was in fact a research paradigm that could be applied to human settlement spaces across time and across space. They believed this model could explain not only the structure of cities in Europe (which had evolved out of a feudal mode of production and with a physical structure very different from that of American cities) but also that of cities in developing nations. According to this theory, residential dissimilarity and segregation among groups (based on religion, ethnicity, caste, or occupation) is universal, and modernization or industrialization will have no effect on this pattern (Mehta, 1969).

Although the evidence from studies of cities in India, Finland, and Egypt was sometimes inconsistent, urban ecologists still believed they had discovered a universal model of urban structure. In "The Factorial Ecology of Calcutta," Brian Berry and Albert Rees (1969) presented an "integrated model of land use" that combined the concentric zone, sector, and multinuclei models of the past and stated their belief that once the additional effects of local geography or history had been taken into account, their model could be applied to any city to explain where any group or business activity is located.

CONCLUSION

All theoretical paradigms are beset with potential problems and contradictions. Theoretical models borrow concepts from other fields of study; they are creatures of the concerns and beliefs of scholars at a particular historical moment. Robert Park wanted to create a new "science of society" and borrowed the model of plant ecology to formulate his model of human ecology. He incorporated the idea of conflict among competing land uses and competition among population groups, although it is unlikely that he envisioned the particular forms of conflict among class, ethnic, and racial groups that beset American society in the twenty-first century. Later ecologists would incorporate new methods of data analysis to answer new and even more challenging questions concerning urban life than the early Chicago sociologists could have imagined. But human ecology and its offspring, social ecology and urban ecology, confront numerous obstacles when studying the complexities of the multicentered metropolitan regions that now characterize urban society in the United States and across the globe.

The human ecology paradigm gives undue prominence to just one factor—technological innovation—to explain urban growth and change. Roderick McKenzie viewed changes in the metropolitan region as the product of shifts in transportation technology. This approach created problems for other human ecologists who followed McKenzie. Amos Hawley, who was McKenzie's student and perhaps the best-known human ecologist, wanted to explain two aspects of change in the postwar period: the massive growth of suburbanization and the restructuring of central city areas away from manufacturing and toward administration. In explaining these changes, he dropped the early ecologists' concern for space itself. He viewed social organization as fundamentally produced by the technologies of communication and transportation. As the technology of these means of interaction changed, so did the patterns of social organization.

The ecological perspective remains active in urban sociology. The core biological metaphor has been retained, as well as the central view that social organization should be understood as a process of adaptation to the environment. Human ecologists avoid any mention of social groupings such as classes or along ethnic, racial, and gender lines. Ecologists see urban life as a process of adaptation to pre-existing conditions, rather than competition over scarce resources that often brings conflict. They have a limited conception of the economy, which is still viewed as simply the social organization of functions and division of labor—a conception that neglects the dynamics of capitalism and the global system. Although they emphasize ecological location, they ignore the real estate industry and its role in developing space, something that the housing crisis of the first decade of the twenty-first century tells us is very important. Finally, urban ecologists have overlooked the important political institutions that administer and regulate society and affect everyday life through the institutional channeling of resources, another very important part of the current housing crisis. Their emphasis on push factors (or demand-side view) neglects the powerful supply-side causes of growth and change in the metropolis. We will examine the factors responsible for the development of the multicentered metropolitan region in the next chapter as we explore the new urban sociology.

KEY CONCEPTS

gemeinschaft / gesellschaft
mechanical solidarity / organic solidarity
modernity
urbanism
rational calculation
blasé attitude
human ecology
concentric zones
sector theory
multiple nuclei
size / density / heterogeneity
Chicago School of urban sociology
social area analysis
factorial ecology
urban ecology

IMPORTANT NAMES

Emile Durkheim
Ernest Burgess

Amos Hawley
Homer Hoyt
Roderick McKenzie
Robert Park
Georg Simmel
Frederick Thrasher
Ferdinand Töennies
Max Weber
Louis Wirth

DISCUSSION QUESTIONS

1. Early sociologists shared a common vision of the consequences of industrialization and urbanization for social organization. What did Georg Simmel, Ferdinand Tönnies, Emile Durkheim, and others see as the consequences of the shift from village life to the modern city?

2. Georg Simmel ultimately felt that urban life would result in greater individual freedom. Why is this likely to be the case?

3. In the text you have examined several competing models of urban structure: concentric zones, sector theory, and multiple nuclei. Explain how each of these models could be used to explain the development of the city that you live in. Which of these models gives the best explanation for the development of your city?

4. Roderick McKenzie wrote about the development and importance of metropolitan regions. Why was this important work overlooked by other human ecologists? How is McKenzie's work similar to the discussion of the multinucleated metropolitan region emphasized in this textbook?

5. In the 1960s and 1970s, human ecologists sought to apply new computer technologies to the study of urbanization. What are some of the results of this research? What did human ecologists see as the limitations of their theoretical model and of its application for studying urbanization in other parts of the world?

CHAPTER 4

CONTEMPORARY
URBAN SOCIOLOGY

At the beginning of this text, we discussed several conceptual changes that are the hallmark of the new urban sociology. These include a shift to a global perspective on capitalism and the metropolis; the inclusion of factors such as class exploitation, racism, gender, and space in the analysis of metropolitan development; an attempt, when possible, to integrate economic, political, and cultural factors of analysis; special attention to the pull factors of real estate investment and government intervention; and the shift to a multicentered, regional approach to cities and suburbs. In the preceding chapters we have used these concepts, which we call the *sociospatial* approach.

In addition to a change in perspective, the new urban sociology involves important theoretical changes in the way human environments are analyzed. The previous chapter discussed classical and current urban sociology of a traditional kind. This chapter considers the new theoretical ideas that have recently invigorated the urban field.

Since the 1970s, a great deal of creative work has been accomplished by numerous writers who have challenged orthodox ideas of city development. One of the most interesting observations about this effort is that much of it has been carried out by people in other fields and even in other countries. Only recently has U.S. urban sociology been affected by new theories. Second, regardless of the international scope and intellectual diversity, most of the new approaches have their origin in the application to city environments of Max Weber's, Karl Marx's, and Friedrich Engels's writings regarding the analysis of capitalism. This chapter concerns this "political economy" approach. While this perspective represents a considerable advance over those discussed in the previous chapter, mainly because the ecological perspective simply ignores the important role of economic and political interests, it has its own limitations. Sociologists have tried to tailor the approach of political economy to the needs of their discipline. In the concluding sections of this chapter, we will discuss such attempts, especially the sociospatial approach of this text.

POLITICAL ECONOMY AND THE CITY: CLASSIC APPROACHES

Marx, Weber, and Engels

The classical sociologists Karl Marx and Max Weber turned to historical analysis to explore their ideas regarding the general laws of social development. Both understood that societies were organized around integrated systems of economics, politics, and culture. Marx emphasized the dominance of economic considerations in analysis, while Weber sought to show how cultural and political factors also affected individual behavior and social history along with economic activity. The two approaches served to complement each other.

While Marx wrote extensively about the new social classes (proletariat and bourgeoisie) created by industrial capitalism, he did not believe there were only two social class groups, as is commonly thought. In his analysis of the failure of the 1848 revolution in France, Marx identified seven social class groups and discussed why each group supported (or opposed) a new government. Industrial workers and small shopkeepers in the cities might support the revolution, for example, because their economic and political interests would benefit from a change in the government, whereas farmers in the countryside and large merchants in the cities might oppose it because their economic and social interests were dependent on maintaining the current government (Marx, n.d.). In this sense, Marx's view of social classes may be seen as a precursor to modern-day thinking about interest groups competing within the political arena.

Marx also recognized that the interests of capital and labor are not one and the same—a radical departure from the economic theory of his time, and the idea that "a rising tide lifts all boats." Because profit results from the difference between the costs of production (raw material, machinery, and labor) and the price for which a commodity can be sold in the market, capitalist producers will look for any way possible to reduce the costs of production (Marx, 1967). Marx's analysis is as relevant for the monopoly capitalism of the present day as it was for the industrial capitalism of his time; in just the last several decades, we have seen the displacement of workers by automation, a dramatic increase in immigration, and the movement of manufacturing to countries in the developing world—all of these the consequence of corporations seeking to lower their labor costs, and all having a tremendous impact on the people and the built environment of urban and suburban settlement space across the world.

Marx wrote very little about the city in his classic *Capital* (1967; originally published in 1867), while Weber included some passages about the nature of the city in a much larger text, *Economy and Society* (1968; originally published in separate pieces beginning in the 1880s). For Marx, the early history of capitalism was a struggle between social relations located within urban areas and those situated in the countryside within feudal manors. For Weber, the city developed because of its political powers—

in particular, the independence of city residents and their local government from feudal relations of authority. In both cases, Marx and Weber showed how modes of social organization, such as feudalism or capitalism, work through a form of space—the city—and social relations situated within that spatial form. It is this perspective that informs the approach of political economy to settlement space.

For example, Weber argued that during the feudal period in the European Middle Ages, traders and craftspeople set up towns and bargained for protection from the king against the activities of local feudal lords. In these towns, capitalism began to thrive through trade in goods and eventually overtook the feudal economy. Thus, as capitalism became a dominating force in Europe, it also created the modern city. The political economy perspective studies social processes within urban space and links them to processes occurring at the general level of society.

While Marx and Weber had comparatively little to say about the industrial city of capitalism, Friedrich Engels devoted some time to the topic. We already mentioned his study of the working-class situation in nineteenth-century England and his field observations of the "great towns," Manchester in particular. For Engels, the large industrial city was the best place to study the general aspects of capitalism as a social system, just as the factory was the best place to study the specific details of the relationship between capital and labor. Engels picked the city of Manchester because it was built up as capitalism developed in England, as opposed to other cities, such as London, which had a longer history.

Engels observed several aspects of capitalism at work within the urban space. First, he noted that capitalism had a "double tendency" of concentration: It concentrated capital investment, or money, and also workers. This centralizing process made industrial production easier because of the large scale and close proximity of money and people. Second, Engels noticed that as Manchester developed, investment moved away from the old center and extended farther out to the periphery. Unlike Burgess, but very much like Harris and Ullman and the sociospatial approach, Engels pictured growth as a multiplication of centers. For him this followed no particular plan, and he observed that capitalism unregulated by government planning produced a spatial chaos of multiplying minicenters.

Third, among other important observations, Engels focused on the social problems created by the breakdown of traditional society and the operation of capitalism. In Manchester, he noticed examples of extreme poverty and deprivation: homelessness, orphan beggars, prostitution, alcoholism, and violence. For him this misery was the result of exploitation at the place of work, which went largely unseen in the factory itself, along with the failure of capitalism to provide adequate housing for everyone. He thus connected conditions in the workplace with those in the living space, or what Marxists call the *extended conditions* of capital accumulation, which involve the reproduction of social relations that ensure the continued use of the working class across the generations. For example, if problems such as poverty and homelessness become too severe, they can threaten the ability of working-class families to produce new generations of workers. This would then threaten the future of the capitalist system. Hence, neighborhood or living-space relations and the quality of daily life are just as important to the survival of capitalism as are relations at the place of work.

In addition to the problems of poverty, Engels observed that the city of Manchester was a segregated space. Rich and poor lived in segregated neighborhoods. Engels concluded that capitalism produces this spatial isolation of the classes. The sum total of all these social problems is described by the term *uneven development*, which conveys both the disparity between rich and poor and their segregation in space by capitalism. We will use this concept frequently in subsequent chapters.

Uneven Development

Urban and suburban settlement spaces grow and develop because of capital investment. The ebb and flow of money determines community well-being. Not only are jobs created, but economic activity also generates tax revenue. The latter is used partly by local government to fund public projects that improve the quality of community life. But spending, both public and private, is not uniformly distributed across metropolitan space. Some places receive much more investment than others. Even within cities there are great differences between those sections that are beehives of economic activity and those that seem scarcely touched by commerce and industry.

Within any given business, there are also great disparities between workers who are well paid and those who receive the minimum salary. Wages are carried home to neighborhoods, and a significant portion is spent in the local area. Hence, the well-being of a place depends not only on the amount of investment it can attract but also on the wealth of its residents.

In the metropolitan region, the variation in the affluence of particular places is called *uneven development*. It is a characteristic of our type of society with its economic system of capitalism, but, as we will see in Chapters 12 and 13, it is also characteristic of other societies, some of which have communist rather than capitalist economies. People with money seek to invest in places and enterprises that will bring them the highest rate of return. Profit drives the capitalist system. But this profit making is usually expected to occur in a short time period and with the largest return possible. Consequently, investors look carefully at opportunities and always try to switch to places where money will achieve its greatest return. This process also causes uneven development. As capital becomes increasingly mobile, it can shift money around more easily with corresponding effects on the quality of life. At present, capital is more mobile than ever before and has the ability to move operations from one country or region to another in search of the lowest costs or highest profit margins. This process, of course, can have immense consequences for individual places.

The changes since the late 1960s in Silicon Valley, the high-tech showcase of California, illustrate this pattern. In the 1960s, when the printed circuit industry was first expanding, all operations, including manufacturing, research and development, and marketing, were located within Silicon Valley. By the late 1960s, one of the leading manufacturers, Fairchild, transferred its manufacturing operations to plants in Mexico, leaving thousands of U.S. workers jobless. Soon after, other electronic assembly plants followed Fairchild's lead, and by the 1970s most of the manufacturing operations of Silicon Valley had been transferred to other countries with cheaper labor. By that time, too, owners of corporations had discovered that operating in Mexico was not as cheap as production in the Orient. Hence, many plants were shut down and work was transferred to Hong Kong, South Korea, and Singapore, then to Malaysia and Indonesia, and more recently to Sri Lanka. In Chapter 5, we will see that at present, Silicon Valley residents lament the rapidity with which the boom-and-bust cycle played itself out in their region. But other areas of the world are caught in a similar process because of the increased mobility of capital.

Silicon Valley residents are well-educated, and they hope that eventually a new round of investment will occur in their space from companies seeking their skills. At that time, their area of the country may once again prosper. When a place is poor, however, such as an urban ghetto, and its people have limited educations, it is highly unlikely that capital will come there and invest, especially when cheaper labor is available in other countries. This remains so even for "small" capital ventures, such as grocery stores. Ghetto areas, such as the Watts section of Los Angeles, have comparatively few places where residents can provide for their needs. Most often, they must travel out of their community to shop because local convenience stores charge excessive prices.

As a result of the inherent desire not to invest in places that are already depressed and offer little incentive for profit, uneven development usually becomes more acute over time. This pattern increases the polarization between those places that are poor and those that are thriving. But places are made of people, so the spatial disparities result in different life chances for metropolitan residents. As Engels observed in Manchester, inequities create a problem of social justice as the less affluent members of the working class find it difficult to raise families that will acquire a reasonable, productive status in society.

Because of uneven development, the society would degenerate into a two-tiered structure, with a select group of people and places that are thriving amid a sea of poverty, except that the U.S. government has stepped in with a safety net of programs that tries to prop up the bottom stratum. Unemployment insurance, welfare, and job training are but a few of the ways government agencies use tax revenues to fight the inherent tendency of capitalist activities to produce uneven development. Over the years, however, despite periods of prosperity, the problems of the poor have been little affected by government programs (Jencks, 1992). New techniques of public policy therefore are sorely needed.

Metropolitan areas today are besieged by the uneven nature of capitalist development. Job security and planning for the future are jeopardized for people in communities across the nation. Extremes of poverty and wealth characterize metropolitan life. This clash between rich and poor in the city was also observed over a hundred years ago by writers in the industrial towns of England. What is new and different today is the global reach of such uneven development and the way in which the cyclical nature of growth affects people and places across the world.

THE REVIVAL OF URBAN POLITICAL ECONOMY: HENRI LEFEBVRE

In the late 1960s and early 1970s, the Marxian tradition was revived in social science. Urban analysis was affected minimally at first in this country but greatly affected in France by the philosopher Henri Lefebvre. Lefebvre is without question the seminal source of new thinking on the city from a critical and Marxian perspective (Lefebvre, 1991). His accomplishments can be broken down into four areas:

1. He went back to the work of Marx and Engels on the city and extracted from their writing an urban political economy. That is, Lefebvre showed how it was possible to use economic categories such as capital investment, profit, rent, wages, class exploitation, and uneven development in the analysis of cities. In effect, he argued that the city development process was as much a product of the capitalist system as anything else—the production of shoes, for example. The same operation of the economy applies in both cases.

2. Lefebvre showed how Karl Marx's work on the city was limited. He introduced the idea of the circuits of capital, particularly the notion that real estate is a separate circuit of capital. For example, we often think of economic activity as involving the use of money by an investor of capital, the hiring of workers, their production of products in a factory, and the selling of the goods in a market for a profit, which can then be used for more investment. Automobile production would be a good example of this circuit. Lefebvre called all such industrial activity the "primary circuit of capital."

   Much of the wealth created in a capitalist society is of this type. But for Lefebvre there was a "second circuit of capital," real estate investment. For example, the investor in land chooses a piece of property and buys it; the land is either held on to or developed for some other use; it is then sold in a special market for land, the real estate market, or developed as housing for a profit. The circuit is completed when the investor takes that profit and reinvests it in more land-based projects. Lefebvre argued that the second circuit of capital is almost always attractive as investment because there is usually money to be made in real estate, although at present a recession is occurring in all economic sectors. As we have seen in the development of the United States, investment in land was an important means for the acquisition of wealth. But in addition, it was investment in real estate that pushed the growth of cities in specific ways.

3. Lefebvre also introduced the idea that real estate is a special case of the dynamics of settlement space. For Lefebvre, all social activities are not only about interaction among individuals but about space as well. Social activities take place in space. They also produce a space by creating objects. The city-building process, for example, creates a certain space. When we visit a city, we experience particular attributes of the space that was created in that area. Other city spaces may be different, although places produced by similar social systems tend to resemble each other, such as the close resemblance of suburbias in California and Virginia or between the United States and Australia.

Lefebvre therefore introduced the idea of space as a component of social organization, as we discussed in Chapter 1. When people discuss social interaction, they are implicitly talking about behavior in space as well. Space is involved in a dual sense (see Chapter 1): as an influence on behavior and, in turn, as the end result of construction behavior because people alter space to suit their own needs.

4. Finally, Lefebvre discussed the role of government in space. The state uses space for social control. Government places fire stations and police departments in separate locations across the metropolis in order to respond to distress relatively quickly. The state controls a large amount of land and utilizes it in its administration of government. It dispenses resources and collects taxes according to spatial units such as cities, counties, individual states, and regions. Government also makes decisions and relays them to individuals across the network of administrative units, that is, from the national level down to the separate regions, individual states, counties, cities, and ultimately neighborhoods.

Lefebvre argued that the way capital investors or businesspeople and the state think about space is according to its abstract qualities of dimension—size, width, area, location—and profit. This he called "abstract space." In addition, however, individuals use the space of their environment as a place to live. Lefebvre called this interactively used space of everyday life "social space." For him the uses proposed by government and business for abstract space, such as in the planning of a large city or suburban development of new houses, may conflict with the existing social space, the way residents currently use space. Lefebvre said that the conflict between abstract and social space is a basic one in society and ranks with the separate conflict among classes, but is often different. With this view, he also departed from Marxian analysis because the latter stresses class conflict as the basic force in the history of capitalism.

In sum, Lefebvre is responsible for a large number of the ideas that inform the sociospatial perspective used in this text. He also heavily influenced a number of critical and Marxian urbanists to develop ideas of their own. In the following sections, we will discuss some of the most contemporary urban approaches and indicate how the ideas of Lefebvre in some cases or those of the classical thinkers Marx, Engels, and Weber in other cases have influenced new theories of urban development.

CLASS CONFLICT THEORIES: GORDON, STORPER, AND WALKER

A class conflict approach to urban development was introduced by the economist David Gordon (1977, 1984). He suggested that the locations chosen by capitalists for factories were affected not only by economic needs but also by the desire to remove their workers from areas of union organizing. According to Gordon, owners of businesses prefer to locate in places where workers are not as militant as they are in cities with a long labor tradition.

To prove his point, he studied a period in U.S. history when workers were especially militant: the latter part of the 1800s to the 1900s. He calculated the number of workers engaged in strikes during those years and matched it with the number of times owners of factories decided to relocate to the suburbs or to more isolated cities. The matchup was significant for the years between 1880 and 1910. Hence, the need to control labor conflict by relocating to the outlying areas of large cities was a very early reason that urban development assumed a regional, multicentered form because it led to the suburbanization of factories (see Chapter 6).

Two geographers, Michael Storper and David Walker, have expanded Gordon's approach (Storper, 1984; Storper and Walker, 1983). They view labor force considerations as the principal locational variable. By doing so they argue against the received wisdom of traditional location theory, asserting that businesses choose to locate in a specific place because of marketing and production costs (including transportation), a view that is similar to that of urban ecologists (see Chapter 3). Walker and Storper's "labor theory of location" argues that the commodity, labor, is unique. Its quality depends not only on the physical attributes of the worker but on his or her training and interest in being a part of a union, that is, in organizing against capital for rights and benefits.

For example, studies of the shift in manufacturing to Asia note that it is caused predominantly by labor force considerations (Peet, 1987). These include not only the presence of cheap labor but also the particular qualities of the workers. In the case of the electronics and garment industries in Asia, the workforce is overwhelmingly female, young, and unmarried. These laborers are advertised by development officials as providing a docile, easily controlled workforce (Fuentes and Ehrenreich, 1987). According to one Malaysian government brochure, "The manual dexterity of the Oriental female is famous the world over. Her hands are small, and she works fast with extreme care" (Fuentes and Ehrenreich, 1987:205). Reports on the condition of these women describe a world where they are kept bound by the conditions of work from living productive family and social lives.

According to the class conflict approach, then, any given nation has regions that vary with regard to the quality of labor. In part, the quality of schools and training facilities is responsible for this. However, the presence of a union tradition in the local area is also considered. Finally, particular cultural conditions, such as extreme patriarchy that subjugates women workers, are also important for creating a docile labor force. Storper and Walker use these ideas to explain the shift of industry to the Sun Belt in the United States, which occurred because the southern and western regions of the country have weak or nonexistent unions. They also suggest that their approach is applicable to the entire globe and that location decisions of multinational companies follow what has been called the "international division of labor" (Frobel, Heinrichs, and Krege, 1980); that is, multinational corporations decide where to locate their activities by choosing places around the globe that have cheap and compliant labor. In short, for these theorists, the qualities of labor are the determining factors in industrial location.

For example, although the garment industry was a staple of employment for many decades in New York City, during the 1960s many factories closed down and moved to the southern states because there were no unions and labor was much cheaper. In another case, the assembly of electronic devices beginning with solid-state TVs vanished quickly from the United States in the 1960s and became a basic industry, as it is today, in Southeast Asia where, among other factors, cheap labor is supplied by young women who are controlled by a patriarchal society. Today, purchasers of low-priced electronics from such chain stores as Walmart or Target, in particular, have no concept of the working conditions in far-flung Asian factories where these products are produced, mainly by young women.

In broadest terms, the contentions of class conflict theorists have merit, especially for the case of shifts in the location of manufacturing in recent years. Since the 1970s, the advanced industrial societies have lost over 8 million manufacturing jobs. At the same time, Latin American and Asian countries have experienced a 6-million job growth (Peet, 1987). During this period, the average hourly earnings for the United States was $8.83; for Mexico, $1.59; for South Korea, $1.35; and for India, 40 cents. These wage differences provide considerable incentive to invest global capital in less advanced countries. Regions with low class struggle and a docile labor force are also attractive.

Class conflict theorists make a mistake common in traditional Marxian analysis: They try to explain *everything* by economic factors alone. In the previous chapter we saw that some traditional ecologists, such as Amos Hawley, commit the fallacy of technological reductionism; that is, they explain everything in terms of changes in technology. Similarly, traditional Marxists such as Storper and Walker are economic reductionists. Thus, while class conflict and the global search for low-wage labor pools may indeed explain many of the moves owners have made to outlying areas of the world since the 1960s, it cannot explain relocations during other periods, and there are certainly additional reasons for such moves, such as the pull factors we discussed in the case of suburbanization: cheap land, distribution considerations that often override the need for cheap labor, low taxes, and other government incentives that subsidize capital.

There is no doubt that labor-force considerations are a major reason for the transfer of manufacturing activity to less developed countries such as Mexico or Malaysia. This approach, however, cannot explain why many multinationals continue to build plants and offices in the United States, Germany, and Japan, which have comparatively high wages. Factors including relative government stability and the desire to remain close to markets are also important considerations. For example, Japanese companies such as Honda, Toyota, and Mazda have recently opened plants in the United States. Most of the popular models from these two companies are made in Ohio, Tennessee, and even Michigan, the traditional stomping grounds for the United Auto Workers and General Motors, where they are close to the important U.S. markets. These factors also play a role in the well-being of places within a global economy. Thus, while the cost and quality of labor count for much in location decisions, other factors, such as government subsidies and distribution considerations, are also relevant.

CAPITAL ACCUMULATION THEORY

When sociologists discuss economics, they usually think in general terms and focus on individuals such as wealthy businesspeople who own companies. Class conflict theories go beyond individuals to discuss group behavior—particularly, the clash between the capitalist class of owners or investors and the class of workers who sell their labor for a wage. In this section we consider other urbanists who use economically based ideas to explain city development, but with a great deal more detail than traditional sociologists.

David Harvey, a well-known geographer from England, started out as a mainstream member of his field, concerned with mathematical modeling techniques. During the late 1960s, however, he was greatly influenced by events in the United States, such as the ghetto riots, and by the writings of Henri Lefebvre. In the 1970s, he wrote a book and a series of articles that applied Marxian economic analysis to the condition of the cities. He was especially influenced by the earlier writings of Lefebvre on the urban analysis of Karl Marx and Friedrich Engels.

Harvey, like Lefebvre, systematically applied the categories of Marxian economic analysis to the study of urban development. He asserted four things. First, he stated that the city is defined in the manner of Engels as a spatial node that concentrates and circulates capital. Second, he applied a conflict perspective to discuss the way the capitalist and the working classes confronted each other in the city (1973, 1976). According to Harvey, and unlike the general way sociologists usually speak about classes, this basic conflict takes many forms as both the capitalist and working classes split up among themselves into various groups or factions as a consequence of protracted struggles for advantage. The capitalist class, for example, can be divided among financial investors (finance capital), owners of department stores and other marketing assets (commercial capital), and owners of factories (manufacturing or industrial capital). Workers can also be split—for example, among factory laborers, white-collar salespeople, and professional financial analysts, all of whom still work for a wage. Each of these factions may want different things from urban development, so that conflict and coalition building are always a part of urban life. However, the basic struggle is still between capital and labor, as Gordon, Storper, and Walker also suggest (see pp. 134–137). As Harvey suggests, "Labor, in seeking to protect and enhance its standard of living, engages in a series of running battles in the living place over a variety of issues that relate to the creation, management, and use of the built environment" (1976:268).

Third, Harvey discusses how the volatile urban mix of economic interests brings about government intervention as a means of quieting things down so that planning can take place and capitalists can get back to their principal task of profit making (1975, 1976). As Harvey suggests, "Capital, in general, cannot afford the outcome of struggles around the built environment to be determined simply by the relative powers of labor, the appropriators of rent and the construction fraction" (1976:272). Therefore, the capitalist class requires government to intervene and aid the profit-making process within cities.

Sometimes, however, investment simply will not flow into districts of the city because they are so run-down or unattractive economically. In such cases, Harvey argues, government must step in to make the areas profitable again. Usually this form of state intervention involves the tearing down or destruction of existing buildings to make way for new construction, such as in the example of government-supported urban renewal programs (see Chapter 13). According to Harvey, "Under capitalism there is, then, a perpetual struggle in which capital builds a physical landscape appropriate to its own condition at a particular moment in time, only to have to destroy it, usually in the course of a crisis, at a subsequent point in time" (1982:14). For Harvey this process of boom and bust, or new construction and urban decay, is basic to urban change in a capitalist system.

Finally, Harvey took a detailed look at the capitalist class and how it made money within the space of the city. He borrowed the concept of circuits of capital from Lefebvre and elaborated on the latter's ideas. In particular, Harvey argued that capitalists involved in the first industrial circuit are principally interested in location within the urban environment and in reducing their costs of manufacturing. Capitalists in the second circuit hold a different set of priorities relating to the flow of investment and the realization of interest on money loaned or rent on property owned. These differences are reflected in the different ways capital investment circulates within the two circuits.

While investment in factories is often located in places with cheap housing, capitalists in the second circuit often refuse to invest in poorer areas and seek out only the higher-rent districts of the city. As a consequence, areas of the city can become run-down and abandoned not because of the actions of industrial capital, the faction that we usually think of as determining city fortunes, but because of actions taken by investors in real estate, as the sociospatial perspective suggests. In the Baltimore study, both suburbanization of the population and central city decay were linked to the priorities of the second circuit of capital as assisted by government programs. Harvey's work bears out the importance of Lefebvre's ideas on the real estate industry and of Engels's central insight into the production of uneven development under capitalism.

In sum, both the class conflict and capital accumulation approaches of the new urban sociology provide impressive improvements over more traditional perspectives. The world today is a volatile one where the predictable accommodations of work, shopping, and residential living characteristic of the industrial city have been shattered. Economic factors such as the ebb and flow of real estate investment and the changing structure of manufacturing in a global system affect the sociospatial features of daily life. So do the activities of workers involved in the struggle lying at the heart of the capital/labor relationship, and the residents of communities who are concerned about maintaining their quality of life. Each of these aspects helps determine the pattern of sociospatial organization.

Until the development of the new urban sociology, the effects of special, powerful interests (such as transnational corporations) on the pattern of growth were ignored by the traditional approach that emphasized biological factors of species competition over territory. But the work of geographers and Marxian analysts places greater importance on economic than on social factors in sociospatial arrangements. As we have discussed, there are several limitations to both the class conflict and capital accumulation approaches. In recent years, therefore, sociologists have added to the new perspective on the city by showing how social factors are also important in the production of settlement space.

APPROACHES BY URBAN SOCIOLOGISTS: THE GROWTH MACHINE VS. THE SOCIOSPATIAL PERSPECTIVE

The Growth Machine

This approach is most closely associated with the work of Harvey Molotch and his recent collaboration with John Logan (Logan and Molotch, 1987). Molotch was dissatisfied with the traditional ecological approach to urban development and highly influenced by new work carried out among French urbanists inspired by Lefebvre and Castells (Pickvance, 1976). Molotch was especially taken with the studies by the Frenchman Lamarche (1976) on the role of property development in the city, although since then this analyst has not been considered important. The focus of urban change involves the activities of a select group of real estate developers who represent a separate class that Marx once called the "rentiers." According to Lamarch, who wrote from an historical, European perspective, it is this class that both prepares land for new development and pushes the public agenda to pursue growth.

For Molotch, the intentions of the rentier class mesh well with the needs of local government. This is so because government is in constant need of new tax revenue sources. As increasing numbers of people enter an urban area, their demand for services strains fiscal budgets. Without new sources of revenue, city governments cannot maintain the quality of life, and the region is threatened with a decrease in prosperity. Property development is a major source of taxes. New people also bring in new demands for city goods and services, which aids the business community and, in turn, increases revenues to local government. In short, according to Molotch, cities are "growth machines" because they have to be. Pushed from behind by demands for community quality and pulled from the front by the aggressive activities of the rentiers, city governments respond by making growth and development their principal concerns.

The growth machine approach is wrong for three reasons: (1) Theoretically it depends totally on hypothesizing the existence of a separate *rentier class*, which is the source of action and behavior in leading urban development. However, in the United States, no such class has ever existed. Logan and Molotch borrowed this term from Lamarche, as we noted, an analyst who has not been influential since writing in the 1960s. In the United States, a free market in land allows all people with money to invest and even speculate in real estate development. The latter quality is an important contention of Lefebvre's theory that sees the boom-and-bust cycles of growth coming from this feature of capitalism. Therefore, and unlike the ideas of Logan and Molotch, the pursuit of growth is as much a danger to the well-being of place as it is a blessing. (2) Logan and Molotch borrowed a simplistic version of Lefebvre's theory of space. They argue that the urban environment can be dichotomized into a social space vs. an "abstract space," with the former category encapsulating all behaviors of residents who live in an urbanized environment. This is a simplistic reduction of a more complex Lefebvrian idea concerning a threefold distinction about environments. They contain lived spaces, spaces of representations, and, third, representations of space (see below). (3) Logan and Molotch's approach is obsessively concerned with growth and fails to explain periods of decline, deindustrialization, and the boom-and-bust cycles of capitalism. They simply assumed that growth would proceed when pushed by the rentier class or growth machine elites in a smooth fashion. They initially ignored the obvious possibility of conflicts produced by growth and change, not to mention the all too real aspect of urban decline and the overreaching, speculative structure of the real estate industry that always leads to boom-and-bust cycles. Later on they attempted to add the possibility of growth conflict to their approach, but they are not convincing, nor is their modified theory useful. Conflicts exist not only between proponents of growth and citizen opponents, as they claim, but also within coalitions that push for it, as

Harvey shows. These internal conflicts point out clearly why a separate rentier class does not exist and why their so-called growth machine is a temporary phenomenon that conceptually misses the deeper understanding that Lefebvre's theory of the second circuit of capital—real estate investment—provides.

In the United States, real estate development is often a contentious matter and there are many factions that conflict when it is proposed. Often these warring parties are mixed and include developers and speculators who are in competition with those who have proposed growth as well as different classes that have joined together to argue for or against development. In short, much of the important political conflicts associated with a changing urban environment cannot be grasped by the growth machine perspective.

The Sociospatial Perspective

How can we make sense of the various ideas offered by new urban theories? This text adopts the sociospatial perspective (SSP), which takes what is best from the new ideas while avoiding the endemic reductionism characteristic of both traditional ecology and recent Marxian political economy. It does not seek an explanation by emphasizing a principal cause such as transportation technology (Hawley), capital circulation (Harvey), or special "rentier classes" that control growth. Rather, it takes an integrated view of development as the linked outcome of economic, political, and cultural factors. At one time, it might have been suggested that such an integrated view derives from the tradition of Weber. However, since the 1950s, even Marxists have looked for ways to advance an integrated perspective (see Althusser, 1971), and this is especially important for the understanding of space (see Lefebvre, 1991).

The sociospatial perspective is inspired by the work of Lefebvre and can be distinguished from other approaches by the following characteristics. First, it considers real estate development as the leading edge of changes in the metropolitan region. While other approaches tend to focus only on economic changes in industry, commerce, and services, the SSP adds to these important dimensions an interest in the way real estate molds metropolitan growth, including how real estate declines. Growth and decline are the seesaw operations of Lefebvre's second circuit of capital, and they affect the general business and economic well-being of their surroundings in periods of bust as well as boom but in different directions. Second, the SSP considers government intervention and the interests of politicians in growth as a principal factor in metropolitan change. Traditional urban ecology and the newer approaches of urban political economy either ignore completely the role of government in channeling growth or treat the state as simply derivative of economic interests. The SSP considers the state as relatively autonomous—that is, with officials having interests of their own—and, more specifically, considers politics as being strongly linked to the concerns of property development (Gottdiener, 1986).

Third, the sociospatial perspective considers the role of cultural orientations as critical for an understanding of metropolitan life. Because of the importance of this subject, culture will be considered in more detail in Chapter 7.

Finally, the SSP takes a global view of metropolitan development. The most local areas today are tied to the activities of multinational corporations and banks. Changes in the way they invest affect each of us. By emphasizing global economic changes, however, the sociospatial perspective also seeks to understand how local and national factors interrelate with international links. All spatial levels of organization are important in understanding metropolitan development. In the following section, let us review some of these features while keeping in mind the differences between the SSP and other sociological perspectives discussed in the previous two chapters. In particular, we will see how the sociospatial perspective is a much more sophisticated and useful approach than either the growth machine or traditional ecology.

According to Kleniewski (2002:43–44):

> The sociospatial perspective is similar to political economy in some ways, but it emphasizes visible space and how space can be manipulated to affect urban life. In contrast with the growth machine perspective, for example, the sociospatial perspective holds that real estate developers and local government officials are much more influential in changing the form and function of cities than are the many other businesses that might be included in a pro-growth elite. Further, in contrast with Harvey's emphasis on the mode of production as affecting city change, the sociospatial perspective emphasizes people's understanding of space, including the ways in which local cultures differ in the symbolic meanings attached to different spaces. Thus, rather than confining the analysis to political and economic factors causing urban change, the sociospatial perspective adds cultural factors such as symbols of meanings to the analysis of urban life.

REAL ESTATE AND GOVERNMENT INTERVENTION

Real Estate Investment as the Leading Edge of Growth

From the earlier chapters on urbanization in the United States, we have seen that interest in real estate profits played a central part in urban development. George Washington was not only the first president of the country but he also participated in the innovative scheme to develop the swampland that became the site of the nation's capital. During the 1800s, great profits were made by businesses as the country industrialized, but they were also made through investment in land. Cyrus McCormick earned millions from the manufacture of his famous reaper, but millions more from his activities in real estate. Railroad tycoons competed with one another by building the infrastructure that opened up the great landmass of the United States to development, but they also established towns and developed real estate as they went along. Finally, over the last few decades, we have seen that the shifts to suburbia and the Sun Belt were fueled in part by the phenomenal expansion of the single-family home industry and the development of lands outside the large central cities of the Northeast and Midwest.

The sociospatial perspective argues that other perspectives have neglected the important role played by investment in real estate in the process of regional development. Traditional urban sociology or ecology, for example, overemphasizes the push factor of technology as an agent of change. Marxian political economy pays special attention to the activities of capitalists and the way changes in industrial investment patterns affect local spaces. The SSP acknowledges push factors such as changes in economic production and transportation innovations, but it also highlights the role of pull factors such as government intervention and the action of real estate—the second circuit of capital—as crucial to explanations of metropolitan growth. Both demand-side and supply-side dynamics are studied in their details.

The sociospatial perspective stresses the human dimension along with structural arrangements. It wants to know who the actors are and how they behave, not just the facts or figures about aggregate levels of growth and change. Activities involve people acting as part of social classes and class factions, or of gender, racial, and ethnic interests. How people come together to struggle over the patterns of development is an important question for the SSP, but this is not viewed as a growth machine.

Joe R. Feagin (1983), for example, discusses the variety of ways real estate developers and speculators create development projects and channel money to real estate investment. Agents of growth include *financial conduits* such as commercial banks and trust or pension funds, savings and loan associations, insurance companies, mortgage companies, and real estate investment trusts; *real estate brokers* and chamber of commerce members; and *public utilities* and other relatively immobile public service agencies that must work to maintain the attractiveness of specific places. Real estate, therefore, is composed of both individual actors and a structure of financial conduits that channel investment into land.

Gottdiener (1977) also demonstrates how both structure and agency are important for an understanding of real estate activities. A case study of suburban Long Island, New York, identifies the following types of social roles assumed by investors in the built environment:

1. Land speculators who purchase land or buildings simply to be sold at a later date for a profit.
2. Land developers who purchase land with or without housing and then develop it by constructing housing or other built structures such as factories or malls. To this type can be added developers who restructure the uses of land and

buildings, such as those who convert rental into condominium units, single-family into multifamily dwellings, and residential housing into office space.

3. Homeowners and individuals who invest in property as part of an overall scheme for the protection of income and not just to acquire shelter.

4. Local politicians who are dependent on campaign funds from the real estate industry, and lawyers or other professionals who make money from government-mandated requirements that necessitate legal services.

5. Individual companies or corporations that do not specialize in real estate but develop choice locations for their respective businesses, such as office towers or industrial plants, and a host of financial institutions, such as savings and loans, that channel investment into land.

The preceding list of institutional and private interests involved in the development of the metropolitan region reveals that growth is not simply determined by economic push factors of production, as both the class conflict and capital accumulation perspectives maintain, or by a special class of people called rentiers, as the growth machine approach emphasizes. Development is caused by the pull factor of people's activities involved in the second circuit of capital, real estate. This sector is not simply a select group of investors, as the growth machine believes, but is composed of both *actors* interested in acquiring wealth from real estate and a *structure* that channels money into the built environment. The latter consists of a host of financial intermediaries such as banks, mortgage companies, and real estate investment trusts, which allow a large variety of people to put their money in land.

Because the second circuit of capital enables anyone, even individual homeowners, to invest money in real estate for profit, it is wrong to separate the people in society into a select few who seek to make money in real estate (exploiting its exchange value) and a majority who seek only to enjoy the built environment as a staging ground for everyday life (the exploitation of space's use value). Instead, space can be enjoyed for its uses and for its investment potential by both business and local residents. In fact, that's what makes the relationship of society to space so complicated. The latter is *simultaneously* a medium of use and a source of wealth under capitalist commodity arrangements.

Because developing the built environment involves so many different interests, growth or change is always a contentious affair. This criticism has vital theoretical and empirical implications for the study of urban sociology, especially the role of the state, as we will see next.

Government Intervention and Political Agency

The sociospatial perspective suggests that metropolitan growth is the outcome of negotiations and contending interests, rather than the product of some well-oiled machine without conflict. Developers, for example, must negotiate with government planners and politicians, citizen groups voice their concerns in public forums, and special interests such as utility companies or religious organizations interject their stakes and culturally defined symbolic visions in metropolitan growth. The end result of these negotiations is a built environment that is *socially constructed*, involving many interests and controlled by the quest for profit.

The absence of a separate class of growth mongers means that the conceptualization of local politics by the growth machine perspective is limited. Feagin (1988) shows how powerful economic interests use the state to subsidize growth; hence development often reflects the direct interests of industrial and financial capital rather than some select, separate class of rentiers. Gottdiener (1977, 1985) indicates how local politicians are intimately involved with development interests. The purpose of this alliance is not growth and increased public revenues per se, as it is viewed by the growth machine, but *profit*. In this sense, growth interests represent both factions of capital involved in the accumulation process and also community interests concerned about growth and the quality of life. It is this melding of profit taking and environmental concerns that is most characteristic of settlement space development, and it involves a second source of complexity in the society/space relationship.

The interests aligned around issues of change in the built environment should be seen as *growth networks* rather than as the monolithic entities suggested by the concept of a "machine" (Gottdiener, 1985). The idea of networks captures the way alliances can form around a host of issues associated with development, often splitting classes into factions. The concept of network captures the diversity of people who may join, often only temporarily, to pursue particular growth paths. What counts is not necessarily the push for growth but both the way different community factions perceive the form growth will take and how they evaluate their own environmental needs. There is a rich complexity of people and interests involved in metropolitan growth and change that is captured neither by ecological or political economy perspectives, because they ignore particular agents, nor by the growth machine approach, which reduces conflict to a simple dichotomy of pro- and antigrowth factions.

For example, each community group may have its own interests which are manifested in local politics. They often join in coalitions to push for some version of growth while opposing other coalitions that have their own vision of the future. Growth is not the result of single-minded efforts by some machine. Rather, development is a contentious process involving many groups in society that push for a variety of forms: rapid growth, managed growth, slow growth, no growth, and so on. Local social movements arise not just because of economic needs but because of racial, religious, ethnic, and community interests concerned with the quality of life.

Development or change is a constant occurrence in the American landscape. Local politics consists of the clashes between all these separate interests as they play themselves out in the second circuit of capital and within the forum of local government.

SEMIOTICS AND URBAN CULTURE

Symbols and behaviors that have meaning are an important topic of study in order to understand life in the metropolitan region. In Chapter 7 we discuss culture in detail including the ways that locations have used symbolic resources to acquire an attractive image that appeals to tourists as well as real estate investors. For now, the present discussion addresses the importance of culture to our sociospatial perspective.

Since the 1970s, our lived environment in all areas of the metropolitan region and its rural hinterland have made an increasing use of symbolic markers by locations as a means of increasing value. Signs appealing to consumers denote places of retailing and attract mobile residents to distinct places like malls. Municipal locations increasingly resort to designing images that will register as attractive to developers and tourists. Areas also manufacture a sense of place for otherwise nondescript, newly built housing tracts by bestowing distinctive names on them, such as "Heather Acres," "Mountainview Estates," "Eagles Trace," and the like. While the names themselves have no direct signifying connection to the places that are tagged, they do connote a certain symbolic value that valorizes a specific location for consumers of housing or investors in real estate. Research on such names that are quite familiar to suburbanites is one important way the dynamics of regional development can be understood (see Gottdiener, 1995). The proliferation of signs makes the urbanized, multicentered region *semiotic* in both culture and character.

Henri Lefebvre, in one of his early books (1996), discusses the French style of semiotics, which owes a great deal to the work of Roland Barthes (Gottdiener and Lagopoulos, 1986). Characteristically, he confines his remarks to the central city, while we argue that there is no reason to do so in the sociospatial approach.

Semiological analysis must distinguish between multiple levels and dimensions. There is the utterance of the city, what happens and takes place in the street, in the squares, in the roads, what is said there. There is the language of the city: Particularities specific to each city which are expressed in discourses, gestures, clothing, in the words and use of words by the inhabitants. There is urban language, which one can consider as a language of connotations, a secondary system and derived within the denotative system. Finally, there is the writing of the city, what is inscribed and prescribed on its walls, in the layout of places and their images, in brief, the use of time in the city by its inhabitants.

More signifiers are spread across the metro region by franchise consumer outlets, like McDonalds, by the land development activities of the real estate industry and by levels of government in planning and transportation schemes. The kinds of signs and "writing" that Lefebvre refers to above come from individuals and groups, such as gangs, who mark territory with signifiers that reflect their own meaningful narratives about space.

For decades global media advertising, especially via television, has leveled the kind of "utterances" that once made individual cities relatively unique. At the same time the media has established in the minds of ordinary people an equation between a suggested need, like the desire for food fast to satisfy an overwhelming hunger, and a particular business that satisfies that desire which can be visited anywhere in the nation through franchising and easily recognized by a few distinctive signs on the facade of the outlets. Branding, packaging, and media marketing are all brought to play at the precise point of consumer choice to promote profits while people line up within virtually the same kinds of environments to purchase food, clothing, or even significantly expensive electronics quickly and easily. The signs of franchised chains that have already become valorized from hours and hours of media advertising make the purchase in these places doubly meaningful—first, the purchased product validates the advertising for it and not a rival product; second, the visit to a particular chain store validates the choice of going there and not to another location. In short, signs work to grease the wheels of a consumer society and to elevate spending (and, by corollary, consumer debt) to ever higher heights.

Gottdiener has argued elsewhere (1995; 2000) that the embodiment of signs in this cycle of marketing and selling for profit, or distribution and realization of capital, makes symbols vehicles for organizing consumer society. Signs are also vehicles for the valorization of specific locations in the pursuit of profit by investors in land and developers of housing and commercial buildings. Intrinsic use of symbols in this way—to make a profit—means that meaning itself is part of the political economy of capitalism, as sign value (Baudrillard, 1981; 1993). Hence, the sociospatial perspective calls attention to this semiotic dimension of the material environment within which we live our daily lives.

From our perspective, in addition, there is another reason why signs and a semiotic landscape are important. The multicentered metro region, as the new form of urban space, spreads out over an area that loses the human, pedestrian scale of the historical, compact central city. It is the automobile rather than public transportation or walking that best characterizes how we experience and how we navigate through this environment. Signs are important to this process. In the metro region, which is multicentered, people are drawn to specific locations quite literally by visible signs (from the highway or commercial strip) that are acknowledged as important just the way locations throughout the increasingly dispersed and differentiated region attempt to draw people to them through the use of meaningful symbols. Perhaps the giant neon landscape of Las Vegas is the extreme case of this kind of signage that is engineered for consumers in cars. Consequently, the semiotic dimension of daily life not only figures into the political economy of consumer-oriented capitalism; it is also the symbolic mechanism that makes it possible to navigate around the metro region in order to provide for needs. In contrast, when people lived in compact, pedestrian-oriented cities—that is, in the previous form of urban space—they went about satisfying their needs without the kind of constant aid from giant signs, franchise cues, and themed environments that have become so necessary to the functioning of the new form of urban space—the metro region—today. Yet such displays have not totally disappeared from the central city when we consider the Ginza district of Tokyo, the riot of neon signage that is Times Square in New York, or the similar burst of colored lights characterizing Piccadilly Circus in London.

THE GLOBAL ECONOMY

Finally, the sociospatial approach agrees with all other perspectives that acknowledge the important role of the global economy, the new mobile or "flexible" arrangements in production, and their effects on the restructuring of settlement space. It argues, however, that the push factors of capital mobility and considerations regarding the international division of labor, discussed earlier, are not the only ones determining growth. Often perspectives identified with the "new" urban sociology simply stress the effect of the global system as the key determinant of metropolitan change (see Smith and Feagin, 1987; Palen, 1991). The pull factors of state policies and the second circuit of capital are also important, particularly as manifested at the local, regional, and national levels.

Hence, the sociospatial approach has a more integrated view of push and pull factors associated with growth. The influence of the global system does have a profound effect on the fortunes of place, but unlike other approaches (see Logan and Molotch, 1987; Sassen, 1991; Smith and Feagin, 1987), the SSP does not believe that it has a sole determining effect.

This feature was illustrated in Chapter 3 with the discussions of suburban and Sun Belt development. At that time, it was pointed out that while the U.S. economy had become integrated into the world system, development patterns of deconcentration to suburbs and Sun Belt regions had been going on for many years, even prior to the 1960s when the restructuring of the global system began to be felt. The shifts to the suburbs and the Sun Belt are the two most important sociospatial changes in U.S. history, but neither can be said to have been produced by the power of the global economy. They have their roots in growth trends that have been going on for years and that involve important aspects of both government intervention and the phenomenal draw of real estate investment.

For example, in Chapter 6 we will study the nature of suburban development after recognizing that the majority of Americans live in suburbs, not central cities. Suburbanization in the United States has been going on since the turn of the century. Development accelerated after World War II when the government initiated special loans to veterans and consolidated the income tax subsidy to homeowners, providing families with a cash incentive to invest in real estate. Suburbanization was also promoted by a variety of federal housing acts passed since the 1930s that revitalized the real estate industry and by the Interstate Highway Act in the 1950s, which promoted the construction of freeways. All of these factors fell into place long before the advent of global economic effects.

We have also seen how the Sun Belt prospered as a consequence of government programs and real estate activity. Government military spending during World War II and later during the Cold War propped up the Sun Belt economy by transferring billions of dollars in tax money from the Frost Belt to this region. Real estate investment found riches in a host of Sun Belt schemes for the development of housing and industry. Other factors, such as the prosperity of agribusiness, also helped growth. In short, the most important spatial changes experienced by the United States are the consequence of many factors operating at all spatial levels, as the SSP suggests, rather than at the global level alone.

Of course, since the 1970s, changes in the global economy have had a profound effect on the built environment. The decline of manufacturing in the United States and the transfer of many production activities abroad have wiped out the traditional relationship between central city working-class communities and their capitalist employers. The economy of our largest cities has restructured away from manufacturing and toward specialization in advanced services and information processing, particularly those business services required by the finance capital faction that coordinates investment activity for the global economy (Sassen, 1991). The record high of the stock market and record low in unemployment through the 1990s have not altered this longer-term trend of restructuring of the urban economy and increasing economic polarization of urban space. All of these changes affect the nature of the local labor force and alter living and working arrangements. We will discuss some of these effects on the people of the metropolis in Chapters 8 and 9. Other effects of the restructuring initiated within the context of a global economy will be considered in Chapters 10 and 11 when we look at metropolitan problems and policies, respectively. Finally, in Chapters 10 and 11, we will discuss the effects of global restructuring on cities in the developing world and settlement spaces in European countries and Japan.

The sociospatial changes produced by the global economy have also been important because of the new spaces that have appeared in recent years. Prior to the 1970s, neither Santa Clara County nor the peripheral areas around the city of Boston were significant employment centers. During the last two decades, they proved to be world-class economic spaces, becoming Silicon Valley and the Route 128 high-tech corridor, respectively. These new spaces produced by high-technology industries earned disproportionately large sums of money on the world market for their employment size. At one time, these results prompted analysts to suggest that other countries follow suit and promote their own export-oriented high-tech corridors as the key to future prosperity (see Chapter 11). Today Silicon Valley and Route 128, along with other such spaces, are experiencing a severe recession. The global economy is now shaky as recession hits worldwide. According to the SSP, alterations and development of new spaces of production and consumption will be produced not by investment directed at the global level alone but also by the logic of real estate development and by other pull factors, such as the quality of government intervention, in addition to factors that operate locally, regionally, nationally, and globally—that is, at all sociospatial levels.

SUMMARY: THE SOCIOSPATIAL PERSPECTIVE

The sociospatial perspective involves ideas that distinguish it from previous sociological approaches.

First, it incorporates a number of different factors, instead of emphasizing just one or two, that can account for development and change. It particularly seeks to provide a balanced account of both *push* and *pull* factors in metropolitan and regional growth.

Second, it considers the role of real estate in development as the combined activities of both agency and structure. Investment in land is a sector of capital accumulation with its own factions and cycles of boom and bust. The categories of political economy, such as profit, rent, interest, and value, are just as applicable to metropolitan development as to any other part of the economy.

Third, the sociospatial perspective strives for a detailed view of politics that emphasizes the activities of individuals and groups in the development process. The SSP focuses on the activities of certain *growth networks* that form coalitions interested in choices that must be made over the direction and effects of change.

The sociospatial perspective considers cultural factors such as race, gender, and the symbolic context of space to be just as important as economic and political concerns (see the following three chapters). It also deals specifically with the special qualities of spatial forms and their role in the organization of society. At present, metropolitan life is played out within the context of an ever-expanding multicentered region. We have discussed the historical significance of this form of settlement space in previous chapters and will discuss its significance for daily life in chapters to come.

Finally the sociospatial perspective, along with other approaches, adopts a global view of development but does not claim that the world economy alone is responsible for the restructuring of settlement space. Global changes are particularly relevant for an understanding of how cities, suburbs, and regions have been affected by the economy in recent years. New spaces of industry, commerce, and services have helped redefine settlement patterns as multicentered regional development. Historically, however, the pull factors of government intervention and investment in real estate have also played an essential part in the restructuring of space.

In the chapters that follow, we examine the development of metropolitan areas in the United States (Chapters 5 and 6) and then examine the role of culture in metropolitan life, addressing everyday life and social problems (Chapters 7–9). We then turn our attention to other countries to compare the U.S. experience with growth and restructuring elsewhere (Chapters 10 and 11).

KEY CONCEPTS

political economy
international division of labor
capital accumulation
uneven development
second circuit of capital
abstract space
social space
labor theory of location
growth machine
use value / exchange value
financial conduits
growth networks
sociospatial perspective

DISCUSSION QUESTIONS

1. The new urban sociology has developed in part from earlier theoretical work in what is known as political economy. Who are some of the earlier sociologists identified with this theoretical perspective? What did they write about? How were their ideas incorporated into urban sociology and into sociological thinking more generally?

2. What is meant by *uneven development?* What causes uneven development to occur within a metropolitan region? What are the effects of uneven development on metropolitan growth? What are some examples of uneven development that you can see within the metropolitan region where you live?

3. Henri Lefebvre stands as the major theoretical figure in the development of urban political economy. What was his contribution to recent work in the new urban sociology? Identify three ideas that Henri Lefebvre wrote about and explain how they are used in urban sociology.

4. There are important differences between the class conflict and capital accumulation approaches of the new urban sociology. Discuss the work of one theorist from each of these approaches and explain the differences in their approaches to studying metropolitan regions.

5. John Logan and Harvey Molotch have suggested that urban development is driven forward by a *growth machine* that emphasizes the "exchange value" of urban property against the "use value" that local residents assign to their property. What are some of the limitations of this approach? How is the idea of the growth machine different from the sociospatial approach more generally?

6. What is meant by the *sociospatial approach* to urban sociology? Pick three features of this perspective and discuss how these are used to study metropolitan regions.

CHAPTER 5

URBANIZATION IN
THE UNITED STATES

Americans have a long-standing distrust of cities and of city life. Thomas Jefferson (1977) suggested that cities were the source of evil and corruption that would threaten the young democracy's political system. Despite such sentiments, the growth of urban centers in the United States has been prolific and, as we saw in Chapter 1, has increased in recent decades. For much of our history, the everyday life of Americans has been defined in urban terms.

In many respects, development in the United States mirrors the same trends and effects of social forces unleashed in Western Europe. We experienced, for example, the same industrial revolution that England did and even contributed significantly to its technological breakthroughs. Everyone has probably heard of McCormick's reaper or Thomas Edison's lightbulb. Such inventions helped the United States compete with industrial giants like England in the nineteenth century.

Yet for all its close links to the Old World, the city-building process in the United States exhibits several features that exaggerate aspects of urbanization found elsewhere. These include (1) the lack of walls or fortifications around cities; (2) real estate development as a major component in the economy of capitalism; (3) the ideology of privatism, which limits the role of the state and emphasizes individual accomplishments as the basis of community; (4) large-scale immigration and population churning within cities; and (5) the regional dispersal of the metropolis. This chapter illustrates these features within the larger context of U.S. urban history.

THE STAGES OF URBAN GROWTH

Many different factors have contributed to urban expansion in the United States. The role of economic forces; transportation, construction, and communication technology; political changes; immigration policy; and success at wars are but some of the major causes for the development of city building. *The best explanation for urban patterns is found when connection is made between the production of settlement space and the society's political economy.* According to the sociospatial perspective, this does not mean that the clearly defined stages of metropolitan growth are directly correlated to exact stages of economic development; rather, it means only that important features of each period in economic development are associated in certain ways with important factors in the social and political change of metropolitan space.

Four distinct stages of urban growth in the United States have resulted in the formation of the multicentered metropolitan region. These are (1) the colonial period, 1630 to 1812; (2) the industrial period, 1812 to 1920; (3) the metropolitan period, 1920 to 1960; and (4) the deconcentration and restructuring of settlement space within the multicentered metropolitan region that has taken place since 1960.

Box 5.1

Stages of Capitalism and Urbanization in the United States, 1630 to the Present

Stages of Capitalism	*Stages of Urbanization*
Mercantile-colonial period	Colonial period: 1630 to 1812
Industrialization period	Industrial period: 1812 to 1920
Monopoly capitalism period	Metropolitan period: 1920 to 1960
Global capitalism period	Multicentered expansion: 1960 to today

---

Urban and suburban settlement space within the United States has developed within a free-market economy based on private property and capital accumulation. We know this type of economic system by the name of *capitalism.* As both Adam Smith and Karl Marx emphasized, capitalism is a dynamic system that brings about changes in the social relations and political systems with which it comes in contact. The stages of urban development correspond to growth periods in the development of U.S. capitalism. These stages of development are often referred to as (1) mercantile capitalism; (2) industrial capitalism; (3) monopoly capitalism; and (4) global capitalism. But these periods do not represent an evolutionary theory of development such as that of V. Gordon Childe in Chapter 2. Although cities in the United States went through these periods, there is no reason that another society has to pass through exactly the same sequence because other countries' economic transformations differ from ours. Furthermore, according to the sociospatial perspective, stages in metropolitan growth and in the political economy are only loosely coupled, as mentioned above. Nonetheless, discussion of separate phases of city building is an effective way to organize our analysis of the connection between developments in the U.S. political economy and the forms of settlement space over time.

THE COLONIAL PERIOD: 1630 TO 1812

The United States was colonized by European capitalist societies operating according to the political economy of *mercantilism*, an early stage of global capitalism. In this system, the nation-states of Europe organized the expansion of their local economies at a time when manufacturing was not industrialized and with the aid of the political apparatus of the nation-state. The wealth of countries, it was believed, depended on the well-being of commerce or trade, while domestic manufacture was protected from foreign competition by government tariffs. Mercantilist theory called for the colonization of resource-rich but undeveloped areas of the globe accomplished through the state's own military and naval power. Wealth would increase if raw materials could be plundered from the undeveloped colonies, while manufactured articles would be produced exclusively in the home countries. By these arrangements, the maximum amount of work would be given to the nation's own laborers and excess population could be drained off to the colonies.

In the 1700s the cities of the United States were little more than colonial outposts of England, France, and Spain located on the shores of a country with a foreboding and unsettled interior. The attention and the energies of the colonists were directed eastward across the Atlantic Ocean toward the colonial powers and events in Europe. The existence of these cities was guaranteed by the might of the colonial power's navy and military organization.

Colonial cities were port cities. The docks and warehouses and the shipping, insurance, and trading companies constituted the focus of urban development. Farther back from the port facilities, merchant and counting houses were located, while behind the port district, the beginnings of residential quarters, principally for the colonial businessmen and their families, were located. Artisans of all kinds who engaged in handicraft manufacture of the simple implements required for daily life were also located in the town. Their shops and residences were situated throughout the port district.

As mercantilism developed, it also became a way of relieving population pressures by promoting immigration to the colonies. This, in turn, stimulated a nascent real estate industry in the port cities. Many U.S. cities, in fact, were laid out to accommodate both mercantile economic functions and residential real estate speculation. Often single entrepreneurs in England were granted permission by the crown to set up their own town as just such a speculative enterprise. The case of Philadelphia, founded in the late 1600s by the Quaker entrepreneur William Penn, illustrates the combined mercantile and real estate venture: "Philadelphia was laid out in 1681 on a plan that was probably the original speculator's design for an American city, a plot that measured one by two miles and was easily divided into lots that might be sold at a distance" (Vance, 1990:265).

The colonial cities of the United States prospered because of the success of British mercantilism. Each of the largest towns filled an economic function connected with

European trade. Boston was the center for colonial provisions; Newport, Rhode Island, specialized in shipbuilding and slave trading; New York trading focused on flour and furs; Philadelphia focused on meat, wheat, and lumber; and Charleston, South Carolina, was known for the export of rice and indigo. Initially Baltimore, Maryland, had few natural advantages, and it lagged behind the growth of these five cities, but in the later 1700s its businesses specialized in the flour-exporting trade, and it prospered. However, towns such as Williamsburg, Virginia, which were laid out solely as political centers, never grew.

Table 5.1 shows the development of cities in the period 1790 to 1850, from the colonial period through the decade just before the Civil War. The table gives us some important information about the growth of early cities under the mercantilist system and the later replacement of these cities by industrial towns in the years following the Civil War. In the early colonial period, we see New York City, Boston, and Philadelphia but also a number of smaller port cities in the northeast. None of these cities were very large by European standards (compare the figures here with those for European cities shown in Table 2.3). Some cities, such as Philadelphia and Boston, remain important population centers today. Most of the others, however, like Newburyport, Stephentown, or Southwark, would never develop into metropolitan centers.

By the time of the Revolutionary War, U.S. cities played a crucial role due to their demographic and economic power. The first confrontations, such as the Boston

TABLE 5.1 The 15 Most Populated Urban Areas in the United States, 1790–1850.

1790		1820		1850	
New York	33,100	New York	123,700	New York	515,500
Philadelphia, PA	28,500	Philadelphia, PA	63,800	Baltimore, MD	169,000
Boston, MA	18,300	Baltimore, MD	62,700	Boston, MA	136,900
Charleston, SC	16,400	Boston, MA	43,300	Philadelphia, PA	121,400
Baltimore, MD	13,500	New Orleans, LA	27,200	New Orleans, LA	116,400
North Liberties, PA	9,900	Charleston, SC	24,800	Cincinnati, OH	115,400
Salem, MA	7,900	North Liberties, PA	19,700	Brooklyn, NY	96,800
Newport, RI	6,700	Southwark, PA	14,700	St. Louis, MO	77,900
Provincetown, RI	6,400	Washington, DC	13,200	Spring Garden, PA	58,900
Marblehead, MA	5,700	Salem, MA	12,700	Albany, NY	50,800
Southwark, PA	5,700	Albany, NY	12,600	North Liberties, PA	47,200
Gloucester, MA	5,300	Richmond, VA	12,100	Kensington, PA	46,800
Newburyport, MA	4,800	Providence, RI	11,800	Pittsburgh, PA	46,600
Portsmouth, NH	4,700	Cincinnati, OH	9,600	Louisville, KY	43,200
Nantucket, MA	4,600	Portland, ME	8,600	Charleston, SC	43,000

SOURCE: Campbel Gibson, *Population of the 100 Largest Cities and Other Urban Places in the United States, 1790–1990*. Washington: U.S. Bureau of the Census, Population Division, Working Paper No. 27, June 1997 (1998).

Tea Party, took place in cities. The wealth concentrated in New York, Boston, Philadelphia, and Newport also financed the revolt. Colonial cities became centers of
propaganda that disseminated antiloyalist views throughout the colonies. At the
time of the revolution, for example, thirty-six newspapers actively operated in the
colonies (not all of which opposed the crown). Finally, cities played a major role because they nurtured new political organizations. These organizations became part of
the colonial militia when war finally broke out. One example was the Sons of Liberty
in the New York colony:

> Founded in the fall of 1765 as a secret organization, the Sons of Liberty became a
> public body with meetings announced in newspapers. . . . In addition to commu-
> nicating with other groups in the New York colony, the Sons of Liberty also kept
> in touch with organizations in such other colonial towns as Boston, Baltimore,
> and Newport. The Sons of Liberty armed themselves and became a paramilitary
> group ready to resist British encroachments. The group also provided an organiz-
> ing function, marshalling two thousand people in October 1765 to prevent the
> landing of stamps to be used for tax purposes. (Hoover, 1971:92)

One legacy of colonial dependency was the absence of autonomous government
and the concomitant lack of political responsibility among the citizens of the cities. As
colonies they were administered by agents of the English king. Precisely this lack of
political influence may have contributed to the revolutionary fervor, because the
growing wealth and population of the colonies had no democratic recourse in the administration of port cities. In any event, the absence of autonomy, according to the
historian Sam Bass Warner Jr. (1962), fostered a "laissez-faire" economic and social
milieu that developed into the culture of *privatism* that so closely characterizes U.S.
cities even today (see Chapter 13).

Privatism, a legacy of our colonial history, refers to the civic culture that eschews
social interests in favor of the private pursuit of individual goals. From the very beginning of our urban experience, residents already believed their principal responsibility
lay in the pursuit of self-interest. Unlike the citizens of ancient Athens, for example,
who were obligated to pledge their indebtedness to the city that gave them birth, residents of the American colonies were not responsible to the city but only to the colonial power. Over the years, this greatly restrained the development of a civic culture
that fosters community values and social responsibility. Instead, the limited vision of
privatism remains in place. According to Warner:

> To describe the American tradition of privatism is not to summarize the entire
> American cultural tradition. . . . The tradition of privatism is, however, the most
> important element of our culture for understanding the development of cities.
> The tradition of privatism has always meant that the cities of the United States

depended for their wages, employment, and general prosperity upon the aggregate successes and failures of thousands of individual enterprises, not upon community action. It has also meant that the physical forms of American cities, their lots, houses, families, and streets, have been the outcome of a real estate market of profit-seeking builders, land speculators, and large investors. (Warner, 1968:4)

A second legacy of colonial dependency was the absence of independent city economic rights. European cities of the late Middle Ages were powerful economic enterprises because they possessed independent charters of governance as well as the legal right to mint their own currency and conduct trade in their name. Colonial America granted no such privileges to its cities, and the cities did not possess chartered rights. There were no city trade monopolies, no special currency, and no city property rights beyond city borders, unlike Western Europe. Trade was organized by the large European conglomerates such as the Hudson's Bay Company. Any individual or group of entrepreneurs could break away from a U.S. city and settle in the hinterland, forming a separate town. The varied reasons for such fragmentation could be religious, political, or economic. What mattered was only the relative ability to split off and settle elsewhere under the protective umbrella of the colonial powers. Laissez-faire, privatism, and the ease of settlement characterized city life during the colonial period. Privatism's obverse was the absence of political autonomy characteristic of the urban community as described by Max Weber. Even after the American Revolution, cities failed to acquire independent political rights except as far as these were granted to them by the states. Hence, the legacy of the colonial period remains very much with us today in the form of weak city government and limited city political power.

A third legacy of colonialism was the physical absence of city walls. Max Weber's ideal city of the Middle Ages possessed defensible fortifications or walls. Elsewhere, forts usually defined the old city center. Thus, the words *Kremlin* in Russian and *Casbah* in Moroccan both mean "fortress." Few U.S. cities built by colonial powers exhibited this trait (although some did have temporary stockades) because the home country provided for the general defense of the region by sustaining a standing army (Monkkonen, 1989). Consequently, unlike the walled cities of Europe in the late Middle Ages, U.S cities provided for immense locational freedom. Land could always be developed at the fringe. To the clean-cut speculators' grid of the colonial port city was added a surrounding fringe that could always grow by accretion and land speculation. This particular pattern remains very much with us today as growth occurs constantly at the fringe of development in a pattern of sprawl.

A final legacy of the colonial city was the role played by land development as a singular source of wealth in the economy. For the residents of the United States—unlike in Europe—land was plentiful and cheap. Very early in the history of this country, it became clear to enterprising Europeans with money to invest that land development was a principal way to acquire greater wealth. But the very nature of exploiting this resource requires concomitant locational activities of a group of people and the ultimate attraction of residential and commercial users. It does little good to stake a land claim, no matter how large, in a wilderness with no friendly residents around, without an attendant scheme for the eventual development of the land, including state protection for the influx of population. Hence, early in U.S. history, land developers adopted the practice of working closely with politicians and colonial authorities to promote the development of select places. This pattern of *boosterism*, involving speculators, developers, politicians, and state authorities, or a *growth network* (Gottdiener, 1985) composed of varied individuals who are like-minded developers of land, was repeated many times in our history and remains characteristic of development today (see Chapter 7). The sheer quantity of undeveloped land presented by the U.S. case represents a graphic contrast to the pattern of urbanization in Western Europe (which has always reined in the interests of developers for the good of the larger society and because of real estate's scarce supply), although it may have parallels in the recent history of countries such as Australia and Brazil that also have abundant land masses.

It is often noted in elementary school lessons that George Washington, our first president, was employed as a surveyor in his youth. In fact, he and his family were active real estate speculators. Surveying was just one aspect of this work. As one historian put it, land was "the real wealth" of the colonies. Perhaps Washington's crowning achievement was his participation in the booster effort to develop Washington, D.C., as the nation's capital. In the 1780s, the district was nothing more than an inhospitable swamp of worthless real estate. All that was to change through the efforts of newly achieved political power and economic investment in land. According to an account of the time: "In 1793 George Washington led a procession with two brass bands and Masons in full costume across the Tiber to a barbecue and land auction at which he purchased the first lots of the new capital's undeveloped swampland. . . . Self-promotion, boosterism, and constant attention to the economic main chance soon came to characterize the young nation's cities" (Monkkonen, 1989:63).

THE ERA OF INDUSTRIAL EXPANSION: 1812 TO 1920

The settlement of the vast U.S. territory following the Revolutionary War constituted a magnificent drama involving individuals representing the very legends of our country itself. As Gary Nash (1974) has observed, this drama was colored in red, white, and black, because it involved a three-way clash among white former colonists, Native Americans, and black slaves. Frontiersmen such as Davy Crockett shouldered hunting muskets and fought the Indian Wars. Native Americans such as the Apache chief Geronimo and his people were driven from their lands, killed in vast numbers, or resettled to make way for the white people's development of the interior.

Industrialists such as J. P. Morgan and Jacob Astor accumulated vast sums of money in trade, banking, and real estate, only to lose power and wealth to other upstarts, such as Jay Gould, with equally ambitious schemes. Politicians such as President Grover

Cleveland mingled with the active boosters of growth during a time when corruption was a way of life in government. In the middle of it all, the fate of the nation was decided in a civil war. Great spokespeople such as Frederick Douglass articulated the pain of suppression under which black people were living as slaves. Eventually slavery was defeated but so too was the rural way of southern life in a society that shifted from plantation agriculture to industrialized farming and manufacture. Technology, industrialization, city government, and land development took over the stage of urban growth.

It is helpful to think of American capitalism as acting like a large land development agency in addition to its role as an industrial enterprise. During the period of formative growth, entrepreneurs singled out choice locations in the advancing path of expansion and built cities. According to the historian Richard C. Wade (1959), city construction took place in many cases *before* population influx; that is, urbanization in the United States was often land speculation that proceeded with the aid of local governments. In a sense, the establishment of a town as a political entity harnessed land to the control of growth interests. As a consequence of political reforms during the presidency of Andrew Jackson, it was comparatively easy for groups of capitalist land developers to declare their projects incorporated cities. Hence, with the aid of home rule, the expansion westward during the century between 1812 and 1920, when the majority of the U.S. population became city residents, was an urban expansion and simultaneously an explosion in the number of governments at the local level. By founding towns, developers also used local governments to provide a civic or community structure for people who came there to live.

The real estate projects that opened the American frontier did not proceed in isolation. Entrepreneurs were also merchants or industrialists. Money was invested in commercial enterprises as well as in land. In fact, capital often flowed back and forth between investments in industry and investments in land. This relation will be explained more fully in Chapter 7. Thus, Cyrus McCormick, the inventor of the reaper, made millions in the 1800s from his factory, but his real wealth came from investment of those profits in real estate (Longstreet, 1973).

In addition, the technology of transport became an explicit means through which investors of capital centered in cities competed with one another to build new cities on the frontier. Thus, railroad entrepreneurs such as Leland Stanford were also city builders. Let us consider the era of urban expansion according to these interrelated links among forms of capital, government policies and politicians, and forms of technology.

Land Development and Technology

Prior to the 1820s, the U.S. urban population remained relatively stable at around 10 percent of the total. After that time, a sudden burst of urbanization took place that did not abate until the 1930s. By the 1920 census, over half of all Americans were already living in cities. In the hundred years after 1820, the United States had been transformed into an urbanized nation.

After the War of 1812, urban development continued in the form of networked cities along the Great Lakes and the Ohio River Valley. At this stage, economic interests located within the large East Coast cities turned an about-face by ignoring the mercantilist needs of trade with Europe and actively pursued the development of the interior. In all respects, early westward expansion was highly dependent both on the development of transportation technology and on the protection of white settlers by government against attacks by Native American residents. Land was realized as a capital investment only after transportation and communication infrastructure could be put in place. Roads had to be built. Tracks had to be laid. Telegraph lines were installed. In addition, the safety of work crews for all these efforts had to be ensured. Land was being taken from Native Americans, an effort that required organized government activity and military intervention.

Hinterland development was not simply the consequence of the application of emerging transportation technology, as might be suggested by human ecology. Local capital had to be organized to bring about development. Often entrepreneurs competed with one another over investments in the interior of the country because at the time, the unity of capital under corporate interests that cut across space and united efforts in different cities had not yet fully matured. Consequently, westward expansion was a characteristic of competitive capital and was often marked by the schemes of single individuals who sought to build up business and build a city at the same time.

For example, the earliest urban rivalry involved local capitalists situated in the important East Coast port cities. Their future fortunes depended on the ongoing success of their respective trade routes to the interior, because the latter was the source of goods for export and raw materials needed by local manufacturers.

Just after the War of 1812, the shortest route to the West lay across either Pennsylvania or Maryland. There were two roads—the "national road" out of Baltimore and the "Pittsburgh Pike" out of Philadelphia—but these links were inadequate for handling the heavy agricultural products of the interior (Rubin, 1970:128). Instead, produce was shipped south on the Mississippi River to New Orleans, making that city the most important export center.

New York entrepreneurs saw their city facing decline as the frontier expanded west. In 1817, they began construction of a canal that linked the Hudson River at Albany 364 miles westward to Buffalo on Lake Erie. In a bold stroke, they hoped to create the most efficient link to the hinterland, with Buffalo becoming an inland port for the Great Lakes region of the Midwest. The canal was completed in 1825 and was so successful that it inspired a craze of canal building across the United States. From its inception, New York City competed effectively with New Orleans as an export point for agricultural produce.

As a result of the successful Erie Canal venture, Philadelphia and Baltimore financial interests faced decline, if not extinction. As the historian J. Rubin (1970:131) notes, they responded with their own schemes, aided greatly by government laws and subsidies. Initially Philadelphia interests demanded that the state proceed with a canal to Ohio. However, construction failed in the Allegheny Mountains and a rail segment was required. This occurred several times, and Philadelphia ended up with a mixed canal and rail portage system that required several transshipments. The route was hopelessly incapable of competing with New York's Erie Canal.

Baltimore interests viewed Philadelphia's problems with trepidation. They saw the difficulty of crossing the Appalachian Mountains via canal. By the 1830s, the steam locomotive had just been perfected in England and, in a venture as bold as the New York effort, they opted for the construction of a railroad line that would connect Baltimore with the Ohio Valley over the mountains. The line was eventually called the Baltimore and Ohio Railroad, and it was remarkably successful. As a consequence of these improvements, New York and Baltimore prospered while Boston and Philadelphia declined. In addition, the links to the interior in the 1830s helped found the midwestern Great Lakes cities of Chicago, Detroit, and Cleveland, which also prospered because of successful rail and canal traffic to East Coast ports.

In the period between 1830 and 1920, the most significant technological innovation was the joint development of the steel rail and steam locomotive that perfected the long haul for commerce, resources, and people. Of the 153 major U.S. cities existing today, 75 percent had been established after 1840 when the railroad matured as an established infrastructure, and only 9 percent of these same major cities were built after 1910 (Monkkonen, 1989:75). It would be simple to suggest that transportation technology alone caused the explosion of urbanization. This would be misleading, however. Technology became the means of growth, but inception and execution were the result both of the quest for wealth among entrepreneurs and of the desires of politicians in government at all levels—local, state, and federal—that joined these ventures, aiding them with political resources. It is precisely this conjuncture of investors, political power mongers, and the dream of wealth that characterizes the second stage of urbanization in the United States. According to the historians Glaab and Brown, for example:

> Earlier rivalries had been limited by nature—by the location of rivers and lakes. But railroads were not bound by topography, by the paths of river commerce, or by natural trade patterns. Railroads could be built anywhere, creating cities where they chose. Since the building of railroads was dependent to a considerable extent on subsidies from local communities, railroad leaders were willing to bargain with competing towns to obtain the best possible deal in stock subscriptions, bond issues, and right-of-ways. . . . The "boosterism" associated with the Midwest and areas further west is largely a legacy of the late nineteenth century era of urban rivalry. (Glaab and Brown, 1967:112)

As we will see as well in our discussion of the last two stages of urban growth, this pattern of capital investment, coupled with government subsidies and competition among separate places, is repeated countless times and characterizes urban growth and change in the United States and possibly elsewhere. As the sociospatial approach suggests, development was a consequence of a combination of economic, political, and cultural factors—the frontier myth and the American Dream of wealth combined with cooperative government officials and venture capitalists to urbanize the nation.

What exactly were the proportions involved in the lure of wealth that accompanied town building? Consider the Illinois Central Railroad. Its promoters were also prolific city builders. In 1850, 10 towns existed in the vicinity of the railroad's route. After expansion ten years later, there were 47, and by 1870 there were 81. When the Illinois Central entrepreneurs could not make subsidy agreements with the politicians of existing towns for their right-of-way, they just built their own towns nearby. Champaign, Illinois, for example, was constructed directly by the railroad adjacent to the existing town of Urbana.

Another example shows us the size of the profit realized from real estate investment alone. The town of Kankakee, Illinois, was built by this same railroad in 1855 at a cost of $10,000, and after just one year the owners had already realized $50,000 in lot sales, or a profit of 500 percent, with more city land remaining. As expansion moved west, a similar pattern recurred involving a host of other promoters and their railroads. In San Francisco, which had developed as the premier city of the West Coast during this period, town lots that could be bought for $1,500 in 1850 were worth from $8,000 to $27,000 just three years later in 1853 (Glaab and Brown, 1967:113, 121).

Manufacturing

So far we have fostered the impression that city building involved exclusively land development schemes combining capital, government, and transport technology. During the period between 1812 and 1920, however, the United States became a world leader in manufacturing. Forces of industrialization unleashed with such effect in England during this time had similar results here. During the period between 1850 and 1900, for example, U.S. production of textiles multiplied 7 times, iron and steel increased 10 times, the processing of agricultural products expanded 14 times, and the production of agricultural implements increased 25 times (Hoover, 1971:180).

The very heart of industrialization was the factory, which was the engine that drove the industrial stage of capitalism. But workers and capitalists were not simply disembodied abstractions. They were people who required places to live, raise families, and spend whatever leisure time they had. Industrialization, therefore, produced the factory town or community that contained workers' families and houses, machinery, and energy sources, all within close proximity.

The first American manufacturing city was Lowell, Massachusetts, which was located on the Merrimack River at a site where the water dropped ninety feet and provided the original power source for its factories. Investors chose this place for a complex of cotton mills and struck on the idea of importing a labor force of young women from the neighboring cities, especially Boston, because they would be easy to control as a source of nonunion labor power. The geographer James Vance gives this account of the city:

> In 1845, thirty-three of the large mill buildings ranged along the canals and banks of the Merrimack, making Lowell the largest cotton town in America and one of its few great industrial cities, with a population of thirty thousand. A full third of the population was engaged as operatives in the mills or their workshops, though female employment remained disproportionate with 6,320 females and 2,915 males. (Vance, 1990:347)

Early industrialization in the United States is associated with the names of entrepreneurs who perfected specific products: Singer sewing machines, Yale locks, Armour hams, McCormick reapers, and Remington typewriters are but some of these innovations. Later on, in most cases, the descendants of the originators carried on the family name and its business. In the 1860s, the leading industries reflected early development of manufacturing and the persisting importance of the United States as a supplier of natural resources. Cotton goods, lumber, boots and shoes, and flour dominated. By 1910, according to Geruson and McGrath (1977:68), the major industries reflected the maturation of manufacturing and consisted of machinery, iron and steel, lumber, clothing, and railroad cars, among other products.

TABLE 5.2 The 20 Most Populated Urban Areas in the United States, 1890–1950.

1890		1920		1950	
New York	1,515,300	New York	5,620,000	New York	7,892,000
Chicago, IL	1,099,900	Chicago, IL	2,701,000	Chicago, IL	3,621,000
Philadelphia, PA	1,047,000	Philadelphia, PA	1,823,800	Philadelphia, PA	2,071,600
Brooklyn, NY	806,300	Detroit, MI	993,100	Los Angeles, CA	1,970,400
St. Louis, MO	451,800	Cleveland, OH	796,800	Detroit, MI	1,849,600
Boston, MA	448,500	St. Louis, MO	772,900	Baltimore, MD	949,700
Baltimore, MD	434,400	Boston, MA	748,000	Cleveland, OH	914,800
San Francisco, CA	299,000	Baltimore, MD	733,800	St. Louis, MO	856,800
Cincinnati, OH	296,900	Pittsburgh, PA	588,300	Washington, DC	802,200
Cleveland, OH	262,400	Los Angeles, CA	576,700	Boston, MA	801,400
Buffalo, NY	255,700	Buffalo, NY	506,800	San Francisco, CA	775,400
New Orleans, LA	242,000	San Francisco, CA	506,700	Pittsburgh, PA	676,800
Pittsburgh, PA	238,600	Milwaukee, WI	457,100	Milwaukee, WI	637,400
Washington, DC	230,400	Washington, DC	437,600	Houston, TX	596,200
Detroit, MI	205,900	Newark, NJ	414,500	Buffalo, NY	580,100

SOURCE: Campbel Gibson, *Population of the 100 Largest Cities and Other Urban Places in the United States, 1790–1990*. Washington, DC: U.S. Bureau of the Census, Population Division, Working Paper No. 27, June 1997 (1998).

Population Churning and Immigration

We have covered several features associated with urbanization in the United States. One of the most distinctive is the phenomenon of population turnover, or churning, which for a time was quite exaggerated here compared to other countries. From the mid-1800s to 1900s, American cities functioned as giant magnets that attracted immigrants from all over the world. Prior to the 1800s, most people came from the British Isles or as slaves captured from Africa. After 1830, many more arrived from Germany, Scandinavia, Central and Eastern Europe, and China. Between 1800 and 1925, over 40 million immigrants entered the United States. Seventeen million arrived during the period between 1846 and 1900 alone (Vance, 1990:359).

These figures alone cannot capture the way cities functioned as entry points for people. In effect, cities such as New York, Chicago, Philadelphia, and Boston processed vast numbers of immigrants from Europe and elsewhere, orienting them to life in America before many made their way into the hinterland. At this time the internal demographic differentiation of cities took on the characteristics commonly associated with their residential patterns, namely, mosaics of little worlds comprising ethnic enclaves of immigrants. The robustness of cultural life found there inspired succeeding generations of urban sociologists in their studies.

During the period of urban expansion, population churned throughout the large cities. By one conservative estimate, half of the residents moved each decade only to be replaced by still more immigrants (Monkkonen, 1989). A study of Boston in the year 1890, for example, revealed that with a total population of approximately 450,000 people, at least 600,000 had moved in a decade before, while somewhat more than 500,000 had moved out. In short, the population size of cities during the formative period of expansion is a static figure that disguises the massive movement of people into and out of those cities.

One way to appreciate population churning is to consider the economic and political opportunities created by the phenomenon. Each new immigrant had to be processed by federal, state, and local officials, which meant more government jobs. School teachers were in constant demand, as were settlement house workers, religious functionaries, and the many specialized businesses that catered to the needs of arrivals from foreign lands. City economies thrived not only because of the influx of population but also because it turned over so frequently, making the same services necessary to new people with similar needs as previous arrivals. Above all, the rapid increase in population provided U.S. industry not only with much needed labor power but also with consumers who could use the products being turned out by the factories. Export trade during this period of U.S. history was not as important as the growing domestic market of consumers. In a subsequent chapter, we will take a closer look at the importance of immigration to American cities. Since the 1980s, a new round of significant immigration, this time from Latin America and Asia, has transformed American urban regions again, in the suburbs as well as the cities. Like the period of rapid industrialization we just discussed, the contemporary phase is also tied to economic needs, but this time it is aimed at feeding the demands of both high-tech industries on the one hand, and minimum wage services on the other. As we shall see, areas that received immigrants between 1970 and 2000 experienced economic growth while those that did not declined.

Population influx had a dramatic effect on the internal configuration of cities. Owners of buildings soon discovered that the voracious demand for housing could be met by converting structures to rental units. Later, new buildings called *tenements* were constructed specifically for rental use. These buildings were designed to squeeze together as many families as possible. The increased density made public health crises common. It also increased the risk of fire. On October 18, 1871, for example, the city of Chicago was almost destroyed by a single fire. Other fires at the turn of the century devastated cities such as Boston and San Francisco. Yet the escalating demand for housing also afforded handsome profits to owners of tenements. According to one estimate, by 1890 as much as 77 percent of all city dwellers were renters, and the annual returns on rentals could be as high as 40 percent (Glaab and Brown, 1967:160).

From our present vantage point, it is simply impossible to grasp the kinds of conditions immigrants lived in during the late 1800s in American cities. The writer Luc Sante published a meticulously researched and now classic book on Manhattan during this time, *Low Life* (1991). Box 5.2 outlines the basic features of these tenements and the astonishing population density and primitive living conditions that characterized them.

The Role of Technology: Building Innovations and Urban Transport

During the 1800s, the spatial organization of the city changed as new forms of building introduced a larger scale to the physical environment, aided greatly by several innovations in construction. The balloon-frame house replaced heavy timber construction in the 1830s and made it possible for building to proceed more rapidly and with greater quantity than in the past. In 1848, James Bogardus introduced the use of cast-iron columns and weight-bearing walls supporting the structure of nonresidential buildings, which eliminated the need for heavy masonry construction and opened the internal spaces of buildings so that factories and warehouses could maximize their unimpeded use of floor space. Elisha Otis invented the elevator, and by 1880 its widespread use enabled taller buildings to work more efficiently. Finally, in 1884 William L. Jenny erected the first skyscraper, the ten-story Home Insurance Building in Chicago, which was also the "first building with a fully iron structure carrying the weight of the edifice" (Vance, 1990:471). The city of skyscrapers was not far away.

Tall building construction, unimpeded floor space allowing for the efficient placement of machinery, and the remarkable innovation of the elevator transformed the city

Box 5.2

Tenement Living in Mid-Nineteenth-Century Manhattan

"The typical tenement of the late 19th century consisted of two buildings, front and rear, and most popularly known as the double-decker. The front structure measured 25 feet by 50, the rear was 25 feet, and they were separated by a 25 ft. court. . . . The interior rooms of the front house got no light or air at all, and neither did the back rooms of the rear, since that structure generally abutted on its counterpart across the block. . . . Below were two subterranean levels, both fully inhabited: basements, thought to be comparable to the upper stories since they lay partly above the ground, and cellers, completely submerged, airless and lightless. In 1864 there were 15,224 such populated cellers. Cellers were the lowest rung of habitation, but this did not prevent landlords from commanding princely sums for them, as much as $200 per month."

Within these confines horrific unsanitary conditions prevailed leading to diseases of all kinds and, by today's standards anywhere, alarmingly high infant mortality rates. Fires were also common and, due to the tinderbox nature of construction, tenements that caught on fire burned rapidly and trapped their inhabitants within.

"The density of population is difficult to imagine by present day standards. . . . There were no residential structures more than seven or eight stories high, and the average was four stories, many of these floors inhabited by a single-family. In 1872, for example, the 17th Ward, bounded by 14th street on the north, Avenue B on the east, Rivington Street on the south, and the Bowery and Fourth Avenue on the west, held 1/40th of Manhattan's total area but 1/10th of its population."

It housed a population equal to that of Richmond, Virginia, and greater than that of Cleveland.

"The successive waves of immigrants from Europe had brought so many people, particularly in the last 20 years of the 19th century, and had dumped them in such dire conditions, that as many as four or five families were routinely housed in apartments intended for one. Yet even these could count themselves as provisionally fortunate. Less so were the numbers of homeless, dispossessed, or those who had never found one, who were legion."

SOURCE: Excerpted from Luc Sante, *Low Life* (New York: Farrar, Straus and Giroux, 1991), 30, 32.

into an arena of concentrated industry during the last half of the nineteenth century. Mobility of the workforce became a paramount concern at this time. The need for mass transport was met by a series of innovations, starting with the horse-drawn omnibus that carried twelve to twenty passengers (Glaab and Brown, 1967:147). By the 1850s, these were replaced by the horse-drawn railway car, which not only facilitated the movement of people into and out of the "downtown" districts but also provided the means by which the middle class could suburbanize (Warner, 1962). In the 1870s, the horse was finally replaced by the steam-powered locomotive. By 1881 the elevated lines, or "Els," of New York City were carrying 175,000 passengers a day!

Surpassing all these advances, a major breakthrough occurred in the 1870s, when Nikola Tesla's discoveries on alternating current were applied to the production of electrical power. The dynamo replaced the battery, and electric trains and trolleys were perfected. Electrification made possible the extensive, nonpolluting trolley system and the underground subway train. This change was remarkable. As Glaab and Brown observe, "In 1890, 69.7 percent of the total trackage in cities was operated by horses; by 1902 this figure had declined to 1.1 percent, while electric power was used on 97 percent of the mileage" (1967:148). The result of all these transformations was the 24–7 city with the *diurnal rhythm* of city life—masses of workers converging on business districts in the morning, only to disperse at day's end with the same great spurt aided by efficient and safe mass transit. By the 1920s, the United States had successfully integrated millions of immigrants from over one hundred countries into an industrial labor force. Its large cities were all built and humming with activity. Industrialization and urbanization had not only settled the frontier but led the country itself to a place among the world's powers.

THE RISE OF THE METROPOLIS: 1920 TO 1960

During the period of urban expansion, economic interests located within cities competed with one another and land development in the West made people wealthy. This stage ended as individual entrepreneurs and small businesses were gobbled up by large corporations, often located in different cities or even states. The phase of *competitive capitalism* slowly gave way to a new era, that of *monopoly capitalism*. In turn, cities grew progressively larger.

City building slowed down considerably in the United States in the 1900s following a series of economic depressions that would culminate in the Great Depression of the late 1920s. Economic activity and urban growth picked up again in the 1930s as government reforms aided economic recovery and the United States mobilized for another world war in the 1940s. During the *metropolitan period*, cities not only grew larger but also spread out beyond the political boundaries of their local governments. New areas of development became, in turn, new cities; in many cases, urbanization simply engulfed the smaller towns adjacent to the large cities through a region-wide process of suburbanization.

In the metropolitan period, it was becoming necessary to think about the urban phenomenon less in terms of the large city and more in terms of a region consisting of a mix of residential, work, recreational, and shopping places. The U.S. Department of the Census introduced the term *Standard Metropolitan Statistical Area* (SMSA—see Chapter 1) to account for the regional nature of development. Large central cities such as New York and Detroit also assumed vast economic importance far beyond their borders because of the businesses that were centered there—finance and cars, respectively. This conjunction of spatial reach and economic might gave the city a new name: the "metropolis" or "mother city." Visions of the immense city outgrowing its boundaries began to appear in many countries. The German film *Metropolis* is one such example. Cities such as Tokyo, London, Paris, Berlin, Rome, Rio de Janeiro, and Calcutta all reached an unprecedented scale of size and population.

The metropolitan pattern of increasing size and geographical territory became characteristic of many cities in the United States. Following the Great Depression, urban scientists became interested in the phenomenon of the metropolitan region, and many studies were carried out to discover its social, political, spatial, and economic characteristics (McKenzie, 1933; Schnore, 1957; Bollens and Schmandt, 1965). Research revealed that two processes contributed most to regional growth: greater differentiation of the system of cities, expressed as changes in spatial, functional, and demographic differentiation; and the process of suburbanization.

Spatial, Functional, and Demographic Differentiation of the City

Metropolitan development and change do not occur because of technological factors alone but are also dependent on political and cultural relations. Economic activities, for example, require a workforce and certain community services, such as adequate schooling and health care, for businesses and their labor pools to survive over time. When there is a proper mesh between the human tissue of family and community life and associated economic activities requiring particular skill levels, both businesses and neighborhoods prosper. The sociospatial perspective emphasizes the fact that the relations among the economy, political structure, and culture are reciprocal.

Accommodations between the social fabric of community life and the needs of business produced the early factory towns, such as Burlington, Vermont, and Birmingham, Alabama, during the early period of family capitalism. One characteristic of this phase was that sources of employment and the labor pool were close together and both were tied to the general fate of the city itself. As the structure of capitalism changed in the 1930s, this equilibrium was shattered, and upheavals in the community paralleled those in business. Neighborhood relations changed when people were thrown out of work after plants closed or businesses altered their skill needs. New demands were placed on school systems, city budgets, and families to aid in the adjustment. In many cases, the success or failure of new ways of doing business depended on how well the community, local government, and families adapted to change. Thus, while economic alterations affect the social fabric, the latter in turn can affect the well-being of the local economy.

Consequently, each time new economic priorities are put in place, they affect the composition of territory and alter community life. The social organization of a particular place—the way it is organized according to locational choices of business, the scale of community, the flows of commuters, definitions of city service districts, the pace and structure of family life, and so on—is affected by the reciprocal relation between the local economy and the social fabric. In this chapter, we will discuss the changes brought about by the Depression restructuring of the 1930s. They involve a process of *horizontal integration* of business activity coupled with metropolitan regional expansion. In the next chapter, we will consider equally important changes that have occurred since 1960.

Changes in Spatial Differentiation

Following the Great Depression, the economic system of the United States changed from a comparatively competitive form of industrial capitalism with a relatively large number of firms in each industry to a concentrated form called "monopoly capitalism" (Baran and Sweezy, 1966), where ownership was consolidated in a few hands. One distinguishing characteristic of the new form was the growth of monopolistic (one firm) or oligopolistic (a select few firms) control of major industries. For example, automobile production prior to the 1930s involved a host of firms such as Studebaker, Hudson, Tucker, and De Soto, along with Ford, Pontiac, and Chrysler. These companies were scattered across much of the United States, and their fates were often intertwined with specific cities and communities. After the 1930s, production of automobiles was essentially in the hands of the Big Four—General Motors, Ford, Chrysler, and American Motors (today it's down to the first three). While these companies also maintained branch plants across the country, their operations were national in scope and their headquarters were no longer tied to the places where they had their major factories. The Detroit area in particular became the headquarters for much of the auto industry, and decisions made there affected towns across the country. This change in the horizontal integration of large businesses to a more dispersed pattern, coupled with greater concentration of ownership, was also repeated in other industries, including steel, the production of consumer durables (such as electrical appliances), and even the consolidation of retailing outlets by giant department stores following branch marketing schemes (such as Sears, Roebuck and Montgomery Ward).

The changes in the scale of economic organization had spatial effects, especially on local community life, and several classic sociological studies documented them (Vidich and Bensman, 1960; Lynd and Lynd, 1937). Concentration of wealth and ownership led to greater horizontal integration of business activities and changes in the spatial relations among community, work, and region. That is, prior to the Depression, most companies had all their functions located together and generally in the same city. These firms were replaced by companies with divisions in any number of locations, and they used dispersal in space to their advantage to cut costs, especially labor costs. For example, a large company that was part of an oligopoly in one industry might have its headquarters in a center such as New York, where it would be close to the headquarters of the other oligopolists in the same industry. It would also be close to banking and related services necessary to the command-and-control function of business administration. Its specialized needs would stimulate the local community to supply laborers with adequate training for the jobs that were created. This same firm might have a branch plant for production located in Newark, New Jersey, a central distribution facility in Philadelphia, and so on, each with its own impact on the local community and labor force. Such a pattern of related functional differentiation and spatial or horizontal integration was replicated in many industries.

Changes in Functional Differentiation

As a consequence, after 1930, a new, functionally differentiated system of urban places had emerged in the United States; that is, different cities were the homes of different aspects of industry or commerce. Instead of competing with one another, as was the case during the previous period of competitive capitalism discussed in Chapter 3, local capital was now organized and integrated by a national system of concentrated wealth. This pattern was not a product of the city itself but was attributable to the powers of institutions and social actors whose activities were deployed *within* the cities that were linked to the national corporations producing most of the country's wealth. Thus, horizontal integration and functional differentiation were two related outcomes in the restructuring of social organization after the 1930s. We call this interlinked complex of functionally differentiated activities located within urban places a *system of cities* (McKenzie, 1933; Berry, 1972; Bourne and Simmons, 1978). In studying this system, it is always important to keep in mind that functional differentiation is a feature of the particular complex of economic activities that are located within a city rather than a characteristic of the city itself. Furthermore, the diverse activities across the nation are horizontally integrated by large corporations that possess "command-and-control" headquarters.

Box 5.3 illustrates the pattern of functional specialization for the largest U.S. cities. We can see that virtually all cities had substantial sectors of service employment. Not surprisingly, Albany, New York, is functionally specialized in government activity. In contrast, Detroit, Michigan, retains a functional specialization in manufacturing. Some cities, such as Los Angeles, Baltimore, and Seattle, also have significant manufacturing sectors despite a large service sector. A more detailed study of these differences would require exploring the kinds of businesses that comprise each sector within each city. Thus, while Boston seems functionally specialized in services, we might also wish to know what *kinds* of services are provided and their respective shares of the total. In addition, we might also ask just how many headquarters are located in that city in order to place Boston within the hierarchy of command-and-control centers. In short, variation in the breakdown of employment among the sectors of the economy within cities provides a great deal of information on how local, national, and global business activities concentrate in particular places.

Box 5.3

Functions of Selected U.S. Cities

Education	Government	Government and Education	Manufacturing	Entertainment/ Recreation
Ann Arbor, MI	Albany, NY	Austin, TX	Birmingham, AL	Atlantic City, NJ
Athens, GA	Carson City, NV	Baton Rouge, LA	Buffalo, NY	Fort Lauderdale, FL
Berkeley, CA	Denver, CO	Columbia, SC	Cleveland, OH	Las Vegas, NV
Bloomington, IN	Harrisburg, PA	Columbus, OH	Detroit, MI	Los Angeles, CA
Boulder, CO	Indianapolis, IN	Des Moines, IA	Evansville, IN	Miami Beach, FL
Champaign, IL	Lansing, MI	Lincoln, NB	Gary, IN	New Orleans, LA
Gainesville, FL	Raleigh, NC	Madison, WI	Milwaukee, WI	Las Vegas, NV
Knoxville, TN	Sacramento, CA	Oklahoma City, OK	Newark, NJ	Reno, NV
Tempe, AZ	Springfield, IL		Pittsburg, PA	Vail, CO
Oxford, MS	Jackson, MS		Toledo, OH	

By the 1960s the U.S. urban system consisted of a select group of large cities with populations ranging from several hundred thousand to over 7 million. This pattern represents *balanced urbanization* that is characteristic of the older industrialized countries such as England (see Chapter 11 for a contrast with less developed countries). Several studies have documented the structure of the urban system in the United States (Pred, 1973; Chase-Dunn, 1985). It is arranged across two different dimensions. On the one hand, cities seem to be distinguished by concentration of business in either manufacturing or services, with the larger cities less specialized. On the other hand, there is specialization in finances or commerce. Furthermore, from 1950 to 1970, the functional specialization of the cities in the U.S. system remained relatively stable (South and Poston, 1982). Cities such as New York, San Francisco, Chicago, and Atlanta, for example, were diverse areas, while cities such as Baltimore, Detroit, and Los Angeles were more concentrated in manufacturing, and Portland, Oregon, Kansas City, and Minneapolis specialized in financial activities and commerce. These specializations and rankings are somewhat different today, as we will see in the next chapter. However, until at least the 1970s they characterized an urban system that reflected the increasing functional integration of the emergent national economy. Until the 1970s they also showed that important business activity remained concentrated within central cities. That is no longer as true today.

The immense economic changes bringing about the concentration of capital in large cities were only one aspect of the metropolitan era. As central cities prospered, they attracted talented people from all over the nation. Metropolises became centers of culture and political power as well. They were the sites of important museums, universities, and symphony orchestras. They housed art movements and literary re-vivals. With their immense populations, they also wielded great political power. In many cases, such as Chicago and New York City, carrying the state in a presidential election depended, in effect, on carrying the city. Much of this confluence of eco-nomic, political, and cultural centrality was to change rapidly beginning with the 1960s (see next chapter). But perhaps the best example of the world-class metropolis during the period prior to this is New York City (see Box 5.4).

Box 5.4

New York City in the Metropolitan Period

By the time of the Civil War, New York City was already the country's most popu-lous city and its banking capital. By the 1920s, New York had replaced London as the financial center of the globe. Its great skyscrapers, such as the Empire State and Chrysler buildings; its museums and cultural institutions, including Tin Pan Alley (Twenty-eighth Street) and Broadway theaters; and its universities, made New York the cultural and intellectual center of the United States as well. At this time, the New York Yankees were the best team in baseball and arguably the best team ever. Their home run hitter, Babe Ruth, was so popular that the owner, "Beer Baron" Ja-cob Rupert, decided to build a large stadium to showcase the team (Allen, 1990). Yankee Stadium, or "the house that Ruth built," with over a 60,000 seating capac-ity, was constructed in the Bronx and instantly sold out for many of its games.

By 1930 New York already had over 7 million people, a figure that is slightly less than the population today. The Depression hit the city especially hard. Although many people suffered and manufacturing began its unimpeded decline, the city en-joyed a renaissance under the mayorship of Fiorello La Guardia. An outstanding pro-gressive leader, La Guardia used government to get things done. Parks were cleaned up and renovated, new highways were constructed, the subway system was consoli-dated and improved, and new housing and commercial construction were promoted. La Guardia built the first international airport for New York (now named after him). His administration peaked with the spectacular New York World's Fair from 1939 to 1940, which was visited by almost 45 million people (Allen, 1990:280).

During the 1950s, New York City became the center for corporate headquarters, if not the monopoly capital center for the globe. Beginning in 1952 with the con-struction of Lever House on Park Avenue, the new, international-style office build-ing took over the skyline with its glass facades and square, flat roof. Midtown became a mass of high-rise corporate towers. At this time the New York School of Art, including Jackson Pollock, Mark Rothko, and Willem de Kooning, assumed the global standard for modern art, and the city became the culture capital of the

continues

Box 5.4 *continued*

world (Walloch, 1988). Arturo Toscanini, one of the greatest orchestra conductors, came to live in the city. The NBC Symphony Orchestra was created just for him, and he appeared on television. The new invention, by the way, had its programming centered in New York City, where all the network headquarters resided. By 1960, when the metropolitan period began its decline, there was still no more dynamic, exciting, culturally stimulating, and prosperous place in the United States.

Changes in Demographic Differentiation

Between 1930 and 1960, the complexion of metropolitan demographics changed. As the metropolitan corporate economy kicked in following the Depression and large cities fought for their functional niche in the world, corporations hired a growing number of white-collar professionals. Many more trained workers found employment in the sophisticated service industries that aided the activities of business headquarters. A growing number of these new urbanites were highly educated and well paid relative to the times. In the 1950s and 1960s, many of these corporate employees preferred to live in the city. A study by Leo F. Schnore (1963) in 1960 revealed that metropolitan regions with comparatively newer core cities (those reaching a population of 50,000 after 1920) had higher family incomes, levels of education, and percentages of white-collar employees in the central city than in the suburban ring. This breakdown is no longer the rule today, as we will see in Chapter 6 when we consider the contemporary changes.

In other respects, central cities began to assume the dimensions of ethnic and racial concentration that we find at present; that is, beginning with the 1950s, demographic differentiation of the metropolitan population began to take on the sharp racial distinctions that are characteristic today. Writing in the 1960s, Bollens and Schmandt remark:

> Within the metropolitan area itself, the ethnic colonies are concentrated largely in the central city. . . . Chicago, an urban complex of many nationality groups, furnishes a typical example. The latest census shows that of the approximately 600,000 foreign born living in the SMSA, 73 percent reside in the central city. (1965:96)

Bollens and Schmandt add about black Americans at the time that:

> The geographical segregation or distribution of ethnic settlements is even more pronounced when the non-white migrants, predominantly Negroes, are considered. . . . As the non-whites have migrated to urban places, they have tended to

gravitate into the central cities of metropolitan areas. By 1960 over one-half of the non-white population lived in such communities, a gain of 63 percent over 1950. Among the whites, on the other hand, there has been a continual shift from the central cities to suburbs with the result that in 1960, 52 percent of the whites in the 212 SMSAs lived outside the central cities compared to 22 percent of the non-white. (1965:97)

The migration of blacks from the South involved a mass exodus. Millions left in the 1950s and 1960s. By the time of the 1960 census, only half the black population still resided in the South. Several factors were responsible, including the extensive use of the mechanical cotton picker by the 1940s and the phasing out of the share-cropper system in the Deep South. Many black Americans went north, west, and east, attracted by the possibility of jobs in the newly booming military industries. Most of these migrants settled in the central cities. Returning to the example of Chicago, Nicholas Lemann notes:

During the 1940s, the black population of Chicago increased by 77 percent, from 278,000 to 492,000. In the 1950s, it grew by another 65 percent, to 813,000; at one point 2,200 black people were moving to Chicago every week. By 1960, Chicago had more than half a million more black residents than it had had twenty years earlier, and black migrants from the South were still coming in tremendous numbers. (1991b:70)

The extensive changes in urban form brought about during the metropolitan period led the way to the end of this era as well. By the early 1960s the movement of white families from the central city to the suburbs was well underway, and invest-ment in areas outside of the central city paved the way for the creation of the multi-centered urban region. Although the central cities would remain the focus of economic and manufacturing activity for another decade or two, their populations were already undergoing a remarkable transformation. Many central cities developed extensive ethnic and minority communities and by the end of the century would be more diverse than they had been a hundred years earlier. Increasingly the cities would become the home of ethnic communities and the white working class, while the white middle class would dominate the suburban areas. The crucial factor in all of this is the process of suburbanization, which is also responsible for the creation of the multicentered urban region.

KEY CONCEPTS

mercantile capitalism / industrial capitalism
monopoly capitalism / global capitalism
colonial cities / colonial dependency
mercantile cities
population churning
immigration
economic organization
spatial differentiation
functional specialization

DISCUSSION QUESTIONS

1. How does urbanization in the United States differ from that of other countries discussed in Chapter 2? Identify three specific differences and explain their significance for urban development in the United States.

2. The legacies of colonialism were important for later urban development in the United States. What are the legacies of colonialism, and how have these influenced the development of American cities?

3. Industrial development led to the rapid growth of cities at the end of the nineteenth century. What are some of the social problems that resulted from this rapid growth? How were these problems dealt with by local governments?

4. What are some of the technological developments that influenced the physical structure of the industrial city at the end of the nineteenth century? How did these technological developments alter the spatial structure of the industrial city?

5. How was metropolitan growth from 1920 to 1960 linked to changes in the nature of U.S. capitalism? How did the urban system in the United States change during this period? Why did metropolitan growth in this period result in increased functional differentiation of cities in the U.S. urban system?

SUBURBANIZATION, GLOBALIZATION, AND THE EMERGENCE OF THE MULTICENTERED REGION

Although the presence of suburbanization is not unusual for industrialized countries, the massive scale of this phenomenon in the United States is quite distinctive among most societies, except for places like Australia and Canada. To be sure, many nations have experienced growth beyond city borders, but in the United States this has assumed the form of single-family home construction for the middle class on an unprecedented scale. Suburbanization of the white middle class to single-family homes accelerated its pace after the 1930s, and especially after World War II, but it was always an important aspect of settlement patterns. As we learned in Chapter 2, U.S. cities did not possess walls. Fringe area development occurred as the city itself grew. In Europe, the walls were essentially torn down or overgrown so that these countries also experienced suburbanization, but at a slower pace and with a different, more working-class-oriented mix of population that was housed in multifamily or apartment buildings.

Growth beyond city borders was a common feature of industrialized societies as early as the nineteenth century. In fact, the desire to live outside the city despite commuting there for work seems to be as old as the city itself. Although we can point to numerous writers who extol the virtues of city living, there has always been an expressed "anti-urban" bias in every urbanized civilization. The historian Kenneth Jackson offers the following excerpt from a letter written over 2,500 years ago as evidence that suburbanization was a process coextensive with urbanization itself: "Our property seems to me the most beautiful in the world. It is so close to Babylon that we enjoy all the advantages of the city, and yet when we come home we are away from all the noise and dirt" (1985:12).

But the presence of a yearning for the country among city dwellers or some anti-urban bias cannot explain the immense scale of suburbanization that is characteristic of the United States. There is a demand-side view of suburbanization that is instructive. By "demand side" we mean the production of a settlement space pattern through the desires of consumers and businesspeople acting in the marketplace. Demand-side theories of urbanization make the assumption that settlement patterns are the result of a large number of individuals interacting competitively in the market to satisfy desires. Often they are simply aided by innovations in transportation technology. Many geographers, such as John Borchert (1967), and urban sociologists, such as Amos Hawley (1981), suggest this approach as an explanation of urban spatial patterns.

To an extent, the demand-side view helps us understand aspects of suburbanization, especially the desire of U.S. residents for a home of their own. Homeownership is a potent cultural symbol in our society. It provides people with their most important social status. Owning a home also links with other aspects of consumerism that express basic values in U.S. culture (Veblen, 1899).

There is also, however, a "supply-side" view to urban patterns. In this approach, what counts in development is less the desires of individuals than the quests of special interests, especially networks of businesspeople aided by allies in government that promote development to acquire profits. Feagin sums up the supply-side view:

> Traditionally most urban analysts and scholars have argued that everybody makes cities, that first and foremost the choices and decisions by large groups of consumers demanding housing and buildings lead to the distinctive ways cities are built. But this is not accurate. Ordinary people often play "second fiddle." In the first instance, capitalist developers, bankers, industrial executives, and their business and political allies build cities, although they often run into conflict with rank-and-file urbanites over their actions. Cities under capitalism are structured and built to maximize the profits of real estate capitalists and industrial corporations, not necessarily to provide decent and livable environments for all urban residents. (1983:8)

The history of suburbanization in the United States is a protracted story of bold quests to acquire wealth through the development of fringe area land and individual or group pursuits of a residential vision that would solve the problems of city living. In other words, an account of this phenomenon must consider supply-side and demand-side factors as intertwined.

In the early 1800s, for example, industrialists who had recently acquired fortunes, such as Leland Stanford in railroads, Andrew Carnegie in steel, and James B. Duke in tobacco (the so-called nouveaux riches), sought symbols of their newfound wealth. One practice was to purchase a palatial home with substantial space for manicured lawns and at some distance from the city. According to Thorstein Veblen (1899), who introduced the term *conspicuous consumption*, space in these suburban homes was used as a symbol of "excess" and the ability to afford it. The fronts of houses were given over to large, manicured lawns labored over by a team of hired gardeners, lawns that were used for nothing except the growing of grass. The mansions themselves had many more rooms than were needed to house family and servants. Guests could always be accommodated on the spot with their own individual bedroom; space was simply held vacant. The backyards were devoted to "suburban" leisure—genteel games such as croquet or badminton, lazing in lawn chairs, or simply walking in the garden. Conspicuous consumption, pastoral delights, and the large, single-family house with generous living space became for many Americans the suburban ideal. This cultural value glorifying a particular space fed the economic aspects of demand for homeownership outside the city. In Chapter 8, we will see that other metropolitan lifestyles are also dependent on their own particular spaces for cultural expression.

Demand-side explanations for suburbanization often stress the importance of transportation technology as its cause (see, for example, Jackson, 1985; Muller, 1981; Hawley, 1981), with each innovation, such as the switch from commuter rail to automobile, signaling a new pattern of land use. Transportation modes, however, served only as the *means* for residential suburban development; they were not the cause. Transport technology was always used to further real estate developer schemes. The demand-side view demonstrates that the desire for the suburban lifestyle may have been active in the minds of urbanites because people emulated the rich and disliked the confines of the large city. But dreams alone did not produce concrete spatial patterns. Rather, suburbanization was generated by the supply-side activities of real estate entrepreneurs and government subsidies responding to and feeding demand-side desires.

Early suburban development leapfrogged over the urban landscape. Suburban housing was built as a separate town removed by several miles from city boundaries. In the late 1800s, Westchester and Tuxedo Park outside New York City, Lake Forest and Riverside outside Chicago, Hillsborough adjacent to San Francisco, Palos Verdes near Los Angeles, Shaker Heights eight miles from Cleveland, and Roland Park outside Baltimore were all private developments built as towns. Most of these places advertised themselves as extolling suburban virtues, which at the time meant racial, ethnic, and class exclusion in addition to low-density residential living. It was not until the late 1940s that suburban development occurred on a mass scale. Hence, the desire for racial, class, and religious exclusion also added to the complex of cultural factors contributing to the desire to suburbanize.

But suburbanization in the United States was not just about developing housing. The early deconcentration of industry followed the same pattern. In the 1800s, owners of large businesses often moved all their operations outside the city by developing a separate town. The classic study of such "satellite cities" was done by Graham Taylor in 1915. Gary, Indiana, for example, was built on sand dunes at the base of Lake Michigan by U.S. Steel in the 1880s. At about the same time, George Pullman moved his railroad car business out of Chicago and built Pullman, Illinois, a few miles away. In 1873 Singer Sewing Machine relocated from Manhattan to an existing city, Elizabeth, New Jersey, and by doing so converted it into a company town, where the factory remained until 1982, when it closed due to foreign competition.

Taylor (1915) gives two main explanations for the creation of satellite cities, which echo aspects of our sociospatial perspective. First, the new ventures represented an important investment in real estate as well as an industrial relocation. More space was needed for industrialized plants, hence the need to move out of the congested central city. But the need for space was coupled with the acquisition of real estate. Pullman, for example, expected to make as much money from the development of land he owned in the new city as from the factory itself. Second, industrialists pulled their plants out of cities because the latter were hotbeds of union activity. Workers in any one plant were invariably in contact with workers in other plants and other industries. The city concentrated unions as well as people. During the sequential recessions in the United States, beginning with the 1870s, strikes and worker activism were especially frequent. The decentralization of industry was an important tool for minimizing union influence, according to Taylor (see Chapter 7).

To be sure, transportation technology eventually played a profound role in suburbanization. After the 1920s in particular, the movement of people to the suburbs was aided greatly by the mass production and consumption of the automobile. Prior to that time, regional metropolitan space was organized in a star-shaped form with the greatest development situated along the fingers of rail corridors. The private automobile enabled developers to work laterally and fill in the spaces between the mainline tracks. In the 1920s, 23 million cars were registered in the United States, and that figure increased to 33 million ten years later. "By 1940, the U.S. auto registration rate exceeded 200 per 1000 population and the average number of cars per capita (which was 13 in 1920) had fallen to less than 5" (Muller, 1981:39).

Turn-of-the-century suburbanization played a great role in determining the patterns of growth that followed during the years between 1920 and 1960. Trolley lines and tract housing laid down in the previous period provided the material infrastructure, such as right-of-ways, sewers, and utility lines, for much of the urban growth that was to follow. It is often suggested, for example, that Los Angeles looks the way it does—spread out in a pattern of immense sprawl—because it was built during the age of the automobile. Actually, the formative period of development for Los Angeles took place prior to the invention of the auto. Los Angeles was a product of electrified trolley lines and very active, aggressive real estate speculation schemes that capitalized on the ease of home construction in the region (Crump, 1962). Today's freeways in Los Angeles simply follow the transit routes of the major trolley lines that once existed. The fact that the latter were pollution free should not be lost on the present generation suffering from smog, nor should we forget Spencer Crump's (1962) case study showing how automobile, oil, and highway construction companies colluded to sabotage the trolley car transit business.

The major thrust of suburbanization in the United States took place after 1920, with a profound acceleration of growth after World War II. Truly it can be said that present-day regional patterns of metropolitan development materialized during this time. Prior to the 1920s, a suburban residence could be afforded only by the more affluent; after 1940, suburbanization became a mass phenomenon. So far in this chapter we have mentioned several supply-side factors contributing to decentralization. On the demand side, we have indicated the profound cultural effect that the style of life associated with affluent suburbia had on the tastes of urban individuals and families. While many Americans may have desired to leave the city, few had the means prior to World War II, especially because of the Great Depression. Here the federal government became crucial in creating a mass housing market because its policies promoted single-family homes, as the sociospatial approach suggests.

In the 1930s, the Depression ravaged the home construction industry. Because a principal asset of banks was (and still is) home mortgages, this economic downslide also had a devastating impact on the banking industry. In one estimate, housing values declined by 20 percent between 1926 and 1932; by 1933 at least half of all home mortgages were in default (Jackson, 1985:191). The Great Depression altered the nature of U.S. capitalism during this time because the federal government changed from an indirect participant in the economy to a direct subsidizer of business. In the 1930s, Washington, D.C., attempted a rescue of the housing industry as a means of saving the banks.

In 1934 Congress passed the National Housing Act, which established the Federal Housing Authority (FHA). Briefly put, for qualified houses, the federal government insured buyers' mortgages. For banks, this took the risk out of private loans. It also pumped needed capital into the housing industry. Foreclosures went from 250,000 in 1932 to 18,000 by 1951 (Jackson, 1985:203). The act also established the Federal National Mortgage Association (Fannie Mae), which facilitated the transfer of funds by banks across geographical and political boundaries in the United States. The Fannie Mae program and later Ginnie Mae (Government National Mortgage Association) helped restructure the banking community and subsidized mortgage lending on a mass scale.

Subsequent housing acts were passed in 1937 and 1941. Along with earlier initiatives, they established the homeowner's tax subsidy. Homeowners could now deduct the interest paid on mortgages from their taxes. This subsidy quite literally made it cheaper to own a home than to rent. Along with this tax subsidy, the Serviceman's Readjustment Act of 1944 had the most direct effects on housing. As the war was ending, Congress pledged to support returning servicemen with a package of welfare measures including subsidized education. One provision of this act established the Veterans Administration (VA) guaranteed loan program. Under the plan, GIs could purchase homes with no money down. The mass exodus to suburbia was now guaranteed.

So we see that mass demand for housing was primed by government programs. Most new construction took place in the suburbs. More than 16 million returning servicemen were eligible for benefits under the 1944 act, and a mass market was created. At this time, and due expressly to the war effort, the United States had perfected mass-production assembly-line techniques that could manufacture vast quantities of goods. All types of consumer durables, including cars, washing machines, vacuum cleaners, toasters, dishwashers, refrigerators, and air conditioners, were being produced on an immense scale after the 1940s. Suburban housing developments featured the new goods, and in the 1950s all aspects of mass production—housing, consumer durables, automobiles—combined to create the characteristic view of suburbia as the epitome of the consumer society. This political, economic, and cultural conjuncture that led to a society *domestically* producing and consuming mass quantities of goods with a large population engaged in assembly-line factory work and active union membership is called *Fordism*, and it is a characteristic of monopoly capitalism. As we will see in the next chapter, under global capitalism the structure of Fordism broke apart as manufacturing activity drained from the United States to other countries.

The beneficiaries of suburbanization were overwhelmingly white. From 1940 to 1960, in two decades, the majority of the white child-rearing middle class left the central cities for the suburbs. In the previous section, we saw that this coincided with a period of mass black migration out of the South. This population transfer of whites and blacks is sometimes referred to as "white flight." Experts on the topic indicate that it is largely a product of the pull factors identified earlier (Frey, 1979). That is, whites did not leave large cities because blacks were moving in or the quality of life was declining; rather, they left because the quality of life was much better in the suburbs and because government programs subsidized them. Racial factors, according to the demographer William Frey (1979), affected less the decision to move than the destination of choice; that is, whites preferred to move to exclusively white areas in the suburbs.

Racism played a more overt role in preventing African Americans from moving to the suburbs themselves. Few were able to make that change in status. Real estate agents blocked black people from buying homes in white areas and banks often denied them mortgages. The results were a dramatic increase in segregation for cities and a concentration of white people in the suburbs beyond national population proportions. Those blacks who did suburbanize could find housing only in other black areas outside the city. The color barrier was strictly enforced by suburban developers. Box 6.1, which contains a case study of Levittown in Long Island, New York, illustrates both the mass phenomenon of suburbanization after World War II and the racial exclusion on which it was based.

Since 1970, population growth has been greater for metropolitan areas outside city centers rather than inside them, which reverses the traditional urbanization process of population concentration. This process is known as *population deconcentration*. Commenting on the 1980 census when the trend was first recognized, a demographer noted, "For the first time in well over 100 years, there was virtually no major nationwide population trend in the direction of concentration" (Long, 1981:11). For a brief time in the 1970s, even small incorporated cities lying outside the major metropolitan

Box 6.1

Profile of 1950s Levittown, Long Island

Prior to the 1940s, most homes were custom built or were renovated farmhouses, and most of this suburban housing remained relatively expensive (Gottdiener, 1977). After the war, voracious demand supported by federal government programs made it possible to build housing in large quantities, but construction techniques had not quite been perfected to build single-family homes that were affordable. Abraham Levitt and Sons was one of the nation's largest builders in the 1940s. Work on many military construction projects had given the company the experience necessary to build inexpensive housing on a mass basis. Levitt built the first large-scale, affordable suburban housing development on several thousand acres of converted potato farms in the town of Hempstead on Long Island, adjacent to New York City:

> After bulldozing the land and removing the trees, trucks carefully dropped off building materials at precise 60-foot intervals. Each house was built on a concrete slab (no cellar); the floors were of asphalt and the walls of composition rockboard. . . . The construction process itself was divided into 27 distinct steps. . . . Crews were trained to do one job—one day the white-paint men, then the red-paint men, then the tile layers. Every possible part, and especially the most difficult ones, was preassembled in central shops, whereas most builders did it on site. Thus, the Levitts reduced the skilled component to 20–40 percent. . . . More than thirty houses went up each day at the peak of production. (Jackson, 1985:234)

Levitt was not sure that government subsidies and the GI bill would prove effective in supporting homeownership on a mass basis, so the first houses were offered only for rent in 1947. Soon after, in 1949 and in response to overwhelming demand, they were sold outright. The two-bedroom Cape Cod boxes initially cost $6,990. The community, now called Levittown, eventually numbered over 17,000 houses and contained more than 80,000 residents. Levitt's organization feared that if they let in blacks, they would run the risk of failing to sell their homes to the white majority. Consequently the developer carefully screened prospective customers for race. Hence, the blue-collar community, which became a symbol for the postwar American Dream, was not integrated.

Unlike large-scale developments of today (as we will discuss in the next chapter), early suburban projects were marketed with a full complement of community amenities. Builders were obligated to supply a community quality of life, not just housing. Levittown came with nine swimming pools, sixty playgrounds, ten baseball diamonds, and seven "village greens," or mini-mall centers, within the development (Jackson, 1985).

During the next few years, Levitt and Sons built communities in Pennsylvania and New Jersey. The modular construction process they innovated was duplicated by builders all over the United States, and the mass construction of suburbia began.

centers grew faster than the large cities, although by the 1980s that rapid growth had already subsided.

Other demographers are just as astounded by the changes of the last several decades. According to Frey and Speare (1988), most of the trends prior to the 1960s that characterized the U.S. population were altered and, in some cases, reversed during the last twenty years. First, there has always been a progressive drift of people from the East, Midwest, and South to the West. After 1960 this shift accelerated, producing rapid growth in the West. The South also grew remarkably during this period. Second, after the 1970s the South gained more than the West, for the first time, in net population growth. By 1980, the Sun Belt region of the West and South together contained the majority of the nation's population—a historical shift indeed!

Third, in the past large cities expanded faster than smaller ones. Since the 1970s this process has been reversed, with growth rates in smaller cities outstripping those of almost all larger ones. In 1970, for example, Phoenix was ranked eighteenth in the country with a population of just over 500,000. By 1994 it was ranked ninth, having grown by an incredible 60 percent. In contrast, with the exception of New York, all large Midwest and East Coast cities lost population between 1970 and 1990. In the most extreme case, Detroit lost a staggering 31.5 percent of its people.

Finally, the shift of metropolitan residents to suburbia accelerated during this time. By 1970, in fact, more people lived in suburbia than in central cities. If, in 1920, we could say with truth that the United States had become an urbanized nation, today we can say with equal confidence that the United States is dominated by suburbanization. Between 1960 and 1990, the United States went from a society dominated by large central cities in the Frost Belt to a nation with the bulk of its population living in the Sun Belt and in suburbia!

DEINDUSTRIALIZATION AND GLOBALIZATION: PROCESSES THAT HAVE CHANGED BOTH CITIES AND SUBURBS SINCE THE 1960s

Beginning with the 1960s, forces other than suburbanization emerged to work both cities and suburbs for change. These added to the phenomenon of deconcentration. On the one hand, the United States began to lose jobs to locations outside the country as labor sourcing led corporations to set up shop in countries where wages were considerably lower and workers were considerably more docile than in America. This process is known as *deindustrialization* and it has led over the decades to a massive decline in manufacturing within the United States. On the other hand, national corporations were bought out or went into partnership with giant multinational companies affecting the behavior of industries and banks, which no longer saw America as their natural home.

In the 1950s, the typical city was an industrial city. Factories filled the air with the smoke of manufacturing activity. Workers in plants lived nearby in so-called blue-collar neighborhoods. Although predominantly white, this population was made up of many ethnic groups—Italian, Irish, Jewish, Polish, Hungarian, German, and Scandinavian. Everyday life was circumscribed by the factory routine for both women and men. A co-ordinated exodus of workers from their homes converged on the plants in the morning, while children ran off to neighborhood schools at about the same time. Schools provided vocational training for most boys and homemaker or secretarial skills for girls as a means of fitting them into a working-class world with limited aspirations that few thought would ever change. Several generations of working-class families grew to maturity within this milieu.

By the 1980s, this pattern of everyday life had changed. Cities no longer were dominated by manufacturing, and working-class family life based on predictable employment opportunities in manufacturing had largely disappeared, producing attendant changes and crises in education and job training. The city of Pittsburgh, for example, was once synonymous with steel. In 1930, over 32 percent of its workforce was engaged in manufacturing. By 1980, only 14 percent of the labor force was employed in manufacturing, and steel production engaged only 5.5 percent. In contrast, service employment had risen to 38 percent, thereby dominating the economy (Jezierski, 1988). Pittsburgh had been transformed from an industrial to a nodal service city. In the process, however, it lost 24 percent of its jobs and 37 percent of its population between 1940 and 1980. Between 1980 and 1990, it lost an additional 12.8 percent of its people. Cities have shifted from an economy dominated by manufacturing to one that now specializes in services and retailing, but with a smaller employed labor force and, in many cases, a smaller population than in the past (Frey and Speare, 1988:4).

In 1950 the proportion of total employment for manufacturing was 26 percent, with the next largest sector, retailing and construction, accounting for 22.6 percent. By the 1980s, the latter proportion was virtually unchanged, but total employment in manufacturing dropped to 22 percent. The largest proportion of workers, or 24 percent, was employed in so-called nodal services: transportation, finance, wholesaling, business repair, insurance, and real estate. Cities shifted in thirty years from an economy dominated by manufacturing to one that specialized in services (Frey and Speare, 1988). For the largest cities, such as New York and Chicago, there is considerable evidence that the sector of capital involved in national and global processes of financial investing has taken over the downtown (Gottdiener, 1985; Sassen, 1991). Employment in the sector of finance capital alone has increased dramatically for the categories of investing services, management consulting, legal services, accounting services, and the like.

GLOBALIZATION AND UNEVEN DEVELOPMENT

As we have already discussed, employment growth was located principally in the service sector, especially in nodal services that were provided to corporations and banks—legal services, printing, business consulting, financial consulting, and related services in communication and transportation. Early observers of this trend toward specialization in nodal services suggested that they would provide the core industry for economic revitalization of cities following the profound decline in manufacturing (Noyelle and Stanback, 1984; Sassen-Koob, 1984). It is now clear that no real renaissance has taken place. What has occurred is that robust activity in advanced services has benefited a relatively small and select group of trained professionals who earn high salaries while leading to modest employment in low-paying service and clerical jobs in activities that aid the work of the highly paid core. The so-called service city actually consists of two layers: (1) a core of nodal services forming the focus of internationally important economic growth that employs highly trained professionals; and (2) a second segment of relatively low-paid service workers who clean the buildings and maintain the landscaped areas around the buildings that contain the command-and-control industries and the relatively affluent professionals they employ. When discussing the effect of globalization on the new service profile of large central cities, Sassen (1994) predicted that this obvious kind of social polarization would result. This contrast between affluence and poverty, between "yuppie" professionals and the working poor or undocumented laborers, seems to characterize many cities today. This "dual city" has been the subject of some debate (Mollenkopf and Castells, 1991). By the 1990s, with immense wealth generated in global finance capital, cities like New York, London, and Tokyo, in particular, possessed an extreme kind of income polarization with the ultra-rich, all connected to investment banking or stocks, and the minimum-wage working poor living and working side by side. The current global meltdown of stocks and financial instruments has done little to close this extreme social gap, and the job losses that have resulted from a decline in liquid wealth have made the conditions of the working poor in the city much worse.

In addition, immense numbers of less affluent, immigrant, and marginalized workers have created within the city a large, *informal* economy. The informal economy is defined as the combination of workers who are "off the books," goods produced in unregulated factories with nonunionized and undocumented laborers, goods and services produced and exchanged for barter (i.e., not cash but in kind), and goods and services sold without regulation on the streets. The informal economy in some countries often rivals the formal sector. Everywhere, this aspect of economic activity has emerged as an increasingly important way in which people within urban areas make a livelihood. One example of the informal economy is the illegal drug industry, which runs into the billions of dollars in sales and is an international operation. And in cities such as New York, illegal factories manufacture "faux" designer fashion items, such as fake Rolex watches, and then use recent or undocumented immigrants to sell them on Manhattan street corners for a fraction of the genuine article's price. Even discounting the major effect of drug dealing, the informal economy in large cities represents a formidable source of jobs and income (see Mingione, 1988). The informal economy is usually not discussed, and its presence clashes with the legitimated image of large cities as centers for multinational business leaders (Boer, 1990).

In sum, cities have changed remarkably since the 1960s. They include a larger minority population, due in part to a growing percentage of immigrants. Except for this group, population growth in the cities of the 1980s has been slow. Today's large cities possess a transformed economy that is more specialized in nodal services and low-wage manufacturing, with a thriving informal economy of drug dealing and illegal factories that employ immigrants. All of these economic and social processes fuel a growing social disparity between the working poor, the underclass, new immigrants, and street vendors on the one hand and affluent professionals on the other (see Chapter 8).

HOW DEINDUSTRIALIZATION AND GLOBALIZATION AFFECTED SUBURBS

In the 1950s and 1960s, suburbs were considered places where urban professionals who worked in the city bought homes to live in and raise a family. They were called "bedroom communities" for this reason (Jackson, 1985). We now know that this image merely represented an early view of such places. Since the 1960s, suburbs have matured (Schnore, 1963). In many ways they have become diverse culturally, economically, and politically, much like medium-size urban areas (Muller, 1981). Places such as Tysons Corner, Virginia, outside of Washington, D.C.; Costa Mesa, California, beyond the boundaries of Los Angeles; and Dunwoody, Georgia, outside of Atlanta, are all important and developed suburbs.

In 1970, the U.S. census noted for the first time that more people were living in suburbs than in other settlement spaces. At that time 37.1 percent of the population was suburban, compared with 31.5 percent that lived in the central city or 31.4 percent in rural areas. By 1990 even more rural areas had been absorbed by suburban growth, and the plurality of that population increased further. According to the figures, 46 percent of the 1990 population lived in suburbia, 40 percent in central cities, and 14 percent in rural areas (U.S. Bureau of the Census, 1990). While virtually all cities suffered from no or slow growth over the past four decades, suburban regions remain the most rapidly growing areas of the country.

The change to suburban dominance in population is reflected in comprehensive statistics on economic activity. In many cases, suburbs have outpaced their adjacent central cities in economic importance since the 1970s. Muller cites, in particular, Philadelphia and its surrounding suburbs (1981:19). In the 1980s, the suburbs outside Philadelphia contained 63 percent of the entire region's employment (i.e., including the central city itself); 67 percent of all manufacturing jobs; 68 percent and 70 percent of all wholesaling and retailing, respectively; and over 50 percent of all regional employment in financial, insurance, and business service sectors.

Suburban Social Characteristics

There is no typical suburb and, just as understandably, no unique suburban lifestyle exists, although there is a typical suburban everyday life associated with single-home ownership, automobile commutation, and low-density neighborhoods that differs from life in the central city. Through much of the postwar era, it was assumed that people who lived in the suburbs would commute to the downtown areas to work and even to shop. In the 1960s and 1970s, human ecologists studied the employment-to-residence ratio, which compared the number of jobs within a suburban community with the number of persons in the labor force. Leo Schnore (1963) was able to categorize suburban communities as bedroom suburbs (perhaps the stereotypical suburb of the era), service suburbs, mixed residential suburbs, and suburbs with more employment than residents. But over the last two decades, the employment patterns of suburban residents have changed greatly. The majority of people who live in the suburbs are now employed at jobs within the suburban region, not in the city. The commute from the suburb to a downtown office has been replaced by the commute to a job in a suburban office complex—or manufacturing plant or shopping mall. While there are important differences among different types of suburban communities, most now represent the mixed residential suburb.

In the main, lower-income as well as more affluent whites have found places to live in the suburban region. Blacks, however, have found it difficult to suburbanize, even to this day. They represent around 5 percent of the total suburban population despite being 12 percent of the general population. Typically, black people suburbanize by moving to areas outside the central city that are directly adjacent to their city neighborhoods (Muller, 1981). As we have seen, therefore, blacks are considerably *over*represented in the central city and *under*represented in the suburbs relative to their total population. In other countries that also have a racially mixed society, such as Brazil, large cities such as Rio de Janeiro have the opposite pattern. There the blacks and the poor live in shantytown suburbs, with the affluent ensconced in the city center (see Chapter 11).

While whites have found suburbs open to them, the uniformity of housing prices within each subdivision has resulted in graphic income segregation within suburban regions. Wealthier suburbs in particular have been successful in keeping blacks and the less affluent out of their areas through the home rule device of *exclusionary zoning*; that is, local control over land use and building codes enables individual communities to prohibit the building of low- or moderately priced housing. This perpetuates the value of higher priced homes, thereby maintaining exclusivity. Years of such practices have made suburban housing increasingly expensive, thus creating a housing shortage in suburbia for first-time buyers.

In sum, suburban regions have taken on diverse socioeconomic characteristics. For the white population, there is considerable diversity of community type, although there are increasing class differences and a housing shortage due to the decreasing affordability of moderately priced units. African Americans remain relatively excluded from suburban living except in designated places. Hence, the vast suburban regions are increasingly segregated by class and race. In its own way, this pattern replicates the division of race and class within the central city. Thus, city problems of residential segregation have been duplicated in the suburbs and are now regionwide.

Economic Deconcentration

For the suburbs, economic deconcentration due to deindustrialization since the 1960s has meant a combined process of both capturing new job growth and decentralizing economic activities from the large central city, as well as the process of their recentralization in minicenters within the suburban region. Let us consider the separate economic dimensions of deconcentration.

Retailing. The total amount of all retailing in the United States is now dominated by malls located in suburban realms of the metropolis. By the time of the 1970 census, the suburban share of MSA sales passed the 50 percent mark for the fifteen largest MSAs. According to Muller:

> Steadily rising real incomes, fueled by the booming aerospace-led economy of the middle and late sixties, created a virtually insatiable suburban demand for durable consumer goods. With almost no pre-existing retail facilities in the burgeoning outer suburbs, huge capital investments were easily attracted from life insurance companies and other major financial institutions. Not surprisingly, regional shopping centers quickly sprang up at the most accessible highway junction locations as their builders strived to make them the focus of all local development. (1981:123)

Suburban shopping malls were so successful that their numbers increased more than tenfold from approximately 2,000 in 1960 to over 20,000 in 1980. Over time this success threatened central city shopping areas and bypassed them as the important places to consume. Sizes of suburban retailing centers increased over time to malls and supermalls. Houston's Galleria complex, for example, is modeled after the Galeria of Milan, Italy. It is several stories high and is built around an Olympic-size skating rink that is open year-round, a feat of some proportions if you consider the warm, humid climate of Houston. The Galleria has three large department stores, more than 200 smaller shops, four office towers, two hotels, over fifteen restaurants and cinemas, nightclubs, and even a health club. Its seven-level parking facility has room for over 10,000 cars. Lately the name *Galleria* has become popular for malls in many other places in the United States, and it usually connotes a large and expansive upscale mall.

This type of spectacular, fully enclosed space for shopping has begun to replace the downtown streets of the central city department store district. As the success of malls has advanced, the scale of their construction has increased. Recently the phenomenon of "megamalls" has emerged as the new suburban focus of retailing. In the summer of 1992 a new, fully enclosed complex was constructed outside the city of Minneapolis that is so large it has room at its center for a seven-acre miniversion of a famous California theme park, Knotts Berry Farm. This "Mall of America," as it is called, contains 2 million square feet of space and enough parking for thousands of cars. Central cities cannot compete with such family attractions in immense suburban spaces.

Manufacturing

We have noted the progressive decline of manufacturing in the United States and its devastating impact on central cities, which has ties to globalization. Over the years suburban areas have changed their bedroom image in part by being the recipients of many new manufacturing industries that have remained active. By the 1980s, the percentage share of manufacturing for the suburban rings of most metropolitan areas nationwide was over 50 percent. Boston and Pittsburgh, for example, have over 70 percent of their manufacturing located in the suburbs; Los Angeles, Detroit, San Francisco, St. Louis, and Baltimore have over 60 percent located in the suburbs.

Suburban developers innovated a form of space called the "industrial park" that is zoned entirely for business, especially manufacturing. Usually local towns or county governments provide significant tax incentives, infrastructure, and other subsidies to attract manufacturing. The presence of such attractive and inexpensive locations in suburbia is one factor in the progressive deconcentration of manufacturing.

Most recently suburbs have focused on attracting high-tech companies. Many, as a result of active land-use planning, agglomerated into *growth polse* or "science parks." These are more specialized research and development centers that are often linked with manufacturing and are located near university facilities. The most spectacular example is Silicon Valley, adjacent to Stanford University in California. A corridor stretching from the city of San Jose to Palo Alto makes up the spine of Silicon Valley and contains over 800 factories that produce state-of-the-art electronics and computer products. This complex is intimately connected to the research resources of Stanford University, where the transistor was invented and where the largest electrical engineering department is located.

While Silicon Valley remains the best known of the new spaces created by high-tech industries, other examples of growth are Route 128 outside of Boston, the San Diego–La Jolla complex associated with electronic medical technology innovators, the Research Triangle complex located near the Duke and University of North Carolina campuses, and the Iowa-to-Minnesota corridor of high-tech medical firms anchored at the Mayo Clinic in Rochester, Minnesota. The area around Irvine, California, is very typical of the new spaces created by high-tech industries. It is anchored by the University of California at Irvine campus and stretches for miles across land that was once used for ranching and farming. This region has been the subject of a study (Kling, Olin, and Poster, 1991) arguing that a new social order has developed there that surpasses the stereotype of suburban life and is based on consumerism, suburbia, professional occupations, and an economic base of knowledge- or information-processing industries. In Chapter 10, we will discuss the emergence of similar spaces located in advanced industrial societies around the globe.

The significance of these high-tech growth poles is that they foster industrial development that is completely independent of the central city. Because of their economic success, they often become the principal places in the society that earn money on the global market, thereby leading the country's growth (see Storper and Walker, 1991). In the past, models of industrial development have placed the city in a dominant role by referring to it as "the core," with the suburbs described as "the periphery." Development of society meant nurturing city-based industry. In this model, which better describes urban growth in the '60s and '70s, manufacturing was believed to originate in the city and then migrate out to the suburbs. All evidence now rejects this concept. The city is no longer privileged as the incubator of most industries, although some new manufacturing, such as textiles and light manufacturing, may still start there. Development begins just as frequently in the suburbs as in the cities, and "suburbia is quickly identified as a major zone of industrial expansion in its own right, in which *self-generated* growth has been primarily responsible for its current eminence" (Muller, 1981:143). Hence, the new patterns challenge the way people once thought about economic development.

In sum, then, the central city has lost its role as the dominating node of a regional economy. In many industries, important businesses are likely to locate in the suburbs and economic development is now a metropolitan regional affair.

Office and Administrative Headquarters

Perhaps the most significant example of the increasing importance of mature suburbs and, conversely, the decline of the central city is the progressive relocation of corporate headquarters to fringe areas. In the past, such headquarters were almost exclusively located in the central city. Today this is much less the case, although many headquarters remain in city centers. During the 1960s, New York City, for example, was host to more than 130 of the Fortune 500 companies. By the 1980s that number had dropped to 73, and it is now fewer than 60, or a loss of over 70 corporate headquarters in 30 years.

According to some recent books, large cities have emerged as the "command-and-control" centers for the global economy (Sassen, 1991; Noyelle and Stanback, 1984). This overstates the case for the economy in general and ignores decentralization to areas outside the city but within the metropolitan region (see Kephart, 1991). As indicated above, the largest cities have become the centers for finance capital activities, while other aspects of capitalism, such as producer services, marketing, and manufacturing, have decentralized. One indicator of this more complex spatial differentiation of functions is the phenomenal thirty-year decline in the number of corporate headquarters located in New York City.

We have seen that the city can no longer be regarded as the dominant location choice for manufacturing or corporate headquarters. But the maturation of suburban areas with regard to administrative employment is even more significant. Despite some predictions that, as metropolitan regions grew, central cities would retain their command-and-control functions (Hawley, 1981), this has not proven to be the case.

In a study of the twenty-one largest MSAs, Ruth Armstrong (1972, 1979) found that, leaving the special case of New York City aside, administrative functions were evenly distributed between large cities and their suburbs in 1960. During the decades following her study, administrative and headquarter employment decentralized in favor of the suburbs as companies such as PepsiCo and General Electric abandoned centers such as Manhattan for the adjacent suburban towns of Purchase, New York, and Fairfield, Connecticut, respectively. Several other studies have verified that this trend is continuing and that command-and-control centers are growing in the suburbs (Quante, 1976; Pye, 1977). In short, administrative functions, like all other economic activities, have been deconcentrating since the 1960s. When people like Sassen (1994) and her followers talk about the "Global City" then, they are mistaken in thinking that specialization is concentrated in "command-and-control" functions. Unfortunately, because it has been the source of confusion for quite some time, global-based employment is largely confined to the sector of finance capital, which is concentrated in only a few of the larger cities of the world.

BEYOND SUBURBIA: THE EMERGENCE OF THE MULTINUCLEATED REGION

By the 1990s, suburban regions in many areas of the United States had so matured that development was occurring in peripheral areas independently of major urban centers. This special and independent mode of regional, multinucleated growth was manifested as the *fully urbanized county*, such as Orange County, California, which is a net employing region with a labor force of over 1 million (Kling, Olin, and Poster, 1991). The most important characteristic of the fully urbanized county is that it does not contain any large cities, yet it functions much like a city by providing jobs as well as housing for its residents.

First studied by Gottdiener and Kephart (1991), the fully urbanized counties appeared in number during the 1980s, although two regions, Orange County in California and Nassau and Suffolk Counties in New York, had already achieved independent MSA status by 1980. Other multinucleated counties lie outside of MSAs. Oakland County in Michigan is typical. It lies adjacent to but outside the Detroit MSA and had a 1980 population of over 1 million people, but its largest city contained only 76,715. It employed virtually all of the people who lived there with an employment-to-residence ratio of .93 in 1980 and grew by 11 percent between 1970 and 1980 (a rapid rate considering that Detroit itself declined in population). Oakland County's labor force was composed of 26 percent in manufacturing, 30 percent in retailing and wholesaling, and 25 percent in services, as well as other industries; that is, it possessed a balanced, diversified economy. Finally, in 1980 Oakland County had a median family income of $28,407—above the national average—and was 93 percent white.

Oakland County in Michigan was very much like at least twenty other multinucleated metropolitan regions located around the country that were identified as a new form of space because of their urban character and their deconcentrated form (Gottdiener and Kephart, 1991).

These and other aspects of regional growth testify to the distinctly new form of urban space that has emerged in the United States and elsewhere, which we call the multicentered metropolitan region. It contains a changing and increasingly maturing mix of city and suburban spaces. The MMR is produced by two linked processes—deconcentration and reconcentration, which are the result of the economic changes as a consequence of deindustrialization and the organizational reordering of world places according to the concentration of new functions, which we have referred to as globalization. As population and societal activities have moved away from historical city centers, in the process of deconcentration, and spread out in more uniform density throughout an ever-expanding metropolitan region, they have also coalesced, or reconcentrated in minicenters, such as malls, office parks, sports complexes, government buildings, airports, and higher density residential developments. All these more concentrated aspects of the region possess their own dynamic of social, economic, cultural, and even political activities. Hence, the new form of space remains urban but has taken on the form of a multicentered mix that is regional in scope.

To be sure, the large, historical urban cores have not died nor lost their dominant place within the regional array. Yet they are not nearly so dominant as in the past and, furthermore, their once concentrated cultural, economic, political, and social functions have spread out and into the regional array of multicenters. It would be a mistake to suggest that our concept of the MMR is meant to replace such important cities as New York, London, or Tokyo, for example. However, according to the MMR perspective, New York no longer refers to the Manhattan centers of finance and business alone, London is not simply the City of London, and Tokyo is one of the most widespread, deconcentrated urban agglomerations on the globe. Only a regional, multicentered conception captures this new, networked, functionally differentiated and megascaled organization of space.

Most every urban sociology text talks about how we live in an increasingly urban world. They point to such figures as "more than half the population of the world lives in urban areas, a figure which is expected to grow by 2% per year during 2000–2015"

(United Nations, *World Urbanization Prospects: The 2001 Revision*, 2002). But their conclusion—that we live in an increasingly urban world—distorts the reality of regional growth around historical city centers. Prior to the 1950s, urbanists compared the city not to the suburbs as might be assumed today, but with rural areas. When the comment is made that "we are living in an increasingly urban world," it is within the context of this old and for most countries obsolete city/rural contrast. Our argument is much different and relies on the recognition that the urban form has evolved. Today people live in multicentered metro regions that include cities, suburbs, and even rural areas. Although it's quite true that in the developing world there are still large areas of rural development that have not been absorbed by expanding urban regions, so that observers can say these countries are still "urbanizing," however, in all areas of the globe, growth around historical city centers has taken on the form of the MMR. Consequently, when observers declare that there is a movement around the globe of population to urban areas, they give people the wrong impression that this represents a move to the inner city, rather than the minicenters and underdeveloped areas within the larger metro region. These less informed urban sociology texts, therefore, fail to capture the dynamics of regional growth and the way populations are absorbed by the new form of multicentered space.

At the same time, the word *city* is interchangeable in these discussions with the words *urban area*. For example: in a recent UN report, "The rapid increase of the world's urban population coupled with the slowing of world population growth has led to a major redistribution of the population over the past 30 years. By 2007, one-half of the world's population will live in urban areas compared to more than one-third in 1972, and the period 1950–2050 will see a shift from a 65% rural world population to 65% urban. By 2002, some 70% of the world's urban population will be living in Africa, Asia, or Latin America." According to this UN report, "The most striking current changes are the levels of urbanization in less developed nations: rising from about 27% in 1975 and 40% in 2000, an increase of more than 1,200,000,000 people." While this statement is an accurate projection, it nevertheless was made without any attempt to differentiate between the historical city and the multicentered urbanized region of which it is a part.

Contemporary research on regional urban spaces has uncovered considerable evidence for our perspective. One example, a study of the Canadian cities of Toronto, Montreal, and Vancouver, shows that multicenteredness for these three metro regions is growing despite the presence of some of the very best urban planning programs in North America (Shearmur, Coffey, Dube, Barbonne, 2007). The authors go on to demonstrate that MMRs, even with the presence of a strong, historical city core, function internally according to different "scales" of linkages.

Different processes—local, citywide, suburban county wide, subregion wide, region wide, other regions wide, statewide, nationwide, global subregion wide, global wide—operate with different effects on people and space, according to this research.

Functioning according to these different scales are distinct linkages within the expanding MMR that produce efficient organization of activities despite the seeming chaos. Thus, depending on the scale of analysis in the way data is considered, organized activities, unorganized dispersal, and chaos are all observed. The authors conclude: "There has been some debate in recent years over whether employment has been poly-nucleating or dispersing, and over whether the development of metropolitan areas is chaotic or ordered. All results seem to suggest that all of these processes are occurring at the same time and in the same places . . . clustering and dispersal can occur simultaneously" within the region. (Note: these are the processes we have referred to above as decentralization and recentralization.) "This does not mean, however, that there are no regular processes at work and that no conclusions can be drawn about what is occurring in Canada's three largest cities. It shows . . . that different processes occur at different scales and that by the choice of scale an object of analysis will bring to the fore one or another of the apparently contradictory trends mentioned above."

Canadian cities have a reputation of being well planned, but this has not prevented the emergence of the new form of space, the MMR. Urbanized places in Western Europe and in Latin America, among many examples, also seem to be assuming a similar, multicentered, regional shape under pressure of the forces of globalization, deindustrialization, and the sprouting of new ways of making money as well as new growth poles, like airports and malls.

RECENT TRENDS IN METROPOLITAN REGIONS

A recent report from the Brookings Institution presents us with a snapshot of demographic trends in affecting metropolitan regions (Frey, Berube, Singer, and Wilson, 2009). These trends include the slowing of migration across states and metropolitan regions, concentration of new immigrants in the suburbs, the rapid increase of racial and ethnic minorities and diversity among younger residents, increase in older populations, increasing regional disparities in education, and the increase in poverty and its spread to suburban locations (see Box 6.2). Several of these trends have been discussed earlier in this chapter, and they all will reshape the multicentered urban regions of the future. For example, over the last two decades there has been a continued increase in immigrant populations, and a majority of the new immigrants have settled in emerging ethnic communities in the suburbs, not in the older ethnic neighborhoods of the central city. Even in cities that have not previously been thought of as immigrant gateways, such as Atlanta, Nashville, Orlando, and Raleigh, there has been a substantial increase in immigrant populations, with many settling into suburban settlement space. In many of the older immigrant gateway cities, the continued growth of racial and ethnic minorities has resulted in an expansion of these populations into suburban neighborhoods. The first suburban Chinatown will be discussed in Chapter 7, but there are many examples of suburban ethnic communities in many metropolitan regions across

Box 6.2

Recent Demographic Trends In Metropolitan America

According to a report by the Brookings Institution, the population trends that are shaping and reshaping metropolitan areas—our nation's engines of growth and opportunity—include the following:

Migration across states and metro areas has slowed considerably due to the housing crisis and looming recession. About 4.7 million people moved across state lines in 2007–2008, down from a historic high of 8.4 million people at the turn of the decade. Population growth in Sun Belt migration magnets such as Las Vegas and Riverside and the state of Florida have experienced a net loss of domestic migrants.

The sources and destinations of US immigrants continue to shift to the southeast and to the suburbs. About 80 percent of the nation's foreign-born population in 2007 hailed from Latin America and Asia; the Southeast, traditionally an area that immigrants avoided, has become the fastest-growing destination for the foreign-born, with metro areas such as Raleigh, NC; Nashville; Atlanta; and Orlando ranking among those with the highest growth rates.

Racial and ethnic minorities are driving the nation's population growth and increasing diversity among its younger residents. Hispanics have accounted for roughly half the nation's population growth since 2000. Racial and ethnic minorities represent 44 percent of U.S. residents under the age of 15 and make up a majority of that age group in 31 of the nation's one hundred largest metropolitan areas.

The next decade promises massive growth of the senior population, especially in suburbs unaccustomed to housing older people. As the first wave of baby boomers reaches age 65, the senior population is poised to grow by 36 percent from 2010 to 2020. Because the boomers were the nation's first fully suburban generation, their aging in place will cause many major metropolitan suburbs, such as those outside New York and Los Angeles, to "gray" faster than their urban counterparts.

Amid rising educational attainment overall, there are wide regional disparities. There are growing disparities across metropolitan areas; in knowledge economy areas such as Boston more than 40 percent of adults have a bachelor's degree, while in metro areas that have attracted large numbers of immigrants, such as Houston, more than 20 percent of adults have not completed high school.

continues

Box 6.2 *continued*

Poverty increased during the 2000s, and spread rapidly to suburban locations. The gap between central city and suburban poverty rates has narrowed as poverty has spread across the metropolis. The suburban poor have moved well beyond older, inner-ring suburbs, and now outnumber the number of central city poor by some 1.5 million.

The continued demographic dynamism of our metropolitan areas raises key policy and program issues. New efforts are required to pursue immigrant integration alongside immigration reform, close educational achievement and attainment gaps, combine transportation and housing planning, and provide needed support for low-income workers and families.

SOURCE: Frey, Berube, Singer, and Wilson, 2009. *Getting Current: Recent Demographic Trends in Metropolitan America,* 2009.

the country, including black and Mexican suburbs in Chicago, Filipino suburbs in San Francisco and San Diego, and the like.

The rapid increase of the elderly population in many cities across the country is an important area of concern. In the past, it was common to draw a distinction between cities and suburbs on the basis of age: younger families settled in the suburbs, while older persons were concentrated in the central city (this was an important part of Herbert Gan's [1968] discussion of compositional factors distinguishing urban and suburban ways of life). Yet recent trends point to the increase of older populations in the suburbs, where the aging Baby Boomers will confront special issues because these communities have fewer services for this population group.

The United States confronts serious and growing issues of social inequality, problems that are made all the more serious because of the decline of education in the inner city and growing class disparities in educational achievement. Some metropolitan areas have a well-educated workforce that can compete in the new global economy (Boston is often cited as an example), while other metropolitan areas are less well suited to compete in the global economy because their workforce has a smaller numbers of college graduates and increasing numbers of persons who lack a high school degree. The increasing gap in education, both among ethnic and racial populations and between metropolitan areas in the north and south raises important questions concerning the future growth and quality of life not just in cities but across metropolitan regions more generally.

Even before the recent global economic crisis, the United States experienced an uncomfortable increase in poverty in the last decade. While in the past it was commonplace to assert that central cities had specific problems of poverty associated with ethnic and racial communities that were not found in the suburbs, over the last decade poverty has spread most rapidly across suburban regions. And while in the past suburban poverty was often thought to be a problem confined to the inner suburbs, this now is a problem not only for many working-class suburbs but even middle-class suburbs, as retail stores have shut their doors, manufacturing companies have closed, and families have lost their homes and savings. Even more important, as urban sociologists shift their focus from the central city to the metropolitan region, the number of poor persons living in the suburbs now far outnumber the number of poor in the cities; one important challenge will be how to increase services available to poor households in the suburbs without cutting back further on services for poor households in the cities.

While the Brookings Institution report was about recent trends affecting all of metropolitan America, it is important to note that several of the trends focus directly on metropolitan regions in the Sun Belt (the loss of population from Los Angeles, Las Vegas, and Florida, which previously were important growth poles for Sun Belt population growth, for example) while other trends have important but less obvious connections to the Sun Belt (the growth of the senior population in suburban regions will create special problems for planners and officials in the coming decades, but this will be especially important for the earlier Sun Belt destinations in the Southwest where much of the growth was fueled by the movement of retired couples from northern cities, and where many communities were established specifically for an older, retired population with active lifestyles that may not continue as these persons age in place). The growth of the Sun Belt was the most important population shift affecting the American urban system in the last decades of the twentieth century, and for this reason we will take a further look at the development of this region. And at the end of this next section, we will return to examine further some of the social, economic, and environmental trends affecting the Sun Belt.

THE SHIFT TO THE SUN BELT

Without question the population and activity shift to the Sun Belt is the most important historical event since the 1950s for the United States. The scale of change is quite spectacular. Although variations exist, most analysts define the Sun Belt as thirteen southern states—Alabama, Arizona, Arkansas, Florida, Georgia, Louisiana, Mississippi, New Mexico, North Carolina, Oklahoma, South Carolina, Tennessee, and Texas—plus parts of two western states: California (southern counties below San Luis Obispo) and southern Nevada (Las Vegas, SMSA) (see Bernard and Rice, 1983). Between 1945 and 1975, the Sun Belt region doubled its population. In the decade between 1960 and 1970, Sun Belt MSAs received 63.8 percent of the total population increase for *all* MSAs (Berry and Kasarda, 1977:168). Between 1970 and 1980, the Northeast lost 1.5 percent of its population, the Midwest gained only 2.6 percent, but the South grew by

21.5 percent and the West by 22.6 percent, including a natural increase for all regions (Frey and Speare, 1988:50). By the year 2007, of the eleven largest cities in the United States, seven—Dallas, Houston, Jacksonville, Los Angeles, Phoenix, San Antonio, San Diego—are located in the Sun Belt. In Table 6.1 during the period between 2000 and 2007, Charlotte, North Carolina, grew by 17.1 percent, and Austin, Texas, by 16.1 percent. Only Las Vegas, Nevada, which had grown an astounding 85.7 percent from 1990 to 2000, failed to grow impressively with only a 2.2 percent increase.

Table 6.2 charts this amazing rate of growth accompanying the shift to the Sun Belt for its major cities beginning with the 1950 to 1970 period and including the years between 2000 and 2007. During the first period of twenty years, growth was explosive with some cities, such as Phoenix and Las Vegas, each gaining over 400 percent. Between the years 2000 and 2007, growth in population remained in double digits with the exception of Las Vegas. Texas alone contributes greatly to the overall population jump in the Sun Belt with five of the twelve cities that were tracked. The table shows that, from the year 2000 to 2007, the multicentered regions of Houston grew by 12.1 percent, Atlanta by 15.4 percent, and Phoenix by 16.3 percent. Only the older metro Sun Belt regions of Los Angeles, Miami, and San Jose, California, failed to reach double digits.

Rapid demographic growth was matched by rapid employment growth in the Sun Belt. Between 1970 and 1980, manufacturing expanded by 12 percent in the North but more than double that, or 24.4 percent, in the South. While service employment grew by 11.5 percent in the North, it increased by 44 percent in the South and 47 percent in the West (Frey and Speare, 1988:92). According to one observer, "Never in the history of the world has a region of such size developed at such a rate for so long a time" (Sale, 1975:166). Massive population and employment growth produced sprawling metro regions, as shown in Table 6.2, not confined to the boundaries of central cities alone.

The movement west and southward has been around for some time. Sun Belt states have been receiving a greater share of MSA population than the Frost Belt since the 1920s (Berry and Kasarda, 1977:168). Indeed, the movement of people westward has been a trend in the United States since the 1800s. The shift to the Sun Belt, however, displaces the economic center of gravity in the United States toward the West from the East Coast and obliterates what was once a core-periphery relation between a formerly agrarian South and West and an industrialized North and Midwest. Today the Sun Belt is more formidable economically than other areas of the country. Between 1970 and 1980, almost three-fourths of all job growth took place in the Sun Belt. By the 1990s, however, the economic recession had hit Sun Belt areas especially hard. California, for example, suffered major job losses as did Texas. By the time of the economic crisis of 2009, the states of California and Florida, which once led the nation in growth, had experienced a total population decline for the first time in over 40 years. Readjustments, due to job loss, fiscal crisis, and other factors, continue as a consequence of current crisis conditions in the United States, although it does not seem

TABLE 6.1 Population Growth for Selected Sun Belt Urban Cities, 1950–2007.

City	1950	1970	1980	1990	2000	2007 est.	Rate of Growth				
							1950–1970	1970–1980	1980–1990	1990–2000	2000–2007
Los Angeles	1,970,358	2,816,061	2,966,850	3,348,557	3,694,742	3,849,000	42.9	5.6	17.5	10.3	10.4
Houston	596,163	1,232,802	1,595,138	1,630,864	1,953,633	2,144,000	106.7	29.3	2.2	19.8	11.0
Phoenix	106,818	581,562	789,704	984,309	1,321,190	1,513,000	444.4	35.3	24.5	34.2	11.5
San Antonio	408,442	654,153	785,880	935,393	1,151,305	1,297,000	60.2	20.2	19.1	23.1	11.3
San Diego	334,387	696,769	875,538	1,110,623	1,223,429	1,257,000	108.4	25.7	26.8	10.2	10.3
Dallas	434,462	844,401	904,078	1,007,618	1,188,589	1,233,000	94.4	11.3	11.4	18.0	10.4
San Jose	95,280	445,779	629,442	782,224	895,193	930,000	367.9	36.7	24.3	14.0	10.4
Jacksonville	204,517	528,865	540,920	635,230	735,617	785,000	158.6	21.7	17.4	15.8	10.7
Austin	132,459	253,539	345,890	465,622	656,562	749,659	91.4	36.4	34.6	41.0	16.1
Charlotte	134,042	241,420	315,474	395,934	557,834	675,229	80.1	30.7	25.5	40.9	17.1
El Paso	130,485	322,261	425,259	515,342	563,657	605,410	147.0	32.0	21.2	9.3	11.7
Las Vegas	24,624	125,787	164,674	258,295	479,639	562,582	410.8	30.9	56.9	85.7	2.2

SOURCE: Population figures from U.S. Bureau of the Census, Census of Population and Housing; 2007: *Statistical Abstract of the United States 2009.*

TABLE 6.2 Population Growth for Selected Sun Belt Regions, 1980–2007.

						Rate of Growth			
	1970	1980	1990	2000	2007 Est.	1970–1980	1980–1990	1990–2000	2000–2007
Los Angeles-Anaheim-Riverside CMSA	998,100	11,498,000	14,531,529	16,374,000	12,875,587	15.2	26.4	12.7	7.9
Dallas-Fort Worth-Arlington CMSA	2,352,000	2,931,000	4,037,282	5,222,000	6,144,489	24.6	16.4	12.6	11.8
Houston-Galveston-Barzonia NECMA	2,169,000	3,100,000	3,731,029	4,670,000	5,629,127	42.9	-2.0	5.2	12.1
Atlanta-Sandy Springs-Marietta MSA	1,684,000	2,138,000	2,959,500	3,431,983	5,271,550	27.0	6.5	6.7	15.4
Miami-Ft. Lauderdale CMSA	1,889,000	2,644,000	5,187,171	5,456,000	4,817,595	40.0	19.6	25.2	8.8
San Francisco-Oakland-San Jose CMSA	4,754,000	5,368,000	6,253,311	7,039,362	4,203,898	12.9	16.3	11.3	6.0
Phoenix-Mesa-Scottsdale CMSA	971,000	1,509,175	2,238,498	2,563,582	4,179,427	55.4	-2.7	3.0	16.3
San Diego-Carlsbad-San Marcos MSA	1,358,000	1,861,846	2,498,016	2,644,132	2,974,859	37.4	15.4	16.9	11.3
San Antonio MSA	901,220	1,088,881	1,302,099	1,592,383	1,997,969	20.8	12.0	12.2	12.5
Las Vegas MSA	304,744	528,000	741,000	1,563,282	1,836,333	73.3	14.0	21.1	11.7
Charlotte MSA	840,346	971,447	161,546	1,499,293	1,650,667	15.6	1.7	92.8	11.0
Austin MSA	398,938	585,051	846,227	1,249,763	1,593,400	46.7	14.5	14.8	12.7

NOTE: Sun Belt Regional Classifications: CMSA, NECMA, MSA.

SOURCE: Population figures from U.S. Bureau of the Census, Census of Population and Housing; 2007: *Statistical Abstract of the United States 2009.*

likely that there will be any significant return of people from the Sun Belt to Frost Belt regions in the North and the Midwest.

Push and Pull Factors in Sun Belt Development

As we have seen, the Sun Belt had an advantage over other parts of the United States because of its comparative economic potential. This represents a potent pull factor. The region has other advantages as well. Energy and tourism are exploitable industries. Cheap energy in particular and the warmth of the Sun Belt climate cut home-maintenance costs drastically compared to the Frost Belt. Low energy costs are a major locational incentive for business, both now and in the future. Lower home-maintenance costs and comparatively lower homeowner tax rates also provide considerable incentives for people to move to the region.

A comparison between Frost Belt and Sun Belt locations reveals advantages for the latter regarding labor costs. Sun Belt places do not have a past history of union organizing, and wages there are comparatively lower for manufacturing industries (although higher for many professional services). Sun Belt cities flaunt what they call a "good business climate." This usually means the absence of unions, tax breaks to business, and a general "hands-off" policy of minimal government regulation.

As in the case of suburbanization, one of the most potent supply-side forces that has developed the Sun Belt as a place to live and work is the operation of government intervention. To the extent that government subsidization of real estate development aided growth, it was instrumental in the population shift to the Sun Belt, where real estate is a major industry. But government involvement goes way beyond this obvious observation. Most of the heavily subsidized government industries in the United States, including agribusiness, energy, and military spending, are pillars of the Sun Belt economy.

Over the years, for example, the heavily subsidized agriculture industry has witnessed an immense shift of population out of farm residence, from over 30 percent in 1920 to around 3 percent today. At the same time, the family farm involved in agriculture has given way to the large land holdings of corporations engaged in agribusiness. Farm production has become more specialized and part of a total conglomerate structure involving the growing, processing, and marketing of food by giant corporations linked to the multinational system of capital (Shover, 1976; Hightower, 1975; Berry, 1972).

An important consequence of the rise to hegemony of agribusiness has been the shift of food production away from the Northeast and Midwest and to the Sun Belt (Sale, 1975; Coughlin, 1979), where large open tracts of land are being used. According to Sale (1975), the shift to agribusiness in the Sun Belt has made the family farm uneconomical, causing many small farmers to sell their land to suburban developers. Finally, agribusiness remains subsidized on a grand scale by the federal government, whose Department of Agriculture is the second largest bureaucracy after the Department of Defense (Shover, 1976).

A second pillar of Sun Belt growth is the energy industry, which is also subsidized by the government. The Atomic Energy Commission and its government affiliates are among the largest employers in the state of New Mexico. In a case study of Houston, Feagin (1988) shows how state supports underpin the energy industry, while at the same time business leaders espouse the virtues of "free enterprise." Feagin observes that when discussing government involvement, a distinction is made between state forms of regulation, which are opposed by business, and state promotion and subsidization of economic activity, which is supported wholeheartedly.

In the case of the alleged "free enterprise" city of Houston, development was aided over the years by active government promotion of projects, while regulation was kept at a minimum. Contrary to the prevailing view of Sun Belt cities as economically backward until recent times, Houston was already a major agricultural center for the Texas cotton industry prior to the growth of the petroleum business. As the latter became the new focus of the local economy, government subsidization went hand in hand with the development of the city through private ventures. The federal government provided funds for the dredging of the Houston ship channel and periodically cleared the important port facility for ship traffic. In addition, oil refining and new petrochemical industries during the 1940s were supported directly by the feds, ranking sixth in receipt of national government plant investment (Feagin, 1988:68). Local businesses were the beneficiaries of these subsidies. As a consequence, Houston developed into the energy capital of the United States, only to be hit by a downturn and restructuring in the 1980s.

The third government-subsidized pillar of Sun Belt growth is military spending. During World War II, 60 percent of the total $74 billion spending effort went to the fifteen states of the Sun Belt (Sale, 1975:170). Major industries in Sun Belt states were established during this time. Los Angeles became an aircraft and shipbuilding center. Kaiser Steel was formed in Southern California, importing many workers from the east. Petrochemical and energy-related efforts were also subsidized, as we have already seen. Armaments industries and arsenals were expanded in the South and West. Huge military bases were constructed in California, Texas, Georgia, Florida, Alabama, and the Carolinas, among other Sun Belt states.

By the 1970s, the fifteen Sun Belt states were receiving 44 percent of all military spending, including over 50 percent of the Defense Department payroll; had the majority of all military installations (60 percent); were employing more scientists and technicians than the rest of the United States; and received 49 percent of "Pentagon research and development funds—the seed money that creates new technologies and industries" (Sale, 1975:171). All of this effort and money has created a new industrial core in the Sun Belt that is supported by government spending. Because taxes are collected across the United States but differentially spent on military-related activities, the federal government has for decades transferred wealth from all other regions of the United States to the Sun Belt.

Military spending in the Sun Belt region continued to grow throughout the 1980s on an immense scale. In 1975 military spending was approximately $90 billion. By 1987 it had increased to $390 billion, a fourfold change taking place after the Vietnam War (Gottdiener, 1990). Arms sales in particular became a key U.S. industry in the 1980s, prompting one observer to suggest that the nation had switched to a permanent war economy (Mandel, 1975; see also Melman, 1983; Stubbing and Mendel, 1986).

With Sun Belt prosperity so closely linked to the well-being of arms sales, cuts in the military budget have had profound effects, leading to a downturn in the economic fortunes of states such as California. For example, in July 1991, the McDonnell Douglas Corporation announced it was laying off about 1,000 workers from its Southern California plant and shifting another 1,600 to its facilities in St. Louis, Missouri. The company cited "defense cutbacks and budget woes" (*Press Enterprise*, July 8, 1991:D-2) for its decision, which benefited the Midwest at the expense of the Sun Belt.

The loss of such military-related jobs has turned the once recession-proof economy of California into another case of Sun Belt boom and bust. Since 1989, California has had economic woes so severe that they are eclipsed only by the days of the Great Depression. In 1991, for example, the state lost more jobs than any other, twice as many as the second worst state, New York. And there is still no sign of an economic reversal. In that same year and for the first time in California's history, more people canceled their driver's licenses because they had moved to another state than applied for one. In short, the population boom in California related to its economic expansion may be over, although low-wage, illegal aliens continue to flock to the state.

Finally, it is important to note that government military spending is a key support of many suburban regions, even in the Frost Belt, and is not simply a Sun Belt phenomenon. Thus, between 1975 and 1980, for example, Suffolk County in New York and suburban Monmouth County in New Jersey, respectively, had 20 percent and 16 percent of their labor force growth in military-related industries. By 1980, only Santa Clara County (in Silicon Valley) had more military-related expansion—31 percent total employment growth.

Recent Sun Belt Trends

The shift to the Sun Belt is a spectacular example of regional realignment experienced by an advanced industrial country. As we will see in Chapter 10, there are parallels to the U.S. case in such countries as England, France, and particularly Germany, which have also undergone regional shifts as a consequence of high-technology industrial restructuring. Yet despite these changes, it is possible to overstate the case of Sun Belt prominence. There are at least three reasons to temper the notion that this region is gaining in autonomy and power at the expense of areas elsewhere: the need to place

Sun Belt economic activities within a national and global context, the boom-and-bust cycle of development, and the enormous environmental costs of growth.

Economic Differentiation and the Global Economy.   Because the U.S. economy has become more functionally specialized, many of the rapidly growing Sun Belt industries are tied administratively and economically to Frost Belt centers. The latter still retain the majority of corporate headquarters, for example. Banking and finance are still controlled by Frost Belt interests (Gottdiener, 1985). In addition, since the 1970s many U.S. firms have been either bought out or heavily invested in by multinational corporations that have headquarters in other countries. Sun Belt factories, no matter how stable in employment, may be only a part of some larger operation that also includes Frost Belt command-and-control centers or worldwide organizations. Hence, splits between the regions are *not* autonomous. They reflect instead a growing regional specialization in the United States and the entire world as multinational interests utilize space and place to improve economic performance.

The Cycles of Growth and Decline.   As we have seen, the best way to describe Sun Belt development is in terms of boom-and-bust cycles that fluctuate relatively rapidly. Sun Belt residents who have been attracted to the region by visions of affluence may have to tolerate a life of feast or famine. At present, the national recession has hit many Sun Belt areas especially hard. The powerful states of Texas and California, once thought immune to downturns, have been in the doldrums since the late 1980s. Unemployment was above the national average for a time. California experienced two straight years of fiscal crises that required cuts in spending, wage freezes, and a reassessment of the state's credit rating. Social services such as education are now besieged due to lack of funds, and the quality of life has deteriorated accordingly.

The characteristic woes of the region are exemplified by Silicon Valley, also known as Santa Clara County, in California. This region was once touted as the exemplary high-tech boom area that even countries should emulate in their development plans. In the 1990s the region was called the "Valley of Gloom" (Smith, 1992) because of the severity of its recession. Much of its heralded job creation has shifted to other places around the globe, and its businesses are besieged because of declining sales, while some have fallen victim to both foreign and domestic competitors. As one newspaper report states:

> Not only has Santa Clara County lost 20,000 manufacturing jobs in the last 18 months, industry analysts estimate that tens of thousands of newly created electronic industry jobs have gone elsewhere in the same period. . . . High-tech manufacturing in this area is no longer competitive with other areas of the country or the world. Even if the economy rebounds, we're not going back to the double-digit job growth we enjoyed the last two decades. (Smith, 1992:A-1)

It may be possible that this area has experienced a revival much like the one in Houston (see above), and the cycle of boom and bust will start up again. But as the newspaper report indicates, a profound sense of pessimism paints the future in more modest growth terms. Silicon Valley is typical of other high-tech growth poles. Its population is both well educated and diverse—37 percent of those over eighteen years old have at least a two-year college degree, and 12 percent of its population is foreign born. These residents have been used to several decades of affluence and growth. At present, they are learning to suffer with the rest of the nation during the current recession.

The Environmental Costs of Rapid Growth. Because it has been the site of rapid and largely minimally planned growth, the Sun Belt region has also encountered monumental environmental problems. In fact, since the 1990s, we may be poised at a point of immense growth difficulties for many areas of the Sun Belt. The environment has long suffered the initial impact of development. Unique and pristine formations, such as the Tampa and San Francisco bays, have been almost destroyed biologically in the wake of change. Clear-cutting of virgin forests, pollution of lakes and streams, fouling of beaches with oil or sewage, and emission of choking smog are but some of the environmental problems already well established in the South and West. After years of uncertainty regarding published accounts of the effects of smog, for example, it was recently reported that constant exposure produces permanent lung damage in both children and adults (*Press Enterprise*, May 17, 1992: AA-1). The population of Los Angeles lives in just such an environment, yet the presence of damaging smog has done little to date to stem the otherwise constant stream of new arrivals to the region (see Chapter 12 for a more detailed discussion of the environment and the sociospatial perspective).

In more recent years, other effects of population growth have appeared. Crime is a serious problem, for example. New York is often stereotyped as an unsafe city. Its murder rate was 26 per 100,000 persons in 1989. Houston's rate, however, was 27 for that year, Dallas's was 35, and New Orleans's was 47. Even Los Angeles had a high rate of 25, less than New York but the same as Chicago and much more than Boston (17). Sun Belt cities may just be the most unsafe and violent in the nation, containing nine of our ten most dangerous metro areas (MacDonald, 1984)—see Chapter 9.

In addition to crime, overcrowding in schools and declining educational quality are a typical Sun Belt lament. These conditions are expected to get worse as the western and southern states encounter intractable budget crises. In 1991 California suffered its largest budget deficit to that date. Now the state's deficit is many times larger, and in 2009, along with many more cuts in social services, a giant garage sale was held by the state to raise money by selling off surplus equipment at bargain prices.

In rapidly growing areas, traffic congestion is so bad that it is fast approaching gridlock. It's not uncommon for commuters in parts of California to travel four hours both ways by car, especially when no other alternatives to commuting are available. Finally, housing prices have soared in the best locations, making first-home purchasing increasingly out of reach. But despite these and other constraints, life in the Sun Belt continues to attract new people, especially highly trained professionals who have the ability to find well-paying jobs (Kephart, 1991). It is expected that the fifteen Sun Belt states will continue to grow in the future. As Table 6.3 shows, the Sun Belt region of the United States now possesses more than half of the nation's population.

Since the 1960s, the relationships among people, spatial living, and working arrangements have profoundly changed. Gone is the highly compact industrial city with a working-class culture and labor-influenced, democratic politics. In its place, everyday life now transpires in multinucleated metropolitan regions across the country. Development is dominated by the population shifts to the suburbs and the Sun Belt, while the vision of unending growth and affluence has been tempered by the experience of living through rapid cycles of boom and bust. These changes have been explained by the sociospatial perspective, which emphasizes the pull factors of economic and technological change (as do other approaches) but also the importance of government intervention, real estate, and the restructuring of sociospatial arrangements in business and residential activities.

KEY CONCEPTS

metropolitan region
federal subsidies for homeownership
Levittown (Long Island)
Fordism
conspicuous consumption
demand-side / supply-side explanations
deindustrialization
population deconcentration
nodal services
uneven development
dual city
informal economy
exclusionary zoning
corporate headquarters
industrial park
fully urbanized county
Sun Belt / Frost Belt
military spending
regional realignment

DISCUSSION QUESTIONS

1. What are some of the explanations for the extensive suburban development that occurred from 1920 to 1960? What are some of the demand-side factors that might be responsible for this development? What are some of the supply-side factors that might be responsible? Explain how the roles of real estate development, government programs, and cultural factors fit into these supply-side and demand-side explanations for suburban growth.

2. Describe and discuss two factors responsible for the shift in population from the Northeast and Midwest (the Frost Belt) to the South and West (the Sun Belt). How do these factors affect cities in both the Frost Belt and Sun Belt?

3. Discuss the changes in large central cities that have accompanied the restructuring of settlement space over the past four decades. Pick two changes that you consider to be representative and explain the causal factors responsible for these changes.

4. Profound changes have occurred in the populations of metropolitan regions. Discuss these changes and explain them by focusing on two factors.

5. Suburban settlement spaces have changed greatly since the 1980s. What are some of the most important changes that have occurred in your metropolitan region? Pick two factors responsible for those changes and discuss their significance and their effects on suburban life.

6. Currently, the Sun Belt, like other areas of the country, is experiencing economic problems. How has the housing crisis affected these areas? How can we measure these effects?

CHAPTER 7

PEOPLE AND LIFESTYLES
IN THE METROPOLIS
Urban and Suburban Culture

In previous chapters, we studied the growth and development of metropolitan regions in the United States. The next two chapters concern the people of the metropolis and explore the relationship between everyday life and local territory. The
sociospatial approach to metropolitan life asserts that diversity in lifestyles and subcultures exists not just within the city but throughout the metropolitan region. This
is especially the case since 1980 as suburban settlement spaces have matured and as a
new wave of immigrants from Asia and Latin America have entered the country
since the 1960s. In this chapter we consider the interplay between the social factors
of income, gender, age, ethnicity and race, and the spatial patterns of population
concentration or dispersal across the metropolitan region.

A basic tenet of the sociospatial approach is that social factors determining the
patterns of population dispersal are also linked to particular spaces. Class or gender
relations, for example, are conducted through spatial as well as social means. Lifestyle
differences are externalized in a specific environment: the ghetto, the street corner, the
mall, the golf course. Furthermore, these places are always meaningful. Interaction is
shaped through the signs and symbols of sociospatial context. In this chapter we will
consider the effect of class standing on lifestyles, gender differences, and everyday life;
racial and minority distinctions; and new patterns of ethnic formation and immigration. The effects of class, gender, and race are so powerful in our society that we will
also consider them in Chapter 9 when we discuss social problems. We will see how
differences in sociospatial factors affect the way people live, their interactions with
others, and their use of space.

CLASS DIFFERENCES AND SPATIAL LOCATION

Class Stratification in the United States

Max Weber believed that an individual's class position is important because it helps determine the life chances that could be expected in the future; in other words, the possible opportunities or constraints for future achievement open to any individual. Weber also suggested that economic factors of class status, such as the type of occupation or monetary resources that an individual possesses, are not the only determining factors of overall social status. One's social standing in the society's hierarchy also depends on particular cultural attributes, such as religion, ethnicity, or symbolic differences, and on the possession of political power. Thus, life chances differ according to economic, political, and cultural factors, but material wealth, as Karl Marx maintained, is clearly the most important of all social variables.

The United States is a stratified society. This means that individuals and households are located within a social hierarchy that determines their access to resources. Stratification is often pictured as a pyramid of social standing. Those at the very top control most of the society's resources; they also enjoy the most symbolic prestige and political influence. Those below are the most numerous and have the least power. The United States, despite an active ideology that preaches equality, in fact has the most unequal distribution of wealth of any industrialized nation (Philips, 1988). The top 1 percent of the population control over 70 percent of the wealth, and the top 5 percent control over 90 percent. Status considerations such as driving an expensive car, living in a large home, taking fabulous vacations, and wearing expensive clothing are greatly influenced by the media images of affluence and what life is supposed to be like at the top of the stratification diamond.

American culture and the lifestyles it supports connects the financial resources of individuals and families, expressed in our hierarchy of social stratification, to patterns of consumption. For this reason, sociologists often study how class differences in our society are expressed by different styles of consumption. Consumption patterns are also supported by credit card debt, housing loans, car loans, educational loans, buying through financing, and other arrangements that enable people to spend more than they earn. As we move through different local spaces within the metropolitan environment, we encounter a tremendous diversity in lifestyles. These differences are a function of relative class standing and, in turn, are expressed through the activity of consumption. While many persons in our society consume at a high level by incurring debt, they do so in distinct ways thereby enabling us to talk about lifestyle differences in the metropolitan region.

Research on the American class structure divides our society into a number of different groups based on what social scientists call SES, or *socioeconomic status*, which is a particular combination of wealth, occupation, education, gender, and race, among other factors (see Robertson, 1987). Many studies will divide the population into five groups: the lower class, the working class, the lower-middle class, the upper-middle class, and the ruling class. Only the ruling class controls enough wealth to be considered independent from economic needs; many persons in the lower class do not have access to regular sources of income because of a lack of jobs in the inner city, while many working class households have discovered that it is necessary for both husband and wife to work to support their families, and middle-class families find it increasingly difficult to maintain their standard of living due to the stagnant wages and a declining dollar in the world economy.

Socioeconomic standing also involves the ability of the household to establish residence in a particular place. Thus, a significant component of socioeconomic status will be determined by one's address and the symbolic reputation of particular neighborhoods within the metropolitan neighborhoods. It means something very different to live in the north shore suburb or oceanfront town than it does to be from the 'hood or to have grown up in the projects. In our society, due to stratification differences, the choice of residential location is not always voluntary. Restrictions of wealth, race, and gender are particularly potent sifters of population across the metropolitan regions. Socioeconomic difference and the system of social stratification therefore manifest themselves both as differences in individual lifestyles and as differences in neighborhood living or local space. Let us consider some of the distinct ways stratification is reflected in this interaction between social relations and territorial practice, as the sociospatial perspective suggests.

The Wealthy

The upper classes often have the advantage of owning many homes because they are able to afford it. Former president George H. W. Bush, for example, for many years maintained residences in Houston, Washington, D.C., and Kennebunkport, Maine. Many wealthy people alternate among townhouse, suburban estate, and rural recreational home. Obviously, at any given time the family can occupy just one of these residences, so multiple home ownership is a symbol of wealth and power that has some meaning and prestige in our society. In the city, the wealthy are associated with the more fashionable districts such as Nob Hill in San Francisco, Beverly Hills in Los Angeles, the Gold Coast near Lake Michigan in Chicago, Beacon Hill in Boston, and Park Avenue in New York City. Their activities take place within certain spaces that are allocated to the particular mix of restaurants, resorts, and social clubs reserved for the upper class.

One important way the wealthy manifest their power and status is by isolating themselves as much as possible from the rest of the population. This type of segregation is voluntary. In the city, voluntary segregation may be accomplished by living in ultra-expensive housing with security guards and controlled entrances. Even though public transportation and taxis are available, the wealthy often utilize private, door-to-door limousine services. Shopping and recreation are all located in heavily policed areas. Maintaining this level of isolation remains somewhat of a constant chore that taxes the resources of surveillance and control, requiring private security guards, apartment buildings with twenty-four-hour doormen, and private schools or academies for children. In the suburbs or at country homes, however, the benefits of isolation are more readily enjoyed in gated communities and exclusive country clubs.

One of the best studies by a sociologist of the upper-class lifestyle is E. Digby Baltzell's *Philadelphia Gentlemen* (1958). This study indicates that while the wealthy require their own segregated space, the areas they choose for their voluntary isolation vary over the years, because, in an effort to remain invisible, the wealthy have had to move as the metropolitan region itself expanded over time. Baltzell distinguishes between the elite and the upper class. The former are "those individuals who are the most successful and stand at the top of the functional class hierarchy. These individuals are leaders in their chosen occupations or professions" (1958:6). Baltzell's book is not about the elite but about the upper class, which he defines in contrast as the "group of families whose members are descendants of successful individuals one, two, three or more generations ago. . . . [Individuals in this social grouping are] brought up together, are friends, and are intermarried one with another; and finally, they maintain a distinctive style of life and a kind of primary group solidarity which sets them apart from the rest of the population" (1958:7).

According to Baltzell, the upper class in Philadelphia restricted itself to a particular location in the city and tried to remain out of sight. Over the years, however, its choice of location varied; that is, it usually did not stay in the same neighborhood generation after generation, but tended to be subject to the same forces of deconcentration and regional drift as were other individuals in the metropolis. Most American cities have a pattern similar to Philadelphia of once fashionable districts that have declined as the wealthy shuffle around the metropolitan region in search of secure enclaves for their lifestyle. The most characteristic area of upper-class life was the Main Line, which stretched westward from the central city of Philadelphia on the commuter railroad to the suburbs of Overbrook, Merion, Wynnewood, Ardmore, Haverford, Bryn Mawr, Rosemont, and other towns out to Paoli, Pennsylvania. The Philadelphia upper-class lifestyle consisted of a withdrawal from civic affairs and the concentration on business by the males; while females were expected to stay close to home minding the household and entertaining when necessary for the husbands' needs. In addition, however, women were expected to be involved in philanthropic enterprises outside the home, such as organizing charity balls or fund-raising activities for the arts. Children were sent to exclusive private schools, and social life meant interacting only with other members of the upper class on the Social Register. Family time for these people was divided between town and country residences. In this way, the upper class maintained its spatial and social isolation from other segments of the society.

Box 7.1

The Upscale Urban Lifestyle

Market researchers have studied yuppies in detail because they spend so much of their income on consumer products. They identify characteristic yuppie areas as located in the more affluent sections of the central city (Weiss, 1988). Many live in high-rise buildings in areas of high population concentration and in newly gentrified housing in suddenly fashionable areas of the inner city. According to one report:

> Almost two-thirds live in residences worth more than $200,000, decorating their living rooms according to *Metropolitan Home*, buying their clothes at Brooks Brothers, frequenting the same hand-starch Chinese laundries. In Urban Gold Coast, residents have the lowest incidence of auto ownership in the nation; these cliff-dwellers get around by taxi and rental car. (Weiss, 1988:278)

Market researchers also note the peculiar, service-dependent nature of yuppie consumer behavior. For the sake of last-minute convenience, they will spend more to eat out or purchase items at nearby grocery stores that charge more than large supermarkets. Convenience is prized by people whose high salaries often require them to devote extra hours to their work. According to Weiss:

> Residents usually eat out for lunch and dinner, and their forays to grocery stores mostly yield breakfast items: yogurt, butter, orange juice, and English muffins—all bought at slightly above-average rates. Compared to the general population, residents buy barely one-fifth the amount of such pedestrian treats as TV dinners, canned stews, and powdered fruit drinks. Where these consumers do excel is at the liquor store: They buy imported champagnes, brandy, beer, and table wine at twice the national norm, possibly to take the edge off stress-filled urban living. (1988:281)

The upper class is not confined to city residence. One of the earliest studies of the affluent in suburbia was Thorsten Veblen's *Theory of the Leisure Class* (1899). Although wealth was behind their behavior, the most important characteristics of the lifestyle were symbolic or cultural. Veblen coined the concept *conspicuous consumption* to refer to this particular aspect of the affluent style of suburban life. This concept refers to an outward display of consumption that demonstrates wealth and power through the wasting of resources and the symbols of upper-class membership. The suburban homes of the wealthy, for example, were endowed with excess. Houses were huge, over 5,000 square feet or more, with many more rooms than were necessary to service the immediate family. Estates had large front and rear lawns that were landscaped and attended to by a staff of gardeners. Conspicuous consumption was symbolized by the landscaping of yards precisely because land was allowed to lie uncultivated as a resource—the lawn was just for show.

The suburban lifestyle of the wealthy is focused on leisure activity as a sign of conspicuous consumption. This is particularly significant because symbols of leisure mean that people do not have to work. The suburban country club, costly to belong to and restrictive in its membership, is an essential component for the exclusive set. The fees usually run into the tens of thousands of dollars, thereby keeping out the working class. In many parts of the country, clubs such as the Everglades Country Club in Florida prevent African Americans and Jews from belonging even if they can afford membership fees. The leisure activity of choice for the affluent is golf, and in recent years this game has come to symbolize suburban wealth and leisure itself, because golf is most often played at country clubs. A second important recreational pursuit is tennis, which also requires outdoor maintenance when played at the country club, although tennis is also played in the city. In a wealthy area such as Palm Desert, California, located about a hundred miles east of Los Angeles, a considerable amount of the town land is devoted to golf courses, which require immense amounts of water and daily care. Because Palm Desert is located in the desert, the presence of so many golf courses is indeed a luxury. For the most affluent families in the largest cities and most exclusive suburbs, membership in the local Polo Club may be the most significant indication that the family has reached the top of the stratification pyramid.

Wealthy suburbanites maintain their isolation through mechanisms similar to those utilized in the city, such as the high price of homes, surveillance and control by private security forces, gate-guarded and enclosed communities, and the separation that comes from spatial dispersal itself. Whether we are dealing with the city or the suburbs, the wealthy tend to use topography to their advantage. Their homes are located at the greatest heights. In the suburbs, this often means that estates are built on the high ground, on hillsides or escarpments. In the city, this "god's eye view" is acquired with apartments at the top of luxury high-rises, where there is intense competition for the condominium with the best views of the city.

In short, the wealthy possess a distinct lifestyle founded on class privilege and symbols of high social status. Their daily life manifests itself in space through unique molding of the environment to create isolation and exclusion. The wealthy also overcome the limitations of space by owning several residences, each with its own locational advantages. Whether living in the city or the country, their lifestyle, like any other, is sociospatial; that is, it is organized around expressive symbols (Fussell, 1983) and particular spaces.

Yuppies, Buppies, Dinks, and the Suburban Middle Class

A large proportion of central city residents are not members of the upper class but do have significant discretionary income because of monetary rewards associated with their chosen field of work. Since the 1970s, as manufacturing has declined in the city, there has been a phenomenal increase in service-related jobs (see Chapter 6). Many of these are professional positions created by the information-processing economy of the city, such as the financial and legal institutions associated with corporate headquarters. In previous chapters, we discussed how certain kinds of economic activity create or help reinforce lifestyles, community relations, and expressive symbols. The shift to information-processing professional services has also affected metropolitan settlement space by reinforcing certain upper-middle-class patterns of behavior. As with all other lifestyles in our society, socioeconomic standing and the financial resources of these groups are expressed through particular consumption patterns.

The term *yuppie*, or young urban professional, has acquired a derogatory connotation, but it is a very useful way to describe relatively young (late twenties to early forties), middle-class professionals who live in the city. The same can be said for the term *dink*—double income, no kids—which describes yuppie couples without children. We should note that yuppies and dinks represent urban subpopulations characterized by their income, occupation, and lifestyle; they are not identified by ethnicity or race. As large numbers of African American college graduates entered the labor force in the 1980s, the term *buppie* was used to identify the black urban professional. Only recently have such components of the middle class achieved the kind of numbers that have attracted attention. According to Sassen (1991), yuppies were responsible for gentrification and the upgraded housing and renovation of older loft buildings in New York and other cities; their culinary demands spurred the opening of many new and often exotic restaurants; and their more specialized everyday needs, such as last-minute food shopping, health and fitness requirements, and reading and cinema tastes, have opened up new sectors of employment for a host of immigrant groups and working-class urban residents looking for entry-level service positions.

In the early 1980s, the leaders of many cities believed that the two-pronged explosion of jobs and spending related to the expansion of the business service sector would replace manufacturing as the key growth industry of urban areas. Indeed, places such as Pittsburgh (Jezierski, 1988) managed to change from centers of industry to focal points for global banking and investment. Restructuring of the financial and corporate business sectors with a consequent decline in the growth of jobs, however, occurred in the mid-1980s, cutting short this expansion. Especially significant were the changes that occurred after the October 1987 "crash" of the New York stock market, which led to greater computerization of financial transactions, the reining in of risky ventures such as junk bonds, and the failure of several investment firms (Minsky, 1989). Throughout the 1990s, corporate downsizing led to the loss of tens of thousands of white-collar jobs in cities across the country. Hence, despite what was once believed, the place of yuppies in the revitalization of central cities may be overrated.

Most households that we would identify as part of the middle class do not live in the city. Decades of white flight for those who could afford to move to the ever-expanding suburbs have emptied the central city of much of the middle class. The majority of middle-class Americans have spread out and prospered across the vast expanses of developed housing tracts located in suburban settlement space throughout the metropolitan region. Middle-class suburban living might be thought of as the upper-class lifestyle within a more modest budget. Symbols of status abound in this kind of environment as well. The typical suburban home is a scaled-down replica of the upper-class estate. It consists of a front yard that is strictly ornamental and a backyard reserved for leisure. In the warmer parts of the country, the desirable backyard may contain a built-in swimming pool, which usually is no more than thirty feet long. The 1990s may be known as the decade of the backyard deck; most new middle-class homes have decks in the backyard where children play and adults cook on the gas barbecue, and home improvement chain stores have spread across the suburban landscape. While the upper-class estate requires a team of gardening and maintenance people to take care of the yard, the middle-class homeowner is a "do-it-yourselfer." Indeed, a stereotypical activity of the suburban male invariably involves fighting crabgrass on the lawn, repairing roofs, and maintaining homeowner appliances. Women in suburbia also have a unique lifestyle, as we will discuss more fully later when we consider the relationship between gender and space.

For suburbanites, leisure activities are confined to the weekend, when there is some free time from work—at least for those households where parents do not have to work overtime or stagger their work schedules during the week so that one parent can stay home with the kids. In many municipalities, tax monies have been used to acquire the kind of public facilities that the affluent enjoy in private. These include public golf courses, swimming pools, tennis courts, and parks. In areas close to the ocean or a lake, suburban municipalities often build and service public marinas for boating and other water sports. Suburban life is family life. Box 7.2 details everyday life in suburbia.

Box 7.2

Middle-Class Suburban Lifestyle

A picture of middle-class suburban life was drawn by the geographer Peter Muller (1981):

> The needs and preferences of the nuclear family unit shape modes of social interaction in middle-income residential areas. The management of children is a central group-level concern, and most local social contact occurs through such family-oriented formal organizations as the school PTA, Little League, and the Scouts. However, despite the closer spacing of homes and these integrating activities, middle-class suburbanites . . . are not communally cohesive to any great degree. Emphasis on family privacy and freedom to aggressively pursue its own upwardly

continues

mobile aspirations does not encourage the development of extensive local social ties. Neighboring (mostly child-related) is limited and selective, and even socializing with relatives is infrequent. Most social interaction revolves around a nonlocal network of self-selected friends widely distributed in suburban space. (1981:72)

This relative isolation of individuals in suburbia and the exclusive auto dependency of the spatial arrangements is particularly hard on teenagers. Ralph Larkin makes these observations about suburban teenagers in a place he calls Utopia:

The most serious complaint among Utopia High School students is boredom. They are restless. Many complain of having nothing to do. They are forced to compete with each other for grades, sexual attractiveness, hipness, and all the other minutiae that are involved in the status race. Since everyone else is struggling for the same, somehow scarcer rewards, friendship has a hollow quality to it. It is a gloss on a relationship in which vulnerabilities are hidden so they won't be capitalized on by others. (1979:60)

In his pioneering study of the suburban shopping mall (1984), Jerry Jacobs discussed how teenagers fight the boredom of their lives by converging on a certain space, the fully enclosed shopping mall. Jacobs took one particular teenager, Julie, as typical and detailed her activities within this environment as follows:

First and foremost she and her friends spend "a lot of time" at the (video game) arcade. They often stop in at the "Gift Horse," a shop featuring "jewelry and design shoelaces and calendars and mugs." They might on these walks stop to visit "The Old Erie Coffee House." Ironically, this is not a place to drink coffee although coffee, tea, and their accoutrements are sold there. However, on these jaunts, Julie and her friends usually have a different agenda in mind, and go there to look at "cute stuffed animals, the little animal farm, animals, mugs and stuff, cards and pins." From there they might move on to "Sweet Temptation" and get some "gum or something." By then, it would be approaching lunch-time and they would go to the "T.J.'s" (a hamburger place not unlike McDonald's) where they would get a large French fries and a coke and sit and talk about a variety of topics. (1984:98)

The Working Class and the Working Poor

In the nineteenth century, life in the city was dominated by factories. Modest working-class housing was constructed in grid-pattern rows nearby. Weekly schedules were centered in this space, which included the few amenities available to the working class—the pub, the association football park (soccer) or the local baseball diamond, and the streets themselves, which served as playgrounds for children (Hareven, 1982). In the period immediately after World War II, U.S. cities contained a prodigious density of such working-class districts. Since the 1960s, however, this pattern has been in decline. One reason is that many factory workers attained middle-class status with the ability to purchase single-family homes in the suburbs (Berger, 1957), often with liberal government-sponsored veterans' benefits. A second, more drastic cause was the decline in manufacturing itself. When the factories closed, working-class life became all the more precarious.

Although working-class families have suburbanized in large numbers since the 1960s, many still remain residents of large cities. They are often referred to as the "working poor" because their standard of living is declining as cities themselves have become expensive places to reside. The quality of life of the working class is dependent on the public services provided by local government. They require mass transportation, for example, which is becoming increasingly expensive. The level of medical care for this less affluent group is seriously deficient and dependent on city-supported hospitals because they work at jobs that do not provide adequate, if any, health insurance. In fact, the Health and Hospitals Administration of New York City, which runs that city's medical facilities, has a yearly budget of about $1.5 billion, as much as the entire budget of several small countries.

Because so much of their standard of living depends on city services, the working poor are often at odds with public administrators. City politics involves clashes between this public and the municipal administration over the quality of services. Since the late 1970s, declining fiscal health of cities has made this political conflict worse because of budget crises and cutbacks (as we will see in Chapter 9). The working poor and their advocates in the city fight a running battle with the mayor over the declines in education, fire and police protection, sanitation, highway maintenance, health care, and recreational amenities.

The Ghettoized Poor

In Chapter 9 we will discuss the serious issue of segregation. Being isolated and poor, living in what is commonly referred to as a ghetto, is not a lifestyle that is chosen. It is a set of circumstances that is forced on people who do not have the economic, political, and social resources to oppose being marginalized. Yet, we must discuss this phenomenon here in order to present a clear picture of the kind of diversity that exists in our metropolitan regions that includes not only poor people but residents who are involuntarily ghettoized by negative attitudes towards race and poverty.

Living in the worst areas of the central city means that the ghettoized poor are subjected to an almost unending list of pathological consequences of city living, including public health crises such as AIDS, child abuse, and tuberculosis, dropouts from education, juvenile crime, drug addiction and the bearing of addicted babies, juvenile motherhood, murder, rape, and robbery. The crime and pathology associated with poverty-stricken ghettos makes city living difficult for everyone and are largely responsible for the continuing levels of violence associated with the inner city.

One way of showing the spatial effects of extreme segregation on daily life is by examining access to adequate food shopping facilities. In an influential UK study (Wrigley, 2002): "Research confirmed that there was a lack of easy access to shops for deprived households and, furthermore, places that did service the low income neighborhoods had higher prices. . . . Adopting the term 'food deserts' first coined by the low-income project team of the nutrition task force, the report argued that 'some areas have become food deserts exacerbating the problems those on low incomes face in affording a healthy diet" (*Urban Studies* 39, no. 11: 2030).

Through the concept of "food desert," then, the health inequalities and spatial exclusion of the poor became firmly linked. Most discussions of extreme isolation for ghettoized Americans point out their segregation in distinct areas of cities, but they fail to connect that exclusion to the everyday effect of failing to find adequate and healthy food and a cost enjoyed by other, more advantaged Americans because they live in a "food desert." Research of this kind of deprivation proves how discrimination and segregation lead to physical and emotional injuries rather than simply a "different way of life" for the poor.

WOMEN, GENDER ROLES, AND SPACE

The issue of gender and urban space is a vast topic on which urban sociologists have largely been silent. As recently as the 1970s, one well-known geographer wrote a book entitled *This Scene of Man* (Vance, 1977) and, not to be outdone, more than a decade later an equally famous urban sociologist published a study of Chicago entitled *The Man Made City* (Suttles, 1990). Feminist scholars would indeed agree that the city is manmade because women had little to do with its planning, less to do with its construction, and received few benefits from being confined within a man made environment. The built environment reflects men's activities, men's values, and men's attitudes toward settlement space. Yet the lives of women are a critical component of urban and suburban activities. Increasingly, with the prodding of feminist observers, urban sociology should gain greater insight into the role of women, and their needs, in everyday metropolitan life.

Women and the Urban Political Economy

During the nineteenth century in the early stages of industrial manufacturing, it was common for entire families to labor; ten and even twelve hours a day, six days a week, was the norm. Home life was second to the needs of the factory, and even children were pressed into the service of wage labor in textile mills and other industries

(Hareven, 1982). Over the years, conditions in these "Satanic mills," as Karl Marx (1967) called them, changed. Child labor laws were passed at the turn of the century in the United States prohibiting school-age youth from full-time employment. Many women continued to work, but the growing number of middle-class families during the 1920s enabled people to copy the upper-class lifestyle with married women remaining at home. This effect of class, which occurred because of successful economic growth beginning last century, resulted in the redefinition of the middle-class woman's role to that of housewife (Spain, 1992).

Over the years, other changes would alter the relationship of women to both the family and the larger society. Status differences were caused by the effects of male social dominance, which dictated women's life chances, and by the effects of the economy. For example, among the middle class during the 1920s, women were expected to remain housewives. During World War II, however, many women returned to full-time occupations, including manufacturing, as in the image of "Rosie the Riveter." After the war and especially during the suburbanization of the 1950s, middle-class women were once again expected to remain home as housewives. But in the 1970s, real wages in the United States began to decline, and participation in the middle-class lifestyle has since grown increasingly expensive. Owning a home in the suburbs typically requires more than one income, and it is common for both spouses to pursue full-time employment. A majority of all adult women now work outside the home, whether single or married.

Recent statistics from the U.S. Department of Labor illustrate the phenomenal changes in the labor force participation of women since the 1950s. In 1950 roughly 30 percent of women worked outside the home, but by 1986 the figure was 55 percent. In 1950 it was relatively rare for married women with children to be employed. Only 28 percent of women in this group with children between ages six and seventeen worked, but by 1986 the figure had jumped to 68 percent (see Hochschild and Machung, 1989). At present, a majority of women return to the labor force within a year after giving birth, and most families represent dual-income households.

Working-class and minority women have always had to secure employment outside the home, even if limited to part-time work. Minority women, for example, have always worked, and many are the main sources of income for families due to employment discrimination against males. Certain industries, such as garment manufacturing, depend almost exclusively on the exploitation of female labor in factories. Women in Asia and Latin America, in particular, are exploited as the source of labor for the electronics and garment industries in countries such as Mexico, Singapore, and South Korea (see Chapter 11). McDowell suggests that male domination of female roles is an integral part of the global economy and a major reason for the success of recent restructuring that has shipped manufacturing jobs to developing countries (McDowell, 1991). In short, gender roles appear to be dictated in part by patriarchal social conventions and, in many parts of the world, by the demands of the global economy.

WOMEN, GENDER ROLES, AND SPACE

Domestic labor is unpaid and has low status. Housework is usually not a family topic of importance. Yet the well-being of the family depends on the cooking, cleaning, nurturing, and monitoring of the household. In most societies, it has been women's lot to bear the responsibility for these tasks. Even when women work outside the home, men expect them to complete a "double shift" of cleaning, cooking, and child care when they return home. According to a classic study of this burden (Hochschild and Machung, 1989), married women who work outside the home still do an average of three hours a day of housework compared with seventeen minutes for their male spouses. Indeed, women usually do not get recognition frm the family for the housework they do, unless the wife is working and the husband—or the husband's family— becomes concerned that she is not doing enough around the house. As one group of observers note:

> As women it is assumed that we will be ultimately responsible for the upkeep and general maintenance of our homes whether we have another job or not. . . . Even when others contribute to this work, the primary responsibility remains with the women. We are conscious of its demands at all times; responsibilities cannot be shut off by retreating into a "room of one's own." (Matrix Collective, 1984)

Domestic or unpaid labor supports child rearing and family life. While these activities are necessary in all societies, the tasks themselves are the primary responsibility of women, who for the most part labor alone. Urban sociologists refer to these activities as the social reproduction of the labor force, because household work along with education and health care combine to nurture children until they themselves enter the labor force. The socialization of women to accept the role of domestic laborer in our society, therefore, is an essential and necessary component of the economy.

The participation of middle-class women in the formal economy has been cyclical but increasing in recent decades. Since the 1970s, women have entered the paid labor force in record numbers. As a result of economic restructuring—that is, with the decline in manufacturing and the rise of service industries (see Chapter 6)—new opportunities have been created for women. Women have responded by returning to college and moving into the professional service sector. One consequence of this shift has been a change in the way both men and women view household tasks, with a greater willingness among middle-class men to share in domestic labor, especially a growing percentage of men who "mother" (Lamb, 1986; Grief, 1985). Another consequence has been the multiplication of service-related jobs created by working mothers. Many of the pressing household tasks have been farmed out to specialized service workers for a fee. Child care, housecleaning, shopping assistance, and lawn care are but some of the services that have taken the place of unpaid domestic labor. In addition, fast foods, restaurants, and take-out shops have expanded their operations greatly over the last twenty-five years. All of these new economic activities have changed the texture of space in both cities and suburbs. Specialty shops and services spring up everywhere to cater to those families with double incomes. Supermarket and giant merchandising stores such as Walmart make shopping more efficient for the consumer although they have other negative consequences for local business. Along with malls, retailers also redefine metropolitan space through the construction of minicenters across the region.

The sociospatial relations of the modern global economy have much to do with gender roles and patriarchy, but they also are a consequence of economic and political factors. When women stayed at home and engaged in full-time but unpaid labor, they were responsible for keeping up the appearance of the neighborhood. Once middle-class women in the United States were encouraged to change their social role, although still expected to do a "double shift," energies and resources were transferred to service industries that catered to domestic needs. Neighborhoods changed to accommodate fast-food and take-out places, restaurants, laundries, and dry cleaners, and supermarkets and malls made shopping progressively more convenient.

Houses in the suburbs required at least two-car garages because both spouses commuted to work, and teenagers required their own vehicles for work, school, and leisure activities. In both urban and suburban settlement spaces, day care and extended child care programs changed the place where children went to play—from city streets supervised by mothers to indoor group play areas supervised by paid day care specialists. Elsewhere in the global economy, young girls comprise the bulk of the manufacturing labor force in electronics and garment industries because patriarchal relations make them docile and low-paid workers. The control of women's bodies is as essential to the sustenance of countries in the developing world as it is to the "first world" patriarchal societies. Everywhere, then, the nature of gender roles has a direct effect on sociospatial relations.

Women and the Environment

The relations between settlement space and gender extend from the home to the community to the larger metropolitan region. The home, for example, is the one space in the environment where people can be themselves. It is the most private and intimate space. Due to the family division of labor, women have been assigned the main task of decorating the home. Through this activity they express their own individuality (Matrix Collective, 1984). Of course housing has several meanings, as we will see, and it is a signifier of class status. But for women, their control over the environmental space of the home has meant an opportunity for self-expression. For the middle class, it also has developed into a restricted domain within which women are allowed to influence their environment. Box 7.3 reviews some of the important aspects of the environment as they relate to women's lives.

If the home space can be viewed in this way, it is partly because women have been socialized to take on responsibility for shelter maintenance. Spatial relations therefore play a great role in the perpetuation of female socialized roles in our society. However,

Box 7.3

Gendered Space in the Built Environment

The sociospatial approach asserts that urban and suburban settlement spaces influence individual behavior; however, this influence is mediated by gender, class, and other individual characteristics. In this way, the meaning of space and the built environment may differ for men and women. Consider the ways in which the structure of settlement space in Sweden and that in the United States have very different consequences for the daily activity and well-being of women.

Suburban developments in the United States usually consist of single-family homes located some distance from the urban center. Local zoning restrictions require that suburban settlement space be low-density (not simply single-family homes instead of apartments but also lot sizes of between one and three acres). Land-use plans also require physical separation of residential areas from business and commercial development. The federal government has spent billions of dollars constructing a highway system for private automobiles, and public transportation is limited.

In Sweden, suburban developments are of moderate density, usually garden-type apartments located in mixed-use districts where stores and businesses are located within walking distance. Extensive public transportation connects suburban settlement space to the city core, and child care and other services (provided through the public sector) are available within the local community (Popenoe, 1977).

The effects of these two very different built environments on women's lives could not be more dramatic. In the United States, women who live in suburban housing developments are comparatively isolated from friends, relatives, their place of employment, and health and other public services. A second family automobile is needed for women to take their children to day care, go grocery shopping, or travel to their jobs. Then there is the cost of travel time to and from each of these destinations (separated from one another by zoning). In Sweden and other Scandinavian countries with similar welfare state structures and urban planning, women in suburban developments are more likely to live near friends, relatives, and their place of employment. If they do not, public transportation is available, eliminating the need for a second automobile. Because day care and other family services are funded by the state and located in the new planned suburban communities, they are readily available. And because friends and even relatives may live within walking distance, it is easier to pool resources to arrange for other family needs (Popenoe, 1980).

The arrangement of suburban settlement space in Scandinavian countries encourages women to become fully integrated into the metropolitan community and to build strong social networks with others in the community. In contrast, the structure of suburban settlement space in the United States—where homes, workplaces, schools, and shopping areas are separated from one another—places a significant burden on suburban women's time needs and isolates them from employment opportunities and daily activities within the metropolitan region.

if the female gender role assigns a certain power to women through control of the home environment, the opposite is the case for the larger physical environment of the city and metropolis. Once out in public space, women have to beware. They are subject to harassment and, quite often, danger. Women living in large cities must acquire "street smarts" early if they are to successfully negotiate public space. As one commentary noted: "Whether you wear a slit skirt or are covered from head to foot in a black chador, the message is not that you are attractive enough to make a man lose his self-control, but that the public realm belongs to him and you are there by his permission as long as you follow his rules and as long as you remember your place" (Benard and Schlaffer, 1993:390).

In contrast to men, women are situated in a constrained space and do not enjoy the same freedom of movement. For example, women are cautioned not to go out alone at night, and with good reason. If they walk or jog around the neighborhood, they usually do so only in secure places. The women's movement has been particularly attentive to the needs of females for safe places, such as "Take Back the Night" rallies. The constricted and confined safe places for women in our society are another form of oppression. By patterning what activities are allowed, what are isolated, what are considered safe or dangerous, and what are connected to other activities, such as the combination of child care and shopping found in the mall or the gender segregation of children in elementary schools (Thorne, 1993), space plays a role in gender socialization.

The secondary status of women is reinforced through spatial design. Community planning invariably assigns the major portion of open space to traditionally male-dominated activities, such as sports. Places for mothering are rarely considered at all and are often restricted to playgrounds. Creating safe environments for children and mothers requires some planning. In Columbia, Maryland, one of the totally planned New Towns in the United States, pedestrian and automobile traffic are separated by the segregation of space. This feature of Columbia makes it easier for mothers to protect children at play. It is not so easy to suggest ways the home and community environments can be improved by taking the needs of women more into account, although some progress through feminist activism has been made in sensitizing planners and architects to the specific needs of women (see Matrix Collective, 1984). Change in the accepted gender roles and the new demands placed upon family life may affect our environment in the years to come (see Chapter 12 for an extended discussion on environmental and planning concerns).

Finally, there is a sharp difference between men and women regarding travel. Men travel more than women, and most, but not all, use transportation solely for work-related purposes. Men, more than women, are drawn away from their homes for business trips. Married women, in contrast, most often seek out jobs close to home and, although they commute, their everyday space is confined to family chores using a car that is close to home as well. Shopping, being a "soccer mom," and picking or dropping off children at school are all circumscribed activities in a more restricted daily space than the one enjoyed by men who occasionally go on business trips many miles from home. Men, whether single or married, are also much more likely to travel significant distances for leisure purposes than women—for fishing or golf trips, for example. In short, there is a large gender gap regarding differences in travel behavior that has an impact on male/female and family relationships.

THE CITY AS A SPECIAL PLACE: NIGHTLIFE, URBAN CULTURE, AND REGENERATION OF DOWNTOWNS

Despite the domination of suburbia in regard to total regional population, there is no doubt that the historical central city retains a pedestrian and consumer-oriented culture that remains relatively unique and attractive to all residents. One way of demonstrating this aspect is by examining the important role downtowns play in nighttime activities of a diverse group of people ranging from young adult bar hoppers, music and theater aficionados of all ages, and tourists looking for a "good time."

Chatterton and Hollands (2003) have written an interesting case study of night-life in the UK. They depict an active scene of young adults who carouse through all hours of the evening. Local bars draw large crowds almost every night and many offer live music, although drinking and hooking up with the opposite sex, in their study, seems to be the major attractions. The popularity of these activities brings people back into the downtown core, which had been abandoned as a place for leisure and consumption by most people due to the suburbanization of the population. For this reason, development of such nighttime businesses as bars and theaters has, in the last two decades, been viewed as a major aspect of urban regeneration that greatly benefits the city, through amusement taxes and the like, as well as local businesses. Keeping the once abandoned downtowns busy with people is viewed as a sign of urban renewal, although there remain permanent residents of these areas who complain about the increased noise and nuisance congestion in the evenings when non-night crawlers simply want to sleep.

An important contribution of Chatterton and Hollands's study is the way they demonstrate how major beverage corporations have targeted locally owned pubs and nightclubs for takeover and for outlets that sell their products. What often started as a revival of small businesses and the welcome attraction of locally financed new ones to downtown leisure districts has turned into a money grab by major international corporations selling beer and alcohol under a variety of simulated names that mimic the appearance of existing small breweries. Packaging and advertising in pubs or bars of these mass-produced beverages exploiting consumer desires for high-quality designer products captures profits. Additionally, once local businesses are progressively bought out, or competing venues built by major developers in league with corporations move into areas, they attract enough nighttime traffic to become profitable. Consequently, the kind of chain marketing with global beverage and product control by transnational corporations that most often characterize suburbia is increasingly found in revived sections of major cities as well, according to the authors' case study.

Another aspect of revived city life exploiting nighttime consumption and leisure has been studied recently by David Grazian (2008) in a renewed and highly popular part of Philadelphia. His case study does not have the range of Chatterton and Hollands's, but it reports interesting findings that supplement the UK reality. The author discovers that restaurants in the newly yuppified inner-city areas resort to various tricks in order to get locals and tourists alike to spend much more money for food and drink than they would otherwise. Wine snobbery by waiters is one important means of doing this. Padding bills with drinks is a key way everyone connected with a restaurant makes money.

Another aspect of his book involves what he calls "the girl hunt." College and young adult males make their way to the so-called meat market city nightclubs in search of pickups and one-night stands. The author writes as if he discovered a major aspect of human life on Earth when he states that, after doing extensive "sociological" research and interviews at these nightclubs, most women out with their friends actually resist pickups and are there only to have a good time and get men to pay for their drinks. This research finding plays into a very depressing and cynical view of what amounts to the major means of socializing among young adults in our society. For Grazian, exploitation and resistance are sex typed and personal. For Chatterton and Hollands, in contrast, the real exploitation, echoed by Grazian's first part of his book, is in the way corporations exploit night club consumers and promote alcohol drinking for profit.

URBAN CULTURE AND CITY REVITALIZATION

In Chapter 1 we discussed the fact that the urban form has changed from one that historically relied on the large, compact central city, to a different spatial array of multicenters that are regional in scale with the historical core becoming only one of several areas of high density. This change does not mean that the old central city has disappeared as important (see following and Chapter 14).

The relative uniqueness and attractiveness of urban culture to suburbanites and tourists as well as people seeking an inner-city address has also been exploited by developers and city officials as a means of revitalizing areas that were abandoned or deteriorated during the period of deindustrialization between the 1960s and 1990s. Research results from around Western Europe report the relative success of this kind of revival model (see Miles and Paddison, 2005). Culture-led urban regeneration started with the U.S. concept of "festival marketplace," an approach to developing once derelict waterfront sites emphasizing consumption and entertainment. One of the most successful developments was built by the American Rouse Corporation for the inner harbor of Barcelona, Spain. Rouse is the same corporation that built harbor revival projects in places like Baltimore and Boston. Signature aspects of their approach involve a large shopping mall and an aquarium. Both aspects were carried over to the Barcelona project with success.

This formula was expanded to include investment in prime global tourist-oriented attractions. Perhaps the best example of this is the Guggenheim Museum in Bilbao, Spain, which was so successful as a magnet for tourists that it aided the revitalization of the entire city.

Culture-led development in the European Union arose out of a 1983 initiative called the ECOC, or the European Cities/Capital of Culture program: "Since its inception, the program has gone through a number of transformations. However the basic structure remains, namely that cities take turns acquiring the name of a European cultural capital which is tied to an investment scheme that promotes the local area. Over time there's been a wide variety of responses by European countries with some pouring in a relatively large amount of investment in a particular city and other countries doing less with the same designation." (Garcia, 2005:843)

Although some researchers have uncovered evidence of success in a lingering outcome of greater community involvement, pride and sense of place, Miles and Paddison also note an important criticism that, for example, Glasgow's ability to put on a major event and gather international acclaim is now considered only a mask aimed at hiding the enduring, embedded problems and contradictions resulting from decades of poverty and related housing, health, and nutrition problems.

Despite the mixed results of the ECOC program, there are other aspects of exploiting urban culture for revitalization that have worked in Europe and Canada as well as the United States. As a consequence of globalization and after the 1980s, cities have been able to place an emphasis on aspects of their local culture that are relatively unique in the quest for economic development in competition with other locations. "What is remarkable here is not just the speed with which culture-driven strategies have become advocated by governments and local development agencies as a means of bolstering the urban economy, but also how their diffusion has globalized. Within the space of little more than two decades, the initiation of culture-driven urban regeneration has come to occupy a pivotal position in the new urban entrepreneurialism. . . . The language of place marketing has become as integral to the Asian city as it has the European or North American city—that, more specifically, the invocation of culture has become central to the ambitions" (Miles and Paddison, 2005) of cities everywhere in maintaining, and enhancing, their regional positions in the world system.

What is new and different about the use of culture by cities for global positioning, such as the development of cultural tourism, is that local distinctiveness of urban places, which have developed often over the course of centuries, has now become commodified and transformed into an adjunct of profit making through consumption of space. No longer does urban culture refer to a particular way of life. In the context of capitalist economic development and global competition, the new way in which culture is exploited often clashes with the old, such as in local neighborhood resistance to grand projects of branding in attempting to acquire world attention. Opposition, for example, to the construction projects that follow a decision to hold the Olympics in a particular location is a perfect case.

A third aspect of investigating the role of culture in urban regeneration involves measuring the relative success of such efforts. After the year 2000, many cities across the globe launched their own projects with a common theme of advancing economic development. Only now has it begun to be possible to measure whether or not culture-led urban revival has been successful and under what conditions. The expansion of facilities for tourists, for example, is very much a form of investment that bypasses local citizen needs in favor of the global tourist. This is especially true for cities that have historically been working class and industrial, no matter how hard hit by deindustrialization and globalization. Investment in cultural resources does not usually translate into a more inclusive, better quality of life for the working class of such cities, and it is unlikely to bring about a large enough increase in tourism to offset declining employment.

The important question that is raised here is whether investment in culture can lead to the continued, sustainable development of a city, or is it tied more clearly to one-shot events and enterprises (Miles and Paddison, 2005:838).

A fourth aspect involves a makeover of the city for tourism. Here the consumer that is being addressed is someone from outside the region. Consumer attractions in this case are different in some respects from the way in which central cities seek to appeal to local white affluent shoppers who were principally from the suburbs. Thus tourism represents a separate case of the consumption of space as well as the production of space for that consumption. Bernadette Quinn (2005) researched the effects of city "festivals" in this regard. The holding of festivals in cities has become a popular way to draw attention and crowds to the inner locations. Quinn argues that city authorities "tend to disregard the social value of festivals and to construe them simply as vehicles of economic generation or as 'quick fix' solutions to the city image problems. While such an approach renders certain benefits, it is ultimately quite limiting." According to her research, art festivals have not worked to include enough local residents and have not led to an improved quality of life for them so that the festivals do not have a lasting effect on the people who live in the city. Quinn also notes that these festivals will continue because they are one way in which cities compete with other urban places.

Another aspect of urban revitalization using culture and consumption is reported in an interesting study of Holland by Bas Spierings (2006). He uses Lefebvre's idea of the "spaces of consumption" to investigate how inner-city areas restructure their businesses in order to attract the more affluent consumers from suburbia as well as tourists. This is a kind of restructuring, much like the type of festival-led one reported by Quinn, that ignores the needs of local, less affluent residents, in favor of profit making from a wealthier market segment that most often commutes from outside the city.

Spierings's research specifically focuses on the attempts by cities to attract a particular consumer: an upper-middle-class mobile and demanding person with money to spend and with an interest in having an experience in shopping as well as finding goods that might be purchased. "The belief in the accompanying mobile spending power has made intricate—urban competition flourish" (2006:189) within multi-centered metro regions because developing the inner city for such consumption competes with suburban shopping malls.

"In so doing, city center actors upgraded the quality of both the functional structure and the physical features of the city center. More specifically, the consumer services, the morphology, furnishings and architecture are changed for the visual consumption of shoppers" (2006:189).

The attractive consumer "is assumed to perform the act of 'shopping the city' to consume consumer services, as well as usually consuming 'the shopping city' itself—that is to say, the shopping environment." Spierings's study uncovered differences in the development schemes according to the different cities; however, every center aimed at its renovation in favor of attracting the contemporary and highly mobile consumer with money to spend and in competition with other places with little regard for the ability of local residents to also enjoy such spaces. Transformations of this kind also change completely the culture of the city because they introduce new sign systems that come from global corporations which are instantly recognizable as chain marketing by high-end consumers and tourists alike.

Developers "created a mix of consumer services in the shopping environment. . . . These contemporary consumers stroll and gaze around the consumption space to find satisfaction. The aim of both the functional and physical upgrading therefore is to enable and encourage 'shopping the city'" (2006:192). This implies that consumers are browsing services such as retailing, catering, and cultural facilities. They also visually consumed the shopping city, which consists of such things as facades, windows, and shop interiors. Finally, developers sought to make their projects visually different from the look of other competing city centers. Some projects have to address a lack of pedestrian mall space; others had to make room through redevelopment and the tearing down of obsolete structures for new shops. The latter examples are referred to as structural changes. In addition, functional changes had to be made in order to attract an appropriate mix of sources that complement high-end consumer shopping, such as places to eat and cultural attractions.

In sum, Spierings's study is important because it highlights three aspects of the sociospatial approach of this text. First, he reinforces the research of Holland and Chesterton by showing how global corporations invade the inner-city space and superimpose their own brands and themes on products, thereby erasing historical local culture and, in the case of consumer developments, historical local space as well. Second, like Quinn's results, Spierings's show how this type of urban redevelopment actually ignores the interests and needs of local residents, which produces significant tension between them and the affluent "invaders"—the tourists and high-end suburban consumers—from outside. Cultural and political conflict emerges from this tension that constitutes an important aspect of local politics and social movements. Third, the kind of projects that Spierings mentions helps illustrate an important dynamic of MMR internal processes—namely, the competition of locations throughout the region for consumer dollars. Unlike the early and now obsolete compact model of the city advocated by the 1930s Chicago School, the multicentered metro region model allows for and even promotes analysis of spatial competition among separate locations within the area that is applicable as well to the study of a similar dynamic among individual global cities for such things as competition over tourist dollars.

ETHNICITY AND IMMIGRATION

Ethnic formation in modern society is the consequence of government policy and intergroup competition within an ethnically diverse society (Omi and Winant, 1992). In relatively homogeneous societies, lifestyle differences may exist, but they usually are not expressed as ethnicity; class, gender, religious, subcultural, and age differences may be more important. When indigenous people, such as mainland Chinese, immigrate to another country that contains people from many different origins, such as the United States, subcultural differences may take on the dimensions of ethnic differences. These are almost wholly "semiotic" or symbolic in nature (see Chapter 4). In particular, ascribed characteristics and inherited beliefs may make individuals with foreign heritages uniquely different. What counts for the dynamics of ethnicity is the extent to which those symbolic differences clash with those of the dominant society or of other ethnic groups in a diverse society.

In the United States, ethnic lifestyles are closely connected to the waves of immigration from abroad. Our understanding of immigration should include a spatial perspective that acknowledges the important role of the globalization of capital as well as the push and pull factors that most often are used to explain why people left their land of origin in the first place. Three distinct waves of immigration to the United States have occurred. The first two waves are discussed in this section, and the third wave, or "new immigration," is discussed in the following section of this chapter.

The First Wave

Many thousands of years ago, Asians immigrated to the Western Hemisphere over a land bridge to Alaska. Beginning with Columbus's fateful voyage in 1492, Western European settlers from the British Isles, Spain, Holland, and France confronted the Native Americans. These European settlers arrived as a consequence of official state policy. Some were convicts taking advantage of an alternative sentence to debtors' prison in their homeland. Others signed on with the promise of free land and other resources. Still others, such as the Puritans who founded the Massachusetts Bay Colony and William Penn and his Quaker community, came in search of religious freedom. At the time of the American Revolution, some 95 percent of immigrants to the United States were Northern European, and nearly 70 percent came from Great Britain (Steinberg, 1996).

During the 1840s, the potato famine in Ireland forced many people from that country to immigrate. The Irish people were the first large group of immigrants who were not Anglo-Saxon Protestants, and they confronted extensive discrimination because they were Catholic (Higham, 1977). By the time they arrived, the earlier groups had entrenched themselves as the ruling class. Many of them, such as John Rockefeller (from Scotland), Cornelius Vanderbilt (whose family had come from Holland), and Leland Stanford (of English origin), had made fortunes in the burgeoning industrial economy of the United States. The Irish were considered less valuable than the African slaves of the South, and they were used for dangerous tasks, such as building railroads, or as the first proletarian factory workers in the northern cities where slavery was not allowed.

The Second Wave

By the 1800s, industrialization was in full bloom and the cities of the United States were expanding. At about that time a second substantial wave of new immigrants arrived here from the countries of Central and Eastern Europe. Most second-wave immigrants made their homes in the city. Many had come from rural backgrounds and had to make adjustments to the urban way of life (Handlin, 1951). As we noted in Chapter 5, the cities of the time were overcrowded. Housing for most immigrants lacked the basic necessities of sanitation and sewage. Public health crises and crime waves were quite common (Monkkonen, 1986). The quality of urban life went into decline. In addition, they found most jobs in the factories of the largest cities, and they had to accommodate themselves to the industrial daily schedule.

It wasn't long before antagonisms developed between immigrant groups organized as workers, and city officials and factory owners. Both the Irish who had arrived somewhat earlier and the second wave of Central and Eastern Europeans were viewed by established residents as threatening to the American way of life. Some second-wave immigrants had already been exposed to radical labor movements in Europe, and these groups, such as the Industrial Workers of the World (IWW), started up in the United States. Because of the large majority of Catholics among the foreigners, particularly the Irish, Italians, and Poles, a popular anti-urban sentiment was that large cities were centers of "Rum, Romanism, and Rebellion."

It may be difficult for us to imagine today, but the older, first-wave immigrants, especially those among the elite of the country, propagated racist ideas about the Irish, Italians, Poles, and Jews in the late 1880s. Among the books published was Josiah

Strong's (1891) racist diatribe that blamed the white foreigners for diluting the "American Race" and for spawning the crises of the city. In another case, during the 1920s, many outspoken anti-Semites operated in the open, including Henry Ford, who would not allow Jewish workers in his factories and financed a successful reprinting of the virulently anti-Semitic forgery, *The Protocols of the Elders of Zion*—a racist book that is still circulated today.

To a great extent, such racist and anti-Semitic attacks appeared alongside others accusing the new immigrants of harboring communist and anarchist or anticapitalist ideas. Thus anti-immigrant racism was a strong weapon used to call immigration itself into question. Around the turn of the century, reaction to the second wave of arrivals was so strong that it eventually led to a restriction of immigration from Eastern and Southern Europe. This was accomplished in a succession of federal acts that established quotas favoring first-wave, Western European and Northern European countries. These quotas actually lasted until the immigration reform bill of 1965.

Fighting between employers and workers was not the only conflict of the time; conflict also took on a spatial manifestation. Areas in the city were marked off by ethnicity, class, race, and religion. For example, most large American cities historically have had two separate Irish neighborhoods—one for Irish Catholics, the other for Irish Protestants. These groups competed with each other over territory and access to public resources. Employers would also pit workers from different ethnic groups against each other in a largely successful effort to prevent union organizing and keep workers' wages low. Thrasher's study of Chicago gangs, discussed in Chapter 3, provides an excellent example of how these "defended neighborhoods" that are a sociospatial phenomenon of ethnicity came into being.

The Third Wave

Earlier ideas about race and ethnicity and the immigrant experience are being challenged by the newest, third wave of immigrants that has arrived since the 1970s. Changes to immigration laws enacted in 1965 replaced the earlier quota system (which had been designed to keep Asians and other non-European groups out of the country) with a preference system based on occupational characteristics. Supporters of the immigration reform legislation could not have anticipated the unprecedented response across the globe. Between 1968 and 1990, some 10 million people immigrated to the United States. Further reforms passed by the first Bush administration limited immigration to some 540,000 persons each year. But after intense lobbying from the U.S. Chamber of Commerce and other business groups, this number was increased to 650,000 legal immigrants each year. This rate has not been observed here since the last great wave of immigration at the beginning of the twentieth century. And just as in the earlier period in our history, increased immigration is supported by business as a way to increase the labor pool—and thereby keep wages from increasing.

The composition of the third wave of immigrant groups is very different from that of earlier periods. During the first and second waves, 75 percent of the arrivals were from Europe. Today a similar percentage of arrivals are from Latin America and Asia. Each year since 1970, more than 55,000 Mexicans and 50,000 Filipinos have immigrated to the United States. In California, for example, 22 percent of new immigrants came from Asia and 43 percent from Mexico during the 1970s (Espiritu and Light, 1991). Also striking is the fact that the majority of new immigrants to the United States are female—and this is true even from countries such as Mexico and the Philippines, where women are often thought to be less independent. As a consequence of this new immigration, the United States of the twenty-first century will be more culturally diverse—and more Asian and Hispanic—than at any time in its history. To understand just how significant these changes will be, consider the fact that Hispanics will outnumber African Americans as the largest minority group in the United States early in the twenty-first century, and that even if immigration were halted completely, the U.S. Hispanic population will still double within the next twenty years, from some 14 million to more than 30 million.

A third distinct characteristic of the new immigration is that it is economically diverse. Many recent immigrants exhibit the classic characteristics of the past: limited education, rural backgrounds, and limited resources. A large number, however, are the exact opposite. These well-endowed immigrants are educated—many have college degrees—they are former city dwellers, and they often come with enough personal financial resources to start their own businesses. In their home countries of India, Korea, the Philippines, and elsewhere, this loss of a young and highly educated population is referred to as a "brain drain." Thus, many third-wave arrivals also achieve success in the United States in a relatively short time. According to Portes and Rumbaut (1990), in the decade between 1980 and 1990, professionals and technicians accounted for only 18 percent of the U.S. labor force but represented 25 percent of the immigrant population.

This "bimodal" distribution—that is, having two peaks: one high income, one low income—of immigration is a consequence of uneven development within the global system of capitalism. In the 1960s and 1970s, many countries underwent crash modernization programs that were not entirely successful. On the one hand, large numbers of the middle and working classes received technical and professional training. But upon graduation, their economies had not expanded fast enough to offer them work. On the other hand, agricultural reform programs and development of interior places forced many impoverished and uneducated rural residents into the cities. They too took a chance by immigrating rather than waiting around in their home countries for work (Espiritu and Light, 1991).

Some of the recent immigrants have not only been successful; they have realized opportunities in new ways. For example, Monterey Park, a suburb outside Los Angeles, became a focal point for new Chinese immigration. Between 1960 and 1988, the population went from 85 percent white to 50 percent Chinese, with other Asians also in residence. Consequently, the city has become known as the first "suburban China-town" (Arax, 1987; Fong, 1991), and it provides an excellent example of why we can no longer consider the ethnic neighborhood in large cities as the prime site for ethnic subcultures. Recent arrivals to the United States have invested over $1 billion of their own money in the suburb, and it is estimated that the Chinese own at least 66 percent of all business and property there (Espiritu and Light, 1991:43). Other areas of the country report a similar phenomenon of immigrant suburbanization, where in many cases new arrivals bypass the large city entirely.

Current immigration to the United States (and other developed nations) reflects changes in the global system of capitalism in another respect. Following the breakup of colonial systems after World War II, many European countries saw an increase in im-migration from their former colonies—Caribbean blacks and Muslim and Hindu In-dians in England, Indonesian and other groups in the Netherlands. At the end of the Second Indo-Chinese War, the United States admitted 300,000 Southeast Asian refugees, and the death squads and political conflicts in Central America in the 1980s brought another 500,000 refugees, despite efforts of the Reagan administration and the Immigration and Naturalization Service to prevent them from entering the coun-try. And as noted earlier, each year some 50,000 people immigrate to the United States from the Philippines, our former colonial outpost in the South Pacific.

Audrey Singer's analysis of immigration to metropolitan regions during the twentieth century suggests that the combination of recent immigration and historical settlement patterns of earlier ethnic groups has produced six types of *immigrant gateway cities* (see Box 7.4). Singer's study of the immigrant gateway cities is important for our understand-ing of the effects of the new immigration on metropolitan regions across the country.

Box 7.4

Six Immigrant Gateway City Types

Former gateway cities: Above the national average in the percentage of immi-grants during 1900–1930, followed by percentages below the national average in every decade through 2000. This category includes cities such as Buffalo, New York, and Cleveland, which were destinations for large numbers of immi-grants in the early 1900s but no longer receive immigrants. Many of these older industrial cities are located in the Frost Belt.

Continuous gateway cities: Above-average percentage of immigrants in every decade of the twentieth century. Includes cities like Chicago and New York, which are long-established destinations for immigrants that continue to attract

continues

large numbers of foreign born. Many of these cities are located in the larger New York metropolitan region.

Post–World War II gateway cities: Low percentage of immigrants until after 1950, followed by percentages higher than the national average for the remainder of the century. Includes cities like Los Angeles and Miami, which were relatively small at the time of the Great Migration but have served as destinations for new immigrants in the past fifty years. Many of these cities are located in the Sun Belt.

Emerging gateway cities: Very low percentage of immigrants until 1970, followed by high proportions in the post-1980 period. Includes cities like Atlanta and Washington, which are located in metropolitan areas that nearly doubled in the 1980s and 1990s. They have experienced rapid immigrant growth in the past twenty years, and the total number of foreign born has increased five times during that period. With the exception of Washington, all are located in the Sun Belt.

Re-emerging gateway cities: Above-average percentage of immigrants during 1900–1930, below average until 1980, followed by rapid increases in post-1980 period. This category includes cities such as Seattle and Minneapolis-St. Paul, which were destinations for immigrants in the early twentieth century and now receive large numbers of immigrants. With the exception of the Twin Cities, all are located in the Sun Belt or in the West.

Pre-emerging gateway cities: Very low percentage of immigrants for the entire twentieth century. This category includes cities such as Salt Lake City, Utah, and Raleigh-Durham, North Carolina, which experienced rapid growth of both foreign-born and native-born populations between 1980 and 2000. They attracted significant numbers of immigrants in the 1990s and appear to be emerging as new immigrant gateway cities for the twenty-first century. With the exception of Salt Lake City, all are Sun Belt cities, and most are located in the Southeast.

There are important differences in demographics and settlement patterns among these six types of immigrant gateway cities. Some are located in fast-growing metropolitan regions in the Sun Belt, while others are located in older and larger metropolitan regions of the Midwest and East Coast that have experienced slower overall population growth. Some of the cities have become multicultural melting pots, while others are dominated by a relatively smaller number of ethnic groups. Singer notes that in the fast-growing emerging gateway cities such as Atlanta and St. Louis, immigrants are settling in communities that are greatly stressed by rapid population growth—a situation different from that of those who have moved to cities with a long history of immigrant settlement.

SOURCE: Singer, *The Rise of New Immigrant Gateways*, 2004:18.

One problem with the analysis—something that is discussed in the report—is the focus on the gateway city, because most of the new immigrants live in suburban towns within the metropolitan region, not in the central city. Our focus on the sociospatial perspective will help us to understand the importance of moving beyond the city and looking at the metropolitan region more broadly when we study immigration and other demographic trends that affect our communities.

Although it is common to speak of ethnic neighborhoods in American cities—and most of us are familiar with Chinatowns, Mexican neighborhoods, Greektowns, and the like—urban sociologists are more likely to talk about the ethnic enclave, a concept that emphasizes the ways in which work, residence, and other forms of social interaction overlap in urban space. Much of this research focuses on the paradox of the ethnic enclave: The positive effects that social networks can provide for new immigrants, and the negative effects of concentration and isolation within the enclave. Increasingly, we must think of ethnic enclaves not as simply ethnic settlements in the central city, as a majority of new immigrants now reside in suburban communities of the metropolitan region (Gorrie, 1991).

The new immigration already has had a profound effect on settlement space within metropolitan regions across the country (Suro and Singer, 2003). Some groups have moved into older ethnic neighborhoods, greatly expanding their numbers and size. In southwest Chicago, for example, the Mexican neighborhood in Eighteenth Street/Pilsen has expanded across the Twenty-sixth Street/Little Village community into suburban communities beyond the city limits, while the older Chinatown area near the Loop has seen extensive redevelopment that has doubled the number of business establishments and dwelling units. In these and other ethnic communities across the metropolitan region, local residents have constructed new settlement spaces rich with symbolic meanings—from Mexican storefronts identical to those found in Monterrey and Aguascalientes, the primary origins in Mexico for immigrants to Chicago and the Midwest, now reproduced in suburban settlement space, to a new riverfront park in the second Chinatown, designed by a Chinese American landscape architect, which reproduces traditional Chinese design elements in this new urban settlement space.

CONCLUSION:
ETHNIC AND CULTURAL DIVERSITY
ACROSS THE METROPOLIS

As this summary of settlement patterns for ethnic groups demonstrates, sociospatial relations continue to play a significant role in the lives of minority groups in the United States. Some groups have been able to move into the mainstream of American society and have gained access to employment, housing, and the quality of life that we believe all Americans should have. Others remain in segregated social spaces—ghettos, barrios, or reservations—where they are isolated from opportunities in the larger society.

In the years to come, these new sources of ethnic formation and ethnic identity will influence U.S. culture in ways we have yet to anticipate, just as the formidable influx of Eastern Europeans did some hundred years ago. At the beginning of the last century, many people feared that foreign workers would take away the jobs of American workers and dilute or destroy American institutions; yet those foreigners are now a permanent part of the American mosaic. In the 1990s, we had the lowest levels of unemployment in nearly half a century at the same time that immigration reached near-record levels, suggesting that immigrant workers need not take the jobs of American workers. Immigration was not a political issue. But in the first decade of the twenty-first century, we entered a period of prolonged economic crisis and one of the consequences has been a reexamining of immigration policy. In fact, some areas of the country, such as the extensive region bordering on Mexico in the Southwest, have local authorities that have become highly mobilized to stem illegal immigration, and the same increased vigilance is now characteristic of the federal government in managing flows of non-citizens into this country.

In a few short decades, the new immigrants of today will become part of an even greater American mosaic, living in ethnic neighborhoods if they choose to or living alongside other groups across the metropolitan region. Only time will tell what form this influence will take. Years ago it was proper to speak of an "urban mosaic" (a term used extensively by Robert Park) to capture the diversity of people and lifestyles in the city. Today the entire metropolitan region, both cities and suburbs, must be described this way. As we have seen, urban and suburban settlement space is stratified by class, race, and gender. They are also differentiated according to ethnicity, race, age, and family status. Each lifestyle manifests its own daily rhythm within the settlement spaces each group has created within the metropolitan region. The built environment displays the expressive symbols of this interaction between social factors and local territory. But settlement space also directs behavior in certain ways. In contemporary societies, it is likely that gender roles are conditioned as much by the spatial restrictions of the built environment as by patriarchal domination. Sociospatial relations among groups and individuals are also conditioned by class and race distinctions ranging from inclusion in neighborhoods of shared interests to the extreme case of ghetto segregation.

In the next chapter we shall examine, in more detail, minority populations in the United States as well as the important concepts of neighborhood and community that are used to understand urban daily life.

KEY CONCEPTS

class stratification
socioeconomic status
yuppies, dinks, suburban middle class
working poor

ghettoized poor
gendered space
women and the environment
waves of immigration
gateways of immigration

DISCUSSION QUESTIONS

1. What are the differences in lifestyles created principally by different access to economic resources?

2. Is there a difference between the middle-class lifestyle in the central city and the suburbs?

3. What are the differences between the working poor and the ghettoized poor and what do studies show about those differences?

4. Discuss the phenomenon of urban night life and its aspects.

5. What is the relationship between urban culture and city revitalization?

6. Discuss the issue of immigration and its consequences. What is the difference between attitudes toward immigrants in the late twentieth and the twenty-first century?

MINORITY SETTLEMENT PATTERNS, NEIGHBORHOODS, AND COMMUNITIES IN THE MULTICENTERED METRO REGION

Urbanized regions in the United States exhibit a wide array of different people, housing arrangements, and lifestyles. Cultural conditions, social constraints, and economic realities intersect to produce shifting patterns of settlement that often involve the movement of large groups. Social forces driving such change push minority populations with little power to resist so that their settlement can be considered involuntary in many cases. When it comes to creating a stable local environment for families and daily interactions that satisfy basic needs, all residents of the metro region have to create a sense of community and neighborhood well-being. These aspects of the human dimension of living in multicentered metro regions are the subject of the present chapter.

VOLUNTARY AND INVOLUNTARY MOVEMENTS OF MINORITIES

African Americans

Africans were forcibly removed from their home countries and brought to the United States as slaves during the 1700s. In 1990, their American descendants constituted 12.4 percent of the total population. Until the twentieth century, the overwhelming majority of blacks, more than 90 percent, lived in the South, and most were located in rural areas. Since the turn of the last century until the 1980s, there was a steady movement of African Americans to the North in general and to cities in particular (Lemann, 1991b). In the 1990s, however, some of this movement was actually reversed, as black people with the means and the education returned voluntarily to the South in significant numbers as part of the more general trend of Sun Belt relocation. In fact, the movement south outscored net gains of black migrants from all three of the other regions of the United States during the late 1990s, reversing a thirty-five-year trend according to recent census reports. Of the ten states that suffered the greatest net loss of blacks between 1965 and 1970, five ranked among the top ten states for attracting blacks between 1995 and 2000. Southern metropolitan areas, particularly Atlanta, led the way in attracting black migrants in the late 1990s. In contrast, the major metropolitan areas of New York, Chicago, Los Angeles, and San Francisco experienced the greatest out-migration of blacks during the same period. Among all ethnic or racial groups, African Americans with the means to do so were more likely than any other to move to the South. Furthermore, college-educated individuals led this new black migration back to the South in the 1990s. Georgia, Texas, and Maryland attracted the most black college graduates from 1995 to 2000, while New York suffered the largest net loss.

In the 1800s, many slaves fled the South for freedom. Using such routes as the Underground Railroad, they arrived in the cities of the North, and some even made it as far as Canada. By the end of the Civil War, several communities of African Americans were already established in northern cities. As a result of discrimination against blacks, however, these areas soon became segregated. A similar pattern of ghettoization occurred in the making of black communities in Chicago (Drake and Cayton, 1945; Spear, 1967), Philadelphia (W. E. B. DuBois, 1899), and New York (Osofsky, 1963).

At the turn of the last century, the mechanization of agriculture, coupled with the immense increase in industrialization with its job opportunities, both pushed and pulled blacks off southern farms and into northern factories. This process accelerated as a consequence of World War I, fell off during the Great Depression, and resumed with full intensity during World War II. As a result, by the 1950s African Americans were almost as urbanized as were whites, with over 60 percent of their total population living in cities. After 1950 a large percentage of whites began an exodus from the cities to the suburbs, which at the time were almost overwhelmingly closed to black migration. As a result, the percentage of African Americans living in central cities rose. By the 1980s, cities such as Los Angeles, Chicago, Atlanta, and Detroit had black mayors, and in the 1990s the list grew to include New York and others.

As we have seen, racial discrimination is still a potent force that prevents African Americans from integrating into society. For blacks, segregation into distinct ghetto areas of most cities still persists despite their large urban numbers. During the last two decades, a growing number of blacks have achieved middle-class status (Wilson, 1987) and live alongside white families in downtown high-rise apartment buildings, upscale city neighborhoods, and a wide range of suburban communities across the metropolitan area. However, much of the African American population remains highly segregated; in Chapter 9, we will discuss the immense problems this segregation poses for the quality of urban life. The sights and sounds of poverty and discrimination and the symbols of political struggle distinguish racial ghettos from other urban settlement spaces.

Hispanics

The Hispanic population in the United States has exploded. In 2002, the census fixed the population at 39 million Hispanics—the fifth largest concentration of Hispanics globally. It is estimated that by the year 2050, Hispanics in the United States will be the third largest Latin American concentration in the world. Although Los Angeles and New York contain the highest number of Hispanics in the United States, in recent decades other cities have experienced the fastest growth of Hispanic populations, including Atlanta; Orlando, Florida; and Charlotte, North Carolina.

Mexican Americans

The most important thing in discussing Mexican Americans is to point out the spatial component of their historical segregation in the United States. Their ghetto is known as "the barrio," and we now have, thanks to the entrance of informed Hispanic urbanists, a subfield analyzing the dynamics of the barrio—especially in the work of David Diaz (2005). He has studied the history of Hispanic residential life in the United States focusing on the Southwest. Because of language barriers and racism, Mexican Americans were confined to barrios and their needs were overlooked by government officials and planners. This state of affairs may finally be changing as Hispanics become the largest minority in the United States.

According to Diaz, "El Barrio—the central space, culture, conflict, and resistance of and within—is the foundation of Chicano/a Urbanism throughout the United States. In terms of spatial relations, it is historically a zone of segregation and repression." Uneven development, inflated rents, low-wage labor, lack of housing, and the worst abuses of urban renewal best characterize barrio life. "Conversely, within the context of everyday life, El Barrio is a reaffirmation of culture, a defensive space, and ethnically bounded sanctuary" (2005:3) and the spiritual center of Chicano/a and Mexicano/a identity.

For Diaz and other students of Mexican American urbanization in the United States, the social structure of the barrio was based on mutual aid. This is a characteristic of a true community and it is a source of obvious strength. According to Diaz, the barrio community exhibits:

> Collective forms of civic administration, construction, agriculture, social welfare, and local defense. Survival depended on the self-reliance and resources of the social network . . . in the mid-1900s, resistance and politicization, while continuing to center on labor issues and land issues, expanded to include education, political access and civil rights. Throughout, El Barrio served as the organizing platform to create networks of solidarity, support, and self-determination. Concurrently, Euro-Americans condescendingly viewed the culture of the barrio as seditious, threatening, and rebellious. These enclaves, in the perspective of racist America,

were 'untamed, revolutionary, conflictive and inferior,' typical terms used in the language of ethnic repression of internal minorities in the United States. (2005:3)

Diaz demonstrates how the neglect by municipal authorities and planners of barrio spaces, while other areas of the urban regions were developed for white Americans, created a permanent condition of uneven development where streets went unpaved, there was a lack of infrastructure—for example, sewer systems, water or gas lines—a lack of park facilities, and the use of barrios as places to locate industrial landfills of a toxic nature much as was the case in poor African American communities. Furthermore, "Inattention to these problems led directly to lower property appreciation rates among minority landowners, constant urban deterioration, private sector manipulation of a limited housing supply, and weak commercial districts. The result was virtually permanent uneven development in the barrios of the Southwest" (2005:5).

Diaz notes that more recent immigration of Mexicans to the United States has bypassed some of these barrios, especially in the largest cities of the Midwest and the Northeast. He mentions in particular Chicago and Kansas City, which quite recently experienced a large influx of immigrants from Mexico. In addition, the civil rights movement had an effect on the quality of life of Mexican Americans in the Southwest. Their greater political organization has led to increased political clout. "Challenges to restrictive housing policies, regressive banking practices, and affirmative action has transformed Chicano urban culture and society in the Southwest." Segregation barriers have broken down recently and an increasing number of Mexican Americans now live throughout the regions of the Southwest metro areas. Diaz also criticizes writers like Mike Davis and Ed Soja who have analyzed the regional development of Los Angeles in terms of global economic restructuring and ethnic demographic trends, but who have given insufficient attention to the ways the Mexican American population has had a land use and labor impact on Southwest cities like Los Angeles.

In particular, Gottdiener offered an explanatory model in relation to LA urbanism that has specific application to Chicano urbanism in Southern California. When addressing wedges, dispersed economic and political locations of different ethnic zones, urban cultural transitions, and political exclusion, along with a number of concurrent themes, the [geographer] proponents of Los Angeles are fundamentally revisiting Gottdiener's explorations of the "poly nucleated pattern of administrative decentralization." His articulations of Henri Lefebvre's new spatial theory in the central construct of how actual users read—create space in their own (cultural) image legitimates the significance of barrio culture in the context of an ethnicity bound to everyday life. (2005:10)

Diaz is especially concerned to criticize two proponents of what has come to be called the "Los Angeles approach to the Postmodern City": Michael Dear and Ed Soja.

Both of these geographers argued for the view in the late 1980s that Los Angeles was the model of a "postmodern" urban style of development. According to Diaz:

> 1980s Los Angeles featured increasing levels of inequality, affordable housing crises, endemic discrimination against minorities, massive corruption (due to a costly subway project), and police repression. Thus, when Soja proclaimed that society had arrived at a "postmodern geography" in 1989, the critical question was what had substantially changed in relation to urban form and social relations during the previous decade to justify his explanation of change? Has racism against Chicanos? Did the underground economy disappear or, rather, did wages improve? Has the LAPD internally reformed its practices? Was sprawl legislated out of existence to improve land-use relationships and sustainable environmentalism? Was LA's planning director fired? (2005:13)

Diaz, in response to these questions, goes on to say that the proponents of an alleged postmodern characteristic for Los Angeles had simply created a fiction. "Inequality and poverty remained at high levels, the affordable housing crisis had worsened, barrios in ghettos continued to deteriorate, sprawl continued unabated, the LAPD continued to practice extralegal violence, Asians were still enslaved in the garment district, and environmental crises were exacerbated. . . . The question thus becomes, what is postmodern about these 20-plus years of LA's urban history?" (2005:13).

In short, for Diaz one of the most important aspects of urban restructuring in the Southwest—from California to Texas—is the way Mexican American barrios have survived to the present period when, after the 1970s, the Mexican American population was able to spread out and inhabit all areas of the multicentered metro region while at the same time increasing its population numbers through immigration, despite the continued presence of the same old story of racism and oppression. It is this increased population presence with its newly realized political clout that is transforming the planning and the governance of southwest metro areas in the United States. Precisely for this reason, Diaz's concept of "barrio urbanism" represents a significant motive explanation for contemporary urban development in the United States.

Puerto Ricans

In 1898, the United States defeated Spain in a war of "manifest destiny" and acquired the former Spanish colonies of Cuba, Puerto Rico, Hawaii, and the Philippines. Since that time, Puerto Rico has been governed as a trust, or dependent territory, of the United States; while the island does not have statehood, Puerto Ricans are citizens of the United States and vote for a representative in the House of Representatives. Like other Caribbean countries, most of the population of Puerto Rico is mestizo—a racial mixture of various European and African ethnic populations—but with large white and black populations as well. For many years there was a small Puerto Rican presence in the United States, largely limited to Miami and New York, but in the decades after World War II this changed dramatically.

In the 1950s, labor shortages led the U.S. government to recruit workers from Mexico and the Caribbean. The Puerto Rican communities in Chicago, Philadelphia, and other cities were formed around this earlier migration of laborers from the island. Although Spanish Harlem in Manhattan may be the best known area of Puerto Rican settlement in the country, in the 1960s there was a large increase in Puerto Rican populations in many cities, especially in the Northeast. Like other ethnic groups, Puerto Ricans often settled into older neighborhoods in the central city. Because most Puerto Ricans are part black, some believe they confront greater discrimination in employment and housing than other Hispanic groups; in fact, Puerto Ricans rank alongside African Americans on many measures of poverty, unemployment, and family disruption.

In the 1980s, sociologists began to study the return migration of Puerto Ricans from the urban centers of the North to the home communities of their parents on the island (Alicea, 1990). Although the Puerto Rican population on the mainland has continued to grow from both natural increase and migration, many households and individuals have chosen to return to the island (a decision prompted by both a loss of basic employment in American cities and the discrimination that darker-skinned Puerto Ricans may encounter). While we often read of the "problems" of immigrant adjustment for ethnic groups arriving in the United States (as discussed earlier in this chapter), researchers have studied the adjustment of people returning to the island. Just as bilingual programs are required to teach immigrant children to speak English in public schools across the country, bilingual programs in Puerto Rico teach children coming from the United States to speak Spanish so that they can complete their education and find employment on the island.

Native Americans

The residential settlement patterns of Native Americans are especially interesting. Some Indian tribes continue to live in the same communities that Spanish explorers first visited in the 1500s; indeed, the Twelve Pueblo communities outside of Albuquerque, New Mexico, are the oldest continuously inhabited towns in the United States. Other Indian tribes were forced from their homelands by the Indian Removal Act of 1830. The Cherokees had by this time established permanent towns and schools but were forcibly removed from their homes in Georgia, Alabama, and Tennessee and relocated to reservation land in Oklahoma. During the 1870s, the United States ceased to recognize these people as belonging to independent nations, and they came under the administration of the Bureau of Indian Affairs.

While we often think of Native Americans as an isolated group living on rural reservations, they too are an urban population. It is estimated that half of the Native

American population lives in cities (with especially large concentrations in Los Angeles, Chicago, and Minneapolis), and in several areas of the country, Indian reservations are located adjacent to large cities (such as the Salt River and Gila Reservations outside of Phoenix) or within the boundaries of cities (such as the Oneida Reservation in Green Bay, Wisconsin). For many years, Native Americans suffered extreme poverty regardless of their residence in cities or rural reservations, and to some degree this is still true. But over the last two decades, many Indian tribes have prospered from economic development associated with casino gambling, although in many ways the patterns of uneven development endemic in the larger economic system have been replicated among Indian tribes across the country.

As we learned earlier, the federal government began cutting funding to states and cities in the 1970s. Instead of raising taxes to cover the additional expense of social programs, many states passed constitutional amendments that allowed them to run state lotteries. As a result, Indian tribes (sovereign nations with rights comparable to states) may run the same type of gambling enterprises (such as lotteries) as state governments. The rise of the Native American casino industry is a direct consequence of the fiscal crises of the federal and state governments. Many Native American reservations located close to urban centers have been able to generate substantial revenues from casinos. The actual development strategies used vary greatly from tribe to tribe. In Phoenix the Salt River Reservation has leased land to a development company that built and manages the largest shopping mall in the metropolitan area, while in Green Bay the Oneida Indian Nation has used profits from gaming to fund new health clinics and elder housing, purchase land within reservation boundaries lost in previous generations, and diversify into retail businesses and manufacturing companies. Many of these reservations have seen a population increase as tribal members living in cities across the country have returned to take advantage of employment opportunities that did not exist just two decades earlier. Yet uneven development may still be the rule; while tribes near urban areas have prospered, those in remote areas of the country have been unable to generate revenue from gaming and remain very poor. And within individual tribes, there still is substantial concern over high levels of poverty, family disruption, and low rates of high school completion.

It is often said that the urban Indian population is largely invisible. Lobo notes that "this invisibility or perceived elusiveness is tied directly to urban Indian community characteristics, including a dispersed, rather than a residentially clustered, population and individual mobility" (2005:1). While there are American Indian cultural centers in most large cities that serve as focal points for community activities, these centers serve households representing many different Indian tribes—groups that often are culturally distinct from one another. Over the last two decades, Indian populations have moved into many different areas of the city and for the most part do not form visible ethnic neighborhoods. For many families there is frequent travel back to Indian reservations to visit or care for relatives. Lobo concludes, "Urban Indian communities may, because they are dispersed and based on a network of relations, for the most part be invisible or misunderstood from the outside and to outsiders, but they are anything but invisible to those who participate in them. They are viable communities, but structured on an American Indian-derived model of community or tribe rather than a European-derived one" (2003:8).

Asian Americans

The Asian American population has increased dramatically over the past several decades; it is concentrated in large metropolitan areas and includes people from India, Pakistan, China, Korea, and Southeast Asia. Thus, this group represents very diverse ethnic populations with distinct cultural differences (language, religion, family structure, foods). Both the Chinese and the Japanese have been living in the United States for over a hundred years. Most large cities in the United States have a Chinatown that reflects the early immigration of Chinese laborers used by the railroads in the 1800s. There were significant Japanese communities in the Pacific states before World War II as well.

Filipinos are likely the most Americanized of the new Asian immigrants (the Philippine Islands became an American colony following the Spanish American War of 1898 and did not achieve independence until after World War II). Most of the Filipino immigrants in the United States are Catholic and speak English, which facilitates their integration into older urban neighborhoods as well as new suburban communities. The same can be said for recent Asian, Indian, and Pakistani immigrants, many of whom are educated professionals who experience little trouble adjusting to life in America.

Other recent ethnic Asians are Vietnamese, Laotian, Cambodian, and Hmong refugees from America's war against Vietnam. Hmong and Laotian people have settled in highly concentrated communities, such as Uptown in Chicago and the Midway neighborhood in St. Paul, Minnesota.

One suburban Asian community that has been studied in some detail is Monterey Park, a suburb outside Los Angeles that became a focal point for new Chinese immigration. In 1960, the population was 85 percent white. By 2000, more than 234,000 Asian persons were counted in the census, and the population was 43 percent Asian, 35.3 percent Hispanic, and just 21.6 percent white. Chinese accounted for 140,000 or 25.8 percent of the total, Vietnamese for 28,000 or 5.1 percent of the total, and Filipinos and Japanese for another 27,000 or 6.2 percent of the total. Much of the Chinese population consisted of new immigrants from China (Logan and Mollenkopf, 2003:67). By 1991, recent arrivals to the United States had invested over $1 billion in the suburb, and it was estimated that Chinese owned at least 66 percent of all businesses and property in the suburb (Espiritu and Light, 1991:43). For a time, the city was known as the "Chinese Beverly Hills," and it was later referred to as the first suburban Chinatown (Arax, 1987).

Timothy P. Fong (1994) studied the growth of the Chinese population in Monterey Park during the 1980s and 1990s. He identified three prominent changes that accompanied the development of this multicultural suburb from the early 1970s to the early 1990s. The first involved the economic transformation of the community that accompanied the influx of Chinese immigrants and capital. Pro-growth advocates welcomed the first groups of Chinese professionals who moved to the community, as well as overseas Chinese investors. This led to land speculation, uncontrolled construction, and increased commercial and home property values. This in turn led to the relocation of many longtime merchants to other communities, the development of strip malls as commercial properties were subdivided, and the replacement of single-family homes with multi-unit apartment complexes. The end result was greater density, increased traffic congestion, a loss of open space, and decreased parking. Fong notes that the new economic investment in Monterey Park included small-scale, low-profit, family-run businesses such as small restaurants, curio shops, and specialty stores owned by Chinese immigrant families with few English language skills; professional services such as medical, legal, accounting, and real estate offices run by college-educated Chinese Americans; and Chinese-owned and -operated financial institutions, including banks and savings and loans. The economic transformation of the community led to a backlash in the larger community and to comments such as, "This feels like a foreign country!"

The second stage in the development of Monterey Park involved the community's response to the challenge that the new Chinese immigrants presented to the dominant cultural values and to community identity more generally. Older residents looked back at what they recalled as the small-town lifestyle of the suburb and felt threatened by the social changes that accompanied economic development and the influx of Chinese immigrants. Other minority populations in the community, including many Hispanic and Asian American households, also felt threatened by the new immigrants. These sentiments were exploited by some in the community through a variety of anti-immigrant, anti-Asian, and English-only movements that were common across the United States in the 1970s. The economic transformation brought about by the new immigrant community was viewed by some in negative terms as the immigrant institutions began to compete for social and political recognition within the established culture of the older suburban community. When a group of progressive Asian, Hispanic, and white activists joined with pro-growth businessmen to promote multicultural issues, many in the community viewed the group as a political cover for developers and speculators. As Fong notes, race and ethnicity were now used as tools for political organizing (1994:175–176).

The third stage involves continuing efforts to deal with complex controversies resulting from racial, ethnic, and class conflict within the community. Older divisions of white against black, majority against minority, and the like are no longer sufficient to encompass the inter- and intra-ethnic differences among long-term residents (many of them minority) and new immigrants, Chinese Americans and immigrant Chinese, Chinese and other Asian American groups, and other divisions. Although Fong describes these as "prominent changes" that took place in the community, we refer to these changes as "stages of development" because they describe the experience of many other suburban communities where new immigrant communities have become established. The process is also described by Logan and Mollenkopf (2003) in their study of political representation in New York and Los Angeles in association with the demographic changes brought about by new immigration. In the first stage, native blacks and Hispanics become the majority or near majority in urban neighborhoods and then in entire cities. In the second stage, new immigrant groups replace native-born blacks and Hispanics to become the majority or near majority in urban neighborhoods. This results in a new, multicultural city where older racial cleavages have been "blurred and transformed" and where new multi-ethnic coalitions must be formed around common issues that unite rather than divide ethnic groups, classes, and immigrant generations within urban and suburban communities and across the metropolitan region.

NEIGHBORHOODS AND COMMUNITY

The Search for Community

Early urban sociologists in the 1920s and 1930s were preoccupied with whether urban settlement space produced differences in behavior, specifically when contrasted with the rural way of life. Hundreds of thousands of people left the farms and small towns of America and moved to the large industrial cities looking for work. At that time, sociologists worked with an idealized image of small-town life that was often expressed as a community in which everyone shared personal friendships. They believed that the intimacy of small-town life was the result of primary social relationships. In contrast, early researchers viewed cities as destroyers of intimacy, forcing secondary or anonymous relations on individuals based on business considerations rather than friendship, with a consequent loss of community feeling. In contrast to the "friendly" rural town, city people were believed to be unfriendly, rushed, uncaring, suspicious, and hard to get to know.

Louis Wirth, of the Chicago School, carried this idea forward. He believed that living in large cities resulted in forms of social disorganization such as increased crime, divorce, and mental illness because of the decline of close community ties. For Wirth it was the city itself, operating through a loss of community and demographic factors such as size and density of population, that produced urban behavior. When we go to a store in a city, we do not have, nor do we seek, a close relationship with the salesperson. We simply want service and wish to buy what we want as quickly as possible. Rural area residents, in contrast, are likely to already have established primary relationships with the employees and even the owners of local businesses and to live in a shared community. The same contrast applies to relations with neighbors in the city and rural areas. The domination of secondary relations in the city, Wirth believed, would result in negative effects such as crime and other problems. This assertion is known as the *social disorganization thesis* of urban life.

Field Research on Community

Following World War II, a number of sociologists decided to challenge Wirth's theory. Studying local neighborhoods within the larger cities, these sociologists discovered communities with strong primary relations among the residents (Whyte, 1955; Gans, 1962). In the 1960s and 1970s, a series of community studies contradicted the social disorganization thesis of the early Chicago School. Researchers discovered evidence of vital, healthy primary relations and an active community life in urban neighborhoods. Ulf Hannerz's (1969) remarkable study of an inner-city ghetto area in Washington, D.C., exemplifies the case study approach to community. This fine-grained analysis depicts ghetto residents as multidimensional human beings, trapped in the ghetto by racism and poverty. Hannerz could not find a single "characteristic" ghetto resident. Rather, he discovered a typology of behavioral patterns reflecting differences in individual character and family organization as each person dealt with racial and economic adversity in his or her own way. These results have been replicated in Elijah Anderson's (1978) ethnographic account of a black neighborhood on Chicago's South Side.

To the outside observer, densely populated inner-city neighborhoods seem chaotic. One sterling accomplishment of field research has been to document the order created out of urban chaos by city residents. Herbert Gans's (1962) classic field study of Boston's East End challenged the view that the area was a "slum" and discovered that life in this working-class community was highly organized around peer groups. Adult males spent leisure time with other males, adult females with their female friends, and so on. Once the form of social organization of the community was understood, it became a familiar place.

Other field research carried out in the 1950s and 1960s showed that primary relations and an intimate community life could be found in suburban areas of the metro region as well, despite a jaundiced view by urban professionals of the alleged anonymity of living in cookie-cutter, massive single-family housing developments, like Levittown. One of the earliest studies of suburban communities was William H. Whyte's *The Organization Man* (1956). Whyte studied the development of Park Forest South, a planned suburban community located twenty-five miles south of the Chicago Loop. His research depicts the classic suburb of the early postwar period as a place where nuclear families were housed in single-family detached homes, where women did not work but spent their time housekeeping and chatting over coffee with neighbors, and where men commuted into the city to corporate professional jobs. For more recent examples, see Baumgartner (1988), Jackson (1985), and Fishman (1987). These studies found that intimacy, friendship, and a sense of community of sorts, while different than the small towns of America, could also be found among the endless tract homes of suburbia. People want primary relations with others and they establish them no matter where they live. Unlike the theory of Wirth, neither the city nor the suburban environment can destroy this need through the social disorganization of mass society.

Box 8.1 describes a particular kind of community centered around a "bohemian" lifestyle that is viewed positively today as supplying the central city with a vibrant, creative culture. As discussed, these kinds of communities, such as Greenwich Village in Manhattan, North Beach in San Francisco, and Wicker Park in Chicago, have been a staple of city life for quite some time in the United States and have provided people pursuing an alternative lifestyle with a place to live and spend time.

Box 8.1

The New Bohemia

Richard Lloyd notes that while cities have always played an important role as incubators of cultural innovation, new ideas about the artist and his or her relationship to the city developed during the course of the nineteenth century, particularly in Paris. The Romantic paradigm viewed artists and poets as "exulted and often tortured geniuses" alienated from and often unappreciated by the larger society. The Latin Quarter in Paris developed from student quarter to intellectual community, described by Balzac in *Un Prince de la Bohème*, with the ideals of the bohemian lifestyle: hedonism and self-sacrifice, rejection of bourgeois values, and the primary of *l'art pour l'art* (art for art's sake). The hillside village of Montmartre would later displace the Latin Quarter as the center of bohemian life in Paris.

In the past, one had to look deeply to find bohemia in the United States; Greenwich Village in New York City was the original bohemian area in the United States, consciously drawing on the European example. After World War II, a new bohemian style developed—the beatnik—along with bohemian districts in San Francisco (North Beach) and Los Angeles (Venice Beach). In the last two decades, however, there has emerged an alternative nation, populated by struggling writers, thrift stores, indie rockers, and the omnipresent coffee house. Richard Lloyd explains how bohemia—once an exotic land confined to the metropolis—has become an ordinary thing in cities large and small across the country.

Bohemia has become an established district in even medium-sized cities and is promoted as a lifestyle amenity that increases property values. Richard Lloyd's

continues

ethnographic study is situated in Chicago's Wicker Park, once home to Frankie Machine, a junkie, in Nelson Algren's *Walk on the Wild Side*, later the site of violent gang warfare in the 1970s and 1980s, and finally the location of Rob Gordon's record shop, Championship Vinyl, in the 2000 film *High Fidelity*. Today Wicker Park is home to fashionable bars, art galleries, and high-tech start-up companies, as well as the people who work in them. Lloyd locates the new bohemia at the intersection of contemporary alternative cultures and the new forces of globalization; the locals are drawn to creative industries like media, advertising, and design and have a tolerance for other nonconformists; they are "creatures of the night" who flaunt thrift store clothes, piercings, and tribal tattoos, and they are the perfect workforce for the new creative industries, willing to work odd hours on a freelance basis at relatively low wages. The bartenders, baristas, and computer designers of Wicker Park have developed a lifestyle and values that are at odds with the suburban lifestyle, and to some degree, with mainstream society as well, as they have traded high wages for more regular jobs in the business world for the romance of bohemia.

SOURCE: Adapted from Richard Lloyd, *Neo-Bohemia* (2006) and *Bohemia* (2009).

Box 8.2 goes further and argues that people with enough energy and belief in the liberating qualities of community can actually produce their own city along the lines of alternative lifestyle. It describes the Burning Man festival, which takes place once a year in the desert of Arizona, where thousands of people practicing a liberated sense of self converge and create, at least for a few days, a complete city in a location that is barren the rest of the year. The report contained in Box 8.2 is important. By implication it asks the question whether people in declining areas of the United States and in other countries can marshal the same kind of energy in order to revitalize their communities without the aid of government programs or plans.

Box 8.2

The Truth About Burning Man

"Really?" the guy at the Alamo Rental Car place said when I'd told him about Burning Man. "I heard it was just a lot of naked people running around on drugs."

Coated in gypsum dust and still high not on drugs but on the altered consciousness of radical creativity and community, I had just tried to describe what Burning Man is, somehow. I think I'd said something like, "It's a temporary city of 50,000

continues

Box 8.2 *continued*

people, devoted to radical self-expression. So you'll find anything you'd find in a regular city—art museums, dance clubs, yoga studios—only in the middle of the desert, with no money, and with more creativity than you've ever seen."

Of the two descriptions, surely Rental Car Guy's is the more familiar. When Adam Lambert revealed that he'd gotten the idea to go on *American Idol* while on mushrooms at Burning Man, America groaned. The image, I assume, was of a drugged-out weirdo coming up with a loopy idea in the middle of a wild, crazy party.

The truth, though, is that Burning Man is an ideal place for self-reflection and self-transformation, whether substance-aided or not, and as someone who's just gotten back from his 8th Burn, Lambert's revelation didn't surprise me a bit. Friends of mine have changed their names, their professions, and their entire lives at Burning Man. And not because they were stoned or tripping, but because Black Rock City—the temporary city (built and erased within a month) where the event goes on every year, the week before Labor Day—has a tendency to expand horizons, reveal possibilities, and question the assumptions most of us make about how we're supposed to live our lives.

Burning Man does this, I think, because of a combination of factors. One of them is the sheer size and scope of the thing. 50,000 people. Hundreds of cars and trucks modified to look like dragons, whales, radios, and steamboats; many breathing fire; most with dozens of revelers dancing on them. It's like *Mad Max* meets *Blade Runner* meets *The Ten Commandments*, and it's real, it's actually happening.

And it's happening without capitalism. There's no vending at Burning Man—it's a gift economy. Entire "theme camps" exist just to give away spaghetti, to serve people free margaritas, to make pancakes. Yes, it does cost a lot to get in (between $150 and $350), but that mostly pays for the rental of the land from the government, the porta-potties and other infrastructure, and grants made to large-scale art projects. No one—not the celebrity DJs who were there this year, like Armin van Buuren and Carl Cox, and not the people who build the solar electrical grid—gets paid. No one is making a buck.

This is incredibly liberating. It's not sustainable, but it is a temporary autonomous zone of bullshit-free living. And just being there, just participating in the creation of an entire city devoted to what we want to do, rather than what we have to do to make money, has the tendency to invite self-reflection like Lampert's. Who am I? What do I really want to be doing? If people can create a twelve-ton sculpture of a bird's nest made entirely out of plumbing pipe, what are the limits on my own creativity? "Once you are free," said Baudrillard, "you are forced to ask who you are."

The temporary erasure of societal, social, and personal boundaries is, for most of us, terrifying. Such boundaries help build the structures of society and self; they

continues

give form to human life, which is often chaotic and unpredictable. Thus they have been the bedrock of religious and civil life for millennia, even before the Furies were imprisoned under Athens, and Moses descended from Sinai.

But if religion creates boundaries, mysticism and spirituality efface them. In the transcendence of ordinary distinctions, peak experiences such as those encouraged at Burning Man give a glimpse of the ultimate, the infinite. It may seem absurd to suggest that Burning Man is a mystical event. But then, if it's just a big party, why is there a temple in the middle of it?

SOURCE: Adapted from "The Truth About Burning Man" by Jay Michaelson, posted at *Huffington Post*, September 8, 2009 (http://www.huffingtonpost.com/jay-michaelson/the-truth-about-burning-m_b_279464.html?view=print).

Neighboring/The Neighborhood

Neighboring studies are important because they are related to the issue of community and territory. There is a conception of everyday life that places individuals within a nurturing neighborhood of friends and relatives. This conjunction of a certain space with an intimate circle of primary relations became the classic image of the community. Yet the terms *neighborhood* and *community* refer to different concepts. A neighborhood can be defined as any sociospatial environment where primary relations among residents dominate. If this connection of intimacy, or primary relations, is absent, such as the possibility of living in large city housing blocks, where apartment dwellers have little connection with one another, we can hardly call such an arrangement "a neighborhood." In contrast, the concept of community is often reserved for a spatial collectivity with an institutional component. That is, it can best be defined as a sociospatial environment that possesses an organized social institution that deals specifically with local matters (see below).

A defining characteristic of the neighborhood is the enjoyment of friendship circles among people living in the same section through the activity of "neighboring." It is a phenomenon that can be found in all sectors of the metro region—city and suburbs, small towns and large, apartment dwellers and single-family tract home developments. Neighboring and community involvement are strongly related to the life cycle—whether individuals are single or married, childless or with children. Most neighboring tends to be done by people raising families. The stereotypical image of suburbia as a place of neighboring may be the result of the fact that families with small children prefer to live there. However, inner cities were once the location for the baby boom with its massive concentration of families and children. Now, as a consequence of several decades of immigration-fueled inner-city growth and the general, explosive arrival of Hispanic populations, neighboring once again is ubiquitous in all metro region locations.

Areas of the metro region with active neighboring and a sense of community are considered important qualities for a sustainable area, whether there is active growth or decline. As we shall see below, when we discuss the characteristic of uneven development, having a quality neighborhood is not enough to ensure a sustainable quality of life.

THE DIFFERENCE BETWEEN NEIGHBORHOOD AND COMMUNITY

It is important to note that although these concepts are most often used interchangeably, they are not the same. As we have already seen, you do not have to be neighborly to belong to a neighborhood, and a community is best described as an area of the metro region with at least one institution that is focused on local well-being. Research on neighborhoods can describe local residential life, but they neglect to indicate connections to community organizations. In contrast, community studies provide evidence of specific links to sociospatial organizations in the area, an approach very much in keeping with the perspective of this text. For example, because of the importance of child rearing in suburban developments, most people living there belong to neighborhoods that they themselves can identify with, and they engage in frequent visits to neighbors. On the other hand, very few suburbanites can identify the "community" within which they live. Instead, they usually mention either their immediate tract home development name or the section of the metropolitan area with the county name. In contrast, people living in the inner city possess a different connection to their location. On the one hand, they may not be living in a neighborhood because they rely on a spatially dispersed network of intimates and most likely do not know their neighbors well. On the other hand, areas of the inner city are invariably provided with a community structure by urban planners and government officials. Commonly they can name their "community" when asked. These parts of the city contain block associations, local planning agencies, political districts, and strong religious institutions. All of these elements contribute to creation of a community with a name and political influence that local residents acknowledge.

Uneven Development: How to Have a Deteriorating Community

Not all communities possess well-being and not all neighborhoods function to provide residents with basic needs and opportunities for personal growth.

Capitalist development processes privilege the affluent and, unfortunately, in a society like our own, where social equilibrating mechanisms are weak, many inner-city and older suburban communities deteriorate due to uneven development. The forces that contribute to decline are important to study because they also operate in the real estate industry to selectively channel investment to some places rather than others, leading to boom-and-bust cycles of growth and decline.

The well-being of neighborhoods and communities in the United States remains important because their public resources are the avenues with which individuals can better themselves and lead a productive life. According to recent research, "Access to decent housing, safe neighborhoods, good schools, useful contacts, and other benefits is largely influenced by the community in which one is born, raised, and currently resides" (Squires and Kubrin, 2005).

Squires and Kubrin say that the opportunity structure of the United States is highly dependent upon the place in which you were raised—in other words, where you live. The authors also say that race matters and they examine the interaction between race and place. They come to the conclusion that uneven development in metropolitan America "is a direct result largely of a range of locational quality decisions made by public officials and policy related actions" in combination with the pursuit of profits by the private sector. They echo the sociospatial approach of this text, which claims that capitalist forces and government programs work in tandem to benefit some people, but not all—generally the well-off and the upper middle class. In the urban scene surveyed by Squires and Kubrin, "The linkages among place, race, and privilege are shaped by three dominant social forces—sprawl, concentrated poverty, and segregation—all of which play out in large part in response to public policy decisions" and the real estate practices of private institutional actors. "This perspective emerges from what has been referred to as 'the new urban sociology' . . . which places class, race, and relations of domination and subordination at the center of analysis" (2005:47). When these three forces are in motion as regional growth working all parts of the urban area, they create a pattern of uneven development that discriminates against less affluent residents by producing deteriorating neighborhoods while other areas grow and prosper. Anyone with the time and access to a car can travel through an American city and discover the pattern of uneven development, of well-being and deterioration, often existing in proximity, that is the material evidence of capitalist investment decisions biased against the less affluent that our society fails to counteract by social programs. Consequently, while the notion of community is believed to benefit people who have it in their neighborhoods, not every area blessed with intimate social relations prospers simply because of it.

For example, "Education has long been regarded as the principal vehicle for ameliorating the chance occurrence of belonging to a low-income family. But in our society, reliance on local property taxes to fund public education nurtures inequality in the nation's schools and this is a feature expressly tied to place. Although some communities have introduced equalization formulas that ensure quality education in all areas regardless of family incomes and value of homes, wealthy communities still provide substantially greater financial support for public schools, with a lesser tax effort, than poor ones" (2005:53).

Educational quality can help individuals, regardless of family circumstances, better themselves. And as we have seen, it is largely dependent on spatial location and the ability of a family to purchase a home in an affluent area with good schools. More directly, "If there is one single factor that is most critical for determining access to the good life, it might be employment. This is particularly true in the U.S. where individuals and households are far more dependent on their jobs to secure basic goods and services than is the case with virtually all other industrialized nations that provide far more extensive social welfare" (2005:54). As of 2000, "No racial group is more physically isolated from jobs than blacks, and those metropolitan areas with higher levels of black-white housing segregation were those that exhibited higher levels of spatial mismatch between the residential location of blacks and the location of jobs" (2005:54). In short, although job creation is an ongoing feature of a growing economy, the exact location of employment openings most often occurs in areas of the multicentered metro region that are difficult to get to for less affluent and often ghettoized residents. Our society, compared to other industrialized nations, has shockingly poor mass transportation. Without adequate means of commuting, the ability of job seekers to find employment, even when openings are plentiful and can be filled by people with limited education, remains highly problematic. Uneven development is not just a spatial issue or characteristic. It is also a product of the failure of a society to overcome the "friction of space" through the production of an adequate mass transportation infrastructure. All those people who wait obscenely long hours for a bus or train or those who commute in cars stuck in traffic jams know full well the negative aspects of American everyday life.

In short, community and neighborhood well-being have always been considered an important even defining quality of a well-functioning society. We can measure the outcome of failed social and private sector patterns of development that work against that quality of everyday life by the evident patterns of uneven development visible in the array of areas within the metro region. Disparities are not a temporary phenomenon where an effort of "catch-up" can solve the dilemma. As we have seen, instead, uneven development is an active part of how our system of political economy operates. In our chapters on other societies later in the text, principally those of Europe, we will revisit the issues of inequality and community well-being. We will see that despite more active government policies to equalize the capitalist tendency of uneven development, not all problems caused by it can easily be solved.

NEW FORMS OF COMMUNITY

Gated Communities

The United States has always had affluent communities that sought to seal themselves off from the general population. In the late 1800s, developments of this type appeared around most major cities as wealthy people used incorporation to create their own exclusive enclaves. Tuxedo Park outside New York City, and Pasadena and Beverly Hills in the Los Angeles area, are just three examples. During the 1980s and 1990s, when affluent seniors began to relocate to the Sun Belt, a different kind of exclusive development emerged using security services and barriers. Places with these arrangements, where visitors and residents alike must stop at a security post in order to gain access, are known as "gated communities." Country clubs and resorts are some early examples but many are retirement developments where security is considered a premium. In 2004 the government estimated that over 4 million people in the United States live in gated enclaves that were both walled and had entryway guards or keyed gates. Exclusive developments that seal themselves off by means of very tight security measures can be found in all parts of the metropolitan region, including areas of the city as well as the suburbs. However, most people associate such communities with Sun Belt suburban living. Researchers such as Sanchez, Lang, and Dhavale (2005) note that the exclusivity of gated communities gives residents a feeling of high status, a sense of community, and a sense of control over local services. Through regular scheduled meetings, residents often have the experience of more direct contact with the neighbors and more involvement in the governance of their local area. According to their report:

> For most people, the term "gated community" conjures up images of exclusive developments with fancy homes and equally fancy lifestyles. Much of the popular and academic literature on TV communities promotes this view. Yet the common perception of jaded communities as privileged enclaves turns out to be only partly correct based on our analysis of the first-ever census survey of these places. There are gated communities composed of mostly white homeowners with high incomes that have a secure main entry—the kind of classic gated community in the public mind. But there are also gated communities that are inhabited by minority renters with moderate incomes. We expected that this dichotomy reflects a distinction between communities, one based on status versus one motivated by concern for security. (Sanchez, Lang, and Dhavale, 2005:281)

Common Interest Developments

Another kind of community that can be found in all areas of the MMR is the common interest development or CID. Basically a CID is an area of housing that requires membership in a homeowners' association. Examples range from condominium associations in central city high-rises and housing quadrants to suburban developments of single-family homes as well as organized associations that have arisen in older sections of the central city in order to defend themselves from such things as crime, deteriorating housing, and a decline in government services. Residents of CIDs often express

greater satisfaction living in such places than residents of either cities or suburbs who
do not have local representation in a homeowners' association. According to Evan
McKenzie in his book *Privatopia* (1996), billions of affluent homeowners have taken
advantage of CIDs and actually secede from urban America "with its endless flux and
permits, its spontaneity and diversity and its unpredictable awards and hazards." Now
they live in "a privatized, artificial, utopian environment where master planning, homogeneous populations, and private governments offer the affluent a chance to escape from urban reality." The downside of such communities is that residents must
live under the rule of the homeowners' association directors who enforce restrictions
that everybody must comply with, such as the inability to alter the outside of their
homes, size restrictions, number restrictions on pets, control of garbage collection,
and late-night noise restrictions. McKenzie is most concerned about CIDs that are
produced by large developers that concentrate people on smaller areas of land than
what area governments mandate in order to realize more profit. Residents accept this
type of zoning because the CID provides them with greater security and more communal amenities than can be found in ordinary housing developments. Critics of this
kind of housing arrangement view it as drastically cutting people off from the regularly governed aspects of the metropolitan region in such a way that the enclave residence no longer needs to have any responsibility for the people living in the larger
society. In this sense CIDs are considered an extreme case of privatization that works
against the public interest as a whole.

Gay and Lesbian Communities and Urban Life

Almost without exception, when the issues of neighborhood and community are discussed in urban sociology textbooks, the overriding assumption is that they are peo-
pled by heterosexual individuals and/or couples. Only recently has that perspective
been challenged by a new generation of researchers concerned about the dynamics of
"queer space." Aside from the presence of gay, lesbian, and transgendered community networks in urban regions, researchers have uncovered differences in the way interaction among people belonging to the "queer" community is structured. "While
gay men have often produced highly visible territorial enclaves in inner-city areas,
lesbian forms of territoriality at the urban scale have been relatively 'invisible' since
their communities are constituted through social networks rather than commercial
sites. Contrasting the patterns produced by these two populations in the inner-city
areas of postindustrial cities during the 'queer' 1990s has created a gender-polarized
and historically specific interpretation of their patterns of territoriality and visibility
that may differ significantly from those of earlier periods" (Podmore, 2006:595).

A key finding of research into gay, lesbian, and transgendered communities
echoes aspects of Lefebvrian theory: such places have to be produced; they do not
appear whole cloth within urban areas. While it is true that sections of cities, such as

the West Village in New York and the Castro in San Francisco, are well known homosexual neighborhoods, in all urban areas, nonheterosexuals must produce the spaces within which they can commune. As one observer notes, "Just as individual persons do not have pre-existing sexual identities, neither do spaces. In other words, space is not naturally authentically 'straight' but rather actively produced and (hetero) sexualized" (Binnie, 1997:223). The production of queer space, then, for these commentators, occurs as a kind of resistance and liberation from heterosexualizing social forces trying to claim space within urban areas for normative activities. The production of gay communities, therefore, is a form of activism.

Keeping in mind the remarks of Podmore on lesbian life, then, we can also observe that the production of queer spaces differs between gay men and women. The latter's mode of liberation and activism is less tied to material neighborhoods and more characterized by active networking, even if both genders, like heterosexual males and females, rely on commercial establishments for socializing outside the home. Social networks are a way of viewing lifestyles that have less need of actual urban spaces. They are sometimes referred to as "communities without propinquity," and they represent another kind of sociality found in urban regions.

SOCIAL NETWORKS AS COMMUNITIES WITHOUT PROXIMITY

In the 1970s, researchers examined the way people connected with others within the expanding metropolitan region. Suburbia provided examples of many middle class residents who had no strong attachments to the places they lived. Yet they participated actively in social networks spread across space that could be considered a kind of community. For some, the local country club provided a grounding point for weekly interaction. But as active consumers, networked people belonging to "communities without propinquity" meet good friends, if not neighbors, in a variety of places and circumstances stretching across the region. The same can be said for city dwellers who were also found to possess a list of intimates with whom they communed without living in proximity to them. What counts in this kind of non-place social structure is not the distance between people but their common interests and their ability to connect with each other whenever they want through transportation, mobile phone, land lines, and the Internet (Fischer, 1975; Wellman, 1979; Koopomaa, 1998).

Current research using network analysis of community relations suggests that while spatial location matters, its effects are not significant. Other factors, such as class, education, gender, and race, are most important when explaining how people choose friends and how they socialize. However, because network researchers look at the role of space in only a very specific way, they miss important influences of the built environment that are derived from external factors such as physical well-being of neighborhoods or the level of crime. Furthermore, research on inner-city neighborhoods reveals that people with limited means, such as the poor and the elderly, require intimates that are close at hand. They are not the kind of far-ranging networkers studied by that group of academics. Thus, network research has a built-in class bias. Even in suburbia, middle-class mothers with children tend to have friends who are in proximity to their house. Children play with other children next door or down the street whether they live in the inner city or the suburbs. Mothers make friends as a consequence of being together while supervising their offspring. Consequently, when networkers talk about the importance of their approach to the study of communities, they often hide a gender bias, in addition to short-changing a focus on the effects of class, especially the way gender and class affect the behavior of women with children.

SUMMARY

In Chapter 7, we surveyed the diversity of metropolitan life. We saw that lifestyles are a consequence of the interaction between compositional social factors, such as class and race, and specific territorial relations that assign particular individuals to particular places within the metropolitan region. In this chapter, we considered how living and working arrangements foster types of community. Many of the discussions about ways of life have suggested that spatial location can influence behavior. Thus, while the previous chapter considered how people are organized into places, this chapter deals with the question of how places influence behavior. Such balanced considerations are in keeping with the sociospatial perspective, which claims that space operates in a dual way as both a product and a producer of behaviors in society.

According to the arguments of urban sociologists, spatial location per se has little effect on lifestyles, which are better explained by compositional factors. Even a person's sense of community has much more to do with his or her network of intimate friends and kin than with where he or she lives. Yet the degree to which a community without place characterizes people's lives varies according to compositional factors such as class and gender, age and race, and ethnicity and religion. Hence the localized, territorially specific community remains important to the way people organize their daily lives. This holds equally true for single, middle-class professional women alone in the city, for poor black men who are disadvantaged because of racial oppression, and for aged central city dwellers, all of whom need the sustaining resources of local neighborhoods and vital community relations.

Space affects behavior in other ways. We orient ourselves in particular places by assigning meaning to space. All objects are meaningful to us. The meanings of space and the objects of the built environment help us organize our everyday lives. This sociospatial process utilizes particular mechanisms in ordering public interaction. We recognize the cues of behavior and acquire street wisdom by repeated use of public space. Our interpretations of behavior require an understanding of spatial context. Spatial context, in short, is a principal component of meaning.

Finally, we have discussed how the metropolitan region is diversified not only with regard to the individuals who live there, but also with regard to the types of neighborhood ties and commitments to community that can be found in particular settings. Sociologists have produced a long list of studies that document the diversity of neighborhood types and community relations in both urban and suburban settlement spaces. An understanding of such differences helps us overcome stereotypical thinking about the people of cities and suburbs.

While the richness of social life across the multicentered metropolitan region was examined in some detail in the last two chapters, metropolitan life also presents problems and challenges. The next chapter considers how metropolitan problems result from the interaction of social, cultural, and spatial factors both within and beyond the metropolis.

KEY CONCEPTS

voluntary and involuntary minority status
African Americans
Hispanic Americans
Native Americans
Asian Americans
the search for community
field research
neighborhood
uneven community development
gated communities
common interest developments
gay and lesbian communities
community without proximity
social networking

DISCUSSION QUESTIONS

1. What is the difference between voluntary and involuntary minority movement?
2. Recently there has been diversity in the locational settlement of African Americans. What are some of the changes?
3. The Hispanic population in the United States is quite diverse. What are some of the differences?
4. What is the significance of the barrio for Mexican Americans?
5. Discuss the new Asian immigration and how it has led to diversity of this population in the United States. How does the evolution of Monterey Park relate to this diversity?

6. What is the nature of community? How do you define "neighborhood"? What is the difference between community and neighborhood?

7. Discuss the pros and cons of gated communities. Why do people choose to live in these communities?

8. Why are cities often the sites of gay and lesbian communities, and why do gay people like to live in them?

9. What have sociologists discovered about the process of social networking? How does social networking relate to the organization of life in the metro region?

10. What is meant by "community without proximity"?

CHAPTER

9

METROPOLITAN PROBLEMS

Racism, Poverty, Crime, Housing, and Fiscal Crisis

Until recently, urban problems were city problems. That is no longer the case as the issues once associated with the large, compact settlement form have spread out, like the metropolitan population and its economic activities, to characterize the entire urban region. In the late 1960s and 1970s, especially during President Johnson's Great Society, urban problems were defined almost exclusively as those involving racial segregation, poverty, violent crime, and drugs. Now, in the first decade of the twenty-first century, poverty, unemployment, foreclosures, and homelessness, as well as the severe economic recession itself, are particular issues of concern. As the attention of the federal government in Washington, D.C., focuses on the major issues of the economy and health care, the nation's state governments seem to be ignored. Consequently, adding to our other urban ills, we currently face more intense fiscal crises and their impact on local public services and infrastructure.

Was there ever a baseline in America against which the problems of today can be measured? As in the other industrialized capitalist countries of Europe, the quality of urban life with the advent of capitalism in the 1800s was severe for all but the wealthy. Early photographic images of American cities at the turn of the last century feature overcrowding: immense traffic jams of primitive Model-T automobiles mixed in with horse-drawn carts, tenements teeming with immigrants, and crowds of children swarming across city streets. Until after World War II, city life in the United States was plagued by frequent public health crises such as cholera outbreaks, high infant mortality rates, alcoholism, domestic violence, street gang activity, and crime. For much of our history, then, city life has been virtually synonymous with social problems. Yet we know now that these same problems—crime, disease, family breakup— are experienced everywhere.

The sociologists of the early Chicago School, in the 1920s and 1930s, believed that the move to the city was accompanied by social disorganization. While subsequent research showed that this perception was inaccurate, people in the United States still rank small and middle-size cities or suburbs as providing the highest quality of life and

209

remain overwhelmingly interested in living in suburbs, especially for couples with small children. The negative perception of the large city provides the basis for varying mental images of place. Yet we have also seen that there are many positive aspects of urban living and that the early belief in the loss of community among migrants to the city was unfounded.

In previous chapters, we have tried to show that problems that appear to afflict individuals are caused in part by factors that we cannot readily see. Consequently, an explanation for the social disorganization often viewed in an individual's fate lies in the particular combination of adverse life decisions, personal circumstances, and more structural social factors, such as lack of adequate education, racism, poverty, and the specific effects of spatial segregation and uneven development. This chapter applies the sociospatial approach to metropolitan problems. One purpose of our discussion is to explore whether or not large cities in particular and metropolitan regions in general possess unique features that might propagate specifically "urban" problems.

THE SOCIOSPATIAL APPROACH
TO SOCIAL PROBLEMS

Social problems are ubiquitous across the metropolitan areas of the United States. Cities do not have an exclusive hold on divorce or domestic violence, and suburbs are now almost as likely as cities to be afflicted with family disorganization, deviant subcultures, drug use, and gang activity (Barbanel, 1992). Many suburban areas have crime rates comparable to those of the central city. As the suburban settlement spaces have matured, differences in poverty levels, crime rates, and other measures of social disorganization have become less. If it appears clear that urbanism by itself is not a generator of social problems, it is also clear that cultural approaches can no longer identify unique differences between city life and life in other developed places.

We know from our earlier explorations of the sociospatial approach that the spatial environment plays an important role in human interaction. The *social background factors* associated with population groups are also important. The variety of lifestyles found across urban and suburban settlement spaces result from social factors such as race, class, and gender. Social problems in particular are caused by poverty, racial exclusion, gender differences, and the severe patterns of uneven development within settlement space that results in differential access to resources and determines a person's life chances. On the other hand, spatial forms still matter. Environments intensify or dissipate these compositional effects of uneven development. In short, ways of life result from an interaction between social factors and spatial organization.

Cities are not unique in having acute social problems, but the spatial nature of large cities and densely populated suburbs makes the uneven development resulting from the inequities of race, class, gender, and age particularly severe. According to the sociospatial approach, the following factors are the most significant.

First, the principal effect of the city as a built environment is that it concentrates people and resources (Lefebvre, 1991; Engels, 1973). Thus, social problems such as drugs and poverty have a greater impact in large central cities and densely populated suburbs than in less dense areas. In confined urban space under the jurisdiction of a single municipal government, it is the sheer numbers, such as the frequency of murders and rapes or the number of "crack babies," that turn social problems into grave concerns.

Second, over the years urban populations have been disproportionately affected by the internationalization of the capitalist economies. For example, large metropolitan regions such as Los Angeles or New York are the destinations of choice for most immigrants from poorer nations who have left their countries in search of a better life. With the flow of immigrants comes specific problems, such as the need for bilingual education, that affect these areas more than other places.

Changes in the global cycles of economic investment also affect metropolitan regions because of the scale of activities in the largest places. For example, after Wall Street stocks plunged in October 1987, more than 100,000 trained professionals were laid off from brokerage and financial service firms in Manhattan, and throughout the 1990s, staggering job losses occurred in many areas as U.S. companies sought to increase their profits and earnings. Job loss on this scale presents a particularly acute problem for cities.

Finally, social problems are caused by the allocation of resources, which may be accentuated in dense, built environments. For example, large cities are major centers of the global economy. Extreme wealth is created within their boundaries, and the signs of that money are highly visible in the city, such as expensive restaurants, upscale department stores, luxury housing, and limousines. Close by, in the concentrated space of the city, are people who suffer the most terrible consequences of abject poverty, such as homelessness, malnutrition, and chronic unemployment. Because this contrast is so visible, the issue of uneven development is particularly oppressive to inhabitants.

In summary, social problems that can be considered uniquely urban derive from the concentrated nature of metropolitan space and the scale of changes in compositional factors. In this chapter, we consider a number of problems often associated with urban life, including racism and poverty, crime and drugs, fiscal problems such as declines in educational quality and infrastructure problems, and, finally, housing inequities and homelessness.

RACISM AND POVERTY

Racism

The most extreme and continuing effects of racism have been felt by African Americans, who have been systematically discriminated against in employment and in the

housing market. As a consequence, their social mobility has been severely constrained. The most powerful indicator of continuing institutional racism in the
United States is population segregation. In Chapters 10 and 11, when discussing
cities around the globe, we will also encounter the phenomenon of population segregation. But nowhere is the racial nature of this sociospatial effect as clear as in metropolitan areas across the United States.

The classic study of segregation is by the Taeubers (1965). They compiled statistics on American cities with regard to the relative locations of whites and blacks. To
measure segregation, they constructed a very useful concept, an "index of segregation." If a city had a 30 percent African American population as a whole, they expected, in the absence of segregation, that the black population would be evenly
distributed across space. The index of segregation refers to the percentage of African
Americans who would have to move in order for all neighborhoods to reflect the 30
percent black composition of the entire city. If a neighborhood were 90 percent
black, 67 percent of the black population would have to move, resulting in an index
of .67.

On the basis of the Taeubers' study, all U.S. cities were discovered to be highly
segregated, that is, with indexes above .50 for African Americans. The Taeubers
replicated their study in the 1970s and found little change in the degree of black
population clustering. Some of the most segregated cities during the 1970s were Detroit; Chicago; Buffalo, New York; Cleveland; and Birmingham, Alabama.

Some have argued that not all of the segregation observed in American cities is the
consequence of involuntary segregation; the spatial cluster of population groups can
also be voluntary. In the case of African Americans, however, we know that the urban
ghettos were created by a form of racism and violence designed to prevent blacks from
moving into "white" settlement spaces, federal housing policies that concentrated
public housing in the inner city while subsidizing "white flight" to the suburbs
through construction of the interstate highway system and home mortgage loans, and
other factors. Bullard and Feagin (1991), for example, discuss various techniques used
by housing-related institutions to prevent blacks from locating where they prefer,
thereby fostering involuntary segregation. This is an example of institutional racism.

Rental and real estate agents also use a variety of methods to prevent blacks from
locating in white-owned areas. One mechanism is called steering. When an African
American couple comes to a rental or real estate agent, the agent will steer the couple
to areas of the city populated by blacks. Agents may also simply refuse to divulge the
existence of housing opportunities in white areas. Despite gains in family income
earnings by a growing number of middle-class blacks, racial segregation remains a
fact of life for the majority of African Americans.

The sociospatial effects of racism on African Americans are also illustrated by
comparing their position with that of other minorities. In metropolitan areas where
minorities were at least 20 percent of the population—that is, where they were pres-

ent in sufficient numbers to perhaps overcome prejudice—Hispanic Americans were highly segregated in only two of the thirty-three metropolitan areas. In contrast, "blacks are highly segregated in 31—two-thirds—of the 47 metro areas where they make up at least 20 percent of residents, including Detroit, Chicago, Miami, Birmingham, Ala." (*USA Today*, "Segregation: Walls Between Us," 1991:A-2).

Since the time of the Taeubers' study, researchers of spatial segregation have developed more precise measures of population clustering. The most sophisticated of these studies combine several different measures to arrive at overall estimates of segregation. They found that black people not only continue to be segregated in significant numbers within central cities, but their exclusion is now extreme. Those that remain ghettoized are extremely isolated because for decades all Americans—black, white, Hispanic—with the means and opportunity to move away from such areas have done so. Consequently, rather than social conditions improving for poor African Americans, their extreme segregation in our nation's cities is now described as "hypersegregation." Douglas Massey and Nancy Denton (1993), for example, used five different measures of population clustering in their study of the causes and consequences of racial segregation in Chicago and other cities while discovering the deteriorating conditions of hypersegregation.

1. *Unevenness:* African Americans may be distributed so that they are overrepresented in some areas and underrepresented in other areas.
2. *Isolation:* African Americans may be distributed so that they have little interaction with other groups.
3. *Clustered:* Black neighborhoods may be tightly clustered to form one contiguous enclave, or they may be scattered about in checkerboard fashion.
4. *Concentrated:* Black neighborhoods may be concentrated within a very small area, or they may be settled sparsely throughout the urban environment.
5. *Centralized:* Black neighborhoods may be spatially centralized around the urban core or spread out along the periphery.

These five dimensions define geographic traits that social scientists think of when they consider segregation. A high score on any single dimension is serious because it removes blacks from full participation in urban society and limits their access to benefits. As segregation accumulates across multiple dimensions, however, its effects intensify. The indices of unevenness and isolation we have discussed so far cannot capture this multidimensional layering of segregation and therefore understate its severity in American society. Not only are blacks more segregated than other groups on any single dimension of segregation, but they are also more segregated on all dimensions simultaneously; and in an important subset of U.S. metropolitan areas, African Americans are highly segregated on at least four of the five dimensions at once, an extreme isolating pattern that they call hypersegregation.

Thus one-third of all African Americans in the United States live under conditions of intense racial segregation. They are unambiguously among the nation's most spatially isolated and geographically secluded people, suffering extreme segregation across multiple dimensions simultaneously. Black Americans in these metropolitan areas live within large, contiguous settlements of densely inhabited neighborhoods that are packed tightly around the urban core. In plain terms, they live in ghettos.

Typical inhabitants of these ghettos are not only unlikely to come into contact with whites within the particular neighborhood where they live; even if they traveled to the adjacent neighborhood they would still be unlikely to see a white face; and if they went to the next neighborhood, no whites would be there either. No other group in the contemporary United States comes close to this level of isolation within urban society. U.S. Hispanics, for example, are never highly segregated on more than three dimensions simultaneously, and in 45 of the 60 metropolitan areas examined, they were highly segregated on only one dimension. Moreover, the large Hispanic community in Miami (the third largest in the country) is not highly segregated on any dimension at all. Despite their immigrant origins, Spanish language, and high poverty rates, Hispanics are considerably more integrated in American society than are blacks. (Massey and Denton, 1993:74–77)

The negative effects of hypersegregation were amply illustrated when Hurricane Katrina hit New Orleans in 2005. Hundreds of thousands of poor black people were living in that city in strict isolation. Their neighborhoods were also the site of the lowlands and landfills that were below sea level and protected only by a series of dikes and channels from being underwater. This area is poor land, a poor person's hyperghetto, and a very risky place to live. Hurricane Katrina devastated this area when the dikes broke, leading to death and dispersal on an unprecedented scale in this country. The total failure of the federal government under former president George W. Bush to deal adequately with this crisis is a frightening example of how little our society cares for poor minorities and the neighborhoods in which they live. Box 9.1 summarizes the tragedy of Katrina and its indictment of our society.

From the information presented in these and other studies, it is clear that the major determinant of racial segregation is not a person's income, social class, or length of time spent in the United States (as suggested by the assimilation model) but rather racial background. African Americans confront the highest levels of segregation while Asian Americans have the lowest levels. Racial background is also important in determining segregation for various ethnic groups within these categories: Puerto Ricans are more segregated than Mexicans, for example. Cultural factors such as language and religion are associated with the level of segregation for particular ethnic groups. For example, Asian Indian and Filipino immigrants are likely to speak English and are familiar with American schools and government and consequently encounter much less segregation than other Asian American populations.

Box 9.1

Hurricane Katrina

Formed on August 23, 2005, and hitting New Orleans on Monday, August 29, Hurricane Katrina was the largest natural disaster in U.S. history with estimated damages at more than $100 billion, and one of the five deadliest. "The federal flood protection system in New Orleans failed at more than fifty places. Nearly every levee in metro New Orleans was breached as Hurricane Katrina passed just east of the city limits. Eventually 80% of the city became flooded and also large tracts of neighboring parishes, and the floodwaters lingered for weeks. At least 1,836 people lost their lives in the actual hurricane and in the subsequent floods."

Initially, hundreds of thousands of residents were displaced, with many having to start new lives in other cities. Four years later, thousands of former residents continued to live in makeshift trailers, some of which were discovered to be giving off toxic fumes. Reports and several books have blasted the Bush administration's handling of this massive disaster along with the dubious choice of former president Bush's appointed head of the Federal Emergency Management Agency, or FEMA, Michael D. Brown.

"In a September 26, 2005, hearing, former FEMA chief Michael Brown testified before a U.S. House subcommittee about FEMA's response. During that hearing, Representative Steven Boyer (R-IN) inquired as to why President Bush's declaration of state of emergency of August 27 had not included the coastal parishes of Orleans, Jefferson, and Plaquemines. (In fact, the declaration did not include *any* of Louisiana's coastal parishes, whereas the coastal counties were included in the declarations for Mississippi and Alabama.) Brown testified that this was because Louisiana governor Blanco had not included those parishes in her initial request for aid, a decision that he found "shocking." After the hearing, Blanco released a copy of her letter, which showed she had requested assistance for "all the southeastern parishes [but not by name], including the New Orleans metropolitan area and the mid-state Interstate I-49 corridor and northern parishes along the I-20 corridor that are accepting [evacuated citizens]." "Brownie, you're doing a heck of job!" is now the famous quote by an oblivious George Bush that captures the incompetence of his administration's response to the great human tragedy.

The disaster response to Katrina redistributed over 1 million people from the central Gulf Coast elsewhere across the United States—the largest diaspora in the history of the United States. Houston, Texas, had an increase of 35,000 people; Mobile, Alabama, gained over 24,000; Baton Rouge, Louisiana, over 15,000; and Hammon, Louisiana, received over 10,000, nearly doubling its size. Chicago received over 6,000 people, the most of any non-southern city. By late January 2006, about

continues

Box 9.1 *continued*

200,000 people were once again living in New Orleans, less than half of the pre-storm population.

Two years after the disaster, criticism of the U.S. government's response to the massive destruction of mostly African-American neighborhoods with their modestly priced homes still reverberates to the detriment of America's reputation. The clear pattern has been to keep displaced poor people from returning by failing to rebuild low-income housing. According to the Association of City Mayors: "Despite Hurricane Katrina causing the worst affordable housing crisis since the American Civil War, HUD is spending $762 million in taxpayer funds to tear down over 4,600 public-housing subsidized apartments and replace them with 744 similarly subsidized units—an 82 percent reduction. . . . HUD plans to build an additional 1,000 market rate and tax credit units—which will still result in a net loss of 2,700 apartments to New Orleans—the remaining new apartments will cost an average of over $400,000 each!"

The removal of poor and black people from New Orleans by an opportunistic government seems to have been for the benefit of real estate interests initially. Private market entrepreneurs have been allowed to operate by constructing nonsubsidized dwellings at a profit, and this past summer New Orleans was reported to be the fastest growing city in the country.

The case study of Hurricane Katrina and the ongoing failure of the federal government to provide adequately for the victims can inspire extreme cynicism, especially in regard to former president George W. Bush's administration. However, it also has important heuristic value. It demonstrates society's lack of commitment to help the less affluent with low-income and affordable housing; it shows how powerful interests in real estate influence the actions, if not the policies of the federal government; and it clearly indicates that when natural disasters strike, it is the poor whose needs are neglected and it is the poor who suffer most. All of these conclusions can be derived from our sociospatial approach. It is not surprising that capital is now flowing back into New Orleans at a substantial rate and that the poor and the black have been replaced by more affluent Americans due to hurricane recovery policies of housing and urban renewal.

In August 2009, the Associated Press ran an article updating the situation in New Orleans. Among its observations, it reported:

> By one estimate, 36 percent of New Orleans' housing is empty, and . . . there is no clear indication when or whether it will be rebuilt. While grace periods for many mortgage holders after the storm helped New Orleans avoid the high foreclosure rates other cities have seen, many homeowners haven't yet decided whether to re-

continues

build or, in some cases, don't have the money to finish the work. . . . New Orleans has regained about 75 percent of its pre-storm population, though a recent report by the Brookings Institution Metropolitan Policy Program and Greater New Orleans Community Data Center said slowing of school enrollment suggests those moving in are single or childless couples. . . . By one recent estimate, less than 20 percent of the Lower 9th's pre-storm population is back. A pocket of new, built-to-last houses in another part of the neighborhood—spearheaded by Hollywood star Brad Pitt and slated to expand—is like a hamlet surrounded by open, vivid-green land.

Overgrown lots and homes that have scarcely been touched since Katrina spill from the cluster of Pitt homes, creating a virtual wilderness. On a recent afternoon, feral chickens scurried across a road that attracted little notice before Katrina but has become a landmark since." The city is recovering but growth is clearly uneven with large areas of the poorest sections comparatively abandoned. Overall, one indicator of recovery is revealing: Prior to the hurricane in the prosperous year the total number of residential addresses actively receiving mail was 188,251. Now, in June of 2009, that number is 154,592 up by slightly more than 8,000 since immediately after the storm. Recovery is happening but, obviously, at a slow pace.

SOURCES: "Four Years After Katrina: The State of New Orleans," AP/*Huffington Post*, August 28, 2009; Dan D. Swenson and Bob Marshall, "Flash Flood: Hurricane Katrina's Inundation of New Orleans." *Times-Picayune*, May 14, 2005; Jed Horne, *Breach of Faith: Hurricane Katrina and the Near Death of a Great American City* (New York: Random House, 2008).

The relationship between racial background and segregation is brought out clearly by research on housing discrimination in suburban communities. Government regulations and real estate agents prevent African Americans from moving outside the large city even if they can afford to do so. Most often this is the result of a kind of racism that is called "exclusionary zoning." Such measures have been confirmed as the cause of segregation by a long research tradition.

According to a report published in 2004:

Much has been written in recent years on continuing high levels of racial segregation and growing income segregation within urban areas in the U.S. Black and Hispanic households tend to live in different neighborhoods than whites, while within these groups high-and low-income households are also spatially separated. Among the factors that contribute to segregated housing patterns are local land-use regulations that tend to exclude lower-income households from suburban communities. The specific regulations that are most often criticized as exclusionary are those that specify a minimum lot size for single-family homes. Large lots artificially inflate the cost of owner-occupied housing within suburban communities, making it difficult for low- and moderate-income households to buy into these communities. In addition to large lot zoning, there are a myriad of other zoning and building regulations that raise home prices and apartment rents within America's suburbs. (Ihlanfeldt, 255)

As a result, there is a scarcity of affordable housing within many communities, and region-wide racial segregation is compounded by poverty. Ihlanfeldt goes on to say, "There are some hard facts obtained by people doing research on exclusionary zoning. It has been found that neighborhood median income increases property value while racial diversity reduces property value. The evidence provided demonstrates that there is a cash payoff to suburban property owners from excluding from their community low-income and minority households."

Recent research on segregation shows that the forces of isolation and discrimination afflicting the black and the poor have deconcentrated just as minority populations have spread out unevenly across the metro region. As a result, an overall locational pattern has emerged with minority communities fragmenting into irregular enclaves throughout the area rather than being confined to specific ghettos. This is even more so for poor Hispanics who have been more successful in overcoming the barriers of exclusionary zoning in suburbia. While affordable housing and mixed communities are not increasingly present, strict ghettoization is giving way to a more dispersed, regional array. Thus research shows that there is an exclusionary and discriminatory dynamic operating at the multicentered metro regional scale rather than the simple dichotomy of city vs. suburb that characterized earlier perspectives on race and income segregation. These results confirm in a different way the emergence of the new form of multicentered regional space than earlier arguments in this text.

In a 2008 study, the author looked at nine metro areas: Atlanta, Chicago, Detroit, Houston, Los Angeles, Miami, New York, San Francisco, and Washington, D.C. He compared segregation in these regions within suburban communities, between suburban communities, between the urban poor and the suburban region, and within the principal cities. In all the regions tested, there was significant segregation within the core cities, between the urban core and the suburban rings in the region, and between suburban communities in the region. Atlanta had most of its segregation within and between suburban communities. Chicago had a large component of segregation within its core area. Detroit possessed a large component of segregation between and within its suburban communities but also within the central city. Segregation in Houston was dominated by its presence in the core central city. Miami's picture was the reverse: Most of the segregation was between and within suburban communities. New York, among the entire sample, had most of its segregation within the principal cities of the region. San Francisco was equally balanced between segregation in the city and in the suburban area of the region, while Washington, D.C., like many of the other cities, was dominated by segregation in the suburban region (Farrell, 2008).

Most metropolitan areas became less segregated during the 1990s, but this effect obscures the more complex and fragmented nature of segregation involving multi-groups and differences in community segregation patterns within the larger metropolitan region. Another reason there is not more fragmentation of minority and poor neighborhoods, especially in the central city, is because of gentrification. In the large cities like New York, young adults are moving into former ghetto areas that were once predominantly black or Hispanic. The same is true in many other large cities; however, it is probably not the case in the smaller cities where there is still room for affordable housing close to the city but located in suburban regions, or in the cities of the south which still maintain racial barriers to locational mobility, such as in New Orleans. We shall discuss gentrification below. Farrell's comparative analysis clearly demonstrates the way discrimination operates to produce variable patterns of settlement for the poor and minorities because of the way those populations have filtered out from central cities according to the different limitations imposed on them by exclusionary practices in the different cities.

At the end of the last century, a growing number of black people have returned to the South, thereby reversing decades of movement north. According to a report by the Brookings Institution (2005), the South outscored net gains of black migrants from all three of the other regions of the United States during the late 1990s, reversing a thirty-five-year trend. Of the ten states that suffered the greatest net loss of blacks between 1965 and 1970, five ranked among the top ten states for attracting blacks between 1995 and 2000. Southern metropolitan areas, particularly Atlanta, led the way in attracting black migrants in the late 1990s. In contrast, the major metropolitan areas of New York, Chicago, Los Angeles, and San Francisco experienced the greatest out-migration of blacks during the same period. Among all ethnic-racial groups, blacks were more likely than any other to move to the South. Both Atlanta and Washington, D.C., were the major recipients of black migrants. Most importantly, college-educated individuals led the new black immigration into the South. Georgia, Texas, and Maryland attracted the most black college graduates from 1995 to 2000, while New York suffered the largest net loss. There was also a large out-migration of African Americans from California. They moved to the "spillover" states of Arizona and Nevada as well as back to the South. Due to the higher level of education and income characteristic of these return southerners, inner-city hyperghettos continue to lose their more affluent residents, assuming, as in the case of New Orleans, there are any left at all.

One effect on U.S. culture of significant segregation is that increasingly whites learn about blacks and blacks learn about whites only from the mass media because they have little direct contact with each other. Styles of dress and language among teenagers, in particular, are highly influenced by the media and the mass-marketing of youth-related fashions in clothing, cinema, and music. In the 1990s, an urban style of ghetto dress among black teenagers that is associated with rap music and inner-city dance styles was marketed nationwide. Many youths in suburbia copy the style that is marketed to them through television and films. At the same time, suburban fashions associated with active leisure wear, especially influenced by Southern California, such as skateboarding and beachwear, are also marketed through the media nationwide. Teenage culture represents a battleground of these and other spatially generated lifestyles that are diffused across the country by the mass media (Chambers, 1986), and it is here, in popular culture, that urban African American culture has had its greatest impact on whites.

Poverty

The issue of poverty is not confined to urban settlement space alone. People throughout the metropolitan region suffer its effects. Poverty is caused by the uneven development of the economy. In the 1950s, despite growing affluence, large numbers of Americans were poor, with some living in appalling conditions (Harrington, 1962). At the time, it was recognized that there were poor people in rural areas as well as urban places. As a result of government antipoverty programs such as the War on Poverty, the poverty rate declined to about 12.1 percent in the 1960s. In the 1970s and 1980s, however, the rate rose again and reached levels comparable to Depression-era statistics; roughly 20 percent of the total population was living at or below the poverty line in the 1980s (Wilson, 1987). Today, as a consequence of our current economic meltdown, unemployment and poverty have hit unprecedented levels and the problem remains our most serious domestic issue.

In 2008 the federal government issued guidelines that defined poverty for a family of four as $21,200 in yearly income for the contiguous United States, with Alaska and Hawaii slightly higher at $26,500 and $24,380, respectively (U.S. Department of Health and Human Services, 2009). It is difficult to figure how a family of four can manage on this budget, particularly for those living in urban areas with high rents and food costs. Today there are many more people living at or below this rate than in 2008; over 40 million, or about 14 percent of the population, in fact. Another indicator of poverty is whether people possess health insurance. In 2007, before the economic crisis hit, almost 16 percent of Americans had none.

Poverty can be considered an urban problem because of its concentration in large city neighborhoods, as the sociospatial perspective suggests, although the range of poverty rates for all cities in the United States is quite broad. Cleveland and Detroit, for example, had rates above 30 percent in 2007, while the rates in their surrounding suburban areas were much less. In general, the city as a spatial form concentrates the poor in record numbers, and that is precisely the sociospatial effect that makes poverty an urban problem. As William J. Wilson has observed, "To say that poverty has become increasingly urbanized is to note a remarkable change in the concentration of poor people in the United States in only slightly more than a decade" (1987:172).

Furthermore, the demographic profile of the poor is cause for alarm. In 2005, 17.6 percent of all children under eighteen years old were living in poverty. This high figure is astounding for a developed country like the United States. During that same year, a higher proportion of black (34.5 percent) and Hispanic (28.3 percent) children under age eighteen were poor than were their non-Hispanic white counterparts (10.0 percent) (http://mchb.hrsa.gov/chusa07/popchar/pages/103cp.html). Because the minority population of the United States is overwhelmingly urban, these figures imply a concentration of poor minority group members, especially children, in the large central cities and represents a major problem for the entire society, not just for those living in central cities.

The spatial effects of concentrating the poor in a few neighborhoods contribute to urban problems. For example, ghetto areas are the sites of the most violent criminal and drug-related activities, so the urban poor are the most likely to be crime victims and suffer the most from crime (Taylor, 1991). In addition, ghetto areas have worse medical care than other parts of the city. A study of infant mortality rates in New York found that the rate was almost twice as high in central Harlem and Bedford-Stuyvesant (23.4 and 21 per 1,000, respectively), both well-known black communities, compared to the city average of 13.3 per 1,000 (the national average was 10 in 1,000 in 1990).

INCREASING INCOME INEQUALITY, UNEMPLOYMENT, AND POVERTY

The current economic crisis has had a number of troubling effects by increasing the problem of poverty in the United States. Because of uneven development, however, the burden of the crisis has fallen most heavily on the working class, not on corporate executives or fully employed professionals. Consequently, as a recent report shows, the income inequality gap has widened considerably. In fact, "Income inequality in the United States is at an all-time high, surpassing even levels seen during the Great Depression" (Saez, "Income Inequality is at an All Time High," *New York Times*, 2009). Since 2000, the top 1 percent of American wage earners have doubled their share of wages. The top 10 percent of employed people pulled in almost 50 percent of all earned wages in 2007, a "level that is higher than any other year since 1917."

As our economic crisis persists, unemployment remains high (it was close to 10 percent in July 2009). According to a federal government report in June:

Unemployment rates were higher in June than a year earlier in all 372 metropolitan areas, the Bureau of Labor Statistics of the U.S. Department of Labor reported today. Eighteen areas recorded jobless rates of at least 15.0 percent, while 9 areas registered rates below 5.0 percent. The national unemployment rate in June was 9.7 percent, not seasonally adjusted, up from 5.7 percent a year earlier.

Among the 369 metropolitan areas for which nonfarm payroll data were available, 352 areas reported over-the-year declines in employment, 16 reported increases, and 1 had no change. (Hall, 2009)

Furthermore, statistics on job loss indicate that the phenomenon is greater in many of our largest multicentered metropolitan regions (not just cities). Thus the economic crisis concentrates the poor and the unemployed in these areas.

Of the 49 metropolitan areas with a Census 2000 population of 1 million or more, Detroit-Warren-Livonia, Mich., reported the highest unemployment rate in June, 17.1 percent. The large areas with the next highest rates were Riverside–San Bernardino–Ontario, Calif., 13.7 percent; Charlotte–Gastonia–Concord, N.C.–S.C., 12.4 percent; Las Vegas–Paradise, Nev., 12.3 percent; and Providence–Fall River–Warwick, R.I., 12.1 percent. Eighteen additional large areas posted rates of 10.0 percent or more. . . . All 49 large areas registered over-the-year unemployment rate increases of at least 2.0 percentage points. (U.S. Bureau of Labor Statistics, 2009)

Loss of a job has negative ripple effects on the economy that bring other jobs into jeopardy. Proposed employment creation to combat this problem so far has not materialized, giving people cause for substantial worry that the economic recovery will take considerable time. Another negative effect of increasing poverty and unemployment is that it impacts the housing market. In fact, because the United States has failed to provide an adequate supply of affordable housing, the banks that provided loans to people who could ill afford them helped pave the way for the present economic crisis. Consequently, the issues of poverty, income inequality, and unemployment are compounded and mixed in with the country's equally large housing crisis.

THE HOUSING CRISIS AND SOCIETY'S FAILURE TO PROVIDE ADEQUATE AFFORDABLE HOUSING

As pointed out in our discussion of community in Chapter 8, family well-being in the United States depends to a great extent on where one's home is located. Differences in wealth and the location of the family home determine the opportunities available to individuals. Where one lives determines the quality of the school one attends, as we have already discussed, but it also determines the safety of the local streets and how much one's property will increase in value. Over the years, the cost of well-situated housing, either owned or rented, has increased substantially as a percentage of income. Consequently, attractive neighborhoods have become beyond the reach of many people.

Since 1965, the cost of housing has risen more rapidly than income. As a result, millions of people either could not afford single-family homeownership or were forced to devote a major part of their income to housing. In 2008 the uneven development of America's market-oriented approach to real estate investment in housing and loans resulted in an economic meltdown with no immediate relief in sight (see below). Yet the present global crisis is only the inevitable outcome of decades of misguided housing policy sacrificed for maximum profit. In the mid-1950s, an average thirty-year-old worker could purchase a median-priced house for just 14 percent of his or her gross earnings. Thirty years later, it would take fully 44 percent of that worker's income to purchase the same house (Levy, 1977). Shannon, Kleiniewski, and Cross (1991) illustrated the rapid increase in housing prices. In 1970, the median monthly rent in the United States was $108; by 1985, it was three times as high ($350). The median sales price of new homes increased by a factor of four, from $23,000 in 1970 to more than $92,000 in 1986. Price increases were most rapid on both the East and West Coasts, becoming almost prohibitively high in places such as Orange County, California, and Nassau County, New York.

Today we are in the midst of a full-blown economic crisis that grew out of our housing dilemma with its lack of affordability and its obsessive emphasis on putting people into single-family suburban tract homes or inner-city high-end condominiums. Since the 1980s, real estate and banking interests in the United States pushed development of housing for the affluent to unprecedented levels. Although little affordable housing was constructed, banks found new ways of placing people into units when they could not afford the expensive housing that was being built. Subprime and adjustable rate mortgages were the principal tools used to keep profits up by tapping into a new market consisting of poorer people who could not afford new housing. Eventually, a speculative and artificially inflated "bubble" of investment and debt was created that came crashing down on the heads of Americans at the end of 2008. However, the warning signs were already there over a decade ago, when bank mortgage lending was deregulated by the federal government and all the watchdogs of land and bank investing somehow went to sleep while mega-profits and mega-bonuses were being made and paid in these industries.

As Lefebvre has argued, the second circuit of investing, namely real estate, is as likely to go through boom-and-bust cycles as any other aspect of capitalism. For several decades, until 2007, average citizens forgot about the dangers of the speculative bubble and focused on the monthly and yearly gains in the value of housing and the steady profit taking it allowed. More significantly for the current economic crisis today, investment banks, which until the Clinton era deregulation, were forbidden from investing in housing at all, cleverly engineered entirely new ways of packaging risky home loans into "assets" that were bought and sold on the global market. The value of these "subprime" derivatives was assured only for as long as the prices of housing continued to rise. It seems astounding now that no one in authority, in either the United States or other industrialized countries, exercised their power to offset such speculation. It is even more astounding that no effective oversight was initiated when not long ago the United States, under President Ronald Reagan during the 1980s, lost billions of dollars in a similar real estate speculation known as the "savings and loan" scandal. That is exactly what happened as a consequence of the deregulation of investment banking activities under President Clinton in the 1990s. In brief, then, the United States has always had an affordable housing crisis because the country has persisted in relying on the private market to supply most of its housing needs.

When the speculative bubble—the nation's housing market—began to burst in 2007, there was ample time for a suitable correction if the government under President George W. Bush had paid any attention. But it didn't. Now the American economy is in the throes of a major, long-lasting plunge. It is extremely important to note that the crisis derives from the government's failure to provide for affordable housing rather than blaming a more complex, less understandable feature of global capital investment and business dynamics. For example, according to an authoritative report, housing markets contracted for a second straight year in 2007.

> Then, the national median single-family home price fell in nominal terms for the first time in 40 years of recordkeeping, leaving several million homeowners with properties worth less than their mortgages. With the economy softening and many home loans resetting to higher rates, an increasing number of owners had difficulty keeping current on their payments. Mortgage performance—especially on subprime loans with adjustable rates—eroded badly. Lenders responded by tightening underwriting standards and demanding a higher risk premium, accelerating the ongoing slide in sales and starts. (Joint Center for Housing Studies, 2008)

By the end of 2008, the foreclosure rate and the drop in stock prices were both equally astronomic and equally painful. The country was well underway into a national banking, employment, and stock depression that people were still suffering from in late 2009.

A recent assessment concluded that a recovery remained unsure and the economic decline was deeply troubling:

> While deep construction cutbacks have begun to pare down the supply of unsold new homes, the numbers of vacant homes for sale or held off the market remain high. Reducing this excess will take some combination of additional declines in prices, a slow-down in foreclosures, further cuts in mortgage interest rates, and a pickup in job and income growth. Until the inventory of vacant homes is worked off, the pressure on prices will persist. Further price declines will not only increase the probability that mortgage defaults end in foreclosure, but also put a tighter squeeze on consumer spending. (Joint Center for Housing Studies, 2008)

Compounding this problem of excess supply, current foreclosure rates are so high that banks still retain excess liabilities (called "toxic assets") and remain in crisis. Continuing high unemployment rates are the major culprit. When people lose their jobs, they often lose their homes as well. According to a recent report, "Economists estimate that 1.8 million borrowers will lose their homes this year [2009], up from 1.4 million last year [2008] . . . and the government, which has already committed billions of dollars to foreclosure-prevention efforts, has found it far more difficult to help people who have lost their paychecks than those whose mortgage payments become unaffordable because of an interest-rate increase" (Merle, *Washington Post*, 2009).

Lack of affordable housing and the irrational way the banking industry, aided by our culture's attachment to the American Dream, pushed the norm of a single-family home, contributed to the bursting of the bubble that is at the heart of the current U.S. economic crisis. By involving such large numbers of people who could least afford homes through subprime loans, the crisis hit African Americans and Hispanic populations particularly hard. Box 9.2 provides a report on the extent of this involvement and the implications it has for an economic recovery.

Box 9.2

The Effect on Minority Populations of the Housing Crisis

Fastest Growing Populations Experiencing Decreasing Wealth

Washington, D.C.—The National Community Reinvestment Coalition (NCRC) has said that the latest report from the U.S. Department of the Census Bureau casts new light on the economic ramifications of the growing foreclosure crisis. The Census report shows that in less than forty years, today's minorities—the disproportionate recipient of subprime loans—will be the majority population in America. This has profound implications on the future of Americans' economic mobility, homeownership attainment, and the nation's global competitiveness.

Hispanics are expected to experience the most dramatic increase in population, according to the report, swelling from 15 percent of the population to 30 percent. African Americans and Asians are projected to grow to 15 percent and 10 percent of the population, respectively.

Disturbingly, Hispanics and African Americans have experienced the greatest rates of subprime lending in recent years, and are being particularly hard hit by the ongoing foreclosure crisis. And African Americans and Latinos already face severe wealth disparities relative to non-Hispanic whites. In large part because of the critical link between homeownership and wealth attainment, African Americans and Hispanics, on average, hold only $10 and $12 of wealth for every $100 of savings of the typical non-Hispanic white household, respectively.

A major driver of wealth disparities is the relatively lower rates of homeownership. Today less than 50 percent of African Americans own their homes, compared

continues

Box 9.2 *continued*

to 75 percent of whites. As minority populations grow, their level of wealth and homeownership, as well as other economic opportunities, continue to lag behind that of non-Hispanic whites.

The ongoing foreclosure crisis threatens to further increase this wealth gap by wiping away billions of dollars in minority communities. According to the nonprofit public policy organization United for a Fair Economy (UFE), the loss of homeownership could translate into a total loss of wealth among African American and Latino households of between $164 billion to more than $200 billion.

Persistent and increasing wealth gaps among communities of color and the broader population represent a problem for America. "Failing to ensure greater financial inclusion of a significant and growing segment of the population is a problem that should not be ignored," said Jim Carr, chief operating officer of NCRC. "As communities of color grow, their economic vitality will be increasingly critical to America's overall competitiveness."

In addition to accessing sustainable homeownership, greater engagement of minority households in the banking and financial system is critical. Nearly 10 million U.S. households are unbanked. A recent report by the Center for Financial Services Innovation estimates that there are 40 million households with limited and tenuous access to the banking mainstream. A disproportionate share of these households is minority. Yet this study showed a full 25 percent of those consumers had prime credit, including 15 percent who had prime-plus or super-prime. These statistics show more can and should be done to bring more consumers into the twenty-first-century banking system.

SOURCE: National Community Reinvestment Coalition, August 20, 2008, http://www.ncrc.org/index.php?option=com_content&task=view&id=331&Itemid=75

In sum, the current and serious economic recession has many intertwined causes. However, at its root, there are just a few and they represent fundamental contradictions of our capitalist system. One factor is the country's inability to provide an adequate supply of affordable housing to all workers. Like the proverbial butterfly that flaps its wings in the equatorial tropics and triggers a world ecological crisis through a series of globally linked events, the scarcity of affordable housing contributed to the economic turmoil that we see today, when unregulated banks were allowed to step in and provide subprime loans to people who then defaulted on them. Solving the protracted recession in the United States is obviously a priority, but attacking the root causes should be an equally important priority.

HOMELESSNESS

One of the first things visitors to a city notice are individuals walking on the street carrying all their possessions. A *New York Times* poll over a decade ago found that roughly 54 percent of Americans see homeless people in the community or on their way to work (Applebome, 1991). While homelessness is related to the above issue of affordable housing, it is not directly related and has multiple causes. To be sure, however, with the current high rate of unemployment and foreclosures of housing, homelessness as an urban phenomenon will increase.

We cannot say for sure how many homeless people there are at present. We do know, however, that the latest numbers have not been seen since the Great Depression of the 1930s (Blau, 1992). The homeless are not found in any single place; they are mobile. Their condition also varies. Some days or nights they may be inside shelters, and at other times they may have enough money for a room in a single-room-occupancy (SRO) hotel. In the mid-1980s, one estimate said there were 350,000 homeless "on a given night" (Peroff, 1987), but other estimates have run much higher, to 3 million or more (Flanagan, 1990:320). In addition, the composition of the homeless population, including married couples with children, is more representative of the entire cross-section of U.S. society than during previous periods such as the Depression.

The current recession coupled with the 2009 housing crisis has produced an unprecedented number of children belonging to families that are either homeless or in temporary living arrangements because they have lost their homes. This terrible plight has put an immense strain on school districts that struggle with a government mandated requirement that all American children, whether living in a home or not, are entitled to an education. In September 2009, 1 million American children were left in distressed conditions due to loss of homes from the foreclosure crisis and the attempts by school districts to comply with federal legislation requiring that young children be given a public education (Eckholm, 2009).

Recent reports indicate that both homelessness and squatting, phenomena once associated with cities in the developing world, have become increasingly common in European as well as American metropolitan areas (Adams, 1986). There are several reasons for homelessness (Flanagan, 1990; Leshner, 1992). Job loss since the 1970s has taken a terrible toll on families. Economic restructuring, as we saw earlier in this chapter, has caused job loss and community decline. In many cases, a loss of income results in an inability to afford housing; for some families, even rental housing can be hard to obtain with limited financial means. But declines in welfare funding have been a principal cause of homelessness: Fiscal austerity and cutbacks in the federal budget have limited the ability of local communities to support people in need.

Finally, homelessness is also caused by the housing problem and the inequities of the second circuit of capital in the United States. Because the real estate market functions both to drive up the cost of shelter and to foster speculation, units may either be too expensive to rent or own or simply be held vacant as a tax loss. The urbanist Carolyn Adams terms this condition one of *maladjustment* rather than a shortage of housing, because in the United States many housing units remain available. As she suggests:

> The term "maladjustment" is more accurate than "shortage" because in many places the number of existing units is theoretically large enough to house the urban population. Yet many households cannot find housing that is both affordable and suitable for their needs. At the same time, large numbers of housing units stand vacant, awaiting demolition or renovation. The presence of empty housing in cities where large numbers of families and individuals need shelter is an invitation to squatting, and that is precisely what has taken place. (1986:528)

But homelessness is not simply a question of social welfare; it is also a matter of land-use issues connected with gentrification, displacement, and the cultural imaginings of what the city should be. Talmadge Wright notes that the "problem" of homelessness in American cities is especially challenging because the homeless, city officials, and other groups have very different visions of how urban space should be used. For low-income persons who cannot afford housing, vacant buildings may be seen as squatter properties. But for most people—including public officials and developers—urban space does not include a place for the homeless (Wright, 1998). This attitude has resulted in the "militarization" of urban space, including such things as concertina wire around dumpsters behind grocery stores and restaurants to prevent homeless persons from obtaining leftover food; park benches specifically designed to prevent people from sleeping; and sprinkler systems in public parks that are turned on during evening hours to prevent homeless persons from sleeping on the ground (Davis, 1990). In Chicago, San Jose, and other cities, homeless populations have mobilized to resist the displacement of their communities, including protests of urban redevelopment projects, squatting activities, and other forms of collective action (Wright, 1998).

Homelessness combines aspects of economic crisis, poverty, and the failures of U.S. health and housing policies. Remedies for this problem require integrated plans that address the root causes. It is clear that with the declining economy, poor people have fewer opportunities to improve their lot, and their relative standing in society is deteriorating. Above all else, it must be noted, not just once but repeatedly, that the failure of the U.S. housing industry to provide affordable housing and the efforts by the banking and investment industry to profit from this failure have been and remain the root cause of the current and deep economic recession. In 2009, the U.S. government provided trillions of dollars as a means of preventing the collapse of these same industries, but when repeated appeals had been made to provide adequate housing for all Americans over the years, the response was indifference. Can such a contradiction in our society persist, even after the present crisis has passed?

No signs so far suggest that the matter is being addressed, and the fact that more than 1 million children have been left in distressed conditions is hard evidence of the consequences for the most innocent victims of the situation.

CRIME

On the night of August 27, 2009, the following incident occurred in Detroit:

> Betty McMahon expected her van to turn up either stripped or dumped from a joyride after she saw someone steal it early today on Detroit's east side. She never expected to spot it with the body of a 22-year-old slumped over the wheel, shot a block from her home, in front of Gleaners Community Food Bank. McMahon heard someone start up her van at 4:20 a.m., and watched out the window as it drove away. She was on her way home from reporting it stolen with her son and daughter-in-law when they spotted the flashing lights of the Detroit Police . . . "I said, 'Go around the corner, let's be nosey and see what all of that is,'" she said. "When I got to the corner, I said, 'Oh my god, that's my van.'" Gleaners' operations manager arriving for work at 5:30 a.m. had called police after spotting the green 1994 Plymouth Voyager in front of one of the food pantry's truck bays. "He saw the van sitting in the street and he saw the window was broken and someone was in it, slumped in it, so he immediately called 911," Gleaners vice president . . . said this morning. McMahon, who had a van stolen and damaged from a joyride about eight years ago, said she's "tore up" about the violence involved with this one. (Battaglia, 2009)

Tragic stories such as this one give the impression that crime is rampant in cities and that cities are unsafe as human environments. When people speak of crime, they usually mean violent crime, which includes murder, assault, rape, and robbery. However, a large amount of property crime—burglary, larceny, and auto theft—occurs every year in both cities and suburbs. White-collar criminals, for example, such as insider traders on Wall Street and the bankers involved in the savings and loan scandal, are responsible for the theft of billions of dollars. But these white-collar crimes are not usually considered when people discuss criminal activity or describe dangerous criminals. White-collar criminals rarely appear in the photographs of the most wanted criminals in post offices or on *America's Most Wanted*. For the most part, the crimes associated with metropolitan areas are of the violent variety such as rape and murder—the stuff of *CSI* and other television shows and movies that continue to fascinate the American public. These crimes affect our view of public safety and the safety of our homes.

Tables 9.1 to 9.3 report crime statistics for metropolitan areas, comparing rates from 2000 to 2007 for property and violent crimes as well as the aggregate city/suburb

TABLE 9.1 Crime Rates in Central City and Suburbs, 2000–2007.

	2000			2007		
	Central City	Suburbs	Metro Areas	Central City	Suburbs	Metro Areas
Property Crime						
Burglary	996.0	598.0	758.0	980.0	605.0	751.0
Auto theft	733.0	402.0	475.0	609.0	290.0	414.0
Larceny	3479.0	2053.0	2628.0	2954.0	1851.0	2280.0
Violent Crime						
Murder	10.2	3.2	6.1	10.4	3.6	6.2
Rape	45.2	25.2	33.1	40.2	23.4	29.8
Robbery	313.5	78.4	173.0	302.5	92.0	174.0
Robbery with gun	118.2	32.2	67.3	129.3	38.4	71.4
Assault	519.8	237.2	351.0	438.8	214.6	301.9
Assault with gun	103.5	34.1	62.4	118.0	36.9	66.4

Cases known to police per 100,000 persons.

SOURCE: FBI, *2008 Crime in the United States,* Table 2, Crime in the United States by Community Type 2008. http://www.fbi.gov/ucr/cius2008/data/table_02.html

contrast. According to Table 9.1, rates per 100,000 people are consistently lower in the suburban areas than in the central city of metropolitan areas with some violent crimes, such as murder, robbery, and assault, occurring about three times more in cities than in suburbs. The three property crimes tracked by national data—burglary, auto theft, and larceny—show the same pattern but only auto theft reflects the same threefold difference. In sum, when average people perceive that cities are, on the whole, more dangerous than suburbs, they are correct and have been so for decades despite fluctuations in the crime rate.

Overall rates of violent crimes—murder, rape, robbery, robbery with gun, assault, and assault with gun reported in Table 9.1—did not change much during the period from 2000 to 2007. Simple assault (without a gun) is the most common violent crime, and the national rate per 100,000 people was 438.8 for cities and 214.6 for suburbs in 2007. Among the three property crimes, larceny is the most common with a rate of 2,954 for cities and 1,851 for suburbs in 2007. Overall, as has been suggested, the United States is more crime-ridden than the societies of Western Europe, Canada, and Japan. We also devote substantially more TV and film programming to aspects of the criminal justice system than other countries. Hence in American culture there is a distinct relationship between the crime that occurs and our apparent hunger for consuming media programming dealing with crime, law, prisons, and the like.

Crime patterns can be examined in more detail for individual metro areas in Tables 9.2 and 9.3. The former reports property crimes. In the case of burglary, for example, the rate ranges from a low of 402 per 100,000 people in 2007 for the Washington, D.C., region to a high of 1,025 for the Dallas metro area.

TABLE 9.2 Property Crime Rates for Largest Metropolitan Regions, 2000–2007.

Largest Metropolitan Regions	2000			2007		
	Burglary	Auto	Larceny	Burglary	Auto	Larceny
New York MSA	442	377	1656	291	188	1351
New York City	463	448	1744	254	161	1403
Suburbs	410	277	1548	310	172	1301
Los Angeles MSA	588	599	1686	523	531	1511
Los Angeles	661	803	2065	507	608	1506
Suburbs	555	488	1383	542	512	1447
Chicago MSA	877	857	3,301	784	528	2653
Chicago	978	1027	3665	876	659	2937
Suburbs	551	349	2498	563	274	2260
Dallas MSA	1003	651	3144	1025	462	2824
Dallas	1708	1509	4272	1814	1113	3850
Suburbs	667	309	2345	710	268	2167
Philadelphia MSA	523	491	2520	530	34	2023
Philadelphia	797	1064	3094	803	774	2728
Suburbs	387	237	1869	404	166	1751
Houston MSA	939	606	2703	1002	552	2556
Houston	1190	1017	3435	1339	897	3449
Suburbs	752	304	2076	791	337	1956
Miami MSA	1160	821	3828	997	543	3127
Miami	2015	1579	5202	1177	945	3042
Suburbs	1049	737	3452	948	503	3006
Washington, D.C., MSA	456	489	2267	402	494	1993
Washington	830	1154	3782	666	1245	2801
Suburbs	410	403	2031	380	421	1894
Atlanta MSA	8534	598	2953	990	550	2326
Atlanta	2223	1765	6550	1782	1412	4093
Suburbs	702	468	2548	906	460	2127
Detroit MSA	720	904	2262	811	729	1852
Detroit	1664	2722	3357	2063	2261	2431
Suburbs	410	355	1824	461	301	1620
Boston MSA	405	443	1595	472	217	1603
Boston	688	1234	2924	644	578	2932
Suburbs	355	330	1359	445	162	1372
San Francisco MSA	617	567	2408	688	861	2195
San Francisco	733	716	3144	692	804	3199
Suburbs	566	428	2068	609	663	1862
Phoenix MSA	1105	1005	3506	975	855	2832
Phoenix	1201	1474	3968	1246	1353	3227
Suburbs	1005	538	2615	856	536	2289

continues

TABLE 9.2 *(continued)*

	2000			2007		
	Burglary	*Auto*	*Larceny*	*Burglary*	*Auto*	*Larceny*
Seattle MSA	889	870	3350	864	793	2787
Seattle	1093	1489	4690	1023	988	3793
Suburbs	783	594	2690	748	604	2162
Minneapolis MSA	557	344	2849	650	309	2553
Minneapolis	1180	989	3865	1660	856	3557
Suburbs	389	197	2507	480	192	2473
San Diego MSA	561	605	1701	570	832	1658
San Diego	549	774	1881	609	1049	1845
Suburbs	558	462	1554	537	675	1527

SOURCE: FBI, *2008 Crime in the United States,* Table 6, Crime in the United States by Metropolitan Statistical Area. http://www.fbi.gov/ucr/cius2008/data/table_06.html

In Table 9.3 we can see that the murder rate for New York City was 6 per 100,000 people in 2007, which is quite low for most cities. The rate for Los Angeles was 10.2; Chicago, 15.7; Dallas, 16.1; and the two murder capitals of the United States in 2007 were Washington, D.C., with 30.8 and Detroit with 45.5. Rape for metro areas ranged from a low of 9.8 for New York to a high of 36.8 for Seattle, which has significantly lower rates for other violent crimes compared to metro areas nationwide. The most violent cities for assault with a gun in 2007 were Detroit at 486.5 per 100,000 people, Dallas at 208.9, Philadelphia at 200.8, Atlanta at 276.7, and Minneapolis at 138.7.

To understand the nature of urban crime, it is necessary to view it as a spatial as well as a social phenomenon. The incidence of crimes varies within any given city by neighborhood. Thus, while all cities have become more dangerous since World War II, there are still places that are as safe as any other place in the country. Conversely, certain neighborhoods are scenes of unremitting terror. Typically, criminal incidents follow the lines of class and racial segregation: The most dangerous places are also the places where the poorest urban residents live. For example, "The typical New York City murder victim is a black man in his late teens or twenties, killed by an acquaintance of the same race with a hand gun during a dispute—most likely over drug-dealing" (Greenberg, 1990:26). In all cities, racially segregated ghettos are the places where violent crimes are committed the most. Furthermore, the majority of incarcerated felons are either black or Hispanic, and virtually all are poor. They come from the ghetto areas of the city, and their crimes usually were committed in those areas. And as the urban environment is partitioned into areas of relative safety and terror, several extreme examples of violent crimes, such as shootings in public schools, indicate that the islands of safety are shrinking in size and availability.

TABLE 9.3 Violent Crime Rates for Largest Metropolitan Regions, 2000–2007.

	2000						2007					
	Murder	Rape	Robbery	Robbery Gun	Assault	Assault Gun	Murder	Rape	Robbery	Robbery Gun	Assault	Assault Gun
New York MSA	5.2	16.4	244.5	66.3	322.7	40.3	4.5	9.8	179.6	34.2	219.6	17.4
New York City	8.4	20.4	406.6	80.6	509.9	55.0	6.0	10.6	265.0	NA	332.0	NA
Suburbs	2.3	12.8	102.6	40.6	161.8	18.4	2.3	8.9	105.9	29.8	124.6	14.2
Los Angeles MSA	8.6	26.4	252.6	99.9	509.9	102.2	7.3	21.6	237.7	84.2	287.3	82.0
Los Angeles	14.9	39.5	420.2	158.2	885.2	176.6	10.2	25.9	348.3	126.8	334.0	117.5
Suburbs	5.6	21.1	169.9	73.9	377.4	64.8	5.7	19.3	187.1	65.7	273.9	64.3
Chicago MSA	18.6	25.2	518.5	40.5	733.4	32.7	13.7	22.8	397.6	38.1	468.8	20.3
Chicago	21.8	NA	668.0	NA	916.6	NA	15.7	NA	546.1	NA	616.9	NA
Suburbs	5.1	19.5	92.5	40.5	262.2	32.7	6.0	18.3	98.6	38.1	181.0	20.3
Dallas MSA	7.5	35.8	209.7	98.9	341.6	98	5.9	31.8	202.0	100.5	264.5	84.7
Dallas	19.4	53.3	592.8	305.0	684.2	268.1	16.1	41.2	582.8	307.2	48.9	208.9
Suburbs	2.6	27.0	52.8	22.1	187.2	26.5	2.3	24.3	68.8	31.5	178.9	33.4
Philadelphia MSA	7.6	29.1	262.3	119.2	355.6	90.1	9.5	30.0	265.5	116.4	325.7	76.3
Philadelphia	21.0	67.3	687.0	298.8	727.9	227.1	27.3	66.6	714.6	319.6	666.9	200.8
Suburbs	1.8	14.0	82.1	34.7	187.2	22.4	2.5	16.3	88.7	35.4	184.9	25.4
Houston MSA	7.2	35.8	222.2	114	413.1	91.1	4.0	30.5	77.4	36.7	265.6	42.9
Houston	11.8	41.6	422.6	220.9	624.1	158.7	16.2	32.0	529.1	272.4	555	170.8
Suburbs	4.0	30.5	77.4	36.7	265.6	42.9	4.0	27.8	103.2	58.3	257.5	47.5

TABLE 9.3 (continued)

	2000						2007					
	Murder	Rape	Robbery	Robbery Gun	Assault	Assault Gun	Murder	Rape	Robbery	Robbery Gun	Assault	Assault Gun
Miami MSA	6.6	41.1	288.6	87.7	582.1	87.2	7.9	29.3	294.0	134.6	472.9	98.2
Miami	18.2	32.6	848.9	N/A	1273.5	N/A	19.0	13.9	618.4	293.2	840.2	184.8
Suburbs	5.2	41.9	224.6	87.2	514.7	88.5	6.6	29.3	249.3	117.4	429.3	89.4
Washington, D.C., MSA	7.5	21.9	174.6	78.6	265.3	45.4	7.7	19.1	207	69.4	212.3	28.8
Washington	41.8	43.9	621.1	238.8	800.4	143.2	30.8	32.6	677.4	N/A	606.2	N/A
Suburbs	2.9	18.9	115.1	57.5	189.4	31.7	5.0	17.6	152.9	72.9	164.3	29.8
Atlanta, MSA	7.9	24.6	214.0	135.8	329.4	88.5	8.7	20.3	233.0	164.4	279.5	83.6
Atlanta	32.2	66.8	1037.8	582.8	1644.5	442.5	25.9	29.8	719.3	465.5	848.8	276.7
Suburbs	5.2	19.8	122.2	70.0	185.6	38.7	6.9	19.1	178.7	124.7	222.8	60.2
Detroit MSA	10.8	42.4	226.9	120.8	471.8	121.6	10.9	31.5	208.5	112.1	458.4	123.3
Detroit	41.6	85.3	827.1	476.7	1,370.50	449.3	45.5	38.9	762.7	452.4	1,439.80	486.5
Suburbs	2.3	29.3	52.9	18.5	172.9	25.6	2.0	28.3	58.5	21.5	188.3	27.2
Boston MSA	2.0	24.9	95.8	25.1	315.5	18.6	2.8	22.0	107.6	27.4	273.4	30.2
Boston	6.6	55.2	416	108.1	765	73.0	11.0	44.4	378.8	94.4	721.0	97.7
Suburbs	1.4	20.3	43.7	8.7	256.1	8.5	1.7	19.3	65.7	17.1	209.6	20.5
San Francisco MSA	5.8	29.7	215.3	60.2	313.5	29.0	8.8	25.2	310.9	117.3	298.9	65.3
San Francisco	7.6	29.5	444.9	77.0	354.7	24.3	13.6	17.0	513.9	123.3	329.5	37.9
Suburbs	3.8	22.9	118.3	38.5	261.0	26.9	5.9	19.8	180.4	70.1	214.9	50.4

continues

TABLE 9.3 *(continued)*

	2000						2007					
	Murder	*Rape*	*Robbery*	*Robbery Gun*	*Assault*	*Assault Gun*	*Murder*	*Rape*	*Robbery*	*Robbery Gun*	*Assault*	*Assault Gun*
Phoenix MSA	7.1	29.4	168.7	79.6	352.3	96.7	8.2	28.4	178.5	95.3	276.9	80.3
Phoenix	11.5	31.9	284.9	137.4	410.1	152.7	13.8	33.0	320.6	173.8	356.4	131.0
Suburbs	3.8	23.8	74.9	32.7	275.6	48.4	5.3	22.5	79.7	37.2	219.6	45.6
Seattle MSA	3.4	49.1	138.5	36.7	256.9	37.4	3.1	36.8	132.0	35.1	214.0	42.5
Seattle	6.4	32.1	293.4	62.7	437.2	56.8	4.1	15.4	260.1	46.1	347.1	46.8
Suburbs	2.3	49.0	71.0	25.4	167.6	33.0	2.4	37.1	75.9	24.6	140.5	26.4
Minneapolis MSA	3.6	46.1	115.7	9.9	191.9	8.2	2.8	20.0	136.1	48.0	191.8	38.2
Minneapolis	13.1	110.3	509.1	N/A	518.5	N/A	12.7	121.8	678.8	230.0	689.9	138.7
Suburbs	1.6	31.9	32.0	10.2	101.4	8.4	1.3	0.8	42.9	13.1	91.8	10.4
San Diego MSA	3.4	28.5	118.9	29.9	337.7	39.5	3.6	24.0	149.5	35.7	288.6	42.4
San Diego	4.4	28.5	145.3	36.1	407.1	46.9	4.7	23.5	166.1	35.5	307.8	54.6
Suburbs	2.7	28.8	94.7	24.5	285.0	33.0	2.6	25.4	133.8	33.4	277.1	33.0

Crimes known to police per 100,000 persons.

N/A = Data not available because reporting by jurisdiction does not meet FBI Uniform Crime Report standard

SOURCE: FBI, *2008 Crime in the United States*, Table 6, Crime in the United States by Metropolitan Statistical Area. http://www.fbi.gov/ucr/cius2008/data/table_06.html

Drugs

According to studies of arrestees, many robberies and burglaries are committed in connection with drug trafficking. In fact, statistics show a disturbing relationship between violent crime and drug use. The National Institute of Justice surveyed arrestees in the twenty largest American cities and found that at least half of them tested positive for the use of illegal drugs. In New York City, as many as 83 percent of males tested positive at the time of their arrest. The range for females was slightly lower but not by much: a low of 44 percent tested positive in St. Louis and a high of 81 percent in Detroit (National Institute of Justice, 1990).

According to this report, the extent of drug use among arrestees varies from city to city, but the use of drugs by people who commit violent crimes is alarming. The most common drug for both male and female arrestees is cocaine or crack. The lack of safety in large cities results from a high crime rate that is compounded by illegal drug use. When city streets are not considered safe, it is difficult for urban areas to attract new residents and businesses. Consequently, the economic life of the city deteriorates further. In addition, when the enjoyment of public space becomes impossible due to crime and drugs, one of the primary enjoyments of urban culture is threatened with extinction.

The Costs of Crime

What effect does crime have on everyday urban life? Perhaps the greatest effect has to do with the use of city space. In less crime-ridden eras, public spaces such as parks, plazas, and streets were enjoyed by everyone. Parks in particular were used by diverse people at all hours of the day and evening; during summer heat waves, families would sleep on the public beaches in Chicago and other cities. Today the use of public space is limited: People are afraid to venture into parks without friends nearby, and children must be supervised and kept away from strangers. The evening use of public spaces and facilities, such as streets and mass transit systems, has also been negatively affected. People leaving their offices late at night now take cabs or cars rather than public transportation. A few years ago, a young woman out for a jog in Central Park was brutally attacked by a group of teenagers. Raped and beaten within an inch of her life, she miraculously survived, but the story of this urban Wall Street professional became a national news story and a symbol of crime's toll on the enjoyment of urban space.

Crime increases the security budgets of private companies as well as public expenditures for security in schools and court buildings. The national criminal justice system supports the largest prison population in the world with its immense costs to taxpayers. Violent crime causes billions of dollars in unnecessary medical expenses. It can also devastate property values. In areas of the city with high crime rates, the value of property remains low and does not rise during times of prosperity (Taylor, 1991).

As a result, innocent households suffer doubly in crime-infested sections because they are victims of crime and because the value of their housing declines. Poor areas remain mired in poverty because high crime levels chase away prospective investment.

Finally, crime makes the city an unattractive place to live, especially for families with small children. Crime repels families from the city, which compounds the problem of population loss and the inability of the city to increase its tax base. This very real cost to communities can be demonstrated by a visit to the "Moving & Relocation Page" at the MSN House and Home website. In an article titled "Best and Worst Cities for Crime," the following blurb rests atop a listing of high- and low-crime cities:

> Feeling safe and secure is especially important to Americans these days. Recent events remind us that the safety of our loved ones and the security of our property can't be taken for granted. . . . So what are America's best and worst cities for crime? Are there certain cities with an especially high rate of violent crime? Where do car thieves thrive? [We] have mined the recently released FBI Uniform Crime Reports to identify those U.S. cities with the highest and lowest rates of crime during 2002.

There are terrible costs to society from white-collar crime as well—criminologists maintain that the monetary cost of white-collar crime is many times that of other crime—but it is not associated with the quality of urban life. Rather, it is violent crime that scares people away from the city. In addition to murder, which usually is committed among people who know one another, mugging is a particularly frightening crime, especially when it involves armed robbery. The frequency of this type of crime in the cities contributes greatly to the image of danger. It is possible to get a sense of the extensive commission of white-collar crime in metropolitan regions by examining Table 9.2 for larceny figures because it is far and away the most common of all property crimes.

The enormous costs of maintaining and running the vast U.S. prison system is another burden of our high societal crime rate. The figure currently is more than $32 billion a year. Each year that an inmate spends in prison costs taxpayers some $22,000. An individual sentenced to five years for a $300 theft costs the public over $100,000. Over the last twenty years, the amount of money spent on prisons has increased by 570 percent while funding for elementary and secondary education was increased by only 33 percent. In several states, more money is spent on prisons than on public universities.

The cost of criminal activity and drugs, which so often go together, can be measured in other ways. In the 2000 presidential election, thousands of voters in Florida were purged from the list of eligible voters because they had been identified (incorrectly) as having a criminal record. A sidebar to the story is the fact that in the African American community, an entire generation has been disenfranchised because of their arrest for drug use and crimes associated with drug use. More than half of the prisoners in the American penal system are incarcerated for these crimes. Denial of the franchise—the right to vote—is a particularly sensitive issue for African Americans, and the events associated with the 2000 presidential election have resulted in a national movement to restore the voting rights of persons convicted of nonviolent crimes. The criminalization of drugs that are legal in many other countries has resulted in increased crime in metropolitan areas, in the breakup of families, and corruption of law enforcement agencies, and it has drawn billions of dollars out of public budgets that could be used to rebuild urban infrastructure, fund public schools, and address many other important metropolitan issues.

The number of women incarcerated for drug offenses has increased 888 times since 1986. More than 1 million women are currently in prison, in jail, or on parole. In many cases, these women were not guilty of committing a crime themselves, but they were caught in the expanding web of the drug war. The expansion of liability laws like conspiracy, accomplice liability, constructive possession, and asset forfeiture laws unfairly punish women for the actions of boyfriends, husbands, and other family members who may be involved with drugs. Not only are families disrupted when women are sent to prison; these women often lose custody of their children and the family gets destroyed.

Caught in the Web: The Impact of Drug Policies on Families and Women, a report from the Brennan Center for Justice at the New York University School of Law (2005), documents the cases of 150 women found "guilty by association" because their husbands or boyfriends were involved in the drug trade. According to Kirsten Livingston, director of the Criminal Justice Program at the Brennan Center for Justice, "This country can no longer ignore the devastation of families and communities when record numbers of women and mothers are locked up for drug offenses. . . . It's time to promote drug policies that work, to stop wasting money, and to use our social systems to help women, not hurt them." Others are aware of the problem. When Martha Stewart was released from the Alderson Federal Prison Camp in 2005, she posted a letter on her website that encouraged American citizens "to ask for reforms, both in sentencing guidelines, in length of incarceration for nonviolent first-time offenders, and for those involved in drug-taking."

Ultimately, the cost of crime is not borne simply by individuals, public budgets, and private security expenditures. The cost of crime is borne by the larger society in ways that are often hidden from view, even though they threaten the well-being of our families and communities. Those costs are increasing with each passing decade.

Suburban Crime

Compared to crime in the large city, little research has been carried out on suburban crime (see Stahura, Huff, and Smith, 1980; Gottdiener, 1982). Most reports on suburban crimes identify the same factors that cause city crimes, that is, racism, poverty, and class conflict. As in the case of urban areas, the rate of suburban crimes has increased dramatically since the 1980s (Barbanel, 1992). However, crimes in the suburbs differ from those in large cities. First, the property crimes of burglary, auto theft, fraud, and larceny dominate suburban crime, although rape is as serious a problem in suburbs as in cities. Thus, while experiencing violent crime in increasing proportion, suburban areas have much less of it than do large cities. In contrast to the city, property crimes are most troublesome.

Second, there is a distinct spatial component to suburban crime that differs from crime in the city. In cities, high-crime areas are associated with urban ghettos. While suburbs have ghettos, they are not all high-crime areas. Instead, according to one study of a mature suburban region outside of Los Angeles (Gottdiener, 1982), police in Orange County, California, associate high crime rates with apartment buildings. These stand out because most residential dwellings in suburbia are single-family homes. In large cities, this distinction would not be effective since most residences are in apartment buildings. According to this study, police in suburbs pay particular attention to apartment dwellings and monitor the activities of their residents. Because of the lower density of suburban areas, surveillance of populations is an easier task than in the large city (see Davis, 1990).

Aside from the above features, however, suburban crime seems very much like crime in large cities, although perhaps not at the same per-capita rate. But given the diversity of suburban communities, ranging from declining industrial suburbs to communities with spillover from adjacent urban ghettos, it is likely that many suburban communities are less safe than many city neighborhoods. While overall crime rates in the United States decreased each year from 1993 to 1998, rates of violent crime remained high, as did the public's perception of and fear of crime. Violent crime, drugs, burglary, rape, and street gang activity have become a significant factor in daily life across the metropolitan region, affecting life in both urban and suburban settlement spaces.

THE FISCAL CRISIS AND PUBLIC SERVICE PROBLEMS

Urban problems are difficult to solve when insufficient money is available to local governments. A fiscal crisis starts when the revenues obtained by government fall short of the expenses necessary to run a city. When this occurs, it is necessary to borrow money and incur debt. Long-term debt involves borrowing to improve resources and finance public works such as bridges. This form of borrowing is usually considered healthy as long as the projects are well thought out. Long-term debt is viewed as an investment in the city's future; if it is successful, the city grows and its economy improves, resulting in an increase in revenues.

In contrast, short-term debt involves borrowing to pay general operating expenses that revenues and money transferred to the city from higher levels of government cannot cover. Occasionally cities must borrow simply to cover operating expenses, such as meeting a payroll, but this tends to happen only in an emergency. However, as a regular practice it can ruin the health of a city by limiting the amount of money invested for future needs.

Fiscal Crisis

The fiscal crisis of cities has two components. During the 1970s, many cities faced budgetary shortfalls because of rising costs coupled with decreasing revenues caused by the decline in manufacturing and the rapid deterioration of urban economies. These cities were forced to resort to short-term borrowing to cover their costs. Compounding the problem was the flight of middle-class families from the cities to the suburbs (traveling on highways built with federal money to homes subsidized by federal housing policies), taking with them potential tax revenue that the cities desperately needed. The lower-income and new immigrant communities in the cities required relatively higher levels of health care, education programs, and housing services. When New York and other cities appealed to higher levels of government for financial relief, they were rebuked, and this precipitated the urban fiscal crisis. Cities responded to this situation by cutting services and systematically laying off personnel. New York City, for example, almost went bankrupt in 1976 and was placed in the hands of a money management panel appointed by the state to bring expenditures back in line with revenues and limit the amount of borrowing. As a result of the changes caused by this fiscal crisis, New York is unable to offer a full range of services to its residents. The closing of firehouses, reductions in the numbers of police officers and the hours of policing, the shortening of library hours, and layoffs and firings at city agencies are some of the austerity measures enacted in response to the urban fiscal crisis.

In the 1980s, many cities, such as Cleveland, which had defaulted in 1978, and New York, which was forced into austerity, regained their fiscal health. The banking community renewed its faith in the obligations incurred by municipal governments. Short-term borrowing was controlled, and many cities prospered. For a time, it appeared that the urban fiscal crisis was resolved (Gottdiener, 1986). However, the problem was simply transferred to higher levels of government. At present, many states face a fiscal crisis; New York and California have been especially hard hit. These and other states have had to cut back on budgets for social programs in education, health, and other areas, with perceptible effects on the quality of life. Because state governments can no longer aid cities, local jurisdictions must increase taxes or cut back services. Hence, the effects of the state fiscal crisis have been especially troubling for local communities, and there is no end in sight for the first decades of the twenty-first century.

The federal government has not been able to help, since it has acquired serious debt problems of its own for the first time in U.S. history. In 1980 the federal deficit was approximately $40 million, an unprecedented but still manageable number. During the 1980s, it rose to more than $150 billion a year. The interest payments on this massive debt made up 14 percent of gross national product (GNP), and the United

States became the world's leading debtor nation. Although President Clinton made deficit reduction of the federal budget a priority, little or no effort has been made to restore either programs or funding cuts during the 1980s. In places such as New York and California, governments at all levels are suffering cutbacks of services and programs as a result of the fiscal crisis. The damaging effects of these cuts cannot be exaggerated. In Los Angeles, the police department and the district attorney's office blame California's Proposition 13, which froze property tax revenues, for cuts in social programs that resulted in increased gang activity and led to Los Angeles becoming known as the gang capital of the United States.

Now the national debt is beyond imagining at many trillions of dollars as a consequence of President Obama's "fiscal stimulation" policy, which aims to jump-start the deep recession economy of 2009 through Keynesian measures of government spending. All lower levels of government have been promised stimulation dollars from this astounding accumulation of fiscal debt. As the fiscal crisis of cities has worked its way up to the state level, California, in particular, has been hit so hard that it would have declared bankruptcy if the massive and damaging cuts in social programs had not been affected in 2008. Yet despite these measures, it still requires either massive help or more massive cuts. As of July 2009, the Obama administration spending proposals have not materialized to any extent, and although they are said to be "in the pipeline," all lower levels of government anxiously await financial relief.

In sum, declines in local government spending on public services can be catastrophic. States as well as municipalities have been fighting fiscal crisis, and cuts—with their damaging results—have become inevitable. One positive aspect of the current response to our national economic crisis by the Obama administration is the promise that critically needed money will be channeled to state and local governments. To date, little of this deficit spending has trickled down to the local level, but there are indications that it eventually will. In the meantime, large states, like California, remain stressed and must continue to cut public resources in order to avoid the unprecedented fiscal failure of bankruptcy. In fact, during the week of August 24, 2009, the state of California ran a massive "garage sale," where anyone could purchase government equipment that was surplus or merely available for the event. The goal of this sale was quite serious, namely to make as much money as possible by selling unwanted items to the public in order to alleviate in a small way California's astronomical fiscal crisis and its need for draconian cuts in public services, employment, and programs.

SUMMARY

It often seems that each month brings new challenges to urban areas in the United States. Part of the problem is that our society, with its ideology of privatism (see Chapter 13), hangs its solutions of pressing social issues, like poverty, health care, and affordable housing, on some variation of mixed private and public interventions. There is no universal health care in our country, as there is in other Western developed societies. Our large demand for affordable housing, once dealt with inadequately by public subsidization, was absorbed by profit-making capitalists in the 1990s as sub-prime mortgage derivative investing and yielded cataclysmic results. Although some violent crime has been reduced in our cities, the overall level remains abnormally high compared to countries in Western Europe and Japan, and we seem to enjoy its media representations because crime and law shows are so popular.

In this chapter we have seen that while many social problems are not typically "urban" anymore, our metro regions play a role specific to their spatial attributes. Cities *concentrate* people, so as a form of space, they also concentrate their problems. City crime rates are higher than in the suburbs. There are more poor people and more concentrated pockets of poverty and racial exclusion in central cities. Consequently, when dealing with many social issues, cities remain important as places that need special consideration from policy makers and municipal governments need resources from higher levels of administration.

We have also seen in this chapter that when the current economic crisis hit, our largest metro regions were affected by unemployment much more severely than other places because of the industries located there. Yet economic downturns, like the present housing crisis, have deep roots in our society's inability to solve its basic social dilemmas. Consequently, as we shall discuss in Chapter 13, public policy can play an important role if it tackles the major issues, some of which, like health care and adequate land-use planning, were resolved in favor of greater public power scores of years ago by comparable countries in Western Europe.

KEY CONCEPTS

social disorganization
public vs. private intervention
racism
segregation and hypersegregation
poverty
unemployment
housing crisis
affordable housing
spatial effects of social problems
fiscal crisis

DISCUSSION QUESTIONS

1. What is social disorganization and how can it explain urban problems?

2. How can you compare the early Chicago School and the sociospatial approaches to urban problems?

3. Why are racism and segregation problems?

4. Why is hypersegregation troubling and how does it relate to the case of Hurricane Katrina?

5. What is the significance of the most recent figures on crime?

6. Why does the space of the city create more problems than the rest of the metro region? Should this result justify an anti-urban attitude in choosing a place to live?

7. Why is unemployment especially worrisome today? How does it affect metro areas?

8. What is the link between the need for affordable housing and the current economic crisis? Why hasn't American society solved its affordable housing crisis?

9. What is meant by a fiscal crisis? What are the implications of a city fiscal crisis? What happens when the fiscal crisis happens at the state level?

chapter 10

URBANIZATION IN THE
DEVELOPED NATIONS

Urban development in the United States at the beginning of the twenty-first century is defined by multicentered regions resulting from the deconcentration of commercial, retail, and government services in the city center and the reconcentration of these land uses in functionally specialized regional minicenters. This spatial pattern is the product of the political economy of American late capitalism, as we show in Chapter 6. Other societies around the world exhibit their own patterns of urban and regional development, the result of historical circumstances, position within the world system, cultural influences, and other factors. Many share a similar fate of increasing regional sprawl characteristic of the United States. Although large cities remain important centers of commerce and culture, particularly in cities of the developed nations, many have reached slow or stable population growth. Redevelopment and gentrification occurs within the central city, but most new development occurs in suburban settlement space. Land use is mixed and shared among densely populated cities, minicenters of various kinds, and expanding suburban regions of residential housing. Metropolitan regions confront problems that are intensified by locational inequities. Income and racial segregation is increasing and, in many cases, has led to serious inequalities in employment, housing, education, medical care, and other aspects of everyday life.

For many years, the study of urbanization in Europe was a relatively predictable affair. This is the oldest part of the globe with fully urbanized societies. In recent years, however, profound transformations have been taking place in Western and Eastern Europe. Shifts in industry to high technology, declines in manufacturing, and growth in the service sector are common to both the United States and Europe. In the past it was assumed (and presented as fact in many sources) that the pattern of urbanization in European countries was substantially different from that found in the United States: With a long history of urbanization, the European city center remained strong, there was a preference for life in the city and correspondingly less development in the urban fringe. But the evidence tells a different story: Since World

TABLE 10.1 Urbanization in Selected European Countries, 1990 and 2005.

Country	Urban Population		% Total Population		% > 1 Million		% Largest City	
	1990	2005	1990	2005	1990	2005	1990	2005
Western Europe								
Belgium	9,600,000	10,200,000	96	97	10	10	10	10
France	42,000,000	46,700,000	74	77	23	22	22	21
Germany	58,300,000	62,000,000	73	75	8	8	6	5
Greece	6,000,000	6,600,000	59	59	30	29	51	49
Italy	37,800,000	39,600,000	67	68	19	17	9	8
Spain	29,300,000	33,300,000	75	77	22	24	15	17
Sweden	7,100,000	7,600,000	83	84	17	19	21	22
United Kingdom	51,100,000	54,000,000	89	90	26	26	15	16
Eastern Europe								
Belarus	6,800,000	7,100,000	66	72	16	18	24	25
Bulgaria	5,800,000	5,400,000	66	70	14	14	21	20
Czech Republic	7,800,000	7,500,000	75	74	12	11	16	16
Hungary	6,400,000	6,700,000	66	66	19	17	29	25
Poland	23,400,000	23,700,000	61	62	4	4	7	7
Romania	112,600,000	11,600,000	54	54	8	9	14	17
Russian Federation	108,800,000	104,500,000	73	73	18	19	8	10
Ukraine	34,700,000	31,900,000	67	68	12	13	7	8

SOURCE: *World Development Indicators 2009*, Table 3.10 (New York: World Bank, 2009).

War II nearly every European city has had a decline in central city population, and there has been a large increase in the suburban population. As we will see below, in most cases the suburban population is several times that of the central city. Metropolitan regions in Europe (and elsewhere) look more and more like the multicentered metropolitan regions described in Chapter 6 (Clapson, 2003). European scholars have labeled these developments as "post-suburban" (Phelps et al., 2006) and have focused on urban sprawl (Richardson and Bae, 2004)—just as in the United States. There are other similarities: the growing inequality among groups living within the city that results from the division between highly paid professionals and low-paid service workers; the growth of immigrant communities from former colonies; and the seemingly intractable problems of poverty resulting from the combination of job loss in manufacturing, segregation, and social exclusion, and more recently, cutbacks in social welfare (Brenner and Theodore, 2003).

Table 10.1 shows four measures of urbanization for selected countries in Western and Eastern Europe: the number of persons living in urban areas, percentage of population living in urban areas, percentage living in regions with a population of 1 million or more, and percentage of the population living in the largest city. Although Europe was part of the first great urban empire under imperial Rome and is one of the most urbanized areas in the world, the figures show substantial differences in the level of urbanization across the region. Two countries in Western Europe (Belgium and the United Kingdom) have 90 percent or more of their population in urban regions, whereas none of the Eastern European countries has more than 75 percent in urban regions. Two countries in Western Europe (Greece and Italy) have lower levels of urbanization, comparable to many countries in Eastern Europe. The highest level of urbanization among Eastern European countries is in the Czech Republic and the Russian Federation.

There are more than 500 cities with populations of 150,000 or more, and relatively few persons live in urban areas with a population of more than 1 million persons (in most countries, the figure is less than 20 percent); Greece has the largest percentage: Athens, with a population of 3.2 million, is four times greater than the second largest city, Thessalonika, with a population of 800,000. This is an interesting case of urban primacy, where the urban system is dominated by one city; Athens accounts for more than half of the total population of Greece. After the unusual case of Greece, the United Kingdom (26 percent) and France (22 percent) have the largest proportion of residents living in large cities. Moscow has emerged as the largest metropolitan region in Europe with a population of nearly 8.3 million persons, moving ahead of London (7.0 million) and Paris (4.7 million). Of the twenty largest cities in

FIGURE 10.1 City Lights of Europe. SOURCE: NASA.

Europe, ten are located in Eastern European countries, including Kiev (2.6 million), Bucharest (2.0 million), Budapest (1.8 million), and Minsk (1.7 million).

Remember that there is substantial variation in the definitions used to determine the urban population in these countries, ranging from a threshold of 10,000 persons (in Switzerland) to the qualitative designation of "towns and settlements of an urban type" (in Poland; see Box 1.2 in Chapter 1). While there is good reason to treat the information in Table 10.1 with some caution, the extent of urbanization in Europe is evident in the satellite photograph reproduced in Figure 10.1. Large urban agglomerations can be seen in the industrial midlands of England and in the Ruhr River valley in northern Germany. Also noticeable are the city lights of the capital cities (Madrid, Paris, London, and Moscow) as well as Milan, Rome, and Naples in southern Italy. These urban agglomerations are similar to those shown in Figure 1.1 when we were looking at the large manufacturing regions along the Great Lakes and urban agglomerations along the East and West Coasts of North America. As noted above, fully half of the largest urban centers in Europe are located in the former Soviet bloc, but here a different pattern of urban development is evident. The large capital cities (Bucharest; Budapest; Minsk, Ukraine) can clearly be seen, but they are distinct from one another and not connected to other large urban agglomerations.

We begin with an overview of urbanization in Western Europe, whose recent history offers many parallels to the U.S. experience. In subsequent sections we discuss Eastern Europe, or the former Soviet bloc countries, to examine urban conditions there. The final section deals with the case of Japan, which exhibits certain similarities to, but also differences from, the restructuring of settlement space that has characterized metropolitan development in the United States.

WESTERN EUROPE

The countries of Western Europe have been urbanized for centuries. There is a well-developed urban hierarchy across the region and within individual countries as well. The United Nations estimated that 74.6 percent of the European population was urbanized at the beginning of the millennium. That number is expected to increase to around 82 percent by 2030 and then stabilize. As we saw in Table 10.1, not all of the urban population lives in large cities; about one-half lives in small towns of 1,000–50,000 persons; one-quarter lives in medium-sized cities of 50,000–250,000 persons; and one-quarter lives in cities of more than 250,000 persons.

In recent decades, Western Europe has experienced a restructuring of population and economic activities similar to those occurring in the United States. The urban population increased at a steady pace during the last decades of the century, and there has been significant sprawl due to the declining housing stock in the urban core, changes in household size, higher household incomes, and increased infrastructure such as public transportation and interurban railroads (the last factor very different from the United States). In many countries the central cities are declining (some have suffered population losses of 40 percent or more, similar to that of older industrial cities in the United States), and there is a marked increase in the development of suburban settlement space. Older towns have experienced rapid growth, and in many European countries new towns (planned communities) have been developed in the suburban fringe. These trends interact with one another to produce multicentered metropolitan regions similar to those found in the United States.

Box 10.1

European Cities Dominate Quality of Life

Europe's cities once more dominate the world's top ten for quality of living. Vienna is the city rated with the best quality of living worldwide, moving up one place in the rankings following improvements in Austria's political and social environment. The rest of the top ten for Europe are dominated by German and Swiss cities, most of them retaining last year's ranking and scores. Zurich, in second place, is followed by Geneva (3), Düsseldorf (6), Munich (7), Frankfurt (8), and Bern (9).

The rankings are based on a point-scoring index, which sees Vienna score 108.6, and Baghdad 14.4. Cities are ranked against New York as the base city with an index score of 100. Mercer's Quality of Living ranking covers 215 cities and is conducted to help governments and major companies place employees on international assignments.

This year's ranking also identifies the cities with the best infrastructure based on electricity supply, water availability, telephone and mail services, public transport provision, traffic congestion, and the range of international flights from local airports. Singapore is at the top of this index (with a score of 109.1), followed by Munich in second place and Copenhagen in third. Japanese cities Tsukuba (4) and Yokohama (5) fill the next two slots, while Düsseldorf and Vancouver share sixth place.

Many Eastern European cities have seen an increase in quality of living. A number of countries, which joined the European Union back in 2004 have experienced consistent improvement with increased stability, rising living standards and greater availability of international consumer goods. Ljubljana in Slovenia, for example, moves up four places to reach 78, while Bratislava moves up three places to 88. Zagreb moves three places to 103.

In the city infrastructure index, German cities fair particularly well with Munich (2) the highest ranked in the region, followed by Düsseldorf (6) and Frankfurt sharing eighth place with London. "German city infrastructure is amongst the best in the world, in part due to its first class airport facilities and connections to other international destinations."

SOURCE: City Mayors—City Rankings (www.citymayors.com/sections/rankings_content.html).

The pattern of urban change is not consistent. Some countries, such as the United Kingdom, Germany, and to a lesser extent, Italy, have experienced decentralization of the population away from the large urban centers. Between 1970 and 2000, for example, Liverpool, Manchester, Birmingham, Belfast, and other cities in the United Kingdom all lost population. The population of Glasgow reached a peak of just over 1 million persons in 1931, remained at this level until 1961, and then began a long period of decline; the population of Glasgow is now just 600,000, but the population of the greater Glasgow region is more than 1,500,000. In Germany, Berlin, Essen, Dortmund, and other central cities also declined even while the larger metropolitan regions grew. Other countries such as Belgium, Luxembourg, and to some extent, France, continue to experience central city growth.

As is the case in the United States, long-term changes in metropolitan regions can be attributed to the restructuring of settlement space as a consequence of government policy and global economic shifts. Manufacturing has declined in many European countries, especially in the United Kingdom. Cities have reduced their labor forces and converted to service economies, but with smaller employment bases than in the past. High-technology corridors, the European equivalent of Silicon Valley, and other "new spaces" of production have emerged (Castells and Hall, 2004). Most prominent in this regard has been the development of "technopoles" and science parks such as the Louvain University Science City in Belgium, the Parc Cientific de Barcelona in Spain, Cambridge Science Park in England, the Sophia-Antipolis international business park near Nice on the Mediterranean coast of France (with some 1,100 companies), Silicon Glen in Livingston, Scotland, and in Russia, the Akademgorodok Science City (Brooker, 2009; Simmie, 1997; Smith, 1997). In Japan, the Tsukuba Science City dates from the 1960s, while the Kansai Science City was developed in the 1980s (Park, 1997).

These have become new sources of employment and growth based on a professional, skilled labor force along with low-wage services. Industrial restructuring has resulted in declining urban cores with considerable unemployment of the working class, while the periphery has grown and developed into an affluent, middle-class population base. Welfare state programs have been cut back, leading to continuing problems with poverty and related issues, just as in the United States. More recently, the global economic crisis has intensified many of these problems, leading to threats of further cuts to government programs, increased agitation against immigrants, and even increases in poverty in the welfare states of northern Europe. A look at individual countries shows the impact of the restructuring of settlement space in greater detail.

United Kingdom

As shown in Table 10.1, more than 90 percent of the population of the United Kingdom was urbanized in 2005, the highest percentage after Belgium, and 26 percent of the population lived in urban areas with populations of 1 million or more. Additional information about the United Kingdom's largest cities and their metropolitan regions is shown in Table 10.2. The prominent role of London in this urban system is quite apparent; with a population of more than 12 million persons, London is some five times larger than the second group of urban agglomerations with populations of 2 million. These include Birmingham, Leeds, and Manchester, the older industrial cities of the midlands and north. There are three other urban agglomerations of 1 million or more but all include small central cities of between 470,000 and 600,000 persons.

It is important to note the extent of urban regional development in the United Kingdom. (Because of the way census data are reported for metropolitan urban areas in the UK, not all of the cities shown include the metropolitan population.) For all but the two largest cities, the population of the metropolitan region is at least twice that of the city center; even in London, with a city population of 7.1 million, the suburban population adds another 4.9 million to create a metropolitan area of nearly 12 million persons. In many of the larger cities, council homes (housing for working-class families built by local municipalities) were built in the suburbs, but the large increase in suburban populations has also been fueled by a move out of the city and the growth of smaller towns in the suburban fringe. This has been a long-term trend, as the development of the suburbs in the UK has followed a pattern similar to that of the United States, with the development of middle-class suburbs in the late 1800s.

The populations of the United Kingdom's ten largest urban areas share certain demographic characteristics typical of a country with slow population growth. About 20 percent of the population is aged 0 to 15 years (the range is 18 percent in the Greater Glasgow Area to 22 percent in the West Midlands of Manchester). More than 15 percent is of pensionable age (65 years and above for males, 60 and above for females, with a range of 15 percent in the Greater London Area to 18 percent in Tyneside). These figures indicate a substantial dependent population (persons 0 to 15 and those of pensionable age), with dependency ratios ranging from 542 in the Greater London area to 672 in the West Midlands urban area (Pointer, 2005). In the United States we have heard much concern about problems with social security because of the aging population (there are relatively fewer persons working to support an increasing dependent population), and the United Kingdom confronts a similar problem, compounded by the recent declines in social welfare programs (see below).

In the United States, one of the most significant changes affecting urban areas has been the increase in immigration and the emergence of new ethnic communities. Immigration has increased in the United Kingdom as well, most noticeably in the Caribbean and Indian populations. But this has been at a very different level from the United States; of the ten largest urban areas in the UK, five are more than 90 percent white, and three others are more than 80 percent white. More than 80 percent of the non-white population in the United Kingdom lives in the Greater London Area (in 2001, Asian or Asian British accounted for 8.1 percent and black or black British accounted for 9.5 percent of the population) where there are sizeable

TABLE 10.2 Most Populated Metropolitan Areas in the United Kingdom, 2000.

	City	Metropolitan Area
London	7,074,265	11,950,000
Birmingham	1,020,589	2,600,000
Leeds	726,939	2,150,000
Glasgow	616,430	1,550,000
Sheffield	530,375	1,275,000
Bradford	483,422	
Liverpool	467,995	1,350,000
Edinburgh	448,850	
Manchester	430,818	2,500,000
Bristol	399,633	
Kirklees	388,807	
Fife	349,300	
Wirral	329,179	
North Lanarkshire	325,940	
Wakefield	317,342	

SOURCE: City Mayors—City Rankings (www.citymayors.com/sections/rankings_content.html).

black neighborhoods (primarily in East London) and Asian neighborhoods (primarily in the Heathrow area). The rich fabric of the ethnic Indian community in London is shown in the popular film *Bend It Like Beckham*, written and produced by an Indian filmmaker who grew up in the United Kingdom.

Deindustrialization, which followed World War II and has accelerated in the past quarter of a century, has had a drastic impact on the United Kingdom. All the older industrial centers have experienced sharp employment declines due to factory shutdowns and wholesale job loss. Between 1978 and 1985 alone, manufacturing in Great Britain declined by 24 percent (Sassen, 1991:131). This followed a decade of comparable job loss in manufacturing. During this same period, employment in business services increased by 44 percent. The loss of manufacturing employment has continued in the new century; between 2000 and 2003, for example, there was a loss of another 2.7 manufacturing jobs (London, 2003). Like the United States, Britain has undergone a shift from manufacturing to service industries.

Statistics for London are most revealing. Between 1960 and 1985, London lost more than 800,000 jobs in manufacturing (Sassen, 1991:210). After 1980 it reaped a harvest of new jobs in the expanding service sector. It was not until 1985, and for the first time in twenty-five years, that net gains in employment finally outstripped net losses. The shift from a manufacturing economy to a service economy can be seen in London, where 27 percent of all jobs were in manufacturing and 69 percent were in services in 1971. Fifteen years later, in 1986, the number of manufacturing jobs had declined to just 15 percent, and the number of service jobs had increased to 80 per-

FIGURE 10.2 Urban Redevelopment Along the River Clyde in Glasgow. Glasgow's population declined from over 1 million in 1961 to just 600,000 in 2005, and most of the shipbuilding industry is gone, allowing for redevelopment along the River Clyde, including housing, office space, museums, and the new city auditorium. SOURCE: MacAteer Photograph Inc., Glasgow.

cent (Sassen, 1991:205). Almost all of the new service employment in London is a result of the city's continued historical role as a global center of financial activities. London, New York City, and Tokyo are today's three global centers for finance capital, and their companies command and coordinate the increasingly dispersed world economy of manufacturing and marketing (Sassen, 1991).

New manufacturing centers tied to high-tech development have also emerged as part of this global restructuring in the United Kingdom. The M-4 highway corridor between London and Reading represents a center for electronics development that is similar to the I-128 peripheral corridor outside of Boston. In Cambridge, the government linked up with private venture capital and with Cambridge University to build a "science park." It contains thirty new enterprises on fifty-five hectares and is similar to the "research triangle" that links Durham, Chapel Hill, and Raleigh, North Carolina (and includes Duke University and the University of North Carolina).

But new employment in the service sector and in high tech has been unable to fully compensate for job loss due to deindustrialization. England has experienced a long-term readjustment that requires retraining of the labor force along with a smaller industrial sector. The need for drastic changes provided support for the Conservative Party in the 1980s. The Conservatives dismantled the British welfare state by increasing private ownership of manufacturing and reducing publicly supported benefits (King, 1990). Although a complete transfer from public financing to market-based services has not occurred in Great Britain, many welfare state programs were partially converted to a pay-for-service basis or simply eliminated during this period (Forrest, 1991). This record is comparable to the downsizing of domestic programs in the United States. The selling off of formerly nationalized companies enabled the Conservative regime in the United Kingdom to avoid massive debt financing of the economy in the 1980s, unlike the case of the United States. Economic policies changed little under the Labor Party with Tony Blair as prime minister (1997–2007), and social welfare programs remain under attack. Chris Hamnett's research shows how the transformation of London led an expansion of high-earning groups and a marked increase in both earnings and income inequality. The growth of the new middle class had major impacts on the nature of the London housing market, particularly in the growth of homeownership, rising prices, and the expansion of middle-class gentrification across much of inner London. This has been paralleled by the growing marginalization of the less skilled, the unemployed, and various minority groups in other areas of the city (Hamnett, 2003).

Privatization has brought increasing misery to many in the British working class. The appearance of uneven development on a national scale has also brought social changes to the entire country. Mellor (1989) notes that shifts in national attitudes involve the replacement of a moral ethos that supported the welfare state and its reliance on redistributive policies to overcome uneven development with a new ethos based on social Darwinism, limited public programs, and a full reliance on the market economy. In current urban research, the trends described here are referred to as neo-liberalism (Brenner and Theodore, 2002).

One outcome of economic restructuring over the past two decades in the United Kingdom is that the police have had to expand their role as controllers of the population as crime and civil unrest have increased (Ball and Webster, 2003). As Mellor notes, "U.K. towns were, in international terms, safe places. Now burglary, often minimal in material effect, violates personal space and enforces discipline in the use of house and effects; assaults and/or harassment limit the freedom of movement of the elderly, children, black people, women and, increasingly, white men" (1989:591). The UK more generally, and London in particular, has led the way in surveillance of urban populations by the installation of cameras on public streets (Goold, 2004); it is estimated that a person traveling through London in the course of a typical day will appear on more than twenty security screens. The consequences of the global restructuring of economic opportunity are graphically shown in *Trainspotting*, a film depicting the lives of young men in Edinburgh, Scotland, when the city had the highest rates of heroin use and, as a result, AIDS infection, of any European city.

There is also evidence that after years of successful redistributive policies under the welfare state, social exclusion, a term similar to our conception of the underclass, has greatly increased. When a family can consistently count on the resources of a single wage earner, it has the resources to support the employment of others, even if their positions are not in high-earning capacities. However, those families suffering from job loss and periodic unemployment are falling behind and floundering in a sea of chronic poverty. One consequence of economic restructuring has been the rise of anti-immigrant and racist groups, particularly among urban youth. Opposition to these neo-fascist groups is brilliantly portrayed in *Rude Boy*, the documentary film by The Clash.

France

The urban population in France and most other European countries has been grow-ing steadily. In the last fifteen years, the urban population of France increased from 42 to 46.7 million persons, and the percentage of the population that is urbanized increased from 74 to 77 percent. The growth that has occurred has not been in large cities: In 1990 just 23 percent lived in the four urban areas with populations greater than 1 million, and this figure decreased to 22 percent in 2005.

The population of the fifteen largest cities in France is shown in Table 10.3. Most notable about this urban system is the large number of cities with populations of 300,000 to 500,000 and the dominant position of the capital city. With a popula-tion of approximately 10.6 million persons, the Paris metropolitan area has nearly seven times the population of Lyon (1.6 million), the country's second largest city. Paris is by far the largest city in this urban system and is an example of how the pres-ence of a single large city can influence the development of other urban centers (see Chapter 11 for a full discussion of the impact of primate cities, as this is called, on urban development). France has long had one of the more centralized systems of ur-ban planning in Europe, reflecting the position and influence of the Paris region.

As in the United Kingdom, an extended period of industrial decline has led the re-structuring of metropolitan regions in France. Coal mining, steel production, and tex-tiles, located in the north and west, have been particularly hard hit by plant closings and layoffs. In one year alone (1982–1983), more than 185,000 industrial jobs were

TABLE 10.3 Largest Metropolitan Areas in France, 2000.

	City	Metropolitan Area
Paris	2,152,000	10,562,000
Lyon	422,000	1,598,000
Marseille-Aix	808,000	1,398,000
Lille	178,000	1,108,000
Toulouse	366,000	917,000
Bordeaux	213,000	882,000
Nantes	252,000	674,000
Nice	346,000	557,000
Strasbourg	256,000	557,000
Grenoble	154,000	505,000
Rennes	204,000	484,000
Toulon	170,000	478,000
Rouen	102,000	470,000
Montpellier	211,000	446,000
Nancy	105,000	396,000

SOURCE: City Mayors—City Rankings (www.citymayors.com/sections/rankings_content.html).

lost (Body-Gendrot, 1987:244). Cities such as Metz, Dunkirk, Nancy, Lille, and Roubaix have taken on the feel of declining Rust Belt cities in the United States. The French government intervened and propped up failing industries to retain jobs and the community quality of life. When these policies were not successful, however, supports were abandoned in favor of a competitive unburdening of unproductive businesses.

Industrial decline has resulted in a social crisis for many working-class families and for French society more broadly. According to one observer, "Austerity brought about a deterioration of the social fabric: . . . racism, demonstrations of workers against arbitrary decisions benefiting other workers, and petty delinquency. At the workplace, competition rose between the working classes: . . . young vs. old, white vs. non-white, men vs. women, all fighting as the size of the pie was shrinking" (Body-Gendrot, 1987:244). The rise of right-wing racists can be attributed in part to this upheaval. Today racism is a major problem in France, and hate crimes target Jews, Arabs, and immigrants from North Africa.

Some French industries were able to respond with modernization programs, especially the French automakers Renault and Citroën. Changes in manufacturing processes, such as flexible production, just-in-time delivery, and computer-assisted manufacturing in the manner of the Japanese industries, were also adopted (see Leborgne and Lipietz, 1988). The French government has been very aggressive in supporting electronics-related industries, software companies, and biotechnology. In conjunction with universities and business venture capital, new technopoles have sprung up in the Grenoble, Montpellier, and Toulouse regions, among others. These resemble the Oxbridge complex in Great Britain (the region of development around Oxford and Cambridge) and the larger university/high-tech industry regions of Silicon Valley and the Research Triangle in the United States.

The push to high-technology industries has affected higher education in the country. As elsewhere, more emphasis is now placed on technologically sophisticated degrees in engineering and science. To date, the changeover to a modernized, flexible, and high-tech economy has met with some success; for example, the French military industries are world leaders. But the older industrialized cities and their problems of decline, unemployment, and renewed racism remain.

In the fall of 2005, French cities experienced two weeks of civil unrest as ethnic minority youth took to the streets to protest high levels of unemployment and discrimination. The disturbances began on October 28, 2005, in the Paris suburb of Clichy-sous-Bois following the accidental deaths of two teenagers who were running from police and tried to hide in a power station. The protests, including the burning of cars and public buildings, spread to other cities, notably Marseilles in the south of France. French rappers and hip-hop artists were blamed for inciting the rioters. A national state of emergency was declared on October 8 and was extended for a three-month period beginning November 16. In total some 9,000 cars were burned, 2,900 persons were arrested, 126 police and firefighters were injured, and one person was killed. Nicolas Sarkozy, the interior minister who declared a "zero tolerance" policy against the protesters, was elected president of France in 2007.

In the United States we are familiar with urban unrest in the cities; what might seem unusual about these events is that they involved ethnic minority youth who lived in the suburbs of French cities. This unfortunate example demonstrates an important difference in the structure of metropolitan regions in France (differences that appear in other European countries as well). Paris and, to a lesser degree, other French cities are surrounded by a ring of older working-class suburbs created in the nineteenth century as the city expanded beyond the central city. In France the traditional word for suburb was *faubourg*, but the term *banlieue* is used to describe areas of low-income apartments and social housing; in the United States we might refer to these areas as housing projects or ghettoes (in England the term would be council homes). These are the areas where both older and recent immigrants have settled.

The Paris riots became signature events in Europe, where the term *suburb* is often equated with immigrant populations, and where problems of unemployment and poverty have taken root. At a broader level, the riots also speak to the problems of inclusion for recent immigrants, who often come from former colonial territories and have a different racial background from the French (Wacquant, 2008). In France, there has been additional conflict because the largest number of immigrants are Muslim (from Morocco, a former colony), and questions of cultural and religious difference have become important social issues. The French census does not collect data on ethnicity, but it is estimated that 6.8 percent of the population is foreign born (some 3.8 million persons), comprising 6.1 percent of the workforce (1.7 million persons). Much of this population lives in the Paris metropolitan region: 2,169,406 or some 19.4 percent of the total.

Germany

Table 10.4 shows the population for the fifteen largest metropolitan areas in Germany; also shown is the region where each is located. Berlin, the capital city, is the largest urban center with a population of some 3.2 million persons—twice that of Hamburg, the second largest city and former center of the Hanseatic League on the North Sea. München (Munich), the largest city in the southern half of the country, is the third largest metropolitan area with a population of more than 1.9 million. The figures in Table 10.4 demonstrate the importance of suburban growth; while the three largest metropolitan regions have more than half of their population in the city core, most of the other urban regions have suburban populations that are about twice that of the city (and in several, the figure is three or even four times greater).

An important feature of the urban system in Germany concerns the Rhine-Ruhr metropolitan area, comprised of five cities in the Northrhine-Westfalia region (Köln, Essen, Dortmund, Düsseldorf, and Duisburg). These are the industrial cities of the

TABLE 10.4 Most Populated Metropolitan Areas in Germany, 2000.

City	Region	City	Metropolitan Area
Berlin	Berlin	3,275,000	4,200,000
Hamburg	Hamburg	1,686,100	2,550,000
München	Bavaria	1,185,400	1,950,000
Köln	Northrhine-Westfalia	965,300	1,850,000
Frankfurt	Hessen	648,000	1,925,000
Ruhr-Rhine			5,800,000
Essen	Northrhine-Westfalia	588,800	
Dortmund	Northrhine-Westfalia	587,600	
Duisburg	Northrhine-Westfalia	513,400	
Stuttgart	Baden-Württemberg	581,100	2,600,000
Düsseldorf	Northrhine-Westfalia	568,900	1,325,000
Bremen	Bremen	527,900	900,000
Hannover	Lower Saxony	516,300	1,025,000
Nürnberg	Bavaria	486,700	1,050,000
Leipzig	Saxony	486,100	N/A
Dresden	Saxony	473,300	N/A
Mannheim	Baden-Württemberg	320,000	1,600,000

SOURCE: City Mayors—City Rankings (www.citymayors.com/sections/rankings_content.html).

Ruhr River valley, forming an urban agglomeration of more than 12 million persons. Fully half of the corporate headquarters for Germany's top one hundred companies are located in Düsseldorf. This urban agglomeration is described further in Box 10.2 and it also is visible in the northern part of Germany in the satellite photograph in Figure 10.1.

Economic restructuring and uneven development has had a pronounced effect on this region. Called the sud-nord-gefülle or the south-north cleavage in Germany, the older, northern industrial cities such as Bremen and Hamburg have been hardest hit by restructuring, while southern towns such as München and Frankfurt have become affluent. This pattern appears to be similar to the way economic changes have affected the United States, where the industrial manufacturing base of the midwestern and northeastern Rust Belt (or Frost Belt) cities such as Buffalo, Detroit, and Pittsburgh has declined, and the "new" Sun Belt cities such as Phoenix, San Diego, and Los Angeles have prospered.

According to Haussermann and Siebel, the north-south split is a consequence of Germany's shift to an export-oriented economy, similar to the case in Italy. In Germany, the southern region contains the automobile industry and also high-tech-based manufacturing—two economic sectors that have done well in the global economy. Steel production and the shipping industry, which are concentrated in the north, have been unable to compete effectively in the world system; consequently, cities based on these sectors have declined. In the 1980s the northern region containing the cities of

Box 10.2

The Rhine-Ruhr Urbanized Region

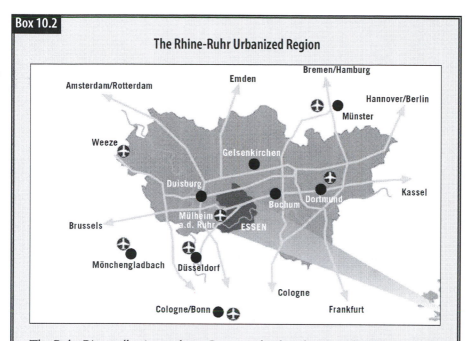

The Ruhr River valley in northern Germany developed as an industrial area in the 1600s as rivers and canals helped transport raw materials and manufactured goods. Rail and road networks in the 1800s led to further expansion during the Industrial Revolution, when the main products were coal, steel production, and tanning of leather. Heavily damaged during bombing raids in World War II, the Ruhr remains Europe's largest industrial zone, and along with the neighboring Rhine-Main industrial area has established Germany as the world leader in mechanical engineering and the world's largest exporting nation at the beginning of the twenty-first century.

The largest city in the Rhine Ruhr region is Cologne (with a population of 990,000). There are four cities with populations of 500,000 or more (Dortmund, Duisberg, Düsseldorf, and Essen) and over twenty cities of 100,000 or more. The entire metropolitan region has a population of over 1.8 million, forming an industrial landscape of unique size and with a population greater than that of the European capital cities. The metropolitan region is often mistaken as a single city because of the continuous urban development that blurs the boundaries of individual cities.

Bremen, Hamburg, and Bonn experienced a decline in employment, while the southern region containing the cities of München, Baden, Frankfurt, and Stuttgart enjoyed an increase in employment (Haussermann and Siebel, 1990:377).

The reunification of West and East Germany has had important effects on German cities. The new German government committed more than $2 billion toward rebuilding the former East Germany, but that region still lags behind West Germany and has been blamed for increasing budget deficits and a slowing of what had been the strongest of the European economies. A poll conducted in 2005 reported that 24 percent of West Germans responded positively when asked, "Would it be better if the wall between east and west still stood?" The same newspaper account noted that stereotypes and resentments persist in both regions of the country, with some West Germans regarding East Germans as backward, while some East Germans regard West Germans as bossy know-it-alls (Associated Press, 2005).

Following reunification, Germany chartered an ambitious agenda to re-create Berlin as the "capital of Europe." The Berlin Wall, which for decades stood as a symbol of the Cold War and divided the city, was removed and open space was redeveloped (particularly in East Berlin, which had suffered under the control of the Soviet Union). There has been extensive redevelopment of areas along the River Spree and of public spaces such as the Potsdamer Platz, which is said to represent a vision of Berlin for the third millennium (see Figure 10.3). Particularly notable are new buildings by world-renowned architects that make forceful statements about the city's renewal (often referred to as resurrection)—an example of the symbolic side of urbanism that has been described as "hypercity" (Nas and Samuels, 2005). Berlin once again hosts a thriving arts community and has become a major tourist city bridging the east and west.

It is expected that populations will shift to centers of increasing employment wherever they are located in the nation. There has been difficulty absorbing the labor force of former East Germany, and there has been migration from other former Soviet countries as well. Unemployment is on the rise, as is racism. Fascist skinheads perpetrating violence and hate crimes against immigrants and Jews threatened to destabilize the government in the 1990s. In May 2005 the celebration of the sixty-year anniversary of the end of World War II brought more than 3,000 neo-Nazis to Berlin's central plaza to protest against German guilt for the war and the opening of a new memorial to Jews killed in the Holocaust. They were opposed by an even larger group of 6,000 protesters, and some 10,000 police were used to keep the two groups separated. As in Italy and France, the renewal of racism in Germany has complex causes, although economic uncertainties following reunification are a contributing factor. Most Germans believe their economy can absorb the population of the former East Germany; nevertheless, the long-term effects of reunification remain unpredictable. Urbanization and conditions of life in the former Soviet bloc countries are examined in greater detail below.

Italy

As we saw in Chapter 2, the historical development of urban life in Europe after 1000 led to the development of a number of very important cities in Italy. By the

FIGURE 10.3 Potsdamer Platz in Berlin. Following the reunification of Germany in 1989, the city of Berlin began an ambitious program to make the city "the capital of Europe." Potsdamer Platz is the historical center of the city. SOURCE: Michael J. Zirbes.

1500s, three of the five largest cities in Europe were located in Italy (Naples, Milan, and Venice). After this period, economic development would focus on Northern Europe, and the great Italian cities of the Renaissance have remained relatively small through recent times. As we saw in Table 10.1, while about two-thirds (67 percent) of the Italian population lives in urban areas, only about 10 percent lives in large cities of 1 million or more persons. Table 10.5 shows the largest cities in Italy and Spain. Rome is the largest city in Italy with a population of 2.6 million, and there are two other cities with populations of about 1 million or more (Milan and Naples). Other great cities of the Renaissance—Florence and Venice—have populations of less than 400,000.

While cities in Italy are notable for the preservation of their historic core—much of the city center of Florence, for example, dates to the sixteenth century and is built around a nucleus of cathedrals dating to the 1300s—they all have experienced significant growth in the suburban region. Table 10.5 shows that for each of the fifteen largest cities, the metropolitan region population is at least two times that of the city, and in several cases the metropolitan population is three or four times larger. This pattern results from migration to the urban centers from urban areas but is also determined by strong preservation laws that in effect prohibit new construction within the city core. Many Italian cities do not appear to have extensive suburbanization because much of the population is housed in apartment buildings that cluster outside the city, but in other cases the metropolitan population has spread to adjacent cities, resulting in the pattern of multicentered regional development that we have become familiar with.

Tourism is important for many local economies and for the nation as a whole, but it has created serious problems for many Italian cities. Some have referred to Florence as an adult Disneyland because of the scale of tourism, and sustainable tourism is an important area of discussion and study. Local residents complain of the high cost of housing in the city center, and there is extensive residential development of more affordable apartment housing along the Arno River valley. Following a devastating series of floods in the 1960s, the population of Venice has declined by half, and it too has been labeled an artificial city (although there are neighborhoods that are residential, much of the workforce employed in the service industry live on the mainland; Davis and Marvin, 2004). The concern over the impact of tourism on Italian cities is a special case of a more general concern with tourism in the Mediterranean region as a whole (Loukissas and Skayannis, 2001).

For decades Italy remained one of the underdeveloped areas of Western Europe. The north was highly industrialized with an urbanized labor force centering on Milan and Turin. The south, in contrast, remained rural and dependent on agriculture (Martinelli, 1985). Population in the south was unstable, as native sons often left home to migrate to cities in the north or immigrated to other countries (including Australia, Argentina, Canada, and the United States) in search of employment.

Since the 1960s, the same force of economic restructuring that has operated in the rest of the industrialized West has changed the sociospatial pattern of development in Italy as well. The middle and southern regions, known as the *mezzogiorno*, developed a vibrant industrial employment base concentrated in the small-craft tradition of the region. This includes apparel, textiles, footwear, wood products such as furniture, metal working, and clay and glass products. Firms in this region have been very successful by adopting custom design and flexible industrial methods. They engage in small-batch production, which can be changed and customized for new orders relatively easily. Many observers believe that these firms would serve as a model for the new type of "flexible" manufacturing (called post-Fordism) that would prosper in the global economy (Scott, 1988; Piore and Sabel, 1984). Because of this, the recent economic crisis has had an important impact on many manufacturing firms in the north, several of which were specialty providers of engine parts for U.S. automobile companies that declared bankruptcy in 2009.

Increased foreign competition, especially in the automobile industry, threatened the northern region, and by the 1990s the cities of Turin and Milan no longer were the employment meccas they had been in the past. Changes were made in the indus-

TABLE 10.5 Most Populated Cities in Italy and Spain, 2000.

	City Population	Urban Region
Italy		
Milano	2,321,552	5,249,727
Roma	1,635,096	4,338,854
Napoli	847,436	3,512,698
Torino	832,204	2,000,018
Firenze	513,826	1,197,190
Palermo	267,210	1,062,993
Bologna	412,102	907,764
Catania	232,456	868,150
Bari	259,753	857,646
Savona	308,393	847,241
Padova	281,440	639,425
Ravenna	267,185	603,327
Venezia	242,980	590,199
Bergamo	252,027	573,215
Taranto	160,196	566,295
Spain		
Madrid	2,618,088	5,877,254
Barcelona	1,949,772	4,386,979
Valencia	713,804	1,724,732
Sevilla	477,277	1,381,084
Bilbao	421,539	1,066,170
Gijón	332,532	922,381
Zaragoza	327,307	780,883
Málaga	261,283	731,162
Las Palmas de Gran Canarias	280,974	710,510
Jerez de la Frontera	201,913	653,980
Alicante	253,810	623506
Murcia	220,970	546,483
Vigo	215,647	538,181
Granada	179,101	533,773

SOURCE: Rafael Boix and Paolo Veneri, *Metropolitan Areas in Spain and Italy* (2009).

trial base to regain the competitive edge of such companies as Fiat Automobiles and Pirelli Tires, and in 1999, Fiat entered into a deal to acquire Chrysler, the U.S. automobile manufacturer. In Turin, existing plants were modernized according to the Japanese style that has also been copied by American automakers. Automation was introduced, and aspects of the assembly line were turned over to robotics. Wholesale use of electronic or computer-assisted manufacturing was also incorporated into production. Finally, the "just-in-time" system was adopted by assembly plants to reduce operating costs by eliminating inventory problems. Under this system, assembly plants do away with holding large inventories of items they require in production. Instead, they work with suppliers outside the plant but within the region to provide what they need at the time they require it in the assembly process. Coordination of supplies is accomplished with the use of computers that monitor all aspects of the distribution and production schedules.

The successful adaptation of Italian industries to changes in the global marketplace stabilized migration patterns within the country. Transformations as a consequence of restructuring have been celebrated by some observers as a new model of growth that other advanced nations undergoing change should copy. The fate of cities depends progressively more on their ability to attract and retain mobile capital investment. Capital, in turn, must restructure and acquire greater flexibility in responding to the increasing demands for small-batch, customized production. Caught by the decline in manufacturing employment and the threat of plant closings or layoffs, workers must settle for less job security and a growing need to work closely with business for the sake of their mutual survival.

Much of Italian industry is oriented toward exports. In the 1990s, the slowdown in the global economy hit Italy hard, especially in the mezzogiorno region. Once again the specter of layoffs and recession has destabilized politics as the standard of living for both working-class and middle-class households is threatened by economic restructuring. Fascist skinheads emerged in the 1980s, and anti-Semitism is on the rise despite the very small Jewish population. Not all of this activity is directly related to the current recession, and other as yet undocumented factors may be playing a role as Italy enters a new period of social transformation.

Spain

During the early Middle Ages, the cities of Spain were the largest in all of Europe; Córdoba, the capital of the Moorish empire, was for several centuries the largest city in the world (see Chapter 2). In the 1500s, Catholic Spain rose to world dominance, and millions of dollars of wealth poured into the country from colonies in the Americas and Asia. But the wealth generated by this mercantilist empire did not produce a well-developed urban system, nor did it lead to industrialization in the 1700s and 1800s. The Spanish Civil War of the 1930s, which resulted in the triumph of the fascist state that survived until the 1960s, created further divisions that made development more difficult. As a consequence, and unlike most other European countries, Spain is not highly industrialized, and agricultural production remains important for a significant proportion of the population. Most of the manufacturing has been centered in the Madrid region, and the urbanization pattern in this country is not as balanced as in the other European nations we have considered so far.

As we saw in Table 10.1, the proportion of Spain's population living in urban areas increased slightly from 75 percent in 1990 to 77 percent in 2005, while the number of persons living in large cities of 1 million or more increased from 20 percent in 1980 to just 24 percent in 2000. The populations of the largest cities in Spain are shown in the bottom half of Table 10.5. Madrid (the capital, with a population of 2.6 million) and Barcelona (1.4 million) are the two largest cities. There are four other cities with populations more than 500,000 and a large number of regional centers with populations ranging from 250,000 to 350,000 persons. This urban system is very different from what we have seen in other areas of Europe, in large measure because the level of industrialization has not led to the concentration of population in large industrial cities. But in recent years, Spain too has been affected by the world-wide restructuring of the global economy.

Older industrial districts, such as Villaverde, have declined and are plagued by job loss and poverty. Small manufacturers, much like the businesses of Italy's mezzo-giorno, have remained successful, especially those involved in metal working, crafts, and printing. In addition, a new high-tech corridor running from Madrid past the airport and toward Barcelona has appeared recently and is expanding in employment. And the city of Madrid itself has been changing from a manufacturing economy to a service economy. A building boom of office towers along La Castellana Boulevard caused by the growing importance of finance-related business services has produced an increase in service-related employment.

Spain is an interesting case because of industrial development during the 1980s under the direction of a socialist government. The 1992 Summer Olympics served to showcase Spain's other large metropolis, Barcelona, as well as to stimulate the nation's economy. The global recession of the 1990s, however, hit the country hard, as it did all other export-oriented economies. Consequently, there has been a slowdown in the sociospatial restructuring of metropolitan areas in Spain even before the recent global financial crisis.

EASTERN EUROPE

The countries in Eastern Europe were occupied by the Soviet Union at the end of World War II and existed under communist domination for seventy years. For the better part of four decades, they were included under the label *second world*, signifying the Cold War distinction between the first world (the United States and the developed Western nations) and the third world (nations in the developing world). They now have joined the capitalist West, but questions about the future development of this heavily urbanized area remain. A United Nations report summarized these concerns in the following manner:

> The countries of Eastern Europe and the former Soviet Union are undergoing an economic, political, and administrative transition which is reflected in shrinking gross domestic products, high unemployment and declining fertility and life

expectancy. While some countries have shown signs of economic stabilization (e.g., reduced rates of inflation and economic contraction), it will take time to establish new institutions and redefine the role of the public and private sectors. . . . Wasteful consumption and productive patterns, long-term neglect, and misdirected policies have led to serious environmental degradation. Toxic industrial pollutants affect health and agriculture. The transition to market economies calls for new regulatory regimes to accommodate greater participation by non-governmental organizations and the private sector. (United Nations Population Fund, 1996)

The complex history of Eastern European countries, and the important social and political issues surrounding their reintegration into European urban history more generally, is described in Box 10.3, which presents the program statement of a 2005 conference titled "Cities After the Fall: European Integration and Urban History Conference."

By 2000, some 68 percent of the population in Eastern Europe lived in urban areas—one of the highest levels of urbanization in the world. But as we saw in Table 10.1, the level of urbanization varies substantially from country to country (54 percent in Romania is the lowest, 73 percent in the Russian Federation the highest). There are seven cities with populations of more than 2 million persons, as shown in Table 10.6. Many Eastern European countries exhibit an uneven pattern of urban development, where one large urban center dominates the country. Only Russia seems to have been able to develop a balanced urban hierarchy.

Table 10.6 shows the population for the largest metropolitan areas in Eastern Europe. There are several distinctive features about this regional urban system. It is dominated by Moscow, the capital of the former Soviet Union, with a metropolitan region population estimated at 15.2 million in 2003 (City Mayors, 2005). The second largest metropolitan area, St. Petersburg, with a population of 6.3 million, is the former capital built in the 1700s as Russia sought to become a world power alongside the European monarchies. These are followed by a group of cities with populations of 1.5 to 3.0 million that for the most part represent the capital cities of older nations in Eastern Europe (Warsaw in Poland, Budapest in Hungary) or the newly independent countries of the former USSR (Minsk in Belarus, Kiev in Ukraine).

In 1970 only six Russian cities had more than 1 million persons. By 2000 there were more than a dozen cities with a population of at least 1 million. The two largest cities—Moscow and St. Petersburg—are the consequence of Russia's long history as a centralized state. Moscow is not only the largest city in Eastern Europe, but it also is larger than any other European city. It accounts for half of all banking activity in Russia, along with one-third of its retail sales and one-third of national wholesale trade. Although there are more than a dozen Russian cities with populations of 1 million or more, the concentration of economic power and political control under the Soviet state means that none of these cities developed as metropolitan centers for

Box 10.3

Cities After the Fall

In his book *Images of the American City*, when Anselm Strauss posed a simple question, "What time is this city?" he was asking about the character of urban temporal orientation and about how it had a formative effect on the character of a city. One could pose the same question in contemporary East Berlin, Riga, Lviv, Vilnius, Minsk, or Wrocsaw, in Gdansk, Kaliningrad, Novgorod, Szczecin, Tallinn, or Odessa; in each case, either storied pasts or supposed European futures would probably insinuate themselves into the contemporary answer. The post-communist projections of the past and the future engender Janus-faced imageries of era and geography in these cities, which, in turn, are strongly influencing their representation and (planned) reconfiguration. A process of cultural reorientation and European integration that began circa 1990 continues.

The reorientations are geopolitical as attempts are made to integrate into a "Western" and "European" context after the fall of the Soviet Union. The transformation of these cities is helping redefine the regions and the modern borders of Europe. One could claim that a "New Europe" takes place and form in these cities, which gravitate to Habsburg, Baltic, Imperial Russian, or Germanic past and propose their own futures in ethnic-national, European, Western, and global contexts. The tourist industry as well as political parties, private heritage societies and government organizations, and other political and economic interests are all involved in this historical and geographical repositioning. Concretely the shift in urban time and place expresses itself in the grand and subtle changes to the urban fabric, which is beginning to accommodate the new order and orientation.

In many cases, there is a strained discourse between the versions of an urban past and the variously envisioned future(s), while the opposing arguments are being set in stone or in steel and glass.

SOURCE: "Cities After the Fall: European Integration and Urban History Conference," Minda de Gunzburg Center for European Studies, Harvard University, Spring 2005.

a larger urban region. This role was reserved for the two cities with former federal status: Moscow and St. Petersburg.

In the past, discussion about Eastern European cities among urbanists focused on whether there is a specific difference in patterns of growth that can be attributed to Communism—was there a particular urban form that might be identified as the Socialist City? But according to Friedrichs, "Except for a short period in the early 1920s, there are no specific socialist types of land use, distribution of new housing, internal organization of residential blocks, or location of companies" (1988:128).

TABLE 10.6 Largest Cities in Eastern Europe, 1975 and 2003.

City	Country	Population		% of Urban Population	
		1975	2003	1975	2003
Moscow	Russian Federation	7,600,000	10,500,000	7.3	10.0
Saint Petersburg	Russian Federation	4,300,000	5,300,000	3.7	5.0
Katowice	Poland	3,000,000	3,000,000	7.7	12.4
Kiev	Ukraine	1,900,000		5.4	8.0
Warsaw	Poland	1,900,000	2,200,000	5.7	9.2
Bucharest	Romania	1,800,000	1,900,000	8.3	15.2
Budapest	Hungary	2,200,000	1,700,000	17.3	26.6
Minsk	Belarus	1,100,000	1,700,000	17.2	24.3
Kharkov	Ukraine	1,400,000	1,500,000	3.0	4.5
Novosibirsk	Russian Federation	1,300,000	1,400,000	1.0	1.4
Nizhni Novgorod	Russian Federation	1,300,000	1,300,000	0.9	1.2
Ekaterinburg	Russian Federation	1,100,000	1,300,000	0.9	1.2
Prague	Czech Republic	1,100,000	1,200,000	11.4	15.4
Samara	Russian Federation	1,100,000	1,200,000	0.8	1.1
Omsk	Russian Federation	900,000	1,100,000	0.8	1.1
Kazan	Russian Federation	900,000	1,100,000	0.8	1.1
Chelyabinsk	Russian Federation	1,000,000	1,100,000	0.8	1.0
Sofia	Bulgaria	1,000,000	1,100,000	13.6	19.5
Rostov-on-Don	Russian Federation	900,000	1,100,000	0.8	1.0
Tbilisi	Georgia	1,000,000	1,100,000	20.8	40.0
Dnepropetrovsk	Ukraine	1,000,000	1,100,000	2.2	3.2
Ufa	Russian Federation	900,000	1,000,000	0.7	1.0
Odessa	Ukraine	1,000,000	1,000,000	2.1	3.1
Volgograd	Russian Federation	900,000	1,000,000	0.7	1.0
Donetsk	Ukraine	1,000,000	1,000,000	2.1	3.1

SOURCE: *World Urbanization Prospects: The 2003 Revision* (www.un.org/esa/population/publications/wup2003).

There was some effort to develop urban structures more friendly to the working population in the years following World War I, when much of Europe was governed by a succession of socialist and left-wing political movements, before the solidification of rightist regimes under Fascism. Consequently, Communist societies have built environments similar to those in capitalist countries. Yet there are fundamental differences between Communism and capitalism, especially with regard to the absence in the former of separate factions of capital and separate markets. There are some peculiarities of land use and population distribution among such cities that differ from patterns in the West. These involve the nature of the central city due to an absence of the finance capital sector, the pattern of population distribution and the housing shortage, and most important, an absence of a capitalist real estate market.

Central City Decline

All Eastern European countries have large capital cities, the result of both historical patterns of development as well as centralization under the Soviet system. Some, such as Hungary and Poland, have very uneven development due to the dominance of their main centers—Budapest and Warsaw, respectively. Others, such as the Czech Republic and Russia, have a more balanced system of cities. In every case, the central sections of the major cities are quite old, dating back several hundred years to their founding. Under the Communist governments, original buildings in the city center were not torn down. They remain standing in many cases and many are in terrible shape. The lack of ambitious office building schemes, characteristic of many Communist cities, stands in contrast to the capitalist city, where finance capital and its associated business services, such as accounting and legal consulting, have taken over the downtown. In most Communist countries, the state directed investment in real estate and economic development; thus, their downtowns do not contain an active real estate market of office buildings that services the needs of corporate and finance capital. As a result, the shift to the service-oriented economy is occurring more slowly in these countries than elsewhere in Europe.

One of the most notable changes in urbanization in the Eastern European countries has been the decline in central city population and increase in the suburbs and urban periphery; this development is common to all countries, and of course similar to that observed in Western Europe. Once the specific state-sponsored incentives that concentrated housing and other development within the urban core were lifted, the population in these countries rapidly moved out of the central cities.

The Demographic Pattern of Land Use

Family and household income differences in Eastern European cities historically were not as disparate as in the rest of Europe or the United States (Ladanyi, 1989). In the United States, both the wealthy and the poorest classes are highly segregated, and in many European cities, working-class families live in the suburbs. In Eastern European cities, such as Budapest, there is some segregation of the wealthy classes and the poor, but the rest of the population is evenly spread out in the city despite some differences in family income.

The reason for this contrast in the Soviet city was the operation of government subsidies for housing, which prevented the poorest people from being concentrated within urban spaces. Thus, a major difference between formerly Communist societies and capitalist ones such as the United States was the active role of government in providing affordable housing for the poor (although, as we will see below, the total volume of available housing is inadequate). In the period following the collapse of the Soviet Union, many of the public housing units were converted to private housing.

Box 10.4

Social Problems in Eastern European Cities

The contraction of state-sector employment without commensurate growth of private-sector employment has led to a decline in real wages, pensions, and social transfers within a general context of high inflation. The breakup of the former Soviet Union generated severe disruptions in the old trading and monetary regimes, which resulted in catastrophic declines in GDP of about 45 percent during the 1990–1996 period.

Over the following decade, the region saw rising income inequalities. Poverty and unemployment also increased significantly. It has been observed that the failure of rapid privatization in Russia, for instance, "was not an accident, but a predictable consequence" of the absence of competition policies and the institutional and legal infrastructure needed to support successful reform efforts. The region's poor housing conditions are reflected in recent slum estimates, which reveal that in transition economies, about one-tenth of the urban population live in slum conditions, without adequate access to basic services, or in crowded housing units. In 2002, about 46 percent of residents of the former Soviet Union and Eastern European countries lived on less than $4 per day, compared to 10 percent in Western Europe. Fifty-three percent of the Russian population, 23 percent in Romania, 28 percent in Latvia, 62 percent in Kazakhstan, and 88 percent in Kyrgyzstan have to survive on even less.

Trafficking and smuggling of human beings operated by organized crime networks in countries whose economies are in transition has become of particular concern to national governments and the international community. Although Asian countries have been the primary suppliers of women to the sex trade for decades, the collapse of the Soviet Union has made former Soviet republics such as Ukraine, Belarus, Latvia, and Russia major source countries of women into prostitution. Trafficked women from this region are delivered into prostitution throughout the world, and there are estimated to be a half million women from Central and Eastern Europe working in prostitution in the European Union alone.

Today the dream for a better life seems to have vanished in the face of the millions of new poor exposed to living conditions that can be similar to those living in the least developed nations. Across Eastern Europe and Central Asia, household poverty has increased fivefold during the last twelve years and its social by-products are discernible everywhere: sharp increases in alcoholism—especially among men—suicide, and mortality, as well as a decline in marriage and a rise in divorce rates.

SOURCE: "Poverty, crime and migration are acute issues as Eastern European cities continue to grow," City Mayors—Urban Society (www.citymayors.com/society/easteurope_cities.html).

Paradoxically, however, under the Communist governments, the more affluent people have also enjoyed considerable state housing subsidies (Ladanyi, 1989). Consequently, it is not the market that has created uneven development in formerly Communist countries, as it does under capitalism, but state intervention itself. This kind of uneven development and privilege produced by state favors for the elite was a common complaint about Communist practice for decades; however, it is comparable to the economic advantages of the capitalist class in the United States.

With the fall of Communism, housing subsidies are declining, and as the market takes over, segregation is increasing. As noted above, much of the public housing has been converted to privately owned housing. The construction of new, privately owned housing represents efforts to alleviate the chronic shortage of housing in these societies. The shift to an active capitalist real estate market has produced the first significant signs of capitalist-style uneven development within urban settlement spaces, such as a growing number of homeless people and a sharp rise in the cost of rental housing, which hits elderly pensioners particularly hard.

The Emergence of Free Markets

Eastern Europe has been the scene of immense social change due to the transition from Communism to a market economy. The most significant change has been the growth of the real estate market and a new, second circuit of capital for formerly Communist countries. It remains to be seen how this restructuring will affect settlement space within urban areas; however, we can use the U.S. case as a guide for future projections. Some early indications suggest that segregation has increased, deconcentration of population has accelerated as suburbanization occurs, and the service economy has begun to replace manufacturing as the principal sector. Old buildings remain, and in many countries there has been little new office construction. This situation most likely cannot last as the capitalist urban land market takes over and the pressures to switch to a service-based economy prevail there as they have in the capitalist West. We can even expect drastic renovation or renewal programs, led by private investment, for the construction of high-rise office towers in the Eastern European cities of the future.

JAPAN

Because of its dominant position in the Pacific Rim and early transition to an industrial power, Japan has contained large cities for hundreds of years. Tokyo, for example, had over 1 million people as early as the 1700s when it served as the capital (called Edo at the time) of the shogun empire. The modernization of Tokyo following the Meiji Restoration resulted in a continuous migration from rural areas to the expanding metropolitan region surrounding the capital city (Bestor, 1985). Since World War II, Japanese cities have developed as large regional agglomerations or multicentered metropolitan regions.

The greater Tokyo metropolitan area is estimated to contain 34 million people, a quarter of the entire population of Japan, while the city of Tokyo alone had more than 8 million persons in 2000. This large urban agglomeration is comparable to that of New York and Los Angeles combined. The overall level of urbanization of the Japanese population, some 80 percent of the total, is comparable to that of many Western countries.

The population of the largest metropolitan areas in Japan is shown in Table 10.7. Two urban centers dominate this urban system. The Tokyo metropolitan area includes the cities of Tokyo (8.1 million), Yokohama (3.4 million), and Kawasaki (1.2 million) and another 20 million persons living in other cities and urbanized areas linked to these cities. The greater Osaka metropolitan area (16.8 million persons) includes the cities of Osaka (2.6 million), Kobe (1.5 million), and Kyoto (1.5 million), and another 11 million persons in the urbanized areas linked to these cities. There is one other great metropolitan area (Nagoya, with a population of 8 million), and two metropolitan areas of more than 2.5 million (Sapporo and Fukuoka). As shown in Table 10.7, the Japanese urban system includes eight other metropolitan areas with populations of more than 1 million, and there is some variation in the structure of these regions: In Hiroshima and Kitakyushu, the city population accounts for more than half of the metropolitan area, while the populations of the cities of Naha and Himeji account for less than a third of their metropolitan regions.

Japanese cities developed trading and commercial centers during the sixteenth and seventeenth centuries. When industrialization developed in the West in the nineteenth century, it was embraced by Japanese business along with the aid of the monarchy. By the beginning of the twentieth century, Japan was already a major industrial power, with extensive manufacturing areas producing textiles and other goods. After the massive loss of labor and industrial production following World War II, Japan initiated ambitious industrialization schemes focusing on exports, which were remarkably successful in establishing Japan as a global economic power (Lee, 1982; Berry, 1989; Honjo, 1998).

Japanese cities have not experienced the deconcentration of population and employment observed in U.S. cities, nor have they undergone a shift to services on the same scale as cities in the United States and older industrialized countries. Today manufacturing remains important to the Japanese economy. Work is highly centralized within city boundaries even though the suburban population is growing. Each day several million commuters ride into the central city by public transportation, often traveling as much as two hours each way. Japan is unlike the United States in other respects as well. Due to a free market in real estate, a general shortage of land in the country, and the centralization of employment within large cities, housing and rental prices are astronomically high, and Tokyo is often rated as the world's most expensive city in which to live. It has become increasingly difficult to own a home in a Japanese city, and most housing space, in terms of square feet, is extremely small by U.S. standards.

The success of Japan's export-oriented industries in the global economy produced important changes in settlement space patterns for the entire Pacific Rim. Japanese industries introduced a number of innovative techniques, such as "just-in-time" methods, that increased their competitiveness. They also embarked on regional schemes of manufacturing in search of cheap labor (much like U.S. companies), which had an impact on other Asian countries, in particular South Korea and Taiwan. But the real impact occurred because of Japan's success in foreign trade earnings, and by the end of the twentieth century, it became a major repository of the world's finance capital.

Several notable trends have characterized Japanese industrial and urban development over the last two decades. Most significant is the profits squeeze from the increasing costs of Japanese labor, coupled with a slowing of population growth that makes labor more scarce. This has resulted in the kind of response adopted by U.S. firms, namely, the shift of some production to other countries with cheaper and more compliant sources of labor. While marketing and control remain located in Japan, there has been an increase in the amount of component-part production farmed out to Taiwan, South Korea, and Singapore (Douglas, 1988; Berry, 1989:203).

Japan is experiencing another trend common to the United States and Europe. Japan has always restricted its immigration, which is why its labor force and urban populations have remained more stable than those in countries such as the United States. Lately, however, illegal immigration is becoming noticeable as the global flow of investment and people integrates the Pacific Rim countries. Typically, such immigration

TABLE 10.7 Largest Metropolitan Areas in Japan, 2000.

	City Population	Metropolitan Area
Tokyo	8,130,000	34,000,000
Yokohama	3,426,000	
Kawasaki	1,249,000	
Osaka	2,598,000	16,750,000
Kobe	1,493,000	
Kyoto	1,467,000	
Nagoya	2,171,000	8,000,000
Sapporo	1,822,000	2,500,000
Fukuoka	1,341,000	2,250,000
Hiroshima	1,126,000	1,725,000
Kitakyushu	1,011,000	1,600,000
Okayama	627,000	1,375,000
Naha	301,000	1,125,000
Himeji	471,000	1,125,000
Kumamoto	662,123	1,100,000
Hamamatsu	582,000	1,100,000
Shizuoka	470,000	1,000,000

SOURCE: Adapted from Thomas Brinkerhoff, Japan: Major Cities (www.citypopulation.de/japan-cities.html).

occurs because the low-wage, menial jobs that are necessary in a developed economy are no longer being filled by the domestic population because of increases in the quality of life and training levels. Sassen (1991:308) notes that since the late 1980s, there has been a rapid increase in the number of illegal aliens working in Japan; typically, they enter the country with tourist visas and overstay their officially permitted time. It is estimated that in the 1990s there were 200,000 illegal male workers in Japan doing manual labor, from construction to restaurant jobs. Almost all of these were from Asia. The largest groups were from Taiwan, South Korea, Bangladesh, the Philippines, and Pakistan.

Japanese cities are not characterized by the kind of social segregation found in the West, although the wealthy are isolated from the rest of the masses. However, they exhibit uneven development with regard to the lack of services and facilities. Extreme housing and space shortages still affect the city's inhabitants. There are few parks, medical facilities, and community centers in Tokyo. The city does contain an extensive mass transit network, as do other Japanese cities, but all Japanese cities suffer from pollution, smog, noise, and overcrowding (Nakamura and White, 1988). Other areas of the country are plagued by extensive pollution resulting from industrial development that the government has not controlled.

Population demographics will have an impact on Japanese cities and metropolitan areas in the coming decades, but in a way very different from other Asian countries (see Chapter 11). The fertility rate is already very low and is expected to decrease rapidly, as we have already seen in some Western European countries. It is estimated that Japan's population in 2050 may be only 100 million—a decrease of 17 percent (Fujii, 2005). Japan generally has not seen the decline of urban centers similar to that of the United States or Europe. Fujii suggests that Osaka may be the most appropriate urban comparison. Osaka reached its peak population of 3 million in 1985 but has decreased since then (to 2.6 million in 1995). Observers suggest that cities in Japan are shrinking for a number of reasons: Port cities such as Nagasaki and Kobe have declined relative to other cities; manufacturing centers such as Kitakyushu are "company towns" vulnerable to the relative success of just one company or economic sector; and in some instances companies have moved out of older industrial cities to locate in the capital. As a consequence, the Tokyo metropolitan region prospers while other cities may decline.

Recent urban development in Japan has involved the construction of technopoles and other spaces that bypass the established urban agglomerations. In the 1980s new technopoles were energetically constructed with massive government support, a feature that differs from the United States, which has yet to undertake such federally sponsored development. Most projects are joint ventures by the state, universities, and private capital, such as the giant Tsukuba "science city" centered on Skuba University outside of Tokyo. More recently, technopoles have been developed in the peripheral regions of Japan—those areas previously bypassed by development—such as

Box 10.5

Japanese Towns Are Disappearing

The world's population may be growing fast and the number of pensioners increasing faster than ever. But the irony of the greying population is not that the world is filling up with people, but rather that huge belts of it are becoming depopulated.

At first sight, Kiyosato doesn't look like a place fighting for its survival. Amid the vast fields of potatoes, sweet corn and beetroot stand rows of pristine houses and a community center. But apart from the distant hum of a tractor, the town is silent and the streets are almost empty. Kiyosato is living on borrowed time. And so, according to the government, are more than 60,000 Japanese towns, at risk of death through depopulation as a result of a twin attack from a declining birthrate and a surging life expectancy—currently 86.05 years for women and 79.29 for men.

Japan has one of the world's biggest proportions of over-65s—22.5 percent of its 127 million people—and one of the smallest of under-15s, at 13 percent. More than two in five people living in rural communities are over 65, and the elderly make up more than half of the population of an estimated 8,000 towns and villages. Demographers expect the current population of 127 million to fall to 100 million over the next 50 years.

About 200 communities have vanished in the past decade. The threat of extinction looms largest in Hokkaido, where almost 10 percent of towns are at risk, with half of those expected to disappear over the next decade. Kiyosato has seen its population plummet from a peak of 11,000 in the early 1960s to just 4,675 today. Almost a third of residents are over 65, 10 percent higher than the national average. Its five primary schools are attended by a total of 318 pupils; the smallest has just 48.

In an attempt to boost its population, Kiyosato is targeting millions of sixty-something salarymen and their families with promises of a post-retirement rural idyll in return for setting up home there. It is allowing prospective residents to live locally for up to a month at vastly reduced rents in spacious new homes. But of the several dozen people to take up the offer since last summer, none has made the move permanent.

Kiyosato's salvation may lie in luring back younger urbanites to rediscover their rustic roots. Yamashita Kengo, who moved to Kiyosato with his wife and two children 10 years ago, says he can't imagine returning to his old city life. "There are plenty of people who want a change in lifestyle, even to quit their jobs and head into the countryside to start again, but it isn't part of Japan's corporate culture to just leave in mid-career. They don't know how to go about it."

SOURCE: J. McCurry, "Japan: Towns Face Extinction," 2009.

Hokkaido, Tohoku, Kyushu, and the area along the Sea of Japan. One of the most ambitious of these projects is the "silicon island" developed on Kyushu, centered in Kumamoto City (Fujita, 1988). This region has become a leading producer of microchips and boasted a population of over 1.8 million in 2008.

Japan exhibits some of the characteristics of Western industrialized countries. Its traditional urban centers continue to grow. At the same time, new urban spaces have been created to house the "knowledge industries." These are similar to technopoles found elsewhere, but Japan's government is energetic in its support of such new development. Japan's urban system shows symptoms of overurbanization and is dominated by Tokyo and other large agglomerations, such as Osaka and Nagoya. Due to the high cost of land and the very high price of housing, there has been little suburbanization or residential construction, and Japanese cities have not grown at rates comparable to Western Europe or the United States. As a result, many Japanese must contend with long commutes from regional towns to work in crowded facilities and cramped living quarters at home.

SUMMARY

Cities and metropolitan regions in the developed nations have undergone significant economic restructuring to service-based economies, with a reduced scale of government aid similar to that in the United States. New techniques of post-Fordist manufacturing have been introduced in the successful industries, including automation and Japanese-style flexible methods of production. High-technology corridors, similar to Silicon Valley in the United States, have also appeared, such as the M-4 corridor in England. Finally, there is an increasing integration of large corporations and transnational firms that, like their American counterparts, conduct business around the globe.

Economic restructuring has also brought an increasing array of urban problems. Crime, poverty, and the declining quality of life, almost unheard of as European concerns, are now becoming serious problems. Hate crimes, anti-immigrant sentiments, and racism are on the rise. Unemployment has increased because of related economic changes that have hit the working class especially hard. Cutbacks in the traditional European welfare state have made the problem of poverty more severe. Since the level of funding for public assistance varies greatly among the countries of Western Europe, despite recent EU programs, fears have been expressed about the migration of poor households to areas with appreciably better social programs than another during a time of economic hardship.

In recent decades, large numbers of workers from the developing world have entered developed societies in the hope of obtaining work. Several million Turks, Kurds, and Greeks, for example, live in Germany. Millions of North Africans have migrated to France, and even the Danes, who have always lived in a homogeneous society, are now concerned about the high Muslim birthrate in their country. It is now quite common to have African, Middle Eastern, or Asian cab drivers in Paris, London, and Berlin (not just Los Angeles and New York). Domestic servants, undocumented workers, and low-skilled, labor-intensive factories or sweatshops composed of developing world workers are increasingly common in all these cities. Even Japan, which restricts immigration, has a growing number of illegal aliens from Asia who come there in search of work.

Global economic restructuring therefore brings an increasingly mobile flow not only of capital investment and goods but also of people. Immigration from developing world countries to Europe has affected the social order of these once relatively homogeneous societies in notable ways. The growing presence of foreigners is reflected in the increasing mix of ethnic restaurants that have sprung up in city centers. This drawing together of the first and developing worlds in a common urban experience is increasingly characteristic of contemporary Western cities.

All of these elements have combined to produce changes in the social order of once homogeneous European societies. Uneven development in wage levels creates a growing disparity between well-off professionals and low-wage service workers. Migration and ethnic cultural influences have met with increasing numbers of hate crimes, racism, and anti-Semitism in a post-Holocaust Europe.

Asian urban development is led by the modern economy of Japan and, more recently, of China (see Chapter 11). It too suffers from uneven development. Japanese housing and real estate issues are worrisome, and the shortage of affordable housing units means that fewer and fewer workers will be able to find places to live within reasonable commuting distance of their place of employment. But many negative effects are outweighed by the success of Japanese economic growth. Industrial expansion brings the growth of multicentered metropolitan regions outside of Japan's traditional manufacturing centers—Tokyo, Osaka, and Nagoya. Financial investment flowing from Japan fuels the economies of the Asian tigers and thereby restructures the entire Pacific Rim (as well as the United States, Canada, and Australia, in addition to the less developed countries of Asia and Latin America) for a new round of growth.

Common problems confront the urban future in Europe, Japan, and the United States, including the growing lack of affordable housing; challenges from the flow of immigrants who are often illegal aliens; declines in manufacturing employment; and the uneven development of economic opportunities for city populations due to the restructuring of the economy and the emphasis on high-tech skills. Despite comparable declines in central city population, extensive suburbanization, and post-suburban development on the periphery, no industrialized country has experienced the kind of inner-city collapse and decline in the conditions of everyday life comparable to the U.S. experience. In this respect the United States presents a unique case to the world—although parallels may be found in cities such as Calcutta and Nairobi in the developing world, as we will see in the next chapter.

KEY CONCEPTS

global restructuring
welfare state
deindustrialization
social exclusion
sustainable tourism
banlieue

DISCUSSION QUESTIONS

1. How is the pattern of urbanization in other industrialized countries similar to that found in the United States? In what ways does it differ from that in the United States? What factors are responsible for these differences?

2. Many of the changes in urban systems and metropolitan areas in other industrialized countries are similar to those in the United States. How have changes in the global economy affected metropolitan areas in Western Europe? Have these changes made these cities more similar to or more different from those in the United States?

3. What are the effects of deindustrialization and other changes in the global economy on cities in Western Europe? What are some of the important differences in the ways in which national governments responded to these changes?

4. How are the patterns of urbanization in Eastern Europe different from those in Western Europe? Explain the effects of the housing shortage and central city decline.

5. How are the history and pattern of urbanization in Japan different from those of other industrialized countries? How have changes in the global economy affected new urban developments in Japan?

chapter 11

GLOBALIZATION AND URBANIZATION
IN THE DEVELOPING WORLD

n the first decade of the twenty-first century, the world's urban population is estimated to be more than 3 billion persons. That is approximately ten times the total population of the United States. That number is expected to increase to 5 billion persons by 2030, representing an annual growth rate of about 1.8 percent (nearly double the increase of the world population as a whole). At this rate of growth, the number of persons living in urban areas will double in three decades. These figures are overwhelming, and not simply because it is difficult to think of 1 million people at anything more than a conceptual level, much less 1 billion people. The figures are overwhelming because almost all of the growth in the world's urban population in the future will take place in the cities and metropolitan regions of the less developed nations.

Figure 11.1 uses imagery from NASA satellite photographs to show the city lights of Asia. There are several notable features about this mapping. Most all of Japan shows up in bright lights, with several large urban concentrations running in a line across the bottom half of the country. India contains many large cities, and the entire country appears to be on an electric grid. In China, we can see the large area of urban development around Hong Kong, and another extensive grouping of cities in the area heading inland from the Pacific Ocean—but much of the remaining space appears undeveloped. Toward the top of the photograph, the cities along the transcontinental Siberian Railroad across the eastern half of Russia are visible. The images from space suggest that many regions of the continent are heavily urbanized but also that there is great variation within and between countries.

Table 11.1 reflects the dramatic changes that have taken place in the world's urban population over the last half-century as increasing numbers of large cities have appeared in the developing world. In 1950 there were just two metropolitan areas with a population of 8 million or more persons—New York and London, reflecting the concentration effects of urban growth under industrial capitalism in the developed nations. By 1970, there were nine metropolitan areas with more than 8 million persons, four in the developed nations (New York, London, Tokyo, and Los Angeles) and five in

FIGURE 11.1 City Lights of Asia. SOURCE: NASA.

the developing nations (Shanghai, Buenos Aires, Mexico City, Beijing, and São Paulo). In 2000 two new metropolitan areas in the developed nations were added to this list, but an astonishing eighteen new metropolitan areas in the developing nations crossed the threshold. Of the twenty-two metropolitan areas with populations of 8 million or more persons in less developed regions, five (Mexico City, São Paulo, Buenos Aires, Rio de Janeiro, and Lima) are located in South America, one (Lagos) is in sub-Saharan Africa, and three (Cairo, Istanbul, Tehran) are in the Middle East. The remaining fifteen metropolitan areas with 8 million or more persons are located in Asia, including six on the Indian subcontinent. Population estimates by the United Nations for 2030 show further growth—overwhelming growth—in metropolitan regions across the developing nations, particularly in Asia.

One way to think of the significance of the increase of large urban agglomerations in the developing world is that most of us would recognize the names of the cities shown in 1970—Mexico City, Buenos Aires (capital of Argentina), São Paulo (capital of Brazil). And many would recognize the cities in 1990—Manila (capital of the Philippines), Seoul (capital of South Korea). But few of us would recognize the cities from many other regions of the globe that by 2030 will take their place alongside these more familiar names. The emergence of these megacities, which are defined by their large size (in excess of 10 million persons), spread over adjacent towns, and the economic, social, cultural, and political dominance that they exert on the regional

TABLE 11.1 Urban Agglomerations with Populations Exceeding 8 million, 1950–2030.

1950	1970	1990	2000	2030
More Developed Regions				
New York	New York	Tokyo	Tokyo	Tokyo
London	London	New York	New York	New York
	Tokyo	Los Angeles	Los Angeles	Los Angeles
	Los Angeles	Moscow	Moscow	Osaka-Kobe
		Osaka-Kobe	Osaka-Kobe	Moscow
		Paris	Paris	Paris
				Chicago
Less Developed Regions				
	Shanghai	Mexico City	Mexico City	Bombay
	Mexico City	São Paulo	São Paulo	Delhi
	Buenos Aires	Shanghai	Shanghai	Mexico City
	Beijing	Calcutta	Calcutta	São Paulo
	São Paulo	Buenos Aires	Buenos Aires	Dhaka
		Bombay	Bombay	Jakarta
		Seoul	Beijing	Lagos
		Beijing	Jakarta	Calcutta
		Rio de Janeiro	Delhi	Karachi
		Tianjin	Lagos	Buenos Aires
		Jakarta	Tianjin	Cairo
		Cairo	Seoul	Shanghai
		Delhi	Rio de Janeiro	Manila
		Manila	Dhaka	Rio de Janeiro
			Cairo	Istanbul
			Manila	Beijing
			Karachi	Tianjin
			Bangkok	Lima
			Istanbul	Seoul
			Tehran	Sante Fe de Bogata
			Bangalore	Lahore
			Lima	Kinshasa
				Tehran
				Bangalore
				Chennai (Madras)
				Wuhan

SOURCE: Adapted from United Nations, *World Urbanization Prospects: The 2003 Revision*; and United Nations, Department of Economic and Social Affairs, Population Division, *World Agglomerations 2003*.

hinterlands, is one of the important characteristics of urbanization across the developing world. Megacities are the centers of innovation and generators of social change that have a significant role in the development of the nation state. Central governments have created regional administrative structures to implement planning and development needs of the new mega-urban regions. At the beginning of the twenty-first century, they appear to have developed a distinctive pattern of organizing economic and social space, with both a densely developed core and extended metropolitan region. Jones and Douglass (2008) note that because the most dramatic changes often are found in areas beyond official metropolitan boundaries, the significance of the mega-urban region has not been fully recognized.

The mega-urban regions found across Asia represent a complex mix of varied settlement types, with important differences due to history, economic, cultural, and technological factors that have influenced their development. Aprodicio Laquian (2005) categorized the new mega-urban regions in Asia into four types:

Technologically advanced East Asian cities: Osaka, Tokyo, and Seoul. These urban regions are characterized by low rates of population growth, homogeneous populations, and planning and governance structures that meet demands for basic services.

Megacities of China: Beijing, Guangzhou, Shanghai, and Tanjin. The newly developed urban regions of China are characterized by low growth rates (resulting from migration and population control policies), high economic growth, with strong pressures on basic services.

Primate cities of Southeast Asia: Bangkok, Jakarta, Manila. These urban regions have moderate rates of growth. Because they are important political centers, there has been regional planning and administrative coordination, but they confront serious problems in housing, water, traffic, and environmental pollution.

South Asian cities: Dhaka, Delhi, Kolkata, Mumbai, and Karachi. The mega-urban regions of Bangladesh, India, and Pakistan are characterized by high rates of growth and are plagued with problems of slums and squatting, inadequate transport, high unemployment, and environmental pollution.

The very different histories and characteristics of the mega-urban regions require more in-depth analysis. Laquian notes that because of this complexity, strategies used in countries in transition from centrally planned economics (such as China and Vietnam) may not prove successful in market-dominated countries (India and the Philippines). Interestingly, it is the mega-urban regions that have emerged from the centrally planned economies that seem better poised for economic growth at the beginning of the twenty-first century than the mega-urban regions that have emerged from market-dominated economies of former colonial regimes, although there are important social costs in both cases, as described later in this chapter.

In Chapter 10 we studied metropolitan regions in Europe and Japan. In many ways the growth of cities in the more developed nations is similar to the postwar development of cities in the United States: There has been extensive growth in the suburban areas, resulting in urban sprawl. Infrastructure development has kept pace with the expansion of the metropolitan area. While there are troubling social inequalities that often are compounded by spatial segregation, most people have adequate housing, with access to basic utilities including electricity, clean water, and sanitary facilities. In the past this pattern of development was sometimes described as urbanization with industrialization, emphasizing the importance of economic development to provide for the needs of a growing urban population.

Despite problems of uneven development and the recent global economic crisis, most people living in cities in the developed nations are well housed and well fed. The majority can find work and pursue careers that offer opportunities for advancement as their communities respond to changes in the new global economy. But in many other parts of the world, cities have a different relationship to society, and people's individual fortunes are plagued by dangers and disparities unheard of in more affluent societies. In this chapter, we examine the urban condition in Asia, Africa, and Latin America. These regions contain three-fourths of the world's population and most of its landmass. The societies range from democracies to totalitarian dictatorships. What they have in common is an inability to sustain economic development and, with some notable exceptions, a declining quality of life for most of their urban residents. In the past, this pattern of development was described as urbanization without industrialization, emphasizing the problems in providing basic needs for an ever-increasing population in cities in the developing world.

CHANGING PERSPECTIVES ON URBANIZATION

In approaching the issue of urbanization in developing countries, a number of misconceptions must be dispelled. First, persons living in the developed nations, and especially persons in the United States, commonly think of these regions as being primitively developed compared to the United States. But in fact countries such as China, Mexico, and Korea are highly industrialized, with factory workers numbering in the millions. Some of the largest cities in the world, such as Shanghai, São Paulo, and Bangkok, not only are located in developing countries but also are dynamic urban centers. As we will see in later sections of this chapter, many of the developing countries are highly urbanized as well. But many of these countries share a pattern of uneven development that is more extreme than that found in the older, developed nations. The prospects for persons living in these cities are very different from those of urban residents in New York, London, or Tokyo.

Second, the ecological theory that continues to dominate mainstream urban sociology argues that developing countries are much like the developed societies, only at an earlier stage of development, and they will "modernize" in time (Kasarda and Crenshaw, 1991). The sociospatial perspective counters this view and considers factors such as the roles of the state, socioeconomic class, global capital investment, and economic changes in the global economy—all of which are neglected by the ecological approach—as critical for an understanding of urbanization in developing countries. Thus the sociospatial perspective suggests that countries having different economic structures will develop in different ways. Close observers of growth patterns in areas such as Latin America (Roberts, 1978) and Asia (Berry, 1989) seem to agree that the explanatory variables stressed by the sociospatial approach are most important, while not necessarily subscribing to the perspective itself. Contrary to what the human ecology and modernization theory would predict, the process of urbanization in the developing nations is different in significant ways from what we have observed in the more developed nations. The key differences involve factors such as elite power, state policies, integration into the global economy, and the effects of class structure (Smith and Timberlake, 1993).

A third change in perspective concerns the increasing relevance of the global economy to understand urban development in both the developed and less developed nations. Prior to the 1970s, there seemed to be a sharp distinction between the economies of these regions. Less developed countries were sources for agricultural goods such as coffee or winter fruits but were otherwise thought to be disconnected from Western society, except perhaps as places for tourists to visit and strategic locations for military bases. Countries such as the United States were still operating under Fordist arrangements of production during this time, meaning that most manufacturing was carried out domestically, and foreign countries were viewed principally as a source of raw materials and as markets for U.S. goods.

Developmental theories of the time proposed the concept of "peripheral urbanization," which emphasized the marginal nature of the developing world (Harvey, 1973; Castells, 1977; Walton, 1982). In other words, countries were seen to be either part of the core of the world system (the developed nations), or they were relegated to the periphery (the developing world).

In recent decades, however, vast changes have occurred in the developed nations as Fordist arrangements of production have been replaced by post-Fordist production and the country underwent deindustrialization. During the 1970s and 1980s, much U.S. manufacturing employment was shipped overseas, and countries such as Mexico, Malaysia, Singapore, Brazil, and the Dominican Republic were used as effective sites for labor. By the 1990s, it had become commonplace for consumers in the United States to find that the products they purchased, whether articles of clothing, sports equipment, or cars, were assembled in foreign places. Thus, a pattern of manufacturing for world markets was established in many areas of the developing world, and people's lives in the United States were connected by multinational corporations to formerly peripheral societies (Peet, 1987). Also in the 1990s, the Chinese government

Box 11.1

The Impact of Globalization on Third World Cities

Globalization at the national level leads to economic restructuring and global linkages of select regions in the nation, select cities in these regions, and select geographical segments within these cities. Thus various levels of dichotomy permeate society. Unfortunately, the globalized population and geographical regions sponge on the population/regions bereft of global links. In developing countries, government policies play an integral role in bridging inequalities. But in their excitement to push rapid global economic integration, governments strengthen the processes of exclusion through fragmentation of employment, housing, and social services.

As nations compete, cities too begin to compete with each other under the neoliberal agenda. These cities differ from those of an earlier era in terms of the way urban space is utilized, governed, contested, and represented. Capital mobility, leading to competition for investment, has forced city governments to adopt innovative and entrepreneurial approaches to local growth. Local governments take up selective projects to improve the urban environment, which end up either displacing or excluding segments of population or, through privatization, leads to fragmentation of housing, infrastructure, and services as well as institutional structures. City plans give priority to business, and scarce city resources are diverted to cater to the needs of business. Many local economies providing employment to the poor are de-legitimized and face eviction from productive locations sought after by elite groups.

An increase in inequality in cities leads to issues of internal security. This pushes the rich to live in enclaves that are well protected. The city gets segmented between the rich and the poor. Segregation may not be total, but some segments of the city would have a concentration of the rich and others of the poor, as observed in the case of Mumbai. In Buenos Aires, one finds rich enclaves cropping up. In Mumbai, the privatization of basic services could exclude poorer areas from receiving an adequate level of services. In Buenos Aires, the rich have avoided contributing to the costs of services at the city level. In the wake of the outbreak of suspected plague in Surat city in 1995, some city planners came up with the idea of bifurcating the Surat Municipal Corporation into two—a corporation consisting of residential areas where the rich and middle classes live, and another where the poor and industrial workers live and where the plague originated. Thus the social and spatial segmentation of the megacity into "citadels" and "ghettos" takes place, and the city's geography changes.

Infrastructure projects based on the principle of public-private partnership or privatization, including those for water supply and sanitation, increase the cost of living for the poor and may altogether exclude the poorest. Land development becomes an intensely contested area. The new environmental agenda, under the concept of Sustainable Cities, also ends up expelling the poor from the city space and economy.

continues

Box 11.1 *continued*

Low-skilled workers in industries or industrial zones, services, and the informal sector, congregate at the fringes where systems are inadequately developed, or in areas of the mega-city that are environmentally stressed or hazardous. The development processes that unwind are exclusionary. Large sections are first expelled from the economic space and then excluded from various city-level social systems. Women in poor communities suffer the most.

The influence of multilateral international development agencies such as the World Bank and Asian Development Bank has increased. Most of these agencies promote privatization in urban areas. The conditions for lending for urban development often include clauses such as allowing transnational or multinational utilities to enter the city. Such policies lead to exclusion in the city through the process of privatization and also increase debt-liability, reducing the city's capability to address the issue of sustainable poverty reduction.

SOURCE: D. Mahadevia, "Inclusive Mega-Cities in Globalising Asia," Info Change Urban India (http://infochangeindia.org/india_10.jsp).

began a series of economic reforms that would lead to the country's emergence as a new industrial nation built upon a manufacturing export economy (Yusuf and Saich, 2009).

Studies of urbanization in the developing nations now reject previous approaches that emphasized world system marginality or dependency (Datta, 1990). Instead, it is argued that these countries are increasingly linked to the global economy. The cycle of investment, manufacturing, consumption, and profit making that leads to greater investment integrates consumers and producers in the developed nations with manufacturing, banking, and consumption activities in other countries, including the developing nations. This effect is often called the "internationalization of capital." The once meaningful "comparative" study of urbanization in developing countries and urbanization in the United States and other developed nations has been replaced by the study of globalization—of the growing interconnections and interdependence between the core and periphery because of government policy, international trade agreements, and other recent developments.

The sociospatial perspective acknowledges the influence of the global system of capital on locality. The case of the Philippines is of some interest in this regard. As one of the capital cities in the Spanish colonial empire, Manila has been part of the capitalist world system since the 1500s. Its position as a regional city within the global system of capital was increased when it became an American colony following the Spanish American War and again in the post–World War II years. Over the past two decades, however, Manila's importance and influence in the Southeast Asian economy has declined. Capital flows and investments in the new system of global capitalism have bypassed Manila in favor of Hong Kong and Singapore and, more recently, Shanghai. While many countries in Southeast Asia have prospered during the past decade, the economy of the Philippines has registered a negative growth rate, and urban development in Manila lags behind that of other cities that have emerged as more important in the global system of capital.

It is important to recognize that urbanization processes in both developed and developing nations often involve combinations of global, national, and local factors that may operate independently of the global economy. The form of government at the national level has played a key role in the success—or failure—of development schemes in many developing countries. China, South Korea, and Singapore, for example, have aggressive national policies in pursuit of growth and governments that actively aid capital investment (Barone, 1983). Other countries, such as many Latin American societies, are plagued by "crony capitalism," government corruption, and dictatorships that squander national wealth.

At the most local level, there are also independent effects that are related to but not determined by the global level. Cities in the developing world are moving rapidly from the stage of developing economies to postindustrial relations, that is, skipping many of the features of industrialization that inform the experience of Western developed nations (Roberts, 1991). Large cities in the developing nations, like their counterparts in the West, are experiencing shifts to a service-oriented employment base due to their increasing role as command-and-control centers of capital investment. As a result of new employment opportunities created for professional workers, there is a growing wage differential between well-paid and working-poor residents. How this increasingly diverse class structure manifests itself politically varies from country to country and involves new patterns of local political activity that are independent of, and in some cases oppositional to, global system needs (see the section on social movements later in this chapter).

The sociospatial perspective on urbanization in developing countries emphasizes global linkages, differences in class structure, the effects of national state arrangements, and differences in local politics as key factors for an understanding of current trends. Urbanization processes in these countries also have many features in common that contrast with the experiences of developed nations. These can be identified by considering the nature of population growth and change, or demography, which we discuss next.

THE DEMOGRAPHIC TRANSITION

When dealing with rapid population changes such as those that affected the United States in the 1800s and affect developing countries today, the science of demography can offer important insights. Demographers track the dynamics of population growth, concentrating on rates of change, such as the frequency of births and deaths and the average number of children per mother. Demographers are also interested in rates of migration, especially changes in the rural and urban populations. For any given population, the rate of increase that depends on the number of births minus deaths is known as the natural increase. Population changes within any given settlement space can arise from natural increase or from migration.

For most of human history, the high birthrate was offset by an equally high death rate, and populations grew very slowly. Following World War II, the introduction of modern medical techniques and preventive measures in developing nations resulted in a population explosion that is called the demographic transition. When new techniques of medical intervention lowered the death rates in these countries, the societies experienced a permanent rise in the rate of natural increase because they maintained a high birthrate. In the developed world, the demographic transition was eventually adjusted by means of a declining birthrate, as the rising standard of living associated with industrialization led to smaller family size. Many European countries now have low or even negative growth rates. That stage has yet to occur in developing nations, although some countries, such as Brazil, have drastically lowered their growth rates in recent years. But for most of the developing world, birthrates still outstrip death rates, and overpopulation is a serious social and environmental problem.

The demographic problems of developing nations are compounded by limited economic development in recent decades. Faced with a population explosion, rural areas have been hard-pressed to grow enough food for domestic consumption, and the standard of living in rural areas has declined drastically since the 1950s in many developing countries. There are simply too many mouths to feed. The dilemma facing families was poignantly depicted in a Mexican film by Luis Buñuel, *Los Olvidados*. A farmer comes to the city with his young son. They move toward a crowd in the center of the city. When the father is satisfied that his son is distracted, he seizes his chance and runs away. Many cities are teeming with such abandoned children, many of whom are exploited by a growing sex industry catering to foreign tourists. As might be expected, many of the abandoned children have a short life span.

The failure of rural agricultural efforts to produce enough to sustain the quality of life has led excess population to migrate to the cities. Despite the hardships of life found there, the move holds out the promise of improvement, and this encourages others to come. As a result, cities in developing nations suffer from a double population explosion: a high rate of natural increase and a high rate of in-migration. In the city, there is little room for poor people's housing. In many cities, urban migrants find space on the outskirts and put up makeshift shelters that lack the basic necessities of homes, such as running water, sanitation facilities, and even adequate ventilation for heating. These shantytowns, or squatter settlements, have many names all over the world—*favellas* (Brazil), *bustees* (India), *barriadas* (Mexico), *poblaciones* (Chile), *villas miserias* (Argentina), *bidonvilles* (Africa), and *Kampongs* (Southeast Asia). But they have many features in common, including frequent public health crises, crime, crushing poverty, and no future for the next generation since few countries provide them with schools. We will discuss shantytowns in more detail later.

A third effect of demographic change in developing countries involves their common experience of social, economic, and political exploitation under European and American colonialism. Western powers took control of underdeveloped countries in Africa, Asia, and South America beginning in the sixteenth century. In 1898 the United States gained control of the former Spanish colonies: the Philippines, Hawaii, Cuba, and Puerto Rico. The principal goal was to acquire natural resources, such as gold and spices, and later, cheaply produced manufactured goods. Because colonialism or imperialism depended on trade with the conquering country, effective links to the global world system were established early. A result of colonialism was the construction of large cities that were usually located near the coast, such as Hong Kong, Manila, Lagos, Singapore, Bombay, and Bangkok. Over the years these cities grew immensely, but few other cities were founded because the colonial powers did not deem them necessary.

Over the years, many developing countries have been able to launch development programs that have overcome the legacy of colonial control. However, the success of these programs has been limited due to changes in geopolitics and the world economy, as well as to national issues such as crony capitalism and civil conflict. These factors hinder the balanced growth of cities in these countries. As a result, many countries today possess a single, gigantic primate city that is overurbanized, or excessively populated, and remains the center for most investment and economic growth, while retaining a relatively underurbanized interior with no large cities. Primate cities are characteristic of an unbalanced pattern of urbanization that remains quite different from that found in the developed countries of the world. Let us examine this unique feature in more detail, as well as other characteristics of urbanization in the developing world, including shantytown development, household coping strategies and the informal economy, and new urban social movements.

PRIMATE CITY DEVELOPMENT PATTERNS

In developed countries such as the United States, there is an even distribution in the number of cities according to size (see Chapter 4). Some, such as New York City with more than 8 million people, are quite large; others fill in the ranks with smaller populations of between 500,000 and 1 million, such as San Francisco, and between 100,000 and 500,000, such as Minneapolis, and so on down the hierarchy. Such a profile constitutes "balanced" urbanization, and it provides a range of urban environments and locational options for both businesses and people.

Primate cities dominate and distort development within their countries. Overurbanization, or the presence of primate cities, is measured by comparing the size of the largest city with other large cities within a given country. In the developing world, the disparities among urban centers may be very great. In Thailand, for example, the population of the capital city of Bangkok was 6,685,000 in 2000, more than thirty times larger than that of the next largest city (the population figure applies to the total urbanized area of the capital city). Countries with primate cities lack locational flexibility: If one is looking for investment opportunities within the country, there typically is only one area that has the population and infrastructure to support development. If one is looking for employment, there is only one area where new jobs are being created. As a consequence, countries that have primate cities are locked in a migratory cycle. Like a magnet, primate cities pull mobile populations from the countryside at the expense of other locations.

The pattern of primate city development not only is inconsistent with models of urban growth based upon location theory but also calls into question the legitimacy of ecological theory. You may recall from Chapter 3 that urban ecologists sought to apply the model of factorial ecology to cities in developing nations with the belief that a single model could explain urbanization in all countries around the world. Another part of this perspective holds that developed nations should be the model for poorer countries, asserting that developing nations should industrialize and urbanize as rapidly as possible. Ecological theory suggests that when they do, those living in industrialized cities will increase their incomes and acquire a better quality of life. By encouraging urban growth, the entire society benefits.

The sociospatial perspective disagrees with this view. Developing countries may grow through industrial development and as part of the new postindustrial economy, but economic growth is likely only when it occurs in conjunction with world system priorities and investment flows. Consequently, rapid urbanization may have negative effects because its principal cause is the needs of global capital and not the quality of life for local populations (Smith, 1985). As a result, countries in the developing world can suffer from extremely uneven development despite impressive modernization efforts, and primate cities are often the consequence. While the average income of primate city residents may be greater than that of rural counterparts, the inequality of income and of quality of life is so severe in primate cities that the standard of living is lower than in rural areas (Bradshaw and Fraser, 1989). Thus, the growth of primate city economies does not help the majority of citizens who are victims of uneven and inequitable development.

SHANTYTOWN DEVELOPMENT

The world's urban population increases by nearly 1 million persons each month. Mexico City, the largest megacity in the developing world, draws more than 20,000 people from impoverished rural states looking for employment each month. The sheer number of urban migrants is too great for either the private or public sector to provide adequate housing or shelter, and thus many families end up in *barriadas*, or squatter settlements. The common conception is that life in these places is totally peripheral to the urban economy of the city. But many shantytowns support robust economies within their informal boundaries—including areas of commercial development and even real estate investment—and many have developed into large residential districts where the working class often lives. There is much discussion about the meaning of the peripheral urbanization in these Fourth World regions; Mike Davis makes this clear in the title of this recent book, *Planet of Slums* (2007). But others have argued that the marginality of shantytown inhabitants is largely a myth (Perlman, 1976), and Howard Husack (2009) has recently referred to them as "slums of hope."

Box 11.2

Rapid Urbanization and Slum Formation

Rapid urban population growth has outpaced the ability of city authorities to provide for housing and environmental health and infrastructure. Cities such as Dhaka in Bangladesh or Mumbai in India are, realistically speaking, metropolitan or urban regions, spanning large territorial areas. Others like Metro Manila in the Philippines or Jakarta in Indonesia are really mega-urban regions. The nature of the governments differs considerably. Jakarta's urban government has the status of a provincial government equal to that of other provinces in Indonesia. The metropolitan government in Manila coordinates among some seventeen local authorities, the majority of which are municipalities with a few town councils.

Squatter and slum settlements have formed mainly because of the inability of city governments to plan and provide affordable housing for the low-income segments of the urban population. Hence, squatter and slum housing is the housing solution for this low-income urban population. In the mega-urban regions or metropolitan areas, part of the problem would lie in the coordination among different authorities that are in charge of economic development, urban planning, and land allocation.

The economically more dynamic regions such as Asia have experienced strong growth because the state sector drives development agendas. National and city governments have generally adopted the position that economic development will take care of basic needs such as housing and environmental and health infrastructure. In cities of higher-income countries such as Malaysia, private sector developers are more interested in building homes for the middle-income market. The proliferation of slum and squatter settlements, however, shows that planned economic growth has to be aligned with the planned development of health services, environmental infrastructure, and housing.

continues

Box 11.2 *continued*

In Ho Chi Minh City in Vietnam, neither the government nor the private developers are able to provide the housing needed for 50,000 migrants per year. An additional 20,000 young urban households are formed annually that enter the real estate market. The resulting growth in squatter and slum settlements now comprises 15 percent of the housing in the city. This kind of housing is associated with lack of sanitation and air pollution. In other low-income cities like Dhaka, only one-quarter of the population in the city is connected to the piped sewerage system with two in three households served with a potable water supply.

In many cities such as Metro Manila in the Philippines and Kuala Lumpur in Malaysia, rapid development of new real estate comprising condominiums and shopping malls has led to gridlocked traffic, severe environmental pollution, and unstable squatter settlements sandwiched between prime commercial complexes and high-class condominiums. With the intensely competitive demand for land in cities, the urban poor will increasingly be marginalized. Many are now settling at the fringe of the most rapidly growing cities. Rapid growth of the larger cities and mega-urban regions in the developing countries is reflected in their being surrounded by dense and generally impoverished shantytowns and numerous other forms of so-called informal or irregular housing. These are characterized by inadequate infrastructure, service provision, and security of shelter and land tenure.

SOURCE: G. Ooi and K. Phua, "Urbanization and Slum Formation," 2007.

The status of shantytowns varies from city to city and country to country. In many places, they are simply illegal settlements built on the outskirts of cities, and they exist under the threat of annihilation by state authorities. In other places, however, shantytowns have acquired legitimate status through political activism, and they constitute working-class suburbs that have many services, including electrical power, running water, and schools. Shantytowns differ not only in location, building materials, and physical appearance but also in the types of groups that live in them. Some settlements suffer from social disorganization and crime, while others provide opportunities for entrepreneurial activity. Charles Abrams (1977) discovered five different types of squatter settlements during his research in cities in South America:

1. *Owner squatters.* This group conforms to our common idea of the urban squatter: The individual or household owns its own building but not the land on which it was built.

2. *Squatter tenants.* This group is composed of new in-migrants to urban centers who do not live in their own buildings but rent this space from other squat-

ters. Because the "landlord" does not pay taxes or for the upkeep of the structure, substantial profit may be realized from this business enterprise.

3. *Speculator squatters.* Like regular landowners, this group understands that occupying land and gaining property rights is a way to make a profit. Squatting is viewed as a business venture in the hope of obtaining title to the land.

4. *Store or business squatters.* This group consists of individuals who operate businesses and often live within the squatter settlement. Because they pay no rent or taxes, they may be able to make substantial profits.

5. *Semisquatters.* Individuals or households in this group construct a building on private land but later come to terms with the owner on the rental or even purchase price for the space. The boundary between the legal tenant and the semisquatter may be blurred, particularly within developing economies.

Some shantytowns possess a robust social order (Aina, 1990; Cooper, 1987; Neuwirth, 2006). They often are the location for small-business enterprises started by urban migrants. Shantytowns may also be the location for small and medium-size factories employing residents from the surrounding area. The penetration of multinational corporations into metropolitan areas in the developing nations as part of the restructuring of the global economy has created new manufacturing jobs and support for local entrepreneurs. In these and other ways, shantytowns may be integrated into the world economy.

In many developing nations, shantytowns may be the only places where the working class can find affordable housing. According to one estimate, a majority of shantytown dwellers actually live in rental housing (Datta, 1990). Individuals who construct housing in these settlements become real estate entrepreneurs and form an important real estate submarket within the larger metropolitan economy. Real estate investment brings in much-needed income for individuals and households living within the shantytown. However, as in the developed nations, there may be problems with this privatized housing market. The increased cost of construction materials has meant that shantytown housing around Mexico City has become excessively expensive, and new pressures have been placed on the Mexican government to address the issue of affordable housing (Schteingart, 1990).

It has been suggested that shantytowns should be viewed as workers' suburbs that require greater attention and services from local government, not as slum areas. But the recent projections of population growth in urban areas of the developing nations raise new concerns and may eclipse the earlier discussions of working-class suburbs. The United Nations reports that more than a third of all urban residents—1 billion persons—now live in slums, most of them in cities in the developing world. By 2030 that figure is expected to increase to more than half—or some 2.5 billion persons living in urban slums (UN-Habitat, 2005). This is likely to be accompanied by increased poverty in urban areas. Of the 14.5 million people living in Metro Manila in 2000, for example, it is estimated that 60 percent had incomes below the poverty line and that 40 percent lived in slums and shantytowns in areas outside of the urban core.

THE INFORMAL ECONOMY
AND COPING STRATEGIES

In previous chapters we noted that many urban sociologists follow the ecological approach. They focus on individual behavior and the aggregation of separate interests in the public and private sectors. The sociospatial perspective, in contrast, recognizes that while society is composed of individuals, a focus on groups, such as classes and networks, is a preferred way of understanding metropolitan dynamics. Homeowner politics and the struggle to control territory and its quality of life are also important political considerations. When studying the cities in the developing world, the nature of class structure and especially the control by select elites through the government and military are important factors. Urban researchers also assert that urban dynamics is not exclusively a class phenomenon and suggest that the appropriate unit of analysis for the study of urban populations in developing nations is the household.

The household and its coping strategies are basic to an understanding of urban life everywhere, that is, in the developed nations as well as the developing nations. Households are collective units that share housing and food, trade clothing and other consumer durables, and are composed of individuals who pool monetary resources. According to Mingione (1988), not all the members of a given household are immediate family. Households may contain distant relatives and even friends. The collective pooling of resources does not preclude differences among household members, such as conflicts between men and women. What counts most with this emphasis is that it conforms better to the reality of urban life in many countries than the focus of mainstream sociology on individual decision making or of Marxists on class alone.

The study of household survival strategies shows that the poor do not accept their adversity in a passive manner. They innovate and find ways to support themselves and others. This dynamism makes shantytown life quite complex and leads to both positive and negative outcomes, such as the reproduction of generations despite poverty and the existence of criminal activity. Households cope with adversity by making collective decisions rather than allowing the burden of poverty to fall on each individual's shoulders alone. To reduce expenses they may engage in self-provisioning, which "includes domestic processing or production of food, making clothes, undertaking repairs, self-construction of housing" (Roberts, 1991:142). Other household coping strategies include reducing the number of members (often children, as in the earlier example of the Buñuel film) and connecting with the informal economy.

The issue of the informal economy is an important focus of urbanization research in developing countries and is increasingly an equally relevant topic for the developed countries (Safa, 1987). In the informal sector, whose activities are considered "off the books" or illegal, people sell everything from drugs, cigarettes, and convenience store items (such as soda) to produce (such as fruits and vegetables)—and even their own bodies for sex. As global restructuring expands in developing cities, bringing with it highly paid professional services, poor people find informal or casual employment as shoe shiners, messengers, delivery persons, and domestic helpers, in addition to the burgeoning demand for restaurant and other commercial laborers. Many laborers, especially domestic servants and babysitters, are hired off the record.

The informal sector is dominated by a market economy, although this is not the same as capitalism because barter or trade as well as monetary exchange prevail, and no formal structures dominate pricing (Korff, 1990). Work is precarious and does not bring the kinds of benefits that people in developed nations identify with full-time employment, such as health insurance or social security. Researchers of this phenomenon note that the numbers of people and activities in the informal sector are growing in all countries, a fact we have noted in connection with the illegal drug industry's role in poor ghetto areas of the United States.

The study of household coping strategies and the informal economy paints a multidimensional picture of shantytown life and illustrates how individuals may take advantage of opportunities in cities that are not usually noted when attention is given only to formal economies and our own limited, culture-bound conceptions of everyday life.

URBAN SOCIAL MOVEMENTS AND POLITICS

Another important topic that is often neglected in discussing urbanization in the developing world is the significance of political struggles within the city (see Castells, 1983; Walton, 1987; Cooper, 1987). According to one observer, urban movements in developing countries are characterized by a gradual transition during the past decade from comprising local movements with limited sociopolitical goals to being more conscious movements making much greater demands on the state and with social and political effects that are no longer limited to the local arena (Datta, 1990:44).

An example of this change concerns the broadening movement for affordable housing (Castells, 1983; Ramirez, 1990) and the drive to make squatter and shantytown settlements legal. Organized efforts of poor people have pitted them against the government with demands for better health, education, and neighborhood services—a phenomenon that is also characteristic of communities in developed nations and that transcends class distinctions. Another recent development is the growing number of class-based union activities that take place in cities. Deindustrialization has meant the decline of manufacturing jobs in the developing nations and with it the drastic decline in the power of unions. But as manufacturing jobs have been shunted to the developing world, an associated rise in union activity and class struggle has resulted.

Countries such as Brazil and India, for example, have formidable industrial labor forces, and with them have come active trade union movements and class-based political action.

Special attention must be given to the role of women in political movements in developing nations. When women migrate to the city, they acquire new opportunities for marriage and male-female relations, "even if social conservatism may also be exacerbated by the novelty and difficulties of urban life" (Coquery-Vidrovitch, 1990:77). African and Latin American studies show that women take advantage both of the informal economy and of shantytown dwellings to earn a living, although some fall victim to male domination and criminal exploitation such as prostitution (Schlyter, 1990). One important measure of the freer status of city women is their important role in urban social movements. Coquery-Vidrovitch suggests that this important representation may be the result of the active involvement of women in voluntary associations connected with urban shantytown life.

Uneven development and the proliferation of shantytowns may lead to political instability. The national government is not viewed as an avenue for solving ordinary people's problems. This makes struggles at the most local level increasingly important as a vehicle for change. According to one African study, the government of Nigeria is seen as no more than the instrument of the dominant class, committed to perpetuating an unbalanced distribution of income and wealth and preserving the dominance of capitalist ideology and political power (Mabogunje, 1990:361). Reports of the performance in government of different groups, whether military or civilian, reveal a cynical use of state apparatus to enrich individuals at the expense of the commonwealth.

Urban social movements are connected to the global economy. Workers in developing countries constitute a complex social order with many different class statuses (Portes and Walton, 1981). Changes in the activities linked to global investment have differential effects on the working class in the developing world. These differences are reflected in different political positions and complex ideological issues among trade union parties, some of whom are active socialist or communist organizations, although there are conservative and reactionary political elements as well. In other words, national and urban politics in the developing nations involves a variety of organized political positions despite the greater presence in many countries of worker-oriented or left-wing movements than in developed nations.

The global economy also affects urban social movements directly through its agents of international control. In the 1970s, for example, the International Monetary Fund (IMF), which controls most of the debt and national financing in the developing nations, called for austerity measures and reductions in state expenditures among all its client countries. In turn, national governments responded by eliminating subsidies on food and other consumer goods. This placed a severe burden on households. In response to the threat of hunger or increased misery, residents of cities began rioting in protest of food subsidy cutbacks. The "IMF riots" (Walton, 1987; Cleaver, 1989), as they came to be called, were powerful political events that affected the stability of state regimes in diverse places around the globe, including Africa, Latin America, and Asia. As summarized by Datta (1990:45), "food riots caused the fall of the Tolbert regime in Liberia in 1979 and threatened the imminent collapse of the regimes in Tunisia and Morocco in 1981, in the Dominican Republic in 1984 and 1985, in Brazil in 1983, in Chile in 1983 and 1985." As a result of organized opposition to global restructuring agents such as the IMF or to multinational corporations and industrial development, urban social movements have broadened their perspectives to deal with issues that affect all levels of society, including the local, the national, and the global.

Urban social movements are important in the developing world and take many forms. In Chile, for example, between 1968 and 1972, 400,000 people converged on the city of Santiago and established free squatter settlements, or *campamentos* (Schneier, 1990:349). Similar self-governing squatter communities can be found in Mexico, where they are a powerful political force in urban areas (Castells, 1983). In Nigeria, shanty-towns have been organized into neighborhoods that have demanded greater political representation. According to one African study, "The mobilization of people at such a level within a city should at least encourage improved information flows and increase the prospect of greater participation by all in the governance (as distinct from the government) of the city" (Mabogunje, 1990:364). Urban social movements are common among city dwellers in both the developed and undeveloped countries of the world.

We have been discussing phenomena that countries in the developing world have in common. These include the presence of primate cities, the complex social order of shantytowns, household coping strategies and the informal economy, and the changing complexion of urban social movements and politics. Much of the research on these topics has been published only since the 1970s, when they were brought into sharper focus for those in developed, Westernized countries.

Above all, studies show that the "comparative" perspective on global urbanization that conceptualized a break between the industrialized West and developing nations must give way to the sociospatial perspective, which acknowledges the growing commonalities and links between metropolitan restructuring patterns in both regions. Along with increasing acknowledgment of global links is the recognition of certain differences that exist among countries. Not everything is determined by global processes alone. National and local differences also add to the complexity of urbanization in the developing world. In the final section of this chapter, we survey briefly these local sources of variation in a region-by-region analysis.

PATTERNS OF URBANIZATION

Latin America

Latin America contains one of the world's largest cities, Mexico City, with a population of 19 million persons in 2007, and several of the world's most rapidly growing metropolises: Rio de Janeiro and São Paulo in Brazil, Buenos Aires in Argentina,

Caracas in Venezuela, and Bogotá in Colombia. The continent of South America, along with Central America and Mexico, was urbanized hundreds of years ago during the period of the Aztec, Mayan, and Inca civilizations, which founded great cities at the time of the European Middle Ages. In the seventeenth and eighteenth centuries, the Spanish and Portuguese conquests founded new towns and administration centers. Uneven spatial development engendered by colonialism created primate cities in most countries. Many of the cities were located on the coast because of the dominance of trade with the colonial power, although Mexico City, the capital of the ancient Aztec empire, remains an inland magnet for migration.

Cities in Latin America share a common form because of their legacy as Spanish colonial history. The *Leyes de Indias* (Laws of the Indies), signed by Charles II in 1573, included 148 ordinances concerning the location and construction of settlements in the Spanish colonies (including the Philippines). These are among the first comprehensive guidelines for the design and development of cities. As shown in Box 11.3, the ordinances specify how public, religious, commercial, and residential spaces were to be designed, including the symbolic placement of the cathedral on a raised area facing the main piazza so that it can be seen from all sides and "acquire greater authority." As a result of the Laws of the Indies, all Spanish cities in Latin America contain a large central plaza, with the main cathedral, city hall, and commercial buildings on the streets facing the plaza. Residential areas spread out from the main plaza, and often these are focused around the many secondary plazas, giving a strong sense of order to the entire city. In addition to the regular patterns established by the ordinances, housing and public buildings are built around open courtyards, following a generic Mediterranean design with houses directly fronting the street, making a sharp divide between the public world of the street and the private space of the house (Leontidou, 2009). In recent decades, some suburban housing has been built with a form more similar to that of the suburbs in the American Southwest, where there is not the same boundary between public and private space.

The development of cities in Brazil is of course different from other countries in Latin America because they were not part of the Spanish empire. But they do share characteristics common to Mediterranean cities more generally, including extensive plazas and housing and government buildings built around open courtyards. The coastal city of Recife in northern Brazil is built along canals and is called the Venice of South America, with much of the older area of the city, built in the 1700s, resembling other European cities. Both Rio de Janeiro and São Paulo have extensive *favelas* (shantytowns) that house millions of persons in the two megacities.

Recent urbanization for Central and South America is shown in Table 11.2. Although Latin America is one of the most urbanized areas in the world, there is substantial variation within the region. Countries such as Argentina, Brazil, Chile, Uruguay, and Venezuela have between 80 and 90 percent of their populations living in urban areas, whereas the figures for El Salvador and Guatemala are less than 60 percent. South

Box 11.3

Urban Design from the Laws of the Indies, 1573

The Laws of the Indies, signed by the Spanish king Charles IV in 1573, specified both the selection of town sites as well as the design of cities and towns in the new world. Here is a sampling of the more than 200 requirements included in the Laws.

112. The main plaza is to be the starting point for the town; if the town is situated on the sea coast, it should be placed at the landing place of the port, but inland it should be at the center of the town. The plaza should be square or rectangular, in which case it should have at least one and a half its width for length inasmuch as this shape is best for fiestas in which horses are used and for any other fiestas that should be held.

113. The size of the plaza shall be proportioned to the number of inhabitants . . . [it] shall be not less than two hundred feet wide and three hundred feet long, nor larger than eight hundred feet long and five hundred and thirty feet wide. A good proportion is six hundred feet long and four hundred wide.

114. From the plaza shall begin four principal streets: One [shall be] from the middle of each side, and two streets from each corner of the plaza; the four corners of the plaza shall face the four principal winds, because in this manner, the streets running from the plaza will not be exposed to the four principal winds, which would cause much inconvenience.

115. Around the plaza as well as along the four principal streets which begin there, there shall be portals, for these are of considerable convenience to the merchants who generally gather there; the eight streets running from the plaza at the four corners shall open on the plaza without encountering these porticoes, which shall be kept back in order that there may be sidewalks even with the streets and plaza.

116. In cold places, the streets shall be wide and in hot places narrow; but for purposes of defense in areas where there are horses, it would be better if they are wide.

118. Here and there in the town, smaller plazas of good proportion shall be laid out, where the temples associated with the principal church, the parish churches, and the monasteries can be built, [in] such [manner] that everything may be distributed in a good proportion for the instruction of religion.

126. In the plaza, no lots shall be assigned to private individuals; instead, they shall be used for the buildings of the church and royal houses and for city use, but shops and houses for the merchants should be built first, to which all the settlers of the town shall contribute, and a moderate tax shall be imposed on goods so that these buildings may be built.

SOURCE: Laws of the Indies, 1573 (http://codesproject.asu.edu/node/10).

America includes several countries with urban populations concentrated in large cities: 40 percent of the urban population of Argentina lives in cities with populations of 1 million or more, and more than a third of the urban populations of both Brazil and Chile lives in these larger metropolitan areas. Table 11.2 also shows the strong presence of primate cities in this urban system. In Chile and Uruguay, 40 percent of the urban population lives in the capital city, and in Argentina, El Salvador, and Peru, the figure is more than 30 percent of the population.

Countries such as Brazil, Argentina, and Mexico have benefited from the global search for cheap labor. Mexico, for example, is host to the successful *maquilladoras* program, which locates primary manufacturing in a band of space along the U.S. border for shipment back to the United States as finished products. The maquilladoras system is similar to enterprise zones in the United States and is becoming increasingly popular with developing nations as deindustrialization continues in the United States and Europe. The enterprise zones allow multinationals in developed nations to retain control of production and marketing while still benefiting from the exploitation of cheap labor in foreign countries with the active support of their governments. The maquilladoras program relies heavily on the use of female labor, which has been made compliant by the culture of paternalism (Fernandez-Kelly, 1991), and enjoys active subsidies from both the Mexican and U.S. governments.

Some Latin American countries, such as Argentina and Brazil, have a long history of industrialization. But to be successful and compete with foreign competition, they

TABLE 11.2 Urbanization in Selected Latin American Countries, 1990–2005.

	Urban Population		(% of total)		Living in cities of 1 million or more (% of urban population)		Living in largest city (% of urban population)	
	1990	2005	1990	2005	1990	2005	1990	2005
Argentina	28,300,000	34,900,000	87	90	39	39	37	36
Bolivia	3,700,000	5,900,000	56	64	25	31	29	26
Brazil	111,700,000	157,000,000	75	84	34	37	13	12
Chile	11,000,000	14,300,000	83	88	35	35	42	40
Colombia	24,000,000	33,200,000	69	73	30	36	20	23
Cuba	7,700,000	8,500,000	73	76	20	19	27	26
El Salvador	2,500,000	4,100,000	49	60	19	22	39	37
Guatemala	3,700,000	5,900,000	41	47	11	28	22	17
Mexico	60,300,000	78,300,000	73	76	32	35	25	25
Peru	15,000,000	20,300,000	69	73	27	26	39	35
Uruguay	2,800,000	3,200,000	89	92	41	36	46	40
Venezuela	16,600,000	24,800,000	84	93	34	37	17	12

SOURCE: Table 3.10, *World Development Indicators 2007* (New York: World Bank, 2007).

must use the most sophisticated techniques to make products that will sell on the global market. In the last decade they have confronted the same competition for manufactured goods imported from China as have American companies. To succeed in the changed economic market, capital-intensive methods, such as automation, are used that require little labor. Consequently, even in countries that have achieved some industrialization, factories are run without significant labor forces. New employment opportunities are not created at a pace that could absorb the excess rural population. The result is the perpetuation of shantytown growth despite industrial development.

Brazil is a prime example of the dilemma presented by world system competition. Historically, Brazil has had a successful indigenous steel industry. It can compete on the world market principally because it is capital intensive and uses the latest techniques of production. But this also means that it employs comparatively few people. Hence it is not a major source of employment, something Brazil desperately needs. In the 1870s England was the world's leader in steel production, reaching the million-ton mark. At that time, England's steel industry employed 400,000 workers. In the 1980s Brazil routinely produced four times that amount of steel but did so using only around 28,000 workers (Cochrane, 1982:16). Modern technology and production techniques make a difference that is surely a mixed blessing to developing countries, and the need to compete in the world system constrains the types of development policies those countries can pursue.

Box 11.4

Economic Insecurity and Polarization in Brazil

Economic disparity in Brazil lends itself to a continued sense of apartheid, as rising conspicuous consumption is positively unabated, regardless of growth rates. São Paulo's economic elite avoid the city's infamous jams and carjackings in favor of journeying by helicopter (there are 240 helipads compared to New York City's 10) and travel around its opulent Daslu mall in golf carts. By Latin American standards, the disparities in Brazil are particularly unnerving, with a political system that in the two decades since the negotiated end of its military dictatorship has been saddled with instability through corruption and inertia. Brazil's elites, in place since colonial times, have remained above reproach throughout its modern history, under both dictatorship and democracy, and have long enjoyed security from commonplace criminality. The rise of gated communities in Brazil, therefore, is a manifestation of a growing middle class, which in itself would ordinarily be taken as a sign of progress were it not for the structural deficiencies that prevent wider economic and social mobility.

continues

Box 11.4 *continued*

The condominium *fechado* (closed estate) can be seen as an extension of the widespread measures put in place by many members of the more affluent working classes, particularly in areas of São Paulo with stable local industries, where private security arrangements are the norm (given a notoriously unresponsive police force).

The 30,000 strong Alphaville community, however, is a particularly interesting and curious example of urban development. The brainchild of the Albuquerque and Takaoka Company, the settlement was founded on farmland in counties 23 kilometers to the west of the city. Its origins lie in a number of co-determinants, namely rising crime in São Paulo, improvements in infrastructure under a massive public works program, and new modes of urban planning around the city. Now in its third decade and comprising 20,000 dwellings in 33 zones, it even boasts its own university and supports 150,000 retail and domestic workers

Alphaville ("first city") residents are not troubled by the widespread kidnappings that take place elsewhere in metropolitan São Paulo—constant surveillance by CCTV and patrols, even around school playing fields, by armed security personnel reassure its compound-dwelling inhabitants. Residents of Alphaville, some executives of multinationals, rebut claims of paranoia and claim that it enables them to live in conventional housing rather than apartment blocks equally as shut off from urban ills and allows children to play freely in the street.

The city is managed by Alphaville Urbanismo, incorporated in 1995. The company provides all utilities and requires no public services. In addition to the monthly residence fees, residents are reliant on private education and health care provision, placing Alphaville living well beyond the reach of the average Brazilian family. Without city governance, ironic given Brazil's 'ungovernable' society in ungated areas, residents are required to participate in communal affairs through regulatory committees. Alphaville's founders, Albuquerque and Takaoka, believe the concept has been a proven success, so much so that they now plan to extend it to lower-income Brazilian families in new affordable in-fill developments amid Brazil's metropolises elsewhere.

SOURCE: Andrew Stevens and Elisangela Fracaroli, "São Paulo's Alphaville Gated Community: An Early Answer to Middle-Class Insecurity," 2009.

Latin America is the scene of some of the most explosive population growth in the world. For example, São Paulo, Brazil, had a population of less than 3 million in 1950, but its population is approaching 24 million today. Brazil is the most populated country in South America, with a census count of 174.2 million in 2000 and a population estimated at 186.8 million in 2005. The Brazilian government estimates that the population will increase to 204 million by 2030, before beginning a slow decline due to an aging population, declining birthrates, and high levels of early mortality due to AIDs (Brazil, Economic Research Institute, 2008). This total is substantially different from estimates made in the 1980s, when the United Nations predicted that the population would increase to 246 million by the year 2025 (United Nations, 1985). But even so, it is estimated that over 90 percent will reside in urban areas. Brazil will become a country of giant cities. To feed these people, Brazil can exploit its arable landmass—but many of these new lands are part of the rain forest. As noted in Chapter 1, the growth of the megacity has been accompanied by serious problems of political and unsustainable pressures on the environment. A potential ecological disaster of global magnitude is in the making.

Unlike Brazil, Mexico is semiarid and lacks appreciable agricultural resources, and it has not been successful in reducing its rate of population growth. It has already cultivated virtually all available land. Population pressures will force people into the cities or to *El Norte* (as the United States is called). At the end of the 1980s, Dogan and Kasarda wrote:

> The urban population is expected to increase from 55 million in 1985 to 131 million in 2025, the equivalent of 13 cities of 10 million each. Is there a limit to Mexico City's growth, this bowl constrained by a circle of pollutant-trapping mountains? Guadalajara and Veracruz might become enormous metropolises. How many new cities of over a million will spring up in the Mexican "desert"? How many Mexicans will head for California, either legally or clandestinely? (1988, 24–25)

In addition to immense population pressures, Latin American countries have shared a history of political instability. They have been controlled for over a century by the dictates of U.S. foreign policy and by the demands of American corporations. Over the years, developmental strategies have been hemmed in by such global constraints. There is a great need to nurture domestic industrial development. In the past, political problems and periodic military coups seem to hamstring such efforts, and while there have been significant advances in democratic rule through much of Central America, instability is also fostered by inequalities in the class system, which is one of the most skewed in the world. Class structure, government control, and global power are prominent factors in understanding development in Latin America.

Asia

The global region of Asia represents great diversity and contains at least half of the world's population. Often overlooked beneath the generic labels such as Asian history or Asian culture, the separate countries have very different histories, as well as very different cultures, so that generalizations as to urban trends are very difficult.

In many Asian countries, primate cities—Tokyo-Yokohama, Pyongyang, Seoul, Taipei, Jakarta, Kuala Lumpur, Manila, and Bangkok—represent the centers of economic growth and development (Yeung, 1988:162). For example, in the 1980s, Tokyo accounted for 60 percent of Japan's elite business leaders and 60 percent of the total capital invested, along with a third of all department store sales; Seoul contained 78 percent of South Korean business headquarters and 90 percent of all large enterprises, while accounting for 27.9 percent of South Korea's GNP; and Bangkok housed one-third of Thailand's manufacturing and almost 80 percent of its banking, and it contributed 26.8 percent toward the country's GNP (Yeung, 1988:162). China's coastal development program, which situates manufacturing activity in planned urban agglomerations, has been different from that of any other country in the region (Newman and Thornley, 2005).

In all of these countries, urban development programs are often given a high profile. Among the issues that must be confronted is the lack of an adequate infrastructure to meet the demands of the growing urban population. The case of urban redevelopment in Manila is instructive. The Philippines suffered from the crony capitalism of the Marcos dictatorship for two decades before electing Corazon Aquino (wife of the political opposition leader assassinated by Marcos's security forces) president of the country in 1986. Millions of dollars from the World Bank and other international agencies lined the pockets of the military leaders, while underdevelopment continued to plague the country; more than 80 percent of its export crops are owned by the Dole pineapple conglomerate, and many Filipinos in rural areas work in a plantation system characterized by Ligaya McGovern (1996) as a "militarized zone." With perhaps the highest birthrate in all of Asia, overpopulation has led many Filipinos to leave rural communities for the capital city of Manila. The result has been uneven development within the metropolitan Manila region, where neighborhoods not much different from those in any modern city exist alongside squatter settlements. For those unable to find employment in rural areas or the cities, overseas labor has become an important safety valve, as the Philippines have one of the highest labor-exporting countries in the world, with substantial communities of Filipino workers, both male and female, in the developed nations (Tyner, 2008).

In recent decades several Asian nations, beginning with Korea, Taiwan, and Singapore, exploded the myth of "third world dependency" and the notion of "peripheral" development by growing rapidly as industrialized countries. They were helped along by the influx of capital investment from Japan and the search for cheap labor by multinational corporations from across the globe. Many of the resulting enterprises are joint domestic and foreign operations. In the 1980s, the "Asian tigers" (Hong Kong, Taiwan, South Korea, and Singapore) led the world in percentage growth of gross domestic product at 7 percent a year (Berry, 1989:176), helped by the continuing demand for consumer goods—especially electronics, textiles, and clothing. This pattern of "export-led" development has also been tried successfully in Spain and Italy (see Chapter

10) among other countries. The economies of the Asian countries suffered in the Asian economic crisis beginning in 1997, but they have since rebounded—although their success has since been overshadowed by the emergence of China as a major industrial power.

An important characteristic of the economic development in Asia has been the dominant role played by the national government in promoting growth. This intervention is not restricted to subsidization of capital investment and development but also includes strong control of unions and, often, harsh methods of regulating the working-class population; unions are not allowed and child labor, low wages, and sweatshop conditions are common (Lee, 1982; Palen, 1990).

While some countries have urban systems dominated by one large primate city, China has embarked on an ambitious program to control urban growth by creating new cities and industrial areas (it is said that China creates twenty new cities each year). The development of the Asian tigers changed the dynamics of global capital investment in the 1980s; more recently China has become as competitive in manufacturing as established economies among the developed nations. While some countries have explosive growth rates that will produce increasing urban populations and environmental pressures in the decades to come, Japan has an aging population and smaller towns are disappearing as the population moves to urban areas. The Asian Pacific Rim, which is linked to Japan (see Chapter 10) as well as the United States, contains economic forces that likely will be the major sphere of power and development in the twenty-first century. We will review information concerning urbanization trends in selected Asian countries, and we will look in more detail at urban development in India and China, the two largest Asian countries.

Table 11.3 gives an overview of urbanization in selected Asian countries. Most of these countries do not show the same high levels of urbanization that we saw in the previous table for Latin America. In 2000, Korea, Malaysia, and the Philippines all had more than 50 percent of their population living in urban areas, but the level of urbanization in other countries, including India, Thailand, and Vietnam, was less than 30 percent. A relatively small proportion of the population lived in large cities of 1 million persons—but in these cases the apparent high level of urbanization is the result of primacy (the case of Manila in the Philippines, Bangkok in Thailand, and the like). Interesting facts not apparent in the table include the following: In 2000, 56 percent of the population of Thailand lived in the capital city (Bangkok), and in three other countries (South Korea, the Philippines, and Vietnam) one-quarter or more of the population lived in the largest city.

India and China exhibit differences in their patterns of urbanization for many reasons, including India's colonial past and China's long history of empire and state bureaucracy. More recently, different national policies have produced rapid change in China's urban system, while India has seen a continuation of earlier urban growth; as in Latin America, the factors of state control and local class structure explain a great

TABLE 11.3 Urbanization in Selected Asian Countries, 1980–2005.

	Urban Population			% living in urban areas		Living in cities of 1 million or more (% of total population)		% of population in largest city (% of urban population)	
	1980	1990	2005	1990	2005	1990	2005	1990	2005
Bangladesh		20,600,000	35,600,000	20	25	9	13	32	35
China	192,300,000	311,000,000	527,000,000	27	40	13	18	3	3
India	158,800,000	216,000,000	314,000,000	26	29	10	12	6	6
Indonesia	32,900,000	54,500,000	106,100,000	31	48	9	12	14	12
Korea		31,600,000	39,000,000	74	81	51	51	33	25
Malaysia	5,800,000	8,900,000	17,000,000	50	67	6	6	13	8
Myanmar	8,100,000	10,100,000	15,500,000	25	31	7	8	29	27
Philippines	18,000,000	29,800,000	52,100,000	49	63	14	14	27	21
Thailand	7,900,000	16,100,000	20,700,000	29	32	11	10	37	32
Vietnam	10,300,000	13,400,000	21,900,000	20	26	13	13	30	23

SOURCE: Table 3.10, *World Development Indicators 2009* (New York: World Bank, 2009).

deal about development. Until the 1980s, China's Communist government restricted the size of China's largest cities, and this effectively controlled the growth of the largest cities. In the last decade, more than 200 million Chinese moved from rural areas into the cities, but this growth took place in many different urban centers and did not result in huge megacities or urban slums as are found in India. The current population figures for the largest cities and metropolitan areas in India and China are shown in Tables 11.4 and 11.5.

Of all the rapidly growing population areas of the globe, only China seems to have controlled the rate of urbanization to match its development potential. China's government pursues a balanced growth process of rural and urban development. Under the *hukou* system, the rural population is prevented by law from moving to cities (Kim, 1988). This prevents the kind of in-migration to the cities from rural areas that is common in the rest of the developing world.

Such balanced growth has had positive effects, and living in one of China's large cities is associated with increased income, access to public services, and an improved quality of life (Bradshaw and Fraser, 1989). Beginning in the 1980s, China launched an extensive drive to integrate into the world economy, particularly by manufacturing textiles and other household and consumer goods. The government adopted rapid modernization policies that included the location of new cities and coastal development zones that have resulted in an even greater balance to urban growth, in contrast to the uneven development that has plagued other countries in the developing world (Yusuf and Saich, 2009).

TABLE 11.4 Largest Urban Agglomerations in India, 1960–2005.

City	1960	1980	2000	2005
Mumbai (Bombay)	4,060,000	8,658,000	16,086,000	18,202,000
Delhi	2,283,000	5,558,000	12,441,000	15,053,000
Kolkata (Calcutta)	5,652,000	9,030,000	13,058,000	14,282,000
Chennai (Madras)	1,915,000	4,203,000	6,353,000	6,918,000
Bangalore	1,166,000	2,812,000	5,567,000	6,465,000
Hyderabad	1,241,000	2,487,000	5,445,000	6,117,000
Ahmadabad	1,181,000	2,484,000	4,427,000	5,122,000
Pune (Poona)	777,000	1,642,000	3,655,000	4,411,000
Surat	311,000	877,000	2,699,000	3,558,000
Kanpur	951,000	1,612,000	2,641,000	3,019,000
Jaipur	402,000	984,000	2,259,000	2,748,000
Lucknow	644,000	993,000	2,221,000	2,567,000
Nagpur	674,000	1,273,000	2,089,000	2,350,000
Patna	359,000	881,000	1,658,000	2,029,000
Indore	389,000	808,000	1,597,000	1,914,000

SOURCE: United Nations, *World Urbanization Prospects, 2007 Revision.*

China and India can also be contrasted with regard to the quality of life in their cities. Just the mention of India's cities (Calcutta, Bombay, Delhi) conjures up images of extreme poverty that became even more familiar following the recent success of the film *Slumdog Millionaire*. To an extent, these images are accurate. The first two cities have large homeless populations, and all possess a declining quality of life. India's cities are surrounded by shantytowns, called *bustees*, that grow each day. Their presence has not prevented the city center from experiencing terrible overcrowding. The population density of Calcutta, for example, has been estimated at 45,000 residents per square kilometer, with the overwhelming majority living below the poverty line. Misery, disease, squalor, and malnutrition afflict the hordes of urban street people. The urban implosion of India is the consequence of rural push factors as well as urban pull. The "green revolution" that modernized India's agriculture has been relatively successful and has led to a decline in the number of people needed to grow food in rural areas. As a result, in recent years more Indians are looking toward the cities for their livelihood.

The uncontrolled migration of people from rural areas to India's cities, on the other hand, only makes a bad situation worse. In the 1980s, one observer noted:

> The most serious problems are related directly or indirectly to the extreme shortage of housing, and to inadequacy of physical and social infrastructures to meet the needs of the urban low- and middle-income groups. . . . The shortages are the principal cause of the progressive deterioration of the urban environment during the past 20–25 years. Proliferation of slums is the most visible symptom of the environmental deterioration. The other major symptom is the rapid increase in the levels of air and water pollution in or near the cities, far above the internationally accepted levels for maintaining human health and safety. (Nath, 1989:264)

From 2000 to 2007, the population of India's five largest cities increased by 7.4 million persons, most of whom moved into the shantytowns of these megacities. The population of India's largest urban agglomerations from 1960 to 2005 is shown in Table 11.4.

Some of India's cities, such as Delhi, have large areas that are middle class and quite prosperous. Bombay was planned by the British as a colonial center and retains its planned streets and residential districts that allow services to be delivered with some efficiency. It is a major center of industrial and service employment. In short, despite their declining quality of life, India's cities are not all mired in extreme poverty and deprivation (Misra, 1978). However, the construction of new middle-class housing estates and efforts to redevelop and improve the appearance of neighborhood areas has had negative effects on many of the urban poor, as described in Box 11.5.

Chinese cities fared comparatively better under Communist rule. One of the first acts of the Maoist regime in the 1950s was to eradicate the poverty and prostitution

Box 11.5

Urban Poor Made Homeless in India's Drive for More "Beautiful" Cities

Large areas of habitation of India's urban poor have been forcefully taken over by city government. The groups of people affected are often the ones who have been employed in informal sectors or are self-employed in the tertiary services sector. Their displacement has as much to do with the space they live in as with the work they perform. The areas that they occupied are being transferred into larger private corporate entities such as commercial complexes and residential developments. These units are also often coupled with labor-replacing devices ranging from automatic tellers and computer-aided machines to vacuum cleaners and home delivery services, thus eliminating the work earlier done by the lower rungs of the urban population. While the driving force behind these changes is manifestly the new globalized economy, it is offered on an environmental platter of "cleanliness" and "beautification."

In Chennai City, 40 percent of the population lives in slums—there are 69,000 families who have been identified to be living on government land—and they are to be relocated to areas far removed from the city. The areas vacated will be taken over by hotel resorts, commercial and residential complexes, and modern businesses. Much of the "clearance" is being undertaken in the name of "beautification" and tourism.

In Kolkata (Calcutta), "Operation Sunshine" evicted over 50,000 hawkers from the city's main streets, and over 7,000 hutments were forcibly demolished along the sides of storm water drains and the metro and circular rail tracks.

In Delhi, where substandard settlements house as much as 70 percent of the city's population, not only have vendors, cycle-rickshaws, beggars, and shanties been "evicted," but also 75,000 families who lived on the banks of the Yamuna River. The resettlement colonies and industrial areas that were once supposed to be at the fringe of the city are now contiguous urban sprawls. Increasing numbers of poor inhabitants continue to live in shantytowns without services. Rapidly shrinking employment opportunities and crusading environmental activism have made the situation significantly worse for them. While the city gets the Clean City Award from far-off California, its own citizens grimly face critical inadequacies of work, shelter, civic amenities, and governance.

In vicious combination, these three trends are changing the urban landscape from "homes" to "estate ownerships" in the name of liberalization, privatization, and globalization. The replacement of housing for poor urban dwellers with commercial and upmarket developments raises several questions about the nature of "planning" itself. Who makes these plans? Who are they made for?

SOURCE: Adapted from Dunu Roy, "Urban Poor Increasingly Made Homeless in India's Drive for More 'Beautiful' Cities," City Mayors—Development (http://www.citymayors.com/sections/development.html).

310

TABLE 11.5 Largest Cities and Metropolitan Areas in China, 2000.

	City Population	Metropolitan Area
Shanghai	8,214,000	12,800,000
Beijing	7,362,000	10.800,000
Tianjun	5,855,000	9,300,000
Hong Kong	6,843,000	6,800,000
Wuhan	4.040,000	5,700,000
Shengyang	4,669,000	4,900,000
Chongging	3,127,000	4,800,000
Guangzhou	3,935,000	3,900,000
Chengdu	2,954,000	3,400,000
Xian	2,872,000	3,200,000
Changchun	2,192,000	3,000,000
Haerbin	2,990,000	2,900,000
Nanjing	2,678,000	2,800,000
Zibo	2,484,000	2,700,000

SOURCE: Adapted from City Mayors, *The World's Largest Cities*; and United Nations, Department of Economic and Social Affairs, Population Division, Urban Agglomerations 2003.

FIGURE 11.2 The Shanghai Tower. The three tallest buildings in the world are located in cities in the developing nations. SOURCE: Rensler Architects.

endemic to the streets of Shanghai, the focal point of global colonial interests. City services throughout China are regulated by the state and function to maintain the quality of life. The Chinese government has also implemented strict measures of birth control, and most families are not permitted to have more than one child. This state policy of restricting population growth in a country of more than 1 billion people has had some success among urban households but has been less successful in the countryside.

There is a visible contrast between cities in India and cities in China, as noted in one of the first books about urbanization in China: "Slums and squatter settlements seemed absent, conspicuous consumption and foreign oriented life styles were not visible, a high degree of economic equality and security seemed to prevail, unemployment seemed absent, close-knit neighborhoods and families seemed to persist, and crime, drug addiction, prostitution, and other forms of deviance seemed minor or nonexistent" (Whyte and Parish, 1984:2–3). Twenty-five years later, despite adding more than 280 million persons to the urban areas in China, there are still low levels of unemployment and there are no slums (World Bank, 2009).

For many decades, a household registration system (*hukou*) kept urban growth in check. Each person in China was assigned a residential location that defines accessibility to state-provided benefits. This policy effectively regulated rural to urban migration—one could move to the city but would not be eligible for health, education, or other services. This policy began to change in 1985 when the Ministry of Public Security authorized new regulations for the "Management of Population Living Temporarily in the Cities," and in 1988 the Ministry of Labor recommended that impoverished provinces in the center of the country export labor to the growing industrial centers of the coastal region (Guthrie, 2010). China's urban strategies, including the important role of the hukou are summarized in Box 11.6.

The urban system in China dates back many centuries, and the current clustering of large cities follows from a pattern of development that was evident during the imperial period (Xeh and Xu, 1984). But it has been strongly influenced by the coastal development strategy—designed in part to decentralize political power away from the more conservative voices in Beijing (Guthrie, 2010). During the 1980s and 1990s, there were a number of important policy shifts that would open China to the global economy, including the development of new industrial strategies, the creation of new economic zones that allowed firms to take advantage of tax incentives targeted to specific types of investment, aggressive export strategies, and (less obvious to the outside) the implementation of regionally specific development strategies within China itself. The 1979 Joint Venture Law was the first series of regulations that allowed foreign capital into China. This was followed in 1980 with development policies that created four special economic zones (SEZs) in Fujian province (Xiamen) and Guangdong province (Shantou, Shenzen, and Zhuhai). The special economic zones were designed to increase investment and foreign trade in the eastern and southern provinces, granting the coastal regions greater autonomy for export trade.

Box 11.6

China's Urbanization Strategies

In the rapidly urbanizing world of the twenty-first century, China is expected to play an important role, chiefly because of its size and the speed at which it is changing. In 1980, China's urban population was 191 million. By 2007, it was 594 million, excluding migrants. About half of China's population now lives in cities. China's phenomenal urbanization has become a focus of policy makers around the world, both in terms of coping strategies and the benefits and challenges the country has experienced. What are some of the strategies that have helped manage the explosive urbanization in China?

A cornerstone of China's urbanization strategy has been the *hukou*, or household registration system to control migration and to try to channel migrants to small or medium-sized cities. There are crowded conditions but not slums in the cities. Increasingly, however, larger cities are relaxing the hukou rules, and there is an ongoing debate about the future role of this system and what it portends for migrants' access to urban services.

There is low urban poverty and unemployment. With the rapid growth of the Chinese economy, urban poverty has been contained and is estimated at between 4 and 6 percent of the population. Despite the rapidly increasing urban population, unemployment is also low, in the 3 to 4 percent range.

Another key element of China's successful urbanization is the devolution of public services and many administrative functions to city governments. In 2005, Chinese citizens' degree of satisfaction with local governments rose to 72 percent—considerably higher than in many other countries, including the United States. China has also been frugal about its use of land space for urban development: Cities now occupy about 4.4 percent of the total land area. But urbanization has increased the income gap between villages and cities, and problems of rural poverty persist. And there are not as yet adequate services for migrants nor safety nets for the poor and elderly.

While China has coped more effectively than many countries with the demands of urbanization, a number of urgent issues need to be tackled. Between now and 2025, another 200 to 250 million people will migrate to China's cities. Providing jobs and infrastructure for this anticipated inflow of people poses major challenges. Rapid economic growth will remain critical. Urban residents use 3.6 times as much energy as rural residents, suggesting that energy use is far from its peak. China suffers from water scarcity, with just over 2,100 cubic meters of water available per person—one-third of the world average. The situation is more precarious in the northern part of the country, where climate change may worsen arid conditions.

SOURCE: Adapted from *China's Rapid Urbanization: Benefits, Challenges & Strategies* (World Bank, 2009).

The economic reforms and industrial policies have produced four main urban agglomerations:

Liaodong Peninsula (Shenyang-Dalian): Shenyang in the north and Dalian in the south are the dominant cities in this region; Shenyang is the major industrial town and Dalian is the major port. Other cities include Anshan, Fushun, Benxi, and Liaoyang.

Beijing-Tianjin: Beijing (the capital city) and Tianjin are the dominant cities of this cluster located in the Yellow River valley. Other important cities of the region include Tanggu and Tangshan.

Yangtze River Delta (Nanjing-Shanghai-Hangzhou): Shanghai (the largest city in China) is the dominant city of this cluster, which also includes the industrial centers of Nanjing and Hangzhou.

Pearl River Delta: The former British colony of Hong Kong and the older Chinese city of Guangzhou are the dominant cities in this region.

Cities located within these clusters are connected by railway, expressway, and canals and are dominated by heavy industry. The Beijing-Tianjin and Liaodong Peninsula regions contain China's metal, machinery, petrochemical, and industrial centers. Newer cities have emerged within these clusters, including Dongguan, Shenzhen, and Zhuhai in the Pearl River Delta, and Changzhou in the Yangtze River Delta. Two other urban agglomerations have emerged in the last two decades:

Shandong Peninsula: Jinan and Qingdao are the dominant cities in this region, with Yantai as the major port of the region.

Fuzhou-Xiamen (Minnan): Fuzhou and Xiamen are the important cities in this region, although they are not as dominant as the major cities in other clusters. Development in this area will depend to some degree on relations with Taiwan.

The cluster city development promoted by the Chinese government has allowed Chinese cities to link with other Asian countries on the Pacific Rim and form urban corridors that are expected to be the major centers of urban growth in the Pacific Rim in the coming decades (Choe, 1998; Yusuf and Nabeshim, 2009). One example of this is the Beijing-Seoul-Tokyo (BESETO) Urban Corridor shown in Figure 11.3. This economic corridor links important manufacturing areas across three countries (China, Korea, and Japan) with emerging world markets across Asia, the United States, and Europe; interestingly, the corridor also links countries with older established manufacturing (Japan), one of the Asian Tigers (Korea), and the new manufacturing giant (China).

As a result of these policies, at the beginning of the twenty-first century, foreign investment in China dwarfed that of Japan in comparable development periods. While many in the West would complain that Chinese markets were closed to foreign

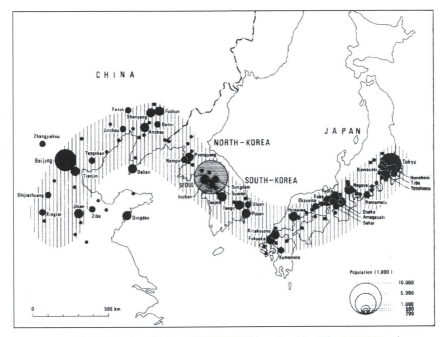

FIGURE 11.3 The Beijing-Seoul-Tokyo (BESETO) Urban Corridor. The BESETO urban corridor links manufacturing areas across three Asian countries, including the industrial zones around the capital cities of Beijing (China), Seoul (South Korea), and Tokyo (Japan). SOURCE: Sang-Chuel Choe, "The Evolving Urban System in North-East Asia," Fu-chen Lo and Yueman Yeung, eds., *Emerging World Cities in Pacific Asia* (New York: United Nations University Press, 1996). http://www.unu.edu/unupress/unupbooks/uu11ee/uu11ee0f.jpg

producers, the foreign investment regime was more liberal than that of either Japan or South Korea, and manufacturers in other Asian countries moved their production to China to take advantage of even cheaper labor (Guthrie, 2010:121). As the film documentary *China Rising* (2006) demonstrates, even older Chinese workers who found stable employment in the factory system of the Communist era have been displaced by low-wage labor in the emerging industrial centers.

Africa and the Arab Countries

Of all the continents, Africa presents the clearest case of the overurbanization/underurbanization dilemma. For the most part, the poverty, overurbanizationization, and political instability endemic to this region reflect a legacy of years of colonial rule (Simon, 1989) and the Cold War policies of the United States and the Soviet Union in the period that followed. South of the Sahara Desert, the primate cities were all founded as trading centers and located near the coasts or with easy access by water to the coast. Some countries, such as Nigeria, have a moderately developed urban hierarchy containing several cities: Lagos, Ibadan, Kano, and Oshogbo. However, most countries, such as Kenya, are classic cases of primate city development. Kenya's capital, Nairobi, with a population of 3 million persons in 2007, contained some 40 percent of the country's urban population. Here, as in most of Africa, the intermediate level of the urban hierarchy (that is, cities with populations greater than 100,000 but less than 1 million) is notably absent.

Africa contains fifty-four separate countries, and it is difficult to generalize about the scale of development or urbanization. The north, which contains Arab countries, is highly urbanized. In 2008, 85 percent of the Libyan population and 59 percent of Morocco's population were living in cities. Egypt contains one of the world's most populated cities, Cairo, with an urban area of nearly 11.9 million people in 2007. Other sub-Saharan countries have rates of urbanization of between 40 and 50 percent, although countries in eastern and central Africa generally have lower levels of urbanization, and in several cases urban growth for the last decade or more has been slowed or even declined due to political instability and conflict in countries such as Ethiopia and Sudan. Table 11.6 provides information on urbanization for selected African countries from the period 1980–2005.

Most African countries have a primate city land-use pattern similar to that of other developing nations. The center consists of wide boulevards loaded with traffic and passing in between high skyscrapers built in the common "international style" of the developed West at the end of the twentieth century. Affluent natives and the foreign community make their home there. Beyond the glitter domes of development, the core is surrounded by mile upon mile of shantytowns—the most depressing agglomeration of ersatz housing imaginable—where entire families follow a precarious existence and play the "life lottery," hoping to acquire some meager portion of the wealth circulating through the center.

Years of dominance and economic exploitation by colonial powers, coupled with political conflict and poor local leadership, have left Africa in an undeveloped state. Many countries continue to rely on natural resources and tourism for economic growth, but political conflicts have discouraged travel to many countries. With the discovery and exploitation of oil, Nigeria acquired considerable capital, as is the case with Libya. However, most countries remain locked in the grip of poverty, with limited industrial schemes and weak rural economies. Without agricultural development in the rural areas, migration to the cities is an inevitable result. Extensive squatter settlements, or *bidonvilles*, have been characteristic of urban development of recent decades (Aina, 1990; Schlyter, 1990).

The Arab cities are also scenes of uneven development. Cairo is known for its cosmopolitan population but also for its squatter settlements, such as the inhabitants of the immense cemetery, the City of the Dead, or the people known as the *zebaleen*,

TABLE 11.6 Urbanization in Selected African Countries, 1980–2005.

	Urban Population (millions of persons)			percent			Living in cities of 1 million or more (% of total population)		Living in largest city (% of urban population)	
	1980	1990	2005	1990	2005		1990	2005	1990	2005
Angola	1,500,000	3,900,000	8,500,000	37	53		15	17	40	33
Cameroon	2,700,000	4,700,000	8,900,000	41	55		14	20	20	20
Congo	7,700,000	10,500,000	18,500,000	28	32		15	17	35	33
Egypt	17,900,000	24,200,000	31,700,000	44	43		22	20	37	35
Ethiopia	40,000,004	6,400,000	11,400,000	13	16		3	4	28	25
Libya	2,300,000	3,400,000	5,000,000	79	85		49	55	44	42
Morocco	8,000,000	11,600,000	17,700,000	48	59		16	16	23	18
Nigeria	19,100,000	31,700,000	63,400,000	35	48		11	14	15	17
Senegal	2,000,000	3,100,000	4,800,000	39	42		17	19	44	45
South Africa	13,300,000	18,300,000	27,800,000	52	59		25	30	10	12
Sudan	3,900,000	6,900,000	14,800,000	27	41		9	12	34	31
Zambia	2,300,000	3,300,000	4,100,000	39	35		9	11	23	31
Zimbabwe	1,800,000	3,100,000	4,700,000	26	36		10	12	34	32

SOURCE: Table 3.10, *World Development Indicators 2007* (New York: World Bank, 2007).

who live off of other people's garbage at the massive city dump (Abu-Lughod, 1969). Most Arab countries have medium-size cities and have not experienced a large rural exodus because their hinterlands have always been sparsely settled. The oil kingdoms of the Middle East have utilized their great wealth to create cities with modern architecture, such as Riyadh in Saudi Arabia and Dubai in the United Arab Emirates. These cities have been designed to showcase the wealth of the Arab states and to attract wealthy tourists from Europe; built with a workforce recruited from other Middle Eastern countries and from southern Asia, they are dependent on the oil industry monoculture.

SUMMARY

Many countries in the developing world have been mired in a vicious cycle of over-urbanization/underurbanization for many decades. The failure of agricultural development in rural areas means future populations face starvation or migration. The limited success of urban economic growth and the toxic effects of the World Bank and other institutions' efforts to install free market trade policies means that cities in the developing nations, particularly in sub-Saharan Africa, will continue to play a marginal role in the global economy. Without balanced policies of development, these countries will face a bleak future. The issue is not simply growth and industrial development financed by developed nations. Rather, there is a need for linked policies that improve agricultural production on the one hand and urban economies on the other. Especially in places such as Asia and Africa, it is essential that rural populations be stabilized so that the migration pressures on cities can be relieved. Yet development that is led simply by global capital investment will not head countries in that much-needed direction.

For example, in the 1980s the World Bank and the International Monetary Fund encouraged developing countries to build enterprise zones of manufacturing that would capture global investment. However, this development has come at a price because much of the labor force in developing countries consists of young women between sixteen and twenty-five years old. The movement of young women from their home villages to secure employment in the city disrupts traditional family structures. These women once constituted the backbone of traditional agriculture. With the young female population working in factories, rural agriculture in many countries is on the verge of collapse. The decline of rural economies pushes more and more people into the cities or, in the case of Mexico, to move across national borders.

Shantytowns are growing rapidly in response to continued population expansion. São Paulo, Brazil, and Calcutta, India, have millions of residents in their *favellas* and *bustees*, while Mexico City's *colonias populares* (irregular settlements) are said to contain as much as 60 percent of the city's population (estimated at 18 million in 2000). The pattern of shantytown/central core uneven development is the exact opposite of what is found in developed nations, where there are maturing and relatively affluent suburbs surrounding a declining urban core. But more important, the gap between the wealthy and the majority of the population is quite enormous.

For the most part, governments in developing nations have failed to achieve a better quality of life for their citizens. As we have seen over the last two decades, domination of the economy and the government by the ruling class leads to harsh measures of social control, hyperaggressive police, death squads, and repressive political dictatorship rather than enlightened policies of social reform. The passion of the people in developing nations manifests itself as a political clash between the fortunate few backed by the government and the afflicted and disadvantaged. As the urban population in these countries grows to some 5 billion persons in the next twenty years, with a majority having incomes below the poverty line and living in massive urban slums, the demands for social reform are likely to increase. While China has charted a separate course for economic development and managed urban growth, it is unlikely that the expansion of global capitalism will be able to meet the needs of persons in developing nations. For the immediate future, the response of people and governments in the developed world will likely focus on repairing the economic turmoil that began with the housing crisis in the United States and that has left national, state, and local governments around the globe with few resources for programs in their own communities, much less in the developing world.

KEY CONCEPTS

uneven development
colonialism
internationalization of capital
demographic transition
primate city
shantytown
informal economy
crony capitalism
overurbanization / underurbanization

DISCUSSION QUESTIONS

1. The global economic system is increasingly important to the developing nations. Discuss the relationship between the two. In what ways has modernization theory changed because of the influence of the global system?

2. Discuss the importance of demographic change in studying urbanization in the developing world. How is urbanization in these countries different from that found in developed nations?

3. Urbanization in developing countries is often characterized by the dominance of a primate city, overurbanization, shantytown development, and the important role of the informal economy. Define and discuss these concepts and give an example of each.

4. Discuss how urban social movements in developing countries have addressed poverty, uneven development, women's rights, and other social issues.

5. What are some of the important differences in urban development in Latin America, Asia, and Africa? What factors might account for these differences? Which theoretical model (dependency theory, modernization theory, world systems theory, or the sociospatial model) might best explain these differences?

6. China has charted a new course for economic growth and management of urban growth. How was this accomplished? What are the consequences for the development of the urban system?

chapter 12

METROPOLITAN PLANNING AND ENVIRONMENTAL ISSUES

In May 2008, the Nobel Prize–winning economist Paul Krugman was in Berlin, and he wrote an Op-Ed piece for the *New York Times* that began, "I have seen the future, and it works." He went on to extol "this marvelous urban environment" with its pitch-perfect public transportation servicing medium height high-rise buildings embedded in a larger urban-scape of commercial service establishments and green areas. He then commented: "It's the kind of neighborhood in which people don't have to drive a lot, but it's also a kind of neighborhood that barely exists in America, even in big metropolitan areas. Greater Atlanta has roughly the same population as greater Berlin—but Berlin is a city of trains, buses and bikes, while Atlanta is a city of cars, cars and cars." The Nobel Prize winner is speaking here not as an objective scientist, but as another tourist from America, and one who subscribes to the subjective bias against suburban sprawl. As any other observant visitor to Berlin can attest, he leaves out other aspects of the experience: the mixed groups of drug addicts loitering around select public places including open-air heroin users and speed freaks; Nazi skinheads roaming the very community transportation corridors Krugman lauds; sectors of the city that could be called slums in the American style, except that the housing is better maintained and the streets are cleaner; and, despite the popularity of Berlin, an increasing and denser development of the region outside the city for the kind of single-family homes that are most characteristic of the United States and that he seems to dislike despite the fact that he probably lives in one back in Princeton, N.J., where he is a professor.

To be sure, Krugman has an excellent point and his comparison between Berlin and Atlanta is well taken. However, any tourist comparing American and European urban development patterns for public consumption, such as this Op-Ed columnist, must be held responsible for pointing out the single most important reason for the contrast. Simply put, European cities have fought sprawl and have a more "rational" public mode of living that includes clustered high-rises and efficient public transportation precisely because in Europe planners have political power and leverage over land use built by profit seekers. America has nothing comparable because Americans dislike public housing and government planning and are generally opposed to government regulation and intervention. The fundamental ideological divide between these societies could not be more different. Witness the frustrating and irrational response average U.S. citizens have made in opposition to government-sponsored health insurance during the summer of 2009. European countries adopted universal health care, in contrast, scores of years ago. At about the same time, in the post–World War II era, they also sanctioned local and national planning schemes for housing and the construction of the kind of public transportation mix of buses, trains, and bike lanes that are so impressive to visitors from the United States like Krugman. In short, Europe's long past commitment to public, government control over land-use planning can only be dreamed about as an American future.

It remains to be stated clearly that the typical U.S. citizen's opposition to government planning ideologically benefits the real estate profit making industry more than it does those same citizens. Such ironies are typical of America because capitalist pursuits of profit have long dominated public discourse and many people possess beliefs about the putative "evils" of government intervention that are actually against their own best interests. Active urban planning and universal health care are, perhaps, the two best examples contrasting American and European societies.

Yet it must also be noted that Krugman and other casual tourists are wrong in their impressions in another context. We have already provided ample evidence showing how the emergent form of urban living and working arrangements is the multi-centered region. This is increasingly true for many European societies as well, even with their strong public planning regulations still in place. Single-family home living, long the norm of housing in the United States, is progressively more attractive to Europeans, not to mention residents of other countries around the globe. Can we really claim today that a majority of citizens in other societies prefer living in high-rises, even if they are only modestly built to four or five stories, rather than pursuing the dream, often referred to as an American one, of owning a single-family home? The public versus private option is currently being debated in many places in Europe that were once unchallenged bastions of government land-use control and planning. To be sure, the historical commitment to the kind of clustered neighborhood development admired by American tourists, like Krugman, continues to define most European cities even after having abandoned the fully fledged welfare state in the twenty-first century. But increasingly, and visibly, areas around historical central cities are being developed for profit and for low density, multicentered metropolitan living, just as it has been ever since the 1920s in the United States.

One excellent example of these contemporary changes is the city of Espoo, Finland, which belongs to the greater Helsinki metropolitan area—a typical multicentered region like those in the United States. Espoo is the second largest city in Finland and has a population of over 240,000. It also has its real estate privatized, despite planning and unlike the larger city of Helsinki, where the municipal government still maintains control over land use and, by contrast, possesses the kind of immense planning powers admired by critics of American urbanism. Espoo itself contains the contradictions that come from changes in welfare state capitalism characteristic of Europe. On the one hand, it envelops the city of Tapiola, a world famous planned "garden city" that was built in the 1950s and is still thriving. Tapiola was designed according to the strict government cluster planning once well known in the United States, during that same post–World War II period, in places such as Garden City, New York (see below for a discussion of this movement). On the other hand, Espoo is home to the new headquarters complex built by the giant electronics corporation, Nokia, which is a private business and no doubt possesses executive and other well-paid high-tech employees who prefer to live in private single-family homes, own cars, and like to drive to work, much as their well-paid counterparts in sprawling and "dysfunctional" Atlanta, Georgia, like to do.

There is a critical difference between Espoo and Atlanta, and one that still marks the difference between the relatively unplanned landscape of the United States and the once highly planned one of Europe. Any person, young, old, healthy, confined to a wheelchair, pregnant, pushing children in a carriage, or walking a dog or bicycle can, if they have the not inexpensive fare, take a bus or a combination bus and tram and travel wherever they like within Espoo, between Espoo and Helsinki, or any of its surrounding areas. And they can do so using a clean, efficient, safe transportation infrastructure with convenient and frequent service. The same certainly cannot, by any stretch of the imagination, be said of Atlanta and almost all other American metro regions where, as Krugman notes, the car reigns supreme.

Critics of the U.S. approach to urban development consider the present pattern evil because of its almost exclusive reliance on cars. This is perceived as wasteful of energy and other resources, a contributor to global warming, and excessively expensive to individuals. But there is another evil equal to the much maligned auto. The multicentered metro form of urban space embodies, at its core, the phenomenon of sprawl. Perhaps this characteristic is the single most targeted aspect of our current way of living that is viewed in a most negative light. We have argued that the multicentered metro region functions, on a much grander scale, just as compact central cities once did by providing locations for jobs, leisure activities, government offices, organized entertainments such as professional sports, which take place in stadiums, educational facilities of all kinds, commercial and retail businesses, and millions of housing units for local residents many of which represent the norm of single-family homes. In order to accomplish this task, social organization that is regional in scale and relies on the car as the main means of transport assumes the perceived pattern of sprawl. For an increasing number of urban professionals in the United States, sprawl is a serious economic and environmental problem that our society can no longer afford.

SPRAWL

In the earlier pages of this text we have argued that the contemporary growth pattern of our urban areas is a new form of sociospatial organization. We call it the "multicentered metro region." Sprawl can be the most serious outcome of this new form, but most critics of it fail to connect the cause to the development of the region, just as Krugman failed in his observations above. Instead they invariably dream of a solution that would bring large compact cities back, and by concentrating significant numbers of people in select spots, they also dream of a return to open, green spaces surrounding these metropolises. We call this a dream because it is. On its most fundamental level it fails to recognize that most Americans, when given a choice, do not want to live that way and that there are important economic forces pushing business locations at a further remove from the historical downtown core. In the United States, sprawl remains the serious problem that it is, not because the centrifugal force pushing out is so much stronger than the centripetal one pulling toward the center, but because so little power has been given to planners and regulators of land use that they have been unable to modify its shape throughout the larger region for more rational conservation of resources and before it has turned into our present pattern of endless ticky-tacky homes and strip zoned highways. To suggest that sprawl can be stopped and that we can return to a city-centered mode of living for everyone, which virtually all critics of sprawl eventually claim, is to ignore the other and even greater causal force operating today in our human environment: the ability, under a capitalist system of land marketing, to supercede municipal boundaries and to spread out. What is needed is not a return to compact city forms, with higher density residential living, but greater power to plan for minicenters and clustered neighborhood development in suburban regions, even if they will remain dominated by the norm of the single-family home.

The recognition that sprawl is a major environmental problem has its own social history. In the 1950s, it was suburbia, rather than sprawl, that drew the ire of critics. As we have seen, a mass movement to single-family living outside the historical central city began during that time. By 1970, only twenty-five years after World War II, more Americans were living in suburbia than in our large cities. As this phenomenon picked up speed and came to define the very nature of growth in the Sun Belt, with its own massive ingestion of population from other parts of the United States, suburban life, despite all its critics in academia and in the architectural and planning professions, became the normative form of American living. Endless sprawl, particularly evident in those same Sun Belt regions or in areas like Long Island, outside our largest and oldest Northeast cities, emerged as a consequence and its critique by the very same group of professionals eventually supplanted complaints about suburbia itself.

Results of unregulated regional growth are quite troubling now. For example, Phoenix, Arizona, one of the fastest growing Sun Belt regions, increases its area about an acre an hour, while Atlanta, Georgia, is now spread out more than the entire state of Delaware. According to a report that was released in 2001, sprawling development claims farmland at a rate of 1.2 million acres a year; an average suburban family now makes ten car trips a day and owns at least two vehicles; and commuting in slow moving rush hour traffic wastes an estimated $72 billion a year in fuel and productivity

(Mitchell, 2001:58). In previous chapters we have also seen that extreme racial and income segregation is a consequence of sprawl. And adding to all these woes is the fact that outward development around metro cores gobbles up open space, grasslands, forests, and farmlands at a pace that threatens the very balance of nature in our country, thereby making it mandatory to import basic food products that were once grown locally and in abundance. In supermarkets today we buy products that have no fertilizer or pesticide information regarding how the garlic, lettuce, tomatoes, and other common vegetables are grown in lands as far away as China.

Fighting Sprawl Through Smart Growth

Fighting sprawl presents society with the inevitable issue of providing planners with more powers. However, few places in our country have been willing to give government greater control over land use. The general term for a more aggressive approach is called "smart growth," and it is a combination of tax incentives, buyouts of farmland (called *land banking*), and better planning of new developments so that they are more concentrated and can be serviced by public transportation. As early as 1967, the state of Oregon, under its governor, Tom McCall, moved to preserve farmland that was being rapidly gobbled up by suburban development by declaring set boundaries for cities and by land banking open areas in order to preserve green space. Portland, Oregon, went even further in the hands of several activist mayors by establishing a metropolitan planning agency that not only maintained its city boundary and green belt, but also by investing heavily in new public transportation in order to make living within the city of Portland more attractive than the surrounding suburbia. For some time, in the 1990s, Portland was lauded as precisely the kind of pedestrian friendly, clustered dwelling, and public transport–using city that could be found in Europe and that has attracted the attention of American tourists like Paul Krugman. Lately, however, the center in Portland has not held. Reports are becoming common about developer violations beyond its growth barriers. The once admired Portland green belt has been breached by building. In sum, aggressive planning to prevent sprawl is still the main tool advocated by opponents, but simply put, it may be impossible in the United States to invoke so-called smart planning without having to live with its daily violations that inevitably lead to the further expansion of the metro area without more rationalized cluster development in minicenters.

A second important component of smart growth is investment in light rail public transportation that competes with automobile commutation. Once again, very few areas in our country have been able to succeed in constructing competitive light rail projects. Although they exist in a number of cities, not enough money has been invested in their passenger capacity in order for them to begin to replace people's reliance on automobiles for commutation. Furthermore, despite some early support in the urban renewal days of the 1960s when the federal government provided cities with funds for public transportation projects, limited funding has been commonplace ever since. Put succinctly, while the federal government is the obvious actor that could bring about the success of light rail projects throughout America, it has provided only piecemeal hit-and-miss support for many decades while abdicating a more aggressive role.

Portland has a successful but very modest facility called the Metropolitan Area Express, or MAX. It services communities within the existing municipal boundary. MAX has succeeded within this context, although it hasn't become a solution to sprawl because it has been combined with strong planning controls on developers thereby pushing growth further outside the core. In contrast, Atlanta also has a light rail facility, called MARTA. Too limited in scope and without any coordination of clustered planning on its route, this version is a failed attempt to provide the region with adequate public transportation. A third example is Metro Rail in the city of Buffalo, N.Y. Under Great Society legislation during the 1960s, adequate federal funds were provided to the region for a showcase project. Yet suburban interests and feuding local politicians worked against this mandate, and eventually the reactionary suburban residents triumphed and blocked the infrastructure of public transport from extending beyond the city line. Heavy auto dependency and sprawl in the now familiar pattern followed quickly. In short, one of the things that makes the study of sprawl such a frustrating problem is that we have the tools to cure many of its ills; however, residents in metro areas other than Portland have rejected the aggressive use of those tools. What's more, even Portland has been so subjected to the powerful centrifugal forces producing a spreading regional pattern that it has failed to stop the hemorrhaging of farmland and forest loss.

A SHORT HISTORY OF
METROPOLITAN PLANNING

The story of sprawl testifies to the fact that land-use planning in the United States is weak, and the responses of tourists to places in Europe where it remains strong confirms this observation. Yet it cannot be asserted that metropolitan planning has not been tried in this country. Just the opposite. Every town, village, municipality, county, city, and state has its own planning authorities. Any budgeted government function must comply with providing such an organizational entity that supervises its assigned oversight duties. Purchasing and planning go along with this activity as does cooperating with private developers and people investing in land for profit.

Most commonly, government presence has been felt in metro areas in order to build and operate public housing or subsidized housing projects precisely because the private sector has been unable to provide the same. As we have seen, the failure of our capitalist society to solve the affordable housing crisis has led, instead, to our current economic meltdown with its use of subprime mortgage lending. In the 1950s the government went into the business of segregating poor people and placing them in high-rise public housing projects. Results of that effort were largely disastrous. In sum, the lack of affordable housing is a central contradiction of American society and has plagued us for centuries, even when local governments were given the authority to plan aggressively for the construction of public housing.

Pruitt-Igoe, for example, was a massive public housing project constructed in the early 1950s in St. Louis, Missouri. It was inspired by the work of the leading architect of the postwar generation, Le Corbusier of France, and executed in design by several famous architects, including Minoru Yamasaki. The project consisted of thirty-three eleven-story buildings with a total of 2,700 apartment units on a site that encompassed almost sixty acres (about one-tenth of a square mile). The project represented the zenith of government-sponsored high-rise/low-income housing construction. Yet residents experienced problems almost immediately after Pruitt-Igoe opened in 1954 (Montgomery and Bristol, 1987). Elevators broke down and were not repaired. Children were injured playing in corridors or stairwells that could not be monitored adequately by adults. Crime began to terrorize residents due to the large scale of design that allowed muggers to remain hidden. People complained of isolation from friends and neighbors.

Within five short years after Pruitt-Igoe opened, occupancy rates were already on the decline despite the subsidized rent. By 1970, vacancy rates in the buildings had reached more than 50 percent.

The St. Louis housing authority made the fateful decision that the problems with the project were insurmountable and ordered its complete demolition. By 1976, the entire project was torn down. Pruitt-Igoe was a combination of architecture design following modernist principles that pursued progress in human/spatial relations and, simultaneously, a type of government intervention that made apartments at subsidized rents available to poor people. Architectural critic Charles Jencks sets this date as the time when modernist ideas about the promise of architecture as promoting social progress gave way to the postmodern period with its abandonment of such lofty aspirations (Holston, 1989).

With the failure of Pruitt-Igoe and other public housing projects came the realization that modernist architecture and government intervention in public housing required reexamination. In Chicago, the Cabrini-Green housing projects are now being dismantled and replaced by single-family town houses (see Box 12.1).

Within the metropolitan region, we find separate agencies devoted to planning that employ significant workforces at each level of government, including each city, suburb, and township within the metropolitan area, plus a countywide and regional planning department! Yet our metropolitan environments seem to be characteristically unplanned. This "planning paradox" (see Gottdiener, 1977) exists because in the United States planners have very little direct power to enact their schemes and for the most part are confined instead to advisory roles. The civic culture of the United States

Box 12.1

Redevelopment of Cabrini-Green

In 1929 Harvey Zorbaugh published his study *The Gold Coast and the Slum*, a description of Chicago's wealthy lakefront neighborhoods along Lake Michigan (the Gold Coast) and of the slum area of tenement housing just half a mile inland. In the 1950s, the slum area was cleared and replaced with some two dozen high-rise public housing units called Cabrini-Green. In the early years most of the occupants were white, but by the 1960s the area was almost entirely composed of poor black families. The film *Cooley High* (1966) was shot at the local high school of the same name. By the 1980s the projects, sometimes called the worst in America, had become symptomatic of all that was wrong with public housing in the United States: All of the residents had incomes below the poverty line; most units were single-parent households; and drugs, gangs, and crime were rampant. In 1996 Dantrell Davis, a seven-year-old boy, was shot and killed while walking to the elementary school across the street from the project, still holding his mother's hand.

For years the site remained not simply a black spot in the city's history but also a controversial area with respect to plans for urban redevelopment. Many floors of the buildings were boarded up and some of the buildings were vacant, while the remainder sported large graffiti showing which gangs controlled the buildings. The *Chicago Tribune* sponsored a design competition for the best redevelopment plan for the area. Neighborhood organizers charged that the city wanted to turn the land over to real estate developers for middle- and upper-class housing close to the downtown area, and city planners looked for ways to relocate low-income households that would be displaced by the removal of the buildings. Finally, in 1998 and 1999, eight of the high-rise buildings were demolished in a scene reminiscent of the earlier destruction of the Pruitt-Igoe projects in St. Louis.

In the area adjacent to the project, new townhouses selling for $180,000 were built by a developer, and in 2003 a Starbucks opened in a strip mall across the street from the projects, seeming to confirm the fears of neighborhood activists. But along with the 65 new units in the Mohawk North condominium development are 16 units of public housing. From the outside, the public housing units are indistinguishable from the private development, and the floor plans of each unit are similar "railroad flats" common to both older and newer housing in this area of the city. By dispersing low-income households and creating, in effect, a mixed-income housing development, the city hopes to eliminate the problems of concentration and isolation of poor families described by Massey and Denton in *Urban Apartheid* (1993). In the coming decade, the high-rise public housing developments will disappear, to be replaced by new row houses—perhaps the end of the slum described some seventy-five years earlier in *The Gold Coast and the Slum*.

has always resisted direct intervention in the market by government. Compounding this restriction is the problem of the urban planning profession in our society. Most schemes come from the private sector, but even when they emerge from public bureaucracies, like Pruitt-Igoe or Cabrini-Green, they most often reflect the ideas of architects who believe they can create successful living and working arrangements for people through principles of design and the control of the built environment alone. Recall that Pruitt-Igoe appeared to be first-rate on paper and represented the highest ideals of the modernist school of architecture but turned out to be a total failure in practice. These limitations to urban planning invite a sociological analysis, which is presented in the next section.

THE SOCIOLOGY OF LAND-USE PLANNING

The Advisory Role of Planners

The most basic kind of planning involves zoning for land use. Based on the principles that like activities should be located near one another and that industrial activities and residential areas should be separated, zoning partitions metropolitan space into distinct areas for each activity. Space is partitioned into zones reserved for residential use, commercial activities, and industrial work, among other functions. Planners use detailed maps to draw up land-use guides that constitute the zoning master plan. In most cases, such a plan needs to be adopted by local residents or their elected representatives. Thus, the ability to plan is restricted by the advisory role of planners. In the end, the public and elected officials determine whether a plan will be accepted and also whether it will be accepted in total or with modifications. Changes and modifications are always a possibility with land-use schemes, and both planners and architects may not like the final result.

Planners also work with elected officials and representatives from the business community to develop new uses of land. They may set aside land or help design an industrial park for factories and businesses, an office tower or city skyscraper complex, a mall, or a large residential development. New developments require infrastructure planning as well as the construction of the buildings themselves. Roads have to be put in along with sewer and utility lines and the like. The impact on the surrounding area also requires careful thought and planning. New developments, just like zoning schemes, must be approved by local political authorities. Sometimes citizens object to new growth, and developments can be blocked or changed according to local resident desires. Most of the time, however, local elected representatives approve growth, since that is the priority of city government. Local communities often feel they must compete against one another to develop new industrial parks, shopping malls, and office centers, adding to the pressures for growth across the metropolitan region.

Physical Determinism

Architects who like to plan for social effects, as well as many planners, believe that optimal living and working arrangements for people can be achieved through the use of construction, design, and landscaping technology. This approach assumes that people's behavior can be controlled or channeled into desirable forms through the manipulation of physical design. As Herbert Gans (1968:28–33) has argued, this commits the fallacy of assuming that physical design will determine personal behavior. As social scientists are aware, behavior is determined by a complex relation of various social processes interacting in and with spatial forms rather than through the influence of the physical environment alone. In practice, planners and architects seem to ignore the social basis of behavior and falsely believe that construction design by itself can bring about desired change, such as increasing the frequency of neighborly interaction. Physical determinism, which privileges the abstract space of the planning professional over social space, has been responsible for some spectacular failures of planning, including the Pruitt-Igoe and Cabrini-Green housing projects, where it was thought that new architectural designs would somehow alleviate the social problems brought about by social exclusion. Perhaps the newest and most important example of the fallacy of physical determinism is the ideology of the "New Urbanism."

The New Urbanism

This contemporary movement of architects and planners includes among its members Andrés Duany, Elizabeth Plater-Zyberk, Jaime Correa, Steven Peterson, Barbara Littenberg, and Daniel Solomon. More so than any other single factor, New Urbanists are opposed to the present-day pattern of metropolitan sprawl and see it as both an immense waste of resources and a blow to the well-being of central cities. Calthorpe and Fulton (2001), for example, critique the existing form of urban planning, which designs zoning areas that separate residential from commercial and industrial use. They see such restrictions as old-fashioned and more relevant to a time when industry was messy and polluting. Now our economy is based on information processing, and most of its economic activities are environmentally clean. For this reason, Calthorpe and Fulton, as New Urbanists, advocate planning for cities that has a mix of residential, commercial, and manufacturing or global economic functions. In their view, plans respecting these new realities would, among other things, do away with regional sprawl.

A major criticism of their approach is that they take as given the activities of both planning agencies and local governments. Their argument centers around the belief that metropolitan regions would look better "if only" planning were better. This belief fails to respect the way private interests in pursuit of profit circumvent and even subvert plans. Real estate interests have a habit of taking what in their view is best about urban planning and disregarding the other recommendations in order to make money.

In short, it is not an outdated form of planning, as Calthorpe and Fulton contend, that is the culprit behind sprawl and inefficient land-use schemes but the relentless pursuit of profit through real estate. The latter is often followed by subverting government regulations and by having planning schemes modified or even discarded.

Another aspect of the New Urbanism is the belief that the behavior of people can be altered for the better through more enlightened architectural design. As the enemy of the present-day sprawl pattern of development, New Urbanists seek, through architectural design, to create residential communities with a high degree of both neighboring and street life. According to their charter, "We are committed to re-establishing the relationship between the art of building and the making of community, through citizen-based participatory planning and design" (Fichman and Fowler, 2003:18).

New Urbanists seek to build up cities by first constructing neighborhoods and communities with active citizen participation that are then connected to larger districts and areas within the metropolitan region. At the most local level, architects like Duany and Plater-Zyberk believe that residential communities can be physically designed to promote neighboring, even though many metropolitan residents prefer networking and possess communities without locality. For this reason, their designs feature houses with porches and emphasize pedestrian pathways rather than streets for automobiles. An excellent example of their ideas put into practice is the new residential development Seaside, a community of 300 homes and 200 apartments on 80 acres located one hundred miles west of Tallahassee, Florida. Its human scale is accentuated by residential housing that is consciously based on the forms of a century ago. All houses have front porches, and most are located on pedestrian paths rather than roads. Lots are small and narrow to facilitate social interaction among neighbors. Communities such as Seaside also incorporate many construction features dictated by architects that play an uncertain role in promoting a new sense of community, such as the mandated use of tin roofs or tall, narrow house windows. The elitism of architectural choice may not appeal to everyone.

New Urbanists, like many architects, believe that social goals such as encouraging neighboring and stemming sprawl can be achieved through the physical means of design and construction. This is a fallacy. Residents of communities do not behave in certain ways simply because well-known architects direct them to do so. Neighboring, in particular, may be facilitated by the presence of porches, but it is not the determining factor. Rather, people create neighborhoods by establishing primary relations with neighbors. They have to want to do so. Many do not because their local reference groups are spread out across the metropolitan region and elsewhere, and yet they can keep in constant communication with these significant others through cell phone and Internet technology. This pattern is known as "community without locality," as we have already discussed. Studies of Seaside and Celebration, another New Urbanist development in Florida, confirm that because the housing is quite expensive, the residents are almost exclusively affluent middle-class Americans. These people prefer their far-flung "communities without locality" to relying on neighbors alone. Furthermore, communities cannot be created merely by facilitating pedestrian traffic. Many people are so dependent on their automobiles that they ignore the role of sidewalks in their daily life. While commercial shopping facilities may be located in New Urbanist developments, residents are more likely to use their cars in order to shop where they please throughout the metropolitan region, as exemplified by the failure of the "Uptown District," a project in San Diego, California.

Some of the most influential planned projects today have come not from contemporary architects and theorists of community development but from utopian thinkers who created coherent plans for growth involving theories of design that are still considered important today. The final section of this chapter addresses these ideas.

UTOPIAN SCHEMES:
HOWARD, LE CORBUSIER, AND WRIGHT

Idealistic thinkers in centuries past lamented the evils of civilization and created a genre of literature known as utopian writing. Plato's *Republic* might be the earliest example, but the consummate vision belongs to Thomas More's *Utopia*. These accounts of some fictional paradise provide us with a means of measuring the prospects of human endeavor by showing how we can perfect ourselves and our society even while exploring our all too frail shortcomings as a species. Over the centuries, utopian literature has provided important inspiration to socially concerned individuals, as has the equally fascinating genre of dystopian writing, especially science fiction's dystopian accounts of life in future cities (such as William Gibson's 1984 book, *Neuromancer*).

Utopia, from the Greek word meaning "no place," and dystopia, a more recently coined expression that means an imaginary place of dread, are examples of places that exist elsewhere in time and space. While the former usually signals the modernist theme of progress, the latter represents our fears about the myth of progress. This yearning for the perfection of settlement space and the realization that it may never be attained due to the limitations of our civilization constitute an important strain in Western literature and cinema. The philosopher Henri Lefebvre (1991) calls all such spaces that exist in our minds as imaginary places *heterotopias*. As mental conceptions, heterotopias have the ability to influence our behavior and to define prospective schemes for architects and planners.

In nineteenth-century Europe, when the evils of industrialization and urbanization became a major social concern, individuals exercised the utopian spirit by conceiving of alternative urban environments. Some of these modernist visions were highly influential in the planning and architectural professions, and indeed by the twentieth century, architects no longer confined themselves to the design of individual buildings but composed manifestos and schemes that addressed the living and working arrangements of the entire city space itself. Among the important conceptualizers of new urban environments are Ebenezer Howard, Le Corbusier, and Frank Lloyd Wright. The modernist vision of each was expressed, respectively, as the Garden City, the Radiant City, and Broadacre City.

The Garden City

Ebenezer Howard, who lived during the turn of the last century, was a social reformer in England. Like others of his time, including Friedrich Engels, he was appalled at the social costs of British industrialization. Some thinkers, such as Robert Owen, responded by founding a utopian movement that advocated the construction of communities (such as New Harmony, Indiana) that would counteract the evils of the industrial city but required a fundamental break with acceptable ways of family or social life. Howard's response was to propose an alternative way of living that everyone could follow, even those uninterested in the utopian movement's social change.

To Howard, the city represented the future of economic growth, but it was, to express it directly, a lousy place to live. In contrast, the rural areas remained in organic harmony with their surroundings, but they were afflicted with limited economic opportunity. Howard's vision combined the two. He proposed that all new industrial growth be channeled to new locations in outlying areas that would combine industrial employment with country living on a moderate, human scale. These "garden cities" would represent the very best of city and country living.

The concept of the garden city proved to be very powerful (see our discussion above of Espoo and Tapiola, Finland). Capitalist industrialization in the nineteenth century knew no bounds. The older cities were crowded and polluted, and large cities gobbled up their adjacent countrysides in a relentless process of accretion. Because planners understood that growth was inevitable, they were attracted to Howard's idea of breaking urban expansion off and aspiring to locate new industry and housing in moderate-size communities.

Howard's ideas influenced the "new town" movement in England, which was responsible for building hundreds of such places, as well as the measured establishment of medium-size cities in Russia, although the latter case does not embody the ideal of the "garden," or suburbanized urban environment. In the United States, a group of architects, notably Clarence Stein, popularized Howard's approach. Working with local authorities and developers, they constructed several places across the country, including Garden City, New York, outside of Manhattan, and Baldwin Hills, California, located in Los Angeles. Ebenezer Howard lived to see the opening of the New York community in 1928. In practice, most of the American garden cities lack their own industry and hence are little more than middle-class suburban housing developments with some interesting features, such as shared public spaces. These ideas, all derivative of Ebenezer Howard's vision, are still put in practice by developers of large suburban residential projects such as planned unit developments, or PUDs.

The Radiant City

Le Corbusier was the professional name of the Swiss-born French architect Charles-Edouard Jeanneret (1887–1965). Along with several German architects, such as Walter Gropius and Ludwig Mies van der Rohe, Le Corbusier is considered the founder of the international style of design and one of the leaders of the modernist movement in architecture. The type of building associated with this movement is familiar to anyone who has seen the skyline of a large city, because the design concepts took over the world of architecture following World War II. International-style buildings are clean, straightforward, rectangular shapes with flat roofs. They are framed in steel and feature large glass windows that are sealed shut. Not until the postmodern architectural revolt of the 1980s were downtown office buildings liberated from the dictates of this concept.

Le Corbusier was influential because he propagated certain ideas about city living instead of confining his practice to building design. He believed in the triumph of technology over social conditions of industrialization. Buildings themselves were to be "machines for living," that is, the most efficient designs for the sustenance of everyday activities. The urban environment would itself have to be changed to conform to the dictates of more enlightened architectural design. Because Le Corbusier lamented the terrible social costs of industrialization, he proclaimed the modernist rallying cry, "Architecture or Revolution," sincerely believing that capitalist countries had little choice but to follow his ideas or confront the revolt of the urban masses.

Le Corbusier's ideas and those of his contemporaries constituted the ideology of modernism, which legitimated the notion of progress and the improvement of human conditions year after year through the intervention of technology. Modernist ideology asserted that the lot of individuals could be improved by the acquisition and application of knowledge—scientific, technological, architectural, social, and psychological. Part of modernist culture was the celebration of architecture and "modern" ideas about city planning.

Le Corbusier's plan for an entire metropolis, the "radiant city," reordered social space across a large, industrial aggregation. Instead of the relatively low density of housing and chaotic land use that was characteristic of the cities at that time, Le Corbusier proposed that buildings should be high-rises. By condensing the living space using building height, open spaces would be liberated, and Le Corbusier envisioned these spaces as parks that would surround residential clusters, thereby transforming the congested, sprawling industrial city into an open, airy, and efficient place of mobility and light.

A second important feature of the new design followed from Le Corbusier's and the modernist belief in the virtues of technology. Le Corbusier believed that the widespread use of public transportation and auto modes of transport would vastly improve the efficiency of urban scale. He proclaimed the "death of the street," that is, the pedestrian thoroughfare characteristic of all cities in the past. He envisioned instead rapid movement facilitated by autos, trains, highways, and feeder roads of people and commodities between the various nodes of urban space, residences, factories, shops, and government buildings.

The lesson of Pruitt-Igoe and Cabrini-Green (see discussion above) illustrates the deeply ingrained physicalist fallacy of Le Corbusier. Construction design, which disregards social process, cannot alone change everyday life. Unfortunately, the modernist ideas of the international style, and especially the concepts of Le Corbusier, were highly influential in urban planning through the 1960s. Along with Pruitt-Igoe, another major tragedy of planning in this vein is exemplified by the case of Brasilia, the capital city of Brazil, which was constructed following Le Corbusier's idea of the radiant city. Designed by the architects Lucio Costa and Oscar Niemeyer in 1960 and located in the interior 600 miles from the Rio de Janeiro coast, Brasilia looks like a giant bird from an aerial view. But on the ground, its limitations have become legendary. The "death of the street" produced an austere, alienating environment in which urban life is shrouded in anonymity. Neighboring and community interaction have all but disappeared because of the inability to overcome the automobile-based lifestyle and the imposing superhuman social scale, which has led to feelings of isolation and anonymity among residents (Holston, 1989).

The city was built to be the country's new capital, and so government administrators and their support staffs find employment there. However, Brasilia has failed to attract the diverse kinds of industry and everyday life that would convert it to a major city. Brasilia, among other austere creations of modernist city planning, reminds us of the perils of physical determinism and the need for architects to work in conjunction with social science to bring about an improvement of urban conditions.

Broadacre City

Frank Lloyd Wright (1869–1959) was the premier American architect for most of the past century. His ideas, unlike Le Corbusier's, are still appreciated today, even if some of his designs have become outdated. Wright was no modernist. In fact, he was much influenced by the crafts movement in the United States and by Asian architecture, particularly the Japanese use of interior space. Wright believed that structures should be organic extensions of natural environments. Houses, for example, should emerge from the crown of the hill rather than being built at the top, since the latter should be reserved for nature. They should embody a fluid connection with the world outside, and their construction should celebrate natural materials and settings, as exemplified by the Kaufmann home, Falling Water House (built in 1936), outside Pittsburgh, Pennsylvania. This summer home is made of concrete that is stacked like pancakes on three levels (called cantilevering) so that it sits on a rock above a forest stream. The water flows under the lower level and out over a falls. Sitting in the living room, one can watch the water flow and hear the stream as it runs over the rock below.

Frank Lloyd Wright was not enamored with the American city that he saw developing after World War II and wrote that with each new skyscraper he saw only the death of the city. Wright's vision of the new city possessed some similarities with that of Ebenezer Howard, especially the desire to merge the city and the country, except Wright thought in modular terms. Instead of a single, human-scale community, Wright envisioned an immense metropolis whose internal structure reduces space to a human scale through modular design. Each family would be assigned a single-family home on an acre of land! The space would enable families to grow their own food and modify their surroundings according to their own personal tastes. Houses would be arrayed on an expansive grid. Wright also liked the possibilities of the auto, and his Broadacre City assumed that the car would be the basic means of transportation. Each place would be accessible by interconnected roads and highways feeding into and out of grids. Commercial shopping would take place in regularly spaced shopping centers, and industry would be isolated in specifically designed factory areas that were zoned exclusively for business.

Wright's scheme seems almost like the massive suburban environments of today—and indeed Wright saw little need for the city. He was one of the earliest architects to envision the concept of the shopping center, and his factory-zoned area is recognizable as the industrial park of the present, a common feature of metropolitan environments. The key element of Wright's vision, however, seems elusive, namely, the one-acre allotment of land that resolved the city/country dilemma at the smallest scale of each individual family. While suburban residences often have ample backyards, these are reserved for leisure activities, including, perhaps, a swimming pool. But Wright's vision of every family providing for its sustenance through backyard farming seems far removed from the realities of metropolitan life.

Our review of architectural visionaries provides us with some alternative ways to think about massive metropolitan environments and reminds us that urbanized landscapes do not necessarily have to assume the form they now possess. The present-day approach to metropolitan development seems oblivious to other ways of building except unending sprawl. But alternatives are possible; only the continuing belief in physical determinism, which wrongly suggests that architecture and urban planning can alter social processes, needs to be abandoned. Developers combining proper design with environmentally aware social science that draws on the legacy of utopian ideas have had some successes, such as the towns of Columbia, Maryland, and Garden City, New York.

PLANNING CRITICS: JACOBS AND KRIER

Ideas about planning have benefited from the work of critics who have taken both architects and the planning profession to task for neglecting the human values embodied within social space (Mayo, 1988). Two of the most influential critics are Jane Jacobs and Leon Krier.

Jane Jacobs

Jane Jacobs (1961) is concerned that we preserve the city as a viable place to live. She believes that the best cities have a vital and active street life. Her critique of urban planning claims that too many projects have ignored the role of human interaction as providing the lifeblood of city culture when most city inhabitants live in apartments with restricted space. For Jacobs, active urban life can never be planned because people invent uses for space. They accommodate the pursuit of their needs to the streets, parks, and playgrounds that they find around them. City planning that discourages this social interaction through the limiting of public or social space results in the destruction of the city itself.

For example, adolescents who live in the city spend a good deal of time out on the streets. Over the years, an incredible variety of street games has arisen using this space, and many of these have been handed down through the generations, such as "Ring-a-Levio," "Johnny on the Pony," hopscotch, rope-jumping games, and stickball. Skateboarders and others make use of urban spaces in ways never envisioned by architects and planners (Bordain, 1999). Projects planned only in terms of efficient automobile traffic (such as Le Corbusier's radiant city or Brasilia) arrange for wide thoroughfares that are heavily traveled. But such efficiency in the name of transportation destroys the ability of children to use the streets for play. Can you imagine active street games in the immense auto corridors of Los Angeles or on the well-traveled two-way streets in your community? In contrast, Jacobs celebrates the streets and advocates blocking them off on a periodic and temporary basis to allow for neighborhood interaction. This is precisely what many cities do when they sponsor neighborhood festivals during the summer months.

According to Jacobs, human-scale public spaces in the city, such as sidewalks, parks, and playgrounds, provide people with a number of resources: (1) They constitute learning environments for children; (2) they allow for parents' surveillance of the neighborhood and their children's activities; and (3) they facilitate intimate, primary relations among neighbors, thereby providing a strong sense of community.

Jacobs's ideas have had a strong impact on the way urbanists and planners think about city life. Local governments encourage park use, street festivals, temporary blocking of community roads, and toleration of sidewalk vendors. But not all of Jacobs's ideas have been accepted. Some of her followers advocated the elimination of elevators in apartment buildings to facilitate neighborly interaction, but the results were disastrous for the residents of these buildings. Planners who emphasize revitalizing streets and city parks must take the high crime rate into account; in many cities, downtown revitalization efforts using Jacobs's ideas have failed due to the fear of urban crime on the part of suburban residents. Jacobs's ideas about community may also be passé. Many city residents socialize with networks of friends and relatives who do not live nearby, as we saw in Chapter 8. Teenagers may prefer to travel to their own friendship networks rather than socialize on the street. On the whole, however, Jane Jacobs's ideas have influenced urbanists because she captured the heart and soul of urban culture. Her importance lies in convincing us that urban culture depends on the relationship between personal interaction and public space. The fact that this culture is in danger of dying today is certainly not the fault of her conception. As we direct our attention to metropolitan regions, it is important to ask whether her ideas are equally relevant for suburban settlement spaces.

Leon Krier

Although Leon Krier is a contemporary architect practicing in Germany, his ideas have been highly influential in the United States in recent years. Like Jacobs, his main concern is revitalizing urban culture. He views this as principally a problem of scale: The contemporary city has grown too large to shelter a livable environment, and it is necessary to return urban building to a human scale. Krier's model of the city is the preindustrial town, and he advocates a return to the type of building characteristic of societies hundreds of years ago. In this sense, Krier is a critic of modernist ideology and one of the inspirations for postmodern architecture.

According to Krier, settlement space should be divided into districts with no more than 15,000 people in each subdivision. Ample use is made of squares, monuments, and public spaces, which should have the proportions of the classical preindustrial towns. These changes, inspired by "retro" thinking, would return urban space to a human scale. Krier also has his critics (see Dutton, 1989). More so than Jacobs, he commits the fallacy of physical determinism. He ignores social process and the larger societal forces that make up the modern city, and the kind of transition in scale that he envisions would be difficult for all but the most affluent residents. Krier's proposal, like those of most architects, also commits the elitist/populist fallacy. He never asks what people want; he only dictates design prescriptions through abstract space.

Despite these drawbacks, Leon Krier's work has had an enormous influence on architects designing new communities in the United States who seek to overcome modernist ideology, especially the New Urbanist movement (see above). Among his most significant disciples is the team of Andrés Duany and Elizabeth Plater-Zyberk. Krier's ideas have been influential because there is a growing sense that typical suburban communities have isolated people unnecessarily. At the same time, these ideas seem destined to be realized by the most affluent but remain unavailable to the average family interested in a suburban home.

OTHER TRENDS IN PLANNING TODAY

In contrast to the New Urbanism and its projects, which dictate a design of human scale, other recent developments in both urban and suburban settlement spaces have embraced projects that are notably large in scale. Projects such as the building of the garden city Columbia, Maryland, and the construction of Battery Park City at the tip of Manhattan are large in scope and encompass many acres. Large tracts of land have been converted from agricultural use in the suburbs or cleared of slums in the city core. These mega-projects usually incorporate mixed-use developments of housing and commercial shops. Due to the influence of planning critics, however, many of these designs incorporate human scaling despite their large size.

Among the most successful developers of large but human-scale projects is James Rouse, whose company built the Baltimore Inner Harbor, Faneuil Hall in Boston, the South Street Seaport in Manhattan, and the Santa Monica Mall. The Baltimore, Boston, and New York projects in particular were constructed on deteriorating, unused land that was revitalized. Rouse's success involved a blending of open spaces, reasonably priced and varied eating places, and upscale shops. Such redevelopment transformed spaces of bleak prospect into vital urban centers with an active public life. The Baltimore Harbor project, for example, consists of a large horseshoe of open space that surrounds the shore of the harbor inlet. Concrete steps lead to benches and play areas. One section is devoted to an array of alternative and moderately priced eateries. Two attractions, the Baltimore Aquarium and the Revolutionary War battleship *Constellation*, also draw visitors.

Another of Rouse's successful developments is Columbia, Maryland, a new town that mixes apartment and single-family home construction with accessible and usable open space and shopping areas. The entire project has been planned to conform to human scale and includes pathways totally dedicated to pedestrian use that link the various sections of the town. As one observer notes:

> In Columbia the size of residential areas was determined primarily by the number
> of households needed to support an elementary school. The Rouse Company, as
> developer, insisted that within a block of the school there be a swimming pool, a
> community building, and a convenience store, and that people be able to walk or
> bike to these facilities without crossing any major streets. Three to five neighbor-
> hoods made up a village, which offered more facilities, including a supermarket, a
> bank branch, and other businesses, also accessible by the community's forty-
> seven miles of walking and biking paths, as well as by car. (Langdon, 1988:52)

The success of the Rouse Company has influenced the way other mega-projects have been designed. In New York City, for example, a ninety-two-acre section of the dilapidated downtown with few residential units was demolished to build Battery Park City. The project consists of high-rise apartments, offices, and shopping facilities. Located at the southern tip of Manhattan, the development makes ample use of its view of the Hudson River. Residential blocks are integrated with an esplanade that includes spaces to sit and socialize with neighbors. Many other projects across the country, such as RiverPlace along the Willamette River in Portland, Oregon, have adopted the successful approach of human-scale residential blocks, mixed commercial and housing land use, and pedestrian amenities to provide a more attractive environment for residents.

SUMMARY OF PLANNING ISSUES

People in the United States regard planning with suspicion. They prefer to defend individual property rights and the home rule prerogative of local government control over land use. Although every jurisdiction, no matter how small, seems to have its own planning department, professional experts are relegated to an advisory role. Planners must maneuver within this politically constrained milieu by exercising their influence on developers, speculators, homeowners, renters, local community activists, and public officials (Weiss, 1987). It is not an easy task. In the main, the professional planners employed by business and government devote their time to working out the ordinary details of mandated land use and construction requirements. They pursue the unglamorous job of drafting site usage plans for developers, reviewing and updating zoning maps for local governments, and assessing traffic studies. They also collect and review demographic information on the present and future growth patterns of individual towns. But this bureaucratic domain of activity remains removed from the active task of fashioning environments in which other people will live.

As we have seen, the limitations placed on professional planners have not prevented individuals from dreaming their dreams of the perfect city. Visionaries and utopian thinkers have tried their best to lead citizens of modern society toward some Eden that actualizes the promise of industrial progress. Some ideas, such as Howard's garden city, have been influential enough to affect future generations. Colossal failures, such as the superhuman building blocks of Le Corbusier's radiant city (actualized in every highrise public housing project, not to mention the ashes of Pruitt-Igoe), have also been helpful because they have shown what we cannot or should not do. Happily, visionary plans are tried sometimes, and even more happily, most of the time on a small enough scale so that the human cost of failure is not dear. We learn from mistakes and successes as our knowledge of planning human environments accumulates.

One important lesson that has recently been learned concerns the yearning for human-scale places in the face of unending metropolitan sprawl and the experience of immense, impersonal city space. Developments today feature an informed use of space. Macro-environments, such as the Santa Monica enclosed mall, are composed of many mini-environments that nurture sociability. The huge Battery Park City project opens itself out to the surrounding urban fabric and natural setting, providing for social interaction through human-scale public spaces and the extended esplanade on the Hudson River. Finally, as we have seen, new towns developed in their entirety (such as Columbia, Maryland) succeed by devoting space to pedestrians and thereby providing alternatives to automobile transportation to perform everyday tasks such as shopping, leisure activities, and commuting to work and school.

A return to human scale alone, however, even through the best efforts of planners, will not save the declining quality of life in either our central cities or our massive, sprawling suburbs. As discussed in Chapter 9, the high level of crime has taken an immense toll on the free use of urban space, not to mention its cost in lives. We can rightly wonder what will happen to the Hudson River esplanade and its pedestrian traffic if it becomes a haven for muggers. How enjoyable would the miles of pedestrian paths of Columbia, Maryland, be if the community were not isolated from the realities of homelessness and destitution characteristic of inner-city districts? The growing problems of land use, congestion, traffic jams, housing blight, environmental pollution, and suburban sprawl spur the public to search for planned solutions to urban growth. These and other problems may yet encourage local citizens to give up their traditional and narrow concern with protecting their property rights in favor of a more coordinated approach to development. Yet the problems of the metropolitan region have societal roots that are not easily addressed by technical recommendations without massive social change.

These contradictions are clearest when we study the impact of environmental pollutants on communities. As we shall discuss, the burden of costs for society's progress seems to fall on poor and minority neighborhoods. Government at all levels participates in producing this pattern of discrimination. In many communities, air pollution affects and endangers the lives of everyone, rich and poor. Environmental problems are found in all metropolitan regions and require economic, political, and social responses in addition to better-quality spatial design.

As sociologists have noted, professional planners, government officials, and architects would probably remain limited by their own outlook even if they were given more power. They preach the fallacy of physical determinism, which holds a blind faith in the power of construction technology and design to alter social relationships. Rarely do they profess what Frank Lloyd Wright saw as the organic, holistic needs of families and households. They are more comfortable with limited prescriptions that conform to the dictates of their professions' focus: building design and construction for architects, landscaping or land-use schemes for planners, or political expediency for politicians. Much more is needed to control the forces of development in the United States, but little public debate seems to be devoted to the issue of planning or the search for alternatives to our deteriorating environment.

ENVIRONMENTAL ISSUES

On October 1, 1980, the Love Canal section of the small town of Niagara, New York, located near the Canadian border, was declared an environmental disaster by President Carter. He ordered the permanent evacuation of all families from their homes. This action followed after two previous evacuations beginning in 1978 (Gibbs, 1981:5). Between 1920 and 1953, the area, an uncompleted canal, was used as a dump site for toxic chemicals from both the private sector and the federal government, particularly the U.S. Army. Homes had been built on top of landfill after the site was no longer used for dumping. Residents who lived along the canal had been exposed for many years to carcinogens from the toxic wastes that leaked into groundwater and oozed to the surface. In the 1970s, some of the 1,000 families that lived near the canal site began to complain about the high incidence of cancer, birth defects, miscarriages, and central nervous system diseases (Gibbs, 1981:3). Once the full extent of the poisoning became known, evacuations proceeded, but this action came too late to save many people from contracting cancer and other environmentally caused health problems.

On April 26, 1986, a nuclear power plant located in Chernobyl, near the Ukrainian capital city of Kiev, exploded. The blast ignited the graphite moderating core of the reactor and resulted in the unleashing of intense radiation across a wide area of the former Soviet Union and Western Europe. Fallout from the disaster was measured as far away as the United States and showed up in the dairy production of countries such as Norway, but the most severe effects were felt by hundreds of thousands of people living in the small towns in the area (Marples, 1988). Had the winds been blowing northward at the time, the Ukrainian people's historic city of Kiev (population 2.4 million) would have been destroyed along with countless lives. Official figures from the Soviet Union listed thirty-one people killed by the accident, but other estimates are as high as 500 (Marples, 1988:42). It was also estimated that as many as 50,000 people may have been directly exposed to excessive radiation, with nearly 500,000 premature deaths predicted over subsequent decades. The disaster forced the permanent evacuation of persons and homes from a thirty-kilometer zone, but over 100,000 children outside this area were also taken from their families to avoid exposure. Thousands of people were treated for radiation sickness. To this day, the region contains "hot spots" that are a threat to life.

Unfortunately, the above examples are not isolated cases. The United States, for instance, had its own potential nuclear catastrophe when the Three Mile Island reactor near Middletown, Pennsylvania, began emitting radioactive steam on March 28, 1979. That emergency was controlled without immediate loss of life or property. Many countries around the world have toxic pollution sites and unsafe radioactive facilities within their borders that compromise the health of citizens every day.

In this chapter, we will use the sociospatial perspective to study environmental issues that result from, and create problems for, the expansion of urban and suburban settlement space. Because the living and working arrangements in modern societies impact the health and well-being of all residents, questions raised about environmental quality have as much to do with spatial issues as they do with economic development. The environmental question and its relation to sociospatial development raise a variety of issues. One set deals with the nature of constructed space, or "second nature," as Henri Lefebvre (1991) calls it. These issues involve the activity of planning, which seeks to obtain the best living and working arrangements in developing cities. The built environment, any built environment, such as a city or a mall, possesses attributes that may enhance or hinder the functioning of its use. Elements of the environmental fabric such as streets, pedestrian pathways, automobile corridors, and housing complexes can be placed in harmony with one another to facilitate the movement of people and vehicular traffic throughout the constructed space. Planning and architectural design address these kinds of issues. In addition, urban and metropolitan governments have sought to incorporate sound environmental principles into future plans. This type of planning is called "sustainable growth," and it has emerged as a very important perspective today.

A separate set of questions involves the inherent quality of the environment. What are the outcomes and by-products of social activities? What effects do the different types of activities, such as manufacturing, have on population groups within their vicinity? Who pays the environmental costs for development? What is the environmental impact of growth on the health and well-being of citizens? These and other questions frame the discussion of urban and suburban settlement spaces as a built environment. Let us explore this topic first and relate it to metropolitan considerations.

Environmental Quality

All societies seek to improve their quality of life through industrial development. Some countries, such as the United States, already possess a heritage of more than one hundred years of industrialization. Although all human activities produce waste products that may adversely affect others, such as the effluent problem in an ancient city like Beijing, the scale and intensity of the environmental costs of industrialization are unprecedented. Manufacturing results in by-products that are toxic to animal and plant life; energy generation affects the temperature and quality of water and air with consequent effects on living things; and the extraction of natural resources, such as gold, results in environmental damage, such as the releasing of toxic metals into forest streams.

Societies around the globe have always put developmental desires above environmental concerns. In places such as China, Brazil, and sections of Europe, the health-related impacts of industrialization weren't even publicly recognized until quite recently, as we saw in Chapter 11's discussion of Shanghai's pollution problem. For many centuries, all societies have held an unwavering belief in the idea of progress. Technology, science, and industrial growth, it is commonly understood, hold the promise of making our lives better and better. At present this assumption has been called into question by some environmentally conscious individuals. According to Murray Bookchin (1990:20), the certainty that technology and science will improve the human condition is mocked by the proliferation of nuclear weapons, massive hunger in the developing world, and poverty in the first world.

Most Americans appreciate the quality of life made available to them by the accomplishments of industrialization, but environmental activists suggest that this comfort for the relative few, globally speaking, has been acquired at a phenomenal cost to the many around the world. Furthermore, the unprecedented scale of human development today has resulted in global effects such as the widening hole in the ozone layer, global warming, acid rain, the eradication of plant and animal species, and the increasing threats to fresh drinking water. In response, environmentalists have called for a new ordering of global priorities that would seek out environmentally enhancing methods of industrial production and safe technologies (Naess, 1989; Gore, 1992). This means redefining the relationship between humans and settlement space on this planet. As the level of awareness about these environmental issues increases across the globe, perhaps the issues of growth and development will be reexamined. New, environmentally sound methods of production and safe technologies such as rechargeable electric cars may usher in a transformed relation between people and the Earth that preserves the well-being of both. Environmental concerns translate into new jobs and industries so that ecologically conscious development can be compatible with saving the planet (Kazis and Grossman, 1982).

The above concerns have been part of the environmental movement in the United States for some time. In the classical phase of activism, which began in the 1800s, Americans sought to protect large areas of the country from development and endangered species from destruction. Naturalists such as John Muir (1838–1914), who won protection for places like Yosemite and led the fight to establish the national parks system, and organizations such as the Audubon Society, which has been at the forefront of the fight to save native birds and other wildlife, are examples of the classical phase of environmentalism (Bullard, 1990). In the twentieth century, the mature phase of activism attacked the unbridled nature of industrialization in the United States. Concerned citizens fought for regulatory agencies, the passage of environmental statutes, and the establishment of industrial standards for control of pollutants. Over the years, regulations and legally binding statutes have been passed by both the federal and state levels of government. In 1970 the mature phase efforts culminated in the establishment of a separate federal agency under the executive branch, the Environmental Protection Agency (EPA), which serves as the public's advocate and coordinates research on environmental issues. In the 1970s, the EPA was granted powers to regulate mileage standards for automobiles, thereby leading to the production of fuel-efficient engines. Although there is still much work to be done and an imminent need for residents of the United States to rethink their relationship with the settlement space of advanced industrial society, the classical and mature phases of environmental activism have accomplished a great deal. This is especially the case when we consider the sensitivity many Americans have acquired in the past several decades to the need for fuel economy, recycling of waste products, and the search for safe technologies.

A third type of activism is grassroots or community efforts. Advocates of grassroots mobilization point out that while social concern about environmental quality is quite high in the United States, there is little appreciation for the social equity and social justice aspects of environmental impacts (Gale, 1983). These impacts are distributed inequitably across settlement space, creating a particular sociospatial dimension to the differential impact of costs. As one observer puts it, "An abundance of documentation shows blacks, lower-income groups, and working-class persons are subjected to a disproportionately large amount of pollution and other environmental stressors in their neighborhoods as well as in their workplaces" (Bullard, 1990:1).

The classical and mature phases of environmental activism have drawn in thousands of people, but the overwhelming majority of them and the concerns they express are those of the middle class. The environmental costs paid by poor and minority people have largely been ignored. This sociospatial pattern of environmental costs is most revealing. Love Canal in New York State was situated within a white, working-class community, and it was these people who paid the price of toxic pollution. In Alabama, the town of Triana was judged to be the unhealthiest in America (Reynolds, 1980:38). The residents of Triana are black, and they have been poisoned by the pesticide DDT and the chemical PCB from a creek whose quality is the responsibility of the federal government. Time and again research shows that society continues to produce toxic pollution and that poor and minority communities are its victims (Bullard, 1990; Berry, 1977; Blum, 1978).

Many of the hazards that differentially affect minorities and the poor are the consequence of industrial location patterns. Factories, chemical plants, mills, and the like are located in areas isolated from middle-class residential space. Because housing costs are lower in settlement spaces constructed around manufacturing areas, this is where poor people are more likely to live. Chemical emissions, spillovers of toxic by-products, unpleasant smells, and loud noises are just some of the hazards that affect these relatively powerless communities. These areas are often selected for unwanted land uses (or LULUs) such as landfills, toxic waste dumps, and effluent treatment plants. Hence, even though regulations have increased for safeguarding environmental quality, they have also led to injustices in the disposal of environmental threats, especially because of the inequitable siting of toxic dumps and landfills. For example: Four landfills in minority zip code areas represented 63 percent of the South's total hazardous-waste disposal capacity. Moreover, the landfills located in the mostly black zip code areas of Emelle (Alabama), Alsen (Louisiana), and Pinewood (South Carolina) in 1987 accounted for 58.6 percent of the region's hazardous-waste landfill capacity (Bullard, 1990:40).

The differential locational impacts of environmental costs and the issues of social equity that they raise have yet to be addressed. Most communities seek to avoid becoming hosts to activities that represent social problems, such as outpatient mental clinics, halfway houses for criminals, and drug treatment centers. They advocate not in my backyard, or NIMBY, politics, which makes location a struggle that the least powerful community loses. The same is true for LULUs such as hazardous waste dumps or landfills. But allowing the stronger to make the weaker pay for all of society's costs violates principles of social justice.

In recent years, grassroots activists have organized poor and minority communities to fight for their rights. They are forcing the larger society to rethink environmental issues. If toxic dumps are unfair to any community, why not design production operations to minimize environmental damage? If landfills are becoming a problem, can't recycling and other, even more imaginative schemes be considered for the ever-increasing volume of garbage we all produce? How can we reorder our priorities to avoid having people pay unfairly for pollution? These and other questions frame the agenda for grassroots organizing and environmental activism in the years to come. This agenda has also become central to the "environmental sustainability" movement.

Sustainable Growth

The concept of "sustainable growth" derives from the environmental movement but it has also had an immense impact on urban planning. For this reason it ties together the two concerns of this chapter.

Local governments deploying this concept frame future growth in terms that also relate to environmental goals. They pursue planning for development that, at the same time, asks the following question: How can we sustain and improve the environmental quality of life defined as a series of concrete planning targets? Another term for this approach is the "livable cities" movement. As noted above in the discussion of planning, while these concepts are all sound, they require strong government controls in order to be put into effect. Now, in the twenty-first century, with environmental concerns increasing and becoming more commonly placed on the public's political agenda, there is some hope that if people do not wish to provide planners with power to control sprawl and suburban development, they may opt to do so for ecological reasons to prevent further decline in the quality of life due to our global environmental issues.

Sustainable development uses concepts from the ecological movement to guide this form of "smart growth." Environmentalists define the impact of any activity as its "ecological footprint." Taken together, the way in which a metro region uses resources and the effects of its activities on the environment define its unique "footprint." The stated goal of sustainable growth is to reduce that footprint to as small an impact as possible. The use of recycling, mass transit, electric or hybrid vehicles, use of solar energy and other renewable energy resources, and citizen activities aimed at cleaning up vacant lots, streets, and highways are but a few of the tools applied in the pursuit of sustainable growth. Sustainable growth has meant a renewed role for local government; in this case, it becomes the manager of environmentally aware development. Activist positions by administrators instigate change and mandate that environmental concerns be addressed. This approach also means that local communities and neighborhoods must be transformed into activist organizations that pursue improvements in environmental quality. In fact, the local community component of sustainable growth is quite critical to its success. One problem emerging in recent years with this movement is that more cities and metropolitan areas claim to be pursuing sustainability than are actually doing so. Consequently, there is a danger that the term may just be used as an election slogan rather than a concrete goal of local administrations. A study by Portney (2003) found that of twenty-five cities in the United States that proclaim they are pursuing sustainability, only eight had actually taken the goal seriously. Furthermore, there is a more serious problem when no apparent linkage is made between ecological measures and planning for smart development. Thus, people might be very enthusiastic about recycling, and most places in America have public sanitation services that support this activity, but there is absolutely no connection made between this activity and reducing the waste of natural resources immediately adjacent to the built environment by greedy developers and indifferent public authorities who both ignore the need for better regional planning to avoid sprawl.

Portney also uncovered a third problem with the putative push to "sustainability." Cities and metropolitan regions vary considerably with regard to what they understand to be sustainable environmental issues. Some places emphasized environmental quality most directly. Others included adequate health care, proper schools, and an acceptable standard of living as goals. According to Portney's study, then, there is no guarantee that pursuit of sustainability necessarily means pursuit of environmental quality. When the term is found as part of a governing agenda, there is also no guarantee that measures deployed will be pursued actively until they are successful. Finally, as we have seen, there is also no direct linkage in virtually all places with environmental programs to stronger land-use planning controls aimed at managing sprawl. Despite these drawbacks, the sustainable development movement is becoming increasingly popular in the United States as public awareness grows regarding serious environmental problems and the costs of growth. As mentioned above, while little sympathy is given to advocates wanting to abandon the so-called American way of life that emphasizes auto use and single-family homes as the norm, increasing environmental issues resulting from that way of living may push us in the direction of significant changes towards more sustainable patterns.

Increased public involvement in the planning process is needed to refocus attention on those issues that affect our daily lives rather than on the profits to be reaped from development and the increased tax revenues that accompany urban growth. It is up to America's leaders and citizens to become more involved in a protracted dialogue regarding the kind of environments they prefer to live in. One last source of reform remains unexamined so far: the activities surrounding the drafting and execution of public policy and state intervention. We will consider this topic in the next chapter.

KEY CONCEPTS

sprawl
smart growth
planning paradox
physical determinism
New Urbanism
sustainable development

IMPORTANT NAMES

Ebenezer Howard
Le Corbusier
Frank Lloyd Wright
Jane Jacobs
Leon Krier
Andrés Duany

DISCUSSION QUESTIONS

1. Environmental problems must be considered as a sociospatial issue. What are some examples of sociospatial inequalities and environmental problems that you are aware of in your community?

2. The textbook suggests that physical determinism and the elitist-populist dilemma are major shortcomings with urban planning. What do these terms mean? What can be done to overcome these limitations?

3. We have discussed three utopian planners—Howard, Le Corbusier, and Wright. How did these planners differ in their ideas for improving urban life? Which has had the most influence on urban development in the United States?

4. What is meant by New Urbanism? Why are some observers critical of this movement? Do you think that New Urbanism can solve the social problems confronting metropolitan regions discussed in Chapter 9?

5. Are there gated communities in the area where you grew up? Do these communities match the description of those in this chapter? In what ways?

CHAPTER 13

METROPOLITAN SOCIAL POLICY

As we have seen, comprehensive planning at the national, regional, and local level can have positive outcomes, although this fact has not convinced Americans to support increased government control over land use. In China, for example, state planning for economic and urban development has established city clusters in coastal areas, created a transitional economy and managed urban growth in part by building twenty new cities each year. This has not come without costs, as pollution from industry and automobiles is of great concern, and environmental policies must now match the economic growth strategies that have been put in place; interestingly, new construction in Chinese cities has taken a lead in this respect, and the second tallest building in the world, the Shanghai Tower now under construction (see Figure 11.2), will showcase environmentally friendly design.

In the previous chapter, we examined both the potential and the limitations of urban planning in the United States. But the effort to fashion a living environment beneficial to all citizens does not end by exhausting planning options. A separate approach, one that is often initiated in conjunction with planning, involves government intervention guided by public policy. The state has the authority to allocate money from tax revenues for social programs and to authorize deficit spending to address social needs. Government actions not only can direct behavior by prohibition, that is, by passing laws that prohibit certain acts, but also can provide incentives and opportunities to channel resources in specific ways. This push-versus-pull feature of public policy is important to keep in mind when examining the issue of political intervention. Although this chapter examines the role of government in improving metropolitan life, it is worth noting that other public interventions, such as the location of toxic waste dumps in poor communities, can also create problems. Just how much intervention is needed and in what forms remain critical issues for any discussion of government policy.

Before beginning our discussion of metropolitan policy, let us consider the following question: What is the urban policy of the United States? One might expect that in a country that has been urbanized for many decades and with many large cities, there would be some form of urban policy that would guide decision-making at the national as well as local level. And when we consider the social issues confronting our metropolitan communities (Chapter 9), the need for comprehensive policies to address these issues would seem obvious enough. The federal agency most involved with metropolitan policy, the Department of Housing and Urban Development (HUD), has responsibility for housing programs, but not for the many other areas affecting our cities and suburban regions, such as transportation and economic development. While the last four Republican presidential candidates have pledged to eliminate HUD, Barack Obama has said that he will make the director of HUD a cabinet-level position. But even this will not give the United States a comprehensive urban policy as we move into the twenty-first century, unlike the situation in many other countries that have had one for some time. The United States possesses a civic culture that is averse to government intervention in the market. In earlier chapters we identified this perspective as *privatism*, the belief that government should restrict its role to supporting the business community (the private sector) and should seek market solutions to social problems. However, this reliance on the market to solve all questions concerning social policy can lead to problems. In the previous chapter, we saw that the desire to plan the development of metropolitan regions was hamstrung by the inability of planners to obtain sufficient power over land-use decisions to implement effective environmental changes. There are other problems with the market as a mechanism to make decisions involving the allocation of resources. These include the difficulty of maintaining the quality of life when public resources are involved and the problems of uneven development that appear to be inevitable in a capitalist society.

THE TRAGEDY OF THE COMMONS

In 1833 William Forster Lloyd presented two lectures on "the checks to population" at Oxford University. The lectures followed Charles Malthus's earlier warnings about overpopulation and likely would be unknown were it not for an analogy that Lloyd presented in the first of the lectures. He asked his readers to consider a village of farmers, each with his own herd of cows in individual fenced pastures. In addition, there is a village commons that the farmers have access to and may use. But if all of the farmers put their cattle in the village commons to graze, the grass will be eaten and the commons will be destroyed. Lloyd asks, "Why are the cattle on a common so puny and stunted? Why is the common itself so bare-worn, and cropped so differently from the adjoining enclosures?" (1833:30).

Because each farmer seeks to use the public resource of the village commons to private advantage, they all will attempt to graze their cows as often and as long as possible on the common green. If the farmers are interested in improving their situation, they have few alternatives. They could each buy a farm that would be owned privately with sufficient grazing land—an expensive move. Or they could band together and create a community scheduling agreement that would recognize the need of each farmer and the need of the field to regenerate itself. Because the users of this public resource might have disputes, the individuals involved would also have to arrange for arbitration in the event of disagreements or abuse.

Lloyd's analogy of the village commons was included in an essay titled "The Tragedy of the Commons" published in 1968. While Lloyd was addressing the problem of overpopulation, Garrett Hardin used the example of the despoiling of the commons to address the problem of public goods and natural resources (Hardin, 1968). This has been said to be one of the most influential scientific articles of the twentieth century; it has been cited in more than 3,400 other articles (Walker, 2009:283). In any retelling of this story, the tragedy of the commons speaks clearly, as it points to the need for the social institution of public authority and local government, which safeguard the benefits to the many from the abuses of the few.

Settlement spaces in modern society contain many public resources such as air, water, streets, public transportation, and parks and recreational areas. Safeguarding these common environmental resources becomes increasingly difficult as the population and frequency of use rise (see Chapter 12). As a consequence, government must develop active public policies to deal with the many problems arising from large populations living in the same settlement space. Often these policies involve laws or regulations that restrict individual rights but are considered necessary to preserve public resources.

Consider one brief example: In New York City during the 1970s, partly as a consequence of a rising crime rate, apartment dwellers purchased dogs in great numbers. The inevitable outcome? Piles of dog excrement made walking the city streets a hazardous affair. It was estimated that the city was drowning in 500,000 pounds of feces each day! The issue pitted civic groups (Children Before Dogs) against pet owners (Pet Owners Protective Association) while city officials proposed a corps of "Envirmaids"— female inspectors who would police the city "night and day." Finally the state of New York passed State Health Law 1310 (1978) mandating that owners clean up after their dogs in public (Brandow, 2008). The "pooper scooper" regulation made it a crime not to comply. To this day, any tourist can observe dog owners from all social backgrounds scooping up after their animals to keep the streets clean. The rule is an infringement on the individual rights of pet owners, but it is sanctioned by society because it leads to a greater public good: the enjoyment of a common resource, public space. Most environmental policy is of this type, and support for such measures requires a public culture that is committed to protecting environmental resources.

In the United States (and many other countries) there are laws that limit the free market to provide for the public good. Some of the most restrictive are the Southern California anti-air-pollution statutes, which are regulated by an independent state agency and affect everything from automobile exhaust systems to emissions from industrial activity, to the burning of trash and the use of outdoor barbecue grills. The air-quality control board has the authority to limit daily activities when air pollution reaches hazardous levels in the Los Angeles metropolitan region. Over the years, Southern California has lost many businesses because they preferred to relocate rather than pay the extra cost of compliance. But that has not diminished public support for air-quality regulation. Rather, in such an environment, where pollution is an ever-present danger to human health, intervention is the only solution until the causes of air pollution are eliminated by other means. Hence, although we dislike government intervention, we find it useful. Sustaining the quality of life in metropolitan regions is an especially difficult task without the aid of government policy and regulation because the free market is incapable of doing so on its own.

UNEVEN DEVELOPMENT AND POLICY: REDISTRIBUTIVE PROGRAMS

In capitalist society, resources tend to flow to those who are most powerful. There are many reasons for this, and not all of them imply wrongdoing on anyone's part. Under pure market conditions, when individuals compete in business with one another, one's prosperity is supposed to spur the others to copy success. Thus the market serves to discipline business people to adopt the best and most efficient means of pursuing a profit. What holds for business, however, does not necessarily apply to individual people. In recent years we have witnessed massive abuse by corporate officials in the Enron affair, a series of scandals on Wall Street involving some of the top brokerage firms, and scandals in the mutual funds industry that bankrupted pension funds and entire investment funds for some cities. Now, as a consequence of the market going completely awry, we confront immense economic problems and must look to the federal government in Washington for all sorts of private sector bailouts. As of September 2009, the public bailout of private business in the United States amounted to about $2 trillion dollars—a sum so immense that it is quite impossible to comprehend. Pharmaceutical companies in the United States operate within the capitalist market; they charge what the market will bear, even for drugs that are required to treat life-threatening conditions. Those people who have the most money can afford the medicine that is needed to keep them healthy. But what happens to people who are too poor to pay for their medication? Why do some people have adequate medical insurance while others do not? Should not all Americans, as a right of citizenship, have equal access to adequate health care? Or should quality of care and access to medicine depend solely on the ability to pay? In the struggle to pass health care legislation, the Obama administration took strong measures to control the health insurance and pharmaceutical companies; the same companies spent millions of dollars on advertisements and campaign contributions to prevent any meaningful reform, and many persons remain strongly opposed to government intervention in the health-care system.

Finally, the housing industry in our society is also part of the market system. Those individuals who can afford a private home can get one. The more you can afford to spend, the better your home will be. But what about those individuals who cannot afford the price? What happens to the poor who cannot even afford rent? In

Box 13.1

Human Rights in the City

The Global Charter Agenda for Human Rights in the City is a declaration (a charter) with an action plan (an agenda). When the local governments adopt the charter, they will commit themselves to develop inclusive public politics in order to protect, respect and implement human rights on their territories, on a local level. The most recent draft of the charter includes the following preamble and provisions:

Whereas all human beings are endowed with the rights and freedoms recognized in the Universal Declaration of Human Rights and the international instruments that build upon it, in particular, the International Covenants on Economic, Social and Cultural Rights, and on Civil and Political Rights and other basic human rights treaties,

Whereas the city is a basic political community in which all its inhabitants participate in a common project of freedom, equality in diversity, and development,

Whereas citizenship, rights and responsibilities are firstly expressed at the level of the city:

All city inhabitants have the right to a city chartered as a local political community that ensures adequate living conditions for all persons, and provides good co-existence among all its inhabitants, and between them and the local authority.

All city inhabitants have the right to the safety of their person and property against any type of violence, including that potentially committed by law enforcement agencies.

All of the city's children, whatever their gender, have the right to living conditions that enable their physical, mental and ethical development and to enjoy all the rights recognized by the 1989 International Convention on the Rights of the Child.

The city ensures all its inhabitants under the age of 18 decent living conditions, in particular, the opportunity to receive normal schooling.

All city inhabitants have the right to a socially and economically inclusive city and, to this end, to access basic social services in acceptable technical and financial conditions.

The city creates, or promotes the creation of, quality and non-discriminatory public services that guarantee the following minimum items to all its inhabitants: training, health, housing, energy, water, and sufficient food.

The city also guarantees all its inhabitants access to sufficient healthy and nutritional food, and that no person is deprived of food for lack of economic means.

The charter-agenda shall become effective in each city after it goes through a consultation process that allows the inhabitants of the city to discuss it and adapt it to local conditions and to the national legal framework, and upon its acceptance by a qualified majority of the city assembly.

SOURCE: *Global Charter-Agenda for Human Rights in the City* (October 2008).

the European Union, the right to medical care and adequate housing is considered a human right, and many cities include these rights in their city charter. Should we in the United States stand apart from other developed societies by sanctioning poverty, homelessness, or the ruination of elderly persons who must pay for health and housing expenses they cannot afford?

Over the years, all capitalist societies have had to face the social costs of uneven development that creates social inequalities within metropolitan regions and between population groups. In the United States, government has enacted legislation at all levels supporting social programs that address social ills. Social welfare programs are designed to pool resources so that all persons have access to them (as is the case with Medicare programs for the elderly) or to redistribute them (in the case of rent vouchers for low-income households). Using a means test to determine who qualifies for specific programs, government officials decide what is needed and who should be eligible to receive assistance. Because these programs are supported by public tax revenues or by special government borrowing, they redistribute wealth from those who are better off to the poor. As we will discuss shortly, such schemes are not without their abuses or critics.

In its most basic form, then, the issue of uneven development and public policy involves a question of money because sustaining the quality of life has both private as well as social costs. Government programs may address problems of hunger and homelessness, which result from low wages among the working poor, but only income redistribution can directly address the problem of poverty. Hence many social programs are destined to fail because they cannot or do not consider the fundamental cause of the problems they seek to address, such as low wages and lack of employment for working families.

Public policy is created by government representatives in conjunction with research staffs and various academic aides. Some policies find the government directly intervening in the production of new resources such as the building of dams, highways, housing, and nuclear energy facilities. These directly aid private-sector business interests as well as the general welfare. In other cases, incentives are created to channel individual behavior in certain directions, such as the tax subsidy provided to people who purchase single-family homes. The enactment of programs often requires new staff and administrators. Government at all levels is a major employer in the United States, accounting for more than 25 percent of the entire workforce. Social programs run by government also support immense bureaucracies, such as the welfare departments in each state. Hence, not only the less affluent but also state workers benefit from public intervention.

There are many ways that government policy redistributes wealth and channels resources toward the public good. Medicaid and Medicare are meant to protect the quality of life among those individuals who are less affluent or whose incomes are restricted because they are single parents or elderly. State boards of education try to equalize school resources among different public districts, regardless of neighborhood family incomes. Public health crises such as the AIDS epidemic are also addressed by government policy. Finally, housing programs exist in a variety of forms; there are even public programs to deal with homelessness.

Government policies also give assistance to and subsidize the private sector. Public programs aimed at helping individuals in need may be co-opted by private-sector involvement toward the pursuit of profit by business. With the introduction of school voucher programs in many states, many new organizations have developed school agendas and sought funding, diverting funding away from the public schools. The largest abuse of federal programs is often by service providers—when, for example, doctors bill Medicare for fictitious office appointments. This co-optation of government intervention is a serious limitation of public policy in the United States, and it alone may be sufficient to cause programs to fail, as the experience with low-income housing programs run by HUD shows.

Most of the examples discussed so far concern the general problems of inequity in our society rather than issues specifically relevant to metropolitan areas, although issues of inequity certainly have major impacts on the quality of life in urban spaces. Let us look more closely at some of the programs aimed at the needs of both cities and suburbs, and the various political, economic, and social ramifications of government policy in metropolitan areas. In the previous chapter, we discussed how the desire for planning is associated with the modernist belief that increased rationality of land use and architectural design can improve our lives and lead to progress for all. Some countries, such as the welfare capitalist societies of Scandinavia, hold a modernist belief in government policy as also aiding progress through rational state intervention. The United States is characterized by a different public ideology called privatism, which requires government to aid business interests through the market. While our approach has had success in some areas, it also leaves public programs vulnerable to co-optation by powerful interests. As we will see next, the pursuit of social justice often fails even when government intervenes with the best intentions.

URBAN AND METROPOLITAN POLICY

There is no escaping the fact that public policy is shaped by fundamental philosophical positions and ideologically held beliefs regarding government intervention. As we have seen, the dominant belief in the United States is that government should always play a limited role in the economy and that market solutions are usually best; however, it is not inappropriate for the government to subsidize private business. This attitude contrasts with those of industrialized countries in Western Europe, for example, which have more active public policy and more publicly supported benefits such as national health-care schemes and family subsidies (although, as we discussed in Chapter 10, some of these countries have begun to limit social welfare programs and restrict which groups are allowed to participate).

The United States, therefore, is ambivalent about government intervention. Different political positions support various points of view in regard to state programs. On the one hand, many liberals lament the takeover of public programs by powerful business interests, faith groups, and voluntary organizations that may replace paid labor. On the other hand, many conservatives oppose the use of government agencies to do work that could be done in the private sector, pointing to the supposed inefficient and deleterious effects of government control. Our discussion of the failure of federal policy to build upon the garden city movement in the 1930s, due to the opposition of the powerful real estate lobby, demonstrates the overwhelming influence of privatism on American public policy.

In addition to the philosophy of privatism, there is a second obstacle to government intervention to improve urban life. Under the federalist arrangements between the national government and the states, the condition of cities is the responsibility of the states, despite the fact that many urban problems, such as poverty and housing affect entire urban regions and are national in scope. Over the years, the respective roles of the federal government and the state government in dealing with these and other urban issues have become a matter of political debate (see the concluding section of this chapter).

The urban renewal program of the 1950s–1970s provides an illustrative case of the evolving relationship between business and government as well as the limitations of policy. Urban renewal grew out of the Roosevelt administration's commitment to rescue the housing and banking industry from the Great Depression, a serious economic crisis indeed. The Housing Act of 1934, for example, established the Federal Housing Authority, which guaranteed home loans. The 1937 Housing Act mandated that the government provide funds for the support of low-income house construction and slum clearance. These powers were amplified in the Housing Act of 1949 under Title I assistance and in subsequent acts passed in 1954, 1961, 1968, and 1970. The Department of Housing and Urban Development grew into a massive bureaucracy that oversaw the many programs associated with urban renewal. Intervention in the housing market has always been viewed as an aid to the real estate industry, one of the three largest industries in the U.S. economy, rather than a showcase of modernist ideas mixing planning with policy, as was the case in the Scandinavian countries during the same period. Providing homes for people and caring for their community needs was only a secondary goal of the many U.S. programs in this area. As a result of this contradiction between public goals and the private market, metropolitan housing policy has had only mixed results. It proved to be a great boon to business but was less effective in attaining its social goals, so that in the first decade of the twenty-first century, the United States had higher levels of poverty, lower rates of home ownership, and more extensive urban blight than the European countries that we studied in Chapter 10.

During the period from 1950 to the present, government intervention aimed at helping cities has gone through three separate phases, each of which reflected the dominant role of business in defining the interventionist agenda. In the earlier period, federal funding targeted slum removal and construction of affordable housing. In the middle period, these social goals were dropped, and the focus turned to the support of economic development for local business. Finally, government funds were used to subsidize economic development for global competition. In all three phases, local government operated less as a vehicle for social justice for all citizens than as an aid to businesses experiencing declining profits in the new global marketplace. And it was during this period that the Clinton and George W. Bush administrations relaxed regulations on the mortgage and security markets, crucial factors that led to the housing crisis and collapse of world markets beginning in 2009.

Support for Slum Removal

In the immediate post–World War II period, urban renewal was aimed at revitalizing the downtown areas of cities and clearing away slums or blighted dwellings. Programs were supposed to replace cleared land with affordable housing and income-earning civic projects. According to some estimates, over 5 million low- to moderate-income housing units in U.S. cities were candidates for destruction and replacement (Flanagan, 1990:292). By the end of 1961, renewal programs had eliminated more than 126,000 substandard housing units, but only 28,000 new dwellings were built (Robertson and Judd, 1989:307). The net result was a decline in the number of dwelling units for low-income households and an increase in housing costs in poor neighborhoods.

By the late 1950s, the amount of federal money allocated for central city slum clearance and renewal increased greatly each year. Combined expenditures were $706 million in 1960, $1.8 billion in 1966, and $3.8 billion by 1970, or an increase of over 500 percent in ten years (Mollenkopf, 1975). There were many reasons for the federal government's spending spree, most of which occurred through the Department of Housing and Urban Development. By the 1950s, central cities were being devastated by the immense outflow of people to the suburbs. This shift, as we already discussed, was made possible by government highway and housing programs. As a result, downtown retailers and their department stores were in danger of being shut down because of the success of suburban shopping malls, while entire residential sections of the city gave way to blight and decline as middle-class people moved out. City politicians appealed to the federal government for help in rescuing downtown areas. A second cause involved the national response to the ghetto riots of the 1960s, which also highlighted the deterioration of inner-city areas. Funding for HUD projects more than doubled after 1966, the year of the worst rioting. While some low-income residents were helped by the ambitious redevelopment schemes subsidized by the federal government, much of the urban renewal involved the clearing away of slums to allow private real estate interests to use downtown land for profit making, including the building of middle- and upper-middle-income housing projects and the regeneration of central city commerce through the construction of plazas, civic centers, and pedestrian malls. At that time, observers noted that the policy seemed to be more effective at removing African American and/or poor residents than at replacing slums with affordable housing. Over 75 percent of all persons displaced by renewal projects were black, and urban renewal became known as "Negro removal" (Robertson and Judd, 1989:3).

Paradoxically, at the same time that HUD programs were intervening in urban renewal projects in the central city, other federal housing policies in the form of tax subsidies to homeowners and war veterans would destroy city neighborhoods by promoting suburbanization. In the United States (but not in most other industrial countries), homeowners are allowed to deduct the interest that they pay for their home mortgages from the amount of taxes they owe to the federal government. The Servicemen's Readjustment Act of 1944, more popularly known as the GI Bill, guaranteed home loans for veterans; by the time the original legislation ended in July of 1953, 2.4 million veterans had purchased new homes with loans backed by the Veterans Administration. These subsidies, which amounted to billions of dollars each year, were responsible for the massive shift to the suburbs, or white flight. By the 1970s, it was already clear that the United States had become segregated by race and class, with middle-class whites dominating the suburbs while the inner cities were increasingly populated by minorities and those whites who either could not afford to move to suburbia or preferred to live in the city in newly built or renovated upper-middle-income housing. Government intervention, working within the confines of the privatism ideology, was no longer rational social policy, and in fact worked against the interests of the larger society in the fight to save the city.

Support for Economic Development

By the late 1960s, the goals of urban policy had changed as a result of political pressures. Commitment to the revitalization of slums was abandoned in favor of using government programs to bolster private business interests in the city. It was now apparent that urban economies, which had been dependent on manufacturing, were in decline. Deindustrialization had taken over the country, and cities needed to retool themselves to compete with other communities within their metropolitan region for new employment. Downtown business interests, along with local politicians, regrouped and worked together to use federal funds for revitalization projects. The focus of renewal shifted from slum clearance to support for economic development, such as the construction of sports stadiums, hotel and tourist complexes, and high-rise service centers.

For example, in the 1960s, the city of Los Angeles used urban renewal funds to bulldoze the blighted section of Bunker Hill near downtown. But instead of replacing the structures with affordable housing and preserving the community, the city and its partners in the business sector constructed a music center, high-rise banking offices, and expensive high-rise apartment complexes. Slightly east of this redevelopment, the city eradicated another blighted residential neighborhood and replaced it with a sports facility, Dodger Stadium, instead of low-income housing (Davis, 1990).

Such projects, backed by powerful political and business interests, were responsible for the eradication of inner-city neighborhoods and small businesses, while the signs of progress greeted residents with visible advertising for the joint government/business ventures. In many cases, city neighborhoods that did not represent high-yield profit making for business were bulldozed despite the objections of local residents. Gregory Squires (1989) illustrated this trend by presenting a dozen case studies drawn from cities around the country in *Unequal Partnerships: The Political Economy of Urban Redevelopment in Postwar America*, and other researchers have presented case studies of public-private partnerships in individual cities (Robertson and Judd, 1989; Stone, 1989; Davis, 1990).

In the 1960s and 1970s, economic development as an urban policy meant that privatism had taken over not just through co-optation as it had in previous periods but overtly as part of city revival schemes. According to the argument, business concerns come first in a period of recession because when business prospers, the tax coffers of the city are also enriched. Housing programs and community redevelopment had to take a backseat, as did the fight against the problems of uneven development and for social justice. As in other periods, while some federal programs directly aided business, others also helped the middle class. City government could not stem the tide of middle-class white flight during this period because the pull of subsidized suburbanization was too powerful (see Chapter 6). Government could try to make the city a better place in which to do business, but it could not make it a better place in which to live. While government subsidies continue to aid business interests in the cities and mostly white homeowners in the city, by the end of the twentieth century the focus of urban development had shifted to a new and higher level, as American cities began to compete against one another, and even against cities in other countries, in the new global marketplace.

Support for Global Competition

The shift to a financial and service economy for the downtown had now turned into global competition. Each place was in competition for limited investment that was attuned to worldwide opportunities within the marketplace of global capitalism. National programs that supported private enterprise would bypass local bureaucracies and downsize the role of government planning. Issues of social justice were ignored. This restructuring of the federal/city government relationship reached its zenith during the eight years of the Reagan administration and resulted in the cutback of urban policy until there was little funding for urban programs of any kind. Several reasons have been advanced for the federal abandonment of HUD program initiatives over the years. Sadly, most are political. In the 1980s Ronald Reagan ran on a platform that de-emphasized the needs of cities. The plurality of active voters lived in the suburbs, and they were attracted by his call to get government "off the backs" of people. This meant that under the Reagan and Bush administrations from 1980 to 1992, there were severe cuts in public welfare programs, which officials explained as the inevitable consequence of the massive buildup in military spending that left large budget deficits (and no money left over for the cities or for urban residents, most of whom voted Democratic and did not support the Reagan agenda). The new regime followed a conservative philosophy that favored market solutions to social problems. It also reaffirmed the political principle of federalism, which made the condition of cities a responsibility of the states. This principle suggests that local and state governments were better able to deal with local problems and that urban revitalization should be market driven rather than pulled along by federally financed and planned projects. Such sentiments were supported by a majority of voters, who backed President Reagan's conservative agenda and later elected George H. W. Bush. The cuts to federal programs that gave assistance to urban areas were unprecedented. Robertson and Judd (1989:314) made these observations about national aid to cities during this period:

> Overall spending dropped from $6.1 billion in fiscal year 1981 to $5.2 billion in fiscal year 1984. The $5.2 billion spent for the fiscal year 1984–1985 amounted to a decline of almost 20 percent when corrected for inflation. By the 1989 budget year, money for urban programs was cut $4.4 billion, a further reduction of about 40 percent when the effects of inflation are considered. Nearly all subsidies for the construction of public housing were ended. Urban mass transit grants were reduced 28 percent from 1981–1983 and were cut another 20 percent by 1986. CETA [Comprehensive Employment and Training Act] funds were eliminated after 1983.

The Clinton administration began with high hopes for the redevelopment of urban regions, but these hopes were quickly dismantled by scandal and bitter partisan politics. Clinton's nomination of Henry Cisneros, the very popular and successful mayor of San Antonio, Texas, to head the Department of Housing and Urban Development was derailed when it was revealed that he had had an affair during his time in office, and Bill Clinton would face similar accusations for much of his second term. The 1990s brought little in the way of new ideas or new aid to urban areas, and the cities and states were left to fend for themselves.

As bad as the 1990s may have been, the situation for cities and metropolitan areas was even worse during the George W. Bush administration. Although the Clinton administration managed to achieve a budget surplus by the end of its second term, which might have been used to shore up local governments in the throes of fiscal crisis, there was no effort to do this under President Bush. Instead, a sizable government surplus was turned into a budget deficit of historical proportions. Much of the spending went to support the U.S. military presence in Iraq, and many credible reports claim that billions of dollars of this effort were unaccounted for and are probably lost forever. While the deficits of the Bush years impacted ordinary citizens, they also had substantial effects on local government. When cities and towns found themselves in fiscal crisis and unable to support services or repair needed infrastructure, they could not turn to the federal government for relief. This might have been possible when the federal government had a surplus, that is, in the latter years of the Clinton presidency, but there were no such opportunities during the Bush years. Instead, city services, investments in infrastructures, funding for housing programs, and much else declined in real dollar amounts during these years.

Local politicians now work directly with business to revive ailing urban economies as their only way out of fiscal distress. Such a strategy only works when the business community has the resources to help. Public/private partnerships in the face of fiscal crisis also represent an extreme example of privatism because the reduction in or elimination of policies aimed at improving social well-being has occurred at every government level since the 1980s. This trend continued through the 1990s as the Clinton administration issued waivers to states that sought to eliminate welfare programs and replace them with a variety of "work incentive" programs. The result has been a substantial reduction in the number of welfare recipients, but this does not mean that former welfare recipients now participate in the paid labor force. Fewer than half of the persons removed from welfare rolls over the last decade have found permanent employment, and the number of families seeking assistance from food pantries and other private-sector charities has increased substantially.

According to Desmond King, local policy has been reduced completely to the subsidization of the private sector through either supply- or demand-side incentives to business (King, 1990). The former consists of tax breaks, rent-free land, and local bond financing designed to attract capital to the area. One such plan commonly used is tax increment financing, where businesses are allowed to forgo local taxes for a specified period of time so that they can recover development costs for new projects in a community. After a specified period of time, the development is placed back on local tax rolls; the creation of TIF zones is described in more detail in Box 13.2. The city of Chicago currently has more than 130 TIF districts that bring in some $500 million in tax revenue (Cook County Clerk's Office, 2009). Demand-side incentives include city (and suburban) development activities to create new industries with the aid of the private sector by underwriting development costs, such as in the creation of high-tech industrial parks. In both cases, the policies commonly used now stand in stark contrast to those of the 1960s, because the emphasis is on the private sector and economic development, without the reference to issues of social equity and injustice that once obscured the emphasis on privatism.

At the close of the first decade of the twenty-first century, we have seen the global economic crisis progress through successive waves that have impacted local governments

Box 13.2

Tax Increment Financing and Urban Development

Tax increment financing (TIF) is a special tool that a city such as Chicago can use to generate money for economic development in a specific geographic area. TIFs allow a city to reinvest all new property tax dollars in the neighborhood from which they came for a 23-year period. "New" revenues arise if new development takes place in the TIF district, or if the value of existing properties rises, resulting in higher tax bills. These funds can be spent on public works projects or given as subsidies to encourage private development. But TIFs can also make it easier for a city to acquire private property and demolish buildings to make way for new construction.

With consistent community participation, TIFs can be a tool for implementing a community-based revitalization plan through encouraging affordable housing development, improving parks and schools, fixing basic infrastructure, putting vacant land to productive use, creating well-paying jobs, and meeting other local needs.

The state law that allows Illinois cities and towns to create TIFs requires that they are only established in areas that are "blighted," or in danger of becoming blighted. To determine if an area is eligible, the city conducts a study of the area and writes a "redevelopment plan" and a "project budget"—an overview of the development priorities for the area and how TIF dollars will be spent during the TIF's 23-year life. The redevelopment plan must be approved by the city council.

TIFs are politically appealing tools because they do not require the city to raise your tax rate. Instead TIFs generate money for redevelopment by raising the value of the property that is taxed. TIF money can be used for: a) planning expenses, such as studies and surveys, legal and consulting fees, accounting, and engineering; or b) acquiring land and preparing it for redevelopment, including the costs of environmental cleanup and building demolition, especially in older areas, where making a site ready for a developer reduces costs and eliminates a major barrier to redevelopment. To aid this process, the TIF law gives the city expanded powers to acquire private property through its power of "eminent domain." If the city can show it is acting for a "public purpose"—a very loosely defined idea—it can force property owners to sell their land to the city at "fair market value." The city then resells the land to a private developer, often at a deep discount, or uses it for a public building.

Under Illinois law, the clerk's office receives and processes a municipality's ordinance establishing the TIF district and directing the clerk to dictate to the Cook County treasurer the allocation of revenues to the TIF. Revenue is generated for the TIF as property values increase within the TIF district. Under state law, the clerk's office must redistribute revenue to the TIF districts according to the amount of the increment or increased value since the initial or frozen value. Parcels are taxed utilizing the current property value of the property, but any taxes collected because of increases to the value beyond the frozen or initial value of the property are diverted from other tax districts and distributed to the TIF.

SOURCE: Adapted from *TIFs 101: A Taxpayer's Primer for Understanding TIFs*, Cook County Clerk's Office (2009).

in several ways. A number of cities lost their entire employee retirement accounts in the collapse of the investment banks. As homeowners have been forced to abandon their homes because of increased interest rates, the cities lose property tax revenue (the largest single source of public school funding for most communities). As state governments confront mounting deficits due to decreased sales tax revenue, the deficit is passed down to the cities in the form of program budget cuts, forcing local communities to cut programs and lay off workers. In many states, state and local governments introduced mandatory furloughs (unpaid days of leave, in effect, wage and salary cuts for workers in the public sector), and some states, such as California, are in such serious financial distress that they seem faced with unprecedented quality-of-life cutbacks in education, infrastructure repair, basic environmental services, and publicly supported health care.

There is little hope for assistance to cities and metropolitan regions in the foreseeable future. The immense and quite incomprehensible level of federal deficit spending had a measurable effect on local communities even before the economic crisis. We now see a very damaging, critically injuring effect on local government. Furthermore, current projections indicate that our foreign entanglements will lead to astronomical deficit spending for many years to come. To be sure, this is terrible news for cities, towns, counties, and even state governments in the United States.

PRIVATISM AND ISSUES OF SOCIAL JUSTICE

Has the support of private enterprise and abandonment of active intervention in cities been successful? Our analysis of metropolitan problems (Chapter 9) shows just the opposite. The limitations of privatism and government subsidy for economic development include the failure to realize benefits from development, especially by low-income residents; the proliferation of beggar-thy-neighbor competition among different cities, which does not benefit local areas; the subsidization of capital investment that is not reinvested locally; and the destruction of public resources without benefit from the public subsidization of private-sector growth (Barnekov and Rich, 1989). What are the limitations of the ideology of privatism and the present constraints on pursuing social justice more broadly?

Lack of Community Benefits from Public Investment

Publicly supported growth does not bring the kind of benefits purported by boosters of public/private partnerships. In Houston, which claims to be a city based on private enterprise, business has used government funds in many ways to develop infrastructure, subsidize industry, and grease the wheels of profit making. During the city's growth, the costs of development were passed along to residents. By maintaining a low tax rate on business, the city failed to plan adequately for highways, sewage systems, garbage collection, water quality, and road maintenance (Feagin, 1988). Future residents will be saddled with the immense public bill to finance the missing infrastructure and the costs of growth. The experience of Houston has been duplicated in other U.S. cities, which now face immense infrastructure problems of their own. This has not prevented cities from spending millions in taxpayer money on "development" projects such as sports stadiums, convention centers, and luxury housing, which provide few benefits for the city as a whole and none for those most in need. The alleged "crisis" of the infrastructure and of public support for the quality of life in our urban areas is not, as some political leaders maintain, a crisis of funding alone, but represents skewed priorities when all available money is spent on civic development projects of dubious value. Other case studies reveal that privatism twists the intent of public/private partnerships to the full benefit of business. Economic development programs are intended to attract private investment in the local community to the benefit of the city as a whole. But increasingly we have seen private businesses turn this process on its head, threatening to leave for other locations unless they are granted special concessions. In some cases cities have been forced to pay significant amounts to keep local businesses in place, and in other instances states have had to step in when the local community lacks the resources.

Case studies have shown how the competition for investment dollars simply forces local jurisdictions to make excessive sacrifices. This is especially true as capital becomes increasingly mobile in the global economy. In the past decade, we have seen cities and states offering incredible tax breaks and other incentives to attract new or relocating industrial plants, another use of public funds to support private business. Between 1996 and 2007, for example, spending by the state of North Carolina doubled from $550 million to $1.3 billion, with $1.1 billion of the total set aside for tax incentives for business (Disilvestro and Schweke, 2008). In 2001, the city of Chicago provided the Boeing Company with $20 million in incentives to relocate its headquarters from Seattle, outbidding Denver ($18 million) and Dallas ($14 million). The deal included payment of $1 million to another company to vacate its lease in the riverfront building that the city had selected for the new corporate headquarters and required the city to develop a downtown heliport (Lyne, 2001). Some observers have called this ruthless competition among places for investment the "new arms race." In the chase after global dollars, social equity programs are cut or abandoned. As a result, cities have a diminished capacity to support socially beneficial programs and to sustain the community quality of life, and the uneven development within and between metropolitan regions is of growing concern.

The Crisis of Local and State Government in the United States

Government policy involves an often unproductive struggle between the dominant priority to support business and the lesser goal, often passionately pursued by social movements, of social justice. Spatial competition among places for limited public and private investment also affects the success of policy because the United States has no overarching national program for metropolitan revitalization. In the 1950s, competition was between central cities and their suburbs; in the 1970s, it was between regions of the country, especially between areas that were not experiencing a decline in manufacturing (such as the Sun Belt) and those that were (for example, the Frost Belt). By the 1980s and 1990s, however, cities large and small had been brought into a universal global competition for scarce resources. These policies pitted place against place to the advantage of capital and at the expense of local taxpayers. In July 2009 President Obama hosted a Metropolitan Summit at the White House, where he announced that he had ordered the first comprehensive interagency review of "how the federal government approaches and funds urban and metropolitan areas so that we start having a concentrated, focused, strategic approach to federal efforts to revitalize our metropolitan areas." (More of his speech at the Metropolitan Summit can be read in Box 13.3). Although the Obama administration has committed itself to forging an active urban agenda, it remains to be seen if the general policy direction and use of public funds to support private enterprise will continue, or if instead a new emphasis on social justice will emerge. As homelessness, housing deterioration, and other urban problems intensify, renewed pressure is being placed on the federal government to intervene once more to stem the decline in the quality of community life. If such a turnaround does occur, it will come only with a renewed debate on the philosophy of intervention.

Box 13.3

Remarks by President Obama at the Metropolitan Policy Roundtable

"It's great to be joined by some of the finest urban thinkers in America for what I understand has been a critical conversation on the future of America's urban and metropolitan areas.

"Now, as you might imagine, this is a subject that's near and dear to my heart. I've lived almost all my life in urban areas. Michelle and I chose to raise our daughters in the city where she grew up. And even though I went to college in L.A. and New York, and law school across the river from Boston, I received my greatest education on Chicago's South Side, working at the local level to bring about change in those communities and opportunities to people's lives.

"And that experience also gave me an understanding of some of the challenges facing city halls all across the country. And I know that those challenges are particularly severe today because of this recession. Four in five cities have had to cut services, just when folks need it the most, and 48 states face the prospects of budget deficits in the coming fiscal year.

"But we're going to need to do more than just help our cities weather the current economic storm. We've got to figure out ways to rebuild them on a newer, firmer,

continues

Box 13.3 *continued*

stronger foundation for our future. And that requires new strategies for our cities and metropolitan areas that focus on advancing opportunity through competitive, sustainable, and inclusive growth. And that's why all of you are here today. And I know that there were a lot of ideas that were shared throughout the morning and afternoon.

"Now, the first thing we need to recognize is that this is not just a time of challenge for America's cities; it's also a time of great change. Even as we've seen many of our central cities continuing to grow in recent years, we've seen their suburbs and exurbs grow roughly twice as fast—that spreads homes and jobs and businesses to a broader geographic area. And this transformation is creating new pressures and problems, of course, but it's also opening up new opportunities, because it's not just our cities that are hotbeds of innovation anymore, it's our growing metropolitan areas.

"We're going to take a hard look at how Washington helps or hinders our cities and metro areas—from infrastructure to transportation; from housing to energy; from sustainable development to education. And we're going to make sure federal policies aren't hostile to good ideas or best practices on the local levels. We're going to put an end to throwing money at what doesn't work—and we're going to start investing in what does work and make sure that we're encouraging that.

"But we also need to fundamentally change the way we look at metropolitan development. For too long, federal policy has actually encouraged sprawl and congestion and pollution, rather than quality public transportation and smart, sustainable development. And we've been keeping communities isolated when we should have been bringing them together.

"So I know that this change is possible. After all, I'm from a city that knows a little something about reinventing itself. In the nineteenth century, after a cataclysmic fire, Chicagoans rebuilt stronger than before. In the last century, they led the world upward in steel and glass. And in this century, under my friend Mayor Daley's leadership, they're helping to lead the world forward in newer, greener, more livable ways.

"Daniel Burnham said, 'Make no little plans.' And that's the spirit behind his bold and ambitious designs unveiled 100 years ago this month that helped transform Chicago into a world-class city. That's the same spirit which we have to approach the reinvention of all America's cities and metropolitan areas—a vision of vibrant, sustainable places that provide our children with every chance to learn and to grow, and that allows our businesses and workers the best opportunity to innovate and succeed, and that let our older Americans live out their best years in the midst of all that metropolitan life can offer. Now is the time to seize that moment of possibility, and I am absolutely confident that, starting today with this conversation, you and I together, we're going to be able to make this happen."

SOURCE: Remarks by the president at Urban and Metropolitan Policy Roundtable, July 13, 2009 (http://www.whitehouse.gov/the_press_office/remarks-by-the-president-at-urban-and-metropolitan -roundtable).

URBAN POLICY: THE POLITICAL DEBATE

Over the past two decades, debate has raged regarding whether traditional liberal or conservative solutions to the urban crisis should be applied. Most analysts of urban problems discuss solutions in terms of precisely this clash of ideologies. In this section, we discuss policy recommendations along ideological lines. In a later section, we will point to a course of action that offers the possibility of rising above this clash of perspectives by addressing the limitations of current public policy arrangements.

Liberal Positions on Urban Problems

Liberals tend to focus on the limitations of existing social institutions and to seek remedies that equalize the ability of all citizens to overcome those limitations. They support government intervention and spending as a means of combating social ills. Most urban problems are caused, in this view, by the inequities of the resource distribution system in our society. Poverty and associated problems of uneven development are the inevitable consequence of the fact that economic rewards and social opportunities are not equally available to all citizens. The liberal agenda uses government intervention as a tool to overcome uneven development. It supports active involvement of policy to identify, address, and help resolve serious urban problems of the less affluent. Economic deprivation and persistent racial segregation are contributing factors in the rise of crime and drug use rates. Programs could be designed, as they were in the 1960s, for job training, long-term unemployment assistance, and even government-subsidized corporate internships that might provide job possibilities for the most disadvantaged city residents. In addition, government-subsidized medical care, family assistance, and aid for the homeless could provide a social safety net below which U.S. citizens would not fall. This would improve the life chances of the less affluent and remove from the city streets some of the worst cases of need that threaten the quality of life for everyone.

Conservative Approaches to Urban Problems

Conservatives, in contrast, believe in limited government intervention and severely restricted government spending. They accuse liberals of squandering society's wealth through excessive public spending. Consequently, they are opposed to the kinds of programs sponsored by liberals precisely because they cost money and must be supported by taxes on private income or corporate profits. Conservatives also address the issue of uneven development. In their view, less advantaged people and places must make themselves more competitive so that they can join in the contest for capital investment. It's up to people and places themselves to become more attractive.

Conservatives believe that many of the problems of the poor reside in their own personalities and family traits. The classic statement of this came from Edward Banfield, who argued that poor people are not motivated to find legitimate jobs and that they prefer not to work (Banfield, 1974). James Murray's influential book *Losing Ground* (1984) argued that welfare and other government programs actually increased poverty and caused the number of unwed mothers to rise. This book was referred to (by conservatives) as the bible of the Reagan administration and would continue to influence urban policy in both Bush administrations. Others have argued that liberals sought to expand welfare programs simply to create more jobs and support the growth of the government bureaucracy.

The conservative position has been taken up by some black critics of liberalism such as Shelby Steele. They argue that urban liberals and their programs, such as affirmative action, have ruined the moral character of blacks while the latter have languished in the ghettos of northern cities. African Americans have been made dependent and are losing the ability to cultivate their own inner resources due to city bureaucracies and their liberal programs of aid. Consequently, the immense problems of the ghettoized poor (formerly called the "underclass") are in effect the outcome of decades of liberal policies that forced blacks to become wards of the state (Steele, 1990). It must be pointed out that even if people favor government intervention for the pursuit of social justice, our study of the record of government metropolitan policy over the past fifty years shows that expensive public programs have continually been co-opted by the business community. Funding that was intended for community development often went to economic development, and funding for social welfare programs has huge administrative costs that support a mostly white, middle-class workforce. Hence there is considerable evidence against returning to the blind faith of some liberals and active public spending to combat the many social ills that plague our metropolitan areas, even if we could do so. The problem may be not so much individual moral character or social programs to provide assistance to those who need it, but rather the uneven development and economic inequalities that give rise to those problems to begin with.

Overcoming the Liberal-Conservative Impasse

What hope exists for the urban future? The lessons of history teach us that either/or choices are unfair. We must look beyond the clash of liberal and conservative ideology and beyond all ideological means of understanding urban problems. What possible solutions might overcome the liberal-conservative ideological impasse? An important but neglected dimension to the debate on urban problems involves recognizing the fact that local governments have only a limited ability to plan adequately for social change. The ideological debate between liberals and conservatives misses an important dimension, namely, the limitations of local government as administrative structures. It also fails to address the particular relationships among the federal, state, and local levels that have always worked against adequate planning and public policy in the United States. Within metropolitan areas, there are so many levels of government, each with its own limited administration, that power is both highly fragmented and weakly applied. Social programs initiated by cities are ineffective because they must tackle problems that are regional in scope. So cities simply control too small a piece of the regional pie to fight the immense problems of uneven development, such as the need for affordable housing. In fact, it can be argued that the city is not the place to initiate programs aimed at social problems of broad scope or at alleviating the inequities of uneven development. Suburbs and cities share similar problems, and the growth patterns of one are linked to those of the other. Hence a metropolitan perspective on improving the quality of life becomes imperative for adequate public policy. Problems that are national in scope, such as crime or the crisis of health care, must be returned to the responsibility of the national and state levels of government, where they belong. By understanding the relationship between spatial and social levels in the study of policy, we can sort out what should and should not be the responsibility of local government. And by adopting a metropolitan, regional perspective, we can design better ways of attacking the problems of social justice and uneven development.

REGIONAL GOVERNANCE

There is strong evidence that the political fragmentation of metropolitan regions in the United States contributes to and may be responsible for uneven sociospatial development. For example, Detroit and Toronto are industrial cities located just 230 miles apart. Detroit, like many other American cities, has long been in the throes of economic crisis. While the metropolitan region contains more than 4 million people (and many wealthy suburbs), the city of Detroit has lost more than half of its population, from a peak of 1.9 million in 1950 to just 912,000 in 2008. One-third of the population lives in a household with an income below the poverty level, and for many years Detroit held the dubious title of "murder city" because it had the highest murder rate in the nation. Most of us are familiar with the Detroit of popular culture—from the vibrant Motown sound of the 1960s to the troubled rap music of Eminem and the film *8 Mile* of the 2000s. The comparison between Detroit of the 1960s and 2000s is of some interest. Detroit of the 1960s was still a booming industrial city. Now entire city blocks are vacant, the housing long since abandoned due to white flight to the suburbs and destroyed by arson. Some of these neighborhoods have actually been reclaimed by "urban forests," and deer have returned to the city. Today Detroit is overwhelmingly black and poor, with apparently few opportunities for economic revival due to the recent restructuring of the auto industry that brought the city to greatness in the 1950s.

In contrast, Toronto has doubled its population since 1950, going from slightly more than 1 million to 2.5 million persons in 2000. The metropolitan region has also grown rapidly, from 3.9 million in 1990 to 5.1 million persons in 2007. Compared to Detroit, Toronto is relatively crime free, with a murder rate lower than any U.S. city with a population of 1 million or greater. While there has been recent concern about increases in poverty, the most recent figure suggests that about 16 percent of the population is below the poverty line. Yet Toronto's residents are a diverse mix of racial, ethnic, and class groups comparable to any major American city. Toronto is also an immigrant city, as more than half of the city's residents are foreign born (more than any American city). One might expect the rapid growth and diverse population to generate a good deal of urban problems.

One thing does much to explain Toronto's success: the enactment in 1953 of a federal form of government for the thirteen previously independent municipalities in the area. The original thirteen have consolidated into six. They are responsible for local affairs, while the metro council handles area affairs, including Metro-wide planning (*The Economist*, May 1990:17).

The metro-wide government consolidates resources in the entire region and coordinates the growth of both the central city and its suburbs. As a result, many of the problems brought about by uneven sociospatial development that have plagued Detroit have been avoided by the Toronto region. Public schools across the Toronto region are well funded, and most students complete their high school career in four years. While there are some good public schools in the Detroit area, these are in the better-off suburbs; nearly half of the students in Detroit's public schools do not graduate from high school.

Regional government has worked in Toronto. In contrast, Detroit cannot possibly find the resources to address its problems because it is cut off from the affluent suburbs. Should society tolerate the extreme forms of deprivation and affluence that can be readily seen in this region, even if all metropolitan Detroit residents suffer from the continued downsizing and outsourcing of the automobile industry? The only metropolitan region in the United States with funding arrangements similar to Toronto is Minneapolis–St. Paul. Enacted in 1972, the fiscal disparities policy was designed to prevent the type of uneven development that we find in many American cities. A portion of the revenues that come into each of the local governments is set aside for a common fund, which then is distributed to communities across the metropolitan region. One might expect that this would result in a transfer of revenues from the suburbs to the central cities, but that is not the case; in the Minneapolis–St. Paul metropolitan region, the northern suburbs are less well-off than those in the south, and they receive the largest transfer of revenue. One of the supporters of this policy is Myron Orfield, who has published a book titled *American Metropolitics*. Box 13.4 presents some of his arguments as to why promoting regional equity is good for all those involved. Interesting given our earlier discussion of privatism, Orfield was attacked as a "socialist" and even "communist" for his support of the fiscal disparities policy while serving in the Minnesota state legislature.

Due to the autonomous home rule of local communities that discourages regional forms of government, suburban settlement spaces have effectively insulated themselves

Box 13.4

Promoting Regional Equity

Policies to reduce physical inequities in metropolitan areas can bring great benefits. They can narrow the disparity in local government's capacities to provide public services; they also can reduce incentives for fiscal zoning and inefficient tax-base competition and the negative consequences of those actions. However, those gains do not always come without costs. Poorly designed policies to reduce inequality can also compromise local autonomy, derail efficient provision of local services, and create incentives for inefficient patterns of migration. Finding policy designs that strike the best possible balance between trade-offs is not a trivial exercise.

Policies that promote equity in the distribution of local taxes can reduce incentives for fiscal zoning and tax-based completion and their negative outcomes in several ways. By ensuring that all local governments can provide the infrastructure and services communities need to function, equity-enhancing policies can guarantee that all residents of a metropolitan area enjoy at least a minimum standard of service for important local public goods like public safety. By reducing the need for local governments to "steal" revenue-generating land uses from each other, such policies allow them to engage in more thoughtful and beneficial land-use planning.

Intrametropolitan competition for a limited tax base harms a region. It is a waste of resources for local governments to engage in bidding wars for businesses that already have chosen to locate in a region. In such situations, public monies are used to improve the fiscal position and services of one community at the expense of another, while businesses take unfair advantage of the competition to reduce their social responsibilities. The mere threat of leaving can induce troubled communities to offer a business large public subsidies to stay.

Greater equity frees local governments from the pressure to base land-use decisions primarily on the need for additional revenues. Instead, they can focus on developing land-use plans that accommodate growth efficiently, reduce the effects of concentrated poverty, and respond to the desires of local citizens without fearing that the resources available to them will be diminished. Furthermore, reducing the incentives for completion allows local governments to focus on cooperative efforts to help build a strong, dynamic region that is attractive to employers and residents.

Public services provided at least in part by local governments in most states (public safety, a healthy environment) are an integral part of what most Americans would regard as an acceptable quality of life. The implication is that all people have the right to a reasonable standard of service—a standard that a highly fragmented and fiscally stratified system with full local autonomy may not always be able to meet.

SOURCE: Myron Orfield, *American Metropolitics: The New Suburban Reality* (Washington, DC: The Brookings Institution, 2002).

from the need to address the problems of uneven sociospatial development. But the contrast is not only one of spatial organization. Canada has a system of health care that is run by the national government; the United States does not. The two federal governments differ regarding what they have chosen to bear as national responsibilities, a decision that affects the quality of life for metropolitan residents. The national concern for social justice cannot be separated from local issues of public policy. We may not know all the solutions to urban decline, but one very good attempt at finding a solution that avoids ideological debates must focus on the structural limitations of city government and the excessive fragmentation of local jurisdictions. Along with these sociospatial concerns are jurisdictional dilemmas among local, state, and national levels that must be faced to determine who shares the burden of responsibility for the quality of life in the United States—the individual alone (as conservative policy dictates), the city, the state, or the federal government. Without metropolitan coordination, and lacking support from higher levels of government, cities simply do not possess the resources they need to address commanding problems of everyday life. At some point in the future, national leaders must provide the vision necessary to share the responsibility for social concerns at the federal and state levels, where it belongs. Until then, the quality of life not only in central cities but across metropolitan regions as a whole will be dependent on the well-being of local business concerns within an increasingly competitive global economy.

KEY CONCEPTS

tragedy of the commons
uneven development
redistributive programs
urban renewal
public housing
public subsidy
liberal / conservative approaches to urban problems
metropolitan government
regional governance
tax increment financing

DISCUSSION QUESTIONS

1. Why is the market system unable to adequately determine the allocation of resources across the metropolitan region? What is the rationale for public intervention in urban planning and metropolitan development?

2. The United States has a federal system of government. What does federalism mean, and what are the consequences of federalism for urban planning and government programs in metropolitan areas in the United States?

3. What is the ideology of privatism? Where did it originate, and what effect does it have on urban policy? What are two of the limitations of privatism? What are some of the consequences of these limitations?

4. What are some of the important differences between liberal and conservative positions as to the causes of urban social problems? How can we overcome the liberal-conservative impasse? What are some of the changes in federal urban policy during the Reagan, Clinton, and Bush presidencies?

THE FUTURE OF URBAN SOCIOLOGY

The beginning of the twenty-first century marks a new era in human history. The world's urban population numbers more than 3 billion persons. For the first time, more than half of the world's population lives in urban areas, and in the next two decades the number will increase by another 2 billion persons to more than 5 billion. In 2030, it is expected that some 70 percent of the total world population will live in urban areas (United Nations, 2007).

We know that these urban areas are linked in exciting and new ways that would have been unimaginable just a short time ago. We are connected by a global economy where the life opportunities of persons in one country may be dependent upon capital flows of new investments from a nation on the other side of the world. The mass media brings us world music from Africa and the Middle East. We use the Internet to keep in touch with old friends who move to other countries and to make new friends in places we have never even heard of. We inhabit a global world, to be sure, but more than that, it is, for the very first time, an urban world.

The people living in this new urban world, the urban world of the twenty-first century, will confront many new and important issues. We know that more than a third of the world's urban population now lives in shantytowns, many with inadequate drinking water or sanitation, substandard housing, and few economic opportunities. The number of persons living in urban slums will increase to more than half of the world's urban population by 2030—some 2.5 billion persons (Neuwirth, 2006; UN Habitat, 2009). Problems of pollution will increase as the less developed nations industrialize and create new urban infrastructures that require the same resources for development that we find in the developed nations. This is already happening in China and India. A changing global climate may lead to major changes in crop production and weather patterns around the world, creating new scarcities of food and water that we have barely begun to consider.

Global society is urban society. And no field of study is more important for understanding these changes than urban sociology. Will urban sociology step up to this challenge?

UNDERSTANDING OUR
NEW URBAN WORLD

Urban studies is a comparatively recent field of study. Perhaps because of the exciting changes—and important challenges—that the new urban world of the twenty-first century presents, urban studies and its related disciplines—urban sociology, urban geography, architecture—have emerged as something of a growth industry in academic publishing for the past decade or more. This work is built around both new and old perspectives in the field and offers some insight as to where urban research will lead in the future. In this final chapter, we explore several topics that are important to our understanding of the new urban world. These topics include globalization, world cities, theming of the urban environment, racialization of urban space, the revanchist city, and cyberspace and the end of the city.

Globalization

First, there is an extensive literature on globalization and world cities. We have discussed some of the important characteristics of globalization and the impact of globalization on urban development in the industrialized countries (Chapter 10) and in the developing world (Chapter 11). But it is important to remember that globalization is not a new phenomenon, nor is it a new area of study in sociology. We usually think of globalization as something that started recently and is just now having important effects on our lives. Although many textbooks seem to suggest that globalization began with the European discovery of the Americas and the development of European colonial empires, there are earlier precedents. The great Chinese empires of the Middle Ages linked trading centers across Southeast Asia with the Chinese urban centers, then the largest cities in the world. Even earlier, Rome, the first truly urban civilization, depended upon wheat grown in Egypt to sustain its growing urban population, and Roman cities across Europe and the Middle East were linked with an extensive road system. Indeed, much of the spectacle of ancient Rome was the product of globalization, from the obelisks brought from Egypt and placed in the Roman Forum to the exotic animals exhibited in the Colosseum that came from countries at the edge of the empire.

The European colonial system connected cities across the world in a new and more systematic fashion. During this period of mercantile capitalism, raw materials (silver from the Americas, spices from the Far East) were brought back to the European trading cities. The neocolonial empires of the twentieth century reestablished and intensified this system of economic dominance (even today the majority of export crops produced in the Philippines is under the control of just one American corporation—Dole). This system of globalization and colonial dependence is described by the world systems theory of the 1970s and 1980s, in which the industrialized countries and the former European colonial powers are seen as part of the core, and countries in the developing world are seen as part of the periphery (Wallerstein, 1976). The current literature on globalization builds upon these earlier models to describe an increasingly complex system of economic competition and urban growth.

Significant issues of economic and social justice associated with globalization have been contested in protests against the International Monetary Fund and the World Bank in cities across the world. We know something about the costs of globalization in terms of job loss and economic restructuring in metropolitan regions across the United States (Chapter 6) and in other industrialized countries. Perhaps less well understood is the impact of globalization on urbanization and urban systems in the developing nations.

The growth of urban centers in China—the number of metropolitan areas with populations of more than 2.5 million persons will increase from a dozen in 2000 to more than twenty by 2025—is largely a consequence of the concentration of industrial production in the urban clusters identified in Chapter 11. In many other countries in the developing world, the growth of urban centers is the result of continuing migration from rural areas as individuals and households are unable to support themselves from simple agricultural work and come to the cities looking for work. Most of the growth of urban populations in the developing nations in the coming decades will be of this type (United Nations, 2007). These urban centers will not be part of the world urban system in the ways currently described in the literature; instead, they are likely to become part of what has been called the Fourth World—areas left behind in the globalization process (Giddens, 2000; Hutchison 2009).

Globalization remains a topic closely studied by urbanists in all countries. One key area of globalization research involves the study of how it affects local labor markets. Changes in the demand for high- and low-tech labor, retail workers, or financial service workers, for example, can directly affect the economic well-being of cities. Commercial growth and housing development are all tied to the ebb and flow of local jobs, including the quality of wages.

American metropolitan regions have been adversely affected by the flight of industry and people from the urban core. Industrial decline has been attributed to the acquisition of local businesses by multinational corporations. Some transnational corporations have purchased American companies just to shut them down or downsize them to increase corporate profits and strengthen market position. These actions have contributed to urban decline. Other places have benefited from new investment, much of it also involving multinationals. Sustained growth in places like Los Angeles, San Diego, and Miami owes a considerable amount to the continuing viability of those cities as sites of global investment (see Box 14.1). Future research on globalization needs to examine the contradictory impacts of this international business activity to determine how they affect different parts of the metropolitan region.

Box 14.1

Miami, Capital of the Caribbean

Miami may well be the most foreign of any large metropolitan area in the United States. Its exotic qualities often invoke images of glamour and splendor, but at times there also is a sense of alienation from mainstream America. The city is above all a showcase of the forces of globalization and of the complexity of those forces. According to some measures, Miami is the most internationalized metropolitan area in the country. The effects of globalization on Miami have been massive, and unprecedented in urban America.

In about forty years, not a long time in the life span of cities, Miami transformed from a quiet resort town at the periphery of the United States to a dynamic metropolis in the center of a growing economic region comprising North and South America and the Caribbean. Between 1960 and 1990, the population of Dade County more than doubled, to approximately 2 million people, and the urban economy grew accordingly. By 1996, Dade County's economy was $56 billion, exceeding the gross national product of Colombia, one of its main trading partners.

Miami's transformation and growth are based on the convergence of two developments: the arrival of very large numbers of Latin American immigrants and the globalization of the world economy. The latter facilitated the intensification of finance and trade flows across political borders, allowing for the emergence of international economic regions, such as the one in which Miami plays a prominent part. Massive immigration, in turn, gave Miami a definitive advantage in terms of the human resources and as a node in the globalizing world economy.

In 1960, on the eve of Miami's transformation, Latinos made up 5 percent of the metropolitan populace. Today, they represent more than half of the city's 2 million people, and approximately 66 percent of all Latinos are Cuban. According to the 1990 census, almost half of Miami's population was born abroad, and over 60 percent speak a language in addition to English at home. Miami's rise to prominence is often attributed to its becoming a multicultural city. The presence of large numbers of relatively skilled and educated bilingual Latinos makes Miami an attractive location for companies that do business in Latin America. However, the influx of immigrants was accompanied by a rapid internationalization of Miami's economy.

Miami handles more than a third of all trade with Latin America and over a half of all trade with Central America and the Caribbean. More than 350 multinational companies have offices in Miami, and it has become the third largest foreign banking center in the United States (after New York and Los Angeles). Miami is the prime example of a world-class trading city in the United States, made possible by the cultural connections created by its binational communities.

continues

Tourism is still a major source of income, but it is increasingly aimed at international markets, especially Latin America and Europe. Besides tourism, international trade and real estate have become leading sectors of the Miami economy. All growth is welcomed, but the city is primarily promoted on the basis of its virtues as an international place. Miami's designation as the capital of Latin America, the Americas, and the Caribbean has been in vogue since the late 1970s.

SOURCE: Jan Nijman, "Globalization to a Latin Beat: The Miami Growth Machine," 1997.

World Cities

Peter Hall's work on *The World City* highlighted seven metropolitan regions—London, Paris, Moscow, New York, Tokyo, Rhine-Ruhr (Germany), and Randstad-Holland (The Netherlands)—and brought attention to cities as places of political and economic power (Hall, 1966). But the study of global cities emerged more directly from world systems theory and political economy models of urban growth (Chapter 4). Friedman and Wolff (1982) introduced the concept of a global network of cities where urbanization was linked to the internationalization of capital, and a later article by Friedman (1986) suggested that the way in which cities are connected to the world economy offers a key to their growth and development. Cities connected to the world economy in similar ways would be alike regardless of differences in history, national policies, and cultural influences. The global city is the site of the concentration and accumulation of world capital and with a large number of professionals in specialized control functions, such as lawyers, computer programmers, and accountants.

Saskia Sassen's study of global cities argues that the presence of global cities has important consequences for the nation and for the global economy (1994; 1999; 2001). Sassen's work is different from the earlier world system theory in that Sassen asserts that the leading global cities, not the nations themselves, have emerged as key structures in the world economy. The global city is characterized by specific forms of urban development, including the redevelopment of the urban core and displacement of the poor, construction of high-rise office towers, and an increasing social and spatial polarization. The transformation of cities into high-tech international business centers privileges global corporations at the expense of other groups, particularly minorities, immigrants, and women. Sassen presents the corporate office building as a metaphor for the polarization that characterizes the global city: During the day, the building is occupied by highly educated, well-paid executives making global transactions; at night it is cleaned by female immigrant workers paid minimum wage. The influence of global firms on urban development raises important moral claims: Whose city is it? (Sassen, 2001).

While this literature has focused on major world cities, other work has emphasized that many cities compete to become global cities. The decline of manufacturing means that cities must find new ways to link to the global economy; they compete with one another to attract corporate headquarters, sports facilities, and new businesses in response to globalization and to achieve world-city status (Short, 2004). Abrahamson (2004) suggests that almost all cities are likely to have some features that make them global and that the focus on a small group of cities—such as Sassen's work on New York, London, and Tokyo—underestimates how widely the global-city construct may be generalized. Chicago and Frankfurt, for example, are significant global cities when concentration of economic activity is used as a measure; Los Angeles figures prominently in cultural activity but is less important in other areas.

In his analysis of global cities, Mark Abrahamson ranks thirty cities on a composite economic index (including the number of stock exchanges, banks and financial institutions, multinational corporations, and services) and cultural industries index (recorded music, movies, and television). The resulting global economic hierarchy puts New York at the top of both indexes, with London, Paris, and Tokyo grouped in a second tier with similar economic and cultural profiles. Abrahamson (2004:164) notes that "everyone else lags substantially far behind them." He finds evidence of regional economic centers—Chicago and Frankfurt—as well as regional cultural centers—Mumbai, Rio de Janeiro, Manila—cities that could move to world-city position by increasing their cultural activities (something that both Chicago and Frankfurt have sought to do) or by increasing their economic potential. These sorts of development activities are the focus of John Rennie Short's work on global cities (2005). He notes that the discourse on globalization leads cities to seek development that will better connect them to the new world economy: the construction of international airports, the establishment of international business centers, the building of world-class sports facilities, and the successful competition for events such as the World's Fair, the Olympics, and the World Cup.

Many scholars have expressed concern with the way "world cities" and "global cities" reify earlier colonial/imperial models of a "world system" with the implied ranking of cities as either modern or in need of development (Fraser, 2006). Although current research gives considerable attention to world cities, from our perspective, the concept of "world cities" is misguided. At times these urban spaces act as cities because some of their global functions are concentrated in their cores. At other times, however, these spaces function as multicentered regions, not cities, and it is necessary to study them in this larger configuration in order to understand them. When speaking of stock and bond trading, for example, the spaces corresponding with these activities would be lower Manhattan, the City of London, and downtown Tokyo, respectively.

Market trading is generally a centralized city phenomenon, although stock markets like NASDAQ are inscribed in telephone and computerized telecommunication links worldwide and have no physical space at all. To be sure, such activities are considered "command-and-control functions," but they are not the only kind. Multinational corporate headquarters are the other major component of the global economy, and these are increasingly located outside the cores of large cities in separate centers. When urbanists speak of "world cities" as if this complex and evolving regional array of urban and suburban settlement space did not exist, they overlook the very significant fact that the "world city" is but a small space embedded within a larger metropolitan region.

Employment in financial services within the City of London, for example, has significantly declined in recent years (Buck and Gordon, 2003) as nationally linked business services have moved into the area. Many corporate headquarters have left Manhattan for areas in the multicentered region of New York, New Jersey, and Connecticut, or for places in other parts of the country. And if we return to the metaphor of the office building in the global city, it should be clear that the maintenance staff and service workers who make these buildings work on a day-to-day basis live their daily lives in very different spaces of the metropolitan region than the office staff who occupy the buildings during the 9-to-5 workday—and the company executives live *their* lives in yet other spaces! The deconcentration and reconcentration of command-and-control centers across regions, the increasing divide—both spatially and socioeconomically—among those who occupy these centers, and similar sociospatial factors make it imperative for future research to take the multicentered metropolitan region as the focal urban form.

Theming of the Urban Environment

The urban environment across the metropolitan region, including cities and suburbs, is increasingly themed and branded because consumerism that relies on franchising and media advertising is so much a part of the way our economy works. In addition, with the decline of manufacturing within American cities, tourism has taken over as one of the major ways downtowns now make money. Theming is the process by which attractions compete for tourist dollars. Increasingly, European cities and even places in China and India rely on theming and branding as their urban economies shift to an emphasis on consumption.

Most of us have visited theme parks (Disneyland, Disney World, Busch Gardens), eaten at themed restaurants (Hard Rock Café, Rainforest Cafe), and even visited themed nightclubs (House of Blues). Research on the role of theming in American culture and, more exactly, the way theming is used to sell products and places that, on their own, may not be markedly different from one another, is a relatively undeveloped area of study (for an exception, see Gottdiener, 1995; 2001; Hutchison and Wright, 1996). In Las Vegas, for example, every casino sells the identical product, gambling, although they might vary slightly according to their house odds. On the outside, however, every casino is different, and each offers a thematic fantasy as an attraction. According to Gottdiener (2001), many of the themes can be bunched together: the

Wild West, the romanticized desert, famous cities of the world, and exotic tropical lo-cales. These motifs work because they have already been well established as familiar symbolic forms by Hollywood cinema and by television.

The success of places like Las Vegas over the decades as a gambling mecca, in con-trast to the decline of American cities with industrial/manufacturing traditions, pin-points both the prospects and problems facing places as they attempt to attract new investment and residents, because not every location can depend on casino gambling for economic stability (Gottdiener, 1994). We have seen the collapse of Atlantic City, an older resort community in New Jersey that was rebuilt as a casino gambling com-plex in the 1980s, in the second wave of the global financial crisis just two decades later. Tourism, on the other hand, which is a more abstract way of looking at the suc-cess of Las Vegas, can be successfully promoted in most places. In 1972 Robert Ven-turi, Steven Izenour, and Denise Scott Brown published *Learning from Las Vegas*, an important book that examined symbolism in the architecture of the Las Vegas Strip and the iconography of urban sprawl. What we can all learn from Las Vegas in this day and age is precisely the way architectural theming can be used to attract people to urban areas. In Las Vegas, theming is the major weapon in the competition for cus-tomers, and casinos have gone to previously unheard-of lengths in the creation of spectacular environments that provide fantasy stimulation and entertainment. When theming is used by other American metropolitan regions in order to attract tourists, however, popular Las Vegas motifs may not work. Consequently, the promotion of lo-cal tourism as a new growth industry requires places to research precisely what themes make sense within the local context. Future research should pay attention to these ef-forts and their variation among urban places.

Racialization of Urban Space

The racialization of urban space refers to the process by which urban and suburban social space is associated with various ethnic and racial groups and to the serious con-sequences of extreme segregation discussed in Chapter 9 that still plague American society. The racialization of space impacts the activities and opportunities of groups and individuals both within and beyond particular urban spaces: For persons living within racialized spaces, there is a stigma attached to the address they include on ap-plications for employment; for persons living outside the racialized space, the racial-ized neighborhood (and its residents) are to be avoided (Hutchison, 2009). The racialization of space is a clear example of how the sociospatial perspective takes us be-yond human ecology to analyze meanings that are given to urban spaces. As we saw in Chapter 1, urban spaces are meaningful spaces—they have specific meanings (some-times contradictory) to persons within and outside of the local community. Racialized spaces often are contested spaces, and groups within the community struggle to de-fine these spaces in particular ways (Wacquant, 2008).

The concept of racialized space is important for understanding particular patterns of development in cities. In the United States, older inner-city neighborhoods, housing projects, and the like have become associated with minority populations and with violent crime. Gotham (2004) describes how racialization was a fundamental part of the debate over urban renewal and the future development of black and white space in Kansas City. City planners painted a picture of the inner-city neighborhoods as racialized spaces, which made the decision to allocate public monies to condemn housing and business the only acceptable plan for development.

When the downtown areas of cities become racialized space, there is a decline in business of all kinds. The redevelopment of the Chicago Loop, highlighted by the very successful development of Millenium Park that turned downtown Chicago into a major tourist destination, required the elimination of downtown movie theaters that featured black films and the removal of other institutions that served this population. This was followed by the development of a new arts district that brings in a very different clientele, including new Borders and Barnes and Noble bookstores. The tourists to the area include not only visitors from other states and even countries, but also persons from the suburbs who avoided the downtown area for decades and viewed Chicago as a "black city." The project has been viewed as a success as the area has become deracialized (Hutchison, 2005).

Although the racialization of space most directly brings to mind the image of inner-city neighborhoods, the concept can also refer to other areas. It has been used by scholars in Europe to study ethnic populations in the multicultural city and by scholars in the United States to study ethnic neighborhoods and populations. One of the most visible and long-lasting of these neighborhoods is the ubiquitous Chinatown; other areas such as Italian or Irish neighborhoods are also prominent features of the American urban environment. In many cases, these neighborhoods were defensive—the Chinese, Italian, and Irish immigrants experienced prejudice and discrimination when they first arrived in the United States, and the ethnic neighborhood provided a safe haven and opportunity for members of the ethnic group (Chapter 8).

Although much of the research on the racialization of space focuses on negative labels that are forced upon the community by members of the dominant group living outside of these spaces, it should be recognized that racialized spaces may also be created from within the neighborhood or group. Street gang graffiti advertises the presence of groups competing for control of urban space and creates racialized spaces that may appear dangerous and mysterious to the outsider. In many ethnic neighborhoods, one finds murals that have been painted to create a racialized space that becomes a source of pride and identity for the group.

There are racialized spaces that have positive images as well. In Chicago and New York there has been extensive gentrification in Bronzeville and Harlem, the former ghetto areas in each of these cities, and in both cases the visitor can take guided tours of the area (for a fee). Tourist bureaus in major cities supply maps that show the location

Box 14.2

Racialization and Tourism in Chinatown

The phenomenon of Chinatown occurs in many major cities in the West, re-creating a small part of the Orient wherever they spring into being. In old American western towns, Chinatown came into existence because of the large-scale immigration of cheap Chinese labor into the states during the building of the railroads. These areas have always been regarded with an element of suspicion and fear by Westerners, together with a curiosity and desire to indulge in the pleasures and vices that frequently seem to occur there, even to this day.

The liner notes to Thin Lizzy's *Chinatown* album capture the air of mystery surrounding the racialized community. San Francisco's Chinatown intrigued tourists from its beginning. One of the main attractions toward the end of the nineteenth century was a group of opium dens that flourished in the warren of underground passages beneath the houses, shops, and restaurants. In 1877 Miriam Florence Leslie, wife of the publisher of *Leslie's Illustrated Weekly*, toured one such den with a group of her friends. She recorded her impressions in her book, *California: A Pleasure Trip from Gotham City to the Golden Gate*. The tour guide was a local police officer. As late as 1974, the popular image of crime and corruption was still real enough to capture public attention as the title of the Roman Polanski film *Chinatown* (even though none of the film actually takes place in Chinatown).

By the end of the twentieth century, Chinatown had become something very different; no longer dark and mysterious, it now was a tourist destination, advertised in city maps and the official tourist Web pages for major cities (not just in the United States but across North America and in other countries as well). While some Chinatowns remain working communities, others have taken on a Disney-like flavor as they shed ethnic culture for tourist business; as is the case with other themed environments, the re-creation of the historic ethnic community means that it no longer is a living ethnic community; the racialized space has been tamed and marketed to the larger society. They also are important economic generators within the community; after 9/11, when many businesses across lower Manhattan were struggling to survive, the mayor held a news conference announcing that the rebirth of the city economy would begin in Chinatown.

of ethnic neighborhoods, such as Chinatown in New York and San Francisco, along with lists of ethnic restaurants and stores. The example of Chinatown, discussed in Box 14.2, is very interesting in this respect; it is an example of how a racialized space that long held negative meanings (opium dens and prostitution) in the popular imagination has been given a positive meaning (an important tourist destination) that has now become part of the city's advertising campaign.

The Revanchist City

When Neil Smith set out to study gentrification in New York in the 1990s, he was struck by the changing political climate that had brought about new laws targeting the homeless, panhandlers, and other groups (Smith, 1999). There were attacks on homeless persons and gays in the streets, and affirmative action and immigration policy was under attack in the courts. Smith coined the term "revanchist city" to describe the new political order. The term comes from the French word *revanche*, which means revenge, but which also has a specific social meaning. *Revanchist* refers to the bourgeois radicals who opposed liberal reforms in the Second Republic and the socialist parties that had put forth women's rights and other social reforms. After the fall of the Second Republic, when the French government surrendered to Prussian forces in the Franco-Prussian War, the people of Paris formed the Paris Commune and refused to turn the city over to the new government. Much of the city was destroyed in the subsequent fighting, and when the Paris Commune was ended, the leaders and their followers were hunted down and a terrible revenge taken: More than 40,000 persons who had defended the city, the enemies of the bourgeois political class, were executed. The *Revanchists* had taken their revenge and restored the conservative political order.

There were similarities, Smith suggested, between the revanchism of nineteenth-century Paris and fin-de-siécle New York City. The liberal climate of the post-1960s had been replaced by paranoia and fear generated by sensational media coverage of immigration, crime, and other hot-button topics. In 1993, Rudolph Giuliani was elected mayor, promising a better quality of life for "conventional members of society." The revanchist policies of the Giuliani administration blamed urban decay on the failures of liberal policy and upon the marginalized populations of the city: Among those identified as major threats to the established order were the homeless, panhandlers, prostitutes, squatters, graffiti artists, squeegee cleaners, and even reckless bicyclists (Slater, 2009). Laws against panhandling, begging, sleeping in the open, and the like were used to remove the homeless from the streets, at the same time that funding for programs for many of the marginalized populations was in decline.

The revanchist city has become very influential in urban studies, but revanchist urban policy was not something entirely new in the United States, nor is it confined to New York City. Metropolitan governments have long imposed harsh penalties on the homeless and other groups who are thought to be threatening to shoppers, commuters, investors, and tourists. Smith's discussion of the revanchist city has been used to describe the 1990s redevelopment of central Glasgow (MacLeod, 2002), the control and management of public spaces in Britain (Atkinson, 2003), and policies directed against Muslims and other ethnic groups in Rotterdam (Uitermark and Duyvendak, 2008).

Even before the economic crisis of the 1990s, there were calls for cuts in spending for social programs of all kinds: With the mounting expenses and growing deficit due to the Iraq War, it would be necessary to cut expenditures for housing, food stamps,

Box 14.3

The Meanest Cities in the United States

While most cities throughout the country have either laws or practices that criminalize homeless persons, some city practices or laws have stood out as more egregious than others in their attempt to criminalize homelessness. The National Coalition for the Homeless and the National Law Center on Homelessness & Poverty have chosen the meanest cities in 2009 based on one or more of the following criteria: the number of anti-homeless laws in the city, the enforcement of those laws and severities of penalties, the general political climate toward homeless people in the city, local advocate support for the meanest designation, the city's history of criminalization measures, and the existence of pending or recently enacted criminalization legislation in the city. Although some of the report's meanest cities have made some efforts to address homelessness in their communities, the punitive practices highlighted in the report impede true progress in solving the problem.

1. Los Angeles
2. St. Petersburg
3. Orlando
4. Atlanta
5. Gainesville
6. Kalamazoo
7. San Francisco
8. Honolulu
9. Bradenton
10. Berkeley

St. Petersburg (ranked second) wasn't even on the list of the twenty meanest communities in 2005, but broke into the top ten in the 2009 listing. Here's why: Since early 2007, St. Petersburg has passed six new ordinances that target homeless people. These include ordinances that outlaw panhandling throughout most of downtown, prohibit the storage of personal belongings on public property, and make it unlawful to sleep outside at various locations. In January 2007, the Pinellas-Pasco public defender announced that he would no longer represent indigent people arrested for violating municipal ordinances to protest what he called excessive arrests of homeless individuals by the city of St. Petersburg. According to numbers compiled by the public defender's office, the vast majority of people booked into the Pinellas County Jail on municipal ordinances were homeless individuals from St. Petersburg.

SOURCE: City Mayors, "Do Not Handcuff the Poor and Homeless," 2009 (http://www.citymayors.com/society/homeless_usa2.html).

and other programs. Similar arguments were made during the 1980s, when high levels of military spending led to increasing deficits; in both instances, Republican administrations used the federal budget crisis as an argument to cut funding for those groups most affected by the declining economy. In earlier chapters, we have noted the increased political activity of groups on the right in periods of economic decline, and we can expect to see much the same in the coming decade as public anger and fear over the declining economy reaches a climax. Revanchist urban policy designed to restore public order and directed against marginalized populations will most likely be an increasing area of study for urban sociologists (Deflem, 2008).

Cyberspace and the Declining Importance of Location

Finally, there is a literature that emphasizes the growth of new technologies and the new information society, resulting in a declining importance of geography and space and, ultimately, of the physical structures of the metropolis. This discussion is connected in some interesting ways to the decline of the public realm: The more time that persons spend online, whether talking with friends, shopping in cyber malls, or trolling websites, the less time they spend participating with fellow citizens in their local community.

Manuel Castells (1998) describes contemporary society as an informational global economy, where the global structure of the world system is based upon a logic of flow, connectivity, networks, and nodes. The core activities of the global economy are linked in real time, and the daily work schedule is now on a planetary scale. While your credit card company may have service lines open from 8:00 a.m. to 8:00 p.m., this means that call operators in India on the other end of the line are working from 8:00 p.m. to 8:00 a.m. on a night shift in their home country. Capital flows in the emerging markets—the urban clusters in Japan and China discussed in Chapters 10 and 11—bypass the corporate headquarters of the West. Global cities are no longer defined by the presence of the corporate headquarters, but by a space of flows.

Castells's view is unsettling. If the new global economy is in fact a system of flows as he describes, there is no longer a geography of spatial location, and social processes will have no particular grounding in the study of cities, suburbs, and metropolitan regions, thereby erasing the importance of urban sociology as a discipline. Clearly, Castells has overstated his case because strategic locations are a necessity for businesses, and the valorization of particular places is exactly how urban landscapes grow. Furthermore, what of all the people left behind by the new global economy? People inhabit lively inner-city neighborhoods, older industrial towns, and growing megacities of the developing world that may not be fully "wired" to the world system but are still connected to it in older ways that have always functioned well for global capitalism in the past—through ordinary trade, manufacture, retailing, and the like located in specific places. A new term has been used to describe the spaces left behind in the new global economy: the Fourth World, but this is clearly no compensation to the millions of people left behind in the empty spaces of Castells's "information economy" (Hutchison, 2009).

Interestingly, it was Karl Marx who wrote that capitalism would destroy space and time by accelerating the production process in the pursuit of profit. This brings us back to the work of Henri Lefebvre, to his concept of the social production of space, the emergence of metropolitan regions, and the origins of the new urban sociology discussed in Chapter 4.

It seems clear that Marx was correct: Modern capitalism has created new technologies that have collapsed time and space; our very casual references to the powerful idea of cyberspace indicate how quickly and pervasively this transformation has taken place. Yet the core of the global economy remains manufacturing, as Marx also asserted, even if people in the United States only have the vaguest ideas of how that key process plays itself out in the obscure regions of China, India, Southeast Asia, and Latin America. The important challenge for urban sociology, of course, is whether the information economy makes the metropolitan region irrelevant.

There is a growing body of literature arguing that urban spaces are still important. Even if we place an online order for goods produced in a country in a different part of the world through Internet shopping, the places where the goods are manufactured are grounded in time and space, as are the locations where the goods are stored and shipped. This suggests that we need to base our understanding of the spaces of flows within those areas where productive activity and social reproduction occur; in other words, we are still interested in specific spatial locations and in the everyday lives of persons who live in multinucleated metropolitan regions of developed as well as developing nations. But it also seems clear that the city, as a physical entity, is less and less relevant as the metropolitan region expands and the new information technologies link nodes of activity across these metropolitan spaces. Louis Wirth would likely struggle to reconceptualize how size, density, and heterogeneity would inform our analysis of the urban world of the twenty-first century!

URBAN STRUCTURE AND URBAN CULTURE

In *Urban Sociology: Images and Structure*, William Flanagan (2010) divides the field of urban sociology into what he labels the culturalist approach and the structuralist approach. In general terms, what Flanagan means by the culturalist approach is the human ecology of the Chicago School and the later development of urban ecology by Amos Hawley, John Kasarda, and others. We have referred to this as the mainstream urban sociology of the past. Under the structuralist approach, Flanagan includes urban political economy, world systems theory, and the related areas of study that began with the revolt against mainstream urban sociology in the 1970s. These theoretical models are structural because they emphasize the importance of social structure (and in some cases, the role of the state) in determining urban development and social interaction within the urban environment. The theoretical models Flanagan identifies under the structuralist approach would view urbanization as a result of factors outside the metropolitan region, whereas the culturalist approach would study urbanization by focusing on factors within the metropolitan region.

As we saw in Chapter 3, the work of the Chicago School of urban sociology was very diverse in subject matter and research methodology, and we drew a sharp distinction between the famous studies by the students of Robert Park and Ernest Burgess referred to as the Chicago School of Urban Sociology (which reflected the ideas of human ecology) and the later applications of human ecology in the work of Roderick McKenzie, Amos Hawley, and others (which we refer to as urban ecology). Flanagan also includes the tradition of community studies, including the work of Robert and Helen Lynd (*Middletown* and *Middletown in Transition*), Herbert Gans (*The Urban Villagers* and *The Levittowners*), and others under the culturalist approach.

In Chapter 4, we described the emergence of a new urban sociology in the work of Henri Lefebvre (*The Production of Space, Critique of Everyday Life*) and others in the 1960s. This also is a diverse area of study, including the Marxist urban sociology of Manuel Castells (*The Urban Question, The City and the Grassroots*), David Harvey (*Social Justice and the City*), the urban growth model of Logan and Molotch (*Urban Fortunes: The Political Economy of Place*), and the like. This work has now merged in what we refer to as the sociospatial model of urban development.

In the final chapter of *Urban Sociology: Images and Structure*, William Flanagan suggests that there is a new unified perspective for urban sociology. The competing models of the past may not have merged into a single model, according to this view, but it seems clear that neither the culturalist approach nor the structuralist approach can adequately explain recent developments in the urban world. The culturalist perspective focuses on events within neighborhoods (community studies) or the city (urban ecology), but it does not place the everyday lives of individuals within the new global society. The research methodology and theoretical models that are used by urban sociologists following the culturalist approach do not make the necessary link between daily life in the metropolis and the larger urban structures that connect persons around the world in the twenty-first century.

The structuralist approach, on the other hand, focuses attention on the global system of capitalism and on the political economy of urban life at the national and sometimes metropolitan level. This approach is necessary for understanding the development of the world urban system, and it helps to explain patterns of economic development and urban change within and across nation states. The importance of this perspective is obvious if we want to understand how environmental policies in the developed nations have led to the migration of industrial jobs to developing nations by companies that do not want to comply, or how the new global economy has created the "dual city" pattern of high technology coupled with a growing service sector in cities in the developed nations. What the structuralist approach cannot do, according to Flanagan, is help us understand the impact of these changes on the everyday lives of persons in cities and metropolitan regions across the world.

Flanagan suggests that a unified perspective for urban sociology will result in a better understanding of both the structural forces that have created our new urban world and the impact of these changes on the lives of individuals in the growing urban agglomerations that now account for more than half of the world's population. The structuralist approach is essential for understanding the powerful forces of global capitalism that have swept across the globe, creating a new urban world in its image. In this new world of growing social inequality and troubling exploitation of the world's diminishing resources, future generations will most likely live in larger and larger urban agglomerations, in a built environment that is far removed from the urban-rural world that our grandparents knew. To understand the new modalities of urban life—whether it be in older metropolises of Europe with urban histories stretching back hundreds of years or the newer and larger megacities of the developing world—we will need the ethnographic accounts and community studies of the culturalist approach.

Flanagan's argument concerning the need of a unified perspective for urban sociology is reasonable. While urban sociology may have started from a common point of applying the European tradition (represented by the work of Töennies and Simmel) to the circumstances of the industrial city at the close of the nineteenth century, the field has become increasingly eclectic. Recent work in what is known as cultural studies offers us glimpses into the lives of persons around the world and emphasizes the ways in which global urban cultures have developed as our world shrinks and our lives become more dependent on other groups and other cultures. At the same time, we know that although there are differences from one area of the world to another and that there are distinctive urban cultures because of historical traditions, religion, and the like, the emerging urban metropolis of the twenty-first century shares some important characteristics regardless of country or region. It is not simply that they are linked with one another in the ever-expanding system of global capitalism. Most importantly, these urban agglomerations increasingly look like the multicentered urban region studied by the sociospatial perspective.

THE FUTURE OF THE CITY

In an earlier work on comparative urbanization, Ivan Light published a drawing from ancient Sumer showing the destruction of a city, with the caption, *The City as an Eternal Death Trap*. This is one view of the urban future, something that we are familiar with from films such as *Blade Runner*, *Logan's Run*, *Robocop*, and *Escape from New York*. The fragility of urban life was brought home to Americans by the great tragedy of 9/11. This event was followed by discussion among urbanists about the future of high-rise buildings—who would want to work or live in one of them? (Interestingly, the three tallest buildings in the world have been built *after* 9/11!)

The apocalyptic view of the urban future is not entirely new, of course. Whether this is depicted as the destruction of the city by divine wrath or by nuclear warfare, human populations have long feared for the survival of the city—the creation that Lewis Mumford considered the greatest achievement of mankind. More recently urban theorists have added to this bleak vision, as we saw above, with prophecies that the city would wither away because of new communication technologies. We know that this is unlikely to happen: While the Internet exists in unbounded space, it requires a concentration of resources in research and development and manufacturing, and while these services and production nodes may be located in different countries, or more likely dispersed across a metropolitan region, they are still grounded in physical space. The idea of urban clusters that have been used so successfully in promoting industrial development and controlling urban growth in China appears to be an appropriate metaphor for this new arrangement of activities across the urban region.

In earlier chapters we have described the multicentered urban region as characteristic of suburban growth in the United States (Chapter 6). As we know from looking at urbanization in the developed nations of the UK and the European Union, this pattern of development is not unique to the United States, and in fact has a long history in both regions. Other terms have been used in other countries—patchwork urbanism in the UK (MacLeod and Ward, 2002), polycentric urban development in the EU (Kloosterman and Musterd, 2001; Parr, 2004)—but the pattern of development is similar to that that found in the United States. While there is room for great concern about the conditions of urban life for persons in the growing slums and vast megacities of the developing world (Chapter 11), the city is not likely to disappear in the foreseeable future. Nor is it likely that the multicentered metropolitan region will be altered by the planning of new urbanism or other policies intended to regenerate the city, and should we return to the future, we most likely will encounter multicentered urban regions very similar to what we see now in the developed nations. So how can we best study the multicentered metropolitan region of the future?

Box 14.4

Report from the 2030 Ideal Home Exhibition

The Ideal Home Exhibition has historically reflected the housing preferences of a substantial proportion of the population, more accurately than the visions of architects and planners. In particular, the exhibition has reflected and perhaps encouraged the trend towards suburbanization that has been a major shaper of the urban and rural landscapes throughout the twentieth century. In this report from the 2030 Exhibition, the trend is shown to have continued, despite the attempts of architects, planners, and politicians to stimulate an "Urban Renaissance."

continues

Box 14.4 *continued*

The suburban ideal, which has been the mainstay of this exhibition since its founding at the beginning of the twentieth century, maintains its appeal. And whilst the model of the suburban house evolves over time, its image of brick walls and pitched roofs with sprinklings of fake half-timbering or rustic weather-boarding remains, in essence, unchanged. Architects have never been comfortable with the success of these houses. And social trends are at issue here, for the appearance of houses says much about the values, hopes, and aspirations of the people who choose to live in them. In the case of the majority of houses shown in the Ideal Home Exhibition, the values expressed are not much liked by architects.

This year's exhibition shows us that despite the great social, environmental, and technological changes we have witnessed over the last twenty years, little has changed in the aspirations and values of Middle England. Despite the pressures of environmental ideology and the exorbitant cost of land and housing, Middle England continues to yearn for the house surrounded by a bit of garden in a landscape, which, in the mind's eye at least, is still bucolic. This has meant that the trend towards urban sprawl and the suburban ideal that many predicted, again perhaps through a little too much wishful thinking, would disappear, is still going strong. And the so-called Urban Renaissance which many architects and urbanists hoped for twenty years ago, has, with the exception of London and a few trendy spots in the northern cities, largely failed to materialise.

One of the consequences of the increasing social polarisation caused by the ever-growing gap between rich and poor is an increase in the process of suburbanization. This 'white flight,' mirroring that which took place in the latter years of the last century in the cities of the United States, began with the middle-class abandonment of inner-city schools, which, at the beginning of the century, were becoming increasingly dominated by immigrant groups, for many of whom English was a second language. However this flight has not only been white. Discrimination against new immigrant groups, made up of illegal economic migrants and environmental refugees, is unfortunately still with us. But going hand-in-hand with this has been a greater acceptance and assimilation of existing immigrant groups who became established, at or before the turn of the last century, into the new citadels of Middle England.

In many ways, it is difficult to maintain the idea that twenty-first century suburbia is suburban in the twentieth century sense at all. The distinction between the urban and the suburban has always been ambiguous. But the transformation of the suburban into the urban has, in the past, been predicated on the annexing of the suburb by the expanding city. In 2023, as cities in the developed world (in marked contrast to those in the developing world) decrease in size, the suburban centres have become more and more physically estranged from the urban centres to which they were once inextricably linked.

continues

Today, the so-called suburban centres have no need to relate to a larger centre at all. The increased tendency to work from home, for people to grow their own food, and even keep animals in their suburban gardens, has reduced the need for a relationship with the city. People living in the suburbs can nowadays find most of what they immediately need within walking distance. What they can't get near to home, they, or their domestic appliances, can order electronically.

Only thirty years ago, those who found themselves contemplating the birth of the Internet age and other new technologies of communication would have found it difficult to imagine that future communities would be like this. For that generation, electronic communication was the force that would bring people together. We were going to be one great "Global Village," not a million little ones. A less predictable consequence of the electronic revolution of the late-twentieth century has been the gradual rebellion against electronic culture. Not that people don't engage with it. On the contrary, the amount of transactions, whether emotional, social, or business, that are carried out electronically or virtually, without any form of human contact, has never been higher. But because of this, people tend to yearn for human contact and seek it out in their communities.

Young people today who have never known a world where public services existed would no doubt be amused to learn that things like transport, health, and education were once provided by local government and other agents of the state. But the communities they live in today might have been very different if past governments had succeeded in delivering their promises on improved public services. Had that happened, perhaps we would have been living in the results of the 'Urban Renaissance' that was much-heralded twenty or so years ago.

SOURCE: Sean Griffiths, *Back to the Future: Staying with the Suburban Ideal,* 2004.

THE FUTURE OF THE URBAN INQUIRY

For many urbanists, analyzing metropolitan phenomena involves a choice between the competing paradigms of human ecology and political economy. While human ecology has been useful because it appreciates the role location plays in social interaction, it under-theorizes this role and adopts one-dimensional, technologically deterministic explanations for sociospatial processes. In contrast, the political-economy approach deals with many important concepts and issues that ecology neglects, such as the role of capital and class in the urban drama. It too is limited, however, because it neglects aspects of culture and politics that cannot be reduced to class phenomena. Unfortunately it also ignores the important features of spatial relations by considering location merely as a container for economic processes.

By adopting the sociospatial perspective, we move beyond the limitations of political economy to explain how the built environment changes and develops. The narrow focus on the restructuring of global capitalism cannot alone explain the changes experienced by metropolitan development in the twenty-first century. Once spatial patterns are altered in one region of the metropolis, this change affects all other parts not just of the metropolis, but also of other cities in the regional as well as national and even international hierarchy of urban regions. The missing element is supplied by a focus on real estate interests as the leading edge of change that channels growth in specific directions. Hence, social space operates as both a product and a producer of changes in the metropolitan environment.

The ecological and political-economy perspectives both assume that the state has only a weak role as an agent of change. Human ecology simply ignores government intervention. Too often, political economists have treated the state as simply the direct agent of capitalist interests. The involvement of the state in sociospatial development of urban space within and across metropolitan regions is both critical and complex. First, government policies help provide the "pull" factors of growth. Second, they are the focus of urban and suburban social movements that aim for a redistribution of both wealth and social costs. Third, government officials are relatively autonomous agents who do not simply follow the needs of capital alone but pursue interests of their own to bring about social change. Finally, national policies of taxation and spending transfer wealth from one region of the country to another; hence, programs such as military spending are critical causes of regional growth or decline, in addition to private-sector investment patterns. As we have seen demonstrated in a variety of contexts, private- and public-sector efforts often work hand in hand.

The sociospatial perspective utilizes a semiotic approach to understand how culture and ideology define sociospatial processes, such as the appeal to progress and modernism in urban renewal or the use of religious belief to structure the ancient cities of the past. The sociospatial approach considers all built environments as meaningful social spaces. Behavior occurs within these social spaces, but our own behavior may change the meaning and use of that space. The sociospatial approach further captures the special articulation between territory and culture that produces lifestyle networks and variation in daily community life within the metropolis. Ethnic, gender-oriented, or racially defined lifestyles enact themselves within the built environment. The street corner, the mall, the coffee house, the local bar, the school cafeteria, and the commuter train, car, or bus are all special venues where social networks interact.

Finally, the sociospatial perspective takes an integrated view of the multicentered metropolitan region. We have considered both urban and suburban settlement space. The traditional field of urban sociology possessed too narrow a focus on the central city. Urban texts invariably treat suburbs only in a special chapter devoted to that purpose, while the remainder of the text specializes in the study of the large central city, even though a majority of population, employment, and business activity is located within expanding metropolitan environments. Urban or suburban concerns are largely metropolitan concerns, and any governmental efforts should begin from a regional rather than a local perspective.

The future of the metropolitan inquiry will require important conceptual changes. In place of the traditional urban sociology, we should have a field called the "sociology of settlement space" that would deal with all forms of human settlement—towns, cities, suburbs, metropolises, the multicentered region, and the megalopolis—so that we no longer privilege the city as the sole urban form of space. In place of a contentious and often confusing clash of different paradigms (ecology for aggregate data analysis, political economy for economic issues, and the culturalist approach for ethnography), we can look forward to integrated discussions at all levels (micro, macro, and meso) following the synthesis of the sociospatial approach. Finally, by critically evaluating the planning efforts of the present and requiring them to recognize the importance of space, we have a means by which we can construct and live in a more humane and enjoyable environment that confronts, rather than hides from, the seemingly intractable issues of environmental, representational, and social justice.

KEY CONCEPTS

cultural approach
cyberspace
globalization
world system theory
world city
racialization of urban space
revanchist city
theming
information society
space of flows
multicentered metropolitan region
structural approach

IMPORTANT NAMES

Manuel Castells
Saskia Sassen

DISCUSSION QUESTIONS

1. What is the relationship between world systems theory and globalization? How did these concepts develop? Have you encountered them in other courses or books

that you have read? How is the use of these terms in urban sociology different from their presentation in other courses?

2. What is the relationship between world cities and global cities? What are some of the factors that might be used to determine whether a city might be included in a list of global cities? Why do the authors critique the recent emphasis on the global city in urban sociology?

3. What is meant by the racialization of space? How is this concept linked to some of the basic propositions of the sociospatial perspective presented in Chapter 1? Can you think of examples of the racialization of space in the community where you grew up?

4. What is meant by "theming" of the urban environment? What examples are given in the chapter? Can you think of other examples of theming in commercial development in your community? In new residential development or in the redevelopment of older neighborhoods of your community?

5. Manuel Castells's work on the new information society and the space of flows might lead some to suggest that cities are no longer important. What do you think of this argument? How would you critique Castells's argument using the concept of the multinuclear metropolitan region and sociospatial theory more generally?

6. What is meant by the revanchist city? Where did the term originate? Can you identify events or policies within your own community that might be included in this discussion of the revanchist city?

BIBLIOGRAPHY

Abrahamson, M. 2004. *Global Cities.* New York: Oxford University Press.

Abrahamson, P. 1988. *Welfare States in Crisis: The Crumbling of the Scandinavian Model.* Copenhagen: Forlaget Sociologi.

Abrams, C. 1965. *The City Is the Frontier.* New York: Harper & Row.

_____. 1966. Report to the U.S. Agency for International Development. Washington, DC: Department of Housing and Urban Development.

_____. 1977. "Squatting and Squatters." In *Third World Urbanization,* edited by J. Abu-Lughod and R. Hay Jr., 293–300. Chicago: Maaroufa Press.

Abu-Lughod, J. 1969. "Testing the Theory of Social Area Analysis: The Ecology of Cairo, Egypt." *American Sociological Review* 34 (April): 313–343.

Adams, C. 1986. "Homelessness in the Postindustrial City." *Urban Affairs Quarterly* 21: 527–549.

Aina, T. 1990. "Shanty Town Economy: The Case of Metropolitan Lagos, Nigeria." In *Third World Urbanization: Reappraisals and New Perspectives,* edited by S. Datta, 113–148. Stockholm: National Research Center of the Humanities and the Social Sciences.

Alicea, M. 1990. "Dual Home Bases: A Reconceptualization of Puerto Rican Migration." *Latino Studies Journal* 1 (3):78–98.

Alihan, M. 1938. *Social Ecology: A Critical Analysis; Ideological and Interest Group Barriers to Reform.* New York: Columbia University Press.

Allen, O. 1990. *New York, New York: A History of the World's Most Exhilarating and Challenging City.* New York: Atheneum.

Anderson, E. 1978. *A Place on the Corner.* Chicago: University of Chicago Press.

_____. 1990. *Streetwise: Race, Class, and Change in an Urban Community.* Chicago: University of Chicago Press.

_____. 1999. *Code of the Street: Decency, Violence, and the Moral Life of the Inner City.* New York: W. W. Norton.

AP/Huffington Post. 2009. "Four Years After Katrina: The State of New Orleans," August 28, http://www.huffingtonpost.com/2009/08/28/four-years-after-katrina_n _270944.html.

Applebome, P. 1991. "Although Urban Blight Worsens, Most People Don't Feel Its Impact." *New York Times,* January 28, sec. A.

Arax, M. 1987. "Monterey Park: Nation's First Suburban Chinatown." *Los Angeles Times*, April 6.

Armstrong, R. 1972. *The Office Industry: Patterns of Growth and Location.* Cambridge, MA: MIT Press.

———. 1979. "National Trends in Office Construction, Employment and Headquarters Location in the United States Metropolitan Areas." In *Spatial Patterns of Office Growth and Location*, edited by P. Daniels, 61–94. New York: John Wiley and Sons.

Atkinson, R. 2003. "Domestication by Cappuccino or a Revenge on Urban Space? Control and Empowerment in the Management of Public Spaces." *Urban Studies* 40, no. 9: 1829–1843.

Bachrach, P., and M. Baratz. 1962. "Two Faces of Power." *American Political Science Review* 56: 947–952.

Bacon, E. N. 1967. *Design of Cities.* New York: Viking Press.

Bairoch, P., J. Batou, and P. Chèvre, 1988. *La Population des Villes Européenes de 800 à 1850.* Geneva: Librarie Droz.

Ball, K., and F. Webster, eds. 2003. *The Intensification of Surveillance: Crime, Terrorism, and Warfare in the Information Era.* London: Pluto Press.

Baltzell, E. 1989. *Philadelphia Gentleman: The Making of a National Upper Class.* New Brunswick, NJ: Transaction Press.

Banfield, E. 1974. *The Unheavenly City Revisited.* Boston: Little, Brown.

Baran, P., and P. Sweezy. 1966. *Monopoly Capital.* New York: Monthly Review Press.

Barbanel, J. 1992. "Robberies on the Rise on Long Island." *New York Times*, February 18, sec. A.

Barnekov, T., and D. Rich. 1989. "Privatism and the Limits of Local Economic Development Policy." *Urban Affairs Quarterly* 25: 212–238.

Barnes, J. 1954. "Class and Committees in a Norwegian Island Parish." *Human Relations* 7: 39–58.

———. 1972. *Social Networks.* Addison Wesley Modular Publications, Number 26.

Barone, C. 1983. "Dependency, Marxist Theory, and Salvaging the Idea of Capitalism in South Korea." *Review of Radical Political Economy* 15, no. 1: 43–67.

Barthes, R. 1973. *L'Empire des Signes.* Geneva: Albert Skira.

———. 1986. "Semiology and the Urban." In *The City and the Sign*, edited by M. Gottdiener and A. Lagopoulos, 87–98. New York: Columbia University Press.

Battaglia, T. 2010. "Detroit Cops Look for Car After Body Found." *Detroit Free Press*, January 19.

Baudrillard, J. 1981. *The Political Economy of the Sign.* St. Louis, MO: Telos Press.

———. 1993. *Simulation and Simulacra.* Ann Arbor, MI: University of Michigan Press.

Baumgartner, M. 1988. *The Moral Order of a Suburb.* Oxford: Oxford University Press.

Bean, F., and M. Tienda. 1987. *The Hispanic Population of the US.* New York: Russell Sage Foundation.

Benard, D., and E. Schlaffer. 1993. "'The Man in the Street': Why He Harasses." In *Feminist Frontiers III*, edited by L. Richardson and V. Taylor, 338–391. New York: McGraw-Hill.

Berger, B. 1960. *Working Class Suburb.* Berkeley: University of California Press.

Berman, M. 1981. *All That Is Solid Melts into Air: The Experience of Modernity.* New York: Simon & Schuster.

Bernard, R., and B. Rice. 1983. *Sunbelt Cities: Politics and Growth Since World War II.* Austin: University of Texas Press.

Berry, B., ed. 1977. *The Social Burden of Environmental Pollution.* Cambridge, MA: Ballinger Publishing Co.

Berry, B., and J. Kasarda. 1977. *Contemporary Urban Ecology.* New York: Macmillan.

Berry, B., and P. Rees. 1969. "The Factorial Ecology of Calcutta." *American Journal of Sociology* 74: 445–491.

Berry, M. 1989. "Industrialization, De-industrialization and Uneven Development: The Case of the Pacific Rim." In *Capitalist Development and Crisis Theory,* edited by M. Gottdiener and N. Komninos, 171–216. New York and London: Macmillan.

Bestor, T. 1985. *Japanese Urban Life.* Palo Alto: Stanford University Press.

Binnie, J. 1995. "Trading Places: Consumption, Sexuality, and the Production of Queer Space." In D. Bell and G. Valentine, eds., *Mapping Desire,* 182–199. London and New York: Routledge.

Blake, W. 1977. "London." In *Songs of Innocence and of Experience,* 150. New York: Oxford University Press.

Blakely, E., and M. Snyder. 1997. *Fortress America: Gated Communities in the United States.* Washington, DC: Brookings Institution.

Blau, J. 1992. *The Visible Poor: Homelessness in the United States.* New York: Oxford University Press.

Bluestone, B., and B. Harrison. 1982. *The Deindustrialization of America: Plant Closings, Community Abandonment, and the Dismantling of Basic Industry.* New York: Basic Books.

Blum, B. 1978. *Cities: An Environmental Wilderness.* Washington, DC: Environmental Protection Agency.

Blumer, M. 1984. *The Chicago School of Sociology: Institutionalization, Diversity, and the Rise of Sociological Research.* Chicago: University of Chicago Press.

Bobrowski, L. 1998. *Collecting, Organizing, and Reporting Street Gang Crime.* Chicago: Chicago Police Department, Special Functions Group.

Body-Gendrot, S. 1987. "Plant Closures in Socialist France." In *The Capitalist City,* edited by M. Smith and J. Feagin, 237–251. Oxford: Blackwell.

Boer, L. 1990. "(In)formalization: The Forces Beyond." *International Journal of Urban and Regional Research* 14: 404–422.

Boix, R., and P. Veneri. 2009. *Metropolitan Areas in Spain and Italy.* Barcelona: Institut d'Estudis Regionals I Metropolitans de Barcelona, IERMB Working Paper in Economics, No. 901.

Bollens, J., and H. Schmandt. 1965. *The Metropolis: Its People, Politics, and Economic Life.* New York: Harper & Row.

Bookchin, M. 1974. *The Limits of the City.* New York: Harper & Row.

———. 1990. *The Philosophy of Social Ecology: Essays on Dialectical Naturalism.* Montreal: Black Rose Books.

Booth, C. 1891. *Life and Labor of the People in London.* London: Williams and Norgate.

Borchert, J. 1967. "American Metropolitan Evolution." *Geographical Review* 57: 301–332.

Bordain, I. 1999. "Speaking the City: Skateboarding, Subculture, and Recomposition of the Urban Realm." In *Research in Urban Sociology*, Vol. 5, edited by R. Hutchison, 135–154. Greenwich, CT: JAI Press.

Bordini, G. 1588. Plan of Rome, *De redus praeclaris gestis a Sixto V p.m.*, 48.

Bositis, D. 2003. *Black Elected Officials: A Statistical Summary 2001.* Washington, DC: Joint Center for Political and Economic Studies.

Bott, E. 1971 [1957]. *Family and Social Network.* New York: Free Press [London: Tavistock].

Boudon, P. 1986. "Rewriting of a City: The Medina of Tunis." In *The City and the Sign*, edited by M. Gottdiener and A. Lagopoulos, 303–322. New York: Columbia University Press.

Bourne, L., and J. Simmons, eds. 1978. *Systems of Cities: Readings on Structure, Growth, and Policy.* New York: Oxford University Press.

Boyte, H. 1980. *The Backyard Revolution: Understanding the New Citizens Movement.* Philadelphia: Temple University Press.

Bradshaw, Y., and E. Fraser. 1989. "City Size, Economic Development, and Quality of Life in China: New Empirical Evidence." *American Sociological Review* 54: 986–1003.

Brandow, M. 2008. *New York's Poop Scoop Law: Dogs, the Dirt, and Due Process.* West Lafayette, IN: Purdue University Press.

Braudel, F. 1973. *Capitalism and Material Life: 1400–1800.* New York: Harper & Row.

Brenner, N., and N. Theodore, eds. 2003. *Spaces of Neoliberalism: Urban Restructuring in North America and Western Europe.* New York: Wiley-Blackwell.

Brinkerhoff, T. 2010. *Principal Agglomerations of the World*, http://www.citypopulation .de/world/Agglomerations.html.

Brooker, D. 2009. "Technoburb." In *Encyclopedia of Urban Studies*, edited by R. Hutchison. Thousand Oaks, CA: SAGE Publications.

Buck, N., and I. Gordon. 2003. *Working Capital.* Oxford: Blackwell.

Bullard, R. 1990. *Dumping in Dixie: Race, Class, and Environmental Quality.* Boulder, CO: Westview Press.

Bullard, R., and J. Feagin. 1991. "Racism and the City." In *Urban Life in Transition*, edited by M. Gottdiener and C. Pickvance, 55–76. Thousand Oaks, CA: SAGE Publications.

Burgess, E. 1925. "The Growth of the City: An Introduction to a Research Project." In *The City*, edited by R. Park, E. Burgess, and R. McKenzie, 47–62. Chicago: University of Chicago Press.

Calthorpe, P., and W. Fulton. 2001. *The Regional City: Planning for the End of Sprawl.* Washington, DC: Island Press.

Castells, M. 1977. *The Urban Question.* Cambridge, MA: MIT Press.

_____. 1983. *The City and the Grass Roots.* Berkeley and Los Angeles: University of California Press.

_____. 1989. *The Informational City.* Oxford: Blackwell.

_____. 1998. *The Rise of the Network Society.* New York: Blackwell.

Castells, M., and P. Hall. 1994. *Technopoles of the World: The Making of Twenty-First-Century Industrial Complexes.* London and New York: Routledge.

Cavan, R. 1928. *Suicide.* Chicago: University of Chicago Press.

Chambers, I. 1986. *Popular Culture: The Metropolitan Experience.* London: Methuen.

Chase-Dunn, C. 1985. "The System of World Cities, AD 800–1975." In *Urbanization in the World Economy*, edited by M. Timberlake, 269–292. Orlando, FL: Academic Press.

Chatterton, P., and R. Hollands. 2003. *Urban Nightscapes: Youth Cultures, Pleasure Spaces and Corporate Power.* London and New York: Routledge.

Chen, X. 1988. "Giant Cities and the Urban Hierarchy in China." In *The Metropolis Era*, Vol. 1, edited by M. Dogan and J. Kasarda, 225–251. Thousand Oaks, CA: SAGE Publications.

Childe, V. 1950. "The Urban Revolution." *Town Planning Review* 21: 4–17.

————. 1954. *What Happened in History.* New York: Penguin Books.

China Rises: A Documentary in Four Parts. 2006. Toronto: Canadian Broadcasting System. Morningstar Entertainment Inc.

Choe, S. 1996. "The Evolving Urban System in North-East Asia." In *Emerging World Cities in Pacific Asia*, edited by F. Lo and Y. Yeung. Tokyo: United Nations University Press, http://www.unu.edu/unupress/unupbooks/uu11ee/uu11ee00.htm#Contents.

————. 1998. "Urban Corridors in Pacific Asia." In *Globalization and the World of Large Cities*, edited by F. Lo and Y. Yeung, 155–173. Tokyo: United Nations University Press.

City Mayors. 2009. "Do Not Handcuff the Poor and Homeless," http://www.citymayors .com/society/homeless_usa2.html.

City Mayors. 2009. "Swiss and German Cities Dominate Top Places of Best Cities in the World," http://www.citymayors.com/features/quality_survey.html.

Clapson, M. 2003. *Suburban Century: Social Change and Urban Growth in England and the USA.* Oxford: Berg Publishers.

Clavel, P. 1985. *The Progressive City: Planning and Participation, 1969–1984.* New Brunswick, NJ: Rutgers University Press.

Cleaver, H. 1989. "Close the IMF, Abolish Debt, and End Development: A Class Analysis of the International Debt Crisis." *Capital and Class* 39: 17–50.

Cochrane, A. 1982. *Patterns of Urban Development.* Unit 29, Block 7. Milton Keynes, UK: Open University Press.

Cook County Clerk's Office. 2009. *TIFs 101: A Taxpayer's Primer for Understanding TIFs*, http://www.cookctyclerk.com/tsd/tifs/Pages/TIFs101.aspx.

Cooper, F. 1987. *On the African Waterfront: Urban Disorders and the Transformation of Work in Colonial Mombasa.* New Haven, CT: Yale University Press.

Coquery-Vidrovitch, C. 1990. "A History of African Urbanization: Labor, Women, and the Informal Sector: A Survey of Recent Studies." In *Third World Urbanization: Reappraisals and New Perspectives*, edited by S. Datta, 75–89. Stockholm: National Research Center of the Humanities and the Social Sciences.

Cortés, H. 1520. Second Letter to Charles V. Modern History Sourcebook, http://www .fordham.edu/halsall/mod/1520cortes.html.

Coser, L. 1971. *Masters of Sociological Thought: Ideas in Social and Historical Context.* Orlando: Harcourt Brace Jovanovich.

Coughlin, R. 1979. "Agricultural Land Conversion in the Urban Fringe." In *Farmlands, Food, and the Future*, edited by M. Schept. Ankeny, IA: Soil Conservation Society of America.

Crary, D. 2005. "Private Prisons Experience Business Surge." *Associated Press*, July 31.

Cressey, P. 1932. *The Taxi-Dance Hall: A Sociological Study in Commercialized Recreation and City Life*. Chicago: University of Chicago Press.

———. 1956. "The Ecological Organization of Rangoon, Burma." *Sociology and Social Research* 40: 166–169.

Crump, S. 1962. *Ride the Big Red Cars: How Trolleys Helped Build Southern California*. Los Angeles: Crest Publications.

Dale, A., and C. Banford. 1989. "Social Polarization in Britain: 1973–1982, Evidence from the General Household Survey." *International Journal of Urban and Regional Research* 13: 482–494.

Darley, J., and B. Latane. 1970. *The Unresponsive Bystander: Why Doesn't He Help?* New York: Appleton-Century-Crofts.

Datta, S. 1990. *Third World Urbanization: Reappraisals and New Perspectives*. Stockholm: HSFR.

Davis, M. 1986. *Prisoners of the American Dream: Politics and Economy in the History of the U.S. Working Class*. London: Verso.

———. 1987. "Chinatown, Part Two? The Internationalization of Downtown Los Angeles." *New Left Review* 164: 65–84.

———. 1990. *City of Quartz: Excavating the Future in Los Angeles*. New York: Verso.

———. 2007. *Planet of Slums*. London: Verso.

Davis, R., and G. Marvin. 2004. *Venice, the Tourist Maze: A Cultural Critique of the World's Most Touristed City*. Berkeley: University of California Press.

Deegan, M. 2007. "The Chicago School of Ethnography." In *Handbook of Ethnography*, edited by P. Atkinson, S. Delamont, A. Coffey, J. Lofland, and L. Lofland, 11–25. Thousand Oaks, CA: SAGE Publications.

Deflem, M., ed. 2008. *Surveillance and Governance: Crime Control and Beyond*. London: Emerald Book Group.

Defoe, D. 1722. *A Journal of the Plague Year*. Reprint, New York: Penguin.

DeLong, J., and A. Shleifer. 1993. "Princes and Merchants: City Growth Before the Industrial Revolution." *Journal of Law and Economics* 36: 671–702.

Diaz, D. 2005. *Barrio Urbanism: Chicanos, Planning and American Cities*. London and New York: Routledge.

DiSilvestro, F., and B. Schweke. 2008. *Business Incentives and North Carolina's Tier 1 Counties: Have They Worked?* Washington, DC: Corporation for Economic Development.

Dogan, M., and J. Kasarda, eds. 1988. *The Metropolis Era*, 2 Vols. Thousand Oaks, CA: SAGE Publications.

Douglas, M. 1988. "Transnational Capital and Urbanization on the Pacific Rim: An Introduction." *International Journal of Urban and Regional Research* 12: 343–355.

Drake, S. 1983. "The Tuskegee Connection: Booker T. Washington and Robert E. Park." *Society* 20: 82–92.

Drake, S., and H. Cayton. 1945. *Black Metropolis: A Study of Negro Life in a Northern City*. New York: Harcourt Brace.

DuBois, W. E. B. 1899. *The Philadelphia Negro*. Philadelphia: University of Pennsylvania Press.

Duranton, G., and D. Puga. 2005. "From Sectoral to Functional Urban Specialization." *Journal of Urban Economics* 57: 343–370.

Durkheim, E. 1933. *The Division of Labor in Society.* Translated by George Simpson. Glencoe, IL: Free Press. First published in 1893.

Dutton, T. 1989. "Cities, Cultures, and Resistance: Beyond Leon Krier and the Postmodern Condition." *Journal of Architectural Education*, 42: 3–9.

Eckholm, E. 2009. "Surge in Homeless Pupils Strains Schools." *New York Times*, September 6, http://www.nytimes.com/2009/09/06/education/06homeless.html?_r=1.

The Economist. 1990. "Toronto and Detroit: Canadians Do It Better," May 19, 17–20.

Egan, T. 2005. "Vibrant Cities Find One Thing Missing: Children." *New York Times*, March 24.

Ehrenreich, B. 1990. *Fear of Falling: The Inner Life of the Middle Class.* New York: HarperCollins.

Eisenstadt, S., and A. Shachar. 1987. *Society, Culture, and Urbanization.* Thousand Oaks, CA: SAGE Publications.

Engels, F. 1973. *The Condition of the Working Class in England: From Personal Observations and Authentic Sources.* Moscow: Progress Publishers.

Espiritu, Y., and I. Light. 1991. "The Changing Ethnic Shape of Contemporary Urban America." In *Urban Life in Transition*, edited by M. Gottdiener and C. Pickvance, 35–54. Thousand Oaks, CA: SAGE Publications.

Euripides, *The Trojan Women.* http://classics.mit.edu/Euripides/troj_women.html.

Fagan, J. 1990. "Social Processes of Delinquency and Drug Use Among Urban Gangs." In *Gangs in America*, edited by R. Huff, 183–219. Thousand Oaks, CA: SAGE Publications.

Faris, R. 1970. *Chicago Sociology, 1920–32.* Chicago: University of Chicago Press.

Farley, R., and W. Allen. 1987. *The Color Line and the Quality of Life in America.* New York: Russell Sage Foundation.

Farrell, C. 2008. "Bifurcation, Fragmentation, or Integration? The Racial and Geographical Structure of U.S. Metropolitan Segregation, 1990–2000." *Urban Studies* 45, no. 3: 467–499.

Fava, S. 1980. "Women's Place in the New Suburbia." In *New Space for Women*, edited by G. Wekerle, R. Peterson, and D. Morley, 125–149. Boulder, CO: Westview Press.

Feagin, J. 1983. *The Urban Real Estate Game: Playing Monopoly with Real Money.* Englewood Cliffs, NJ: Prentice-Hall.

———. 1988. *Houston: The Free Enterprise City.* New Brunswick, NJ: Rutgers University Press.

———. 1992. "Why Not Study the American 'Overclass'?" *Contemporary Sociology* 21, no. 4: 449–451.

Feagin, J., and M. Smith. 1987. "Cities and the New International Division of Labor: An Overview." In *The Capitalist City*, 3–36. Oxford: Blackwell.

Fernandez-Kelly, M. 1991. "Labor Force Recomposition and Industrial Restructuring in Electronics." Paper presented at symposium, "Crossing National Borders: Invasions or Involvement," Columbia University, New York, December 6.

Fichman, M., and E. Fowler. 2003. "The Science and Politics of Sprawl." Unpublished paper. Toronto: York University.

Firey, W. 1945. "Sentiment and Symbolism as Ecological Variables." *American Sociological Review* 10: 140–148.

Fischer, C. 1975. "Toward a Subcultural Theory of Urbanism." *American Journal of Sociology* 80: 1319–1341.

———. 1976. *The Urban Experience*. New York: Harcourt Brace.

———. 1982. *To Dwell Among Friends: Personal Networks in Town and City*. Chicago: University of Chicago Press.

Fishman, R. 1987. *Bourgeois Utopias: The Rise and Fall of Suburbia*. New York: Basic Books.

Flanagan, W. 2010. *Urban Sociology: Images and Structure*. 5th ed. New York: Rowman & Littlefield.

Foderaro, L. 1991. "The New Immigrants: Reshaping the Region/A special report; Wider Mosaic: Suburbs' Jobs Lure Immigrants." *New York Times*, December 7, metro edition, 11, http://www.nytimes.com/1991/12/07/nyregion/new-immigrants-reshaping-region -special-report-wider-mosaic-suburbs-jobs-lure.html?pagewanted=1.

Fong, T. 1991. *The First Suburban Chinatown: The Remaking of Monterey Park, California*. Philadelphia: Temple University Press.

Form, W. 1954. "The Place of Social Structure in the Determination of Land Use." *Social Forces* 32: 317–323.

Forrest, R. 1991. "The Privatization of Collective Consumption." In *Urban Life in Transition*, edited by M. Gottdiener and C. Pickvance, 169–195. Thousand Oaks, CA: SAGE Publications.

Frazier, E. 1932. *The Negro Family in Chicago*. Chicago: University of Chicago Press.

French, R., and F. Hamilton, eds. 1979. *The Socialist City: Spatial Structure and Urban Policy*. New York: John Wiley and Sons.

Frey, W. 1979. "Population Movement and City-Suburban Redistribution: An Analytic Framework." *Demography* 15: 571–588.

———. 2003. "Melting Pot Suburbs: A Study of Suburban Diversity." In *Redefining Urban and Suburban America: Evidence from Census 2000*, edited by B. Katz and R. Long, 155–179. Washington, DC: Brookings Institution.

Frey, W., A. Berube, A. Singer, and J. Wilson. 2009. *Getting Current: Recent Demographic Trends in Metropolitan America*. Washington, DC: Brookings Institution.

Frey, W., and A. Speare. 1988. *Regional and Metropolitan Growth and Decline in the United States*. New York: Russell Sage Foundation.

Friedmann, J. 1986. "The World City Hypothesis." *Development and Change* 17: 69–84.

Friedmann, J., and G. Wolff. 1982. "World City Formation: An Agenda for Research and Action." *International Journal of Urban and Regional Research* 3: 309–344.

Friedrichs, J. 1988. "Large Cities in Eastern Europe." In *The Metropolis Era*, Vol. 1, edited by M. Dogan and J. Kasarda, 128–154. Thousand Oaks, CA: SAGE Publications.

Fuentes, A., and B. Ehrenreich. 1987. "Women in the Global Factory." In *International Capitalism and Industrial Restructuring*, edited by R. Peet, 201–215. Boston: Allen and Unwin.

Fuji, Y. 2005. "City Shrinkage Issues in Japan." Fuji Research Institute Corporation, Urban and Regional Issues. http://www.mizuho-ir.co.jp/english/knowledge/shrinkage 0405 .html.

Fujita, K. 1988. "The Technopolis: High Technology and Regional Development in Japan." *International Journal of Urban and Regional Research* 12: 573–581.

Fussell, P. 1983. *Class: A Guide Through the American Status System.* New York: Summit Books.

Gale, R. 1983. "The Environmental Movement and the Left: Antagonists or Allies?" *Sociological Inquiry* 53: 179–199.

Gans, H. 1962. *The Urban Villagers: Group and Class in the Life of Italian-Americans.* New York: Free Press.

———. 1968. "Urbanism and Suburbanism as a Way of Life: A Reevaluation of Definitions." In *People and Plans: Essays on Urban Problems and Solutions,* 34–52. New York: Basic Books.

———. 1990. "Deconstructing the Underclass: The Term's Dangers as a Planning Concept." *American Planning Association Journal* 56 (Summer): 271–277.

Geruson, R., and D. McGrath. 1977. *Cities and Urbanization.* New York: Praeger.

Gibbs, L. 1981. *Love Canal: My Story.* Albany: SUNY Press.

Gibson, C. *Population of the 100 Largest Cities and Other Urban Places in the United States, 1790–1990.* Washington, DC: U.S. Bureau of the Census, Population Division, No. 27, June 1997 (1998).

Giddens, A. 2000. *Runaway World: How Globalism Is Reshaping Our Lives.* London and New York: Routledge.

Girouard, M. 1985. *Cities and People: A Social and Architectural History.* New Haven, CT: Yale University Press.

Glaab, C., and A. Brown. 1967. *A History of Urban America.* New York: Macmillan.

Glazer, N., and P. Moynihan. 1963. *Beyond the Melting Pot: The Negros, Puerto Ricans, Jews, Italians, and Irish of New York City.* Cambridge, MA: MIT Press.

Global Charter-Agenda for Human Rights in the City. Synthesis Document. 2007. Conclusions of the Expert Group. Nantes, France: Droits de l'homme et gouvernements locaux, http://www.spidh.org/uploads/media/CHARTER-AGENDA_V5_EN_feb2009.pdf.

Goffman, E. 1963. *Behavior in Public Places: Notes on the Social Organization of Places.* New York: Free Press.

———. 1971. *Relations in Public: Microstudies of the Public Order.* New York: Basic Books.

Golledge, R., and G. Rushton, eds. 1976. *Spatial Choice and Spatial Behavior.* Columbus: Ohio State University Press.

Goodman, P., and P. Goodman. 1974. *Communitas: Means of Livelihood and Ways of Life.* New York: Vintage.

Goold, B. 2004. *CCTV and Policing: Public Area Surveillance and Police Practices in Britain.* Oxford: Oxford University Press.

Gordon, D. 1977. "Class Struggle and the Stages of Urban Development." In *The Rise of the Sunbelt Cities,* edited by A. Watkins and R. Perry, 55–82. Thousand Oaks, CA: SAGE Publications.

———. 1984. "Capitalist Development and the History of American Cities." In *Marxism and the Metropolis,* 2nd ed., edited by W. Tabb and L. Sawers, 21–53. New York: Oxford University Press.

Gordon, M. 1964. *Assimilation in American Life: The Role of Race, Religion, and National Origins.* New York: Oxford University Press.

Gore, A. 1992. *Earth in the Balance: Ecology and the Human Spirit.* Boston: Houghton Mifflin.

Gorrie, P. 1991. "Farewell to Chinatown: An Era of Isolation Ends with the Transition to Toronto's Suburbs." *Canadian Geographic* 111 (August/September):16–28.

Gotham, K. 2002. *Race, Real Estate, and Uneven Development: The Kansas City Experience, 1900–2000.* Albany: State University of New York Press.

Gottdiener, M. 1977. *Planned Sprawl: Public and Private Interests in Suburbia.* Thousand Oaks, CA: SAGE Publications.

———. 1982. "Suburban Crime: Testing the Police Hypothesis." *Journal of Police Science and Administration* 10, no. 4: 425–434.

———. 1985. *The Social Production of Urban Space.* Austin: University of Texas Press.

———. 1986. *The Decline of Urban Politics: Political Theory and the Crisis of the Local State.* Thousand Oaks, CA: SAGE Publications.

———. 1990. "Crisis Theory and State Financed Capital." *International Journal of Urban and Regional Research* 14: 383–403.

———. 1995. *Postmodern Semiotics: Material Culture and the Forms of Modern Life.* New York: Blackwell.

———. 2001. *The Theming of America*, 2nd ed. Boulder, CO: Westview Press.

Gottdiener, M., and J. Feagin. 1988. "The Paradigm Shift in Urban Sociology." *Urban Affairs Quarterly* 24: 163–187.

Gottdiener, M., and G. Kephart. 1991. "The Multinucleated Metropolitan Region: A Comparative Analysis." In *Postsuburban California*, edited by R. Kling, S. Olin, and M. Poster, 31–54. Berkeley and Los Angeles: University of California Press.

Gottdiener, M., and N. Komninos. 1989. *Capitalist Development and Crisis Theory.* New York: Macmillan.

Gottdiener, M., and A. Lagopoulos. 1986. *The City and the Sign: Introduction to Urban Semiotics.* New York: Columbia University Press.

Gottdiener, M., and N. Neiman. 1981. "Characteristics of Support for Local Growth Control." *Urban Affairs Quarterly* 17: 55–73.

Gottdiener, M., and C. Pickvance, eds. 1991. *Urban Life in Transition.* Thousand Oaks, CA: SAGE Publications.

Grazian, D. 2008. *On the Make: The Hustle of Urban Nightlife.* Chicago: University of Chicago Press.

Greenberg, J. 1990. "All About Crime." *New York Times Magazine*, September 3, 20–32.

Grief, G. 1985. *Single Fathers.* Lexington, MA: Lexington Books.

Griffiths, S. 2004. *Back to the Future: Staying with the Suburban Ideal.* Project report. London: CABE/RIBA. http://westminsterresearch.wmn.uk/4850/1/griffiths2.pdf.

Guthrie, D. 2010. *China and Globalization: The Social, Economic, and Political Transformation of Chinese Society*, 2nd ed. London and New York: Routledge.

Habermas, J. 1989. *The Structural Transformation of the Public Sphere: An Inquiry into a Category of Bourgeois Society.* Cambridge, MA: MIT Press.

Hacker, A. 1992. *Two Nations: Black and White, Separate, Hostile, Unequal.* New York: Scribner.

Hall, K. 2009. "What Rebound? Foreclosures Rise as Jobs and Income Drop." *McClatchy Newspapers*, August 20, http://www.mcclatchydc.com/2009/08/20/74106/what-rebound-foreclosures-rise.html.

Hall, P. 1966. *The World City.* London: Weidenfeld and Nicolson.

_____. 1988. "Urban Growth and Decline in Western Europe." In *The Metropolis Era*, Vol. 1, edited by M. Dogan and J. Kasarda, 111–127. Thousand Oaks, CA: SAGE Publications.

Hamnett, C. 2003. *Unequal City: London in the Global Arena*. London and New York: Routledge.

Handlin, O. 1951. *The Uprooted*. Boston: Little, Brown.

Hannerz, U. 1969. *Soulside: Inquiries into Ghetto Culture and Community*. New York: Columbia University Press.

_____. 1980. *Exploring the City: Inquiries Toward Urban Anthropology*. New York: Columbia University Press.

Hardin, G. 1968. "The Tragedy of the Commons." *Science* 162: 1243–1248

Hareven, T. 1982. *Family Time and Industrial Time: The Relationship Between the Family and Work in a New England Industrial Economy*. New York: Cambridge University Press.

Harrington, M. 1962. *The Other America: Poverty in the United States*. New York: Macmillan.

Harris, C., and E. Ullman. 1945. "The Nature of Cities." *Annals of the Academy of Political and Social Science* 242: 7–17.

Harrison, R., and D. Weinberg. 1992. "Changes in Racial and Ethnic Residential Segregation, 1980–1990." Paper prepared for the meeting of the American Statistical Association in Boston, August.

Harvey, D. 1973. *Social Justice and the City*. Baltimore: Johns Hopkins University Press.

_____. 1975. "Class-Monopoly Rent, Finance Capital, and the Urban Revolution." *Regional Studies: The Journal of the Regional Studies Association* 8: 239–255.

_____. 1976. "Labor, Capital, and Class Struggle Around the Built Environment." *Politics and Society* 6: 265–295.

_____. 1982. "The Urban Process Under Capitalism: A Framework for Analysis." In *Urbanization and Urban Planning in Capitalist Society*, edited by M. Dear and A. Scott, 91–122. New York: Methuen.

_____. 1985. *The Urbanization of Capital: Studies in the History and Theory of Capitalist Urbanization*. Baltimore: Johns Hopkins University Press.

_____. 2007. *A Brief History of Neoliberalism*. New York: Oxford University Press.

Haussermann, H., and W. Siebel. 1990. "The Polarization of Urban Development in the Federal Republic of Germany and the Question of a New Municipal Policy." *International Journal of Urban and Regional Research* 14: 369–382.

Hawley, A. 1950. *Human Ecology: A Theory of Community Structure*. New York: Ronald Press.

_____. 1956. *The Changing Shape of Metropolitan America: Deconcentration Since 1920*. Glencoe, IL: Free Press.

_____. 1981. *Urban Society: An Ecological Approach*, 2nd ed. New York: J. Wiley and Sons.

Hayden, D. 1981. *The Grand Domestic Revolution: A History of Feminist Designs for American Homes, Neighborhoods, and Cities*. Cambridge, MA: MIT Press.

Hayner, N. 1936. *Hotel Life*. Chapel Hill: University of North Carolina Press.

Henslin, J. 1972. "What Makes for Trust?" In *Down to Earth Sociology*, edited by J. Henslin, 90–102. New York: Free Press.

Hero, R., and R. Durand. 1985. "Explaining Citizen Evaluations of Urban Services." *Urban Affairs Quarterly: A Comparison of Some Alternative Models* 20: 344–354.

Higham, J. 1977. *Strangers in the Land.* New York: Atheneum.

Hightower, J. 1975. *Eat Your Heart Out: Food Profiteering in America.* New York: Crown Publishers.

Hilkevitch, J., and P. Kendall. 1999. "Infrastructure Rust Never Sleeps: Aging Roads, Utilities, Sewers Are Reaching the Breaking Point." *Chicago Tribune,* February 8.

Hobbs, F., and N. Stoops. 2002. "Demographic Trends in the 20th Century." Census 2000 Special Reports, Series CENSR-4. Washington, DC: U.S. Census Bureau.

Holston, J. 1989. *The Modernist City: An Anthropological Critique of Brasília.* Chicago: University of Chicago Press.

Honjo, M. 1998. "The Growth of Tokyo as a World City." In *Globalization and the World of Large Cities,* edited by L. Fu-chen and Y. Yeung, 109–132. Tokyo: United Nations University Press.

Hoover, D. 1971. *A Teacher's Guide to American Urban History.* Chicago: Quadrangle.

Horne, J. 2008. *Breach of Faith: Hurricane Katrina and the Near Death of a Great American City.* New York: Random House.

Hoyt, H. 1933. *One Hundred Years of Land Values in Chicago.* Chicago: University of Chicago Press.

Hughes, E. 1928. "A Study of a Secular Institution: The Chicago Real Estate Board." PhD diss., University of Chicago.

Hummon, D. 1986. "Urban Views: Popular Perspectives on City Life." *Urban Life* 15: 3–36.

Hutchison, R. 1988. "The Hispanic Population in Chicago: A Study in Population Growth and Acculturation." In *Research in Race and Ethnic Relations,* edited by C. Marrett and C. Leggon, 193–229. Greenwich, CT: JAI Press.

_____. 2005. "The Racialization of Urban Space." In *International Making Cities Liveable Conference on True Urbanism and the European Town Square.* Venice, Italy, June 2005.

_____. 2009. "Racialization." In *Encyclopedia of Urban Studies,* edited by R. Hutchison, 629–631. Thousand Oaks, CA: SAGE Publications.

Hutchison, R., and M. Prodanovic. 2009. "Caravanserai." In *Encyclopedia of Urban Studies,* edited by R. Hutchison, 112–114. Thousand Oaks, CA: SAGE Publications.

Hutchison, R., and T. Wright. 1996. "Socio-Spatial Reproduction, Marketing Culture, and the Built Environment." In *New Perspectives in Urban Sociology,* edited by R. Hutchison, 187–214. Greenwich, CT: JAI Press.

Ihlanfeldt, K. 2004. "Exclusionary Land-Use Regulations: A Suburban Phenomenon." *Urban Studies* 41, no. 2: 255–261.

Jackson, K. 1985. *Crabgrass Frontier: The Suburbanization of the United States.* New York: Oxford University Press.

Jacobs, J. 1961. *The Death and Life of Great American Cities.* New York: Random House.

_____. 1970. *The Economy of Cities.* New York: Vintage Books.

_____. 1984. *The Mall.* Prospect Heights, IL: Waveland Press.

Janowitz, M. 1956. *The Community Press in an Urban Setting.* Chicago: University of Chicago Press.

Jefferson, T. 1977. *Notes on the State of Virginia.* Edited by B. Wishey and W. Leuchtenberg. New York: Harper & Row.

Jencks, C. 1992. *Rethinking Social Policy: Race, Poverty, and the Underclass.* Cambridge, MA: Harvard University Press.

Jencks, C., and P. Peterson, eds. 1991. *The Urban Underclass*. Washington, DC: Brookings Institution.

Jezierski, L. 1988. "Political Limits to Development in Two Declining Cities: Cleveland and Pittsburgh." In *Deindustrialization and the Restructuring of American Industry*, edited by M. Wallace and J. Rothschild, 173–189. Greenwich, CT: JAI Press.

Joint Center for Housing Studies. 2008. "The State of the Nation's Housing—2008." Cambridge, MA: Harvard University.

Jones, G., and M. Douglass, eds. 2008. *Mega-Urban Regions in Pacific Asia: Urban Dynamics in a Global Era*. Singapore: National University of Singapore Press.

Judd, D. 1995. "The Rise of the New Walled City." In *Spatial Practices*, edited by H. Ligget and D. C. Perry, 146–166. Thousand Oaks, CA: SAGE Publications.

Justice Policy Institute. 2005. "Fact Sheet: Ganging Up on Crime." April 11. http://www.justicepolicy.org/images/upload/05-04_FAC_GangCrime_GC-JJ.pdf.

Kanter, P. 1987. *The Dependent City: The Changing Political Economy of Urban America*. Glenview, IL: Scott Foresman.

Karp, D., G. Stone, and W. Yoels. 1977. *Being Urban: A Social Psychological View of City Life*. Lexington, MA: D. C. Heath and Co.

Karp, D., and W. Yoels. 1986. *Sociology and Everyday Life*. Itasca, IL: Peacock Publishers.

Kasarda, J. 1988. "Economic Restructuring of America's Urban Dilemma." In *The Metropolis Era*, Vol. 1, edited by M. Dogan and J. Kasarda, 56–84. Thousand Oaks, CA: SAGE Publications.

Kasarda, J., and E. Crenshaw. 1991. "Third World Urbanization: Dimensions, Theories, and Determinants." *Annual Review of Sociology* 17: 467–501.

Kazis, R., and R. Grossman. 1982. *Fear at Work: Job Blackmail, Labor, and the Environment*. New York: Pilgrim Press.

Keller, S. 1968. *The Urban Neighborhood: A Sociological Perspective*. New York: Random House.

Kephart, G. 1991. "Economic Restructuring, Population Redistribution, and Migration in the United States." In *Urban Life in Transition*, edited by M. Gottdiener and C. Pickvance, 12–34. Thousand Oaks, CA: SAGE Publications.

Kervella, G. 2003a. "The 50 Largest French Cities." City Mayors, http://www.citymayors.com/gratis/french_cities.html.

————. 2003b. "Largest French Urban Areas: Montpelier Is Growing Fastest." City Mayors, http://www.citymayors.com/france/france_urban.html.

Kim, J. 1988. "China's Modernizations, Reforms, and Mobile Population." *International Journal of Urban and Regional Research* 12: 595–608.

King, D. 1990. "Economic Activity and the Challenge to Local Government." In *Challenges to Local Government*, edited by D. King and J. Pierre, 265–287. London: SAGE Publications.

Kleniewski, N. 2002. *Cities, Change and Conflict*. Belmont, CA: Wadsworth Publishing.

Kling, R., S. Olin, and M. Poster. 1991. *Postsuburban California*. Berkeley and Los Angeles: University of California Press.

Kloosterman, R., and S. Musterd. 2001. "The Polycentric Urban Region: Towards a Research Agenda." *Urban Studies* 38, no. 4: 623–633.

Koopomaa, T. 1998. *The Cell Phone Society*. Helsinki, Finland: Helsinki University Press.

Korff, R. 1990. "Social Creativity, Power, and Trading Relations in Bangkok." In *Third World Urbanization: Reappraisals and New Perspectives*, edited by S. Datta, 168–185. Stockholm: National Research Center of the Humanities and the Social Sciences.

Kruse, K., and T. Sugrue. 2006. *The New Suburban History*. Chicago: University of Chicago Press.

Ladanyi, J. 1989. "Changing Patterns of Residential Segregation in Budapest." *International Journal of Urban and Regional Research* 13: 556–566.

Lagopoulos, A. 1986. "Semiotic Urban Models and Modes of Production: A Semiotic Approach." In *The City and the Sign*, edited by M. Gottdiener and A. Lagopoulos, 176–201. New York: Columbia University Press.

LaGory, M., and J. Pipkin. 1981. *Urban Social Space*. Belmont, CA: Wadsworth.

Lamarche, F. 1976. "Property Development and the Economic Foundations of the Urban Question." In *Urban Sociology: Critical Essays*, edited by C. Pickvance, 85–119. New York: St. Martin's Press.

Lamb, M., ed. 1986. *The Father's Role: Applied Perspectives*. New York: John Wiley and Sons.

Langdon, P. 1988. "A Good Place to Live." *The Atlantic* 261, no. 3: 39–60.

Laquian, A. 2005. *Beyond Metropolis: The Emergence of Mega-Urban Regions in Asia*. Baltimore: Johns Hopkins University Press.

Larkin, R. 1979. *Suburban Youth in Cultural Crisis*. New York: Oxford University Press.

Laws of the Indies, 1573 (http://codesproject.asu.edu/node/10).

Lawson, C. 1991. "A Writer Reveals the 'Dark Underside of Suburbia': Car Pools," *New York Times*, sec. C, September 12.

Leborgne, D., and A. Lipietz. 1988. "Two Social Strategies in the Production of New Economic Spaces." *CEPREMAP Working Papers* #8911. Paris: CEPREMAP.

Lee, E. 1982. *Export-Led Industrialization and Development*. Geneva: ILO.

Lefebvre, H. 1991. *The Production of Space*. Oxford: Blackwell.

_____. 1996. *The Right to the City*. In *Writings on Cities*, edited by E. Kofman and E. Lebas, 147–159. New York: Wiley-Blackwell.

Leitner, H., J. Peck, and E. Sheppard, eds. 2006. *Contesting Neoliberalism: Urban Frontiers*. New York: The Guilford Press.

Lemann, N. 1991a. "Four Generations in the Projects." *New York Times Magazine*, January 13, 16–21, 36–38, 49.

_____. 1991b. *The Promised Land: The Great Black Migration and How It Changed America*. New York: Alfred A. Knopf.

Leshner, A. 1992. *Outcasts on Main Street: Report of the Federal Task Force on Homelessness and Severe Mental Illness*. Washington, DC: National Institute of Mental Health.

Levingston, K. 2005. *Caught in the Web: The Impact of Drug Policies on Families and Women*. New York: New York University School of Law, Brennan Center for Justice.

Levy, F. 1987. *Dollars and Dreams: The Changing American Distribution*. New York: Russell Sage Foundation.

Lewis Mumford Center for Comparative Urban and Regional Research. 2000. *Metropolitan Ethnic and Racial Change, Census 2000*. Albany: State University of New York–Albany. http://mumford.albany.edu/census/report.html.

Lieberson, S. 1962. "Suburbs and Ethnic Residential Patterns." *American Journal of Sociology* 67: 673–681.

_____. 1980. *A Piece of the Pie: Black and White Immigrants Since 1880.* Berkeley and Los Angeles: University of California Press.

Lieberson, S., and M. Walters. 1988. *From Many Strands: Ethnic and Racial Groups in Contemporary America.* New York: Russell Sage Foundation.

Light, I. 1983. *Cities in World Perspective.* New York: Macmillan.

Lin, J. 1998. *Reconstructing Chinatown: Ethnic Enclave, Global Change.* Minneapolis: University of Minnesota Press.

Lindio-McGovern, L. 1997. *Filipino Peasant Women: Exploitation and Resistance.* Philadelphia: Pennsylvania State University.

Lineberry, R. 1977. *Equality and Urban Policy: The Distribution of Municipal Public Services.* Thousand Oaks, CA: SAGE Publications.

Lineberry, R., and I. Sharkansky. 1978. *Urban Politics and Public Policy,* 3rd ed. New York: Harper & Row.

Lipsky, M. 1976. "Toward a Theory of Street-Level Bureaucracy." In *Theoretical Perspectives on Urban Politics,* edited by W. Hawley et al. Englewood Cliffs, NJ: Prentice-Hall.

Lloyd, R. 2006. *Neo-Bohemia: Art and Commerce in the Postindustrial City.* London and New York: Routledge.

_____. 2009. "Bohemia." In *Encyclopedia of Urban Studies,* edited by R. Hutchison. Thousand Oaks, CA: SAGE Publications.

Lloyd, W. F. 1833. *Two Lectures on the Checks to Population.* London: Oxford University Press.

Lo, F., and Y. Yeung, eds. 1998. *Globalization and the World of Large Cities.* Tokyo: United Nations University Press.

Lobo, S. 2003. "Urban Clan Mothers: Key Households in Cities." *American Indian Quarterly* 27, no. 3: 505–522.

_____. 2005. *Census Taking and the Invisibility of Urban American Indians.* Washington, DC: Population Reference Bureau.

Logan, J. 2002. *Metropolitan Ethnic and Racial Change, Census 2000.* Albany: State University of New York–Albany, Lewis Mumford Center for Comparative Urban and Regional Research.

Logan, J., and J. Mollenkopf. 2003. *People and Politics in America's Big Cities.* New York: Drum Major Institute.

Logan, J., and H. Molotch. 1987. *Urban Fortunes: The Political Economy of Place.* Berkeley and Los Angeles: University of California Press.

Logan, J., and G. Rabrenovic. 1990. "Neighborhood Associations: Their Issues, Their Allies, and Their Opponents." *Urban Affairs Quarterly* 26, no. 1: 68–94.

Long, J. 1981. *Population Deconcentration in the United States.* Washington, DC: Bureau of the Census.

Loukissas, P., and P. Skayannis. 2001. "Tourism, Sustainable Development, and the Environment." In *Mediterranean Tourism: Facets of Socioeconomic Development and Cultural Change,* edited by Y. Apostolopoulos, P. Loukissas, and L. Leontidou, 239–256. London and New York: Routledge.

Lyman, S. 1991. "Robert E. Park's Congo Papers: A Gothic Perspective on Capitalism and Imperialism." *International Journal of Politics, Culture, and Society* 4: 501–516.

Lynch, K. 1964. *The Image of the City.* Cambridge, MA: MIT Press.

Lynch, S. 2009. "America's Most Stressful Cities." Forbes.com, http://www.forbes.com/2009/08/20/stress-unemployment-homes-lifestyle-real-estate-home-values-stressful-cities_slide.html.

Lynd, R., and H. Lynd. 1929. *Middletown: A Study in Contemporary American Culture*. New York: Harcourt, Brace and World.

———. 1937. *Middletown in Transition: A Study in Cultural Conflicts*. New York: Harcourt Brace and World.

Lyne, J. 2001. "$63 Million in Incentives, Last-Second Space Deal Help Chicago Land Boeing." http://www.siteselection.com/ssinsider/incentive/ti0106.htm.

Mabogunje, A. 1990. "Organization of Urban Communities in Nigeria." *International Social Science Journal* 42: 355–366.

MacDonald, M. 1984. *America's Cities: A Report on the Myth of Urban Renaissance*. New York: Simon and Schuster.

MacLeod, G. 2003. "From Urban Entrepreneurialism to a 'Revanchist City'? On the Spatial Injustices of Glasgow's Renaissance." In *Spaces of Neoliberalism: Urban Restructuring in North America and Western Europe*, edited by N. Brenner and N. Theodore, 254–276. New York: Wiley-Blackwell.

MacLeod, G., and K. Ward. 2002. "Spaces of Utopia and Dystopia: Landscaping the Contemporary City." *Geografiska Annaler. Series B, Human Geography* 84:153–170.

Mandel, E. 1975. *Late Capitalism*. London: Verso.

Marples, D. 1988. *The Social Impact of the Chernobyl Disaster*. New York: St. Martin's Press.

Marshall, D. 1990. "Continuing Significance of Race: The Transformation of American Politics." *American Political Science Review* 84: 611–616.

Martinelli, F. 1985. "Public Policy and Industrial Development in Southern Italy." *International Journal of Urban and Regional Research* 9: 48–56.

Marx, K. 1967. *Capital*. New York: International Publishers.

———. n.d. *The 18th Brumaire*. Moscow: Progress Publishers.

Massey, D., and N. Denton. 1993. *Urban Apartheid: Segregation and the Making of the Underclass*. Cambridge, MA: Harvard University Press.

Mathews, F. H. 1977. *Quest for an American Sociology: Robert E. Park and the Chicago School*. Montreal: McGill-Queen's University Press.

Matrix Collective. 1984. *Making Space: Women and the Man-Made Environment*. London: Pluto.

Matzer Jr., J. 1986. "Local Control of Fiscal Stress." In *Cities in Stress*, edited by M. Gottdiener, 63–80. Thousand Oaks, CA: SAGE Publications.

Mayhew, H. 1851–1862. *London Labour and the London Poor*. 4 vols. London: George Woodfall and Son.

McCorkle, R., and T. Miethe. 1998. "The Political Organizational Response to Gangs: An Examination of a Moral Panic." *Justice Quarterly* 15: 41–61.

McCurry, J. 2009. "Japan: Towns Face Extinction as Young People Desert Roots and Head for Cities." *The Guardian*, http://www.guardian.co.uk/world/2009/jul/20/japan-towns-face-extinction.

McGovern, L. 1997. *Filipino Peasant Women: Exploitation and Resistance*. Philadelphia: University of Pennsylvania Press.

McKelvey, B. 1968. *The Emergence of Metropolitan America, 1915–1966.* New Brunswick, NJ: Rutgers University Press.

McKenzie, E. 1996. *Privatopia.* New Haven, CT: Yale University Press.

McKenzie, R. 1923. "The Neighborhood: A Study of Columbus, Ohio." PhD diss., University of Chicago.

———. 1924. "The Ecological Approach to the Study of the Human Community." *American Journal of Sociology* 30: 287–301. Reprinted in *The City*, edited by R. Park, E. Burgess, and R. McKenzie, 1967, 63–79.

———. 1933. "The Rise of Metropolitan Communities." In *Recent Social Trends in the United States: Report of the President's Research Committee on Social Trends*, 443–496. New York: McGraw-Hill.

———. 1944. *The Metropolitan Community.* Chicago: The University of Chicago Press.

McKeown, T. 1976. *The Modern Rise of Population.* London: Edward Arnold.

Mehta, S. 1969a. "Patterns of Residence in Poona (India) by Income, Education, and Occupation, 1937–1965." *American Journal of Sociology* 73: 496–508.

———. 1969b. "Patterns of Residence in Poona (India) by Caste and Religion, 1822–1965." *Demography* 6: 473–491.

Mellor, R. 1989. "Transitions in Urbanization: Twentieth-Century Britain." *International Journal of Urban and Regional Research* 13: 579–592.

Melman, S. 1983. *Profits Without Production.* New York: Knopf.

Merle, R. 2009. "Unemployment Spike Compounds Foreclosure Crisis." *Washington Post*, August 18.

Michaelson, J. 2009. "The Truth About Burning Man." *Huffington Post,* September 8, http://www.huffingtonpost.com/jay-michaelson/the-truth-about-burning-m_b _279464.html?view=print.

Miles, S., and R. Paddison. 2005. "The Rise and Rise of Culture-Led Urban Regeneration." *Urban Studies* 42, nos. 5/6: 833–840.

Miller, J. 2000. *One of the Guys: Girls, Gangs, and Gender.* New York: Oxford University Press.

Mingione, E. 1988. "Urban Survival Strategies, Family Structure, and Informal Practices." In *The Capitalist City*, edited by M. Smith and J. Feagin, 297–322. Oxford: Blackwell.

Minsky, H. 1989. "Financial Crises and the Evolution of Capitalism: The Crash of '87." In *Capitalist Development and Crisis Theory*, edited by M. Gottdiener and N. Komninos, 391–403. New York: Macmillan.

Misra, R., ed. 1978. *Million Cities of India.* New Delhi: Vikas Publishing House.

Mitchell, J. 2001. "Urban Sprawl: The American Dream." *National Geographic* (July): 54–73.

Mollenkopf, J. 1975. "The Postwar Politics of Urban Development." *Politics and Society* 5: 247–296.

Mollenkopf, J., and M. Castells. 1991. *The Dual City: Restructuring New York.* New York: Russell Sage Foundation.

Monkkonen, E. 1986. "The Sense of Crisis: A Historian's Point of View." In *Cities in Stress*, edited by M. Gottdiener, 20–38. Thousand Oaks, CA: SAGE Publications.

———. 1988. *America Becomes Urban.* Berkeley and Los Angeles: University of California Press.

Montgomery, R., and K. Bristol. 1987. *Pruitt-Igoe: An Annotated Bibliography*. Chicago: Council of Planning Librarians.

Morawska, E. 1990. "The Sociology and Historiography of Immigration." In *Immigration Reconsidered: History, Sociology, and Politics*, edited by V. Yans-McLaughlin, 187–238. New York: Oxford University Press.

Muller, P. 1981. *Contemporary Suburban America*. Englewood Cliffs, NJ: Prentice-Hall.

Mumford, L. 1961. *The City in History*. New York: Harcourt Brace Jovanovich.

Murray, J. 1984. *Losing Ground: American Social Policy, 1950–1980*. New York: Free Press.

Naess, A. 1989. *Ecology, Community, and Lifestyle: Outline of an Ecosophy*. New York: Cambridge University Press.

Nakamura, H., and J. White. 1988. "Tokyo." In *The Metropolis Era*, Vol. 2, edited by M. Dogan and J. Kasarda, 123–156. Thousand Oaks, CA: SAGE Publications.

Nas, P., and A. Samuels, eds. 2005. *Hypercity: The Symbolic Side of Urbanism*. New York and London: Kegan Paul.

Nash, G. 1974. *Red, White, and Black: The People of Early America*. Englewood Cliffs, NJ: Prentice-Hall.

Nash, N. 1992. "Latin America's Shantytowns Grow as People Flock to Cities." *Press Enterprise*, November 15, sec. A.

Nath, V. 1989. "Urbanization and Urban Development in India." *International Journal of Urban and Regional Research* 13: 258–269.

National Community Reinvestment Coalition. 2008. "Latest Census Projections Give New Significance to Foreclosure Crisis." August 20, http://www.ncrc.org/index.php?option =com_content&task=view&id=331&Itemid=75.

National Institute of Justice. 1990. *Drug Use Forecasting, Annual Report, 1988*. Washington, DC: U.S. Department of Justice.

National Council of Black Mayors (NCBM). 2005. www.ncbm.org.

Neuwirth, R. 2006. *Shadow Cities: A Billion Squatters, a New Urban World*. London and New York: Routledge.

Newman, P., and A. Thornley. 2005. *Planning World Cities: Globalization and Urban Politics*. London: Palgrave-Macmillan.

Nijman, J. 1997. "Globalization to a Latin Beat: The Miami Growth Machine." *ANNALS of the American Academy of Political and Social Science* 551: 164–177.

Noyelle, T., and T. Stanback Jr. 1984. *The Economic Transformation of American Cities*. Totowa, NJ: Rowman and Allanheld.

Oakes, J. 1985. *Keeping Track: How Schools Structure Inequality*. New Haven, CT: Yale University Press.

Obama, B. 2009. Remarks by the President at Urban and Metropolitan Policy Roundtable, July 13. http://www.whitehouse.gov/the_press_office/Remarks-by-the-President-at -Urban-and-Metropolitan-Roundtable.

O'Connor, A. 1978. *The Geography of Tropical African Development*, 2nd ed. Oxford: Pergamon Press.

Ogunwole, S. 2002. *The American Indian and Alaska Native Population 2000: Census 2000 Brief*. Washington, DC: U.S. Department of Commerce, Economics and Statistics Association, Bureau of the Census.

Olin, S. 1991. "Intraclass Conflict and the Politics of a Fragmented Region." In *Postsuburban California*, edited by R. Kling, S. Olin, and M. Poster, 223–253. Berkeley and Los Angeles: University of California Press.

Omi, P., and H. Winant. 1992. *Racial Formation in the United States: From the 1960s to the 1990s.* London and New York: Routledge.

Ong, P., H. Sung, and D. Houston. 2003. *The Status of American Indian Children in Los Angeles.* Los Angeles: University of California–Los Angeles, Ralph and Goldy Lewis Center for Regional Policy Studies, Policy Brief, Paper 3.

Ong, P., H. Sung, A. Uchida, and J. Heintz-Mackoff. 2004. *American Indian Adults in Los Angeles, California, and the U.S.* Los Angeles: University of California–Los Angeles, Ralph and Goldy Lewis Center for Regional Policy Studies, Policy Brief.

Ooi, G., and K. Phua. 2007. "Urbanization and Slum Formation." *Journal of Urban Health* 84, no. 1: 127–134.

Orfield, M. 1997. *Metropolitics: A Regional Agenda for Community and Stability.* Rev. ed. Washington, DC: Brookings Institution.

———. 2002. *American Metropolitics: New Suburban Realities.* Washington: Brookings Institution Press.

Osofsky, G. 1963. *Harlem: The Making of a Ghetto, Negro New York, 1890–1930.* New York: Harper & Row.

Palen, J. 1990. "Singapore." In *International Handbook of Housing Policies and Practices*, edited by W. Van Vliet, 626–640. New York: Greenwood Press.

———. 1991. *The Urban World.* New York: McGraw-Hill.

Park, R. 1915. "The City: Suggestions for the Investigation of Human Behavior in an Urban Environment." *American Journal of Sociology* 20: 577–612.

Park, S. 1997. "The Japanese Technopolis Strategy." In *Innovation, Networks and Learning Regions*, edited by J. Simmie, 133–155. London and New York: Routledge.

Parr, J. 2004. "The Polycentric Urban Region: A Closer Inspection." *Regional Studies* 38, no. 3: 231–240.

Pedley, J. 2005. *Sanctuaries and the Sacred in the Ancient Greek World.* Cambridge: Cambridge University Press.

Peet, R., ed. 1987. *International Capitalism and Industrial Restructuring: A Critical Analysis.* Boston: Allen and Unwin.

Perlman, J. 1976. *The Myth of Marginality: Urban Poverty and Politics in Rio de Janeiro.* Berkeley: University of California Press.

Peroff, K. 1987. "Who Are the Homeless and How Many Are There?" In *The Homeless in Contemporary Society*, edited by R. Bingham, R. Green, and S. White, 33–45. Thousand Oaks, CA: SAGE Publications.

Perry, M., and P. Macun. 2001. *Population Change and Distribution, 1990–2000: Census 2000 Brief.* Washington, DC: U.S. Department of Commerce, Economics and Statistics Administration, U.S. Census Bureau.

Phelps, N., N. Parsons, D. Ballas, and A. Dowling. 2006. *Post-Suburban Europe: Planning and Politics at the Margins of Europe's Capital Cities.* London: Palgrave Macmillan.

Philips, K. 1990. *The Politics of Rich and Poor: Wealth and the American Electorate in the Reagan Aftermath.* New York: Random House.

Pickvance, C., ed. 1976. *Urban Sociology: Critical Essays.* New York: St. Martin's Press.

Piore, M., and C. Sabel. 1984. *The Second Industrial Divide: Possibilities for Prosperity.* New York: Basic Books.

Podmore, J. 2006. "Gone 'Underground?' Lesbian Visibility and the Consolidation of Queer Space in Montreal." *Social and Cultural Geography* 7, no. 4 (August): 595–625.

Polsby, N. 1980. *Community Power and Political Theory.* New Haven, CT: Yale University Press.

Popenoe, D. 1977. *The Suburban Environment: Sweden and the United States.* Chicago: University of Chicago Press.

————. 1980. "Women in the Suburban Environment: A U.S.–Sweden Comparison." In *New Space for Women*, edited by G. Wekerle, R. Peterson, and D. Morley, 165–174. Boulder, CO: Westview Press.

Population Reference Bureau. 1990. *1990 World Population Sheet.* Washington, DC: Population Reference Bureau.

Pornchokchai, S. 1993. *Bangkok Slums: Review and Recommendations.* Bangkok, Thailand: Agency for Real Estate Affairs.

Portes, A., and R. Rumbaut. 1990. *Immigrant America: A Portrait.* Berkeley: University of California Press.

Portes, A., and J. Walton. 1981. *Labor, Class, and the International System.* New York: Academic Press.

Portney, K. 2003. *Taking Sustainable Cities Seriously.* Cambridge, MA: MIT Press.

Pred, A. 1973. *Urban Growth and the Circulation of Information: The United States System of Cities, 1790–1840.* Cambridge, MA: Harvard University Press.

Press Enterprise. 1992a. "School Integration into Revenge." January 19, A1, A7.

————. 1992b. "Our Altered Planet." May 17, AA1.

Pressman, J., and A. Wildavsky. 1973. *Implementation.* Berkeley: University of California Press.

Pye, R. 1977. "Office Location and the Cost of Maintaining Contact." *Environment and Planning* 9: 149–168.

Quante, W. 1976. *The Exodus of Corporate Headquarters from New York.* New York: Praeger.

Quinn, B. 2005. "Art Festivals and the City." *Urban Studies* 42, nos. 5/6: 927–943.

Quintus, S. 2002. *Posthomerica.* Edited by G. Pompella. Hildesheim, Germany: Georg Olms Verlag.

Ramirez, R. 1990. "Urbanization, Housing, and the (Withdrawing) State: The Production-Reproduction Nexus." In *Third World Urbanization: Reappraisals and New Perspective*, edited by S. Datta, 204–234. Stockholm: National Research Center of the Humanities and the Social Sciences.

Raushenbush, W. 1979. *Robert Park: Biography of a Sociologist.* Durham, NC: Duke University Press.

Reckless, W. 1933. *Vice in Chicago.* Chicago: University of Chicago Press.

Reynolds, B. 1980. "Triana, Alabama: The Unhealthiest Town in America." *National Wildlife*, August 18.

Rhodes, R. 1995. *Architecture and Meaning on the Athenian Acropolis.* Cambridge, UK: Cambridge University Press.

Richardson, H., and C. Bae. 2004. *Urban Sprawl in Eastern Europe and the United States.* London: Ashgate.

Riposa, G. 1992. "Urban Empowerment: The Cambodian Struggle for Political Incorporation in California." Working Paper, Department of Political Science, Long Beach State College, Long Beach, CA.

Roberts, B. 1978. *Cities of Peasants: The Political Economy of Urbanization in the Third World.* Thousand Oaks, CA: SAGE Publications.

_____. 1991. "Household Coping Strategies and Urban Poverty in a Comparative Perspective." In *Urban Life in Transition*, edited by M. Gottdiener and C. Pickvance, 135–168. Thousand Oaks, CA: SAGE Publications.

Roberts, S. L. 2004. "The Spatial Dispersion of Native Americans in Urban Areas: Why Native Americans Diverge from Traditional Ethnic Patterns of Clustering and Segregation." MA thesis, Columbia University.

Robertson, D., and D. Judd. 1989. *The Development of American Public Policy: The Structure of Policy Restraint.* Glenview, IL: Scott Foresman.

Robertson, I. 1987. *Sociology.* 3rd ed. New York: Worth.

Rondinelli, D. 1988. "Giant and Secondary City Growth in Africa." In *The Metropolis Era*, Vol. 1, edited by M. Dogan and J. Kasarda, 291–321. Thousand Oaks, CA: SAGE Publications.

Roy, D. 2005. "Urban Poor Increasingly Made Homeless in India's Drive for More 'Beautiful' Cities." City Mayors, http://www.citymayors.com/development/india_urban1.html.

Rubin, J. 1970. "Canals, Railroads, and Urban Rivalries." In *Urban America in Historical Perspective*, edited by R. Mohl and N. Betten, 127–139. New York: W. and T. Publishers.

Russell, J., and J. Cox. 1972. *Medieval Regions and their Cities.* Bloomington: Indiana University Press.

Saez, E. 2009. "Income Inequality in the United States Is at an All-Time High." *New York Times*, August 14.

Safa, H. 1987. "Urbanization, the Informal Economy and State Policy in Latin America." In *The Capitalist City*, edited by M. Smith and J. Feagin, 252–274. Oxford: Blackwell.

Sale, K. 1975. *Power Shift: The Rise of the Southern Rim and Its Challenge to the Eastern Establishment.* New York: Random House.

Sanchez, T., R. Lang, and D. Dhavale. 2005. "Security Versus Status? A First Look at the Census's Gated Community Data." *Journal of Planning Education and Research* 24: 281–291.

Sante, L., 1991. *Low Life.* New York: Farrar, Straus, and Giroux.

Sassen, S. 1989. "New Trends in the Socio-Spatial Organization of the New York Economy." In *Economic Restructuring and Political Response*, edited by R. Beauregard, 69–114. Thousand Oaks, CA: SAGE Publications.

_____. 1991a. *The Global City: New York, London, Tokyo.* Princeton, NJ: Princeton University Press.

_____. 1991b. "The Informal Economy." In *The Dual City: Restructuring New York*, edited by J. Mollenkopf and M. Castells. New York: Russell Sage Foundation.

_____. 1994. *Cities in a World Economy.* Thousand Oaks, CA: Pine Forge Press.

_____. 1998. *Globalization and Its Discontents: Essays on the New Mobility of People and Money.* New York: New Press

_____. 2000. *Guests and Aliens.* New York: New Press.

Sassen-Koob, S. 1984. "The New International Division of Labor in Global Cities." In *Cities in Transformation: Class, Capital, and the State*, edited by M. Smith. Thousand Oaks, CA: SAGE Publications.

Schlyter, A. 1990. "Housing and Gender: Important Aspects of Urbanization." In *Third World Urbanization: Reappraisals and New Perspectives*, edited by S. Datta, 235–246. Stockholm: HSFR.

Schmidley, D. 2003. "The Foreign-Born Population in the United States: March 2002." *Current Population Reports*, P20–539.

Schneier, G. 1990. "Latin America: A Tale of Cities." *International Social Science Journal* 125: 337–354.

Schnore, L. 1957. "Metropolitan Growth and Decentralization." *American Journal of Sociology* 63: 171–180.

_____. 1963. "The Socio-Economic Status of Cities and Suburbs." *American Sociological Review* 28: 76–85.

_____. 1965. *The Urban Scene.* New York: Free Press.

Schteingart, M. 1990. "Production and Reproduction Practices in the Informal Sector: The Case of Mexico." In *Third World Urbanization: Reappraisals and New Perspective*, edited by S. Datta, 105–117. Stockholm: National Research Center of the Humanities and the Social Sciences.

Schwartz, D., P. Ferlauto, and D. Hoffman. 1988. *A New Housing Policy for America: Recapturing the American Dream.* Philadelphia: Temple University Press.

Schwirian, K., ed. 1974. *Comparative Urban Structure: Studies in the Ecology of Cities.* Lexington, MA: D. C. Heath and Co.

Scott, J. 1972. *Comparative Political Corruption.* Englewood Cliffs, NJ: Prentice-Hall.

Sennett, R. 1994. *Flesh and Stone: The Body and the City in Western Civilization.* New York: W. W. Norton.

Serrin, W. 1992. *Homestead: The Glory and Tragedy of an American Steel Town.* New York: Times Books.

Shannon, T., N. Kleiniewski, and W. Cross. 1991. *Urban Problems in Sociological Perspective.* 2nd ed. Prospect Heights, IL: Waveland Press.

Shaw, C. 1930. *The Jackroller: A Delinquent Boy's Own Story.* Chicago: University of Chicago Press.

Shaw, C., H. Zorbaugh, H. McKay, and L. Cottrell. 1929. *Delinquency Areas.* Chicago: University of Chicago Press.

Shearmur, R., et al. 2007. "Intrametropolitan Employment Structure: Polycentricity, Scatteration, Dispersal and Chaos in Toronto, Montreal and Vancouver, 1996–2001." *Urban Studies* 44, no 9: 1713–1738.

Shevky, E., and W. Bell. 1955. *Social Area Analysis: Theory, Illustrative Application, and Computational Procedures.* Westport, CT: Greenwood Press.

Shevky, E., and M. Williams. 1949. *The Social Area of Los Angeles: Analysis and Typology.* Berkeley: University of California Press.

Short, J. 2004. *Global Metropolitan: Globalizing Cities in a Capitalist World*. London and New York: Routledge.

Shover, J. 1976. *First Majority-Last Minority: The Transformation of Rural Life in America*. De Kalb: Northern Illinois University Press.

Simmel, G. 1950. "The Metropolis and Mental Life." In *The Sociology of Georg Simmel*, edited by K. Wolff, 409–424. Glencoe, IL: Free Press.

Simmie, J., ed. 1997. *Innovation, Networks and Learning Regions*. London and New York: Routledge.

Simon, D. 1989. "Postcolonial Africa and the World Economy." *International Journal of Urban and Regional Research* 13: 68–92.

Singer, A. 2004. *The Rise of New Immigrant Gateways*. Washington, DC: Brookings Institution, Center on Urban and Metropolitan Policy. http://www.brookings.edu/reports/2004/02demographics_singer.aspx

Sjoberg, G. 1960. *The Pre-Industrial City*. New York: Free Press.

Slater, T. 2009. "Revanchist City." In *Encyclopedia of Urban Studies*, edited by R. Hutchison. Thousand Oaks, CA: SAGE Publications.

Sleeper, J. 1990. *The Closest of Strangers: Liberalism and the Politics of Race in New York*. New York: W. W. Norton.

Smith, C. 1985. "Theories and Methods of Urban Primacy: A Critique." In *Urbanization in the World Economy*, edited by M. Timberlake, 87–117. Orlando, FL: Academic Press.

Smith, D. 1992. "Valley of Gloom." *Press Enterprise*, October 15, A1, A7.

Smith, D., and M. Timberlake. 1993. "World Cities: A Political Economy/Global Network Approach." In *Urban Theory in Transition*, edited by R. Hutchison, 179–205. Greenwich, CT: JAI Press.

Smith, H. 1997. "National Laboratories and Regional Development: Case Studies from the UK, France, and Belgium." In *Innovation, Networks and Learning Regions*, edited by J. Simmie, 207–228. London and New York: Routledge.

Smith, M. 1994. "Hernan Cortes on the Size of Aztec Cities: Comment on Dobyns." *Latin American Population History Bulletin* 25 (Spring): 25–27.

Smith, M., and J. Feagin. 1987. *The Capitalist City: Global Restructuring and Global Politics*. Oxford: Blackwell.

Smith, N. 1996. *The New Urban Frontier: Gentrification and the Revanchist City*. London and New York: Routledge.

South, S., and D. Poston. 1982. "The United States Metropolitan System." *Urban Affairs Quarterly* 18: 187–206.

Sowell, T. 1981. *Ethnic America*. New York: Basic Books.

Spain, D. 1992. *Gendered Spaces*. Chapel Hill: University of North Carolina Press.

Spear, A. 1967. *Black Chicago: The Making of a Negro Ghetto: 1890–1920*. Chicago: University of Chicago Press.

Spierings, B. 2006. "Cities, Consumption and Competition." PhD diss., Radboud University of Nijmegen, The Netherlands.

Squires, G. 1989. "Public-Private Partnerships: Who Gets What and Why." In *Unequal Partnerships: The Political Economy of Urban Redevelopment in Postwar America*, edited by G. Squires, 1–11. New Brunswick, NJ: Rutgers University Press.

_____. 1991. "Partnership and the Pursuit of the Private City." In *Urban Life in Transition*, edited by M. Gottdiener and C. Pickvance, 196–221. Thousand Oaks, CA: SAGE Publications.

_____. 1992. "Economic Development Is Killing Education." *In These Times*, December 28, 28–29.

Squires, G., and C. Kubrin. 2005. "Privileged Places: Race, Uneven Development and the Geography of Opportunity in Urban America." *Urban Studies* 42, no. 1: 47–68.

Stahura, J., K. Huff, and B. Smith. 1980. "Crime in the Suburbs." *Urban Affairs Review* 15: 291–316.

Steele, S. 1990. *The Content of Our Character: A New Vision of Race in America.* New York: St. Martin's Press.

Stevens, A., and E. Fracaroli. 2009. "Sao Paulo's Alphaville Gated Community: An Early Answer to Middle-Class Insecurity." City Mayors, http://www.citymayors.com/development/alphaville-sao-paulo.html.

Stone, C. 1989. *Regime Politics: Governing Atlanta, 1946–1988.* Lawrence: University of Kansas Press.

Storper, M., and R. Walker. 1983. "The Theory of Labor and the Theory of Location." *International Journal of Urban and Regional Research* 7: 1–41.

Storper, M., and R. Walker. 1984. "The Spatial Division of Labor: Labor and the Location of Industries." In *Sunbelt/Snowbelt*, edited by L. Sawers and W. Tabb, 19–47. New York: Oxford University Press.

_____. 1989. *The Capitalist Imperative.* Oxford: Blackwell.

Strauss, A. 1976. *Images of the American City.* Somerset, NJ: Transaction Publishers.

Strong, A. 1971. *Planned Urban Environments.* Baltimore: Johns Hopkins University Press.

Strong, J. 1891. *Our Country.* New York: Baker and Taylor.

Stubbing, R., and R. Mendel. 1986. *The Defense Game.* New York: Harper & Row.

Sullivan, M. 1991. "Crime and the Social Fabric." In *The Dual City: Restructuring New York*, edited by J. Mollenkopf and M. Castells, 225–244. New York: Russell Sage Foundation.

Suro, R., and A. Singer. 2003. "Changing Patterns of Latino Growth in Metropolitan America." In *Redefining Urban and Suburban America: Evidence from Census 2000*, edited by B. Katz and R. E. Long, 181–210. Washington, DC: Brookings Institution.

Susser, L. 1982. *Norman Street: Poverty and Politics in an Urban Neighborhood.* New York: Oxford University Press.

Suttles, G. 1972. *The Social Construction of Communities.* Chicago: University of Chicago Press.

_____. 1990. *The Man Made City.* Chicago: University of Chicago Press.

Swanson, K. 2007. "Revanchist Urbanism Heads South: The Regulation of Indigenous Beggars and Street Vendors in Ecuador." *Antipode* 39, no. 4: 708–728.

Sweetser, F. 1965. "Factorial Ecology: Helsinki, 1960." *Demography* 2:372–385.

Swenson, D., and B. Marshall. 2005. "Flash Flood: Hurricane Katrina's Inundation of New Orleans." *Times-Picayune*, May 14.

Taeuber, K., and A. Taeuber. 1965. *Negroes in Cities: Residential Segregation and Neighborhood Change.* Chicago: Aldine.

Taylor, G. 1915. *Satellite Cities: A Study of Industrial Suburbs.* New York: Appleton.

Taylor, R. 1991. "Urban Communities and Crime." In *Urban Life in Transition*, edited by M. Gottdiener and C. Pickvance, 106–134. Thousand Oaks, CA: SAGE Publications.

Thin Lizzy. 1984. *Chinatown*. Warner Records. LP BSK 3496.

Thorne, B. 1993. "Girls and Boys Together . . . But Mostly Apart: Gender Arrangements in Elementary Schools." In *Feminist Frontiers III*, edited by C. Richardson and V. Taylor, 115–126. New York: McGraw-Hill.

Thrasher, F. 1927. *The Gang: A Study of 1,313 Gangs in Chicago*. Chicago: University of Chicago Press.

Tobio, C. 1989. "Economic and Social Restructuring in the Metropolitan Area of Madrid: 1970–1985." *International Journal of Urban and Regional Research* 13: 324–335.

Töennies, F. 1957 [1887]. *Community and Society [Gemeinschaft und Gesellschaft]*. Edited by C. Loomis. East Lansing: Michigan State University.

_____. 1971. *Ferdinand Töennies on Sociology: Pure, Applied, and Empirical*. Edited by W. Cahnman and R. Heberle. Chicago: University of Chicago Press.

Tyner, J. 2008. *The Philippines: Mobilities, Identities, Globalization*. London: Routledge.

Uitermark, J., and J. Duyvendak. 2008. "Civilising the City: Populism and Revanchist Urbanism in Rotterdam." *Urban Studies* 45, no. 7: 1485–1503.

UN Habitat. 2009. *Slums of the World: The Face of Urban Poverty in the New Millennium?* New York: United Nations.

United Nations. 1985. *Estimates and Projections of Urban, Rural, and City Populations, 1950–2025: The 1982 Assessment*. New York: United Nations, Department of Economic and Social Affairs.

_____. 2002. *World Urbanization Prospects: The 2001 Revision*. New York: United Nations, Department of Economic and Social Affairs, Population Division.

_____. 2003. *World Urbanization Prospects: The 2003 Revision*. New York: United Nations, Department of Economic and Social Affairs, Population Division.

_____. 2007. *World Urbanization Prospects: The 2007 Revision*. New York: United Nations, Department of Economic and Social Affairs, Population Division.

United Nations Population Fund. 1996. *Changing Places: Population, Development and the Urban Future*. New York: United Nations.

U.S. Bureau of the Census. 1970. *Census of Population*. United States Department of the Commerce, Bureau of the Census. Washington, DC: Government Printing Office.

_____. 1980. *Census of Population*. United States Department of the Commerce, Bureau of the Census. Washington, DC: U.S. Government Printing Office.

_____. 1990. *Census of Population*. United States Department of the Commerce, Bureau of the Census. Washington, DC: U.S. Government Printing Office.

_____. 2000. *Census of Population*. United States Department of the Commerce, Bureau of the Census. Washington, DC: U.S. Government Printing Office.

_____. 2009. *Statistical Abstract*. United States Department of the Commerce, Bureau of the Census. Washington, DC: U.S. Government Printing Office.

U.S. Department of Health and Human Services. 2009. The 2008 Poverty Guidelines. http://aspe.hhs.gov/poverty/08Poverty.shtml. Accessed August 25, 2009.

U.S. Immigration and Naturalization Service. 1985. *Statistical Yearbook*. Washington, DC: U.S. Government Printing Office.

_____. 1988. *Statistical Yearbook*. Washington, DC: U.S. Government Printing Office.

_____. 1993. *Statistical Yearbook*. Washington, DC: U.S. Government Printing Office.

_____. 1998. *Statistical Yearbook*. Washington, DC: U.S. Government Printing Office.

_____. 2003. *Yearbook of Immigration Statistics*. Washington, DC: U.S. Government Printing Office.

Usdansky, M. 1991. "Segregation: Walls Between Us." *USA Today,* November 11, A1–3.

Vance, J. 1977. *This Scene of Man: The Role and Structure of the City in the Geography of Western Civilization*. New York: Harpers College Press.

_____. 1990. *The Continuing City: Urban Morphology in Western Civilization*. Baltimore, MD: Johns Hopkins University Press.

Veblen, T. 1899. *The Theory of the Leisure Class*. New York: Viking Press.

Venturi, R., S. Izenour, and D. Brown. 1972. *Learning from Las Vegas*. Cambridge, MA: MIT Press.

Vidich, A., and J. Bensman. 1958. *Small Town in Mass Society: Class, Power, and Religion in a Rural Community*. Princeton, NJ: Princeton University Press.

Vigil, J. 1988. *Barrio Gangs: Street Life and Identity in Southern California*. Austin: University of Texas Press.

Wacquant, Loïc. 2008. *Urban Outcasts: A Comparative Sociology of Advanced Marginality*. Cambridge: Polity Press.

Wade, R. 1959. *The Urban Frontier: The Rise of Western Cities, 1790–1830*. Chicago: University of Illinois Press.

Walker, P. 2009. "From 'Tragedy' to Commons: How Hardin's Mistake Might Save the World." *Journal of Natural Resources Policy Research* 1: 283–286.

Wallerstein, I. 1976. *The Modern World System*. New York: Academic Press.

Walton, J. 1982. "The International Economy and Peripheral Urbanization." In *Urban Policy Under Capitalism*, edited by N. Fainstein and S. Fainstein, 119–135. Thousand Oaks, CA: SAGE Publications.

_____. 1987. "Urban Protest and the Global Political Economy: The IMF Riots." In *The Capitalist City*, edited by M. Smith and J. Feagin, 364–386. Oxford: Blackwell.

Warner Jr., S. 1962. *Streetcar Suburbs: The Process of Growth in Boston*. Cambridge, MA: Harvard University Press.

_____. 1968. *The Private City: Philadelphia in Three Periods of Its Growth*. Philadelphia: University of Pennsylvania Press.

Weber, A. 1899. *The Growth of Cities in the Nineteenth Century*. New York: Macmillan.

Weber, M. 1958. *The Protestant Ethic and the Spirit of Capitalism*. New York: Scribner.

_____. 1966. *The City*. New York: Free Press.

_____. 1968. *Economy and Society*. New York: Bedminster Press.

Weiss, M. 1987. *The Rise of Community Builders: The American Real Estate Industry and Urban Land Planning*. New York: Columbia University Press.

_____. 1988. *The Clustering of America*. New York: Harper & Row.

Wellman, B. 1979. "The Community Question." *American Journal of Sociology* 84: 1201–1231.

_____. 1988. "The Community Question Re-evaluated." In *Power, Community, and the City*, edited by M. Smith, 81–107. New Brunswick, NJ: Transaction.

Wellman, B., and B. Leighton. 1979. "Networks, Neighborhoods, and Communities." *Urban Affairs Quarterly* 14: 363–390.

Whitt, J. 1982. *Urban Elites and Mass Transportation: The Dialectics of Power.* Princeton, NJ: Princeton University Press.

Whyte, M., and W. Parish. 1984. *Urban Life in Contemporary China.* Chicago: University of Chicago Press.

Whyte, W. F. 1955. *Street Corner Society: The Social Structure of an Italian Slum.* Chicago: University of Chicago Press.

Whyte, W. H. 1956. *The Organization Man.* Garden City, NY: Simon & Schuster.

_____. 1988. *City: Rediscovering the Center.* New York: Doubleday.

Williams, T., and W. Kornblum. 1985. *Growing Up Poor.* Lexington, MA: D. C. Heath and Co.

Wilson, J. 1992. "Anarchy Spreads on Day 2." *Press Enterprise*, May 1, A1.

Wilson, W. 1987. *The Truly Disadvantaged: The Inner City, the Underclass, and Public Policy.* Chicago: University of Chicago Press.

_____. 1996. *When Work Disappears: The World of the New Urban Poor.* New York: Random House.

Wirth, L. 1928. *The Ghetto.* Chicago: University of Chicago Press.

_____. 1938. "Urbanism as a Way of Life." *American Journal of Sociology* 44: 3–24.

Wohl, R., and A. Strauss. 1958. "Symbolic Representation and the Urban Milieu." *American Journal of Sociology* 63: 523–532.

World Bank. 2009. *World Development Indicators, 2009.* New York: World Bank.

Wright, T. 1998. *Out of Place: Homeless Mobilizations, Subcities, and Contested Landscapes.* Albany: State University of New York Press.

Wrigley, N. 2002. "'Food Deserts' in British Cities: Policy Context and Research Priorities." *Urban Studies* 39, no. 11: 2029–2040.

Yago, G. 1984. *The Decline of Transit: Urban Transportation in German and United States Cities: 1900–1970.* New York: Cambridge University Press.

Yeh, A., and X. Xueqiang. 1984. "Provincial Variation of Urbanization and Urban Primacy in China." *Annals of Regional Science* 23, no. 3: 1–20.

Yeung, Y. 1988. "Great Cities of Eastern Asia." In *The Metropolis Era*, edited by M. Dogan and J. Kasarda, 155–186. Thousand Oaks, CA: SAGE Publications.

Yusuf, S., and K. Nabeshima. 2009. "Optimizing Urban Development." In *China Urbanizes*, edited by S. Yusuf and T. Saich, 1–39. New York: The World Bank.

Yusuf, S., and T. Saich, eds. 2009. *China Urbanizes.* London: The World Bank.

Zhou, M. 1992. *Chinatown: The Socioeconomic Potential of an Urban Enclave.* Philadelphia: Temple University Press.

Zhou, Y. 1991. "The Metropolitan Interlocking Region in China: A Preliminary Hypothesis." In *The Extended Metropolis: Settlement Transitions in Asia*, edited by N. Ginsburg, B. Koppel, and T. McGee, 89–111. Honolulu: University of Hawaii Press.

Zorbaugh, H. 1929. *The Gold Coast and the Slum: A Sociological Study of Chicago's Near North Side.* Chicago: University of Chicago Press.

INDEX

Fiscal crisis, 239–241
Fisk University, 60
Flanagan, William, 388–390
Florence (Italy), 260
Fong, Timothy, 193–194
Ford, Henry, 178
Fordism, 128
Foreclosure rates, 224–225
Fourth world, 291, 377, 388
Frankfort, as global city, 380
French Revolution, 49
Frey, William, 128
Fully urbanized county, 138–139
Functional specialization, 117–118

Galleria (Houston), 135
Gang, The, 67–68
Gans, Herbert, 195
Gary (Indiana), 125
Garden City, 323, 333
Gated communities, 202–203
Gemeinschaft und Gesellschaft, 38, 49–50
gender roles, 165–168
Gendered space, 168–171
Gentrification, 219, 383
Germany, 257–260
    reunification, 259–260
    Rhine-Ruhr District, 257–259
    urbanization, 258–259
Ghetto, 221
Ghetto, The, 56
Ghettoized poor, 164–165
Ginnie Mae (Government National
    Mortgage Association), 127
Giulini, Rudolph, 383
Global capitalism, 13–15, 128
Global Charter on Human Rights, 353
Global cities, 379–381
Global city, 138
Global competition, 359–363
Global economy, 95–96, 137–138,
    150–152, 375, 284
Globalization, 123–130, 131–132,
    376–377, 285–286
Gold Coast and the Slum, The, 65–67, 328
Gordon, David, 84
Gottdiener, Mark, 90–91, 94, 138–139

Gottman, Jean, 2
Government, role of, 15–16, 81
Government intervention, 91–92,
    355–357
    subsidies, 147–149
Great Britain (see United Kingdom)
Great Depression, 127, 227
Growth machine, 86–88
Growth networks, 92
Growth poles, 136–137

Hall, Peter, 379
Hannertz, Ulf, 195
Harden, Garrett, 351
Harris, Chauncy, 64
Harvey, David, 84–86, 389
Hawley, Amos, 72, 124
Health care, 323
Henderson, Charles, 58
Heterotopia, 332
Hispanic population, 179, 187–190,
Home mortgage, 127–128
Home ownership, 225–226
Homelessness, 227–229
    children, 277
    India, 304
    mobilization, 228
Homeowners, subsidies, 358
Household coping strategies, 294–295
Housing, affordable, 218
    crisis, 222
Housing discrimination, 217–218
Housing policy, 212
Houston, 148, 363–364
Howard, Ebenezer, 333
Hoyt, Homer, 64
Hukou system, 307, 311
Human ecology, 69–72, 72–73
Human rights, 353
Hutchison, Ray, 382
Hypersegregation, 212–214
Hyperurbanization, 13

Immigrant gateway city, 180–182
Immigration, 176–180, 251–252,
    256–257, 176–180
    first wave, 176–177

ABOUT THE AUTHORS

Mark Gottdiener is the recipient of the 2011 Robert and Helen Lynd Lifetime Achievement Award. He is professor of sociology at the State University of New York-Buffalo. He received his Ph.D. from the State University of New York-Stony Brook and taught at the University of California-Riverside before moving to Buffalo. Mark is the author of more than sixteen books and edited volumes in urban sociology, urban semiotics, and urban theory, including *Life in the Air*; *Key Concepts in Urban Studies*; *Las Vegas: An All American City*; *The Social Production of Urban Space*; *The Theming of America*; and *Postmodern Semiotics*. He teaches courses in urban sociology, contemporary theory, and cultural studies. Mark is married and has two children.

Ray Hutchison is professor and chair of urban and regional studies at the University of Wisconsin-Green Bay. He received his Ph.D. in sociology from the University of Chicago and taught at the University of California-San Diego and the University of Nevada before moving to Green Bay. Ray is series editor of *Research in Urban Sociology* (now in its tenth volume) and editor of *The Encyclopedia of Urban Studies* (2009). In 2008 he received the International Award of Merit from the Romualdo Del Bianco Foundation in Florence for his participation in international seminars and workshops, including The Tourist City (2008) and Everyday Life in the Segmented City (2010). Ray is the author of more than twenty-five articles and book chapters on urban sociology, immigration and refugee populations, and street gangs. He teaches courses in urban sociology, the city through time and space, and ethnic and racial identities. Ray is married and has three children.